Analog and
Digital Electronics
for Scientific Application

DENNIS BARNAAL
Luther College

Breton Publishers
a division of Wadsworth, Inc.
North Scituate, Massachusetts

To Doris, Erik, Hans and Kari

ANALOG AND DIGITAL ELECTRONICS FOR SCIENTIFIC APPLICATION was prepared for publication by the following people: Shirley Pitcher, copy editor; Comprehensive Graphics, interior text designer; Wayne Williams, illustrator. Ellie Connolly supervised production. The book was set in Times Roman by Arabesque Composition; printing and binding on the Cameron Belt Press was by The Book Press. The sponsoring editor was Ed Francis.

The initial version of this book was prepared with the support of Luther College and National Science Foundation LOCI grant No. SER77-02795.

Breton Publishers
A Division of Wadsworth, Inc.

Library of Congress Cataloging in Publication Data

Barnaal, Dennis, 1936-
    Analog and digital electronics for scientific
application.

    Also published separately under titles: Analog electronics for scientific application, and Digital and microprocessor electronics for scientific application.
    Includes index.
    1. Electronics. 2. Electronics—Scientific
applications. 3. Digital electronics.
4. Microprocessors—Scientific applications.
I. Title.
TK7816.B338   621.3815   82-1196
ISBN 0-534-01044-X   AACR2

Printed in the United States of America
1 2 3 4 5 6 7 8 9 — 86 85 84 83 82

Contents

DIGITAL AND MICROPROCESSOR ELECTRONICS FOR SCIENTIFIC APPLICATION

Preface

This book could be subtitled "A course in modern electronic techniques for students in physics, chemistry, computer science, engineering (other than electronic), biology, medicine, experimental psychology, geology . . . ." Such a title would illustrate the wide-ranging influence of electronic instruments and techniques in contemporary science. A laboratory in any area of science uses electronic instruments to study much of the phenomena under investigation. Indeed, electronics is pervasive throughout modern society.

People working in the areas listed above need an acquaintance with electronics for a number of reasons: to make proper use of instruments; to understand instruments including new instruments becoming available; to conceive of new possibilities and techniques and convey them to designers; and, on occasion, to save time and keep the operations going by fixing the instrument or building it oneself!

Because of these needs electronics courses have been taught in physics departments for many years. However, they have typically been "scaled-down electrical engineering courses" that emphasize the design of various amplifier types from transistors. This approach is not well suited to the needs of scientists, for there is little time to consider the *overall design of instrument systems*. For most laboratory applications we need not concern ourselves with complex amplifier design, particularly now with the sophisticated linear and digital integrated circuits available. Students in biology, chemistry, and medicine in particular can solve almost all amplifier problems with that powerful function block, the *operational amplifier*.

Therefore this book relegates discrete active devices to the last chapter of the analog electronics section. The design of function blocks around integrated-circuit devices and their implementation into instrumentation for representative tasks in science and medicine are emphasized. Application of the various electronic techniques in the laboratory are frequently outlined; in general I have tried to avoid simply presenting a catalog of circuit types.

Approximately the first half of this book deals with analog electronics, while the second half deals with digital and microprocessor electronics. A comment on analog versus digital is in order here. In the era of the 1980s, almost everyone has an idea of the difference between the two. People are familiar, for example, with the widely used digital watch that now often replaces the "analog watch" on wrists. The term *digital* implies the use of discrete numbers and electronic circuits that are just "on" or "off" like a switch. The term *analog* implies the use of a needle (such as a watch hand) along the range of a scale and electronic circuits wherein currents and voltages may be any of a range of values.

A good understanding of Ohm's Law and dc circuits, as well as basic ac circuits, remains important in electronics. Chapter A1 reviews and occasionally extends these basic areas for the student. Chapter A2 describes some important features of various kinds of measuring equipment and instruments used in electronics and the laboratory. Electronics is useful because of its contact with the physical world through appropriate transducers, and Chapter A3 introduces a selection of these devices. After diodes and basic power supplies are discussed in Chapter A4, some general features of amplifiers and amplifier use are examined in Chapter A5. Then Chapters A6 and A7 represent the kernel of the analog section as they survey the uses of linear integrated circuits, especially the operational amplifier. Finally, Chapter A8 presents various transistor types and a basic understanding of their characteristics and use.

For a long time scientific electronics courses included a modest section dealing with pulses and counting circuits. However, since digital logic integrated circuits became available in 1965, the performance and low cost of these devices have promoted digital techniques to equal importance with analog electronics as a tool for scientists. For example, the digital voltmeter and the microcomputer are now commonplace in the laboratory.

The first *minicomputer*—the PDP-8/E from Digital Equipment Corporation—was introduced in about 1965 for approximately $20,000. This price permitted the minicomputer to become an element of laboratory instrumentation. However, the computer revolution continued as Intel Corporation invented the first 4-bit *microprocessor* in 1971. Within a few years more sophisticated 8-bit and 16-bit microprocessors were developed and incorporated into *microcomputers* that rival the minicomputer in capability. Furthermore, microprocessor chips can be purchased for less than $8 and make possible "intelligent" scientific equipment as well as new digital approaches to data acquisition and analysis.

Microprocessor design has replaced detailed logic design in many of the more complex digital electronics applications. However, a study of digital logic is still very useful for several reasons: to design digital logic elements into various types of electronic instrumentation; to understand and occasionally repair existing digital instrumentation; and to interface microprocessors or minicomputers to laboratory equipment and industrial processes. Therefore the first half of the digital portion of this book is devoted to digital logic concepts and techniques.

Chapters D1 and D2 present digital logic elements and circuits, while Chapters D3 and D4 introduce flip-flops and counting circuits. The level and selection of topics are designed especially for the scientist and general engineer; advanced design techniques typical of a text intended for a professional digital designer are avoided. The digital logic chapters culminate with Chapter D6, which discusses how digital instruments can be developed from these concepts.

The last half of the digital section examines the characteristics and application of an important microprocessor, the 6502. In this concise course, no attempt is made to survey the many types of microprocessors available. Because it is often necessary to program a microprocessor in its *machine language* for high-speed *real-time* laboratory applications, a basic instruction set and essential machine language programming techniques for the 6502 microprocessor are developed in the microprocessor chapters. It is *not* assumed that the reader has studied machine language programming previously, although previous work with computer programming in a higher-level language such as BASIC is helpful. The goal of the four microprocessor chapters is to provide the scientist with a training in microprocessors sufficient to develop and apply microprocessor-based laboratory instrumentation.

As background for the course, the book assumes only that the student has studied electricity in the context of a noncalculus college physics course. However, the first chapter provides a reasonably self-contained review of these topics, and the preliminary version of this book has been used in a general nonprerequisite course at one institution. Higher mathematics has been completely avoided; almost all derivations require only Ohm's Law and some algebra.

At Luther College, the analog and digital electronics sections of this book are taught as a pair of 2-credit courses; these are generally elected by physics majors and pre-engineering students as a 4-credit semester-long course (3 lectures and one 3-hour laboratory each week) in the first semester of their second year. The study of electronics early in the curriculum of physical science permits this important tool to be realistically exploited throughout later laboratory work. Nonphysics majors typically elect one or both of the minicourses during their third or fourth year in college. The analog and digital sections of this book are available as separate paperback books to serve the latter students.

Laboratory work remains crucial to the art of using electronics. Merely reading about it is not enough; a certain intuition needs to be developed through *doing*. To assist the student in developing this intuition, electronics diagrams in this book often include values for components; furthermore, "nitty-gritty" problems and practice of real-world electronics as used in the laboratory are often mentioned. A laboratory manual with a selection of analog, digital, and microprocessor experiments to complement this book is available. The experiments utilize inexpensive breadboard techniques for analog and digital experimentation, together with commonly available electronic instruments. The KIM and SYM microcomputer boards are used for the microprocessor experimentation and are used in the microprocessor examples in this book.

Finally, it should be mentioned that a number of my colleagues reviewed the manuscript during the various stages of its development. Thanks for their helpful comments and suggestions are extended to Charles Duke, Grinnell College; Mark J. Engebretson, Augsburg College; Roy Knispel, University of Wisconsin; and Thomas I. Moran, University of Connecticut. A special word of thanks goes to Ed Francis of Breton Publishers who inspired me to develop my original work into a textbook suited to a broad, national audience. And Ellie Connolly of the Breton production staff is to be commended for her many contributions to the final product.

Dennis Barnaal
Luther College
Decorah, Iowa

Analog Electronics
for Scientific Application

ANALOG

Passive Components and Networks

The first chapter deals with elements of electronics that do not "amplify"; that is, they do not cause an increase in the power level of the signal. Much of the material is at least touched upon in a first-year physics course (considered a prerequisite to this book). Although the presentation is reasonably self-contained, the first chapter functions primarily as a review. Nonamplifying elements, however, are the foundation of electronics, and any rusty memories must be reoiled. Further, working with electronics is applying Ohm's Law again and again; therefore, the student must understand basic circuits very well.

In the course of the chapter we review electrical concepts such as charge, current, resistance, voltage, and electrical power. We consider how to analyze the behavior of dc circuits and simple ac circuits. The important passive elements are reviewed; these include the resistor, potentiometer, battery, capacitor, inductor, and transformer. However, we do discuss important characteristics of the real components used in electronics, and this may not be review material. Also, the emphasis with respect to ac circuits is on frequency filter circuits. Finally, a remarkable property of electrical circuits called Thevenin's Theorem is discussed. This theorem is the basis of an approach to electronics that is emphasized in this book—that is, the black box model of amplifiers and system components. Although the contents of the boxes may change over the years, this approach promises general and quite timeless utility.

Summary of Basic Concepts

Electricity begins with the Coulomb Law for the force F between point electrical charges Q_1 and Q_2 that are a distance r apart. In MKS or SI units it is

$$F = k\left(\frac{Q_1 Q_2}{r^2}\right) \qquad \text{(A1-1)}$$

where $\quad k = 8.987 \times 10^9 (\approx 9 \times 10^9) \text{Nm}^2/\text{C}^2 = 1/(4\pi\epsilon_0)$

The unit of charge is the *coulomb,* which is defined through current in the MKS system. We have the familiar story that unlike charges attract and like charges repel. We imagine that a charge experiences a force because of the electrical field at that point due to other charges. If F is the force on a charge Q, then the electric field E at that point is

$$\vec{E} = \frac{\vec{F}}{Q} \qquad \text{(A1-2)}$$

Combining Equations A1-1 and A1-2 quickly shows that the magnitude of electric field due to an isolated point charge Q is

$$E = \frac{kQ}{r^2} \qquad \text{(A1-3)}$$

where r is the distance from the charge. The total electric field from a group of charges is the vector sum of individual contributions given by Equation A1-3.

If one moves a charge Q between two points A and B in an electric field, *work W* is generally done (a force is exerted through a distance). We speak of the *potential difference* or the *voltage difference* V_{AB} between two points; that is,

$$V_{AB} = \frac{W}{Q} \qquad \text{(A1-4)}$$

Thus the voltage between two points is the *"work per unit charge"* to move the charge between the two points, and the units are joules/coulomb $\equiv$ volts in the MKS system. Since these are the "practical units" of the electrician, MKS units have become dominant in electronics and, indeed, throughout science. One of the remarkable features of electric fields is that the work done in moving a charge between two points is independent of the path followed. This permits us to speak of a *conservative field* and to use the term *potential.* Kirchhoff's second law follows directly from this fact, as we note shortly.

Charges in motion constitute electric current. The net charge passing through a surface per second is the current in amperes. If $\triangle Q$ is the net charge that flows in a time $\triangle t$, then the current I is

$$I = \frac{\Delta Q}{\Delta t} \qquad \text{(A1-5)}$$

It follows that 1 ampere = 1 coulomb/second.

The direction of conventional current flow is the direction that positive charges move (or at least would move if they were there). Negative charge moving in the opposite direction is counted as equal to positive current moving in the conventional direction. Thus, ions of opposite sign in an electrolyte solution move in opposite directions, but these currents add when calculating net current.

Review of dc Circuits

The first section of our review covers circuits and circuit elements for the case when the current is nearly constant and in one direction only—that is, the *direct current* or *dc* case.

Ohm's Law

If a voltage difference exists between two points on a length of wire or other material, the difference is due to the existence of an electric field between the two points. Any charges—that is, *charge carriers*—that are free to move in the material will do so because of the push of the electric field. The charges move at a *drift velocity* that is limited by frictional effects in the material, and a certain current results. The current is proportional to the push of the electric field that in turn is proportional to the voltage difference between the two points. On the other hand, it is inversely proportional to the frictional effects, or *resistance R,* to current flow between the two points. We write this as Ohm's Law:

$$I = \frac{V}{R} \quad \text{or} \quad V = IR \qquad \text{(A1-6)}$$

The unit of resistance is the *ohm* and Equation A1-6 shows 1 ohm = 1 volt/ampere.

The resistance of a length of wire is proportional to its length L but inversely proportional to its cross-sectional area A. We have

$$R = \frac{\rho L}{A} \qquad \text{(A1-7)}$$

where the proportionality constant ρ is called the *resistivity* of the material used for the wire. Table A1-1 gives resistivities for several metals, alloys, and insulators at room temperature.

TABLE A1–1. *Some Resistivities*

Material	Resistivity (ρ) in 10^{-8} ohms $\times$ meters
Silver	1.5
Copper	1.7
Aluminum	2.6
Manganin	44.0
Constantan	50.0
Nichrome	100.0
Carbon	350.0
Silicon (pure)	625.0
Glass	10^{20}

Batteries

Batteries serve as electrical elements that by chemical action maintain a potential difference (voltage) between two terminals whether a current is flowing or not. A single cell consists of two electrodes made from different materials that are inserted in some electrolyte. The potential or *emf* of the cell is determined by the composition of the electrodes and the electrolyte concentrations, not by the physical size of the cell. Strictly speaking, batteries are cells that are connected in series to increase the voltage; however, the term is often used for single cells as well. Figure A1–1 shows the conventional circuit symbols for a cell and a battery.

Batteries have regained popularity in electronics because of the low power requirements of contemporary solid-state circuits. They are necessary for equipment used in remote places and useful when equipment must be isolated from power line (wall socket) noise. It is desirable for the circuit designer and the user to have a basic knowledge of different cell characteristics.

The *lead-acid storage battery* is the common car battery in the United States and has been in use for many years. It has an emf of 2.06 V to 2.14 V when charged, requires a liquid (acid) electrolyte, is heavy because of the lead, and is capable of high currents (up to hundreds of amperes). It is rechargeable by reversing the current through the battery and thus is reusable for a few years. A sealed form is now available.

FIGURE A1–1. *Conventional Circuit Symbols for a Cell and a Battery*

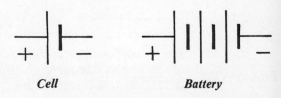

Cell   **Battery**

The *carbon-zinc battery* is the familiar flashlight battery of many years use. It is called a *dry cell* because of the paste electrolyte used and has a fresh emf of about 1.55 V. It is inexpensive but has poor performance at low temperatures and a shelf life only of a year or so; that is, even if unused (or left on the shelf), it becomes useless after a period of time because of the internal discharge that takes place. The battery can be only partially recharged over a period equaling the shelf life.

The *alkaline-manganese battery* is another paste electrolyte cell with an emf of about 1.5 V. It has a higher current capability and longer shelf life than the carbon-zinc, but at approximately four times the price. It is not rechargeable.

The *nickel-cadmium battery* is a rechargeable battery that has been used in Europe for many years but is perhaps twice as expensive as the lead-acid type. It uses a liquid electrolyte, but is available in sealed form in smaller sizes (for example, for use in calculators). It is capable of high discharge and charge rates and has a long service life. The cell emf varies from 1.4 V at full charge to about 1.25 V for most of the discharge period.

The *mercury battery* is popular in scientific instruments because its voltage remains very constant at 1.35 V over the discharge period of the battery. It uses a paste electrolyte, but is considerably more expensive than other paste types and does not perform well at low temperatures. See the forms of discharge curves for several battery types in Figure A1–2.

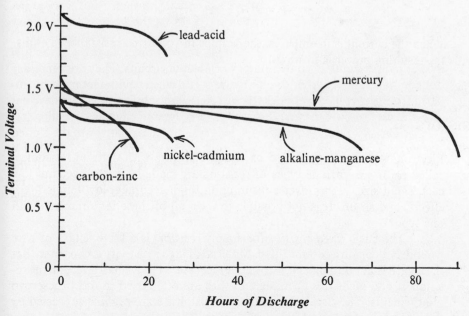

FIGURE A1–2. *Discharge Curves for Several Battery Types*

For all battery types it is important to use a battery that is physically large enough to handle the current drain. Large plate area implies a lower internal resistance and less heat dissipated in the battery, as well as a smaller drop in terminal voltage. Batteries are rated in *ampere-hours,* or in *milli-ampere-hours.* This rating is simply the product of current drain times the discharge period that we may expect from the battery, and is basically a unit of energy. Eveready (Union Carbide) has a substantial handbook listing properties of their large line of dry cells.

Power in Electrical Circuits

The *voltage* of a battery is the work per unit charge to move the charge from one terminal to the other. If positive charge Q moves from the positive terminal to the negative terminal, the battery performs work W equal to VQ. *Power P* is the time rate of doing work. Dividing by the time involved quickly gives (for steady current)

$$P = \frac{W}{t} = V\left(\frac{Q}{t}\right) = VI \qquad P = VI \qquad \text{(A1–8a)}$$

as the power delivered when a current flows between a voltage difference V. If the voltage appears across a resistance R, Ohm's Law gives two alternate ways to compute the power (in the form of heat dissipated in the resistor):

$$P = I^2 R \qquad P = \frac{V^2}{R} \qquad \text{(A1–8b)}$$

When the current is in amperes, the voltage in volts, and resistance in ohms, the resulting power is in *watts.*

Resistors

Electronics makes regular use of circuit elements with definite resistance, called *resistors.* Various types of resistors are made to fit the needs of low cost, small size, high power consumption, high accuracy, low-temperature effects, and so on. It is not possible to meet all of these requirements with one type.

The basic *fixed resistor* (or simply *resistor*) is a large length of wire wound as a coil on a ceramic tube. Material of high resistivity is chosen so that the length is not outlandish. Further, temperature has a small effect on the resistance, and nichrome or manganin wire are often used to meet these two requirements. The circuit symbol for a resistor is a zig-zag line suggested by the side view of a coil of wire (see Figure A1–3).

FIGURE A1–3. *Schematic Symbols for Fixed and Variable Resistors*

Fixed   Variable

If a sliding contact is arranged so the length of wire is effectively variable, we obtain a *variable resistor.* In general there are three terminals available from this device; they are from the two ends of the fixed resistor and from the slider or tap. Only one end terminal and the slider terminal need to be used for a variable resistor. This two-terminal device is called a *rheostat,* although the term rheostat is encountered primarily for large variable resistors capable of dissipating 10 watts or more. The symbol for a two-terminal variable resistor is shown in Figure A1–3 as a zig-zag line with a cross arrow to suggest variability.

The three-terminal variable resistor is commonly called a *potentiometer* because all three terminals are put to use when it is employed in a variable potential divider (or voltage divider). The circuit symbol for a potentiometer is shown in Figure A1–3 as a zig-zag line with an arrow to the edge; this arrow suggests the sliding contact connection. Almost all variable resistors used in electronics are in fact potentiometers, with the electrical connections then made to the slider terminal and to one end terminal.

The *wirewound resistor* is commercially available virtually as already described for the fixed resistor. It can be made with high precision (for example, 1% for $.50 and 0.1% for several dollars each) and is usually put on a ceramic form for high power. Five-watt, 10-watt, 20-watt, and even 50-watt sizes are quite common, with size proportional to the ability to dissipate power as heat. When operating at capacity, it is hot to the touch. Manganin is the alloy usually used to obtain a small-temperature effect on the resistance (temperature coefficient). The wire is usually folded back on itself to obtain a *noninductive winding,* but even so, a wirewound resistor does not work well at radio frequencies (100 kilohertz and above) because of its inductance.

Certainly the workhorse resistor of electronics is the *carbon composition resistor* with its hallmark color coding. Because of the high resistivity of carbon, wires may be inserted into opposite ends of a cylinder of carbon to give resistances between about 1 ohm and 22 megohms. This resistor has a low inductance, a fairly small temperature coefficient, and a small size. Power capabilities available are 1/8, 1/4, 1/2, 1, and 2 watts. The commonly used tolerance is 10% (silver band), with price on the order of $.05 per unit, although 5% (gold band) is becoming similarly priced and is often preferred. See Figure A1–4 and Table A1–2 for the color code scheme.

The first to third color bands on the resistor provide the digits that represent the resistance. The first and second bands give the first two digits and the third band is the multiplier that shows how many zeros to add to the first two digits. For example, if the bands were brown, red, and yellow, the

TABLE A1-2. *Carbon Color Code*

Color	Digit	Color	Digit
black	0	green	5
brown	1	blue	6
red	2	violet	7
orange	3	gray	8
yellow	4	white	9

resistance would be 120,000 ohms. The fourth band gives the tolerance. A fifth band, if present, gives the reliability of the resistor. Reliability is used for military specifications.

For precision resistors with low inductance and moderate power capabilities, the *thin film resistor* is a good choice. A thin film of metal, carbon, or metal oxide is deposited on a glass or ceramic cylinder with a manufacturing tolerance of usually 1%. The metal type is the best because it has the lowest noise and a low temperature coefficient, but each metal resistor costs $.50 to $1.00. The value of resistance is usually stamped on the metal film units, although color coding is common for the carbon film resistors.

Figure A1-5 illustrates a number of common resistor types: power wirewound (Figure A1-5a), carbon composition (Figure A1-5b), and metal or carbon film (Figure A1-5c).

The most common *potentiometer*—that is, three-terminal variable resistor—used in electronics has a sliding contact moving over a circular segment of carbon resistive film. The interior construction and exterior appearance are shown in Figure A1-6a. It is typically rated at 2 watts, and the center lug (of the three available) is the sliding contact. For higher resolution *multiturn potentiometers* are available that typically have a linearity of 0.1%. The interior construction of the popular small rectangular *trimmer* type is

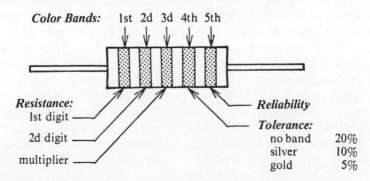

FIGURE A1-4. *Color Code for Carbon Composition Resistors*

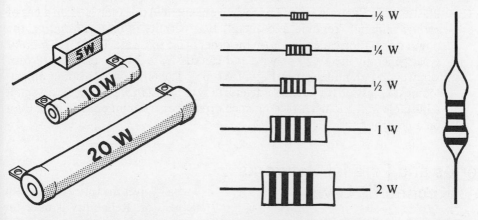

(a) Power Wirewound Resistors

(b) Carbon Composition Resistors
   (Actual Size)

(c) Metal or
   Carbon Film
   Resistor

FIGURE A1–5. *A Sample of Types of Common Resistors*

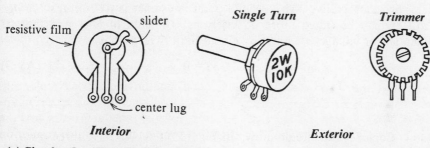

(a) Circular One-Turn Potentiometers

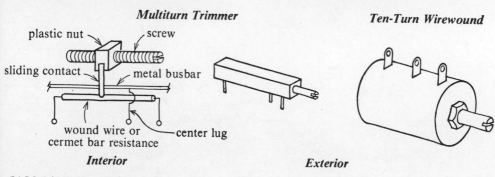

(b) Multiturn Potentiometers

FIGURE A1–6. *Common Variable Resistors or Potentiometers*

illustrated in Figure A1–6b. The resistive element in this type is often a bar of *cermet* material (ceramic and metal) that permits *infinite resolution;* the power dissipation capability is on the order of 0.5 to 1 watt. The larger *tubular* types generally use a coil of wire and can dissipate 3 watts (see the 10-turn wirewound potentiometer in Figure A1–6b). The term *pot* is a common colloquial expression for potentiometers; thus the term *trim pot* refers to a small adjustable potentiometer often placed directly on a circuit board rather than on a control panel.

Series and Parallel Networks and Kirchhoff's Laws

In solving problems where resistors are interconnected in quite general ways to form networks, the first point to remember is the relationship between relative polarity of voltage across a resistor and the direction of current through it. The more positive end is always the end at which current enters, as pictured for resistor R in Figure A1–7.

The second point is that the voltage computed between two points is the same no matter what path is chosen between the points (because electric fields are conservative). This second point in essence is *Kirchhoff's Voltage Law.* It may be stated more concisely as: The sum of rises and falls of potential (or voltage) around any closed path is zero; that is,

$$\sum_{\substack{i \\ \text{closed} \\ \text{loop}}} V_i = 0 \qquad\qquad \textbf{(A1–9)}$$

Consider the circuit shown in Figure A1–8. We have three *resistors in series* (because the same current must flow through each) that are connected to a battery of voltage V. The voltage at B compared to A, $(V_B - V_A)$, must

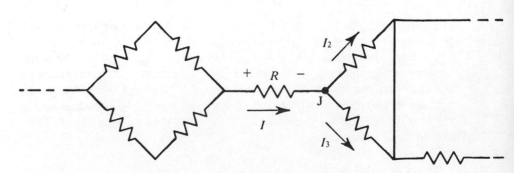

FIGURE A1–7. *Polarity and Current Direction in a Resistor*

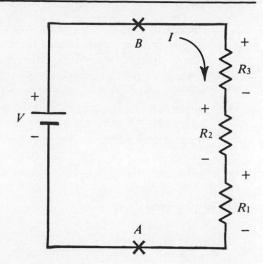

FIGURE A1–8. *Series Resistance*
Circuit

be equal to V when considering the left path from A to B. Going up the right side involves successive voltage rises of V_1 across R_1, V_2 across R_2, and V_3 across R_3. The total potential rise is $V_1 + V_2 + V_3$, which must be the same as V. Therefore,

$$V = V_1 + V_2 + V_3 \qquad \text{(A1–10)}$$

However, Ohm's Law requires that $V_1 = IR_1$, $V_2 = IR_2$, and $V_3 = IR_3$. Substituting into Equation A1–10 results in

$$V = IR_1 + IR_2 + IR_3$$

Solving for I gives

$$I = \frac{V}{R_1 + R_2 + R_3} = \frac{V}{R_s}$$

if we let

$$R_s = R_1 + R_2 + R_3 \qquad \text{(A1–11)}$$

The three resistors in series behave as one equivalent resistance R_s, and Equation A1–11 is the familiar *additive rule for resistors in series*.

Note that direct application of Equation A1–9 results in the same equation as Equation A1–10. Suppose we begin at A and travel counterclockwise around the circuit, adding potential rises and falls. We go up through R_1 an amount V_1 (since we go $-$ to $+$), again up V_2 and again up V_3, but then down $-V$ for $+$ to $-$ through the battery as we return to A. Then adding these voltage changes gives

$$V_1 + V_2 + V_3 - V = 0$$

which is the same as Equation A1–10 if V is moved to the other side. We may show the same happens if we think of going clockwise from A and back to A (or again, if B is chosen as the starting point).

Before reviewing parallel resistors, the third fundamental point about electric circuits—called *Kirchhoff's Current Law*—should be mentioned. When there is a junction of current paths (a fork in the road) such as J in Figure A1-7, the current into the junction must equal the current out. (Otherwise net charge would accumulate there and literally explode from coulomb repulsion.) Therefore $I = I_2 + I_3$ in Figure A1-7. A neater way of stating the same thing is the algebraic sum of currents into a junction must give zero; that is,

$$\sum_i I_i = 0 \qquad (A1\text{-}12)$$

Here a current is reckoned positive if going into the junction and negative if leaving it.

Consider now the circuit shown in Figure A1-9. We have three *resistors in parallel* since there are three current paths literally parallel from A to B. Applying Kirchhoff's Current Law to the junction at A gives

$$I = I_1 + I_2 + I_3 \qquad (A1\text{-}13)$$

The voltage between B and A must be V when the battery path is followed, but it must be $V_1 = I_1 R_1$ or $V_2 = I_2 R_2$ or $V_3 = I_3 R_3$ when moving through the respective resistors from B to A. Solving for the currents in these three statements and substituting into Equation A1-13 gives

$$I = \frac{V_1}{R_1} + \frac{V_2}{R_2} + \frac{V_3}{R_3} = V\left(\frac{1}{R_1} + \frac{1}{R_2} + \frac{1}{R_3}\right)$$

We see that

$$I = V\left(\frac{1}{R_p}\right)$$

where $\qquad \dfrac{1}{R_p} = \dfrac{1}{R_1} + \dfrac{1}{R_2} + \dfrac{1}{R_3}$ $\qquad (A1\text{-}14a)$

Thus the three resistors in parallel behave like one equivalent resistance R_p, which is given by Equation A1-14a. This equation is the familiar *rule for the equivalent resistance of parallel resistors*. Note that the parallel resistance is always *less* than the smallest resistor in the group.

It should be clear how to generalize the series and parallel resistance formulas of Equation A1-11 and Equation A1-14a, respectively, for the case of more than three resistors: Add more R_i or $1/R_i$ terms in each respective formula. If only two resistors are involved, the parallel resistance case becomes

$$R_p = \frac{R_1 R_2}{R_1 + R_2} \qquad (A1\text{-}14b)$$

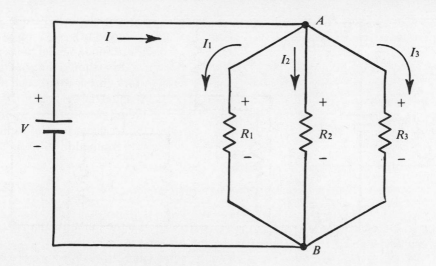

FIGURE A1-9. *Parallel Resistance Circuit*

We next review by example circuits consisting of resistor combinations that can be considered in series or parallel.

Example: Consider the circuit given in Figure A1-10a. Suppose both the *current drain* from the battery and the *current through the 5-ohm resistor* are desired. Our goal is to replace the circuit with one equivalent resistance connected to the battery.

Solution: The 1-ohm and 2-ohm resistors are clearly in parallel and, in fact, are in parallel with the 3-ohm resistance, too. We compute their effective resistance:

$$\frac{1}{R_{p1}} = \frac{1}{1\ \Omega} + \frac{1}{2\ \Omega} + \frac{1}{3\ \Omega} = \frac{11}{6\ \Omega} \qquad R_{p1} = 0.545\ \Omega$$

The parallel combination is now replaced with a single 0.545-ohm resistor to obtain the simpler circuit of Figure A1-10b. We now see the 0.545-ohm resistor in series with the 4-ohm resistor, which gives an equivalent resistance of 4.545 ohms. This in turn is in parallel with the 5-ohm resistance to give a resistance (using Equation A1-14b)

$$R_{p2} = \frac{(4.545\ \Omega)(5\ \Omega)}{4.545\ \Omega + 5\ \Omega} = 2.38\ \Omega$$

and the circuit then reduces to the one shown in Figure A1-10c. Now there are three resistors in series that have the equivalent resistance of

---

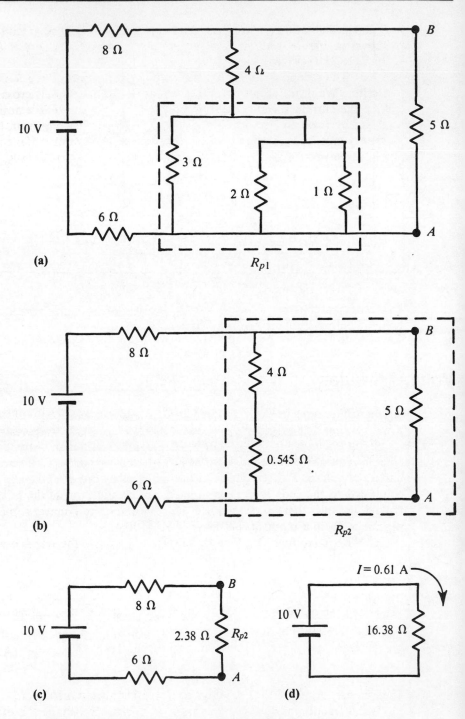

FIGURE A1-10. *Combination of Series and Parallel Resistors*

$8 \ \Omega + 6 \ \Omega + 2.38 \ \Omega = 16.38 \ \Omega$. The completely simplified circuit is shown in Figure A1–10d. The *current drain* from the battery is $I = 10 \ V/16.38 \ \Omega = 0.61 \ A$.

The second quantity desired is the current through the 5-ohm resistor. We need to figure out the voltage V_{AB} that appears across it; then the current through it is simply $V_{AB}/5 \ \Omega$. We can follow points A and B down to Figure A1–10c. The 0.61-ampere current from the battery must pass through the 2.38-ohm equivalent resistor that is connected between A and B. Then the voltage between A and B must be

$$V_{AB} = IR = 0.61 \ A \times 2.38 \ \Omega = 1.45 \ V$$

Finally

$$I_{5 \ \Omega} = \frac{V_{5 \ \Omega}}{5 \ \Omega} = \frac{V_{AB}}{5 \ \Omega} = \frac{1.45 \ V}{5 \ \Omega} = 0.29 \ A$$

It is important that the student be thoroughly familiar with this sort of circuit analysis before studying electronic circuits.

Voltage Divider

So many situations in electronics are quickly understood in terms of *voltage divider action* that a review of this circuit and concept is important. Basically the circuit is a poor person's way to make a lower voltage source out of a battery. In Figure A1–11a we have two resistors in series that are connected to a battery of voltage V. Let us think of the circuit as placed in a box, and wires connected to the ends of one resistor, R_2, are brought out of the box. The voltage between these wires is called V_{out}. We intend to connect some *load resistance R_L* in a moment, but leave it off at first.

We wish to find V_{out}. First the current I flowing in the loop is given by

$$I = \frac{V}{R_1 + R_2}$$

The voltage across R_2 must be this current times its resistance, and the output voltage is the same:

$$V_{out} = V \left(\frac{R_2}{R_1 + R_2} \right) \tag{A1–15}$$

The quantity $R_2/(R_1 + R_2)$ in Equation A1–15 is always a fraction, so that V_{out} is this fraction of the battery voltage V. In fact, the voltage V is divided between R_1 and R_2; hence the name *voltage divider*.

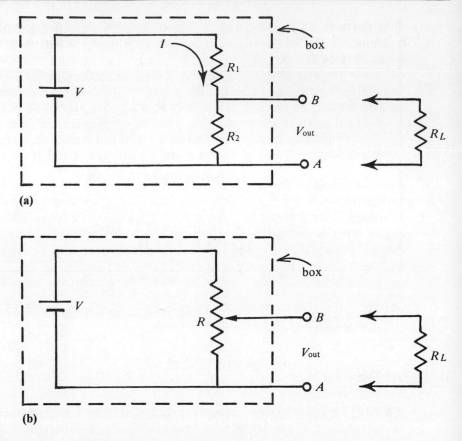

FIGURE A1–11. *Voltage Divider*

If a variable resistor is used as illustrated in Figure A1–11b, the resistance $R_1 + R_2$ is a constant R and the fraction R_2/R becomes the fractional setting of the slider along the potentiometer. This is a quick and easy way to produce a continuously adjustable voltage. However, the voltage V_{out} is *not* independent of the current drawn by R_L (as it would be for a good battery). If R_L is connected we have a parallel resistance combination between A and B. This resistance is always less than R_2 was alone, and we can easily evaluate V_{AB} in this case and find it to be *less than* the voltage V_{out} before R_L was connected (the so-called open-circuit voltage).

Review of ac Circuits

Until this point the voltage sources discussed were constant, which is the case for good batteries, and the resulting currents are then also constant, or direct currents. But many electronic applications deal with voltages and currents that change with time and may even alternate in direction or polarity. Such changing currents are called *alternating currents* or *ac*. This section of our review covers basic ac circuits and properties of important elements other than resistors used in ac circuits. This section concludes with a discussion of ac filter circuits, which may be new rather than review material.

Basic Concepts

A source of voltage that is changing in time is represented schematically by a circle as shown in Figure A1–12a. This changing-voltage source is called an ac voltage. Time graphs of some common types of ac voltage are shown in Figure A1–12b along with the common names for these waveforms. The shape of one cycle of the waveform is generally drawn within the circle that represents the ac voltage source.

The *sinusoidal waveform* is very basic; indeed, more complex forms can be thought of as the combination of many sinusoidal frequencies (called Fourier analysis). The mathematical expression for this voltage $v(t)$ as a function of time t is

$$v(t) = V_p \sin (\omega t + \phi)$$

where $\omega = 2\pi f = 2\pi / T$, V_p is the peak value of the voltage, ω is the circular frequency in radians per second, ϕ is the phase angle in radians, f is the frequency in cycles per second or hertz, and T is the period in seconds.

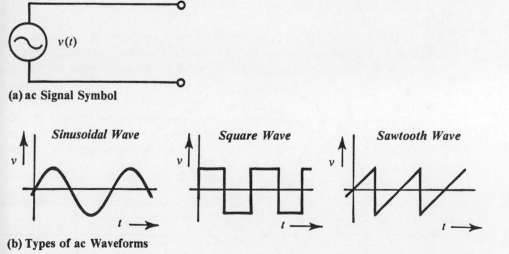

(a) ac Signal Symbol

(b) Types of ac Waveforms

FIGURE A1–12. *ac Signal Source Symbol and Common Waveform Types*

Note: Lowercase letters are used for time-varying values, while capital letters are used for peak or constant values.

If $\phi = 0$ we have the simplest sine function graph, and we think of this as the *reference case*. If ϕ is a negative number, the graph shifts so that peaks occur later, and we say the voltage now *lags the reference*. Conversely, if ϕ is positive the voltage *leads the reference* (see Figure A1–13). Note that if $v(t)$ leads by $\pi/2$ radians (or 90°), the peak occurs at $t = 0$ and we have a cosine graph, whereas if it lags by 90°, a negative or inverted cosine results.

If an ac voltage is applied to a resistor as shown in Figure A1–14, the instantaneous current follows the instantaneous voltage faithfully. Ohm's Law applies at every instant:

$$v(t) = i(t)R \tag{A1-16}$$

In the sinusoidal case for $v(t)$, this law becomes

$$V_p \sin \omega t = i(t)R$$

so

$$i(t) = \left(\frac{V_p}{R}\right) \sin \omega t \tag{A1-17}$$

The peak value of current I_p is clearly the multiplier of the sine function in Equation A1–17 so that

$$i(t) = I_p \sin \omega t$$

where $\qquad I_p = \dfrac{V_p}{R}$ $\hfill$ (A1-18)

The power $p(t)$ dissipated in the resistor at every instant is changing in time:

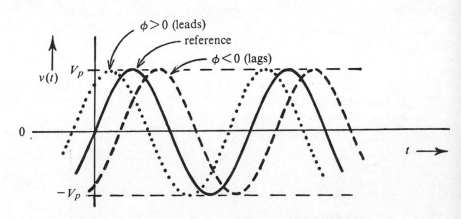

Figure A1–13. *Reference, Leading, and Lagging Sinusoidal Waves*

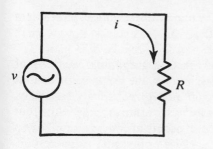 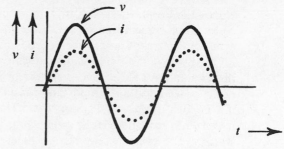

FIGURE A1–14. *ac Signal Applied to Resistor*

$$p(t) = v(t)i(t) = \left(\frac{V_p^2}{R}\right) \sin^2 \omega t \qquad \text{(A1–19)}$$

The *time-average power* $\bar{p}$ determines the heating of the resistor and is given by

$$\bar{p} = \overline{\left(\frac{V_p^2}{R}\right) \sin^2 \omega t} = \left(\frac{V_p^2}{R}\right) \overline{\sin^2 \omega t} \qquad \text{(A1–20)}$$

since a constant may be factored from an average. But a trigonometric expansion states that

$$\sin^2 \omega t = \tfrac{1}{2} - \tfrac{1}{2} \cos 2 \omega t \qquad \text{(A1–21)}$$

Since the average of the cosine in Equation A1–21 is zero, we see the average of $\sin^2 \omega t$ is $\tfrac{1}{2}$. Then

$$\bar{p} = \frac{V_p^2}{2R} = \frac{(V_p/\sqrt{2})^2}{R} = \frac{V_{rms}^2}{R} \qquad \text{(A1–22)}$$

if

$$V_{rms} = \frac{V_p}{\sqrt{2}} \qquad \text{(A1–23)}$$

The average power is given by a familiar dc-like formula *provided* the rms (root-mean-square) voltage, V_{rms}, is used; this voltage is 70.7% of the peak voltage (Equation A1–23) for the sinusoidal waveform.

Alternatively, we can examine the power using $i^2(t)R$ and find

$$p = \left(\frac{I_p}{\sqrt{2}}\right)^2 R = \frac{I_{rms}^2}{R} \qquad \text{(A1–24)}$$

where $\quad I_{rms} = \dfrac{I_p}{\sqrt{2}} \qquad \text{(A1–25)}$

Again the formula is a dc-like formula for power. In fact, most ac meters for voltage and current give the rms values rather than peak values. But a word of caution: The rms current and voltage are in general related by a factor $\sqrt{2}$ to the peak values *only* for the sinusoidal forms. For example, such meters usually do not tell the true rms current for a sawtooth waveform.

Two additional important circuit elements for ac circuits need to be reviewed: *capacitors* and *inductors*. The analysis of ac circuits with these elements is most powerfully done using the concepts of complex impedance, voltage, and current. However, to meet the objectives of this short book we content ourselves with the limited *vector approach* (such as is done in the typical college physics prerequisite course).

Capacitors and Capacitance

The *capacitor* (*condenser* is an older term) of common use consists basically of two parallel metal plates, usually with an insulator or *dielectric* in between. When a battery of voltage V is connected between the plates, equal and opposite charges $\pm Q$ very quickly flow onto the opposite plates (see Figure A1-15a). The charge Q on one plate—that is, on the capacitor—is proportional to the applied voltage through the proportionality constant C, which is called the *capacitance* of the unit (see Figure A1-15b). We write

$$Q = CV \qquad\qquad \text{(A1-26)}$$

where Q is in coulombs, V is in volts, and C is in farads (after Michael Faraday). If d is the distance between the plates, it can be shown that the electric field E that is in this region is given by

$$E = \frac{V}{d} \qquad\qquad \text{(A1-27)}$$

If the area of each plate is A, it is not difficult (with Gauss's Law) to show the capacitance is given by

$$C = \frac{\epsilon A}{d} \qquad\qquad \text{(A1-28)}$$

where ϵ is the *permittivity* of the dielectric material between the plates. The permittivity of vacuum is ϵ_0, which may be calculated through the expression

$$\frac{1}{4\pi\epsilon_0} = 9.0 \times 10^9 \left(\frac{\mathrm{N\,m^2}}{C^2} \right) \qquad\qquad \text{(A1-29)}$$

Air is very close to this value, but other materials have a larger ϵ and enhance the capacitance by some factor k, which is called the *relative dielectric constant*.

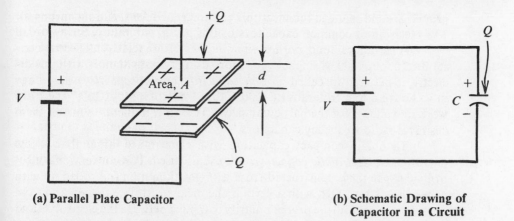

(a) Parallel Plate Capacitor

(b) Schematic Drawing of Capacitor in a Circuit

FIGURE A1–15. *Essential Parallel Plate Capacitor and Schematic Drawing*

We have

$$k = \frac{\epsilon}{\epsilon_0} \qquad (A1\text{–}30)$$

so that

$$C = \frac{k\epsilon_0 A}{d} = \frac{kA}{4\pi 9 \times 10^9 d} \qquad (A1\text{–}31)$$

A large area produces a large capacitance (and a physically large capacitor); a small distance d between the plates also produces a large capacitor, but increases the chance for a spark to jump through the dielectric (*voltage breakdown*). Capacitors have printed on them the maximum safe *working voltage*.

One Farad is a very large capacitor. Typical values range from one picofarad (1 picofarad = 1 pF = 10^{-12} F or 1 $\mu\mu$F) to some thousands of microfarads (1 microfarad = 1μF = 10^{-6}F).

Paper, mica, mylar plastic, and polystyrene plastic are common dielectrics. They have relative dielectric constants of the order of 2 to 3. Capacitors between 50 picofarads and about 5 microfarads often use these materials. Paper is common and cheap, mica is high quality but expensive, while the plastics have a good combination of price and quality. The term *high quality* in this instance refers to such factors as *low leakage* of charge through the dielectric, stability of capacitance against time and against temperature changes (low *temperature coefficient*), and low ac power absorption (low *power factor*). Usually sheets of aluminum foil with a dielectric sheet in between are rolled up to make a compact cylinder. Wires protrude from the ends; the wire connected to the outside sheet is often marked with a bar printed around that end (connect this end to ground for shielding purposes). The precision of common capacitors of this group is typically ±10%.

A certain ceramic, *barium titanate,* has a high relative dielectric constant of about 1000. Compact capacitors using two small discs with this dielectric in between are called *ceramic capacitors* or *disc capacitors,* and range in value from 5 microfarads at 1000 V to 0.1 microfarads at 25 V (these are working voltages for the particular sizes). Their low inductance makes them desirable radio frequency capacitors.

To obtain compact capacitors with capacitance larger than a few microfarads, *electrolytic capacitors* are usually used. The conventional electrolytic capacitor is constructed from a *single* aluminum foil rolled up with paper that is saturated with a certain chemical electrolyte. When an initial *forming voltage* with the proper polarity is applied between the electrolyte and the foil, an extremely thin oxide film forms on the foil; this becomes the very thin dielectric or insulator. The electrolyte/paper is in contact with the outer aluminum housing and becomes the one plate of the capacitor, while the aluminum foil is the other plate. Because of the very thin dielectric film, the capacity of the device is very large for its size.

However, an electrolytic capacitor can only be used with one end more positive than the other. The required positive terminal is marked (+), and the device is called a *polarized capacitor.* If the voltage should be reversed to an electrolytic capacitor, the electrolyte decomposes into gases that can cause the unit to explode! Heat and age also cause deterioration of the electrolytic film, and these capacitors are often the culprits in the radio or stereo that gives out a loud buzz after a few years of use (or even nonuse). The precision of electrolytic capacitors is typically −10% to +100%; note the large possible excess capacity. Also, the capacity decreases sharply below −20°C.

In recent years, *tantalum electrolytic capacitors* have become available that have a precision of ±10%. This type of electrolytic capacitor also has lower inductance, smaller leakage current, and better aging and temperature characteristics than the conventional electrolytic type. Since these features are provided along with large capacity in very small size, tantalum electrolytic capacitors are becoming quite widely used. However, they have been significantly more expensive than conventional electrolytic capacitors. For both electrolytic types, the maximum operating voltage is often quite low in order to obtain small size; this limitation must be carefully observed for a particular unit.

To obtain *variable capacitors,* two sets of parallel plates are often made to move by each other as a shaft is turned (thus changing the effective area A of the capacitor). Some small *trimmer* units have plates squeezed together by a screw; turning the screw causes C to be variable through the variable distance d between plates. Trimmer capacitors are used to make small adjustments to the fixed capacitance in an electronic circuit.

Figure A1-16 illustrates commonly encountered shapes for the various types of capacitors: ceramic (Figure A1–16a), mica (Figure A1–16b), paper and plastic (Figure A1–16c), and electrolytic (Figure A1–16d).

When capacitors are connected in series and to a battery, the same charge must accumulate on each capacitor (see Figure A1–17a). It is left as an exercise to show that the group behaves like a single capacitor with the effective capacitance given by Equation A1–32.

$$\frac{1}{C_{eff}} = \frac{1}{C_1} + \frac{1}{C_2} + \frac{1}{C_3} \qquad (A1–32)$$

The effective capacity is *smaller* than any contributing value. On the other hand, when capacitors are connected in parallel, the effective capacity is simply the sum as given in Equation A1–33 (see Figure A1–17b). This is reasonable if we think of the larger effective area that results.

$$C_{eff} = C_1 + C_2 + C_3 \qquad (A1–33)$$

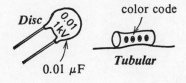

(a) Ceramic Types

(b) Mica Type   **(c) Paper, Plastic Type**

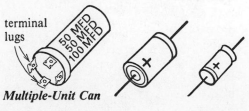

(d) Electrolytic Types

FIGURE A1–16. *Various Common Capacitors*

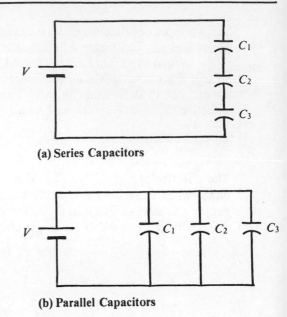

(a) Series Capacitors

FIGURE A1-17. *Series Capacitors and Parallel Capacitors*

(b) Parallel Capacitors

RC Circuit

When a battery is connected through a resistance R to a capacitance C, the charge accumulates exponentially in the capacitor and the voltage across the capacitor grows toward the battery voltage accordingly. The *characteristic time* involved is equal to the product RC; this is the time to reach 63% of the final charge or voltage. This feature is the basis for most timing circuits used in electronics.

Figure A1-18a illustrates a battery connected through a single-pole–double-throw (SPDT) switch to the series connection of a resistor R and capacitor C. The switch is alternately moved from position (1) to position (2) and back. Then the voltage v_{AB} that appears between points A and B in the circuit has a time graph as shown in Figure A1-18b. In fact, the graph shows that the circuit within the dotted box in Figure A1-18a can be thought of as a form of *square-wave generator* (also see Figure A1-12b).

The voltage waveform v_C that develops across the capacitor is shown in Figure A1-18c. Notice that while the switch is in position (2) and the capacitor is charging, the v_C voltage grows exponentially (with time) toward the battery voltage V. When the switch is in position (1), the capacitor discharges exponentially toward 0 volts. The characteristic time RC is illustrated for the charging and discharging curves.

Note that the mathematical expressions for the respective charging and discharging curves are shown in Figure A1-18c in conjunction with the curves. For their derivation, the interested reader is referred to the supplement to this chapter. The expressions apply to this case if the square-wave period

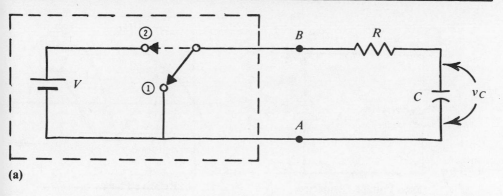

(a)

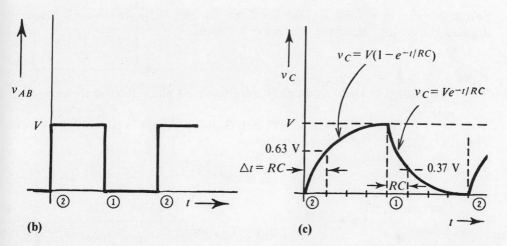

(b) (c)

FIGURE A1–18. *Response of Capacitor-Resistor Combination to Applied Square-Wave Voltage*

is sufficiently long enough to permit complete charging or discharging in each half cycle. As a rule of thumb, the time for nearly complete charging or discharging can be taken to be $4RC$, since the capacitor voltage moves within 1.8% of its asymptotic value in this time interval.

Capacitive Reactance

When an ac voltage is connected to a capacitor as illustrated in Figure A1–19a, the capacitor alternately charges in opposite senses as the polarity of the applied voltage changes. Consequently, an ac current flows. An important feature of this analysis is that the voltage applied to the capacitor is required to be sinusoidal. We then find that the ac current flowing is also

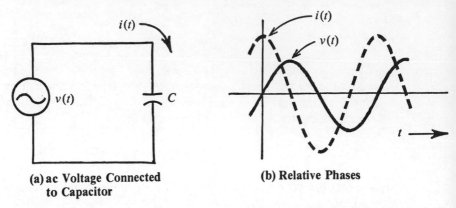

(a) ac Voltage Connected
to Capacitor

(b) Relative Phases

FIGURE A1–19.   *ac Voltage Applied to a Capacitor and Phase Relationship Between Applied Voltage and Resulting Current in a Capacitor*

sinusoidal in time, although it is shifted in its phase relative to the applied voltage.

At every instant $v(t) = q(t)/C$. If the voltage is sinusoidal, we have $V_p \sin \omega t$ as this voltage, so that

$$V_p \sin \omega t = \frac{q(t)}{C}$$

or

$$q(t) = CV_p \sin \omega t \qquad \text{(A1–34)}$$

In general, instantaneous current $i(t)$ is the rate that charge moves past a point in the circuit. That is, if an increment of charge Δq flows in a time interval Δt about the instant in question, the instantaneous current is the ratio $\Delta q/\Delta t$ in the limit that Δt approaches zero. In the circuit of Figure A1–19a, this instantaneous current (or charge movement rate) must also be the rate that the charge on the capacitor is changing. Then it follows from differential calculus that the current $i(t)$ is the derivative with respect to time of the time-dependent expression for charge on the capacitor:

$$i(t) = \lim_{\Delta t \to 0} \left(\frac{\Delta q}{\Delta t} \right) = \frac{dq}{dt} \qquad \text{(A1–35)}$$

(The reader without a differential calculus background may skip to the conclusion for $i(t)$, which is obtained in Equation A1–36.) The current in the circuit is the time derivative of Equation A1–34.

$$i = \frac{d}{dt}(CV_p \sin \omega t) = \omega C V_p \cos \omega t$$

or

$$i = \left(\frac{V_p}{(1/\omega C)}\right) \sin\left(\omega t + \frac{\pi}{2}\right) \qquad \text{(A1-36)}$$

Note that the current is not in phase with the voltage, but leads it by 90°, as evidenced by the $+\pi/2$ radians in Equation A1-36. The relative phases are illustrated in Figure A1-19b. Letting

$$X_C = \frac{1}{\omega C} \qquad \text{(A1-37)}$$

we see that the peak current is the multiplier of the sine function in Equation A1-36:

$$I_p = \frac{V_p}{X_C} \qquad \text{(A1-38)}$$

X_C is called the *reactance of the capacitor* and has the dimensions of ohms. Equation A1-38 shows that an expression similar to Ohm's Law holds for the voltage across a capacitor in relation to the current through it; that is,

$$V_p = I_p X_C \qquad \text{(A1-39)}$$

We can also divide Equation A1-39 by $\sqrt{2}$ to find

$$V_{\text{rms}} = I_{\text{rms}} X_C \qquad \text{(A1-40)}$$

Notice that increasing either the frequency or the capacitance lowers the reactance and therefore increases the current in the circuit of Figure A1-19.

Inductors

The basic *inductor* is a coil of wire wound on a tube as shown in Figure A1-20a. When current passes through the wire, a magnetic field B is produced that threads through the interior of the coil. If the current is changing in time, the magnetic field in the coil's interior is also changing. Now the *magnetic flux*—that is, the number of magnetic field lines—in the coil is proportional to the field strength, which is in turn proportional to the coil current. A changing current thus implies a changing magnetic flux in the circuit and, by Faraday's Law of Electromagnetic Induction, an emf is induced around the circuit. Mathematically, Faraday's Law states:

$$v_{\text{emf}} = -\frac{d\phi_B}{dt} \qquad \text{(A1-41)}$$

where ϕ_B is the magnetic flux. Since ϕ_B is proportional to the current i flowing, we write

$$\phi_B = Li \qquad \text{(A1-42)}$$

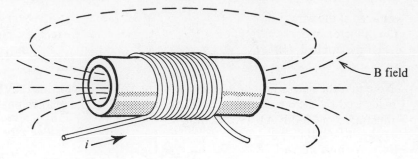

(a) Basic Inductor

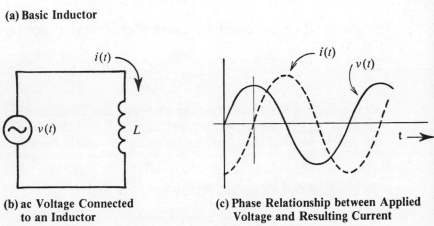

(b) ac Voltage Connected
to an Inductor

(c) Phase Relationship between Applied
Voltage and Resulting Current

FIGURE A1-20. *The Inductor and Its Basic Circuit Behavior*

where the proportionality constant L is called the *inductance of the coil*. In MKS units, ϕ_B is in webers, i in amperes, and L is in henries. Substituting Equation A1–42 into Equation A1–41 gives

$$v_{\text{emf}} = -L\frac{di}{dt} \qquad \text{(A1–43)}$$

The minus sign indicates that the induced voltage is a *back emf*—that is, an induced voltage that opposes the current change and the voltage that caused it.

Inductive Reactance

Consider now that an ac voltage is connected to an inductor L, as shown in Figure A1–20b. (This figure also shows the conventional circuit symbol for an inductor; the symbol is suggested by the side view of a solenoid such as the one shown in Figure A1–20a.) We assume an ideal inductor where the resistance of the wire composing the solenoid is negligible; only the back emf of the inductor opposes current flow, and this only if the current is changing. Then the applied voltage equals the induced emf:

$$v = V_p \sin \omega t = L \frac{di}{dt} \tag{A1-44}$$

To solve for the current, we *separate the variables* by multiplying each side by the differential dt and take the indefinite integral of each side of the equation. We also move L to the other side; that is,

$$\int di = \int \frac{V_p}{L} \sin \omega t \, dt \tag{A1-45}$$

Then

$$i(t) = \frac{V_p}{L} \left(\frac{-\cos \omega t}{\omega} \right) + \text{CONST} \tag{A1-46}$$

where CONST is the constant of integration. We'll discard this constant on physical grounds: If it were not zero, the current would have a dc component—that is, it would be larger in one direction than the other without any cause. Using $-\cos \omega t = \sin (\omega t - \pi/2)$, Equation A1–46 can be written:

$$i(t) = \frac{V_p}{\omega L} \sin \left(\omega t - \frac{\pi}{2} \right) \tag{A1-47}$$

We see the current *lags* behind the applied voltage by 90° because of the $-\pi/2$ radians. This is diagrammed in Figure A1–20c.

The peak current is again the multiplier of the sine function in Equation A1–47; that is,

$$I_p = \frac{V_p}{\omega L} = \frac{V_p}{X_L} \tag{A1-48}$$

where $\quad X_L = \omega L \tag{A1-49}$

is called the *reactance of the inductor*. Again an Ohm's Law relationship is seen in Equation A1–48; that is,

$$V_p = I_p X_L \tag{A1-50}$$

Indeed if ω is in radians/second (that is, 2π times the frequency in hertz or cycles per second) and L is in henries, the reactance X_L is in ohms. Notice that if either the frequency or the inductance is increased, the inductive reactance increases and the ac current that flows in the circuit of Figure A1–20b decreases.

Practical inductors range from radio frequency suitable units of a few microhenries up to audio frequency units of several henries. The radio frequency inductors are often wires wound on ferrite (iron oxide) cores that enhance the magnetic field and therefore the inductance. Laminated iron core is used to make large inductors, but the iron is frequency responsive only in the audio region. In either case the wire is chosen so that the resistance is small compared to the reactance at frequencies of use; resistance also determines the current handling capabilities. The resistive heating must remain within safe levels. Figure A1–21 illustrates some common inductors.

When inductors are placed in series, the inductances add in the same way as resistances; that is,

$$L_s = L_1 + L_2 + \ldots \tag{A1-51}$$

There is also a corresponding rule for parallel inductors:

$$\frac{1}{L_p} = \frac{1}{L_1} + \frac{1}{L_2} + \ldots \tag{A1-52}$$

RL Circuit

Suppose a battery V is connected through a resistor R to an inductor L as shown in Figure A1–22a. After the switch in the circuit is closed, the current in the circuit does not begin flowing immediately. The inductor's back emf proportional to di/dt (the rate of change of current) prevents this. It can be shown that the current grows exponentially to the value determined by the inhibiting resistance R. The graph of current versus time for the circuit is shown in Figure A1–22b along with a mathematical expression for the current. The characteristic time for the exponential growth is given by the ratio L/R. Although this behavior could be the basis for timing circuitry, the

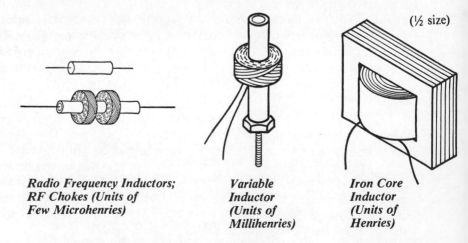

(½ size)

Radio Frequency Inductors; RF Chokes (Units of Few Microhenries)

Variable Inductor (Units of Millihenries)

Iron Core Inductor (Units of Henries)

FIGURE A1–21. *Common Inductors in Electronics*

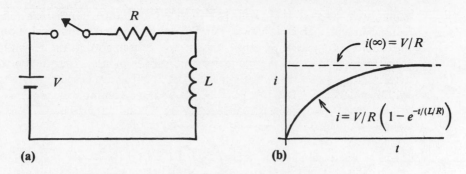

FIGURE A1–22. *Series* RL *Circuit Response to dc Voltage*

RL circuit is seldom used because of the inconvenient size and weight of the inductors generally required. In fact, the contemporary use of inductors is primarily in radio frequency circuitry (100 kilohertz and above) where the reactance of a millihenry is significant.

Transformers

If two coils of wire are placed near each other, a changing current in one coil produces a changing field that threads through the other. Faraday's law of induction then requires that an emf be induced around the circuit of which the second coil is a part. The coils are usually wound so that all the field produced by the first coil (which we call the *primary winding*) passes through the second coil (the *secondary winding*). The applied emf, V_p, across the primary is proportional to the magnetic flux through it, which in turn is proportional to the number of turns of wire in it (N_p). Similarly, the emf V_s across the secondary is proportional to the number of turns N_s of the secondary. Therefore, the simple rule for ideal transformers is that the ratio of secondary voltage to primary voltage is just the same as the ratio of the windings:

$$\frac{V_s}{V_p} = \frac{N_s}{N_p} \tag{A1-53}$$

Such a coil arrangement is called a *transformer*. In this way ac voltages can easily be *stepped up* or *stepped down* to meet various requirements.

The coils of a transformer for low frequencies are wound on a laminated-iron core to increase the inductance of the windings. In this way, if no load is connected to the secondary, very little current will flow in the primary windings. Indeed for an ideal transformer, the power into the primary should equal the power passing out from the secondary:

$$V_p I_p = V_s I_s \tag{A1-54}$$

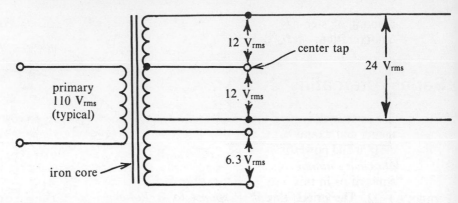

FIGURE A1–23. *Schematic Representation of a Multiwinding Transformer with One Tapped Winding*

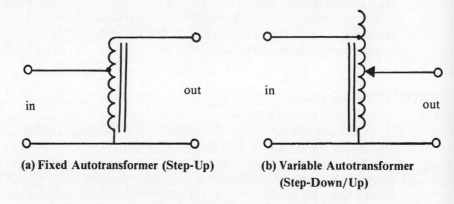

(a) Fixed Autotransformer (Step-Up)   (b) Variable Autotransformer
(Step-Down/Up)

FIGURE A1–24. *Fixed and Variable Autotransformer Schematic Symbols*

      The schematic representation of a transformer suggests the coils and the iron laminations (see Figure A1–23). It is also possible to have several separate windings to achieve several voltages simultaneously. If the voltages can have a common potential in a given application, the windings need not be separate, but can be portions of the same coil; that is, wire *taps* may come out from the coil. A *center tap* is illustrated in Figure A1–23.

      Autotransformers use a single winding for both the primary and the secondary. These are cheaper but the secondary is *not* then electrically isolated from the primary circuit. Figure A1–24a shows the schematic symbol for a *fixed autotransformer*. Notice a fixed tap position is made to the coil winding; the ratio of output to input is therefore also fixed. A *variable autotransformer* (Variac is a common trade name) uses a sliding tap to produce a convenient variable ac voltage. See Figure A1–24b for the schematic symbol of a variable autotransformer. In fact, the unit diagrammed implies that a small amount of step-up is possible, as well as step-down. This is a common configuration.

Series Alternating-Current *RC* Circuit

We next wish to consider series connections involving *reactive circuit* elements and examine how they respond to an applied ac voltage. The most elegant and powerful approach uses the notion of complex impedance and the *imaginary number* $\sqrt{-1}$. However, for the series ac circuits that primarily concern us in this book, it is possible to use an easier approach.

The principal complexity of ac circuits over dc circuits is that the current through a capacitor or inductor is *not* in phase with the applied voltage, as already reviewed. Consider the case of a resistor R and capacitor C connected in series to a sinusoidal voltage V as shown in Figure A1-25a. The following is true about this circuit:

1. At every *instant* the voltage v_R across the resistance and the voltage v_C across the capacitance is equal to the applied voltage v_{in}; that is,

$$v_{in} = v_R + v_c \tag{A1-55}$$

2. At every instant, the current i is the same in the resistor as in the capacitor; that is, they have the same frequency, phase, and amplitude.
3. If the applied voltage is sinusoidal, the current flowing is expected to be sinusoidal in time.
4. The voltage across the resistor is in phase with the current, but the voltage across the capacitor lags behind the current (or the current leads the voltage) by 90°.

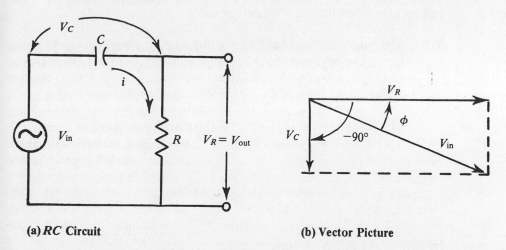

(a) *RC* Circuit   (b) **Vector Picture**

FIGURE A1-25. *Series RC Connection with Output Connection for High-Pass Filter*

The central point we now make is that when two sine waves of the *same* frequency (but differing in *phase*) are added together, another sine wave of the same frequency results. With a bit of trigonometry, it is possible to show that the amplitude of the resultant sine wave is given by a *sum of vectors rule*. The two component vector amplitudes should be the same as the two respective sine wave amplitudes, and the angle between the two vectors should be the same as the phase angle between the two sine waves. The resultant of these vectors then tells the amplitude and phase of the sine wave that results.

If V_R and V_C represent the peak voltage across the resistor and capacitor, respectively, then the magnitude of the total voltage across the two elements is the magnitude of the vector sum of V_R and V_C vectors. This in turn is equal to the input voltage V_{in} in Figure A1-25a. The angle between the vectors should be chosen the same as the phase angle between the time-varying voltages. The voltage across the capacitor lags the voltage across the resistor by 90° according to point 4 above. Consequently, the vector picture is as shown in Figure A1-25b.

By the Pythagorean theorem, the hypotenuse V_{in} is given by

$$V_{in} = \sqrt{V_R^2 + V_C^2} \qquad \text{(A1-56)}$$

However, $V_R = IR$ and $V_C = IX_C$. Substituting these into Equation A1-56 and solving for I gives the current flowing:

$$I = \frac{V_{in}}{\sqrt{R^2 + X_C^2}} \qquad \text{(A1-57)}$$

We let

$$Z = \sqrt{R^2 + X_C^2} \qquad \text{(A1-58)}$$

where Z is called the *impedance* of the circuit. Then $I = V_{in}/Z$ or $V_{in} = IZ$, and an expression like Ohm's Law results.

NOTE: Since peak and rms values are proportional, Equation A1-57 holds for rms voltage and current as well. However, the total impedance is somewhat more complicated than the simple sum of R and X_L that we might expect for a series circuit from the dc resistance analog.

The phase angle of the current in this circuit (compared to the applied voltage) is the same as the angle between V_{in} and V_R in Figure A1-25b. Since V_R is at an angle $+\phi$ relative to V_{in}, the current *leads* the applied voltage by

$$\phi = \arctan \frac{V_C}{V_R} = \arctan \frac{X_C}{R} \qquad \text{(A1-59)}$$

This "leading" feature is characteristic of capacitive circuits (recall $\phi = 90°$ for the case of capacitor only, mentioned earlier).

No power is dissipated in ideal capacitors or inductors—only in resistors. The power dissipated in the RC circuit of Figure A1–25 is therefore

$$P = I^2 R = IIR = \left(\frac{V_{\text{in}}}{\sqrt{R^2 + X_C^2}} \right) IR$$

$$= V_{\text{in}} I \left(\frac{R}{\sqrt{R^2 + X_C^2}} \right) = V_{\text{in}} I \cos\phi \qquad \textbf{(A1–60)}$$

where the *power factor* $\cos\phi = R/\sqrt{R^2 + X_C^2}$. The current and voltage must be in rms to give the proper average power. Notice that the power expression is more complicated than the simple VI product of Equation A1–8a (the dc case) due to the phase angle and power factor. Indeed, if $R = 0$ we have $\phi = 90°$ and $\cos\phi = 0$, so the power is zero; this is correct since the circuit is then purely capacitive. If the frequency is such that $X_C = R$, we can show (assigned problem) that the power is half of what it is at very high frequencies. Recall that at high frequencies the capacitive reactance is small and the current is greatest. This frequency is called the *half-power frequency* of the circuit.

Low-Pass/High-Pass *RC* Filters

The voltage appearing across just the resistor R in the series RC circuit of Figure A1–25 can be put to good use. In fact, wires are pictured as connected to these points and leading to the right. We call the voltage between these points V_{out} or the *output voltage* from the circuit; the wires could well lead to other electronic circuits, meters, or whatever.

The voltage V_{out} is just the current flowing times the resistance:

$$V_{\text{out}} = IR = \left(\frac{V_{\text{in}}}{\sqrt{R^2 + X_C^2}} \right) R = V_{\text{in}} \left(\frac{R}{\sqrt{R^2 + X_C^2}} \right) \qquad \textbf{(A1–61)}$$

In general the output voltage is less than the input voltage because of the voltage divider type action that occurs between the resistance R and the reactance X_C.

It is useful to consider the behavior of the output voltage as the frequency of the input voltage is varied from very low to very high frequencies. Since the capacitive reactance X_C decreases with increasing frequency as shown in Figure A1–26a, the output voltage V_{out} as given by Equation A1–61 must go from nearly zero to essentially V_{in}. Then the ratio of the output to the input voltage, $V_{\text{out}} / V_{\text{in}}$, goes from zero to one as the frequency is changed from zero to very high frequencies, as shown in Figure A1–26b. At high frequencies the voltage out is the same as the voltage in, whereas at low frequencies the input voltage is virtually blocked from passing to the output. This feature is very useful in a situation where an unwanted low frequency is mixed in with a

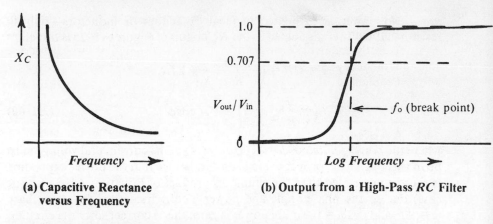

(a) Capacitive Reactance versus Frequency

(b) Output from a High-Pass *RC* Filter

FIGURE A1–26.   *Behavior of the High-Pass* RC *Filter*

desired high-frequency signal. The circuit can be used to filter out the unwanted low frequencies and pass only the desired higher frequencies; hence the name *high-pass filter*. See Figure A1–27 for a diagram of this feature.

The frequency that divides the high-pass region from the low-frequency (reject) region is usually taken to be that for which $X_C = R$. This is the half-power frequency mentioned earlier and is also referred to as the *breakpoint frequency* f_0. From Equation A1–61 we can see that

$$\frac{V_{out}}{V_{in}} = \frac{1}{\sqrt{2}} = 0.707$$

at the breakpoint frequency, and f_0 is so indicated in Figure A1–26b.

A "*low-pass filter*" may be obtained by interchanging R and C in Figure A1–25a. In other words, take the output from across the capacitor rather than the resistor. In this case, unwanted high frequencies may be removed from the signal.

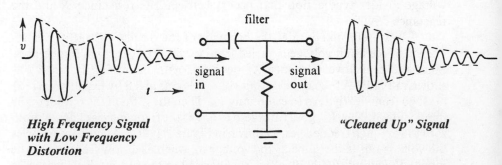

High Frequency Signal with Low Frequency Distortion

"Cleaned Up" Signal

FIGURE A1–27.   *Action of a High-Pass Filter to Reject Low Frequency Distortions in a Signal*

It is also possible to construct low-pass and high-pass filters from series combinations of resistors and inductors. In all cases the frequency behavior is easily understood qualitatively by thinking of voltage divider action and the frequency behavior of the reactance. Circuits and derivations are left to the Problems at the end of the chapter.

Network Analysis

This last principal section of the chapter may not be review material. It considers some techniques for analysis of electrical networks that cannot be analyzed by elementary series/parallel arguments. However, we will find the notions developed to be of general utility in our work with electronic amplifiers and systems. The techniques that may be applied include use of Thevenin's Theorem, the Superposition Theorem, Norton's Theorem, and others. Only Thevenin's Theorem is discussed here, but the Superposition Theorem and Norton's Theorem are briefly considered in the Problems at the end of this chapter for the interested reader.

Thevenin's Theorem

There is a remarkable theorem about circuits containing *linear electrical elements*—namely, elements for which current is directly proportional to voltage—that is, used again and again in doing electronic work. The theorem is called Thevenin's Theorem and is simply this: If two connections lead away from an arbitrary connection of batteries and resistors (we may think of the batteries and resistors as being in a box, either real or imaginary), then the electrical effects of the circuit in the box on whatever is connected to the box is just the same as if in the box were merely a single battery connected in series to a single resistance (and connected to the leadout wires).

We speak of finding the Thevenin equivalent circuit for the given circuit, which consists of the Thevenin equivalent voltage, V_{Th}, and the Thevenin equivalent resistance, R_{Th}. Figure A1–28 illustrates the concept. Although dc batteries are drawn in the figure, the theorem is also valid for a collection of ac voltage sources and resistors. (If capacitors are present, the theorem applies only at sufficiently low frequencies.) This diagram should impress on us the fact that although a box may contain a complicated voltage/resistor circuit, the electrical behavior of the two terminals from the box is just the same as if the circuit were very simple: merely a voltage source in series with a resistor. Chapter A5 exploits this remarkable fact; it is basically what permits us to characterize and work rather easily with integrated circuit amplifiers (indeed any amplifier) that may in fact contain a complicated voltage/resistor circuit. The actual interior design of these devices does not greatly concern us.

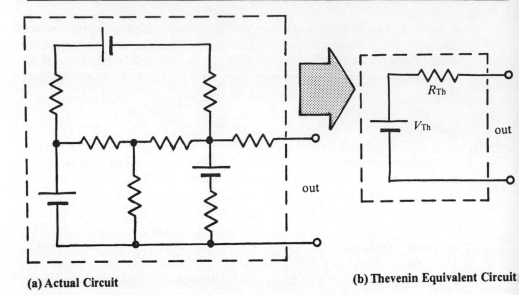

(a) Actual Circuit   (b) Thevenin Equivalent Circuit

FIGURE A1–28. *Conceptual Equivalence of Thevenin's Theorem*

However, Thevenin's Theorem can also be a very effective technique for analyzing or understanding circuits. Thus, later in this section Thevenin's Theorem is demonstrated in contrast to the rather traditional circuit analysis technique based directly on Kirchhoff's Laws of Networks.

The question immediately before us is: How do we find the voltage of the single battery (the Thevenin equivalent voltage) and the resistance of the single resistor (the Thevenin equivalent resistance) that are in the Thevenin equivalent box?

We may be faced with (1) a theoretical circuit, for which the Thevenin equivalent is desired; or (2) a laboratory situation where a circuit is literally in a box and the elements of the equivalent circuit must be found by experimental measurements. The rules for the two situations will now be considered.

Theoretical case

1. Replace all batteries in the circuit with wires and compute the theoretical resistance that appears between the two output terminals. This is the Thevenin equivalent resistor R_{Th}.
2. Compute the voltage that appears between the output terminals when no load is connected; that is, the voltage as would be measured by an ideal voltmeter connected to the terminals. This is the Thevenin equivalent voltage V_{Th}.

We will not prove the theorem or even this approach to finding the equivalence elements. However, notice that if the actual circuit is as simple as a battery in series with a resistor, this approach clearly gives the correct answer; namely, the circuit itself. It should be noted also that for a circuit as complicated as the one drawn in Figure A1-28a, it may be no easy task to find the solutions. Kirchhoff's laws may need to be applied to a multiloop circuit.

Experimental case

1. Connect a very high impedance voltmeter (approaching the ideal) to the output terminals. Its reading is the Thevenin equivalent voltage V_{Th}.

2a. Connect a very low impedance (approaching the ideal) ammeter to the output and measure the *short circuit current* I_{short}. The Thevenin resistance must be given by

$$R_{Th} = \frac{V_{Th}}{I_{short}}$$ (A1-62)

2b. *Alternate way.* Connect a variable resistance across the output, and monitor the voltage across this resistance with the quality voltmeter. Adjust the resistance until the voltmeter reading is half the open circuit reading of step (1). The value of the attached resistance now equals the Thevenin equivalent resistance. This method is the technique most commonly used.

The generality of these experimental techniques can be proved by assuming Thevenin's Theorem is true. Then the box behaves like the circuit of Figure A1-28b—only a battery in series with a resistance need be imagined. A very good voltmeter will indeed measure the battery voltage since no voltage drop occurs across R_{Th} (no current flows through it). Further, when a load is connected to the equivalent circuit, it should be clear that voltage divider action occurs. The output voltage is reduced to just half the battery voltage V_{Th} when the load resistance equals R_{Th}.

Networks Requiring Kirchhoff's Laws or Thevenin's Theorem for Solution

Consider the circuit shown in Figure A1-29a. We wish to find the current flowing from the 4-volt battery. This is *not* a problem that can be solved by elementary techniques. That is, it is not possible to replace certain resistors with a parallel equivalent or a series equivalent so that a simple circuit is obtained. The circuit *can* be solved by applying Kirchhoff's laws; that is, by obtaining several simultaneous equations from application of Kirchhoff's laws. It can also be solved by use of Thevenin's Theorem, and both approaches are illustrated.

1. *Example:* (Solution by application of Kirchhoff's laws) A current must be chosen for each circuit leg and a direction assumed (see Figure A1–29a). (If a direction is in fact wrong it does not matter; the solution for that current will come out negative.) This is done in Figure A1–29b. Next, Kirchhoff's Current Law is applied to junction J in Figure A1–29b.

$$I_1 + I_3 = I_4 \qquad\qquad \text{(A1–63)}$$

To solve for the three unknown currents (even if only the current in the 3-ohm resistor I_3 is desired) we must find two additional simultaneous equations. These are obtained by applying Kirchhoff's Voltage Law for voltages around two different loops in the circuit. These loops are shown as dashed lines in Figure A1–29b. First consider the left-hand loop that goes counterclockwise around the circuit. Beginning at point B and traveling entirely around and back to B, we have potential rises and falls as follows:

$$+I_4 4\ \Omega + I_1 1\ \Omega - 2\ \text{V} = 0 \qquad\qquad \text{(A1–64)}$$

For the right-hand loop, beginning at point A and moving counterclockwise again, we have

$$+4\ \text{V} - I_3 3\ \Omega - I_4 4\ \Omega = 0 \qquad\qquad \text{(A1–65)}$$

Notice that the trip through the 4 Ω resistance is from (−) to (+) for the path chosen from B, while it is the opposite for the path chosen from A. Thus the signs of the $I_4 4\ \Omega$ term differ in the two equations. Eliminating I_1 and I_4 from the three equations A1–63, A1–64 and A1–65 now gives the solution for I_3. More generally, the three equations can be solved by the method of determinants. The final numerical solution from this method is left to the student to solve in the exercises for this chapter.

2. *Example:* (Solution by application of Thevenin's Theorem) This problem can be solved rather quickly by application of Thevenin's Theorem and serves to illustrate the method and utility of this approach. Imagine that all of the circuit of Figure A1–29a is placed in an imaginary box, *except* for the 4 V battery. This is drawn in Figure A1–30a.

First we work on the Thevenin equivalent resistance. The battery in the box is replaced by a short, and the resistance between points A and B should be calculated, as diagrammed in Figure A1–30b. We see 1 ohm in parallel with 4 ohms (equivalent to 0.8 ohms), which is in turn in series with 3 ohms to give a Thevenin equivalent resistance of 3.8 ohms. Next the Thevenin equivalent voltage is obtained by calculating the voltage appearing between points A and B in Figure A1–30c. This calculation is trivial. The voltage at B relative to A must be the *same* as the voltage at J relative to A (no voltage drop occurs across the

3-ohm resistance since no current flows through it in *this* circuit). But the voltage at J is clearly just 4/5 of 2 V because of voltage divider action between the 1-ohm and 4-ohm resistors. Hence the Thevenin equivalent voltage $V_{Th} = 1.6$ V.

Finally, the current that flows from the 4 V battery in the original circuit is found by connecting the 4 V battery to the simple Thevenin equivalent box as shown in Figure A1–30d. There we see two opposing batteries. Applying Kirchhoff's Voltage Law around this single loop gives

$$4 \text{ V} - I_3 3.8 \ \Omega - 1.6 \text{ V} = 0$$

or

$$I_3 = \frac{4 \text{ V} - 1.6 \text{ V}}{3.8 \ \Omega} = 0.63 \ A$$

The solution here certainly comes more quickly than by Kirchhoff's laws/simultaneous equations approach. We can almost work out I_3 in our heads!

NOTE: The solution of a network problem by use of Thevenin's Theorem is particularly time-saving when only one network current is required, as in the case of the example above. The use of Kirchhoff's laws and solution of the associated simultaneous equations may be equally effective if *all* network currents are desired.

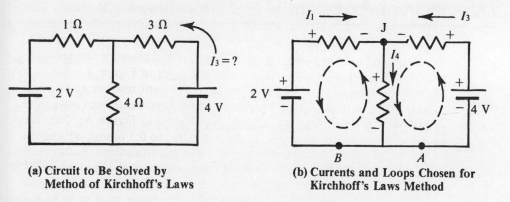

(a) Circuit to Be Solved by
Method of Kirchhoff's Laws

(b) Currents and Loops Chosen for
Kirchhoff's Laws Method

FIGURE A1–29. *Circuit with Application of Kirchhoff's Laws*

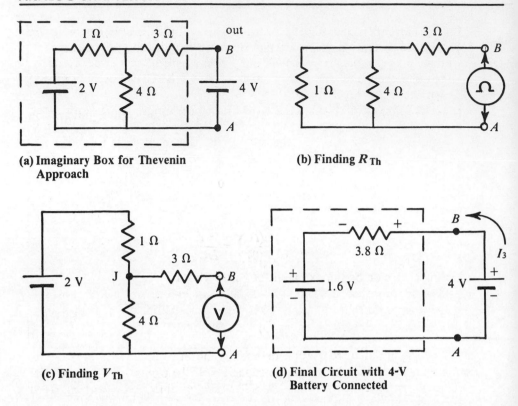

(a) Imaginary Box for Thevenin Approach

(b) Finding R_{Th}

(c) Finding V_{Th}

(d) Final Circuit with 4-V Battery Connected

FIGURE A1-30. *Application of Thevenin's Theorem to a Circuit Problem*

Supplement to Chapter: Derivation of Exponential *RC* Charging Law

We now derive the exponential charging character of an *RC* circuit such as that shown in Figure A1-18a. Suppose the switch is moved from position (1) to (2) in that diagram at time $t = 0$. A time-varying current $i(t)$ then begins to flow through R, and a charge q consequently begins to accumulate on the capacitor. We can write Kirchhoff's Voltage Law around the circuit at any time:

$$V = v_R + v_C \qquad \text{(A1-66)}$$

$$= iR + \frac{q}{C} \qquad \text{(A1-67)}$$

But the current i is the rate that charge arrives on the capacitor, or $i = dq/dt$. Taking the derivative of Equation A1–67 and substituting for i gives

$$0 = R\frac{di}{dt} + \frac{i}{C} \qquad \text{(A1–68)}$$

Now we separate the variables i and t and perform the definite integral on both sides:

$$\int_0^t \frac{di(t)}{i(t)} = -\int_0^t \frac{dt}{RC}$$

which gives

$$\ln\left(\frac{i(t)}{i(0)}\right) = \frac{-t}{RC}$$

Letting each side be the exponent of e now yields

$$\frac{i(t)}{i(0)} = e^{\frac{-t}{RC}} \qquad \text{(A1–69)}$$

The initial current $i(0)$ is determined by Equation A1–67 in conjunction with the initial charge on the capacitor. If the capacitor is initially discharged, we have $i(0) = V/R$. Then $i(t)$ is determined and, working from Equation A1–66, we have

$$v_C = V - v_R = V - iR = V - Ve^{\frac{-t}{RC}}$$

or

$$v_C = V\left(1 - e^{\frac{-t}{RC}}\right) \qquad \text{(A1–70)}$$

This is the voltage across a charging capacitor as indicated in Figure A1–18c. The student should check that it has the correct behavior by mentally substituting $t = 0$ and $t = $ infinity into the equation (to note v_C goes from 0 to the steady battery voltage V).

To find the solution for the case that the switch is moved from (2) to (1) in Figure A1–18a, we notice that we can regard the problem as the same as before but with $V = 0$. But the differential equation A1–67 would still be the same, so that the $i(t)$ solution must again be that of Equation A1–69; only the initial condition $i(0)$ will be different. If the capacitor had become fully charged so that $v_C = V$, then from Equation A1–66 we have at this new initial time that

$$0 = v_R + v_C = i(0)R + V \qquad \text{or} \qquad i(0) = -\frac{V}{R}$$

A43

Then at later times

$$v_C = -iR = Ve^{\frac{-t}{RC}} \tag{A1-71}$$

The expression of Equation A1-71 just represents an exponential decay beginning at V and is also shown in Figure A1-18c. When $t = RC$ (the characteristic time), we have $v_C = Ve^{-1} = 0.367\ V$ and the capacitor voltage has fallen to 37% of its initial value.

REVIEW EXERCISES

1. (a) What is the volt a measure of?
    (b) What are its fundamental units?
2. Criticize the following statement: "The common automobile battery has an emf of 12 V, therefore the lead-acid cell emf is 12 V."
3. Consider the battery types: A. alkaline-manganese, B. carbon-zinc, C. lead-acid, D. mercury, E. nickel-cadmium.
    (a) Which are readily rechargeable?
    (b) Which is noted for a stable terminal voltage during discharge?
    (c) Which is the inexpensive "flashlight" battery?
    (d) Which use paste electrolytes?
    (e) Which has a 2.0 V emf?
    (f) Which has a 1.35 V emf?
    (g) Which types might be used in applications requiring currents of 10 amperes?
    (h) Which type exhibits a quick initial fall in emf while discharging, but remains quite constant for most of the remaining discharge?
4. (a) What is a voltage drop?
    (b) How is it always related to current direction?
5. Which of the following is not expressed in volts? A. potential drop, B. emf, C. potential difference, D. power, E. standard cell voltage.
6. A certain resistor is marked with 3 orange stripes, followed by a gold stripe. Its resistance can be expected to be between what values?
7. Consider the resistor types: A. carbon, B. wirewound, C. metal film, D. oxide film.
    (a) Which two are commonly color coded?
    (b) Which two are used for high precision and stability?
    (c) Which one is not appropriate for radio frequencies?
    (d) Which one is readily available with power ratings over 5 watts?
    (e) Which two have lowest electrical noise?
    (f) Which one is often 10% precision?
8. Select the false statement:
    (a) The resistance of 3 resistors in parallel is less than that of any of the resistors.
    (b) The resistance of 3 resistors in series is less than that of any of the resistors.

(c)   The resistance of 4 identical resistors in parallel is less than that of 3 of said resistors in parallel.

(d)   The resistance of 4 identical resistors in series is more than that of 3 of said resistors in series.

9.   (a)   State Kirchhoff's Current Law.
     (b)   State Kirchhoff's Voltage Law.

10.   (a)   What is the difference between an emf and a voltage drop?
      (b)   Can a voltmeter detect which is which?

11.   Which term does not belong? A. potentiometer, B. transformer, C. rheostat, D. variable resistor.

12.   What happens to the capacitance of a capacitor if:
      (a)   The area is doubled.
      (b)   The distance between the plates is doubled.
      (c)   The dielectric constant of its dielectric is doubled.

13.   Consider the following capacitor types: A. ceramic, B. electrolytic, C. mica, D. mylar, E. paper, F. polystyrene, G. tantalum.
      (a)   What does the term for each type refer to?
      (b)   Which types can be found with a capacitance of 500 microfarads?
      (c)   Which types are polarized (proper voltage polarity must be used)?
      (d)   Which type is useful because of its low inductance (and is not polarized)?
      (e)   Which types are useful for low leakage and low price?
      (f)   Which often has a disc shape?

14.   What is the most common electrical circuit that is the basis for timing (causing certain time delays, and so forth) in electronic circuits?

15.   Consider the circuit shown in Diagram A1-1. Each resistor is 10 Ω, the capacitor is 1 μF, and the battery is 2 V. The switch is closed and we wait a few seconds before reading the voltmeters. What do voltmeters V_1 and V_2 read?

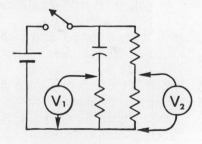

DIAGRAM A1-1.

16.   Name the electrical quantity corresponding to each of the following units:
      (a)   coulomb   (e)   watt
      (b)   ampere   (f)   farad
      (c)   volt   (g)   henry
      (d)   ohm

17.   Why does increasing the number of wire turns in a coil (with length and diameter held constant) increase the inductance of the coil? (In fact, the inductance is approximately proportional to the square of the number of turns.)

18.   (a)   If the frequency of the voltage that is applied to a capacitor is doubled, what happens to the current through the capacitor? (Assume other factors remain constant.)

    (b)   Substitute inductor for capacitor in part (a).

19. (a)   What is the effect of an ideal inductor in a dc circuit?

    (b)   What is the effect of an ideal capacitor in a dc circuit?

20. (a)   What is the difference between a standard transformer and an autotransformer?

    (b)   Why might you risk touching *one* output lead from a 200-V secondary of a standard transformer, but not a lead from even a 2-V autotransformer secondary?

21. A transformer (alone) cannot "transform" a dc voltage to another dc voltage. Why not?

22. (a)   What is the phase relationship between the ac current passing through a capacitor and the voltage across it?

    (b)   Substitute inductor for capacitor in part (a).

23. The concept of capacitor reactance may be applied directly for the voltage-current relationship of a capacitor in which situation? A. sinusoidal applied voltage, B. square-wave applied voltage, C. sawtooth applied voltage, D. dc applied voltage.

24. Consider a resistor and capacitor connected in series, with 3 ac voltmeters connected as shown in Diagram A1–2. A certain ac current is flowing.

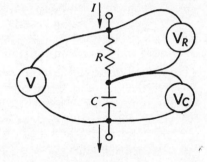

    (a)   It is *not* true that $V = V_R + V_C$, where the Vs here are voltmeter readings. Discuss briefly why it is not.

    (b)   Write a correct relationship between the three voltmeter readings.

DIAGRAM A1–2.

25. Where is the term *half-power frequency* used? What does it refer to?

26. What type of filter is represented by the circuit drawn in Diagram A1–3? Make a verbal (qualitative) argument to justify your answer.

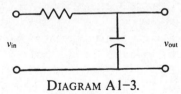

DIAGRAM A1–3.

27. Sketch the output/input voltage versus frequency for a low-pass filter. Identify the half-power frequency f_o quantitatively in the sketch.

PROBLEMS

1. What is the resistance of a rod of carbon (to be used in a carbon composition resistor) that has a diameter of 2 mm and a length of 1 cm?

2. At times it is useful to wind your own resistor from nichrome wire. If a 0.100-ohm

resistor is to be made from number 22 wire-gauge nichrome wire, what length should it have? Look up the diameter of number 22 wire in a reference such as *The Handbook of Chemistry and Physics* or *The Radio Amateur's Handbook*. It is useful to note the various standards of the past; assume AWG (American Wire Gauge), which is the same as B&S (Brown and Sharp).

3. This exercise suggests the use of an OEM (original equipment manufacturer) electronic catalog. (Indeed, thumb through it to note the range of items available.) Examples in the United States are the Newark, Allied, Cramer, and Hamilton-Avnet electronics catalogs. Look up the prices for the AA-size ("penlight") battery for each of the types listed below. You may need to find AA dimensions and use them for some types. Compute the price ratio of each of the others to carbon-zinc.

   (a) carbon-zinc   (c) alkaline
   (b) nickel-cadmium   (d) mercury

4. What is the (warm) resistance of a 100-watt light bulb that operates from 110 V?

5. An inexpensive and widely used resistance box contains 1-watt 10% carbon resistors. A switch selects the desired resistor.

   (a) What is the maximum current that may pass respectively through the 47-ohm and 47-kilohm resistors within it?
   (b) What is the maximum voltage that may be applied respectively to the 47-ohm and 47-kilohm resistors?

6. Suppose 3 resistors of 1 kΩ, 2 kΩ, and 3 kΩ are connected in series to a 6-V battery.

   (a) Diagram the problem (schematic diagram).
   (b) What current flows from the battery, and what power is delivered by it? (Express in mA and mW, respectively.)
   (c) What is the voltage across each resistor?
   (d) Verify that they add up to the applied voltage.

   NOTE: Volts = milliamps × kilohms; it is usually convenient in electronics to work in mA and kΩ units for current and resistance, respectively.

7 Suppose 3 resistors of 1 kΩ, 2 kΩ, and 3 kΩ are connected in parallel to a 6-V battery.

   (a) Draw the schematic circuit for the problem.
   (b) What is the effective resistance connected to the battery?
   (c) What is the battery current drain?
   (d) Find the current in each resistor and verify that they sum up to the answer in part (c).

8. (a) Consider the circuit pictured in Diagram A1–4. Find the current in the 3-Ω, 6-Ω, and 5-Ω resistors. Also find the voltage across each.

   (b) Multiply each resistance in the figure by 1000; that is, change from Ω to kΩ. Again find all currents and voltages.

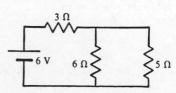

DIAGRAM A1–4.

9. Consider the circuit pictured in Diagram A1–5. Find the current flowing in each resistor. Note all resistances are in *kilohms*.

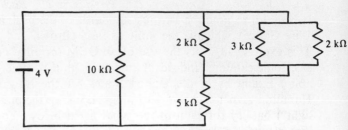

DIAGRAM
A1–5.

10. The 3 resistors pictured in Diagram A1–6 are in some op-amp circuit, but the details of the rest of the circuit are not drawn and do not matter here.
    (a) What are the readings of the 3 voltmeters?
    (b) Diagram the circuit and show the more positive test prod of each voltmeter (this is conventionally the red test prod).

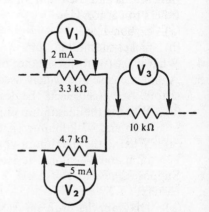

DIAGRAM A1–6.

11. An electronic device of some sort is connected in the circuit shown in Diagram A1–7. The milliammeter *A* reads 12 mA. What is the reading of the voltmeter *V*?

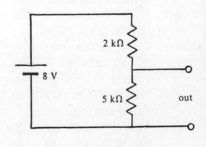

DIAGRAM A1–7.

12. Two resistors are connected to form a voltage divider as shown in Diagram A1–8.
    (a) What is the voltage out when nothing is connected to it?
    (b) Assume a 6-kΩ resistance is connected to the output. What voltage appears across the output?
    (c) When an unknown resistance is connected to the output, its

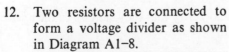

DIAGRAM A1–8.

voltage is observed to decrease to 80% of the value in part (a). What is the value of the resistance?

13. Suppose a paper capacitor is to be constructed with a capacitance of 0.01 μF. If the thickness of the paper is 0.1 mm and its (relative) dielectric constant is 2, what area is required for each plate?

14. Suppose a disc-ceramic capacitor is to be constructed with a capacitance of 0.01 μF. The thickness of the ceramic is 0.1 mm and its relative dielectric constant is 1000. What area is required for each plate?

15. Suppose a 10-kΩ resistor, a 2-μF capacitor, and a switch are connected in series to a 20-V battery, as shown in Figure A1−18a. Also suppose the switch has been in position (1) for a long time and is switched to position (2) at $t = 0$. Calculate and plot the voltage across the capacitor v_C for the time interval from 0 up to 3 characteristic times. Perhaps a dozen points will do. You should obtain the rising part of the charge/discharge plot in Figure A1−18c.

16. An important integrated circuit discussed in Chapter A7 (the 555 timer) makes use of an RC charging circuit. In one connection, it performs a test on a charging capacitor, asking "When does the capacitor's voltage reach 2/3 of the charging voltage?" Thus, in the circuit pictured in Diagram A1−9, what time is required for the capacitor voltage to reach 6.00 V after switch S is opened?

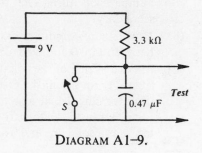

DIAGRAM A1−9.

17. A certain voltage is characterized by the expression

$$v = 5 \text{ V} \sin (0.0628 \text{ sec}^{-1} t)$$

The argument of the sine function is in radians. Give the following characteristics for it:

(a) average voltage
(b) peak voltage
(c) peak-to-peak voltage

(d) rms voltage
(e) frequency
(f) period

18. Consider the circuit pictured in Diagram A1−10. Make a moderately accurate sketch of the voltage between the terminals versus time.

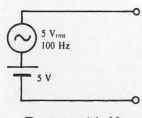

DIAGRAM A1−10.

19. Write out a derivation for the effective capacitance of 3 capacitors connected in series; that is, derive Equation A1–32 for Figure A1–17.
    NOTE: The same charge flows onto each capacitor.

20. (a) Assume that a 1-μF capacitor is connected to a 6.3-V_{rms} voltage. Find the rms current flowing through the capacitor if the frequency is 60 Hz, and also if it is 10 kHz.
    (b) Assume a 1-mH (millihenry) choke is connected instead to the 6.3-V_{rms} source. Find the currents for the two frequencies.

21. Consider the transformer with the primary and secondary windings pictured in Diagram A1–11. Tap B is actually connected to the earth and is a true ground.

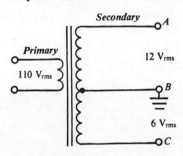

DIAGRAM A1–11.

    (a) If there are 5000 turns on the primary, what is the total number of turns in the secondary?

    (b) How many windings exist between tap B and lead C?

    (c) Make a sketch of the voltage (relative to ground) versus time for tap A and also for tap C. Draw the voltage from tap A as a solid line and from C as dashed, and on the same graph.
    NOTE: The voltage at C is 180° out of phase with the voltage at A.

22. Assume that a resistance R_s is connected to the secondary of a transformer, that Equation A1–53 is valid for the transformer, and that the transformer is ideal; that is, all power presented to the primary of the transformer is passed to the output of the secondary. Show that the impedance R_p, presented by the primary to any ac voltage source connected to it, is given by

$$R_p = \left(\frac{N_p}{N_s}\right)^2 R_s$$

    where R_s is the resistance connected to the secondary
    NOTE: Evaluate the ratio of the primary voltage to primary current. This ratio is the *input impedance* of the transformer; we see that a transformer may be used to "transform impedance" in ac circuits (but not for dc circuits). R_p may be smaller or larger than R_s.

23. Consider an RC high-pass filter such as shown in Figure A1–25. Assume that $V_{in} = 10\ V_{rms}$, $C = 0.01\ \mu F$, and $R = 10\ k\Omega$.
    (a) If the voltage frequency is 1 kHz, find:
        (1) current flowing
        (2) voltage across the resistor
        (3) voltage across the capacitor
        (4) ratio V_{out}/V_{in}
        (5) power factor angle

(6)   average power delivered by the ac voltage source

(b)   What is the half-power frequency for this circuit?

24.   Suppose we construct an RC high-pass filter from a 0.01-μF capacitor and a 4.7-kΩ resistor.

(a)   Diagram the circuit.

(b)   What is the half-power frequency for this filter?

(c)   At what frequency is V_{out}/V_{in} equal to 0.1?

(d)   At what frequency is V_{out}/V_{in} equal to 0.9?

(e)   Could this filter be used to reduce 60-Hz line frequency interference in a signal?

25.   (a)   Consider an RC high-pass filter such as shown in Figure A1–25. Give an argument to support the fact that the maximum power delivered by the constant voltage source must occur at high frequencies. Deduce a formula for this maximum power in terms of just V and R.

(b)   Show that when the frequency is such that $X_C = R$, the power delivered by the constant voltage source is half of the value given by the formula in part (a).

26.   (a)   Design an RC high-pass filter circuit that has $V_{out}/V_{in} = 0.5$ at 5 kHz. At very high frequency, the filter is to present an impedance of 1000 Ω at its input.

(b)   What is the phase of V_{out} relative to V_{in} at this frequency (5 kHz)?

27.   (a)   Design an RC low-pass filter that has $V_{out}/V_{in} = 0.707$ at 1 kHz. At very high frequencies, the impedance at the filter input is to be 500 Ω.

(b)   What is the phase of V_{out} relative to V_{in} at this frequency?

28.   Consider an inductor connected to a resistor as shown in Diagram A1–12.

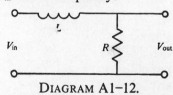

V_{in} R V_{out}

DIAGRAM A1–12.

(a)   Make a qualitative argument for the type of filter this is.

(b)   Derive an expression for V_{out} in terms of V_{in}, R, and X_L. Include a diagram similar to Figure A1–25b in your derivation.

NOTE: Although it does not influence the expression deduced here, V_L should point upward, rather than down as V_C does. Why?

29.   Solve the simultaneous equations A1–62, A1–63, and A1–64 to find the unknown currents in Figure A1–29. The current I_3 should agree with that found in the text by application of Thevenin's Theorem.

30.   Find the Thevenin equivalent circuit for the circuit pictured in Diagram A1–13.

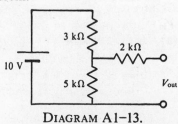

3 kΩ

2 kΩ

10 V

5 kΩ V_{out}

DIAGRAM A1–13.

31. Consider the circuit of Figure A1–29.
   (a) Calculate the current through the 2-V battery by applying Thevenin's Theorem. Assume the 2-V battery to be outside an imaginary box that contains all the other circuit elements (properly connected).
   (b) Finally, assume the 4-Ω resistor is outside the Thevenin box. Calculate the current through it. Now all the circuit currents have been obtained.
32. Consider the circuit drawn in Diagram A1–14.
   (a) Find the Thevenin equivalent circuit for the circuit in the box in Diagram A1–14. Make a drawing of the equivalent circuit, with the values of the components specified.
   (b) Find the current through the 1-V battery. Is the battery charging or discharging?

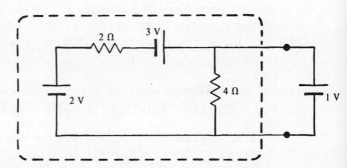

DIAGRAM
A1–14.

33. The *superposition theorem* for electrical circuits is rather simple and makes a problem like that in Figure A1–29 rather easy to solve. The theorem is this: "The current in each leg of a circuit can be obtained by calculating the current in each leg, assuming only one battery in the entire circuit is active at one time; all the others should be shorted. Then the actual current in any particular leg is the algebraic sum of the contributing currents in that leg, caused by all the batteries simultaneously." For example, in Figure A1–29 the current in the 1-Ω resistor is the sum of the current that would flow in it if only the 2-V battery were present (and the 4-V battery replaced by a short) plus the current if only the 4-V battery were present. Solve for the 3 currents in Figure A1–29 by use of the superposition theorem. These solutions may be checked with earlier solutions.

34. (a) An ideal battery is a constant voltage source. Show that a large voltage source in series with a very large resistor (as shown in Diagram A1–15) performs nearly like a constant current source. (For example, show that the current that passes from the source is nearly constant no matter what resistance (with-

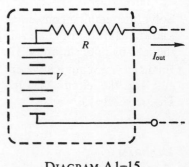

DIAGRAM A1–15.

in limits) is connected as load to the source.)

(b) What determines the value of the constant current?

(c) What limits the resistance of the load for proper operation?

(d) Are there limits on any voltages that may be present in a circuit connected to this constant-current source?

35. *Norton's Theorem* is a close relative of Thevenin's Theorem. It states that a circuit containing an arbitrary connection of batteries and resistors (and also constant-current sources) between two terminals will behave as though just a resistance in parallel with a constant-current source is connected between the two terminals (see Diagram A1–16). The circle with enclosed arrow represents the constant-current source, and I_N is the Norton equivalent current. R_N is the Norton equivalent resistance. Find the Norton equivalent circuit of a battery V in series with a resistance R (that is, for a Thevenin equivalent circuit). Justify your answers.

NOTE: Consider short-circuit output current and open-circuit output voltage of both the actual circuit and the Norton equivalent circuit.

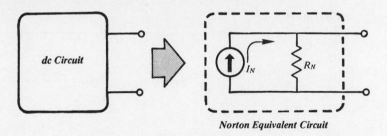

DIAGRAM
A1–16.

Norton Equivalent Circuit

36. (a) Consider an *RC* filter (either high-pass or low-pass) that is well beyond the breakpoint frequency and into the attenuation region in terms of frequency. Show that V_{out}/V_{in} changes by a factor of 10 for every factor-of-10 change in frequency.

(b) Suppose we make a plot of $\log(V_{out}/V_{in})$ versus $\log f$. Base-10 logarithms are used. This log-log plot is often called a *Bode plot*. Show that well into the attenuation region, the plot is a straight line with slope -1 for a low-pass filter and slope $+1$ for a high-pass filter.

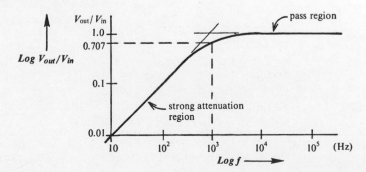

DIAGRAM
A1–17.

NOTE: Then the Bode plot is simple to draw over most of the "curve." The drawing (Diagram A1–17) shows the Bode plot for a high-pass filter with a breakpoint frequency of 1 kHz. Note that the straight-line asymptotes cross at this frequency.

37. Suppose two *RC* filters are cascaded as pictured in Diagram A1–18. The buffer represents a factor-of-1 amplifier that simply passes the voltage from the output of the first filter to the input of the second. (We learn in Chapter A6 how simple it is to design one of these with an op amp.) The buffer has no effect on the output voltage of the first filter. Show that in the low-frequency attenuation region, the attenuation of the overall filter changes by a factor of 10^2 for every factor-of-10 change in frequency. This is an example of a *second-order filter*. What is its advantage?

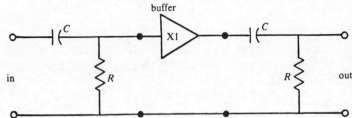

DIAGRAM
A1–18.

Important Electronic Instruments

There are a number of electrical and electronic instruments that are routinely used in electronics practice and in electronics-based laboratory experimentation. Much of this equipment is used to measure the voltage, current, or resistance presented by an electronic circuit or by the actual laboratory phenomenon being studied. Thus, various electronic measuring devices are commonly used for testing electronic circuits either in the design phase or after they are being used in the laboratory. Moreover, an experimental phenomenon may also be measured or monitored with this equipment. If the phenomenon is not inherently electrical, it is often made so through the use of *transducers*—the topic of Chapter A3.

Consequently, it is very desirable to have a basic understanding of the principles of operation, operating techniques, and capabilities and limitations of the various common electronic measuring instruments. These aspects are discussed in this chapter for the various types of meters available, such as the VOM, FTVM, and DVM. The Wheatstone bridge is discussed in some detail, since this circuit is widely used to measure phenomena that are manifested through a changing resistance. Particular attention is paid to the modern triggered-sweep oscilloscope, since this is a very versatile laboratory instrument with a number of operating modes. The chapter also considers electronic equipment that is used to generate various forms of ac voltage. Instruments to measure the frequency of ac waveforms are then discussed. The chapter concludes with a discussion of the practical techniques used to electrically connect measuring instruments to electronic circuits; however, these methods are also important because they are used to interconnect electronic equipment generally.

Basic Meters

D'Arsonval Meter

The student should already be familiar with the essentials of the moving coil or *d'Arsonval meter*. Though now being replaced by digital (all electronic) meters, it still has a place as an inexpensive and handy device. The movement responds to current. When current flows through the windings of the armature or coil, the coil experiences a force due to nearby permanent magnets. Actually, a torque is produced on the coil that turns it against the counter-torque of a coil spring, or a *taut band* suspension. A twist of the suspension proportional to the current results, and an attached needle moves over a scale. The meter is characterized by its resistance and by the current required to move the needle to a full-scale reading or the *full-scale sensitivity;* for example, a 50-microamperes movement, or a 1-milliamperes movement. If the meter is used only in its basic form (often with zero at the center of scale of travel for the needle), it is called a *galvanometer*.

Ammeter

Frequently the "bare" d'Arsonval meter is too sensitive for common current measurements. A bypass or *shunt* resistance R_{sh} is then arranged around the meter as shown in Figure A2–1. In essence, a galvanometer is shunted to increase its range (see Figure A2–1a). The desired full-scale reading I is related to the shunt current I_{sh} and movement current I_m by

$$I = I_{sh} + I_m \qquad \text{(A2–1)}$$

The full-scale sensitivity I_m and resistance of the movement coil R_m must be known to proceed in a design. The voltage across the movement V_m for full-scale deflection is calculated to be

$$V_m = I_m R_m \qquad \text{(A2–2)}$$

This voltage also is responsible for the shunt current I_{sh}. We have

$$V_m = I_{sh} R_{sh} = (I - I_m) R_{sh} = I_m R_m \qquad \text{(A2–3)}$$

Then

$$R_{sh} = \frac{R_m}{(I/I_m) - 1} \qquad \text{(A2–4)}$$

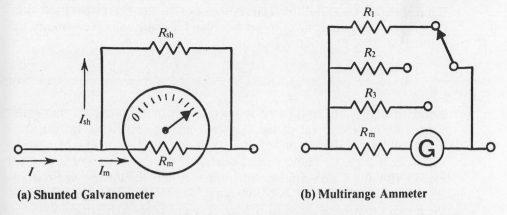

(a) Shunted Galvanometer　　　　　　(b) Multirange Ammeter

FIGURE A2–1　*Construction of an Ammeter from a Sensitive D'Arsonval Meter*

A switch can be used to make a more versatile multirange instrument as shown in Figure A2–1b. There will typically then be several rows of numbers along the scale; an appropriate row is used (with the markings) depending on the switch setting.

Voltmeter

The d'Arsonval meter is basically an ammeter, but it may be used to measure voltages if the movement is quite sensitive. A series resistance R_s is connected to the movement such that the desired voltage must appear across the meter when the full-scale current I_m passes through the meter (see Figure A2–2a). Let the desired full-scale voltage be V. We have $V = I_m(R_s + R_m)$ from which the required series resistance in terms of the known I_m, R_m, and V is obtained; that is,

$$R_s = \frac{V}{I_m} - R_m \qquad \text{(A2–5a)}$$

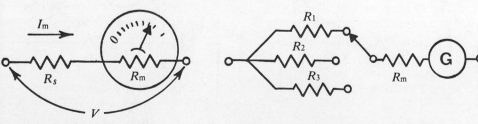

(a) Series "Multiplier" Resistor
　 Added to Movement

(b) Multirange Voltmeter

FIGURE A2–2.　*Construction of a Voltmeter from a D'Arsonval Meter*

But it is useful to examine the total resistance of the voltmeter when used with the proper multiplier resistor to get a certain full-scale voltage capability. It is obtained from Equation A2–5a as

$$R_s + R_m = V\left(\frac{1}{I_m}\right) \qquad \text{(A2–5b)}$$

Notice that the total resistance is obtained by multiplying the full-scale voltage by the reciprocal of the full-scale current sensitivity. In fact, this reciprocal has the dimensions of ohms/volt. Thus if $I_m = 50$ microamperes, the meter is a 20,000 ohms/volt voltmeter. If such a movement is used to make a 10 V full-scale voltmeter, the resistance between the *testing prods* of the voltmeter will be 10 V $\times$ 20,000 ohms/volt = 200 kilohms. Notice that the higher the voltage range is, the larger is the meter resistance.

To construct a versatile meter with several ranges, a switch that connects to one of several multiplier resistors is commonly used, as shown in Figure A2–2b.

Ohmmeter

If a known voltage is placed across an unknown resistance and the resulting current through the resistor is measured, the resistance may be calculated from Ohm's Law: $R = V/I$. Typically, ohmmeters use a carbon-zinc battery to supply the voltage and the movement responds to the current. A scale is then marked off to read resistance directly; however, the scale is not linear, since the resistance is proportional to the reciprocal of the current.

Carbon-zinc dry cells show a marked decrease in terminal voltage over their useful life. Therefore a potentiometer is typically placed in the circuit to *zero adjust* the meter (see Figure A2–3a and b). When the leads of the ohm-

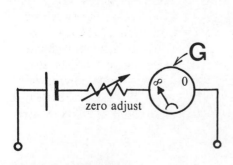

(a) Basic Circuit with Galvanometer G

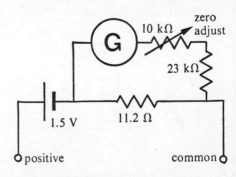

(b) Simpson VOM Ohmmeter for $R \times 1$ Scale

FIGURE A2–3. *Ohmmeter*

meter are connected together, the zero adjust knob should be used to cause the needle to point to zero ohms (full-scale current). Note that leaving the leads shorted for a length of time will drain the ohmmeter batteries. If the zero adjustment cannot be made, the batteries are probably old and need replacement.

Measuring Instruments

VOM, FTVM, and VTVM

The volt-ohm meter, commonly called a VOM or a multimeter, is a handy combination ac/dc voltmeter, ohmmeter, and ammeter with switch selectibility. A sensitivity of 20,000 ohms/volt is quite common and implies a 50-microamperes movement so that we can expect the most sensitive current range to be 50 microamperes as well. Resistors of 1% accuracy are typical, and a 2% overall dc accuracy is therefore common. D'Arsonval-type meters with an accuracy of 1/2% exist, but are rare.

To obtain a much higher resistance—and thus approach the ideal more closely—electronic amplifying circuits are used to obtain the *vacuum tube voltmeter* (VTVM) or the more modern *field-effect transistor voltmeter* (FTVM). A maximum *grid-leak resistor* or *gate-leak resistor* of about 10 megohms is typically found in the input amplifier of these units; it is literally connected between the two test prod inputs and determines the input impedance of these meters. Therefore it is constant on most ranges. These voltmeters typically can measure a wide range of dc or ac voltage, but not current.

The typical scheme for ac voltage measurement in both VOMs and VTVMs is to rectify and filter the ac voltage to produce a dc voltage equal to the peak-to-peak ac voltage. Indeed, a *peak-peak ac scale* typically exists on VTVMs. However, the rms scale is simply set to be 0.707/2 times the peak-peak scale; this is correct for the sinusoidal waveform, but will be wrong for other waveforms. The peak-peak scale, however, is correct for any waveform.

VTVMs require some minutes for the tubes to warm up after turn-on. Furthermore, a zero adjust occurs for use on all scales, not just the ohmmeter scale. There is also an *infinity adjust* for the ohms setting on VTVMs. Even though VTVMs must be plugged into a wall socket for tube power, they typically have a battery for the ohmmeter circuit. FTVMs are battery-operated and therefore free of the bothersome line cord; they also have little warm-up drift.

Wheatstone Bridge

For more precise measurement of resistance than the few percent afforded by an ohmmeter, the *Wheatstone bridge* has been commonly used since the turn of the century. A square of four resistors is used, with one resistor being the unknown R_x. An *excitation voltage V* is connected across one diagonal, and galvanometer or sensitive voltmeter is connected across the other diagonal as shown in Figure A2–4. Measurement of the unknown R_x uses a null comparison approach and assumes that the other three resistors are known and that one is adjustable.

The bridge is balanced by adjustment of R_3 until no current flows through the galvanometer G. When balanced or nulled, no current flows through G because the voltage at point A (relative to ground gnd, for example) is the same as the voltage at B. But we have two voltage dividers and thus have

$$V_A = \frac{R_2 V}{R_1 + R_2} = V_B = \frac{R_x V}{R_3 + R_x}$$

so that

$$R_x = R_3\left(\frac{R_2}{R_1}\right) \qquad\qquad \text{(A2–6)}$$

For precise work the resistors can be 0.1% or even 0.01% with the adjustable resistance being an accurate decade resistance box. Notice that in the *balanced condition,* a change in the excitation voltage V will have no effect.

NOTE: A *decade resistance box* uses a series of switches in order to provide an accurate variable resistance. Each switch S selects one of ten precision resistances for its decade of range. These ranges are connected in series so that a resistance such as 347.6 ohms may be readily selected by adjusting the four corresponding switches.

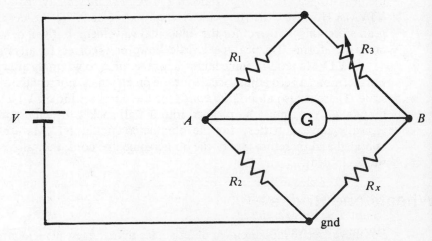

FIGURE A2–4. *Schematic Diagram of the Basic Wheatstone Bridge*

However, many contemporary applications of the Wheatstone bridge use it in an *out-of-balance* mode. (Accurate measurements of resistance are now made more quickly with a good digital voltmeter.) Many experimental parameters can be monitored through a resistive effect, as discussed in Chapter A3. That is, a change in the parameter causes a change in the resistance of a *resistive transducer*. For changes in R_x of up to 10%, the bridge voltage V_{AB} is quite linearly proportional to $\triangle R_x$. Furthermore, suppose the transducer is susceptible to a second parameter such as temperature. The effect of such variations can be minimized by making R_2 an identical device that experiences the same extraneous effect—for example, temperature— but not the actual parameter to be measured. We can see that even though R_2 and R_x may vary due to this same parameter, they will do so to the same extent, and no out-of-balance condition will result.

Suppose that the resistances R_1, R_2, and R_3 in these three arms of a Wheatstone bridge are all equal to R. Then it is readily seen that at balance the resistance R_x is also equal to R. This is a simple and convenient bridge configuration for use and for analysis of the out-of-balance mode of operation. Suppose the transducer resistance changes by an amount $\triangle R$, and the excitation voltage is V. The chapter Problems show that the out-of-balance voltage (or signal) V_{out} from the bridge output is given by

$$V_{\text{out}} = V_B - V_A = \left(\frac{V}{4}\right)\left(\frac{\triangle R}{R}\right) \tag{A2-7}$$

provided $\triangle R/R$ is much less than one. Thus the output signal is proportional to the fractional change in the transducer resistance. Also notice that the signal depends on the excitation voltage; therefore, this voltage must be stable for accurate out-of-balance operation.

Potentiometer

The *potentiometer* is a null comparison device that measures voltage and has been in use where high precision is needed since the turn of the century. It has now been largely replaced by the *digital voltmeter*, which is just as accurate and a good deal faster to use. However, voltage standardization still often uses a potentiometer. Also, the potentiometer has the interesting characteristic that at null, no current is drawn from the source being measured. In this sense it becomes an ideal voltmeter. (It does draw or deliver current when off balance, however.)

The circuit for the basic potentiometer is shown in Figure A2–5. The R_A *working current* adjustment potentiometer is adjusted until the voltage at point T is, for example, 1.500 V. Then the unknown voltage V_x is connected through a galvanometer to the movable contact of the main potentiometer R (from which the name *potentiometer* derives). The contact is then moved

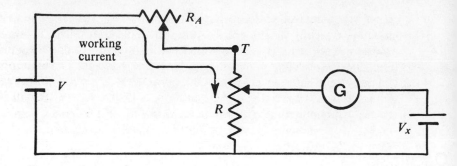

FIGURE A2–5. *Basic Potentiometer Voltage-Measuring Circuit*

until G reads zero. At this balance the unknown voltage V_x must equal the voltage at the movable contact; this is the reason no current flows through the detecting meter.

If the potentiometer R has high linearity, the fractional position of the slider can be used to calculate the voltage at its position by taking this fraction of the known voltage at T. There is one problem remaining, and that is to adjust the voltage at T accurately by adjustment of R_A. This may be done by connecting a *standard cell*—that is, a standard single cell battery for which the voltage is accurately known—to the *unknown* V *terminals* V_x. However, in this case V_x *is* accurately known. Then the potentiometer R is set to the fraction corresponding to this accepted voltage, and R_A is adjusted until G reads zero. The potentiometer is now calibrated. An unknown voltage may be determined by connecting it to the V_x terminal in place of the standard cell and balancing the potentiometer as discussed above.

Digital Voltmeter (DVM)

If for no other reason, the d'Arsonval meter is limited in accuracy by the degree to which the scale can be read by the eye (of course, bearing friction, nonlinearity of the magnetic field or of the coil spring are other likely problems). *Digital voltmeters* (DVM) use electronic circuits to convert a voltage or current to a number that is then read from a numeric display. Any number of digits can in principle be read by the eye in this case. The trick is to design electronic circuits of sufficient accuracy and linearity.

Details of the way a voltage or current can be digitized are part of a digital electronics course; however, certain features should be mentioned here. Since the voltage to be measured is presented to the input of an amplifier, the resistance of the voltmeter is generally independent of the range used. Ten megohms is a typical value. Some DVMs have *autoranging,* meaning the measuring range—or decimal point—is selected automatically to keep the number in the range of the display. *Autopolarity* is quite common: A plus or minus sign lights up to indicate the polarity of the voltage. The DVM accuracy is typically on the order of the least significant digit. However, the accuracy of the ac range is almost always less than that for dc. When using the ohmmeter capability, a definite current (for example, 1 milliampere) is generally sent through the unknown resistance. The meter then reads the voltage across the resistance; for example, if 1-milliampere current is used, the voltage is numerically equal to its resistance in kilohms.

Oscilloscope

Perhaps the most versatile single electrical instrument is the *oscilloscope*. With it one can measure dc voltage and ac voltage quite readily with an accuracy of a few percent. However, its greatest service is drawing a time graph of an arbitrary voltage waveform from which we can see relative voltage levels as they occur in time. Inherent in this application is the ability to measure the time interval between voltage changes that can occur as quickly as a fraction of a microsecond.

Figure A2–6 illustrates the essential parts of the *cathode-ray tube* (CRT) that is the heart of an oscilloscope. Beginning at the left, a heater or filament glows red-hot and boils electrons out of a cathode structure. These electrons are accelerated toward two accelerating anodes that are at rather high positive potentials. However, a negative voltage applied to the grid close to the cathode repels some electrons back toward the cathode and in this way controls the number of electrons that strike the screen at the far right; this in turn controls the spot brightness or intensity. The relative voltages of the two accelerating anodes determine the sharpness of *focus* of the spot formed.

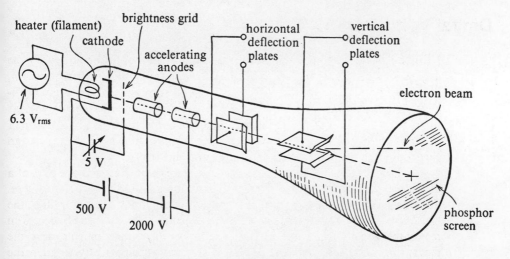

FIGURE A2–6. *Basic Components of a Cathode-Ray Tube*

The anodes are cylinders and consequently the electrons can zip on through toward the deflection plates. If a voltage is connected between a given set of plates, the electrons are attracted toward the more positive plate and the beam is deflected from the straight-through course. When the electrons strike the end of the tube, a phosphor coating on the end emits visible light at the spot of electron bombardment. Figure A2–7 is representative of the controls commonly found on a laboratory-quality oscilloscope. The assortment can be bewildering at first, but they are actually quite understandable.

Most contemporary oscilloscopes are of the *triggered-sweep* variety, with the vertical axis calibrated in volts and the horizontal axis calibrated in time. A *vertical* control selects the desired volts/centimeter for the vertical scale, and a *horizontal* control selects the microseconds/centimeter (or perhaps milliseconds/centimeter or seconds/centimeter) for the horizontal scale. The consequence is that the spot of the electron beam is deflected upward—or downward if the polarity is reversed—by say 1.5 centimeters if a 1.5-V battery is connected to the VERT IN jacks. Meanwhile, a sawtooth voltage generated inside the scope is applied to the horizontal deflection plates, causing the spot to move from left to right at a definite rate of so many centimeters/second.

NOTE: The rate that the spot moves across the screen is the reciprocal of the scale setting selected by the horizontal control knob.

There are usually several knobs that control the *triggering mode* of the scope, and these are a bit more elaborate to understand. The central point to appreciate is that a triggered-sweep scope causes the horizontal sweep of the spot to occur at the same point of the voltage waveform time after time. Only in this way is a stable picture drawn on the scope face (no double exposure or ghost-like traces). When the TRIGGERING MODE is set to one of the *internal modes*—for example, ac, dc, or auto—a monitoring circuit within the scope measures the incoming voltage. Only when the signal reaches a certain *triggering level* selected by the LEVEL knob does it instruct the sweep circuit to begin a sweep. The graph of the waveform then begins at the left of the scope display at this *trigger point*. These features are illustrated in the scope picture of Figure A2–8a. During the *retrace* of the spot from right to left, a *blanking* circuit in the scope extinguishes the unwanted trace. Figure A2–8b shows the sawtooth-like HORIZONTAL SWEEP voltage V_H generated within the scope; this produces the desired horizontal motion of the spot to trace out the graph of the input voltage waveform.

If the LEVEL knob is examined in Figure A2–7, a (+) and a (−) will be noted to either side of a zero. When the LEVEL knob is set to zero, triggering will take place near the point of zero voltage on the input waveform. Turning the knob toward (+) moves the triggering point to a higher (more +) voltage on the waveform, while turning toward (−) moves it to a lower point.

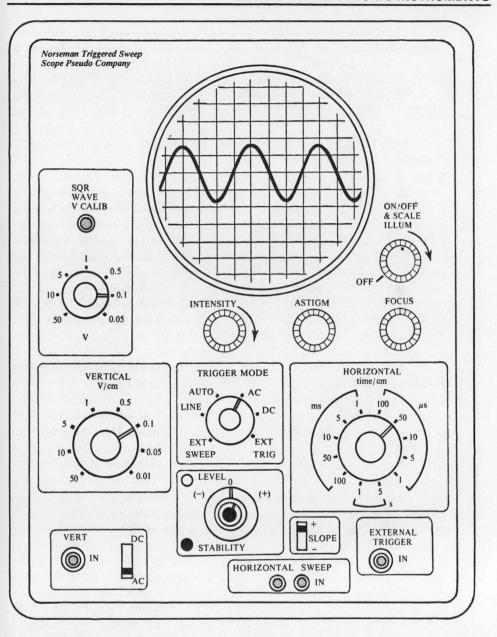

FIGURE A2–7. *Controls Commonly Found on a Laboratory-Quality Triggered-Sweep Oscilloscope*

In addition, most scopes have a (+), (−) SLOPE switch. With this switch, we can choose to begin the trace on the upward (+) slope of the waveform, or the (−) downward slope. Note the (+), (−) indicated points in Figure A2–8a. The scope picture shown assumes that the SLOPE is set to (+).

We now consider the meaning of the various TRIGGER MODE settings.

1. If the mode is in ac or dc, no sweep occurs—that is, the scope is dark—until a voltage with an amplitude above the triggering level is at the scope vertical input.

2. The AUTO mode is convenient in that a trace—that is, a line—is present even with no signal in. It can be reassuring to see that the scope is active and just where the trace is; the absence of vertical deflection shows that there is no substantial signal in the circuit to which the scope is connected. However, we usually lose control over the triggering level in this mode because the scope automatically triggers at somewhere near the middle of the waveform. For some waveforms the trace may be unstable.

3. When the mode is placed to LINE, the sweep occurs in synchronism with the 60-hertz line voltage coming to the scope through the power cord. This is only useful if the signal being observed is itself somehow derived from the domestic power lines, so that it will be stabilized on the scope.

4. In the EXTERNAL TRIGGER mode, the sweep sawtooth is triggered *not* by the signal into the vertical input jack, but rather by whatever waveform is presented to the EXTERNAL TRIGGER IN jack. The triggering level knob now operates relative to this signal. For example, a voltage pulse into a *pulsed nuclear magnetic resonance* (PNMR) spectrometer trig-

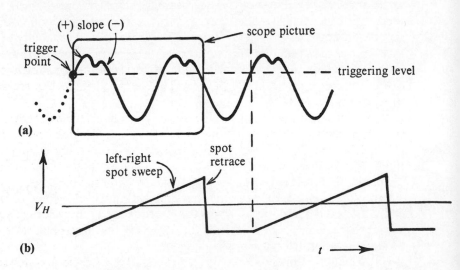

FIGURE A2–8. *Sweep Timing of a Triggered-Sweep Scope*

gers a chain of events that ultimately causes a *transient signal*—that is, a decaying voltage—to be produced by the sample being studied. The signal can be reliably displayed on a scope by connecting the voltage pulse also to the external trigger input and using external trigger mode. The sample signal is input as usual to the vertical input and the sweep will display it nicely. The horizontal time/centimeter knob is still operative.

5. When the TRIGGER MODE is set to EXT SWEEP (external sweep), the horizontal deflection system is disconnected from the sawtooth oscillator and its time/centimeter knob control. Rather it is connected to the HORIZONTAL SWEEP IN jack, and the spot will now move horizontally in the X direction in response to this input signal (in the same manner as the vertical Y motion is controlled by the voltage to the VERTICAL IN jack). The scope is then being used in the X-Y *mode*.

In fact, a true X-Y mode scope has a volts/centimeter knob for the horizontal direction in addition to the one for the vertical direction. It is fun to connect two sine wave oscillators to the vertical input and horizontal sweep inputs and watch the so-called *Lissajous figures* on the scope. See pp. 31–34 of Malmstadt, Enke, and Toren (1963) for a careful pictorial justification of the various figures.

Dual-trace scopes can display time graphs of two different signals simultaneously. Then two vertical input jacks are present, each controlled by a vertical volts/centimeter knob. For example, a dual-trace scope is desirable for displaying the signal into a system and its signal output simultaneously for comparison. It is rather like two scopes for the price of one. However, the two traces are actually displayed alternately one above the other—*alternate sweep*—which works well for signals occurring at rather high frequency so that no flicker is evident. For low-frequency signals the *chopped mode* can be used, where the trace rapidly moves up and down and shows a sample of each input as it moves across the scope face. An additional nice capability of most dual-trace scopes is that the two volts/centimeter controls and jacks are used in the X-Y mode to give true X-Y scope performance (again, the time-base sawtooth is then internally disconnected from the Y axis). The scope pictured in Figure A2–7 is *not* a dual-trace scope.

Triggered-sweep scopes sometimes also have a *stability* control that sets the sensitivity of the sawtooth oscillator. If set too high, the oscillator produces a continuous sawtooth without waiting for a synchronizing trigger point. The sweep then shows a confusing multiple exposure of the waveform connected to its vertical input. In fact, this is the way less-expensive *recurrent-sweep* scopes operate; a stable trace results only if the frequency of the incoming signal is a multiple of the sawtooth frequency, or more correctly, if the sawtooth frequency is so adjusted. Unfortunately, the horizontal scale is not accurately calibrated on this type of scope.

Finally, comment should be made about the *ac/dc mode* switch for the vertical input. For example, it is *not true* that the switch must be set to ac to make measurements on an ac voltage. When set to dc, the spot (trace) will move through a proper vertical deflection even when a dc voltage such as a battery is connected to the vertical input. The trace will also respond to an ac signal presented to the vertical input. However, when set to ac, a capacitor is inserted in series with the input line within the scope. The capacitor serves to block dc voltage but pass ac voltage on through to the amplifiers and scope face. Therefore, in the ac input mode, the scope trace will *not* deflect in response to a battery or other dc voltage that might be connected to the vertical input.

The purpose of the ac mode setting is to permit the vertical scale to be set to a sensitive level so that a small ac voltage "riding atop" a large dc voltage remains on the scope display to be observed. Figure A2–9a illustrates the scope display for a scope in the dc input mode; the scope is receiving an input voltage with both an ac part and a dc part as shown. The dashed line at the bottom of the display represents the trace for zero input voltage. Suppose we want to magnify the display in order to examine the small ac signal more carefully. Unfortunately, if the scope is left in dc input mode and the vertical setting is changed from 5 V/centimeter to 0.5 V/centimeter to accomplish the magnification, the trace will disappear off the top of the visible display. But switching the input mode to ac blocks the offending large dc voltage from reaching the oscilloscope amplifiers, and the enlarged ac voltage is nicely displayed as shown in Figure A2–9b. To summarize: When set to dc, the scope can be used to measure both ac and dc waveforms, but when set to ac, the scope can be used to measure only ac waveforms.

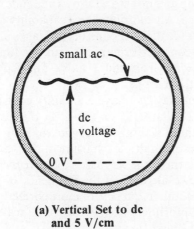

(a) Vertical Set to dc
and 5 V/cm

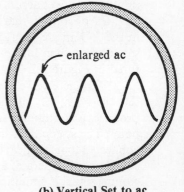

(b) Vertical Set to ac
and 0.5 V/cm

FIGURE A2–9. *Use of the ac/dc Switch on a Scope*

Recorders

There are many circumstances in both science and industry that require a continuous recording over a period of time of some parameter; example parameters are voltage, pressure, temperature, and speed. The recorded data may be analyzed later for an understanding of the phenomenon, or it may be reviewed to be confident that the parameter was maintained within certain tolerances. Frequently, it is helpful to have a time graph of the phenomenon in order to literally see what is going on.

The oscilloscope provides such a time graph, but it is useful primarily for recording rapid phenomena, that is, processes that occur in a time interval of less than a few seconds. For a permanent record, a photograph may be taken of the scope display with a camera designed to be attached to the oscilloscope display bezel. However, for processes that occur over longer time periods, other techniques are generally used.

A recording measuring instrument that has been commonplace for many years in the laboratory is the *strip-chart recorder*. This instrument draws a time graph of the input voltage on a moving strip of paper. Some units use several pens to draw several time graphs simultaneously to the respective input voltages.

A related instrument is the *X-Y recorder*. In this case, the pen moves independently in two dimensions over a fixed piece of paper. The pen moves in the perpendicular X and Y directions in response to two voltages that are input to the respective X and Y inputs. This recorder is often used to present a graph of how one parameter varies in an experiment as a function of some other parameter.

A *magnetic tape recorder* permits the scientist to record data on magnetic tape. In contrast to the recording techniques just described, magnetic tape recording does not produce a graphic picture. On the other hand, it has the advantage that the information is in a *machine-readable form*—that is, the parameter behavior can be later read by an electronic instrument like a computer for further analysis. In contrast, the techniques that directly graph the data on paper generally require a human to read the data in preparation for analysis.

Strip-Chart Recorder

Most strip-chart recorders use a pen to draw a graph of the input voltage on a strip of graph paper as it is dispensed from a roll. The pen is moved laterally across the paper as the paper moves past the pen at a constant rate (see Figure A2–10).

The paper movement rate is often determined by a *synchronous ac motor*. The same type of ac motor is used in the common electric wall clock, and derives its rate from the quite stable frequency of the 60-hertz house power. The user may select gear ratios in the chart-drive mechanism in order to obtain a chart speed that may range from as slow as 1 centimeter/hour to as fast as 10 centimeters/second. However, some more recent recorders use a *stepper motor* to advance a fixed gear train. The stepper motor is an interesting recent motor-type that rotates its shaft through a fixed angular increment in response to each input power pulse. The pulse rate can be produced by accurate digital circuitry, and thus the paper advancement can be accurately selected and controlled.

The lateral pen position must be automatically adjusted by the recorder in proportion to the input voltage. This is generally accomplished with some type of *servomechanism*. A servomechanism is a control system that monitors the position or state of a system in the process of moving the system into the desired position or state. The most common way this is accomplished in a strip-chart recorder is with the aid of a potentiometer; such recorders are generally termed *potentiometric recorders*. The pen of the recorder is

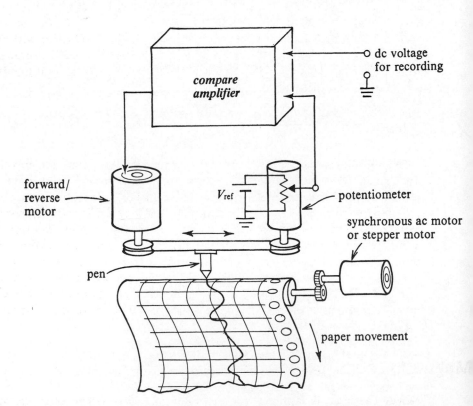

FIGURE A2–10. *System Diagram of a Strip-Chart Recorder*

attached through a cord and pulley system to an electric motor that may turn in either forward or reverse directions. The cord system also turns a multiturn potentiometer. This system is diagrammed in Figure A2–10. The motor receives power to move the pen as long as the pen is not at the proper position corresponding to the input voltage. This is done by having an amplifier compare the voltage from the potentiometer with the dc input voltage. If these two voltages are not the same, the amplifier produces an output with a polarity appropriate to turn the motor and move the pen toward the desired null position. Notice that the servosystem functions as a self-balancing potentiometer voltage-measuring system.

The typical full-scale sensitivity of the basic strip-chart recorder is 10 millivolts dc. If the input parameter is not a dc voltage, it must be converted to one by appropriate electronic circuitry. Some strip-chart recorders include this circuitry internally in order to measure current, resistance, and ac voltage. A control knob very similar to that on a VOM or multimeter is then present in order to permit selection of the function and the full-scale response. The accuracy of the pen position is typically a few tenths of 1 percent, and the response time for the pen to move full scale is generally a few tenths of a second for the motor-driven type.

More rapid response is available in recorders that used special techniques to draw the trace. One approach is to use the needle of a specially designed d'Arsonval meter as the drawing mechanism. Recorders with fast response are generally called *oscillographic recorders.* These recorders can follow a sinusoidal input signal with a frequency of up to several hundred hertz with good fidelity.

X-Y Recorder

The *X-Y* recorder, or plotter, uses two independent servomechanisms that are similar to that just described for the strip-chart recorder. These move the pen in perpendicular directions over a fixed sheet of graph paper or other paper (see Figure A2–11). The full-scale response for each direction is selected by respective control knobs. The response time of the servomechanism and accuracy of the pen position is similar to that just described for the strip-chart recorder. The *X-Y* recorder can also be used to draw a time graph (rather like a strip-chart recorder) if a voltage that increases linearly with time is presented to the *X*-axis input. Some instruments incorporate within them a *ramp voltage* source of this type in order to conveniently permit what is called the *Y-t* mode of operation.

Magnetic Tape Recorder

Nearly everyone is familiar with the common *cassette-type magnetic tape recorder* that was introduced about 1970. Many are also familiar with the high

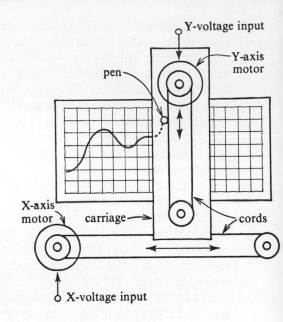

FIGURE A2–11. *Simplified Diagram of an X-Y Recorder*

quality *reel-to-reel magnetic tape recorder;* this type of recorder has been available since about 1960 for high-fidelity music recording. These devices can conveniently record ac voltages that range in frequency from about 50 hertz to 15 kilohertz (namely, the audio frequency range) and can sometimes be used in scientific applications.

NOTE: The recorder should *not* incorporate *automatic gain control* or AGC if the ac playback signal is to faithfully follow the amplitude of the original input signal. AGC automatically adjusts the amplitude of the recorded signal in order to maintain an approximately constant audio level.

Very high quality magnetic tape recorders called *instrumentation recorders* are often used in scientific work. These may be used in *direct recording mode* to record ac voltage signals with frequencies from 50 hertz to as high as 200 kilohertz (the latter frequency is *ultrasonic*). However, they may also be used to record dc voltage or low frequency ac voltage by use of an *FM recording mode.* (The FM mode is discussed later in this chapter.) The FM signal is the signal recorded on the magnetic tape. When the tape is played back, internal electronic circuitry converts back, or *demodulates,* the recorded signal to a voltage signal that corresponds to the original input voltage. Instrumentation recorders can often record several channels simultaneously; four-channel or eight-channel instruments are commonly available.

Signals that have been recorded on magnetic tape may be input to a computer through the use of one of several techniques. In one technique the voltage output from the instrumentation recorder may be input to an *analog-to-digital converter* or *ADC*. This device produces as output a number that is proportional to the input voltage, and this output number is in the form of digital voltages with which a computer works internally. (The ADC is discussed in *Digital and Microprocessor Electronics for Scientific Application*.) Another technique uses FM recording of the signal essentially as described above. At the time of playback, the frequency of the signal recorded on tape may be measured with a frequency counter. As mentioned, the frequency is proportional to the original input voltage. The frequency counter should output a number in the form of digital voltages appropriate for input to a computer. Frequency counters are briefly discussed later in this chapter, and also in detail in the *Digital and Microprocessor Electronics for Scientific Application* by Barnaal.

Other Instruments and Instrument Aspects

Signal Generator

Although not used of themselves to measure electrical quantities, instruments that generate voltage waveforms of various frequencies and amplitudes are often useful for testing equipment, as well as for incorporation into various experiment systems. It was mentioned earlier that the sinusoidal waveform is fundamental, and units that produce this form as output have long been available. Some sort of oscillating circuit is involved, and the sine-wave generator is therefore frequently referred to as an *oscillator*. A given circuit is usually limited in the range of frequencies over which it will operate; therefore, a given oscillator is usually an *audio oscillator* (frequency range about 1 hertz to 100 kilohertz), or a *radio frequency oscillator* (frequency range about 100 kilohertz to 100 megahertz).

Range and dial switches choose the frequency, and it is desirable that the voltage output be constant as the frequency is changed. Stability of amplitude for generators is generally stated in decibels (dB), and the dB will be considered later in this chapter. It is also desirable that the selected frequency be accurate (1% is typical for dial units) and stable in time (0.1% fluctuations are typical). For high-frequency stability a *crystal-based oscillator* is desirable, although this type is fixed in frequency and only available in the radio frequency range. Stability of 1 in 10^6 is then quite possible.

Oscillators may be obtained that permit internal or external manipulation of the output signal. Sine-wave oscillators with these additional capabilities are generally called *signal generators*. For example, the amplitude may vary, or be *modulated,* in proportion to some waveform of lower frequency; this is called *amplitude modulation* or *AM*. Or the frequency of the waveform may be modulated in proportion to some waveform of lower frequency; this is called *frequency modulation* or *FM*.

In recent years *waveform generators* have become available that can produce *square-wave, sawtooth* or *ramp,* and *triangle* waveforms in addition to the sine wave. A nice feature in some of these units is the *sweep frequency* capability. Often it is desirable to study the behavior of an instrument or experiment as a function of frequency. These units can continuously sweep the frequency of the output waveform from some low frequency to a high value; for example, across the audio spectrum. Then the outcome of the experiment should typically be recorded on a strip-chart recorder or other record-producing means, such as a computer. For large frequency ranges, even a logarithmic sweep is available on some units.

If the internal sweep ability is not present, a *voltage-controlled frequency input* often is. This means that the frequency out is proportional to a voltage in at this control input. Connecting a *second* waveform generator in the sawtooth mode to the control input of the first will then sweep frequency.

Finally, a relative of the waveform generator is the *pulse generator.* These units can produce a rectangular pulse of adjustable amplitude and duration, as shown in Figure A2–12. The pulses may be continuously generated at an adjustable rate or frequency, or each pulse may be produced only in response to a timing pulse supplied externally to a *trigger input.* The pulse waveform or pulse train is characterized by the length in time of each pulse, or *pulse duration,* and by the frequency of occurrence of the pulses, or *pulse frequency.* These times are illustrated in Figure A2–12. The term *pulse repetition rate* is often used on the control for the pulse frequency on a pulse generator instrument.

An important feature of any signal generator is its *output impedance.* A signal generator behaves like the Thevenin equivalent circuit shown in Figure A2–13. Consequently, when a load resistance R_L is connected to the output, only a fraction of the generator voltage V_{gen} appears across R_L. For example, if the output impedance of an audio oscillator is 600 ohms and an 8-ohm impedance loudspeaker is connected to it, the output voltage drops to only 8/608 times the signal output when a very large load resistance is connected; that is, 8/608 times the *open circuit output voltage.*

Frequency Counter

Integrated circuitry has made the *frequency counter* as inexpensive as the voltmeter, and they can now be readily found in the lab. Better types can be used in two modes: frequency and period. Consider a waveform input similar to that in Figure A2–12. In the *frequency mode,* the counter will count the number of pulses that come to its input in a fixed time duration—for example, 1 second. The number of counts is then clearly the frequency. For low frequencies, more significant digits can be obtained in a short time by measuring

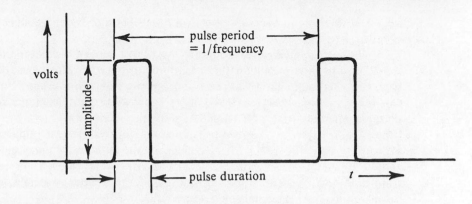

FIGURE A2–12. *Output of a Pulse Generator*

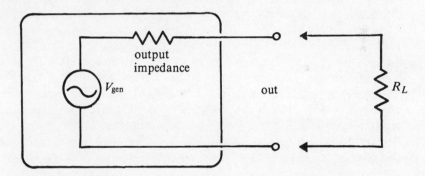

FIGURE A2–13. *Equivalent Circuit of a Signal Generator*

the time interval between two pulses. This "stop watch" approach is the *period mode* because the period of the waveform is then being measured. If we actually want the frequency, we simply calculate the inverse of this period. To count an arbitrary waveform accurately, triggering controls very similar to those on a scope are found on better frequency counters.

Attenuator

Sometimes we are fortunate to have a voltage larger than desired; then an *attenuator,* not an amplifier, is needed. A voltage divider such as the one pictured in Figure A1–11 is the simplest attenuator. Accurate attenuators use fixed resistors and a multiposition switch; for continuous adjustability a potentiometer could be used. The output voltage is clearly reduced or attenuated from what is put to the input.

However, the output impedance of the simple voltage divider is *not* constant and this may be undesirable in some applications. This fact can be seen by simply applying Thevenin's Theorem to Figure A1–11a. The output impedance is R_2 in parallel with R_1 (simply think battery-shorted to deduce this), and this value changes as the potentiometer *tap point* changes. Further, the resistance presented to the voltage source (the battery in the figure) changes when different potentiometer settings are used.

There are several clever resistance networks and switching schemes that produce an attenuator with a constant input impedance and a constant output impedance, even though the voltage reduction factor is changed. It is quite common for these units to be put in a box with a row of switches. If all switches are *down,* the voltage passes from input to output without reduction. Each switch flipped *up* causes the voltage to be reduced by a certain factor, and the factors multiply together.

It is quite common for attenuators to have the reduction factors labeled in decibels, or dB. The following section discusses this concept.

Decibel

The *Bel* is a logarithmic scale that was originally introduced in connection with sound levels because the ear perceives relative sound power levels logarithmically. One Bel contains 10 *decibels* (dB).

The decibel (and Bel) always involves a *ratio* of two power levels that we will call P_1 and P_2. Then the level of P_2 compared to P_1 in decibels is given by

$$\text{Relative Power in decibels} = 10 \log_{10}\left(\frac{P_2}{P_1}\right) \qquad \textbf{(A2–8)}$$

Example: Suppose P_2 is 100 watts while P_1 is 0.1 watts. What is the level of P_2 relative to P_1, expressed in dB?

Solution:

$$\text{Relative Power} = 10 \log_{10}\left(\frac{100 \text{ W}}{0.1 \text{ W}}\right) = 10 \log_{10} 10^3 = 10 \times 3 = 30 \text{ db}$$

We say P_2 is 30 dB *above* P_1.

Example: Suppose P_2 is 0.1 watts while P_1 is 100 watts. What is the level of P_2 relative to P_1 expressed in dB?

Solution:

$$\text{Relative Power} = 10 \log_{10}\left(\frac{0.1 \text{ W}}{100 \text{ W}}\right)$$

$$= 10 \log_{10} 10^{-3} = 10 \times (-3) = -30 \text{ dB}$$

Here we say P_2 is 30 dB *below* P_1.

If the two power levels occur across a certain resistance R, we may substitute $P_1 = V_1^2/R$ and $P_2 = V_2^2/R$ into Equation (A2–8). Then the dB ratio in terms of the two *voltages* becomes

$$\text{Relative Power or dB ratio} = 10 \log_{10}\left(\frac{V_2^2/R}{V_1^2/R}\right) = 20 \log_{10}\left(\frac{V_2}{V_1}\right) \quad \text{(A2–9)}$$

Example: Suppose V_2 is 10 V while V_1 is 1 V (same resistance assumed). What is the ratio of power levels for V_2 relative to V_1?

Solution:

$$\text{dB ratio} = 20 \log_{10}\left(\frac{10}{1}\right)$$

$$= 20 \log_{10} 10^1 = 20 \text{ dB}$$

From the preceding example, we can see that *voltage* ratio and *dB ratio* are related by the rule: 20 db for every factor of 10 in voltage. This relationship is presented in Table A2–1.

Strictly speaking, the correspondence between a voltage ratio and this ratio expressed in dB, as presented in Table A2–1, is only valid when the two voltages involved appear across the same value of resistance. However, this restriction is frequently ignored in electronics practice. When large voltage ratios are encountered, it is common to express them in dB even if the two voltages appear across different resistances. This practice then simply represents a compact way to express large ratios.

TABLE A2–1. *Voltage Ratios Expressed in dB*

Voltage Ratio	0.01	0.1	1	10	100	1000
Ratio in dB	−40 dB	−20 dB	0 dB	+20 dB	40 dB	60 dB

Interconnecting Cables

Virtually all electronic and electrical equipment must be interconnected by wires or cables of some sort. Simple insulated wires or *leads* constructed with banana plugs at both ends are convenient and effective for signals with rather low frequency (dc to audio frequencies) and substantial voltage and/or current levels (tenths of a volt or more and milliamperes or more). The name *banana plug* obviously derives from the appearance of the flexible metal parts that constitute the plug (see Figure A2–14a). The plug mates with a jack that is normally insulated from the panel in which it is installed. (The 4-way jack can also be used with simple stripped-end wire or with leads using *spade lugs* or *crocodile clips* at the ends.)

At lower voltage and current than listed above, *electrical interference* can cause problems. External oscillating electric and magnetic fields (electromagnetic fields) couple to the electrical leads and introduce spurious voltages and currents. The origins of these fields can be the 110 V_{ac} house wiring and transformers, fluorescent lights, nearby computers and electrical machinery (e.g., electric motors), and radio and television stations.

The induced emf from electromagnetic induction (changing magnetic fields) can be reduced by avoiding large area circuit loops. For example, the two signal leads normally connecting two instruments can be twisted together. However, the electric fields that terminate on the connecting wires still introduce interference. The conducting wires and components in an electrical circuit literally act like aerials, receiving the radiated signals.

Electric field pick-up is eliminated (or greatly reduced) by placing the components of an electronic circuit within a metal *chassis box,* and connecting the box to earth potential (grounding the box). The electric field lines then terminate on the box, and we say the circuit is *electrostatically shielded.* Often, one point in the electronic circuit within the box is also connected to the box ground and becomes the *ground* of the circuit. Electrostatic shielding for the signal connecting wires between electronic boxes is also important and can be achieved through the use of shielded cables. A commonly used type is *coaxial cable,* which is simply a wire passing down the center and insulated from a flexible metal cylinder. The metal cylinder is often a metal braid, which is in turn enclosed in insulation (see Figure A2–14b). As with the electronic chassis box, the coaxial shield should be grounded in order to provide electrostatic shielding. Since the electronic circuit within the chasis is also usually grounded, the "coax" shield generally serves as the return path for the signal. (A complete round trip path for the electrical signal must be provided, of course.) If the signal return path must be different from ground, a shielded cable with two inner signal wires may be used, or two separate coaxial cables may be used.

A popular quick connect/disconnect connector for coaxial cables is the *BNC-series connector.* The cable plug and panel jack for this type are shown in Figure A2–14c. The outer metal shell of the plug is connected to the

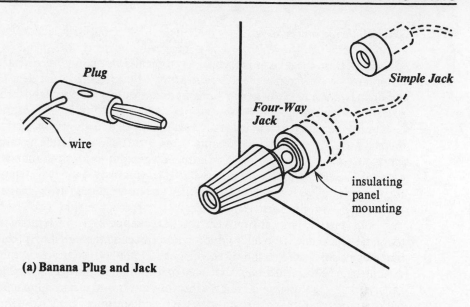

(a) Banana Plug and Jack

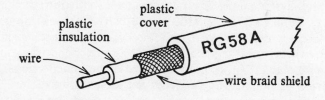

(b) Coaxial Cable

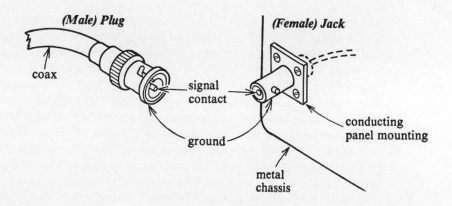

(c) BNC Plug and Jack

FIGURE A2–14. *Two Popular Quick-Connect Cables*

coax shield and mates to the metal shell of the BNC panel jack. Since the braid is to be grounded, the BNC jack is normally mounted on the metal chassis surface. In turn, the chassis is connected to earth or ground by electrical connection to the ground pin of the 3-pin ac house plug for the instrument. Thus the chassis and coax shield are both automatically grounded and provide electrostatic shielding.

This important practical fact means that one of the two signal leads for the many electronic instruments using BNC connectors (e.g., oscilloscopes, frequency counters, radio frequency generators) is automatically at ground. For example, it is *not* possible to directly connect the typical modern oscilloscope to measure the voltage that appears between two points in a circuit, if *both* points are at a voltage different from ground (we often say "are off ground"). Thus, the ground lead of the scope coax must be connected to the ground of the electronic circuit to be tested, and the signal wire from the scope coax connected to a desired off-ground point (electrically *hot*) of the circuit. If the reverse is done, the electronic circuit would be shorted to the ground, and the possible large current flow can damage components. (The author remembers well the smoke that resulted when a fellow *graduate* student in physics damaged a high quality VTVM through this error!)

At radio frequencies (100 kilohertz and above), the use of coaxial interconnecting cables become quite necessary for distances of more than a few centimeters. This is done because of electrical standing waves that can be set up on the conecting wires due to electrical wave reflections. These reflections can be eliminated by assuring that each end of the coaxial *electrical transmission line* is connected to an effective resistance equal to the *characteristic impedance* Z_o of the cable. The characteristic impedance of a coaxial cable is determined by its radial dimensions and the dielectric constant of the interior insulation. For example standard RG58/A coax has a characteristic impedance of 50 ohms, while RG59/A coax has a 75-ohms characteristic impedance. Thus, a radio frequency oscillator connected to RG58/A coax should have an output impedance of 50 ohms.

This book will not generally be concerned with signals above 1 megahertz, and therefore these features of characteristic impedance are not of great concern. Coaxial cables do not need to be properly terminated with characteristic impedances for dc or audio frequency signals. However, it is true that the capacitance of the cable itself can cause loading problems if the cable is rather long. For example, the capacitance between the central wire and the shield is about 90 picofarad per meter for RG58/A coax. A 6-meter cable of RG58/A coax thus has a capacitance of about 600 picofarad between the central wire and shield. At 100 kilohertz, this presents an impedance of only 2600 ohms, which is a shunt between the signal wire and ground. The signal reduction due to loading when connected to a 100 kilohertz signal generator with 600 ohms output impedance, for example, becomes very significant.

To reduce the problems of capacitive loading by the connecting cable and by the scope itself, *attenuating input probes* are often used to connect oscilloscopes (also frequency counters) to high frequency circuits. Thus a typical *10-to-1 probe* uses an internal voltage divider to reduce the voltage by a factor of 10 before presenting the signal to the actual vertical input jack of the scope. The volts/centimeter setting of the vertical deflection must be multiplied by 10 for proper interpretation of the display. Sometimes this voltage reduction is necessary in order to accommodate high voltage signals to the scope. However, the real purpose for these probes is that they present a low capacitive shunt load—only about 13 picofarad—to the circuit to which the probe is connected. However, to faithfully transmit square waves (and also radio frequencies) to the scope input, a small *compensation capacitor* within the voltage divider of the probe itself must be properly adjusted. This is usually done by adjustment of the probe capacitor while observing the scope presentation as the probe is connected to a square wave source known to be "very square."

REVIEW EXERCISES

1. (a) An ammeter A and voltmeter V are connected in series to a battery as shown in Diagram A2–1a. Are either likely to be damaged? Why?

   (b) The ammeter and voltmeter are shown connected in parallel to a battery in Diagram A2–1b. Are either likely to be damaged? Why?

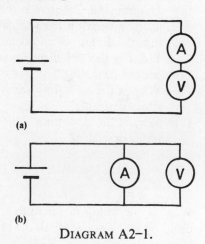

(a)

(b)

DIAGRAM A2–1.

2. (a) What do VOM, VTVM, FTVM, and DVM stand for?
   (b) Which is likely to have the lowest resistance when used as a voltmeter?
   (c) Which type can usually measure current?
   (d) What is the typical input resistance of a VTVM or DVM?
   (e) Although many VTVMs can be operated from "the mains"—that is, a wall socket—they also often contain a battery. What is the purpose of the battery?

3. You have just constructed a light-duty extension cord by connecting a 2-contact plug and receptacle to the opposite ends of a 2-conductor lamp cord.
   (a) Diagram three connections that you could make with a VOM to test the integrity of your product *before* connecting the cord to the mains.
   (b) What function of the VOM would you use?
   (c) Describe what possible problem is being eliminated in each case.

4. (a) Suppose you are considering the purchase of a VOM. You find a 1000 Ω/V meter and a 50,000 Ω/V meter with similar features, accuracy, and price. Which would you probably choose and why?
   (b) Suppose the voltmeter were to be used primarily to test batteries. Why might you consider the other choice from the one made in part (a)?

5. It is quite common to make an in-circuit test of resistance between two points in an electronic circuit, using an ohmmeter for the measurement.
   (a) Why must all voltage sources be turned off or removed from the circuit before making the test?
   (b) Suppose the ohmmeter is connected across some resistor to test it. Why is it likely that the ohmmeter's reading is less than the value of the resistor?

6. What is meant by a balanced bridge or a balanced potentiometer circuit?

7. (a) What electrical standard is required for the adjustment of a precision potentiometer?
   (b) Why is this standard not required for a precision Wheatstone bridge?

8. (a) Diagram A2–2 illustrates the ac/dc switch on the vertical input of an oscilloscope. What is the switch position for the ac setting?
   (b) Why is the ac setting sometimes desirable?
   (c) Why is the dc setting sometimes desirable?

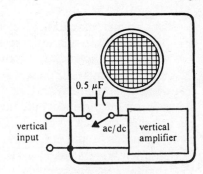

DIAGRAM A2–2.

9. What is the utility of the auto setting of the TRIGGER MODE switch of an oscilloscope? Contrast with the behavior of the scope when the triggering mode is ac or dc. What is a disadvantage of using auto mode?

10. Which one of the following is *not* true about a triggered-sweep laboratory-quality oscilloscope?
    (a) The peak-to-peak voltage of an ac waveform may be measured to within a few percent.
    (b) The voltage of a battery may be measured to within a few percent.
    (c) When the vertical input is set to dc mode, the voltage of an ac waveform cannot be measured.
    (d) When the vertical input is set to ac mode, the voltage of a battery cannot be measured.

11. Explain the difference between the external-trigger input and the horizontal-sweep input of an oscilloscope.

12. The level-control knob has a (+) and (−) associated with it. The slope switch also has (+) and (−) positions. What do (+) and (−) refer to in each case? A diagram of some waveform should be used in connection with the explanation.

13. When an oscilloscope is operated in X-Y mode, the scope's triggering circuitry is not required. Explain why.

14. (a) What is meant by a dual-trace oscilloscope?
    (b) Why is it evident from the front panel of Figure A2–7 that the oscilloscope pictured is not a dual-trace type?

15. (a) What is a servomechanism?
    (b) What is a stepper motor?
    (c) Most strip-chart recorders are effectively self-balancing potentiometers. Briefly explain this statement.

16. (a) The term X-Y occurs in both the X-Y oscilloscope and X-Y recorder. What do these two devices have in common?
    (b) What is the general nature of application of the X-Y feature?
    (c) Under what circumstances should one device be selected over the other in part (a)?

17. Give a relative advantage and disadvantage for each in regard to the use of the strip-chart recorder and the magnetic recorder in recording applications.

18. (a) Compare the upper frequency limits of an entertainment cassette recorder and an instrumentation recorder.
    (b) Describe the technique used by an instrumentation recorder to record slowly varying dc signals.

19. What is a principal difference between a waveform generator and the traditional audio oscillator?

20. A typical pulse generator has at least 3 control knobs. Give a possible control panel name for each of the 3.

21. What is meant by the output impedance of a signal generator?

22. Suppose you have at hand a resistance box (a selectable resistance with many known values) and a voltmeter. Describe a simple method for determining the output impedance of an audio generator that is presented to you.

PROBLEMS

1. A d'Arsonval movement with a resistance of 500 Ω and a full-scale sensitivity of 200 μA is used to construct an ammeter with 0.1-ampere full-scale capability.
   (a) Diagram the construction of the completed meter, including resistance values.
   (b) What is the voltage drop across the meter when placed in a circuit and reading full scale?

2. The d'Arsonval meter of the preceding problem is used to construct a 15-V full-scale voltmeter. Diagram the construction of the completed meter, including resistance values.

3. Suppose the needle position of a d'Arsonval meter is to be read to an accuracy of ±0.5% of full scale. If the full-scale deflection is 110°, what is the angular accuracy required (±△)? Draw two lines 4 cm long with the angle 2 △ between them.

4. What will be the reading of the voltmeter in Diagram A2–3? It is a 100 Ω/V meter set to the 15-V scale.

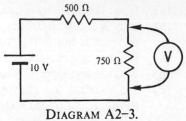

DIAGRAM A2–3.

5. Assume that the circuit shown in Diagram A2–4 is constructed to produce an ohmmeter. The galvanometer resistance is negligible.

   (a) Zero resistance is printed (as usual) at the full-scale position for the needle of the meter. What resistance R is required?

   (b) What value of resistance should be printed at the middle of the scale?

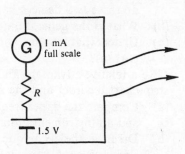

DIAGRAM A2–4.

6. (a) Suppose an ohmmeter is connected to a good capacitor (initially discharged) with a capacitance of some microfarads. What should be the behavior of the ohmmeter reading?

   (b) It is not unusual to test an electrolytic capacitor for a short by using an ohmmeter. However, what precautions should be considered? (Certainly one precaution, and possibly a second.)

7. Justify the statement made in the chapter: If 1-milliampere current is established through an unknown resistance, a voltmeter connected across the resistance shows a reading (in V) equal to the resistance in kilohms.

8. Consider the Wheatstone bridge pictured in Diagram A2–5. What is the reading of the DVM connected? Does the DVM indicate (+) or (−) voltage?

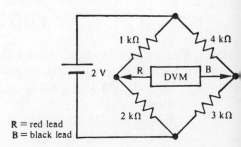

DIAGRAM A2–5. R = red lead
B = black lead

9. Suppose the known resistances in a balanced Wheatstone bridge are each accurate to $\pm 1.0\%$. What is the precision of determination of the unknown resistance?

10. (a) Show that the bridge pictured in Diagram A2–6 is in balance. K is an arbitrary constant.
    (b) Find the Thevenin equivalent circuit that presents itself to the detector terminals. (This is important in considering the impedance of the detector to use.)

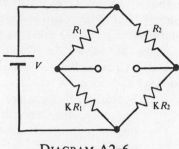

DIAGRAM A2–6.

11. Justify that if a Wheatstone bridge is in balance and R_2 and R_x (in Figure A2–4) both change with temperature in the same way, the bridge will remain in balance. You may assume that $R_x = R_x^0 (1 + \alpha T)$ and $R_2 = R_2^0 (1 + \alpha T)$. Here T is the temperature in Celsius, α is the temperature coefficient of resistance at $0°C$, and R_x^0 and R_2^0 are the respective resistances at $0°C$.

12. (a) Consider a Wheatstone bridge as diagrammed in Diagram A2–7a that is used in the out-of-balance mode to monitor the change in resistance R_x. Derive an expression for V_{out} in terms of V, R, and $\triangle R$. For small $\triangle R$, show V_{out} is equal to $(V/4)(\triangle R/R)$.

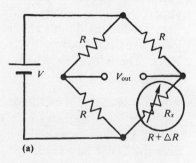

(a)

    (b) Suppose it can be arranged that while one transducer increases its resistance by $\triangle R$ a second transducer decreases its resistance by $\triangle R$ (in response to the given external stimulus). These may be placed in a bridge as shown in Diagram A2–7b; the configuration that results is called a *half-active bridge*. Show that V_{out} (the output signal) is twice that obtained in part (a).

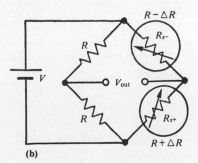

(b)

DIAGRAM A2–7.

13. Many Wheatstone bridge applications are used in the out-of-balance mode. But if a balance is not required, why not save the expense of two resistors and simply put the resistive transducer R_x in a voltage-divider connection as shown in Diagram A2–8? Criticize this "money-saving" approach.

    NOTE: Typically, the change in transducer resistance is a small fraction of its resistance.

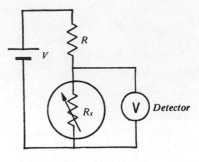

DIAGRAM A2–8.

14. A typical oscilloscope display is 6 cm high by 10 cm wide. The vertical control knob is set to 0.5 V/cm, and the horizontal control knob is set to 0.5 msec/cm. A 1-V_{rms} sinusoidal signal at 1-kHz frequency is input to the scope. Sketch with some accuracy the appearance of the scope display.

15. Suppose the scope triggering level is set for the voltage waveform as shown in Diagram A2–9. Justify that a double exposure will appear on the scope screen. Sketch what the double exposure looks like on the scope.

    NOTE: The slope switch is set to (+).

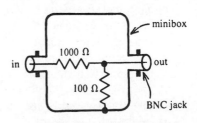

DIAGRAM A2–9.

16. A widely used audio oscillator has an output impedance of 600 Ω. Suppose the oscillator is adjusted to 1 kHz, and a DVM connected to its output reads 5 V_{rms}. Then a 0.33-μF capacitor is connected to the oscillator output. What voltage does the DVM now read?

17. A simple attenuator is constructed from 1% 1000-Ω and 100-Ω resistors. These are placed in an aluminum minibox, as shown in Diagram A2–10, for convenience in connection to cables in the lab.

    (a) Assuming an open-circuit output, the output voltage will be what fraction of the input voltage (to within 2%)?

    (b) Suppose the attenuator is connected to the output of an audio oscillator that has an output impedance of

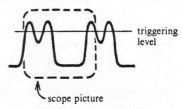

DIAGRAM A2–10.

600 Ω. The open-circuit voltage of the oscillator was 4.0 V p-p. What is the open-circuit voltage out of the attenuator?

(c) What will be the output impedance of the overall oscillator plus attenuator? Diagram the problem to help justify your work.

18. Suppose the voltage across a certain resistance changes from 4.5 V to 7 V, what is the power change in dB?

19. Suppose the power into a loudspeaker changes by -12 dB.
    (a) What is the (fractional) ratio of the power after to the power before?
    (b) What is the ratio of the voltage after to voltage before?

20. VOMs and VTVMs often have a *dBm scale* that may be used in certain situations; they actually monitor the voltage, however. A reference level of 1 mW (10^{-3} W) developed in 600 Ω is assumed, and this situation is called *0 dBm* on the meter scale.
    (a) What is the voltage across a 600-Ω resistor if a VTVM connected to it reads 0 dBm? (This voltage in fact appears across from 0 dBm on the associated voltage scale.)
    (b) Suppose the voltage across the 600-Ω resistor is 3.0 V. What is the dBm reading?

21. Consider a filter (either high-pass or low-pass). Show that at the breakpoint frequency (half-power frequency), the output voltage is down 3 dB from the unattenuated value. (Thus this frequency is also often referred to as the *−3 dB point*.)

22. The attenuation of the common commercial attenuation box is set by switches. Let 3 switches be marked F_1, F_2, and F_3, respectively. If each attenuation factor F_i is expressed as a simple ratio, the total attenuation is the product $F_1F_2F_3$ when all 3 switches are set. (It is just F_iF_j if two switches i and j are set.) However, if the attenuation factor for each switch is expressed in dB, show that the total attenuation is $F_1 + F_2 + F_3$. Thus, the simple rule is to add together the dB values for all set switches. This is an advantage of the dB scheme.

23. (a) Consider an *RC* filter (or an *LR* filter) that is well beyond the breakpoint frequency and into the attenuation region in terms of frequency. Show that V_{out}/V_{in} changes by a factor of 10 for every factor-of-10 change in frequency. Account for the statement that the filter rolloff is -20 dB/decade.
    (b) An octave (for example, in music) is a factor-of-2 change in frequency. Account for the statement that a simple *RC* filter may also be called a -6 dB/octave attenuator when well beyond the breakpoint frequency.

24. Consider the second-order filter of Problem 37 in Chapter A1. Show that the attenuation region may be characterized as -40 dB/decade.

25. Consider the T attenuator shown in Diagram A2−11. Assume a voltage source characterized by V and R is connected to one set of attenuator terminals, and a load resistance also with resistance R is connected to the other set of attenuator terminals as shown in the diagram. In terms of this resistance R, the attenuator has been designed with R_1 and R_2 as defined in the diagram and assuming some fraction B.

(a) Show that $V_{out}/V_{in} = \beta$. β is thus the attenuation factor for the *terminal* voltages.

(b) Show that $V_{out}/V = \beta/2$, however. (Due to loading, V_{in} is just half of the open-circuit voltage V of the voltage source.)

(c) Show that the impedance seen between the input terminals of the attenuator is just R. A load R should be assumed connected at the attenuator output.

(d) Show that the output impedance of the network (voltage source plus attenuator) to which the load is attached is also R.

(e) Illustrate how an attenuator that reduces its input terminal voltage by β^n (n is any integer) could readily be constructed and that it has the input and output properties of parts (c) and (d).

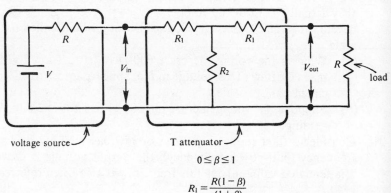

voltage source ⤴   T attenuator ⤴

$$0 \le \beta \le 1$$

$$R_1 = \frac{R(1-\beta)}{(1+\beta)}$$

DIAGRAM
A2–11.

$$R_2 = \frac{R2\beta}{(1-\beta^2)}$$

CHAPTER
A3

Transducers

The term *transducer* has become quite fashionable since the mid-1960s as a general term for a host of devices that link the physical world to the world of electronics. Of course, it is the possibility of making this interconnection that permits electronics to become so pervasive in science, technology, and even the household.

Various physical effects in themselves are often not electrical. For example, temperature may be monitored by a human observing the length of the mercury column in a conventional thermometer. But if temperature is converted into some proportional electrical effect, the power and versatility of electronic circuitry may be used to condition the corresponding *electrical signal* in a variety of ways. We may achieve greater sensitivity, or automatic recording over extended periods, or even analysis of information. If a computer is to be used for analysis of the measurements, it is often desirable for the computer to make the measurements automatically rather than to require a human intermediary. But this procedure requires conversion of the physical effect such as temperature to the electrical domain used internally by the computer.

For these reasons, the application of electronics to a problem may begin with a transducer, and the success of the application may depend on the selection of an appropriate transducer. In this chapter, we consider the general possibilities and limitations of a modest selection of commonly used transducers. These basically respond to one of the following effects: temperature, light intensity, strain in an object, movement of an object, position of an object, and ion concentration. However, it is useful to notice that these effects may often be used to monitor other phenomena; therefore some examples are briefly pointed out in the chapter.

One scheme for classifying transducers is through the electrical effect that is output by the device. Thus, the physical effect may produce a change in some resistance, capacitance, or inductance; or it may actually generate a voltage (emf). Since most transducers discussed in this chapter are of the resistive or the voltage type, two principal chapter sections are devoted to them. However, it is helpful to first put the general elements of an electronic system in perspective. This perspective is given in the first section of the chapter

General View of Electric Systems

It is useful to our understanding of laboratory electronics to organize the typical electronic instrument or application into a few general blocks. This arrangement is illustrated in Figure A3–1. As we have mentioned, there is first some parameter that we want to study or monitor in some physical system. Because typically the parameter is not in itself electrical, a transducer is employed to generate an electrical effect that is related to the particular parameter. If the electrical effect is not already voltage, such a transformation is usually made, and this voltage is then sent to an *amplifier* that increases the typically small and feeble voltage level to some robust value. Finally, the latter voltage is put to an *output device* such as a meter, oscilloscope, strip-chart recorder, loudspeaker, fluid valve, motor, and so on. At times the desired end result may be an effect back on the original system; this is typical of experiment control or industrial process-control situations.

We speak of input transducers and output transducers. An *input transducer* causes an electrical effect in consequence to some physical parameter at its input. The transducer block pictured in Figure A3–1 is actually an input transducer. Generally speaking an input transducer converts or *transduces* energy from some form in the physical world into electrical energy. Conversely, an *output transducer* converts electrical energy into some other form

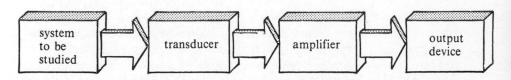

FIGURE A3–1. *Typical Electronic Application in Science*

of energy and causes a desired physical effect in the process. The output device block in Figure A3–1 is actually an output transducer. Only a few output transducers will be discussed in this chapter.

A simple example that uses both transducer types is a public-address (PA) system. The input transducer is the microphone into which someone speaks. The *air vibrations*—that is, sound energy—are converted to a small voltage by either a crystal or a dynamic microphone. The PA amplifier increases the voltage and power level to a magnitude (or degree) that is sufficient to operate or *drive* the output transducer, which is the loudspeaker system. In the output transducer, electrical energy is converted back into sound energy again—hopefully at a level heard throughout the auditorium. Of course, the additional power in the sound amplified must come from somewhere. It comes from the *power supply* or voltage source for the amplifier. This source could be a battery or, more likely, a nearby electrical power generating station connected through the 115-V line cord.

Resistive Input Transducers

Photoresistor

The *photoresistor* is a resistor made of a semiconducting material that changes its resistance in response to the intensity of *light* falling on it. Ordinarily, a semiconductor does not conduct electricity well because of the relatively small number of charge carriers that are free to move. However, when photons of light strike a semiconductor, electrons are kicked away from host atoms into a mobile condition and the conductivity of the material increases. Conversely, resistivity decreases.

The resistance R depends on the intensity I_* of the light according to

$$R = R_0 I_*^{-K} \qquad \text{(A3–1)}$$

where R_0 is a multiplying constant and K is a constant in the range of 0.5 to 1.0. Thus the dependence is not linear but follows a power law. The change in resistance does *not* occur instantly with change in light level; delays of microseconds to milliseconds are typical, depending on the particular photoresistor type. Figure A3–2 shows a typical photoresistor.

The resistance of a typical photoresistor may vary from 50 megohms in the dark to 9 kilohms in an illumination of 2 footcandles or 20 lux.

NOTE: 1 footcandle = 1 lumen/foot = 10.7 lumens/meter^2; 1 lumen/meter^2 = 1 lux.

For comparison, the proper *illuminance* in a building hallway is about 30 lux; in a classroom, about 400 lux; direct sunlight is about 10^5 lux.

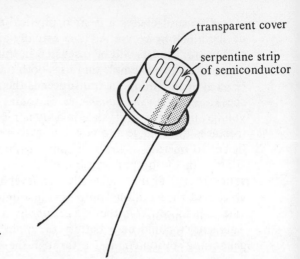

transparent cover

serpentine strip
of semiconductor

FIGURE A3–2. *Typical Photo-resistor (Twice Normal Size)*

Photoresistors can be used in a number of ways, and a few applications are sketched here to give an idea of the possibilities. Some of the applications are rather novel; notice that light itself is often not the physical quantity of basic interest.

1. Photoresistors may obviously be used to monitor light intensity when this quantity is of direct interest. Thus, a typical contemporary light-meter for photographic applications is essentially a photoresistor connected to an ohmmeter. The ohmmeter scale is calibrated in appropriate photographic units.

2. The passage of an object can be detected. The passing object may block a light beam that normally illuminates a photoresistor; this event can be detected by monitoring the voltage variation across the photoresistor while it is connected in a voltage divider circuit, and the voltage signal may be passed to an electronic counting circuit. Thus, we may monitor the number of persons passing through a door, or the number of items passing on a conveyor belt, or the number of times an animal is in part of an enclosure.

3. Rather tiny movements of objects can be monitored. A movable opaque vane should only partially block a light beam that falls on the sensitive area of a photoresistor. Suppose that the vane is connected to a frog muscle; tiny movements of the stimulated frog muscle can be detected by the variation in resistance of the photoresistor. Similarly, finger tremor can be measured by using a person's finger as the vane.

4. The heart rate of a person can be monitored. A small light source and a photoresistor can be placed on opposite sides of the earlobe. At each heart beat, blood pumps into the capillaries and momentarily renders the flesh slightly more opaque. The light reaching the photoresistor then changes, and the change in resistance of the photoresistor may be detected and monitored by an electronic circuit. In fact, an electronic system for this application is described as an example system in Chapter A7.

5. The level of translucent fluid in a container can be monitored. A light beam can be arranged to shine from the top toward a photoresistor installed at the bottom of the container. As the fluid thickness increases, less light reaches the photoresistor. The fluid level could be indicated on the scale of an ohmmeter, or more elaborate automatic electronic recording circuitry could be used.

Thermistor

Like the photoresistor, the *thermistor* is a resistor made of a semiconducting material; but it makes use of the fact that *increasing temperature* rapidly decreases the resistivity of semiconductors. Increasing temperature generates more carriers by thermally shaking electrons loose from host atoms and consequently decreases the resistivity of the material. The resistance depends approximately exponentially on the temperature:

$$R = R_0 e^{+E/kT} \tag{A3-2}$$

where R is the resistance of the thermistor (at temperature T), R_0 and E are constants for the given unit, k is Boltzmann's constant (1.38×10^{-23} joules/molecule °K) and T is the absolute temperature. In one sense it is inconvenient to make a thermometer from a thermistor, because it is not linear. On the other hand, the exponential behavior implies a rapid change with temperature and therefore a sensitive element. At room temperature the resistance of a thermistor may decrease by some 5% for each degree Celsius rise in temperature.

Standard thermistors may be used over the temperature range $-100°$C to $+300°$C and have a resistance specification of $\pm 10\%$ at 25°C. However, selected (more expensive) types are interchangeable and accurate to $\pm 0.2°$C over a 100°C range. Note that very high *relative* accuracy is possible with even standard units; 0.0005°C changes are quite readily detectable with appropriate circuits.

Table A3-1 shows sample resistance-temperature data for a typical thermistor, the Fenwall GB32J2 thermistor. One may typically purchase a thermistor that has a certain resistance between 10 ohms and 10^5 ohms at 25°C. The thermistor will then have a resistance at other temperatures in nominal proportion as given in Table A3-1.

TABLE A3-1.   *Resistance Vs. Temperature for a Typical Thermistor*

Temperature (°C)	0	25	50	100	150	200
Resistance (ohms)	5700	2000	810	185	59	25

> **Example:** A thermistor is specified to have a resistance of 10,000 ohms at 25° C. What is expected to be its resistance $R(0)$ at 0° C? Assume the thermistor material is the same as that for the thermistor of Table A3–1.
>
> **Solution:** By ratios from Table A3–1 we have
>
> $$\frac{R(0)}{10,000 \ \Omega} = \frac{5700 \ \Omega}{2000 \ \Omega} \quad \text{or} \quad R(0) = 28,500 \ \Omega$$

Thermistors may be used in simple ohmmeter circuits or in a Wheatstone bridge circuit. The dial of the ohmmeter type of circuit can be calibrated to indicate the temperature directly. The bridge circuit is often used to detect small temperature variations. The bridge output may be amplified before being sent to a meter, and sensitive thermometers may be constructed in this way.

Thermistors come in various shapes and sizes to accommodate different experimental situations. Some are much smaller than a pinhead. Figure A3–3 illustrates some typical forms.

NOTE: There is one precaution in using thermistors. If a significant current is passed through a thermistor in the measuring process, it will *self-heat* from $I^2 R$ and indicate a temperature higher than the actual temperature.

The self-heating effect can, however, be put to use in a number of ways. Two examples are given here.

1. A self-heating thermistor can be used as the basis of a simple but effective *liquid-level sensor*. If a fluid is to be pumped into a tank, the pump should be stopped when the fluid reaches a certain level. Therefore, a yes/no (or binary) liquid-level sensor is required. We can exploit the fact that a self-

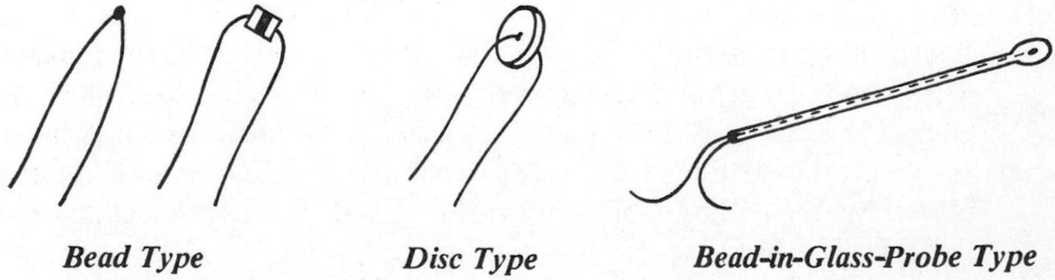

| *Bead Type* | *Disc Type* | *Bead-in-Glass-Probe Type* |

FIGURE A3–3. *Typical Thermistors*

heating thermistor is cooled by conduction and convection more effectively when immersed in liquid than in air. Consequently, when the liquid level reaches a thermistor suspended in the tank, its resistance increases significantly. The thermistor can be connected in a voltage divider circuit, and the change in voltage across the thermistor can be used to distinguish whether the liquid is above or below the particular level.

2. A self-heating thermistor can be the basis for a rugged *vacuum gauge* that measures intermediate vacuum pressures between about 10^{-4} and 1 torr. If the thermistor is placed in the vacuum to be measured, it will be cooled more effectively at higher pressure than at lower pressure. The corresponding change in its resistance can be used as a measure of the vacuum. Of course, it must be calibrated against an absolute vacuum measurement instrument such as the McLeod gauge. The Pirani gauge is a similar vacuum gauge technique that has been used for many years; however, the conventional Pirani gauge uses the self-heating of a *metal* resistor.

Platinum Resistance Thermometer

The resistivity of any metal increases in an approximately linear fashion from the small value it has when near absolute zero temperature. Therefore the resistance of a metal wire can be used as a temperature indicator; however, near 0°C the resistance can be expected to change by a fraction only on the order of 1/273 or about 0.4% per degree Celsius. For reasons of linearity and stability, platinum has become the metal of choice and in fact the *platinum resistance thermometer* is the world standard for temperature measurement from −270°C to +660°C. High-purity platinum wire with a resistance of the order of 100 ohms is typically wound on a ceramic core in a manner to relieve wire stresses. The size of the resulting sensing element can be expected to be larger than that for a thermistor, and instrumentation using the platinum resistance thermometer is generally more elaborate than for a thermistor. However, if performance approaching that of laboratory standards is required, this approach may be necessary.

Strain Gauge

If a metal or semiconductor wire is stretched, its resistance increases because of its longer length and smaller cross-section. Provided the stretch is not too great, the elasticity of the material causes it to return to the original shape and resistance if the force of stress is removed. The amount of stress (expressed as a fraction of its length) that a rod undergoes is called the *strain,* and fine wire used expressly to measure or "gauge" small amounts of elongation is called a *strain gauge.* One scheme is to bond fine wire to an elastic insulating sheet, as shown in Figure A3–4. The resulting strain gauge is

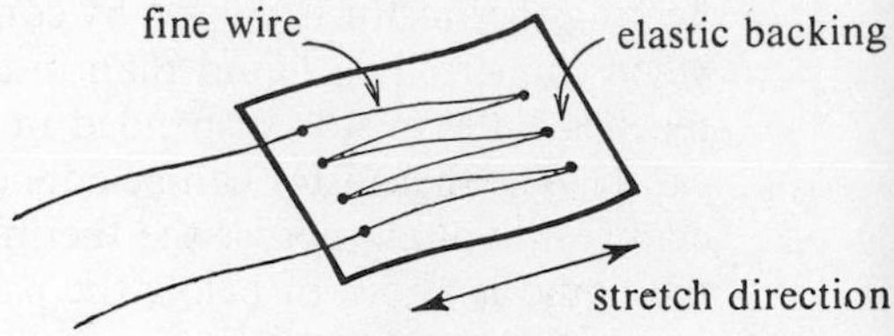

FIGURE A3-4. *One Form of Strain Gauge*

bonded to the object to be studied. As the portion under the gauge strains slightly, the wire in the strain gauge must stretch or compress by an equal strain. The resistance change of the gauge is then a measure of the strain in the object.

Unfortunately, the resistance change with strain is small and the resistance change with temperature can readily be large. A desirable approach to minimizing the temperature problem is to use two strain gauges—one *active* and one a *dummy*—in a Wheatstone bridge. The dummy strain gauge is placed as resistance R_2 in Figure A2-4 and is arranged to experience the same temperature as the active strain sensor, but not the strain. Then, as discussed in Chapter A2, the output of the bridge should change very little with change in temperature of the sensors.

Using strain gauges constructed from metal wire, we may expect bridge outputs on the order of 0.01 V for strains of 10^{-3}; that is, 10^{-3} centimeters stretch per centimeter of length. Amplification of this small voltage is typically required and quite possible, so that rather small displacements are accurately measurable. *Load cells* are available that use strain gauges in order to obtain transducers for force and weighing applications. For example, the weight of a container as it is being filled during a manufacturing process may be monitored electronically with the aid of a load cell. A second strain gauge application is used in electronic measurement of fluid pressure. The pressure transducer incorporates a thin diaphragm with a strain gauge mounted on it. The diaphragm bulges slightly under the pressure of the fluid, and the strain gauge resistance changes accordingly.

Conductivity Cell

Pure water has a very high resistivity and, conversely, low conductivity (because H_2O dissociates rather little into H^+ and OH^- ions). Ions in solution increase the conductivity rapidly and ion concentration can be obtained by measuring the resistance between a pair of conductors immersed in the solution. To be quantitative, a *conductivity cell* is constructed with plates and dimensions such that the resistance measured is related to the resistivity of the liquid (in ohms × meters) by a simple factor like 0.1, 1 or 10. Also, to prevent the ions coming out of solution at the respective electrodes, an ac current should be used in the measuring process. Figure A3-5 illustrates a typical

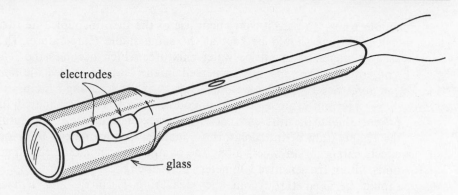

FIGURE A3–5. *Typical Conductivity Cell (Immersion Type)*

conductivity cell that is intended to be dipped into a liquid in order to measure its resistivity.

Voltage Input Transducers

Thermocouple

The *thermocouple* is a junction between two different metals, and represents a temperature-to-voltage transducer. For measurement purposes, the two metals are usually in the form of two fine wires that are welded or soldered together at one end to form a junction. The junction is effectively the sensor. The thermocouple combines the virtues of good accuracy, stability, low cost, broad temperature range, and small size; consequently, it has been widely used in science and industry for temperature measurement.

What may be called the *thermocouple effect* is actually the combination of two effects:

1. An emf or voltage develops between the ends of any wire that has its two ends at different temperatures. The voltage produced increases with increasing temperature difference between the two ends and is different for different metals.
2. An emf develops across the junction between two different metals. This emf depends on the metals used and on the temperature of the junction.

If a sensitive voltmeter is connected between the "free ends" of the thermocouple wire pair, it senses a small voltage that depends on the temperature of the thermocouple junction and also on the temperatures of the two junctions that are now formed between the voltmeter and the two thermocouple wires. To permit convenient use of the thermocouple, the two "free end" junctions should be kept at the same stable temperature. They are usually immersed in an ice water mixture, which becomes the *reference temperature*. The junctions immersed in the bath are called the *reference junctions*. See Figure A3–6 for a diagram of the resulting system.

The emf around the thermocouple circuit is approximately linearly proportional to the difference between the reference junction temperature and the temperature of the monitoring junction. Unfortunately, thermocouple effects can occur anywhere along the circuit path, including circuit connections within the sensitive voltmeter. To reduce these problems, copper wire should be used throughout the measuring circuitry, and temperature gradients should be avoided within this circuitry.

The thermocouple voltage developed is quite small. For example, the commonly used *copper-constantan* junction develops about 40 microvolts per Celsius degree. A potentiometer or good DVM is required for such measurements. Tables of thermocouple emf vs. temperature can be found in the *Handbook of Chemistry and Physics,* although thermocouples actually must be calibrated to be relied upon for accuracies better than 1C°. Copper-constantan thermocouples may be used in the temperature range of $-183°$C (boiling point of oxygen) to $+400°$C. *Chromel-constantan* units may be employed up to 1000°C, while some tungsten alloy units are usable to 2800°C.

Ion-Selective Electrode and pH Measurement

The rapid and convenient measurement of concentrations of ions in solution is important in many contexts; for example, the testing of fluoride ion content in fluorinated water. Scientists, as another example, are particularly interested in the concentration of hydrogen ions $[H^+]$ or *pH measurement*

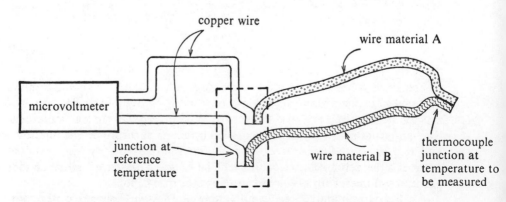

FIGURE A3–6. *Thermocouple Temperature Measurement*

because it measures the *acidity* or *alkalinity* of a solution. To review briefly, since the concentration of H^+ ion can range over many orders of magnitude, the pH measure of acidity/alkalinity is defined as

$$pH = -\log_{10} [H^+] \tag{A3-3}$$

where $[H^+]$ is the *molar concentration* of H^+ ion (in moles/liter). Pure water has $[H^+] = 10^{-7}$ molar so that its pH = +7. An *acidic solution* has a pH of less than 7, while an *alkaline solution* has a pH of more than 7.

Membranes have been developed that exhibit a voltage between the two sides when the concentrations of a selected ion type are different on the two sides of the membrane. The behavior is as though the membrane is permeable only to the one ion, so that diffusion from the high-concentration to low-concentration side by the selected ion would set up a potential difference that depends on the concentration ratios. The actual mechanism is generally much more complex, but in any case, charge transfer through the membrane material is involved, and the resistance of the membrane material is often quite high. For example, the selective membrane of the common *pH-indicating electrode* is made of a type of glass, and the resistance of the probe is typically on the order of 100 megohms.

Suppose then that the concentration of a certain ion in a solution is to be measured. The solution of unknown ion concentration is arranged to be on one side of the ion-specific membrane, while a *reference solution* of known ion concentration is placed on the other side. The emf or voltage V that develops between the two solutions must be measured, because this provides a measure of the relative ion concentrations. This voltage difference must be measured with a pair of electrodes. One electrode, the *reference electrode*, is placed directly in the solution with the unknown concentration, while the other electrode is placed within the reference solution that in turn is contained in the *indicating electrode*, or *selective-ion electrode*. The indicating electrode incorporates the selective membrane and is placed into the solution to be measured. Figure A3–7 is a diagram of the general configuration of a selective-ion measurement.

The voltage difference V is expected to obey Nernst's Law

$$V = V^{\circ} + \frac{kT}{ne} \ln\left(\frac{a_1}{a_2}\right) \tag{A3-4}$$

where V° is a constant depending on the particular ion, k is Boltzmann's constant, T is the absolute temperature, e is the charge of the electron, and n is the number of electrons in excess or in deficiency for the particular ion. The quantities a_1 and a_2 are the so-called *activities* of the ion in the unknown and the known solutions respectively. For dilute solutions, the activities approach the actual ion concentrations and can be expressed either in ions per unit volume or in moles/liter (molar concentration).

Suppose in particular we are interested in the pH-sensitive electrode. Then $n = 1$ and we have from Equation A3–4

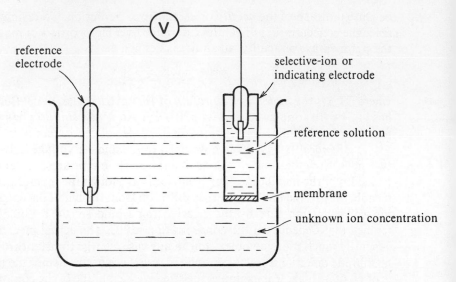

FIGURE A3–7. *Diagram of a Selective-Ion Electrode and Reference Electrode Placed in a Solution to Determine the Concentration of Ions in the Solution*

$$V = \left(V^\circ - \frac{kT}{e} \ln [H^+]_2 \right) + \frac{KT}{e} \ln [H^+]_1$$

$$= K + \frac{2.3\, kT}{e} \log [H^+] \qquad\qquad \text{(A3–5)}$$

where we have grouped the constant quantities together as K and have changed to common logarithms as desired for the pH definition. Finally, at a temperature of 25°C, we have from Equation A3–3 and Equation A3–5 that

$$V = K - 0.05915 \left(\frac{\text{volts}}{\text{pH}} \right) \text{pH} \qquad\qquad \text{(A3–6)}$$

We see that the voltage difference between electrodes in a pH meter changes by about 59 millivolts for each unit change in pH (or each order of magnitude change in hydrogen ion concentration). Accurate measurement of this small voltage through an impedance of 100megohms is a difficult assignment. Thus, if a voltmeter with an impedance of 10 megohms is used (for example, a conventional digital voltmeter of good quality), a factor-of-ten error results because of voltage divider action. This practical difficulty will be addressed in Chapter A6.

Electromagnetic Induction Transducers

We reviewed in part of Chapter A1 the fact that a changing magnetic flux within a coil of wire induces an emf or voltage in the coil circuit. The value of the emf is given by Faraday's Law as Equation A1–41. A number of input transducers that are sensitive to movement make use of this effect and are called *electromagnetic induction transducers.* The magnetic field is typically produced by a small permanent magnet in proximity with the sensing coil, so that a movement of the magnet relative to the coil produces the change in magnetic flux and consequently the voltage in the coil circuit. Note that a voltage is induced only while the magnetic flux through the coil is changing, so that this transducer approach is most suitable for detecting oscillating movements; the voltage out of the coil is then an ac voltage at the frequency of oscillation.

Figure A3–8 shows schematically several applications of this transducer type. Figure A3–8a shows the principle of construction for a *dynamic microphone.* A coil is attached to a flexible diaphragm that is in turn held fixed at the edges. As sound waves strike the diaphragm, it flexes and vibrates; then the coil attached to the diaphragm also oscillates in the field of the fixed permanent magnet. Consequently, the magnetic field through the coil oscillates and an ac voltage proportional to the amplitude of the oscillation and having the same frequency is induced in the coil. Voltage on the order of tenths of volts may be expected, with a relatively low output resistance because of the relatively few number of turns of the coil.

Figure A3–8b shows one type of *magnetic phonograph cartridge.* As the stylus oscillates from side to side in the record groove (very slightly in modern microgroove records), a small permanent magnet attached to the stylus cantilever oscillates between the iron core tabs that pass through a stationary coil. The iron core serves to "gather" the magnetic field through the coil from the air in the vicinity. This is due to the low *reluctance* of the iron; that is, the magnetic field prefers to pass through it. Thus an oscillating magnetic flux occurs in the coil and an ac voltage is generated in response to the audio recording.

In prospecting for oil and mineral deposits, geophysicists routinely use seismic reflections from underground rock structures. These scientists set off a near-surface explosion or vibration of some sort and measure the time for the seismic wave thus generated to return to the earth's surface. Transducers to measure these vibrations are termed *geophones,* and the type commonly used on land relies upon electromagnetic induction. Figure A3–8c shows that a movable permanent magnet is suspended by springs from the case of the geophone. As the earth vibrates, the magnet is set into oscillation relative to the coil (which is fixed to the geophone core) so that a voltage is induced in the coil

Piezoelectric Transducer

When certain crystals (for example, quartz or Rochelle salt) or ceramics (for example, barium titanate) experience a mechanical strain or pressure, a voltage develops between the opposite faces of the crystal or ceramic during

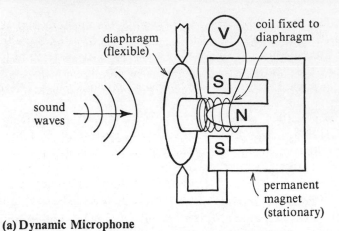

(a) Dynamic Microphone

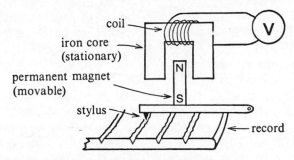

(b) Magnetic Phonograph Cartridge

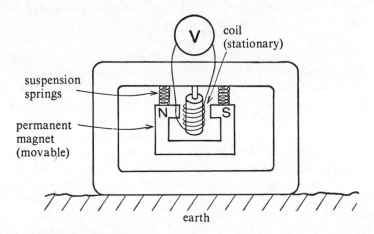

(c) Electromagnetic Geophone

FIGURE A3-8. *Schematic Illustration of Three Transducers That Use the Electro-magnetic Induction Principle*

the distortion process. Materials that exhibit this phenomenon are called *piezoelectric*. Metal plates can be attached to the opposite sides; the voltage measured between these plates can then be used as a measure of the force that is producing the distortion of the crystal or ceramic. A number of force-to-voltage transducers use this effect and may be classified as piezoelectric transducers.

In a *ceramic phonograph cartridge* the stylus is attached to a small piezoelectric slab. The output from this type of pickup can be in the range of tenths of volts and thus needs less voltage amplification than the magnetic type; however, the output impedance of the device is quite high: approximately 1 megohm. Also, the fidelity to input amplitude tends to fall above about 15 kilohertz. *Crystal microphones* are sound transducers that use a piezoelectric element and therefore operate on much the same principle as the ceramic phonograph cartridge and with similar advantages and disadvantages. Similarly, geophones for use underwater in offshore explorations generally use piezoelectric elements to sense the water pressure variations associated with a seismic signal.

Photovoltaic Cell and Photodiode

The *photovoltaic* cell can be used to convert light energy directly into electrical energy and thus has aroused considerable interest during this energy-conscious era. Space satellites have used these *solar cells* to generate their electrical energy requirements. Scientists are further interested in them as a light transducer that generates a voltage or current in relation to the light irradiating the cell. The *photodiode* is essentially a small photovoltaic cell that is especially constructed to be useful as a light sensor.

The construction of a photovoltaic cell or photodiode is basically the same as that of a normal diode. The *semiconductor diode* is discussed in some detail in Chapter A4, but the *silicon photovoltaic cell,* invented at Bell Telephone Laboratories in 1953 by D. Chapin and C.S. Fuller, is described here. The description uses some of the terms from semiconductor physics that will be clarified in Chapter A4.

A thin layer of P-type silicon is formed near the surface of a slab of N-type silicon, thereby developing a *PN junction* as shown in Figure A3–9a. A silicon semiconductor diode is therefore constructed. When light photons strike the PN junction region, charge carriers (holes and electrons) are produced that move under the electric field that exists in the junction. Electrons move to the N region and the positive-charge-acting holes move to the P region so that a voltage difference is produced in the contacts to the cell. That is, metal contacts to the opposite sides of the cell exhibit this voltage and carry current sustained by the process to an external circuit. If very little current I is drawn from the cell—that is, *no load*—the voltage V of the cell increases with the light intensity but approaches a *saturation level* of about

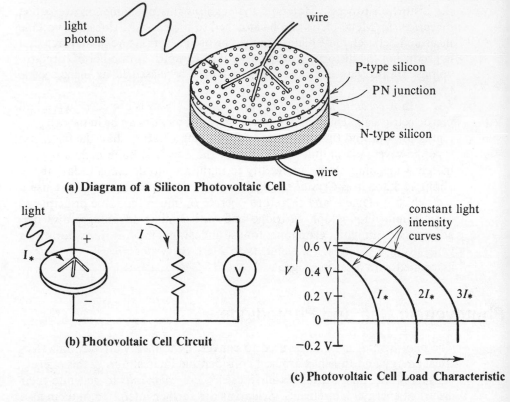

(a) Diagram of a Silicon Photovoltaic Cell

(b) Photovoltaic Cell Circuit

(c) Photovoltaic Cell Load Characteristic

FIGURE A3-9. *Silicon Photovoltaic Cell*

0.6 V that cannot be exceeded. Thus the voltage increases with light intensity *I** but in a very nonlinear fashion. This voltage versus current behavior is illustrated in the *load characteristic plot* of Figure A3-9c by the intersection points on the *V* axis of the various curves of constant light intensity. (Note the crowding together near 0.6 V.) However, the *short-circuit output current* is directly proportional to the light intensity, *I** (note the even spacing of the intersections along the *I* axis). That is, the current through a very low resistance (such as a good ammeter) connected across the cell is directly proportional to the light intensity striking the cell and provides a convenient linear light transducer.

However, it should be realized that the cell is responsive to light only over a certain range of light wavelengths. For silicon cells this *spectral response* ranges from about 400 nanometers (4000Å) to about 1100 nanometers (11,000Å). The amount of current depends upon the area of the cell and its efficiency of light energy conversion; therefore, no units are placed along the *I* scale of Figure A3-9c. However, when a cell is placed in full sunlight, an output current on the order of 20 milliamperes per centimeter^2 of cell area can be expected.

The PN junction may also be conveniently used in a different mode. An *external* voltage may be applied to *reverse bias* the junction: positive applied to N-type side (the cathode) and negative applied to P-type side (the anode). Then the current that flows is again directly proportional to the light intensity falling on the diode junction. This behavior is illustrated in Figure A3–9c by the constant intensity curves as they extend to the negative quadrant in terms of voltage. Generally only a tiny chip of semiconductor material is used for devices designed to be operated in this mode, and they are termed *photodiodes*. An important feature of photodiodes is their rapid response times to changes in light intensity. Thus the Texas Instruments TIED80 is rated with a 15 nanosecond (15×10^{-9} seconds) response time, while special *P.I.N.* photodiodes can respond in a fraction of a nanosecond.

Other Transducers

Snap-Action Switch

Detecting the presence of an object (perhaps a rat's paw or some moving mechanism) can sometimes be accomplished quite simply by a little switch that is activated by a small force acting through a small distance. For example, a psychologist may want to measure the number of times that a rat presses a bar and obtains a portion of food; or a physicist may want a small motor to be turned off when a zone refiner heating element passes a point in its travel. The small switch that is convenient for application in both cases is called a *snap-action switch*, although the term *microswitch*, which is a trade name, is also commonly used.

Pressing a small button on the snap-action switch either causes the switch to close a pair of *normally open* (NO) contacts or open a pair of *normally closed* (NC) contacts. Both types are available and operate with a *common* contact in the single-pole–double-throw (SPDT) type of switch. Often a hinged lever is attached to increase the mechanical advantage. An operating force in the range of 10 grams (0.35 ounces) to 100 grams is typical, with a current handling capability on the order of 5 amperes at 115 V. Removing the force causes the switch to snap back to its normal contact state. Figure A3–10a illustrates a typical switch of this type. Figure A3–10b shows a circuit that might be used with an electromechanical counter to monitor the number of times the switch has been pressed. Counters requiring a pulse of current (perhaps 300 milliamperes) at 24 V to turn the number wheels up one unit are commonly available, and such a counter is assumed in Figure A3–10b.

Magnetic Reed Switch

Another simple but useful switch that has many applications is the *reed switch;* it is especially useful in situations where we want to sense the

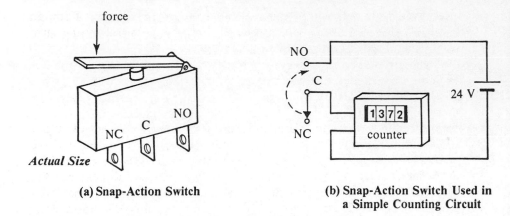

(a) Snap-Action Switch

(b) Snap-Action Switch Used in a Simple Counting Circuit

FIGURE A3–10. *Snap-Action SPDT Switch*

proximity of an object without physical force or contact. The switch consists of overlapping reeds constructed of a ferromagnetic material that are placed inside a hermetically sealed glass tube perhaps 3 centimeters long. If the reeds are normally slightly separated (normally open), bringing a small permanent magnet near the reeds causes them to snap together and close the switch; removing the magnet will permit the reeds to flex back to their normally open configuration. These switches will work reliably for millions of operations at rates up to several hundred operations per second and can typically control currents of the order of a hundred milliamperes at up to 50 V. (Various ratings are available.)

Figure A3–11 illustrates a typical reed switch in a simple circuit in an application that requires counting the number of revolutions of a shaft. As the shaft turns, the magnet closes the switch and increments the counter.

A *reed relay* is constructed by placing a wire coil around the reed switch. Passing a current of perhaps 20 milliamperes through the coil pro-

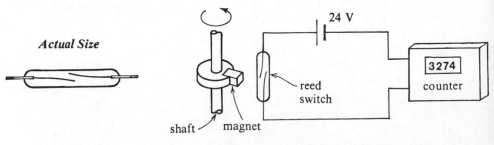

(a) Reed Switch

(b) Reed Switch Used in a Simple Circuit

FIGURE A3–11. *Reed Switch*

duces a magnetic field within the coil that closes the reed switch. Thus, an electrically operated switch is obtained; this is what is meant by the term *relay*. (Relays are discussed in the next section.)

Electromagnetic Relay

The *electromagnetic relay,* or simply *relay,* can be considered a type of output transducer. It is simply an electrically operated switch and has been a staple of electrical circuits for many years. In recent years, the *solid-state relay* (discussed in Chapter A8 and presented in Figure A8–29) has replaced the electromagnetic relay in a number of applications. However, the "old-fashioned relay" still enjoys a great deal of usage. It is a simple solution to the situation that calls for a small current to control—that is, turn on and off—a large current in some circuit.

The schematic symbol for the electromagnetic relay strongly suggests its construction (see Figure A3–12). The *relay coil* is in fact an electromagnet. When a current greater than the *pull-in current* for the particular relay passes through the coil, its magnetic field pulls the iron *armature* of the relay to a position nearer the coil. Conversely, when the coil current falls below the *drop-out current,* a spring attached to the armature snaps it back to the "dropped-out" position. But the *pole* of a switch is an integral part of this armature; often it is the pole of a *single-pole–double-throw* (SPDT) switch. Therefore, we have a SPDT switch that operates in response to an electrical input. The SPDT switch configuration is illustrated for the relay in Figure A3–12.

Sensitive relays may have a pull-in current of a few milliamperes in response to a coil voltage on the order of 12 V. Typically, the coil's resistance and voltage for pull-in are given by the manufacturer. A second important rating is that of the switch contacts. The contacts of a sensitive relay are typically capable of switching 1 ampere at about 120 V. Heavy-duty relays

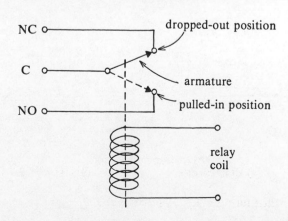

FIGURE A3–12. *Conventional Electromagnetic Relay*

often require coil currents of some hundred milliamperes at a coil voltage of 24 V and can switch tens of amperes at hundreds of volts. However, pitting of the switch contact points can be a problem. A significant resistance can develop between the closed points and thus inhibit current flow in the target circuit. Pitting results from the arcing between the points at the moments of "make" or "break." Life expectancy may range from 100,000 operations to several million, depending on the design.

Solenoid and Solenoid Valve

The pull-action *solenoid* is an output transducer that converts electrical energy to a mechanical movement. This device is useful when a small physical motion is desired as an output process. Push-pull–type solenoids are also available. These devices use an electromagnet in the form of a hollow solenoid to pull an iron plunger through a stroke that is typically about 1.5 centimeters (see Figure A3–13). The pull on the plunger exists as long as the solenoid (coil) receives sufficient current, which may be ac or dc depending on the type. The force exerted on the plunger ranges from a few ounces (~0.5N) for miniature units with exterior dimensions of about $1.5 \times 1.5 \times 4\,cm^3$, to three pounds (~15 N) for larger units with $3.5 \times 3.5 \times 4\,cm^3$ dimensions. The power required by the electromagnet coil ranges from 3 W to 24 W for these respective capabilities and may be from 12 V or 24 V_{dc} sources, or 120 or 240 V_{ac} mains.

For on/off control of fluid flow through tubing, a *solenoid valve* may be used. This output transducer is an electrically operated valve. It uses an internal solenoid to move a plunger which opens a flow path. 120 V_{ac} coil voltage at a current on the order of 0.2 A is a typical requirement to operate the valve, which may be normally open or normally closed. These valves are common fixtures in any automatic clothes washer or dishwasher machine.

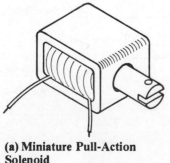

(a) Miniature Pull-Action Solenoid

(b) Diagram

coil

stroke

closed position

ferromagnetic plunger

FIGURE A3–13.   *Pull-Action Solenoid*

REVIEW EXERCISES

1. (a) Does the resistance of a photoresistor increase or decrease as it is brought from a dark room to a well-lit room?
   (b) Explain briefly the direction of the effect.
2. Select from the choices given for a characterization of: A. a thermistor and B. a platinum resistance temperature detector (RTD).
   (a) Its resistance increases with temperature increase.
   (b) Its resistance decreases with temperature increase.
   (c) Its resistance has approximately exponential dependence on temperature.
   (d) Its resistance has approximately linear dependence on temperature.
   (e) It has high absolute accuracy.
   (f) It has high sensitivity.
3. Describe how a thermistor may be used to give a measure of wind speed or of fluid flow in a tube. It thus becomes the essential element in a flow meter.
   NOTE: Consider wind chill.
4. Diagram a Wheatstone bridge with one active strain gauge, and one dummy gauge. Label these gauges. Describe the purpose for this arrangement and, in qualitative terms, how it achieves the purpose.
5. What is the difficulty expected with using a conventional ohmmeter with a conductivity cell?
   NOTE: This difficulty holds true even for high-accuracy, wide-range ohmmeters found in many quality DVMs.
6. What is the difference in the electrical output from a thermocouple compared with that from a thermistor?
7. The voltage output from a pH indicator/reference cell pair is 59 mV/pH near room temperature. The majority of DVMs on the market can measure voltage with 0.1-mV resolution or better. Nevertheless, the majority cannot be used as the voltage measuring component in a pH meter. Why not?
8. Why are electromagnetic induction transducers (which do not use an external ac voltage) suitable only for measuring an oscillating motion?
9. Briefly contrast the operating principle of the dynamic microphone to that of the crystal microphone.
10. The photoresistor and the photovoltaic cells are sometimes confused. What are the essential differences between these devices?
11. Some computer circuits are being interconnected with fiber-optic ("light-pipe") cables for high-speed, electrical-interference-immune communications. The light intensity into a cable can be modulated (turned on and off) at a rate of many megahertz. For use as a detector at the receiving end, we might consider a photoresistor or a photodiode. Which would we choose and why?
12. We wish to use a photovoltaic cell to obtain an output that is directly proportional to the light intensity falling on it. What should be the mode of operation of the cell?
13. Describe the principle of operation of a reed-type electromagnetic relay.
14. (a) What are meant by the NO, C, and NC contacts, respectively, on an elec-

tromagnetic relay? Make a diagram to illustrate your discussion.

(b)   What are meant by the pull-in and drop-out currents of an electromagnetic relay?

PROBLEMS

1.   Suppose a photoresistor has a resistance of 2000 ohms at an illuminance (light intensity) of 400 lux. What would be its resistance in direct sunlight, where the illuminance is about 10^5 lux? Assume that the photoresistor obeys a power law with an exponent of 0.7.

2.   A simple calculation can be made to test how accurately the thermistor of Table A3–1 (in the chapter text) follows exponential behavior. For accurate exponential change, the device should show the same *percentage* change in any identical temperature intervals.

   (a)   Evaluate the percentage change in resistance for the four 50°C temperature intervals in Table A3–1.

   (b)   Is the thermistor accurately exponential?

   (c)   Is there a trend in the data?

3.   The thermistor of Table A3–1 is used in the bridge pictured in Diagram A3–1.

   (a)   What is the magnitude of the voltage V_{out} at 0°C, 25°C, and 50°C?

   (b)   What point (A or B) is more positive at each temperature in part (a)?

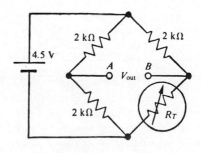

DIAGRAM A3–1.

4.   A certain thermistor has a resistance at 25°C that is a factor of 19.8 more than its resistance at 125°C.

   (a)   Assume exponential behavior over the temperature range. What is the value of E in Equation A3–2 for this unit? What are its dimensions?

   (b)   Suppose the resistance for the thermistor is 2000 ohms at 25°C. What will the resistance be at 100°C?

5.   Suppose a resistance thermometer is used in a Wheatstone bridge wherein the three other arms have equal resistances. The excitation voltage to the bridge is 6 V, and the bridge balances at 25°C.

   (a)   If the resistance thermometer is a pure metal, the temperature coefficient for its resistance can be expected to be about $(1/300)(C°)^{-1}$. What is the magnitude of the output voltage when the temperature of the thermometer is 26°C?

(b) Assume that the resistance thermometer is a thermistor with a temperature coefficient of $-5\%(C^\circ)^{-1}$. What is the magnitude of the bridge output at 26° C?

6. The fractional change in resistance $\Delta R/R$ of a strain gauge is proportional to the strain $\Delta L/L$ that it experiences (for $\Delta L/L$ less than about 10^{-3}). We write $\Delta R/R = G\Delta L/L$, where G is the *gauge factor* for the particular gauge. For most metals, G is on the order of 2, but for semiconductors it can be on the order of 200.

(a) Assuming a single active strain gauge in a Wheatstone bridge with equal arm resistances, find an expression for the output from the bridge in terms of bridge excitation voltage, gauge factor, and strain.

(b) Argue that other things being equal, the output from a bridge with a semiconductor strain gauge is much greater than for the case with a metallic strain gauge. However, what rather serious problem can be expected with a semiconductor strain gauge?

NOTE: Recall what a thermistor is.

7. Diagram A3–2 illustrates a force transducer that is based on strain gauges. The diagram shows a bar (originally straight) with strain gauges *A* and *B* mounted on the opposite sides (by use of an adhesive). One end of the bar is fixed, while a force applied to the opposite end causes the bar to bend, as shown in Diagram A3–2.

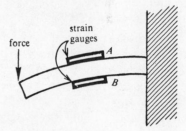

DIAGRAM A3–2.

(a) Which gauge is in extension and which is in compression?

(b) Discuss how this arrangement can be used to advantage in a half-active Wheatstone bridge.

NOTE: When a strain gain is made to compress, its resistance decreases.

(c) Discuss how a platform (weighing) scale with electrical readout could be constructed using this force transducer. (This is a form of load cell.)

8. Assume that a copper-constantan thermocouple is used to monitor the temperature of a sample. Approximately what voltage resolution is required to observe 0.1C° variations in temperature?

9. Given the definition of pH (Equation A3–3) and Nernst's Law (Equation A3–4), justify the numerical value: 59 mV per unit change of pH at 25°C.

10. A displacement transducer based on the variable capacitance of two metal plates can readily be imagined. We could consider having a capacitor with the displacement changing the distance between the plates, or changing the overlap area of two parallel plates. Select and justify the case:

(a) Which would be most sensitive to small displacements?

(b) Which would have capacity approximately proportional to displacement?

11. Suppose that a ferrite rod or a laminated iron rod is free to slide into a solenoid.
    (a) Describe how this arrangement could be a transducer for measuring linear position.
    (b) What property of the solenoid could be measured? Can this be a dc measurement?

12. A certain sensitive electromagnetic relay requires 5 V at a coil current of 20 mA for pull-in operation.
    (a) What is the coil resistance of the relay?
    (b) What is the input power required to operate the relay? (This is a valid measure of relay sensitivity.)

13. Electromagnetic relays that require less than 5 V at perhaps 20 mA to operate the relay are rare.
    (a) Why is it not possible for a single photovoltaic cell (solar battery) to operate a relay?
    (b) How might several photovoltaic cells be interconnected to operate a relay directly? What would be an approximate minimum number, assuming silicon photovoltaic cells and a sensitive relay as described?
    (c) Why is the area of each photovoltaic cell also of importance?

14. We wish to regulate the temperature of a warm box using a thermistor R_T, a sensitive electromagnetic relay, and a 100-W heater operated from 110 V. (The heater could be a 100-W bulb.) The relay's characteristics and the circuit are shown in Diagram A3–3. Of course, the thermistor and heater are both placed in the warm box.
    (a) Justify qualitatively that if the temperature of the box and thermistor are sufficiently high, the system behavior is such that the heating will stop. However, as the temperature then falls, heating will resume at some temperature.
    (b) We desire the system to stop heating at 30°C. What should be the thermistor resistance at 30°C to achieve this behavior?
    (c) As the temperature falls, what is the thermistor resistance when heating again resumes?
    (d) Assume that the thermistor resistance changes by −5%/C° near 30°C. At what temperature does the unit begin heating again? Note that the temperature is maintained only within a certain interval, often called the hysteresis of the regulator. The regulation is *not* particularly good for this simple circuit.

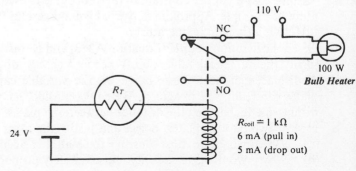

110 V

NC

100 W
Bulb Heater

R_T

NO

$R_{coil} = 1\ k\Omega$
6 mA (pull in)
5 mA (drop out)

DIAGRAM
A3–3.

24 V

CHAPTER
A4

Diodes
and Power Supplies

We begin the study of electronic devices and their utilization in this chapter. The principal actor in this study is the diode—a device that permits electrons to flow through it in only one direction. Since the diode does not actually achieve amplification of electrical signals, it is generally placed in the class of the passive devices that were studied in Chapter A1. Yet an understanding of the mechanism by which diodes operate is a direct precursor to the understanding of amplifying devices. Thus, in this chapter we study briefly the vacuum tube diode; this study permits the essential behavior of the vacuum tube triode to be quite readily understood in Chapter A8. Then our study moves to the solid-state diode.

The term *solid state* has quickly become a part of everyday language. Consider for example advertisements for the "all solid-state television." Whereas electrons are controlled as they move through a vacuum in the vacuum tube, it is their rather special behavior in *semiconducting solids* that is exploited in the solid-state diode and in various forms of transistors. In this chapter a basic account of semiconductor behavior is given that is then used to understand the solid-state diode; semiconductor behavior is later used to understand the essential features of transistor action (Chapter A8). Since transistors and diodes are fundamental constituents of integrated circuits (ICs), the story of modern miniaturized electronics properly begins in this chapter.

Although the diode itself has a surprising number of applications, in this chapter the diode will be applied only to the process of *rectification;*

A113

that is, any process that changes an alternating current to a direct current. Rectification is central to the theme of the chapter: techniques for making an electronic battery from an ac power source. The formal term for an electronic battery is *power supply*. Power supplies are important to the scientist because dc power is required, at least internally, for the operation of virtually all electronic equipment.

Ideal Diode

The *ideal diode* is a circuit element that passes current only one way. It is a "one-way street" for electrons. Figure A4–1a shows the circuit symbol for a diode, and Figure A4–1b and c show the voltage polarity that results in *current flow* and *no flow,* respectively. The arrow of the symbol points in the direction of permitted *conventional* current flow. If the anode of the diode is made more positive than the cathode, current will pass through and the diode is said to be *forward biased.* Figure A4–1b, therefore, shows a forward-biased diode, while the diode in Figure A4–1c is *reverse biased.*

The diode is a *nonlinear* device. The reason for this statement becomes clear when we look at the contrasting graphs of current versus voltage for an ideal resistor and an ideal diode. Figure A4–2 shows such graphs, which are called the *current-voltage characteristics* for the two devices. On the horizontal axis is the voltage across the device, while the current flowing through it is on the vertical axis. Notice that both negative and positive voltage (as well as current) possibilities are graphed; these correspond to one voltage sense or the other across a device similar to Figures A4–1b and c.

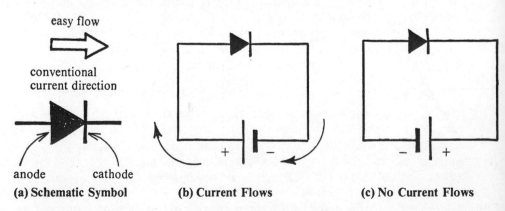

easy flow

conventional
current direction

anode   cathode

(a) Schematic Symbol   (b) Current Flows   (c) No Current Flows

FIGURE A4–1.   *Diode Symbol and Current Flow Sense*

The positive voltage axis in Figure A4–2b corresponds to a forward-biased condition for the diode. The current that then flows is called a *forward current*. Notice the large forward current that flows as soon as the *ideal diode* is even minutely forward biased. The negative voltage axis in Figure A4–2b represents a reverse-biased condition for the diode. Any current that then flows is called a *reverse current* or *leakage current*. Figure A4–2b shows the reverse current is zero for any reverse voltage across an ideal diode.

Real Diodes

Vacuum Diode

The *vacuum diode* has been in existence since about 1900 and for many decades was the diode most widely used. It is reviewed here very briefly because it is not used in new designs; however, it is still encountered in the lab in older equipment that uses vacuum tubes. Examples include vacuum tube voltmeters, oscilloscopes, and oscillators.

The vacuum diode consists of a filament, cathode, and plate inside an evacuated glass tube as shown in Figure A4–3a. The schematic symbol for a vacuum diode is shown in Figure A4–3b. The *filament* or heater is typically operated from 6.3 V or 12.6 V and glows red hot. (When the filament burns out or opens, similar to the filament of a light bulb, it is useless.) The very hot filament heats the metal cathode structure and literally boils electrons out of

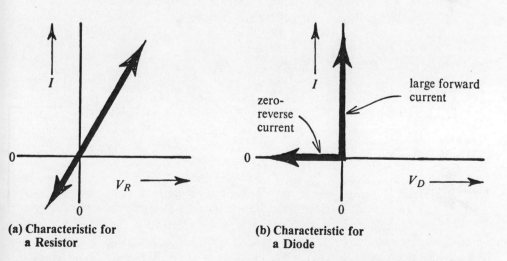

(a) Characteristic for a Resistor

(b) Characteristic for a Diode

FIGURE A4–2. *Current-Voltage Characteristic Graphs for an Ideal Resistor and an Ideal Diode*

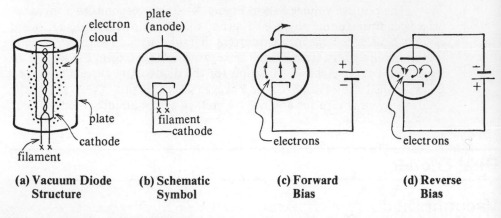

FIGURE A4–3. *Vacuum Diode*

it. The *cathode* is covered with a special oxide that promotes the emission of electrons at lower temperatures.

Surrounding the cathode cylinder is a second cylinder called the *plate*. If the plate is made positive with respect to the cathode, as shown in Figure A4–3c, the electrons are attracted toward it and current flows through the tube. If the plate is made negative relative to the cathode, the electrons are simply repelled back nearer the cathode and no sustained flow of charge or current results. The device acts like a one-way street for electrons.

NOTE: The term *diode* derives from the fact that just two elements—plate and cathode—are principally involved.

Semiconductor Diode

Like the vacuum diode, the *solid-state diode* has actually also been around since about 1900. The "cat whisker" of an old-time crystal set is a solid-state diode; it was a *point-contact diode* that utilized the curious one-way conducting behavior of the contact between a wire and a semiconductor crystal, but this was a temperamental diode that was not easily mass produced.

When pure semiconductor behavior and fabrication became well understood in the 1940s, the semiconductor diode became possible. *Silicon* and *germanium,* which both have 4 valence electrons, are the commonly used semiconductors of electronics. Each electron is shared with a neighbor's electron to form covalent bonds as diagrammed in Figure A4–4; a group of 8 electrons is thus in the outer shell of each atom. The simple picture, sufficient for our purposes, is that these electrons are quite tightly bound in place and not free to move around; thus, the charge carriers are not available and

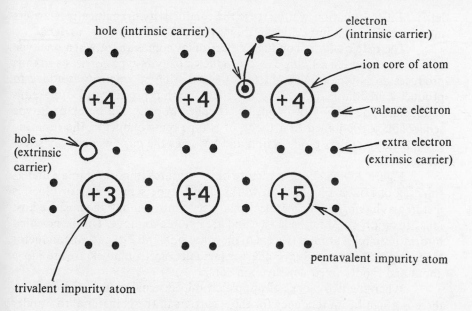

FIGURE A4–4. *Representation of Silicon or Germanium Atoms Showing Bonding Electrons and Impurity Atoms*

an insulator material would result if it were not for the mechanisms discussed next.

Thermal agitation will shake a few electrons free; these electrons can move under an electric field and thus be charge carriers. One such electron is circled at the top of Figure A4–4 and labeled an *intrinsic carrier;* because it is negatively charged, it is called an *N-type charge carrier.* A *hole* is left where the electron was, and neighbor electrons are inclined to jump into it. When one does, the hole moves to a different atom and charge motion is involved. The charge motion behaves as though a positive charge is jumping along with the hole; thus, we may think of a positive or *P-type charge carrier* as having also been broken loose by thermal agitation.

Not many of these intrinsic carriers are present at room temperature in pure silicon or germanium (about one per 10^{12} atoms in silicon and one per 10^9 atoms in germanium), therefore, they are poor conductors, or *semiconductors.* However, even tiny amounts of an impurity can change the situation. If a pentavalent impurity such as phosphorus is present, the fifth electron is not needed for bonding and becomes quite free to roam around the lattice. The fifth electron is a negative or N-type carrier, and such an atom is diagrammed in the bottom segment of Figure A4–4. On the other hand, if a trivalent impurity like boron is present, a missing bonding electron or hole automatically exists. A neighbor electron can quite easily jump into it and, as the process continues, a hole or positive-acting P-type carrier hops about the lattice. Either situation will increase the conductivity dramatically. Carriers introduced through impurities in this way are called *extrinsic carriers.*

The magic of semiconductor electronics comes about when one type of impurity is added *on purpose* to produce mostly N-type carriers and thus produces an N-type semiconductor or else a different impurity is added to produce a predominance of P-type carriers and thus produces a P-type semiconductor. The adding of impurities is called *doping.* If a block of P-type semiconductor is joined to a block of N-type semiconductor, the resulting *PN junction* exhibits diode action and becomes the curious one-way street for current.

Figure A4–5a shows a picture of the features important to an understanding of how a PN junction works. The N-type semiconductor block is pictured as having − charges (electrons) free to move about; the positive host ions are rigidly fixed in the lattice and are not free to move. This is indicated by drawing circles around the +. On the other side, the P-type semiconductor block is pictured as having + charges (actually electron holes) free to move about and rigidly fixed negative ion cores.

When the two blocks of oppositely doped semiconductors are joined, there is a significant tendency for the − carriers in the N material to wander or *diffuse* over into the P block, and also for the + carriers in the P material to diffuse into the N block. This tendency is very similar to the tendency in nature for different gases in a volume to distribute themselves uniformly throughout the volume. Suppose two adjoining rooms are first filled with pure oxygen and nitrogen gas, respectively, and then a door between the two rooms is opened. The oxygen molecules will diffuse into the room with no oxygen concentration, and the nitrogen molecules will diffuse in a similar manner. After a short time both rooms are filled with an oxygen and nitrogen mixture.

We may similarly think of the − and + carriers in these semiconductor blocks as charged gas-like particles bouncing about in rooms. When the

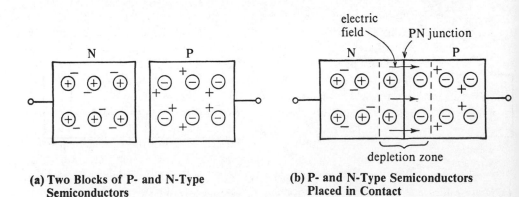

(a) Two Blocks of P- and N-Type
    Semiconductors

(b) P- and N-Type Semiconductors
    Placed in Contact

FIGURE A4–5. *P- and N-Type Semiconductors*

blocks are joined, the − carriers in the N block will wander into the P block for some distance. There each soon encounters a + carrier (a hole); the electron drops into the vacant bond represented by the hole, and both carriers disappear as a normal bonding arrangement results. However, the − carriers do *not* achieve a uniform distribution throughout the two blocks by any means, because they leave behind bare or *uncovered* + stationary host ions in the N block near the junction, and these ions set up an electric field tending to pull the wanderers back. Similarly, some of the + carriers in the P block diffuse into the N block, but they leave behind uncovered − host ions in the P block near the junction that inhibits other + carriers from diffusing over. The result is a *depletion zone* of primarily host ions—that is, a zone depleted of carriers—near the junction, and this situation is shown in Figure A4–5b.

An electric field develops in this depletion zone between the + and − ions near the junction (much as between the plates of a capacitor), and the push of this field will keep most of the − and + carriers on their respective sides of the junction. This field is sketched in Figure A4–5b. Because of this field there is a voltage difference V_0 that develops between the two blocks of semiconductors after they are joined; this voltage difference is called the *barrier voltage*.

Now the remarkable diode action of this device can be explained. Consider a battery connected with its plus terminal to N and minus terminal to P as shown in Figure A4–6a. The − carriers in the N material will initially be attracted toward the plus terminal and move some distance toward it. However, more uncovered + ions then appear near the junction, and soon an equilibrium tension develops between the attractions to these two positive elements. Similarly the + carriers in the P block are attracted initially toward the minus battery terminal, but soon stop due to the attraction back toward the additional − ions that appear near the junction. The end result as shown

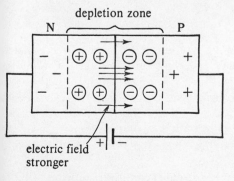

(a) Reverse-Biased PN Junction

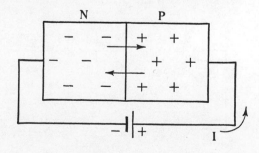

(b) Forward-Biased PN Junction

FIGURE A4-6. *Reverse- and Forward-Biased PN Junctions*

in Figure A4–6a is a widening of the depletion zone (and an even greater electric field barrier to diffusion across the junction) but no sustained current flow. We have a *reverse-biased diode*. Actually, a tiny *reverse-leakage current* flows because the very few minority intrinsic − carriers in the P block diffuse over to the junction and are swept across by the field there (the field direction does *not* inhibit minority carriers) so that they continuously neutralize some of the retarding + host ions and permit a like number of − carriers to flow out the end of the N block to the plus battery terminal. A similar flow of minority intrinsic + carriers out of the N block occurs in the opposite direction. This current is essentially constant no matter what the battery voltage is.

On the other hand, if the plus terminal of the battery is connected to the P material (and minus terminal to the N material) as shown in Figure A4–6b, the carriers in each block will initially be repelled from the battery terminals and propelled toward the junction. The width of the depletion zone is decreased and the barrier presented by the electric field there is lessened. Now many carriers have the energy to pass through the depletion zone and into the other side (where they soon neutralize with carriers of the opposite type). The continuous neutralization of the carriers in the vicinity of the junction causes more carriers to be supplied by the battery at the ends of each block, where they then move toward the junction. (Electrons enter from the wire at the N end; they depart from the P-end wire, but leave + holes in the process that then move toward the junction.) Thus, a continuous current flows, and we have a *forward-biased diode*. In fact, if the applied battery voltage is as large as the barrier voltage (about 0.3 V for germanium diodes and about 0.6 V for silicon diodes), the barrier is removed and the current becomes very large; that is, limited only by the actual resistance of the semiconductor blocks.

Characteristic of a PN Junction: Real Devices

The current-voltage characteristic of a PN junction is not the perfectly sharp angle graph of an ideal diode, where even an infinitesimal forward-bias voltage results in a very large current. However, it is much closer to the ideal than the old vacuum diode. When forward biased, the current does not begin rising appreciably until the battery voltage is of the order of the barrier voltage V_0, and V_0 depends on the semiconductor used in construction. As was just mentioned, the barrier voltage is about 0.3 V for germanium, and about 0.6 V for silicon.

A graph of the semiconductor diode characteristic is shown in Figure A4–7. It will be observed that the current appears to increase steeply after the *knee* of the diode curve is reached. This knee is at about 0.2 to 0.3 V for diodes constructed from germanium and at about 0.6 V to 0.7 V for silicon

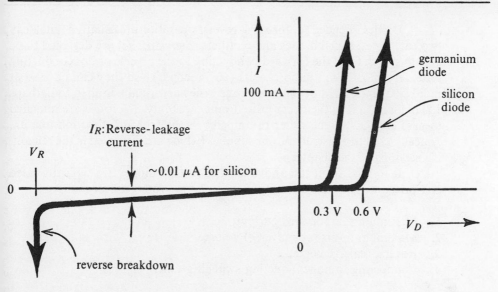

FIGURE A4–7.   *Semiconductor Diode Characteristic*

diodes. In fact—especially for applied voltages below the knee—the curve follows a theoretical exponential curve quite well (derived in solid-state physics). The theoretical relation is often called the *diode law:*

$$I = I_R \left(e^{\frac{|e| V_D}{kT}} - 1 \right) \tag{A4-1}$$

Here I is the current passing through the diode, I_R is the reverse-leakage current, $|e|$ is the magnitude of the charge on the electron, V_D the voltage across the diode, k is Boltzmann's constant, and T is the absolute temperature. The reverse-leakage current is a few hundredths of a microampere for silicon diodes; for germanium it is much larger, perhaps 50 microamperes. This leakage current increases with temperature because of the increase in thermally generated intrinsic carriers and increases more rapidly for silicon than for germanium. The ideal diode would have zero reverse-leakage current, of course.

In addition, the characteristic graph of real semiconductor diodes in Figure A4–7 shows that they do *not* withstand a reverse voltage or back-bias voltage to arbitrarily high values. There is a limit, called the *reverse-break-down voltage, V_R*. At this limit, reverse current then begins to flow, and if it is not limited in some way, the diode can be destroyed. The value at which this breakdown occurs can fluctuate from diode to diode in even one production batch. However, the limit is sharply defined for a given diode and put to good use as a voltage reference in *zener diodes* that are manufactured to have this reverse knee at a low-to-moderate voltage. (Zener diodes are briefly discussed within the Problems at the end of the chapter.)

Diodes intended for forward/reverse operation are usually available in two categories: signal diodes and rectifiers. *Signal diodes* are designed to be able to switch from the forward-conducting to the reverse or nonconducting state very rapidly—in nanoseconds (10^{-9} seconds)—so they can be used at radio frequencies and beyond. However, they are usually limited to perhaps 100 milliamperes in their forward-current capability. *Rectifiers* are intended to pass currents of the order of amperes in the forward direction and are typically used to construct power supplies (which are discussed in the remaining sections of the chapter).

It follows from the above discussion that diodes are typically rated and priced on the basis of three and sometimes four parameters:

1. Maximum safe forward current,
2. Maximum reverse (or inverse) voltage,
3. Reverse-leakage current,
4. Conducting to nonconducting switching time.

Figure A4–8 shows some typical diode shapes and identification features.

A longtime standard germanium signal diode is the 1N34, which has a maximum average forward-current capability of 50 milliamperes (though 1-second surges of 500 milliamperes are withstood), a maximum continuous-reverse voltage of 60 V, and a maximum reverse current of 50 microamperes at −10 V. A popular silicon switching diode (a *computer diode*) is the 1N914, which has nearly the same maximum characteristics as the 1N34 except that the reverse-leakage current is less than 0.025 microamperes. The 1N4001 to 1N4007 family of epoxy-case silicon rectifiers are widely available for use in power supplies and other applications where high currents must be passed. The maximum average forward current for these devices is 1 ampere, although 0.1-second surges of 10 amperes are possible. The maximum continuous reverse-voltage ranges from 50 V for the 1N4001 to 1,000 V for the 1N4007. Notice that the prefix 1N occurs with all these diodes and indicates a *JEDEC-registered diode.* Many semiconductor manufacturers produce them. The prefix *2N* indicates a *JEDEC-registered transistor.* JEDEC is the abbreviation for the Joint Electron Device Engineering Council.

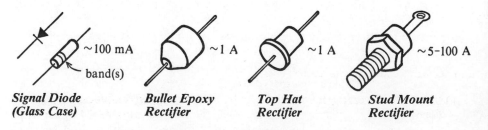

**Signal Diode
(Glass Case)**   **Bullet Epoxy
Rectifier**   **Top Hat
Rectifier**   **Stud Mount
Rectifier**

FIGURE A4–8. *Common Diode (Rectifier) Types*

Rectification and Filtering

Perhaps the most common application of diodes is in *rectification* of ac current/voltage to produce dc current/voltage. In many cases, rectification is done in a module that amounts to an "electronic battery"; that is, an ac voltage goes in and a dc voltage, such as from a battery, comes out. However, an appropriate filter circuit is required to approach a true dc voltage.

Half-Wave Rectification

First, the negative swings of the ac voltage must be blocked from passing to the output, and the diode is needed in order to do this. Consider the connection of transformer and diode shown in Figure A4–9a. To use a specific illustration, a transformer with a 12 V_{rms} secondary is illustrated. A time graph of the voltage between the leads of the transformer secondary is shown in Figure A4–9b. When the transformer lead at A swings positive in voltage compared to G, the diode becomes forward biased and conducts current easily, like a closed switch. But when the voltage at A goes negative with respect to G so that current would like to flow *into* terminal A, the diode will

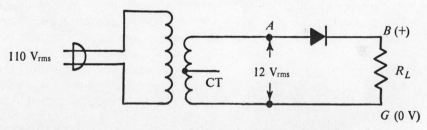

(a) Half-Wave Rectification Circuit with Load Resistor Attached

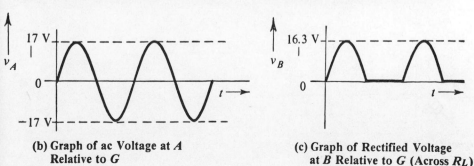

(b) Graph of ac Voltage at A Relative to G

(c) Graph of Rectified Voltage at B Relative to G (Across R_L)

FIGURE A4–9. *Half-Wave Rectification Circuit and Characteristic Graphs* not permit current flow in this sense. The diode reverts to acting like an open switch that disconnects the transformer at point A from the load at point B.

Thus, only the positive voltage swings appear across R_L, and current surges through R_L from B toward G only during these times. The current flows in only one direction through R_L, and point B is only made *positive* relative to G. The peak voltage appearing at B is the peak voltage from the transformer, which is $12 \text{ V}_{rms} \times \sqrt{2} = 17 \text{ V}$ in this case. Actually, a little less appears at B due to the nominal 0.7 V drop across the diode while conducting (assuming a silicon diode). Figure A4–9c shows a time graph of the voltage v_B that appears across R_L. The voltage curve v_B has the shape of half of the sine wave from the transformer; therefore the action of the circuit is called *half-wave rectification*.

Notice that during the half cycle that no current is flowing, no voltage appears across R_L; therefore the peak transformer voltage $V_p = 17 \text{ V}$ must appear as reverse bias across the diode. The existence of this reverse bias across the diode means we must use a diode with a minimum reverse breakdown of V_p in this circuit.

Although the voltage between B and G is unipolar, it is by no means steady and cannot yet be used as a battery replacement; it is satisfactory as a battery charger, however. If a battery of less than 16 V is connected between B and G as shown in Figure A4–10a, the current passes through the battery in only one sense (in surges) and the battery charges. Connecting the battery to just the transformer as shown in Figure A4–10b does *not* work since the current would pass in one sense just as much as the other. (Actually, the battery would discharge through the resistance of the secondary windings.) Charging current flows in Figure A4–10a whenever the instantaneous output voltage exceeds the battery voltage.

Full-Wave Rectification
Using a Center-Tapped Transformer

Let us consider the battery charger of Figure A4–10a again. The current flows during half of each cycle; during the remaining time nothing is ac-

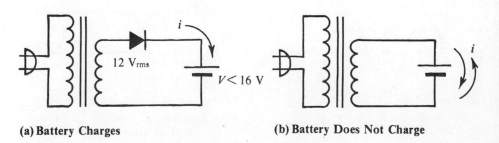

(a) Battery Charges   (b) Battery Does Not Charge

FIGURE A4–10. *Simple Battery Charger*

complished. The battery would charge more rapidly (in half the time) if we could arrange for current to flow from (+) to (−) through the battery during each half of a cycle. This can be done, and making full use of each cycle is called *full-wave rectification*.

One scheme for full-wave rectification requires a *center-tapped* (CT) *transformer* and two diodes. Figure A4–11a shows the diagram with only the secondary drawn. For illustration we assume that the same transformer as in Figure A4–9a is used (notice it was diagrammed as a CT transformer, although not needed there). The voltage between each end of the transformer and the CT ranges up to 8.5 V_{peak}, and the polarities alternate. First assume the "top end" (labeled T) of the transformer is (+) and the "bottom end" (labeled B) is (−) relative to CT as shown in Figure A4–11a. Then diode (1) is forward biased and conducts current, while diode (2) is reverse biased and blocks any current flow through it. During this half cycle, the current flows from the top (+) end through diode (1) and R_L to the center tap as shown by the dashed line. A peak voltage of about 8.5 V − 0.7 V = 7.8 V develops across the R_L load resistor as shown by the dashed half sine wave in Figure A4–11b. During the next half cycle, the polarities of the top and bottom ends of the transformer reverse relative to the midpoint (the top end goes negative compared to the bottom end). Now the bottom diode (2) is forward biased, since positive voltage is applied to its anode. Current flows from end B through diode (2) and the load resistance R_L to the CT as shown by the dotted line. Notice that the current flow is through R_L in the *same* sense as for the

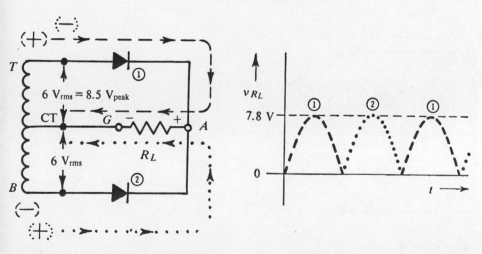

(a) Full-Wave Center-Tapped Rectification   (b) Voltage Waveform Appearing across R_L

FIGURE A4–11.   *Full-Wave Center-Tapped Rectification Circuit Showing Alternate Voltage Polarities and Current Loops along with the Voltage Waveform Appearing across R_L*

first half of the cycle, and the voltage across R_L follows the dotted half sine wave (2) in Figure A4–11b. A full-wave rectified waveform is pictured there. Notice that the peak voltage is only half of what was obtained in the half-wave case. However, the peak reverse voltage that the diodes must sustain is just as much as if the transformer were used in a half-wave circuit. This fact can be seen by noting that when point A is positive at $+7.8$ V, the voltage at the bottom of the transformer (point B) is at -8.5 V (relative to the CT); thus nearly 17 V develops across diode (2).

Full-Wave Rectification
Using a Bridge of Rectifiers

It is possible to obtain full-wave rectification without a center-tapped transformer, but at the expense of using four diodes. Today diodes are so cheap that using four diodes is the common approach.

Four diodes are arranged in a square with the load resistance connected across one diagonal and the transformer connected across the other as shown in Figure A4–12a. The name of the scheme—full-wave bridge rectification—derives from this bridge arrangement (like the Wheatstone bridge).

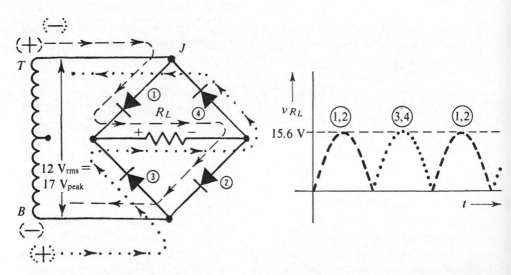

(a) Full-Wave Bridge Rectification   (b) Voltage Waveform Appearing across R_L

FIGURE A4–12.   *Full-Wave Bridge Rectification Showing Alternate Current Paths along with the Voltage Waveform Appearing across R_L*

Again assume the top of the transformer secondary is (+) and the bottom is (−) first. Current will attempt to flow out of T of the transformer to the junction J. Diode (1) will permit the current to progress through it while (4) will not (note the arrow senses of these two diodes). The dashed-line current then comes to a second junction with a choice of diode (3) or the load resistance R_L. Diode (3) says *no* (note its arrow) and the current passes left to right through the load resistance. Finally the current passes through agreeable diode (2) down to the negative bottom terminal of the transformer B. Note that the current would not go back "uphill" in voltage through diode (4).

Half a cycle later the secondary winding polarity has reversed to the bottom (+) and top (−). The student should justify that the current now follows the dotted path from B through diode (3), R_L, and diode (4) to the negative top T. Again note that the current passes in the same direction through the load resistor so that the left end is more positive and the right more negative. The voltage across R_L is full-wave rectified as illustrated in Figure A4–12b, with a peak value of approximately $17\,V - 0.7\,V - 0.7\,V = 15.6\,V$. With the same transformer, the voltage in the full-wave case is virtually the same as the voltage in the half-wave case. The student should justify why 0.7 V is subtracted twice in this case. The peak reverse voltage appearing on the diodes is also about 16 V.

Filtering to Obtain dc

The rectified waveform obtained in the circuits just described works fine for charging batteries, but such a device is a poor battery eliminator. Using one on a transistor radio, for example, would result in a loud 60-hertz or 120-hertz buzz from the radio. The peaks need to be "smoothed out." The easiest way to manage this need is with a simple *capacitor (C) filter*. A large capacitor (typically electrolytic) is connected across the rectifier output and thus is in parallel with whatever load resistance R_L is connected, as shown in Figure A4–13a.

To understand the smoothing process, assume the transformer is plugged in at instant $t = 0$ in Figure A4–13b. Then the voltage swings positive and the diode is forward biased; it conducts current like a closed switch to the load R_L and capacitor C. The capacitor charges and the voltage across it follows the waveform input up to point (1). At this time the voltage from the transformer begins dipping, and the capacitor should like to discharge through the diode (as well as through R_L). However, this current direction through the diode is the wrong way. The diode will not permit it and becomes back biased as the transformer voltage drops toward zero and beyond. Therefore, between points (1) and (2) in Figure A4–13b, the diode behaves like an open switch, and the capacitor must discharge (we hope, slowly) through the load resistance R_L. The voltage decreases exponentially with characteristic

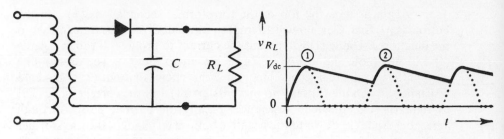

(a) Filtered Half-Wave Rectifier   **(b)** Smoothed Voltage Appearing across R_L

FIGURE A4–13. *Half-Wave Rectifier with Simple C Filter and Smoothed Voltage Appearing across R_L*

time RC between times (1) and (2). When the transformer voltage again rises to more than the voltage across the capacitor, the diode becomes forward biased, and the capacitor again charges to the peak voltage from the transformer. This process continues, and if the time to discharge (roughly RC) is much more than the time between voltage pulses, a quite steady voltage is sustained across the load resistor.

Notice that the dc voltage that develops is just the same as the peak voltage of the rectified waveform. There is always some *ripple* with a sawtooth-like shape riding atop the dc voltage. The ratio of the peak-peak voltage V_r of this sawtooth to the dc voltage is a measure of the quality of the dc voltage (ideally it would be zero). To calculate this ratio, it is sufficient for a rule-of-thumb design to imagine that the capacitor discharges linearly toward zero over a time RC as shown in Figure A4–14a. In fact, this approximation becomes precise in the case of small ripple.

The triangles with which we shall work in Figure A4–14b are obtained from the ripple and rectified ac waveforms (see Figure A4–14a). From the similar triangles we see that

$$\frac{V_r}{V_{dc}} = \frac{T}{RC} = \text{ripple ratio} \qquad \text{(A4–2)}$$

The time T in this expression is approximately the period between half sinusoids. If the transformer used in the power supply operates from the United States power lines, this time is $1/60$ seconds (see Figure A4–15a).

Now we are able to appreciate the advantage of smoothing out a full-wave rectified form. Again a capacitor may be placed directly across R_L for the job. The discharging now takes place over only $1/120$ seconds however, as shown in Figure A4–15b, and this value for T should be used in Equation A4–2. The ripple is reduced by a factor of two (for a given C and R_L) because the capacitor has only half as long to discharge.

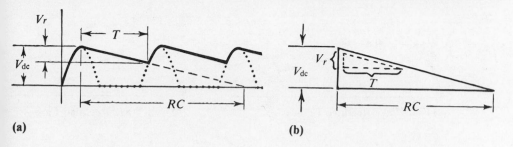

FIGURE A4-14. *Approximate Calculation of the Peak-Peak Ripple Voltage V_r*

Figure A4-15c shows a dc *power supply* or battery eliminator using a simple *C* filter in conjunction with a full-wave bridge rectifier circuit.

Example: Suppose in Figure A4-13 a 60-hertz, 12-V_{rms} transformer and capacitance of 500 microfarads are used. What is the dc voltage and ripple if this power supply is used with a load resistance of 100 ohms? What dc current is drawn from the supply?

Solution: The dc voltage will be $V_p = \sqrt{2} \times 12$ V = 17 V and the dc current drawn is 17 V/100 ohms = 170 milliamperes; next

$$V_r = \frac{V_{dc}T}{RC} = \frac{17 \text{ V}(1/60 \text{ s})}{100 \ \Omega \times 500 \ \times 10^{-6}\text{F}} = 5.6 \text{ V}$$

This is a lot of ripple (33%) and a larger capacitor should be used. Using the bridge rectifier of Figure A4-12 with this transformer would reduce the ripple to 2.8 V (16%).

Other Filter Schemes

The problem at hand is to reduce the ac voltage and retain the dc component of the voltage coming from the rectifier output. Clearly, a low-pass filter is an appropriate tool. We can use a resistor and capacitor—that is, an *RC filter*— as shown in Figure A4-16a, or better (though more expensive and bulky), an inductor and capacitor—that is, an *LC filter*—as shown in Figure A4-16b. Because of the ⌐ shape of the schematic drawing of the filter they are called *L-section filters*.

We examined the action of a filter in Chapter A1. Again, think of the ac ripple as being reduced by ac voltage divider action. We have impedance elements shown as boxes in Figure A4-17. The "dc part" of the rectified ac

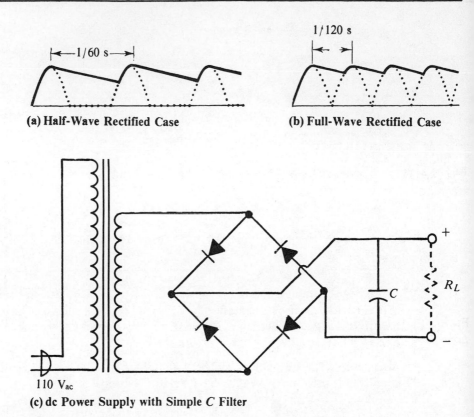

(a) Half-Wave Rectified Case

(b) Full-Wave Rectified Case

(c) dc Power Supply with Simple C Filter

FIGURE A4-15. *Reduced Ripple from a Filtered Full-Wave dc Power Supply*

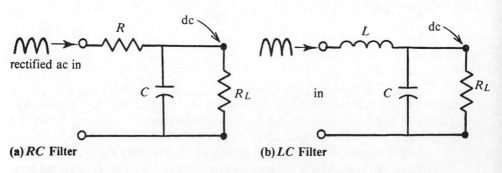

(a) RC Filter

(b) LC Filter

FIGURE A4-16. *L-Section Filters to Reduce Ripple*

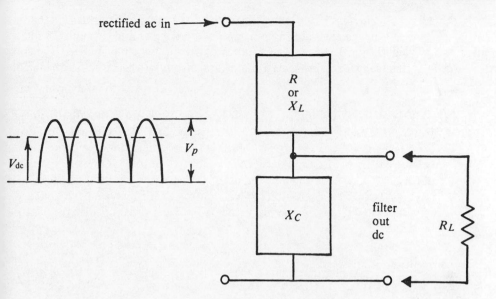

FIGURE A4–17. *Reduction of Ripple by ac Voltage Divider Action in the L-Section Low-Pass Filter*

voltage waveform—that is, the average value of the rectified ac waveform—passes to the output easily. The dc voltage from the output of the filter works out to be about $(2/\pi)V_p$ or $0.64\ V_p$ for the full-wave rectified input. The ac component is reduced greatly if $R \gg X_C$ or if $X_L \gg X_C$. Then the ripple voltage out is of the order of X_C/R times $V_{ac,in}$ ($V_{ac,in}$ is approximately V_p) for the resistor L section; or X_C/X_L times V_p for the inductor L section.

The resistor input L-section filter is not as desirable if there are variations in the load current because there will be variations in the dc drop that develops across it. The dc voltage out then varies also.

Electronic Voltage Regulators

The ripple remaining after filtering may be in excess of what is tolerable in a scientific application. There are two other problems:

1. *Line voltage variations:* If the power company voltage fluctuates by 10%, for example, this fluctuation also appears in the transformer output and ultimately in the dc voltage.

2. *Load current variations:* When the load resistance changes, changes occur in the current drawn from the transformer and through the diodes and filter. Because of resistance in these elements, increased current results in a drop in the dc voltage (and also typically results in an increase in ripple).

Electronic circuits may be used to greatly reduce the fluctuations in dc voltage due to ripple, line voltage variations, and load current variations; these circuits are called *voltage regulators.* The general voltage regulator can be adjusted to provide the desired dc voltage as output. However, many applications simply require one or more of the standard voltages used with integrated circuits. Therefore, we will confine the discussion here to a group of widely used fixed-voltage regulators, also called three-terminal regulators.

Three-Terminal Regulators

Electronic techniques to regulate against variations in line voltage or load changes have long been available but were relatively expensive. However, integrated circuits (ICs) have now made this elegant approach as cheap as a banana split! One handy type of unit—the *three-terminal regulator*—takes as its input any voltage a few volts higher than the design dc output voltage and *reduces* it to a certain steady dc voltage out (see Figure A4–18a). There is also an upper limit to the voltage that the device can take as input voltage.

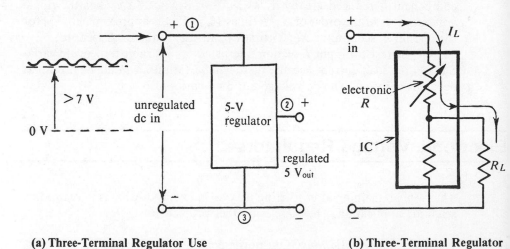

(a) Three-Terminal Regulator Use

(b) Three-Terminal Regulator Operation

FIGURE A4–18. *Three-Terminal Electronic Regulator*

Manufacturers' specifications sheets should be consulted for the capability of a particular device.

A simple view of how the task of reducing the voltage to the steady dc voltage out is accomplished is shown in Figure A4–18b. An electronic variable resistor (a transistor in the IC) is continuously adjusted by a sensing circuit in the device so that the voltage drop across it is just right to subtract from the instantaneous voltage in and yield the desired voltage out. Even the ripple is canceled out this way, as long as the voltage in does not drop below the output voltage. This eliminates the need to purchase very large electrolytics to produce ultra low ripple dc.

NOTE: Heating will occur in this series resistance due to the load current through it, and regulators capable of handling currents over 100 milliamperes typically must be *heat sinked;* that is, they are bolted to aluminum fins to give off the heat. Most units will automatically shut down if overheating occurs due to excessive current (and thus save themselves).

Figure A4–19a illustrates the LM109/209/309 positive 5-V, 1-ampere regulator in the TO–3 metal case that has now been available for a decade. The LM prefix is often used by the National Semiconductor Corporation to designate their various *Linear Microcircuit* (integrated circuit) products. Many other manufacturers also produce the LM309. The 1XX, 2XX, 3XX numbering system is used by National to designate *military temperature range* (−55°C to +125°C), *industrial temperature range* (−25°C to +85°C)

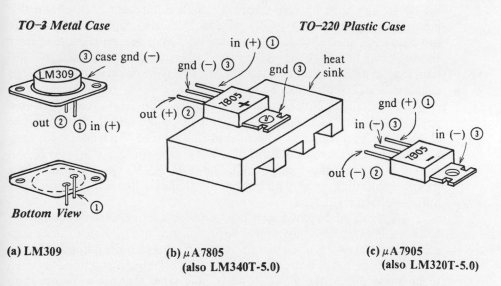

(a) LM309

(b) μA7805
(also LM340T-5.0)

(c) μA7905
(also LM320T-5.0)

FIGURE A4–19. *Packages of Three Widely Used Fixed Voltage Regulators*

and *commercial temperature range* (0°C to 70°C) devices. As might be expected, the larger temperature range commands a higher price. The in (1), out (2), and ground (gnd) (3) pins are labeled in Figures A4–19a, b, and c and the corresponding connections are numbered in Figure A4–18a. Notice that the case is ground or negative, while pin (1) is positive; the pin usage establishes the device as a positive voltage regulator (unless the case is insulated from the ground or chassis of the power supply; then it may be used in a negative regulated supply).

Figure A4–19b illustrates the μA7805 5 V, 1.5 ampere *positive voltage regulator* in the TO–220 plastic case with heat-sink tab, which is in turn screwed to a heat sink. A variety of fixed voltages are available in the μA78XX group. Thus the 7806 is a +6 V unit, 7815 is a +15 V unit, and so on. There is a corresponding fixed *negative voltage regulator* family, designated μA79XX. The μA prefix is used by Fairchild Semiconductor to designate their microcircuit devices, but again many other manufacturers now produce this family of devices.

NOTE: In Figure A4–19c that the pin functions are defined differently on the negative regulator. Thus, the tab is NOT grounded!

Regulated Power Supplies

As we will discuss in the following chapters, most electronic circuits require a source of dc power (dc voltage and current) for operation; in some cases the dc voltage must be very stable. Portable equipment must obtain this power from batteries (or possibly photovoltaic cells), which are already dc sources of course. Although mercury batteries may be used because of their excellent stability, they are expensive. Rather, an electronic voltage regulator may be used with some battery that has a less desirable voltage discharge characteristic (and also may be rechargeable).

To eliminate batteries altogether in the laboratory, most electronic apparatus use a *regulated dc power supply* that plugs into the ac mains. The constituents for a regulated power supply have already been discussed. They are brought together in the form of a block diagram in Figure A4–20. Although a fixed-output-voltage regulator (e.g., +5 V) would suffice for a specific application, general purpose power supplies often employ adjustable-output-voltage regulators.

A regulated dc power supply is often built into electronic equipment, but sometimes the dc voltages must be provided by one or more exterior supplies. The latter case is often true of "home built" electronic equipment for the lab. When external dc power is required, the most effective approach is often to purchase one of the many power-supply types that are available com-

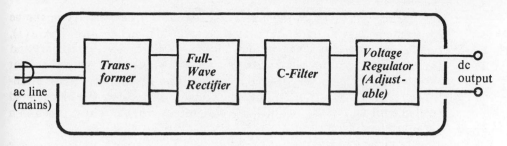

FIGURE A4–20. *Block Diagram of a Regulated dc Power Supply*

mercially. These range from *open frame* units designed to be incorporated into equipment, to more expensive general purpose *laboratory bench supplies*. The latter generally provide one or more adjustable output voltages and meters to monitor output voltage and current.

A modern bench supply also often provides adjustable *current limiting* at the dc output, which protects both the supply and the electronic equipment from catastrophic large currents in the event of a short circuit. This current limit should be adjusted to a value perhaps 30% greater than is expected to be required by the electronic circuit and is done by first actually connecting a shorting lead across the power-supply output. (This sight could have provoked heart failure in a laboratory in 1960!) Then the current-limit control knob should be adjusted for the desired current reading on the supply's current meter.

Because of the low cost of integrated circuits, almost all modern scientific power supplies are regulated. The quality of the regulation is specified relative to the three problems mentioned in the beginning of this section. They are:

1. *Ripple regulation:* Generally the maximum percent ripple is specified. This is the ratio of the rms-ripple voltage to the dc voltage present at the output.
2. *Line regulation:* Generally the maximum percent change in the output voltage is specified for a 10% change in the ac line voltage into the supply.
3. *Load regulation:* Generally the maximum percent change in the output voltage is specified for a change from zero current to the maximum rated output current for the supply.

In addition, stability of the output voltage against changes in ambient temperature and long term stability (or voltage drift) are specified for quality supplies.

REVIEW EXERCISES

1. Diagram the electrical characteristic for an ideal diode.
2. (a) Which element in the vacuum diode is the source of electrons within the device?
   (b) What should be the polarity of the voltage of the anode relative to the cathode for current to flow through the vacuum diode? Why?
3. (a) What is the difference between an intrinsic carrier and an extrinsic carrier in a semiconductor?
   (b) Which is a better insulator: a doped semiconductor or a pure semiconductor?
   (c) What is the difference between N-type semiconductor and P-type semiconductor?
4. (a) What is the depletion zone in a semiconductor junction diode? (Basically, why does it form?)
   (b) Why is there a barrier voltage in a semiconductor junction diode? What is it between, and what does it come from?
   (c) Which material in a PN junction should be more positive to produce significant current flow? Briefly explain why.
5. Consider the PN junction shown in Diagram A4–1. Reproduce the little drawing and name the two terminals. Also draw the corresponding diode symbol beside it.

DIAGRAM A4–1.

6. (a) What is the reverse-leakage current for an ideal diode?
   (b) Compare the typical reverse-leakage currents for silicon and germanium diodes.
7. (a) What is meant by the knee of a real diode characteristic?
   (b) Give approximate values for this knee for silicon and for germanium diodes.
8. Name the three important electrical parameters that are commonly specified for diodes by their manufacturers.
9. Which of the circuits shown in Diagram A4–2 will certainly ruin the real diode, and why? In each of the other cases, explain why the diode is not likely to be ruined.

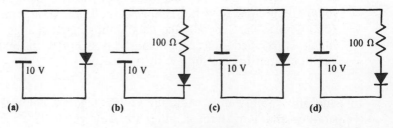

DIAGRAM A4–2.

10. Consider the two diodes con-
    nected in series to a voltage source
    as shown in Diagram A4–3.
    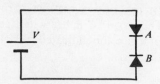
    (a) If the two diodes are ideal,
        does any current flow? Why?
    (b) For real diodes, there is cer-
        tainly a tiny current flowing,
        and there is the possibility of
        a large current. Explain what
        diode characteristic is in-

DIAGRAM A4–3.

volved in each case and to
which diode in the circuit it
applies.

11. (a) What specification is typically given by manufacturers for signal diodes,
        but not for rectifiers?
    (b) Give order-of-magnitude forward-current capabilities for signal diodes and
        for epoxy-case rectifiers.
    (c) Three widely used diodes are the 1N34, 1N914, and 1N400X. Designate
        each as silicon or germanium and signal diode or rectifier.
    (d) What is the difference between the 1N4001 and the 1N4007?

12. A signal diode is placed in two
    circuits as pictured in Diagram
    A4–4. In which case will a sig-
    nificant current flow?

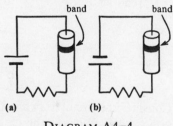

DIAGRAM A4–4.

13. Sketch the voltage output from a half-wave rectifier and a full-wave rectifier.

14. Consider Diagram A4–5.
    (a) Which diode connection will
        correctly produce rectifica-
        tion of the polarity indicated
        on the load resistor?
    (b) Which connection(s) will
        probably burn out all diodes?

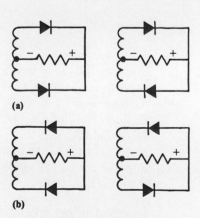

DIAGRAM A4–5.

15. In the bridge rectifier shown in Diagram A4–6, draw in diodes to produce the indicated polarity on the resistor.

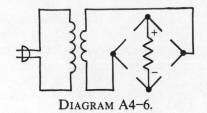

DIAGRAM A4–6.

16. What is the difference between a battery charger and a battery eliminator?
17. Describe how a simple shunt-capacitance filter is able to produce an "almost dc" voltage from a rectified ac voltage.
18. (a) Draw an L-section filter constructed from a capacitor and an inductor, as well as from a resistor and a capacitor.
    (b) What type of filtering action is desired, high pass or low pass?
    (c) Which L-section filter displays better load regulation, the LC or the RC? Why?
19. Which power supply is superior, one with 1% line and load regulation, or one with 5% line and load regulation?
20. Briefly, tell the purpose of each of the following elements of a power supply:
    (a) transformer   (c) filter
    (b) rectifier   (d) regulator

PROBLEMS

1. Consider the circuit drawn in Diagram A4–7. What is the current drain of the battery? (Include approximate diode drop for silicon.)

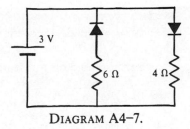

DIAGRAM A4–7.

2. (a) Consider the diode law. Show that the quantity $|e|/kt$ is equal to 39.6 V^{-1} at room temperature (20°C). Justify both the number and the units.
   (b) Assume a reverse-leakage current appropriate to silicon of 0.01 μA. Evaluate the diode law to find the currents for respective forward biases of 0.1 V and 0.45 V.
   Note that the change in current certainly does not follow Ohm's Law.

3. (a) Suppose the ac voltage $v_{in}(t)$ shown in Diagram A4–8(a) is input to the circuit diagrammed in (b). Sketch the graph of the output voltage

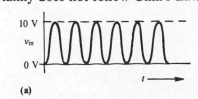

(a)

$v_{out}(t)$. Include a voltage scale.

(b) Suppose instead the voltage $v_{in}(t)$ is input to the circuit diagrammed in (c). Sketch the graph of the output voltage $v_{out}(t)$. Include a voltage scale.

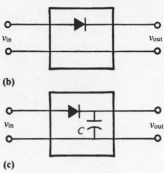

DIAGRAM A4-8.

4. (a) Why must we be concerned about the reverse-voltage rating of diodes to be used in a rectifier circuit?

   (b) What minimum reverse-voltage rating is required for the diode used in a half-wave rectifier circuit that is used in a 20-V_{dc} power supply?

   (c) What minimum reverse-voltage rating is required for the diodes used in a full-wave rectifier circuit with center-tapped transformer, if the circuit is used in a 20-V_{dc} power supply?

5. Draw a complete half-wave battery charging circuit. If the battery to be charged is 6 V, what is the minimum rms voltage from the transformer output?

6. Consider Diagram A4-9: What is the dc voltage out of each power supply?

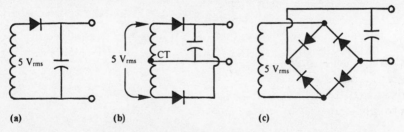

DIAGRAM A4-9.

7. (a) Consider the power supply shown in Diagram A4-10. Sketch the voltage appearing across R_L, $v_R(t)$ versus t, if the switch S is open. Include a scale on your two axes and use a dashed line for this $v_R(t)$.

   (b) Suppose $R_L C = 0.01$ s. Sketch with some accuracy $v_R(t)$ when the switch is closed. Use a solid line for this $v_R(t)$.

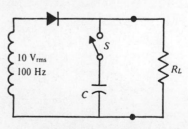

DIAGRAM A4-10.

   (c) Comment on the performance of this power supply.

8. Suppose you want to build a battery eleminator for a small portable radio. It operates from 4 AA (penlight) cells in series. With a VOM you measure the battery current drain to be 30 mA when the radio is on. You accept a ripple voltage (peak-to-peak) of 0.1 V and plan to use a bridge rectifier scheme.

   (a) What voltage transformer (rms) should you purchase?

   (b) What size filter capacitor should you obtain for simple C filtering? What type of capacitor should it be?

9. Consider the L-section filter shown below in Diagram A4–11.

   (a) What dc voltage is expected out?

   (b) What is the approximate value expected for the ripple voltage?

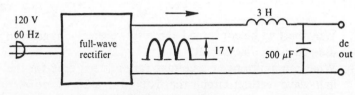

DIAGRAM A4–11.

10. (a) An LM309 three-terminal regulator is operated from a 12-V automobile battery to produce a $+5$ V_{dc} supply for a portable computer circuit. Suppose a 10-Ω load is connected as shown in Diagram A4–12. What is the power (heating) dissipated within the LM309?

    (b) Why would a 6-V automobile-type battery in principle be a better choice? (In practice, the input voltage should be about 2 V greater than the regulated output voltage, however. This rules out the 6 V battery.)

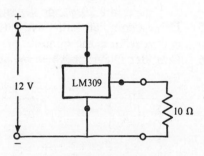

DIAGRAM A4–12.

11. The load regulation of a power supply can be characterized by the power supply *output impedance*. This is simply the Thevenin equivalent resistance, R_{out} from the output terminals. Suppose the output voltage from the supply changes by an amount ΔV_{out} when the load current changes by ΔI_{out}. Show that $R_{out} = \Delta V_{out}/\Delta I_{out}$.

12. An *inverter* is a device that converts from one dc voltage level to a higher dc level. This is done with the aid of an oscillator that operates from the lower dc voltage and a transformer.

    (a) Make a block diagram of a possible inverter design. Why is an oscillator required?

(b)   The frequency of the oscillator is usually chosen to be well above 60 Hz (for example, 400 Hz). Why does this permit the use of small-capacitance filtering?

13.   Zener diodes are manufactured specifically to be operated in reverse-breakdown mode and to take advantage of the well-defined voltage at which it occurs for a given diode. Provided the power dissipated in the diode does not exceed the power rating of the zener, the diode is quite safe and operates with a nearly constant *zener voltage* across it.

Note that in normal operation the zener diode cathode is positive. A zener diode may be operated in a simple voltage-regulating circuit, typically providing about 1% line and load regulation.

(a)   Consider the zener regulator circuit shown in Diagram A4–13 (which illustrates the zener diode symbol). If the zener voltage is 6 V, find the current in the 1-kΩ resistor, the 6-kΩ load resistor, and finally the zener diode. What is the power dissipated in the zener diode?

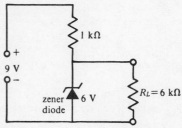

DIAGRAM A4–13.

NOTE: This problem can be worked out in your head.

(b)   Suppose the load resistor R_L is reduced from 6 kΩ to 2 kΩ. Again find the current in the 1-kΩ resistor, the load resistor, and finally the zener diode.

(c)   The load used in part (b) is the minimum value (and draws the largest load current) for which the voltage across the load resistor is nearly constant. For smaller R_L, the voltage across it is simply determined by voltage-divider action between the 1-kΩ and the R_L resistors. Justify this statement.

CHAPTER
A5

Amplifier Behavior

ndamental Amplifier Properties

In an electronics application we are often faced with a source of small voltage that is not capable of producing the desired end results; therefore, an amplifier of some sort is needed. Actually, it is not only the voltage capability of the source that is of concern, but also the current capability. At times a source produces a quite satisfactory voltage but can supply only a small amount of current. These features must be considered in the system design, as we see shortly.

In dealing with amplifiers there are a number of amplifier properties that are always the same, no matter the design or manufacturer of the unit. These properties should be appreciated before examining specific amplifier designs in later chapters; they can be indicated in a fairly simple *black-box model* of the amplifier. Also, black-box models are useful for the input and output devices that connect to the amplifier. Note that this amounts to putting some equivalent circuits into the boxes of the system model in Figure A3–1.

ack-Box Models: Input Transducer,
nplifier, and Output Transducer

By Thevenin's Theorem we expect typical *input transducers* to behave like a voltage source (in some cases dc, while in others ac) that is in series with a certain resistance called its *output impedance*. The input transducer may then be represented by a box with contents *source voltage* $v_s(T)$ and source resistance R_s (see Figure A5–1). The source voltage depends on the parameter of the system being studied; we use T for temperature, but the parameter could be any measurable quantity.

Next the *amplifier* has two terminals called the *input port* that appear to have an *input resistance* R_{in} (also called an *input impedance*) between them as far as any external circuit is concerned. The amplifier monitors whatever voltage appears across the input resistance R_{in} and generates a voltage that is larger by the factor A_v. A_v is the *open circuit voltage gain* or *voltage amplification* of the amplifier. This voltage is represented by a voltage generator with voltage $A_v v_i$ that in turn is in series with an *output resistance* R_{out}. The voltage generator in series with the resistance R_{out} is connected to the two output leads—that is, the *output port* or output of the amplifier. Note the Thevenin equivalent nature of the amplifier output circuit.

Finally the amplifier is connected to an output transducer, which is the *load* for the amplifier. This load has a certain resistance R_L. A voltage develops across this resistance and power is dissipated in it. In fact, the name of the game is to begin with a low power P_{in} produced by the input transducer into the input of the amplifier and produce a large power P_{out} into the output transducer. Generally (but not always) this involves an increase in the voltage level of the signal. The *power gain* or *amplification of power* A_p is defined through the equation:

$$A_p = \frac{P_{out}}{P_{in}} \tag{A5–1}$$

Expressed in decibels it is equal to $10 \log A_p$.

To predict the voltage that appears across R_L, the source voltage v_s, the four resistors R_s, R_{in}, R_{out}, R_L, and the voltage gain A_v must be known. The situation is perhaps best discussed by example.

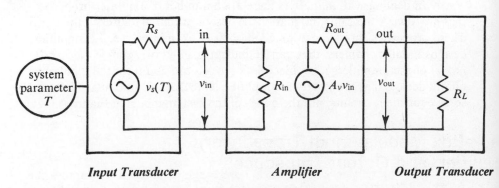

Input Transducer   **Amplifier**   **Output Transducer**

FIGURE A5–1. *Black-Box Model of an Electronic System*

Example: Suppose a microphone with an output impedance of 10,000 ohms is connected to an amplifier with an input resistance of 1,000 ohms. The voltage gain of the amplifier is 2,000 and its output impedance is 200 ohms. The amplifier is connected to a loudspeaker with a resistance of 8 ohms. If the microphone produces an *open circuit* voltage of 0.2 V_{rms}, what voltage appears across the loudspeaker and what power is dissipated in it? What is the overall voltage gain and power gain of the system? The situation is diagrammed in Figure A5–2.

Solution: We must work from input to output in the system. Although the voltage from the microphone is a time-varying or ac voltage, we may work with the rms value of the microphone voltage. Consequently, the other voltages throughout the electronic system are also developed as the respective rms values, and the uppercase letter V is used for V_{in} and V_{out} rather than the lowercase v of Figure A5–1.

1. A voltage V_{in} appears between the input terminals of the amplifier that is less than 0.2 V because of the voltage divider action. We see

$$V_{in} = 0.2 \; V_{rms} \left(\frac{1 \; k\Omega}{1 \; k\Omega + 10 \; k\Omega} \right) = 0.0182 \; V_{rms}$$

2. The signal generator within the amplifier generates a voltage

$$2000 \; V_{in} = 2000 \times 0.018 \; V_{rms} = 36.4 \; V_{rms}$$

3. The voltage out of the amplifier that appears across the loudspeaker is less than this, however, because of voltage divider action between the 200-ohm and the 8-ohm resistances. We see

$$V_{out} = 36.4 \; V_{rms} \; \frac{8 \; \Omega}{8 \; \Omega + 200 \; \Omega} = 1.4 \; V_{rms}$$

4. The power developed in the loudspeaker is

$$P = \frac{V^2}{R} = \frac{(1.4 \; V_{rms})^2}{8 \; \Omega} = 0.245 \; W$$

5. The power generated by the voltage source in the microphone is

$$P = \frac{V^2}{R} = \frac{(0.2 \; V_{rms})^2}{(10,000 + 1000) \; \Omega} = 3.6 \times 10^{-6} \; W$$

6. The voltage gain of the *system* is the voltage 1.4 V_{rms} across the speaker compared to 0.2 V_{rms} in the microphone, for a ratio of only 7.

7. The power gain of the *system* is

$$\frac{0.245 \text{ W}}{3.6 \times 10^{-6} \text{ W}} = 68,000$$

In decibels it is

$$10 \log 68,000 = 48 \text{ dB}$$

8. The power gain of the amplifier is much more than that in (7). The power into the amplifier itself P_{in} is

$$P_{in} = V_{in}I_{in} \text{ or } \frac{V_{in}^2}{R_{in}} = \frac{(0.0182 \text{ V}_{rms})^2}{1000 \text{ }\Omega} = 3.31 \times 10^{-7} \text{ W}$$

(Note that this is only about 1/10 the power delivered by the voltage in the microphone, but it *is* the power delivered by the microphone into the amplifier.) The power delivered by the amplifier to the loudspeaker was obtained in (4) above. Then using Equation A5–1 we get

$$A_p = \frac{P_{out}}{P_{in}} = \frac{0.245 \text{ W}}{3.3 \times 10^{-7} \text{ W}} = 7.42 \times 10^5$$

Expressing this in decibels we have

$$\begin{aligned} \text{dB ratio} &= 10 \log (7.42 \times 10^5) \\ &= 10 (5 + \log 7.42) \\ &= 10 \times 5.87 = 58.7 \text{ dB} \end{aligned}$$

We say the amplifier itself affects a 58.7 decibel power again.

NOTE: The power delivered by the voltage generator inside the amplifier is considerably more than the power delivered to the load—in fact, about 20 times more—but about 95% of this is lost in the 200-ohm resistor.

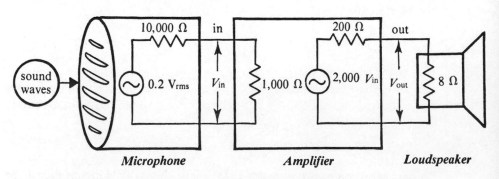

Microphone   *Amplifier*   *Loudspeaker*

FIGURE A5–2. *Example of Black-Box Electronic System*

Several important features of electronic systems are evident in this example. First notice that the voltage V_{in} appearing at the input of the amplifier is greatly reduced by voltage divider action from the 0.2 V_{rms} developed *within* the microphone. And the amplifier can only amplify the signal V_{in} appearing between its input terminals, so that we have a case of "2 steps backward before making 4 steps forward." This is an example of *impedance mismatch.*

Instead of having R_{in} be much less than R_s (here 1,000 ohms and 10,000 ohms, respectively), R_{in} should be much greater than R_s. Then little voltage divider action would take place and the amplifier would develop an internal voltage of $2,000 \times 0.2$ $V_{rms} = 400$ V_{rms} (rather than 36.4 V_{rms}). It should now be clear that *an ideal amplifier has an input impedance of infinity* (similar to a voltmeter).

The second feature to notice in this example is that the output voltage across the loudspeaker is greatly reduced because of the voltage divider action that takes place between the 200-ohms R_{out} and the 8-ohms R_L of the loudspeaker. We say the loudspeaker *loads down* the amplifier output. If the output impedance of the amplifier were very low (approaching zero) the full voltage would appear across R_L irrespective of its value. Therefore, we can see that *an ideal amplifier would have zero output impedance.*

The third feature to notice is that although the voltage amplification in this example is only 7, the power amplification is very much more: 68,000. This is because the impedance of the microphone and loudspeaker are so different. In fact, the voltage generated in the microphone is rather substantial as transducers go, but because of its high output impedance, the microphone is capable of delivering only a small current and, therefore, power to the outside world.

To demonstrate this: Suppose the microphone were connected directly to the loudspeaker. Then the current flowing from the microphone and through the loudspeaker is

$$I = \frac{0.2 \text{ V}_{rms}}{10 \text{ k}\Omega + 8 \text{ }\Omega} \simeq \frac{0.2 \text{ V}_{rms}}{10 \text{ k}\Omega}$$

The power delivered to the speaker is given by I^2R or

$$P_{speaker} = \left(\frac{0.2 \text{ V}_{rms}}{10 \text{ k}\Omega}\right)^2 8 \text{ }\Omega = 3.2 \times 10^{-9}\text{W}$$

This is indeed a tiny amount compared to that delivered to the loudspeaker with the help of the amplifier (0.234 watts calculated in part 4). We say there is a *large impedance mismatch* between the microphone and the loudspeaker.

Power Gain with an Ideal Voltage Follower

The fact that there was a large power gain with only a small voltage gain in the microphone/amplifier/loudspeaker system may have been surprising.

Actually, there can easily be power gain when there is no voltage increase; this accounts for the utility of that rather odd "amplifier," the voltage follower. The *voltage follower* is an amplifier with an open circuit voltage gain A_v of unity. Then the output voltage (at least if it is unloaded) is just the same as the input voltage. The output voltage *follows* the input voltage in that at every instant the voltage between its output terminals is a copy of the input voltage.

Let us consider the case where an ideal voltage follower has been interposed between the microphone and loudspeaker of Figure A5–2. Recall that by ideal we mean its input impedance R_{in} is very large ($\approx\infty$) and the output impedance R_{out} is very small (≈ 0). This system is diagrammed in Figure A5–3.

Because of its very large input impedance, the voltage divider action at the input to the ideal amplifier is negligible, and V_{in} is just 0.2 V_{rms}. This voltage is copied by the voltage generator in the black-box model of the voltage follower and passes unattenuated to the 8-ohm loudspeaker resistance. The power expended in the loudspeaker is then

$$P = \frac{V^2}{R} = \frac{(0.2 \text{ V}_{rms})^2}{8 \text{ } \Omega} = 5 \times 10^{-3} \text{W}$$

The result is power over a million times greater than the power delivered to the loudspeaker if the microphone is connected directly to it. Thus, although there is no voltage gain, there is a very great power gain, and the voltage follower deserves the title of amplifier. The voltage follower is developing a rather respectable power (relative to the world of electronics) by maintaining 0.2 V_{rms} across the rather small resistance of the loudspeaker.

NOTE: If the voltage follower can sustain this same voltage across a very small resistor, the power delivered becomes very large.

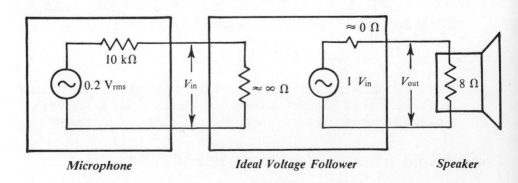

FIGURE A5–3. *Ideal Voltage-Follower Amplifier*

Impedance Matching
and Maximum Power Transfer

Suppose we have a certain amplifier as a given—in particular, a certain output voltage and output impedance—but we have the choice of various impedance values for the load. For example, suppose that in the Figure A5–2 the amplifier's 200-ohm output impedance is something we must live with, but imagine we can choose the impedance of our loudspeaker. (This is not close to reality for loudspeakers, but it can be true for other output transducers.) The question now is: What value for load impedance maximizes the power delivered to the load? How do we obtain *maximum power transfer* to the load?

We first write down a general expression for the power delivered to the load and treat the load resistance R_L as a variable. Figure A5–4 illustrates the situation at hand. The power delivered to R_L (as a function of R_L) is

$$P(R_L) = \frac{V_{R_L}^2}{R_L} = \frac{[VR_L/(R_L + R_{out})]^2}{R_L}$$

$$= \frac{V_{R_L}^2}{(R_L + R_{out})^2} \qquad \text{(A5-2)}$$

Notice that in the limit of very small load resistance ($R_L \to 0$) the power goes to zero due to the zero R_L in the numerator. (The power is all dissipated inside the amplifier in the resistance R_{out}.) At the other extreme, as R_L becomes very large ($R_L \to \infty$), the power also goes to zero because of the infinity in the denominator. (No power is delivered to the load because the current flowing drops to zero.) There apparently is some R_L between these extremes that accomplishes the maximum power transfer.

From calculus we know that the slope of the function is zero at the maximum of the function. Therefore, to find the maximum of the function $P(R_L)$, we take the derivative of Equation A5–2 with respect to R_L, set the result equal to zero, and solve for R_L; that is,

$$\frac{d}{dR_L} P(R_L) = \frac{V^2}{(R_L + R_{out})^2} - 2V^2 R_L (R_L + R_{out})^{-3} = 0 \qquad \text{(A5-3)}$$

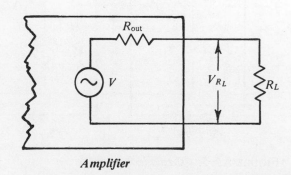

FIGURE A5–4. *Pertinent Circuit for Solving for Maximum Power Transfer*

Amplifier

A149

Cancel the V's and multiply through by $(R_L + R_{out})^3$. Then we get

$$R_L + R_{out} - 2R_L = 0 \quad \text{or} \quad R_L = R_{out} \quad \textbf{(A5–4)}$$

This is the condition for maximum power transfer: that the load resistance be equal (or match) the output impedance of the power source. It is a bit surprising since clearly half the power delivered by the voltage generator in the source of power is dissipated in the R_{out} of the source itself.

A common example of impedance matching occurred in the past for vacuum tube high-fidelity (hi-fi) amplifiers. The output of the amplifier was available through several impedance-value outputs: for example, 4 ohms, 8 ohms, 16 ohms. To obtain maximum power transfer to a 16-ohm speaker, for example, the speaker should be connected to the 16-ohm post. This impedance matching was done by using a step-down transformer with several taps on the secondary to provide various impedance levels.

Cascaded Amplifiers

Suppose we have several amplifiers, each with an *unloaded voltage gain* of 10, but there is need for a voltage amplification of 1,000. What can be done? The answer is quite clear: Connect the output of the first into the input of a second, and so on, in a sequence. The result is a *cascaded amplifier* as illustrated in Figure A5–5.

The output of the first amplifier becomes the input of the second, and so on. In general we must be concerned about the loading of the second amplifier on the output of the first amplifier in order to predict the output voltage of the first, which then becomes the input voltage to be amplified by the second. This concern carries on down the line.

If each amplifier were ideal ($R_{in} = \infty$; $R_{out} = 0$), then it is easy to see what the voltage out of the system should be, compared to v_{in}; that is, the overall voltage gain of the cascaded amplifier. The output voltage of the first

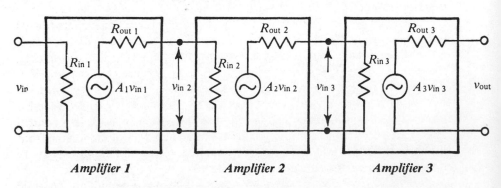

FIGURE A5–5. *Cascaded Amplifier*

amplifier would then be $v_1 = A_1 v_{in}$. This is amplified by the second amplifier to become $v_2 = A_2(A_1 v_{in})$. Finally, the third amplifier receives this as input and produces as output $v_3 = A_3(A_2 A_1 v_{in})$. We see the overall gain of ideal amplifiers would be the product of the individual amplifications:

$$A_{\text{total ideal}} = \frac{v_{out}}{v_{in}} = A_3 A_2 A_1 \qquad \text{(A5–5)}$$

The examination of a more realistic case is left to the problems. There the student is asked to derive a formula for overall gain if the three amplifiers are identical.

Fundamental Amplifier Types

There are a number of fundamental variations or types of amplifiers that are discussed in the remaining sections of this chapter. These types are introduced here and their properties and terminology are discussed. To aid this understanding we first consider a simple electrical model for the operation of a basic amplifier building block or stage.

Amplifier-Stage Model

The basic amplifier is constructed around one transistor or vacuum tube (as we see in Chapter A8) and can be characterized by a certain input impedance, output impedance, and voltage gain. In other words, a basic amplifier behaves like the amplifier black box that we have already examined. Typically the voltage gain from one basic amplifier is not enough for a task; thus several basic amplifiers must be cascaded as shown in Figure A5–5. Each basic amplifier in the overall chain of amplifiers is then referred to as an *amplifier stage.*

We see also in Chapter A8 that it is in the nature of amplifiers for the output voltage to tend to be midway between the negative and positive terminal voltages of the battery (or batteries) supplying the power to the amplifier. The reason can be understood from a voltage divider model of the amplifier as shown in Figure A5–6a. In an amplifier stage, the *active device*—that is, the transistor or vacuum tube—behaves like an electrically controlled variable resistor; it changes its resistance in response to an input voltage to a control input. The output voltage from the amplifier is then the output voltage from this voltage divider and can range between the voltage levels present at the top and at the bottom of the voltage divider.

Figure A5–6b emphasizes the connections that are made to the basic amplifier box of Figure A5–6a. Notice that there are actually just four wires

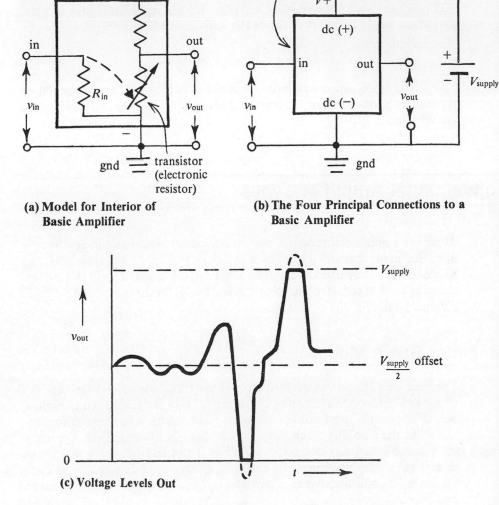

(a) Model for Interior of Basic Amplifier

(b) The Four Principal Connections to a Basic Amplifier

(c) Voltage Levels Out

FIGURE A5-6. *Connections and Behavior of a Basic Amplifier*

that lead from the box itself. There is a single signal input wire, a single signal output wire, a power supply wire $V+$, and a (bottom) wire that serves in both the input and output circuits. This last wire is often referred to as the *ground* (gnd) of the amplifier, although it may not actually be electrically connected to "true ground" (that is, to the earth). The term *common* would be a better term; it serves as a reference voltage level for both the input and the output. The negative terminal of the *power supply battery* is connected to this ground or common, while the positive battery terminal is connected to a dc (+) power-in or $V+$ terminal. The battery is drawn explicitly in Figure A5-6b, but to simplify the drawing the battery itself is usually omitted, and only the $V+$ and gnd connections are drawn, as in Figure A5–6a. For portable equipment, batteries may actually be used, but otherwise electronic power supplies (battery eliminators) are generally used. Some source of dc electrical power to the amplifier is always necessary.

The voltage out of the *electronic voltage divider circuit* must then vary between the $V+$ supply voltage and ground as shown in Figure A5–6c. Often what is of interest is the changing of the output signal, or what is called the *ac component* of the signal. The average value of the output signal is called the *dc component* of the signal. In Figure A5–6c the ac component signal is seen riding atop a dc voltage of about half the supply voltage. We see shortly why it is desirable that the design have this average voltage level (or *resting level* if there is no signal input) midway between the power supply voltages.

The ac component of the output signal is larger than the voltage signal in v_{in} by the factor of the amplifier voltage gain (provided the amplifier is not loaded down). Notice two places in the output voltage v_{out} of Figure A5–6c where the signal is distorted or *clipped off*. To faithfully follow the input voltage shape, the output signal should have gone higher and also lower in voltage. But it is physically impossible for the amplifier—that is, the voltage divider—to produce a voltage more positive than the $+$ supply voltage or more negative than the $-$ supply voltage. There is *no* source of voltage in the amplifier itself (for example, no batteries) to produce a higher voltage. It should be clear that to get an output with no clipping, the input signal peak-to-peak voltage must be smaller than the power supply voltage used by the amplifier by a factor equal to the amplifier's voltage gain. Also, for symmetrical input signals, a dc or resting-level output set midway between the supply voltages will accommodate the largest peak-to-peak output *swing*.

ac and dc Amplifiers

When we need to cascade two or more of these basic amplifiers in order to make an amplifier with higher gain, the large dc offset voltage of the output causes a severe problem in the next stage. The next stage will attempt to amplify this large dc input voltage, and its output will simply become stuck or *latch up* at the limiting supply voltage. A simple cure is to connect *blocking capacitors* as shown in Figure A5–7 between stages. These *interstage coupling capacitors* then pass or *couple* the ac signal on to the next stage to be amplified but *block* the offending dc. There is a penalty to be paid, however. The amplifier loses the ability to amplify dc voltages. It becomes an *ac-only amplifier* or as commonly stated, an *ac amplifier*. For example, the voltage produced by a copper-constantan thermocouple at $10°C$ is only about 0.4 millivolts; it needs to be amplified before being observable on most voltmeters. But it would do no good to connect this small dc voltage into an amplifier like the one shown in Figure A5–7. Connecting it into stage 1

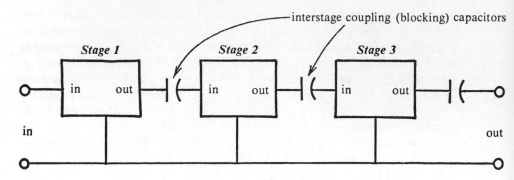

FIGURE A5–7.   *Capacitively Coupled (ac) Amplifier*

causes that output to increase some amount, but this increase is blocked from influencing the input of the next stage by the capacitor (except for a brief charging interval).

A *dc amplifier* retains the capability of amplifying dc input voltages as well as ac voltages. In general, this is accomplished by operating the amplifier from two supply voltages that are equally plus and minus with respect to the ground of the amplifier. The situation is shown in Figure A5–8. Then the general rule that the output voltage be halfway between the two supply voltages puts it normally at—or at least near—the ground. The amplifier is also arranged so that the input voltage should be relative to the connection between the two supply voltages. This point is labeled gnd (ground) in Figure A5–8, and it is convenient to think of it as such, although *common* is

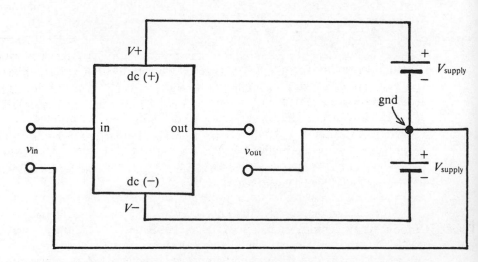

FIGURE A5–8.   *Dual Voltage Supply, dc Amplifier*

again a better term. If v_{in} is zero ("in" lead shorted to ground), v_{out} should also be zero ("out" lead at same voltage as ground) for the perfect dc amplifier.

For example, if $V+$ is $+12$ V and $V-$ is -12 V, halfway in between is zero volts. The dashed output offset line of Figure A5–6c thus gets moved to zero volts. Now there is no dc component in the output signal, and several stages of this type of amplifier can be cascaded without blocking capacitors between stages. The overall amplifier then retains the ability to amplify dc voltage.

Because of this *dual supply voltage* arrangement, it is possible for v_{out} to go both above and below ground if the input voltage is positive or negative. This is often desirable. The output can typically go positive by nearly V, or negative by nearly V, where V is the voltage of either battery in Figure A5–8. Generally the output of the dc amplifier is *not* zero when the input is shorted for real amplifiers. This voltage is called the *output offset voltage* for the amplifier and is usually *referred to the amplifier input;* that is, the amplifier behaves as though a phantom tiny battery, called the *input offset voltage,* exists in the input wire to the amplifier. This input offset voltage is equal to the output offset voltage divided by the voltage gain of the amplifier.

Amplifier Bandwidth

Because of coupling capacitors, an ac amplifier is clearly limited with respect to the lowest frequency that it can amplify well. In addition, all amplifiers have some upper limit frequency beyond which they begin to fail. The high frequency failing comes about because capacitances in the tubes or transistors themselves begin to *short-circuit* the currents at high frequencies. The consequence is that the voltage gain A_v of the amplifier is a function of frequency. A plot of the logarithm of A_v versus the logarithm of signal frequency $\log f$ results in a fairly simple graph that tells the story (see Figure A5–9).

The voltage gain for this particular example is constant at 1000 over a frequency range of about 5 hertz to about 500 hertz. The frequency range of $500\text{ Hz} - 5\text{ Hz} = 495\text{ Hz}$ is called the *bandwidth* of the amplifier, while the value of 1000 is called the *midband gain* of the amplifier. The end points for the bandwidth are taken to be when A_v is decreased by the factor 0.707 (similar to the case for filters).

If the plot in Figure A5–9 were for a dc amplifier, there would still be some high-frequency limit, but the line would extend straight to the left to zero hertz or dc as shown by the heavy dashed line. The dashed line is precisely how a dc amplifier differs from an ac amplifier.

Noninverting and Inverting Amplifiers

We will define what is meant by noninverting amplifier and inverting amplifier. A *noninverting amplifier* produces an output in the same sense as its

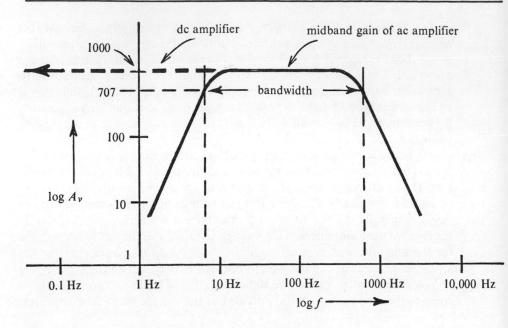

FIGURE A5-9. *Bandwidth of ac and dc Amplifiers*

input, as shown in Figure A5-10a. There the input signal is seen to change more positive, and the output changes in the positive sense, too, although it is greater by the factor A_v. If the input swings more negative, the output also swings more negative. On the other hand, an *inverting amplifier* has an output that changes in the opposite sense to any change in the input, as illustrated in Figure A5-10b. For example, if the input is made more positive, the output goes more negative. In both cases, the input and output voltages are between those respective leads and ground.

Several other conventions are introduced in Figure A5-10. First, rather than representing the amplifier by a rectangle (which reminds us of a black box), a *triangle* is used. The amplifier output extends from a triangle corner, while the amplifier input wire goes to the opposite triangle side; indeed, with this convention it is not actually necessary to label input or output. Second, if the amplifier is noninverting, the input is labeled with a +; if it is inverting, the input is labeled with a −.

NOTE: These lines are *not* + or − power supply connections. The power supply connections are actually left off the diagram for simplicity, although in fact power must be supplied, of course.

Difference or Differential Amplifiers

There are a number of situations, especially in chemistry and the life sciences, where it is desirable to have two inputs into an amplifier *besides* ground. For

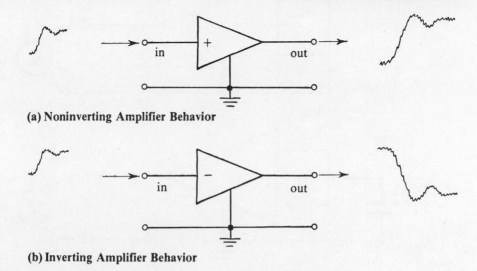

(a) Noninverting Amplifier Behavior

(b) Inverting Amplifier Behavior

FIGURE A5–10. *Noninverting and Inverting Amplifier Behavior*

example, every electrocardiogram instrument requires these two inputs, and we see why in the next section of this chapter. Such amplifiers produce a non-zero output voltage if there is a *difference* in the voltages presented to the two inputs, and this output voltage is independent of whether or not both inputs are *off ground*—different in potential (or voltage) from ground potential—by any amount.

Thus the *difference or differential amplifier* has two signal inputs; they are inverting and noninverting inputs and are labeled with the − and + convention, respectively, in Figure A5–11. The behavior of a dc differential amplifier with a voltage gain of 20 is illustrated in the figure by showing the output resulting from various connections to the inputs. The student should study the various consequences.

First, Figure A5–11a shows that the output of an ideal difference amplifier is zero if both inputs are grounded, which is certainly no surprise. However, Figure A5–11b shows that the output is still zero if both inputs are brought off ground by the *same* voltage; that is, a *common-mode voltage*. The output is only nonzero if a voltage *difference* occurs between the two input terminals, as happens in Figures A5–11c, d, and e. Notice the output voltage is 20 times the input voltage difference of 0.1 V in these three cases, although a common-mode input voltage of 1 V occurs again in the case of Figure A5–11e. Also notice that the output voltage swings positive if the + input is more positive than the − input, but it swings negative if the − input is the more positive (see the case in Figure A5–11e). This behavior is in accord with the noninverting and inverting character of the inputs. We can write:

$$v_{out} = A_{vd}(v_{in+} - v_{in-}) = A_{vd}v_{id} \qquad \textbf{(A5–6)}$$

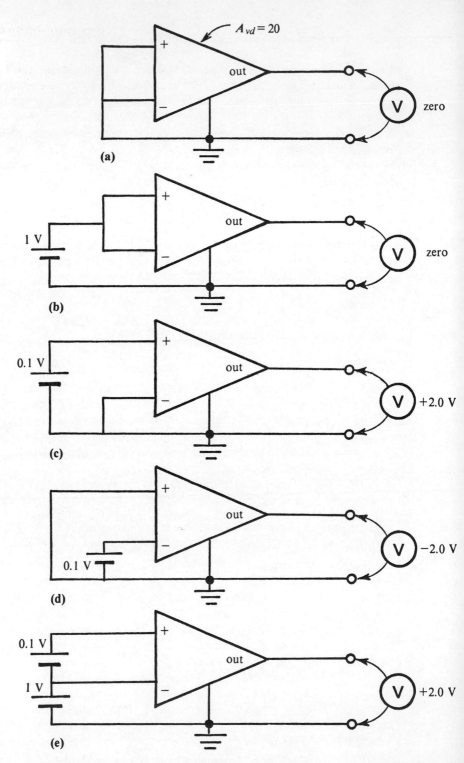

Figure A5-11. *Output of an Ideal dc Difference Amplifier with a Voltage Gain of 20 for Various Input Voltages*

where v_{out} is the output voltage; v_{in+} and v_{in-} are the voltages into the $+$ and $-$ inputs, respectively, with respect to ground; A_{vd} is the *difference voltage gain;* and we let the *input difference voltage* $(v_{in+} - v_{in-}) = v_{id}$. In the example of Figure A5-11, A_{vd} equals 20.

Real difference amplifiers would show a nonzero output voltage in Figure A5-11b, even though both inputs have a common (or the same) voltage. If v_{oc} is the voltage out for a common voltage v_{ic} in, the *common-mode voltage gain* A_{vc} is

$$A_{vc} = \frac{v_{oc}}{v_{ic}} \qquad (A5-7)$$

We want this ratio to be small compared to the desirable difference voltage gain of the amplifier. If v_{od} is the voltage out for a voltage difference of v_{id} between the input terminals, the *difference voltage gain* is

$$A_{vd} = \frac{v_{od}}{v_{id}} \qquad (A5-8)$$

The ratio of A_{vd} to A_{vc} is called the *common-mode rejection ratio* (CMRR). That is

$$CMRR = \frac{A_{vd}}{A_{vc}} \qquad (A5-9)$$

It is quite common for this ratio to be 10^4 or more (the larger the better). Actually manufacturers usually quote the ratio in decibels. Since the ratio refers to voltage, we have 20 decibels for every factor of 10.

Example: Suppose for a realistic amplifier in Figure A5-11b, the connection gives an output voltage of 0.005 V. Find its CMRR.

Solution: We have

$$A_{vc} = \frac{0.005 \text{ V}}{1 \text{ V}} = 0.005$$

The difference voltage gain is clear from Figure A5-11c as

$$A_{vd} = \frac{2.0 \text{ V}}{0.1 \text{ V}} = 20$$

$$CMRR = \frac{A_{vd}}{A_{vc}} = \frac{20}{0.005} = 4000$$

In decibels we would have

$$CMRR = 20 \log 4000 = 20 \times (3.6) = 72 \text{ dB}$$

A Differential Amplifier Application

The differential amplifier is a very desirable part of the electrocardiograph that is routinely used in medical practice to diagnose certain heart diseases. Heart muscle action is initiated by an electrical pulse that passes around the heart. The body is a conductive volume, and the electric fields associated with each pulse support small currents and attending voltage drops out to the body surface. Voltage pulses on the order of 10-millivolts (10^{-2} V) amplitude and 0.1-second duration may be observed between the limbs of the body.

It is common to find oscilloscopes in science laboratories that can display 10-millivolt pulses quite satisfactorily. However, if a student connects a scope probe between his or her two hands, the scope display will almost certainly show a rather "noisy" appearing signal of perhaps 1 V in amplitude and 60 hertz in frequency. The 60 hertz is the telltale sign (in the United States) that the signal comes not from the heart but from the electric utility company! The problem is that the 60-hertz voltage in the wiring to lighting fixtures and so forth produces electric field lines that end on the person's body. In effect, there is a capacitive coupling C_1 between the wires and the person, as is diagrammed in Figure A5–12a. There is also capacitively coupling C_2 between the person's limb and ground, and the pair of capacitors constitutes an ac voltage divider that establishes a 60-hertz voltage between the limbs; this rather large voltage completely masks the electrocardic potential. Notice in the diagram that the one input signal lead for most oscilloscopes is connected to ground (true earth) through the ground prong of the three-prong power plug.

The solution is to connect the leads from the two limbs into a differential amplifier, where neither of the input leads is grounded. This is illustrated in Figure A5–12b. We can expect the noise voltages induced in the two parts of the body to be about equal and *in phase* with each other. The signals v_{arm} from the arm and v_{leg} from the leg are diagrammed in Figure A5–12c where we see the desirable bioelectric signals are an *out-of-phase modulation* (for clarity, shown here relatively large) on the constantly oscillating 60-hertz signal that is "in common" to both signals. The differential amplifier subtracts v_{arm} from v_{leg}; this largely eliminates the 60-hertz common-mode signal and the desired bioelectric signal emerges as output. The bioelectric signal may be displayed on an oscilloscope (electrocardioscope) or drawn on a fast-response strip-chart recorder (electrocardiograph).

Noise in Electronic Systems

When the magnitude of the voltage from a transducer is small—for example, less than 1 millivolt—electrical noise can be a problem. Several cases of electrical noise are familiar to almost everyone. For example, a hiss is heard

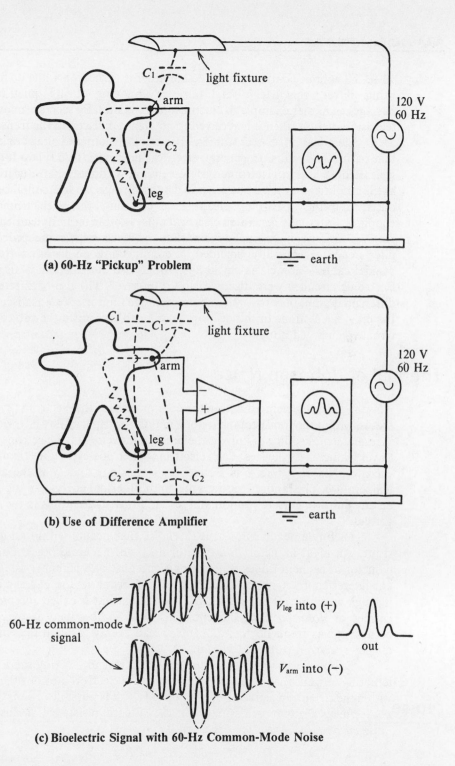

(a) 60-Hz "Pickup" Problem

(b) Use of Difference Amplifier

(c) Bioelectric Signal with 60-Hz Common-Mode Noise

FIGURE A5–12. *Rejection of 60-Hertz Common-Mode Signal by Use of a Differential Amplifier in Electrocardiography*

when the volume control of a stereo amplifier is turned up while no music is being played; this background noise is annoying during quiet musical passages. Another example of electrical noise is literally seen as "snow" in a television picture when it is received in an area remote from the transmitter.

Electrical noise is unwanted or spurious electrical voltage or current that occurs in circuits. In general, electrical noise is of two types: It may be generated *within* the electronic system—that is, within the transducer as well as the amplifier—or it may be generated by some *external* source and be introduced into the system by electrostatic coupling or by electromagnetic coupling. Externally generated electrical noise is often termed electrical *interference,* and we have already discussed ways to reduce the problem of interference. Electrically shielded interconnecting cables—for example, coaxial cables—as well as shielding through use of a metal chassis for the electronic circuitry were discussed in Chapter A2. The use of difference or differential amplifiers to reduce common-mode interference was discussed in the previous section. In this section we want to introduce the subject of internally generated noise.

Thermal or Johnson Noise

Noise is always generated within the components of the electronic system—that is, within the transistors, resistors, inductors, capacitors, and even wires. A fundamental source of noise is the random movements of electrons as they travel within these devices. Each electron carrier possesses a thermal kinetic energy $(3/2)kT$, where k is Boltzmann's constant and T is the absolute temperature. The random motions due to this thermal energy are superposed on any uniform current motion and result in tiny fluctuations in the flowing current.

Of fundamental interest is the noise that occurs within an ideal resistor. An ideal inductor or capacitor does not generate noise; but a real inductor or capacitor does generate noise because of inherent resistance. We are interested then in the fluctuations that occur in the current flowing through a resistor. The random part of the current is called *thermal noise* current or *Johnson noise* current. This noise is described as *white noise* because it has frequency components spread evenly through the entire frequency *spectrum* from dc to about 10^{13} hertz.

Suppose we simply short the ends of a resistor. A tiny randomly alternating current that is caused by the random electron motions then flows within the circuit. In a given frequency band Δf, it is possible to show that the *noise power* P_N that is dissipated in the shorted resistance R due to the *noise current* I_{Nrms} that flows is given by

$$P_N = I_{Nrms}^2 R = 4kT\Delta f \tag{A5-10}$$

Notice that the power is proportional to the absolute temperature T and this is basically because the thermal energy of the electron is proportional to kT; further, the noise power is directly proportional to the frequency band Δf because a larger bandwidth includes more of the noise frequencies that are present across the entire spectrum. As we have stated, the noise current is a *randomly alternating* current, and some sort of average measure is required; therefore it is not surprising that the root mean square or rms measure of the noise current must be used. It is interesting that the value of the *power* does *not* depend on the resistance.

When dealing with amplifiers in electronics, it is the voltage present that is often of particular interest. We may think of an equivalent *noise voltage* V_{Nrms} that appears within any resistance R; the noise voltage is con-sidered to cause the noise current that flows. The noise voltage may be modeled as a voltage generator V_{Nrms} that is in series with a noiseless resistance R, as shown in Figure A5–13. Let the terminals of the model resistor be shorted. Then the power dissipated in the resistance must be given by V_{Nrms}^2/R. The noise power is given by Equation A5–10, and it therefore follows that the noise voltage must be

$$\frac{V_{Nrms}^2}{R} = 4kT\Delta f \qquad (A5\text{--}11)$$

or

$$V_{Nrms} = \sqrt{4kTR\Delta f} \qquad (A5\text{--}12)$$

Let us consider the implications of this result through an example.

Example: A 50 kilohm resistor at 20°C is connected to an ideal dc amplifier with a voltage gain of 3000; however, the amplifier has an upper frequency response limit of 1000 hertz. The system is diagrammed in Figure A5–14. What is the noise voltage expected at the amplifier output?

Solution: Since the amplifier amplifies voltage over a bandwidth of 1000 hertz, this is the bandwidth for which noise from the resistor is relevant. The equivalent noise voltage present in the resistor is then given by

$$V_{Nrms} = (4 \times 1.38 \times 10^{-23} \times 293 \times 50 \times 10^3 \times 1000)^{1/2} \text{ V} = 0.9 \text{ } \mu V_{rms}$$

Since the amplifier is ideal—the resistor is connected to the amplifier—there is no loading on this noise voltage source. (Note that the output impedance of the resistor is its own resistance R.) The rms noise voltage V_{Nout} appearing at the amplifier output is then

$$V_{Nout} = A_v V_{Nrms} = 3000 \times 0.9 \text{ } \mu V = 2.7 \text{ mV}_{rms} \qquad (A5\text{--}13)$$

NOTE: If an oscilloscope is set to 5 mV/cm and is connected to the out-put of the amplifier here, the scope trace shows a hash of jiggles like those in Figure A5–13. The scope picture of thermal noise looks like grass, and "grass" is one slang term for it. Due to its random nature, the peak-to-peak voltage of the noise signal is *not* a well-defined quantity. Nevertheless, it is possible to make a visual estimate on the scope display of the *p-p* noise, and we can expect it to be on the order of three times the rms voltage value, or about 9 millivolts in this case.

Several features of thermal noise that are of particular interest to the scientist practitioner of electronics may be rather quickly inferred from this example. First, if the 50 kilohm resistance were the output impedance of a transducer, we may expect a noise output from the transducer of at least 0.9 μV_{rms}. If the true output signal of interest from the transducer were on the order of one microvolt, then the desired signal would be almost hidden by the noise signal. In fact, we speak of the ratio of the signal voltage to the noise voltage as the *signal-to-noise ratio* (S/N) from the source. The ideal amplifier would amplify both the desired signal as well as the noise, so that the desired signal is still obscured when it immerges from the amplifier output.

Second, a larger resistance produces a larger noise voltage. Therefore, a transducer with a large output impedance has two strikes against it: The large resistance implies a larger inherent noise value, as well as a possible problem with excessive loading due to the input impedance of a nonideal amplifier. Actually, the Johnson noise given by Equation A5–12 represents a lower bound on the noise that may be expected from any real resistance. For example, metal wire or metal film resistors may approach this theoretical limit, but carbon composition and carbon film resistors are significantly more noisy. This noise is related to the granular structure of the conducting path in the carbon-type resistors.

Third, lowering the temperature of the resistor lowers its thermal noise output. In some scientific applications where the signal-to-noise ratio

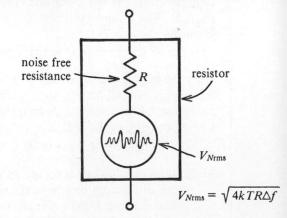

FIGURE A5–13. *Model for Thermal Noise or Johnson Noise from a Resistor*

$$V_{Nrms} = \sqrt{4kTR\Delta f}$$

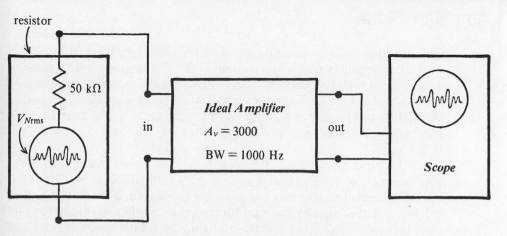

FIGURE A5-14   *Resistor Connected to Ideal Amplifier*

is critical, the transducer temperature is lowered to the temperature of liquid nitrogen or even liquid helium in order to improve the S/N.

Fourth, the effective input noise voltage depends on the size of the bandwidth that passes the signal—the *pass bandwidth*. An important technique that is used to improve the signal-to-noise ratio is to use an amplifier with a bandwidth that is as small as possible. For example, if the bandwidth in the previous example were reduced by a factor of 64 (to 15 hertz), the noise voltage would be reduced by the factor $\sqrt{64} = 8$. However, the bandwidth of the amplifier should be chosen large enough to pass without attenuation the range of frequencies that is present in the desired signal. If the transducer signal is a dc or low-frequency signal, a low-pass *RC* or *LC* filter may be placed at the amplifier output in order to reduce the effective amplifier bandwidth and therefore the noise.

NOTE: What are called *tuned amplifiers*—such as those present in radio and television receivers—use the narrow bandwidth (or filter) character of resonant (or tuned) inductance-capacitance circuits. In this way the receiver can achieve a narrow bandwidth for the radio frequencies that are of interest in this application. However, in this book we avoid the topic of resonant *LC* circuits since they are most appropriate for circuitry operating at radio frequencies; we are generally not considering the subject of radio-frequency circuitry. At audio frequencies it is possible to use *bandpass* filters that are constructed from resistors and capacitors. For a discussion of these more advanced *RC* networks, refer to the texts by Brophy, Jones, or Malmstadt, Enke, and Toren that are listed in the Reference section.

Amplifier Noise

The previous example assumed an ideal noiseless amplifier. But any real amplifier introduces noise of its own into the signal that immerges from the amplifier output. The most important noise sources in an amplifier are usually those present in the first stage of amplification in an amplifier. The quality of the first stage is important because the noise generated in later stages is generally well below the amplified noise that they receive as input from the first stage.

One useful measure of the noise generated within an amplifier is the *equivalent input noise voltage* V_{Nin} that may be modeled as present at the amplifier input. This amplifier noise voltage appears added to the signal (and the noise) that is input by the transducer to the amplifier. It should be quite clear that for a good—that is, high—signal-to-noise ratio from the amplifier, we desire that the equivalent input noise voltage V_{Nin} be much less than the signal voltage from the transducer.

Since the bandwidth of the amplifier may be adjustable, the equivalent input noise voltage is often quoted as an input noise–voltage *density,* with units of $V_{rms}/\sqrt{hertz}$. This reflects the fact that for frequencies above about 100 hertz, the internal amplifier noise is generally quite uniform (or white) in terms of its frequency dependence, similar to the noise from a resistor. From Equation A5–12, we see that the rms-noise voltage is proportional to the square root of the frequency bandwidth. To obtain the actual equivalent noise voltage at the amplifier input, we must multiply the noise-voltage density value by the square root of the amplifier bandwidth.

The input noise–voltage density for an amplifier was introduced as being uniform above approximately 100 hertz. Unfortunately, below this

---

Example: The OP–07 type of operational amplifier is quoted to have a typical input noise–voltage density of $10\,nV/\sqrt{hertz}$. An OP–07 is used to construct an amplifier with a voltage gain of 50 and a bandwidth of 10 kHz. What is its equivalent input noise voltage?

Solution: Although operational amplifier design is discussed in the next chapter, we may nevertheless use the quoted values of noise-voltage density and bandwidth to compute

$$V_{Nin} = \text{noise density} \times \sqrt{BW} = 10\,\frac{nV}{\sqrt{Hz}} \times \sqrt{10^4 Hz} = 1.0\,\mu V_{rms}$$

Note that the voltage gain is actually not needed here.

NOTE: If a noise-free 1-microvolt signal is input to this amplifier, the signal out of the amplifier will be almost obscured by noise, with a poor signal-to-noise ratio of 1.

---

frequency the amplifier-noise density generally increases approximately in proportion to the quantity $1/f$, where f is the frequency of interest. This noise regime is termed *1/f noise* or *flicker noise* and originates in the transistors or the tubes of the amplifier. For example, in the frequency range of 0.1 to 10 hertz the OP–07 operational amplifier mentioned in the previous example is specified to have a typical peak-to-peak noise voltage of 0.35 μV. Notice that this is significantly more than what would be obtained from the input noise–density value for the operational amplifier, 10 nV/$\sqrt{\text{hertz}}$, since from the latter value we obtain

$$V_{N\text{rms}} = 10 \; \frac{n\text{V}}{\sqrt{\text{Hz}}} \times \sqrt{(10 \text{ Hz} - 0.1 \text{ Hz})} = 30 \; n\text{V}_{\text{rms}}$$

The *approximate* peak-to-peak noise voltage is then about $3 \times 30 \; n$V $= 90 \; n$V $= 0.09 \; \mu$V, which is only about one-fourth the flicker noise that appears in this frequency interval.

We see that in practice, noise voltages of several origins are effectively present simultaneously at an amplifier input. But the magnitude of the total noise voltage present is *not* obtained by merely adding the noise voltages together. The total noise voltage is calculated by finding the square root of the sum of the squares of the contributing noise voltages. (This rule is characteristic for the probable value of the sum of random variables and evolves quickly here from the fact that the total noise *power* is the simple sum of the contributing noise powers.)

Example: A transducer with a noise voltage of 0.5 μV$_{\text{rms}}$ over the frequency range of dc to 100 hertz is input to an amplifier constructed from an OP–07 operational amplifier. The amplifier has been designed with a bandwidth of dc to 100 hertz. What is the total effective input noise to the amplifier?

Solution: We must properly add the transducer noise, the OP–07 flicker or $1/f$ noise, and the broad-spectrum noise of the OP–07. The transducer noise is given as 0.5 μV$_{\text{rms}}$ in the total frequency interval. The broad-spectrum noise in the frequency interval of 10 hertz to 100 hertz is given by

$$V_{N\text{in}} = \left(\frac{10 \; n\text{V}}{\sqrt{\text{Hz}}}\right) \sqrt{(100 - 10)\text{Hz}} = 95 \; n\text{V}_{\text{rms}}$$

The rms value of the OP–07 internal noise in the interval 0.1 hertz to 10 hertz including $1/f$ noise is approximately one-third of the peak-to-peak value, or 0.35 μV/3 $= 0.12 \; \mu$V. Then the total rms noise that effectively appears at the amplifier input is given by

$$\text{total } V_{N\text{in}} = \sqrt{(0.5)^2 + (0.095)^2 + (0.12)^2} \; \mu\text{V} = 0.52 \; \mu\text{V}_{\text{rms}}$$

Summary

Basic properties of amplifiers and principles for their use have been considered in this chapter. Especially with the miniaturization of electronics, it is important to appreciate that although the circuit within the chassis or the integrated circuit may be very complex, the scientist is often primarily interested in a relatively few properties of the box for its application in the laboratory. The black-box model for an amplifier is very useful for predicting and understanding amplifier performance. The notion of amplification or gain enters through this model, and the utility of impedance matching also becomes apparent.

The behavior of ac, dc, and difference amplifiers are important. It is useful to appreciate the essential nature of an amplifier stage through the voltage-divider model for it and the process by which the consequent dc offset problem in the stages of a cascaded amplifier can be solved with coupling capacitors. However, the capacitors limit the amplifier to ac performance, and indeed the general notion of amplifier bandwidth entered there.

The simple voltage-divider model for an amplifier stage also illustrates why the power supply voltage(s) limit the peak-to-peak voltage that can be output by an amplifier and why dc amplifiers usually require two supply voltages for their operation. The general consideration of input, output, and power supply connections to an amplifier are also illustrated in this model. The nature of the difference or differential amplifier, including its property of common-mode rejection, is an important final consideration.

REVIEW EXERCISES

1. Draw the black-box model for an amplifier. Label the ports and resistors. In what quantity does the voltage amplification appear?
2. (a) Define mathematically the open-circuit voltage gain A_v of an amplifier.
   (b) Define mathematically the power gain A_p of an amplifier.
3. (a) What should the input impedance be for an ideal amplifier? Why?
   (b) What should the output impedance be for an ideal amplifier? Why?
4. Suppose we connect an audio generator to one input of a stereo amplifier and an 8-Ω (power) resistor to the corresponding output. Then we measure the input voltage to be 0.01 V_{p-p} and the voltage across the 8-Ω resistor to be 4.0 V_{p-p}.
   (a) Explain why the open-circuit voltage gain for the stereo channel is not 400.
   (b) Should it be more or less than 400? Why?
5. (a) What is a voltage follower?
   (b) Can its voltage gain be greater than one?

    (c)   Can its power gain be greater than one?

6.   A high quality voltage follower is often inserted between a voltage source and a load. It is then often called a *buffer amplifier*. Comment on the reason for the term *buffer* here.

7.   Suppose we decide to heat a cup of water for tea by connecting a power resistor to the output of the stereo in Question 4 and dropping it into the cup. (This is not an exaggeration of their power.) Is there an optimum value for the resistor? Explain.

8.   In general, it is not possible for the peak-to-peak voltage from an amplifier output to exceed a certain voltage. What is the determining voltage? Explain briefly. (However, if inductors or transformers are used, this rule can be broken for ac signals.)

9.   (a)   What is meant by the clipping of the signal out of an amplifier? What is its cause?

    (b)   Describe how to make a square wave, given a large-amplitude sinewave source, and an amplifier with substantial voltage gain.

10.   (a)   What is the reason (in terms of amplifier construction) that a high-gain ac amplifier cannot amplify dc voltages?

    (b)   Why can't these offending items simply be replaced by wires within the amplifier?

11.   (a)   What is meant by the offset voltage of a dc amplifier? Describe how it can be measured.

    (b)   Make a black-box model of a dc amplifier, including the input offset voltage in the model.

12   Give a definition of the bandwidth (BW) of an amplifier using the term *midband gain*.

13.   The human ear is responsive to frequencies from about 60 Hz to 15 kHz. The bandwidth of the amplifier in a phonograph prior to 1955 was generally less than 10 kHz, with the low-frequency limit at about 100 Hz. What did this bandwidth do to the phonograph sound? (Actually, the bandwidth of the pickup and loudspeaker were also limited.)

14.   (a)   Generally, what sort of power supply configuration is required for a dc amplifier?

    (b)   Name two desirable features of dc amplifiers that result from this power supply configuration.

    (c)   Which feature is virtually necessary if several dc amplifiers are to be cascaded? Why?

15.   A differential amplifier could well be marked with two leads each marked + and two more each marked −. However, in each case the two should be distinguished as to use. Explain.

16.   (a)   What is meant by *common-mode rejection* of an amplifier? What general type of amplifier does this term apply to?

    (b)   What is the definition of CMRR?

17. (a) In electrocardiography, how can the 60-Hz interference problem be modeled electrically?
    (b) What can be done to reduce the 60-Hz interference problem?
18. (a) What is meant by white noise?
    (b) What is the origin of thermal noise or Johnson noise in a resistor?
    (c) How does flicker noise differ from white noise?
    (d) Which resistor type is superior in terms of noise: carbon composition or metal film?
19. Which amplifier type is likely to have the greater problem with flicker noise: a dc amplifier or an ac amplifier? Explain.
20. (a) Explain why an amplifier with the minimum possible bandwidth is generally preferable in terms of noise problems.
    (b) What generally limits a scientist from using an amplifier with exceedingly small bandwidth?

PROBLEMS

1. A certain amplifier is specified by its manufacturer to have a power gain of 45-dB when used with a 50-Ω load. Its input impedance is 1000 Ω. If 0.1 V_{rms} is established at its input, what voltage appears across the 50-Ω load connected to its output?

2. (a) It is not unusual to express virtually any voltage ratio in dB, according to dB = 20 log (V_1/V_2). Argue that according to the fundamental definition of dB, the two voltages should appear across identical resistances (if not actually the same resistor). What should be the voltage-ratio-to-dB relation for nonidentical resistances?

   (b) A certain amplifier is characterized by an input impedance of 1000 Ω and an open-circuit voltage gain of 100. Argue that strictly speaking, it is improper to say that its open-circuit voltage gain is 40 dB. (Nevertheless, when voltage ratios are quoted, it is common practice to ignore the resistances involved and simply use the simple voltage-ratio-to-dB relation. Then 40 dB is correct.)

3. It is possible to purchase voltage calibrators for calibrating VOMs, DVMs, and oscilloscopes. One such device was available quite inexpensively for a number of years from a well-known "kit" company. Although it provides only a dc output with 1% precision, it remains a convenient device. The calibrator produces 1.00 V out with no load; however, when 5 kΩ is connected to the output, the output decreases to 0.9 V. Show that the output impedance for this dc signal source is 555 Ω.

4. Suppose the voltage calibrator of the above problem is set to 10 mV *on its dial* and connected into a certain dc amplifier. A 100 Ω/V_{dc} voltmeter is connected to the output of the dc amplifier and the 1.5-V scale of the voltmeter is used.

The dc amplifier has a voltage gain (open-circuit) of 50, an input impedance of 1 kΩ, and an output impedance of 20 Ω.

(a) Make a diagram similar to Figure A5–2 for this problem.

(b) Find the reading that will appear on the voltmeter.

5. A certain audio oscillator has an output impedance of 200 Ω. It is connected to a good oscilloscope, and its output is adjusted to 0.2 V_{p-p}. Then the oscillator is connected to an amplifier that has an input impedance of 400 Ω, an output impedance of 50 Ω, and an open-circuit voltage gain of 100. A 100-Ω resistor is connected to the output of the amplifier.

(a) Diagram the problem using a black-box model for the parts of the system.

(b) Find the peak-to-peak voltage that develops across the 100-Ω resistor.

6. Suppose we have an audio oscillator with a 50-Ω output impedance and another with a 600-Ω output impedance. They each present an open-circuit output voltage of 20 V_{rms}. What is the maximum possible power that may be output by these respective generators to some (proper) load connected to each?

7. A certain audio power amplifier has an output impedance of 2 Ω and is connected to an 8-Ω loudspeaker. Compute how much the power output to the loudspeaker would increase if the amplifier operated into a matching loudspeaker.

NOTE: Calculate the percentage increase in power.

8. Suppose 3 identical ideal ac amplifiers are cascaded, each with a voltage gain of 20. A signal source of 0.1 V_{p-p} is connected to the input of the overall amplifier.

(a) What is the voltage expected from the output of the overall amplifier?

(b) What minimum power supply voltage is required for each stage of the overall amplifier?

9. Consider the 3-stage cascaded amplifier of Figure A5–5. Assume the three stages are identical, each with input impedance R_{in} and output impedance R_{out}. Solve for the open-circuit voltage gain of the amplifier; that is, find a formula for v_{out}/v_{in}.

10. Consider an amplifier constructed by cascading 3 ideal amplifiers with voltage gains A_1, A_2, and A_3. Show that if A_1, A_2 and A_3 are expressed in dB, the overall voltage gain in dB is $A = A_1 + A_2 + A_3$. Thus the voltage gains are simply additive when expressed in dB.

11. We have on the lab bench an ac amplifier and also a dc amplifier. Each has a voltage gain of 4.

(a) Suppose a 1.5-V battery is connected to the respective amplifiers. What is the voltage out of each?

(b) Suppose a 1.5-V_{rms} ac voltage is connected to the respective amplifiers. What is the voltage out of each? What frequency assumption is made?

12. Let us consider the low-frequency bandwidth limit of ac-coupled amplifiers. Suppose two identical amplifiers are capacitively coupled as shown in Diagram A5–1. For each the output resistance is considered to be ideal, the input resistance is 1 kΩ, and the voltage gain is 10. They are coupled with a 0.1-μF capacitor. An *ideal* signal generator with 0.1-V_{rms} output signal is attached to the input A of the overall amplifier.

    (a)   Suppose the frequency of the signal generator is very high. Find the voltages appearing at ports B and C, respectively.

    (b)   Suppose the frequency of the signal source is 500 Hz. Find the magnitude of the voltages appearing at ports B and C, respectively.

    (c)   Argue that the frequency response of the overall amplifier is determined by a high-pass filter behavior. What resistor and capacitor compose the filter?

    (d)   What is the low-frequency end (-3 dB point) of the amplifier?

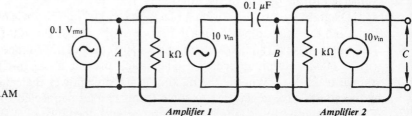

DIAGRAM
A5–1.
                          Amplifier 1   *Amplifier 2*

13.   Consider the high-frequency bandwidth limit of cascaded amplifiers. Suppose two identical amplifiers are cascaded as shown in Diagram A5–2. The input resistance of each is considered to be ideal, but there is an internal shunt capacitance of 200 pF. The open-circuit voltage gain is 10, and the output resistance is 10 kΩ for each amplifier. An ideal signal generator with 0.1-V_{rms} output signal is attached to the input A of the overall amplifier.

    (a)   Suppose the frequency of the signal source is very low. Find the voltages appearing at ports B and C, respectively.

    (b)   Suppose the frequency of the signal source is 1 MHz. Find the magnitude of the voltage appearing at ports B and C, respectively.

    (c)   Argue that the frequency response of the overall amplifier is determined by a low-pass filter behavior. What resistor and capacitor compose the filter?

    (d)   What is the bandwidth for this amplifier?

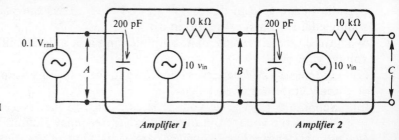

DIAGRAM
A5–2.
                          Amplifier 1   *Amplifier 2*

14. A_v can be positive or negative, depending on whether an amplifier is noninverting or inverting.

    (a)   Justify this statement.

    (b)   Which is positive?

15.   A 0.1-V battery is connected to a dc noninverting amplifier and also to a dc inverting amplifier, as shown in Diagram A5–3. The magnitude of A_v for each

amplifier is 5. Three DVMs are connected with the red lead placed as indicated by R in each case. When the red lead is more positive, the DVM reading shows a + sign. What is the reading, including sign, for each DVM?

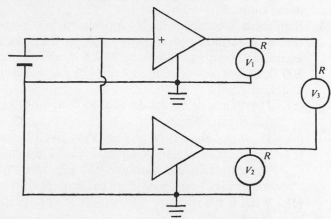

DIAGRAM
A5–3.

16. (a) An ideal differential amplifier with a difference-mode gain of 20 has +50 mV applied to its + input and −100 mV applied to its − input. What is the output signal?

(b) What assumption about common-mode gain did you make in part (a)?

17. Consider an ideal difference amplifier that is connected as pictured in Diagram A5–4. The voltage gain of the amplifier is 20. What is the voltage reading, including sign, of the DVM? (Note the "red" DVM lead R.)

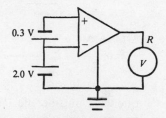

DIAGRAM A5–4.

18. Consider the difference amplifier shown in Diagram A5–5. A 0.5-V battery is connected to it in the two ways shown.

(a) What is the difference voltage gain for this amplifier?

(b) What is the common-mode voltage gain for this amplifier?

(c) What is the CMRR for this amplifier in dB?

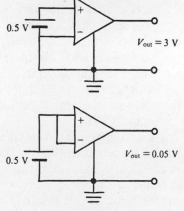

DIAGRAM A5–5.

19. A difference amplifier (or differential amplifier) has a difference gain of 100 and a common-mode rejection ratio of 60 dB. Suppose a 1-V_{p-p} signal is applied to both inputs simultaneously with respect to ground. What signal will appear at the output?

20. Suppose a Wheatstone bridge is operated in out-of-balance mode in conjunction with an ideal noninverting amplifier that has a voltage gain of 160. The excitation voltage to the bridge is 4.5 V, and the arms of the bridge are each 300 Ω, except for the transducer resistance, which we write as 300 Ω + Δ. See Diagram A5–6.

    (a) The source of excitation voltage to the bridge must *not* be grounded in this circuit. Why?

    (b) Show that the output V_{out} (in V) is given by $+0.6\Delta$, if Δ is in ohms.

    (c) Suppose the excitation voltage must be grounded at the negative terminal. We still desire the output signal V_{out} to be relative to ground. Draw a circuit illustrating how it can be accomplished using a difference amplifier.

    (d) What is the nominal common-mode voltage into the difference amplifier of part (c)?

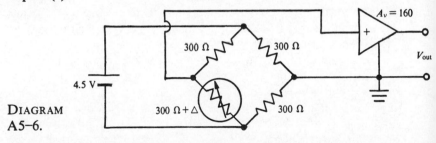

DIAGRAM A5–6.

21. (a) An ideal *bandpass filter* passes no signal from input to output for frequencies outside the bandwidth or *pass band* of the filter; however, it passes all signals unattenuated if their frequencies lie within the pass band. Let v_{in} and v_{out} be the input and output frequencies, respectively, for a bandpass filter, and let $A_v = v_{out}/v_{in}$. If f_1 and f_2 are the lower and upper frequencies of the pass band, draw a graph of A_v versus frequency f for the ideal bandpass filter.

    (b) Suppose a metal film resistor with a resistance of 100 kΩ is connected to a noise-free ideal bandpass filter for which the band-limit frequencies are 4000 Hz and 6000 Hz. What is the rms noise voltage expected at the filter output? The temperature of the resistor is 25°C.

    (c) Repeat part (b) except change the band-limit frequencies to 29 kHz and 31 kHz.

22. A 1-kHz signal is input to an amplifier that has a bandwidth of 100 Hz about the 1-kHz center frequency. The signal-to-noise ratio from the amplifier output is 20. A bandpass filter with a 10-Hz bandwidth about a 1-kHz center frequency is connected to the amplifier output. What is the signal-to-noise ratio expected for the signal from the bandpass filter output?

23. A transducer with a noise voltage output of $8\,nV_{rms}/\sqrt{Hz}$ is connected to an amplifier that has an equivalent input noise voltage of $4\,nV_{rms}/\sqrt{Hz}$. The voltage gain of the amplifier is 3000 and its bandwidth is 100 kHz. What rms noise voltage is expected from the amplifier output? What is the minimum desired voltage signal from the transducer output for a signal-to-noise ratio of 20?

CHAPTER
A6

Operational Amplifier and Electronic Function Blocks

Until about 1962, amplifiers were constructed from *discrete active devices;* that is, from tubes or transistors that could be used in conjunction with passive elements and a power supply to increase the power level of a voltage signal. Since that date it has been possible to produce a number of transistors interconnected with resistors and perhaps capacitors on a single small *chip* of semiconductor. An amplifier is produced all at once by techniques used to manufacture single transistors. Such an electronic circuit is termed an *integrated circuit* (IC) because transistors and resistors are combined or integrated together on one chip.

The focus for this analog electronics book is the study of one versatile type of amplifier called the *operational amplifier* (OA or *op amp*). The operational amplifier was first constructed in the 1940s from vacuum tubes and used in analog computers to perform various mathematical operations such as addition or multiplication of voltages. This function is the reason for the term *operational.* However, the operational amplifier has great versatility and has since been put to use in all sorts of applications. It is probably fair to credit Malmstadt, Enke, and Toren with popularizing the op amp among scientists with their book *Electronics for Scientists* published in 1963. At that time, the op amp was still a vacuum tube design.

The revolution in electronic system design caused by the op amp began in earnest when a young electronic engineer named Bob Widlar (three years out of college) designed the "702" integrated circuit operational amplifier for Fairchild Semiconductor in 1963. In 1965 he designed the improved "709" that quickly became a classic IC and is manufactured by almost all important sources of solid-state devices. Fairchild introduced the "741" in 1968, and this unit is a widely used "workhorse" (and the one used in most of our discussion). It is an amplifier containing 20 transistors. By 1972 the price of these units was about $1.00—less than the single price for many transistors or tubes. Subsequently, the price declined to about $.25.

Properties of the Operational Amplifier

An *operational amplifier* is any high-voltage-gain dc amplifier with high input impedance and low output impedance, usually having differential inputs. *High* is a relative term and is qualified later on. The op amp is universally represented as in Figure A6–1a; that is, as a triangle with an output at one corner and the noninverting and inverting inputs marked plus (+) and minus (−), respectively. Most units are operated from positive and negative voltage supplies so that the amplifier output may swing either positive or negative. The power supply connections are usually omitted from the symbol.

The operational amplifier may be modeled as in Figure A6–1b. The similarity of the op-amp model in this figure to the general amplifier model given earlier in Figure A5–1 should be quite evident. The *output impedance* R_{out} of the op amp corresponds directly; however, the *input impedance* R_{in} for the op amp is between its + and − input terminals since the op amp is a difference amplifier. Notice that v_d is the *difference voltage* between the two input terminals of the actual operational amplifier. Then the size of the voltage generator in the model is given by $A_{vo}v_d$, where A_{vo} is called the *open-loop voltage gain* of the operational amplifier. A_{vo} corresponds directly to the A_v of Figure A5–1, but the subscript o is added to emphasize or distinguish that this is the voltage gain of the op amp *itself*. (The reason for the term *open loop* will become clear shortly as we consider amplifier circuits that incorporate op amps.) If no load is connected to the op-amp output, we see that the output voltage is the same as the voltage of the internal voltage generator, so that

$$v_{out} = A_{vo}v_d \qquad (A6-1)$$

This relationship simply says the output voltage v_{out} of the op amp is more than its input difference voltage v_d by the factor of the open-loop voltage gain A_{vo} of the op amp.

NOTE: Arrows are used in Figure A6–1b and also in the remainder of the book to indicate points between which a given voltage is defined; notice the v_d and v_{out} arrows in Figure A6–1b. The "tail" of the arrow tells the reference point for the voltage. If the point at the arrow's "head" is the more positive of the two, the designated voltage is a positive quantity.

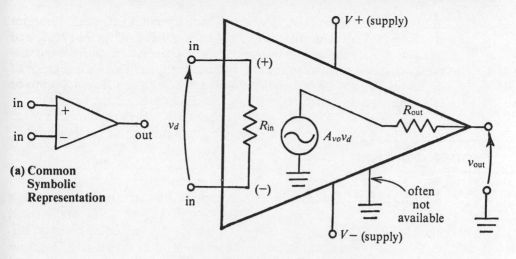

(b) Model of Operational Amplifier

FIGURE A6–1. *Operational Amplifier*

Let us consider some values for the parameters in the model of Figure A6–1b for an actual operational amplifier. For the popular 741 IC op amp, the resistance between inputs R_{in} is typically 2 megohms, the output resistance R_{out} is 75 ohms, and the *open-loop voltage gain* A_{vo} is 200,000 (106 decibels). However, this gain begins to fall for frequencies greater than about 10 hertz. The maximum supply voltage is ± 18 V (use of ± 12 V to ± 15 V is common). The dc power supply connections are made to the $V+$ and $V-$ leads as diagrammed earlier in Figure A5–8.

Ideal Operational Amplifier and Basic Circuits

If the operational amplifier has a very large (approaching infinity) input resistance R_{in} and also very large (approaching infinity) voltage gain A_{vo}, it has the essential ingredients of being an *ideal op amp*. Two more requirements should be added: (1) If the voltage between the inputs v_d is zero, the output voltage should be exactly zero (the extent to which this is not true is called the *input offset-voltage error* and is discussed later under real op-amp considerations; and (2) the voltage gain should remain large independent of frequency.

The operational amplifier is almost always used with a large amount of *negative feedback;* that is, some of the output signal is fed back to the input in a way that tends to negate or counteract the original signal into the amplifier. The case of *positive feedback* is usually much less desirable. Most students have encountered a case of positive feedback: When the microphone of a PA system is placed in front of the loudspeaker, positive feedback from the loudspeaker output to the microphone input causes a loud squeal.

If the two requirements hold true, the analysis of various amplifier configurations is quite straightforward and the amplifier behavior turns out not to depend on the character of the op amp itself. The behavior of the resulting amplifier in general depends only on the values of the components connected to the op amp. If these values are accurately known, the behavior of the constructed amplifier is just as accurately predictable; herein lies the beauty of the approach. Actually, this sort of situation has long been true of amplifiers that include a high gain element and a large amount of feedback. Enough said; let us see by example.

Inverting Amplifier

Certainly the basic configuration and prototype illustration of how the op amp may be put to use is the *inverting amplifier* shown in Figure A6–2a. Only two resistors are involved: a resistor R connected between the amplifier input and the op-amp inverting (or $-$) input, and a resistor R_f connected between the op-amp output (as well as the amplifier output) and the op-amp $-$ input. The noninverting (or $+$) input is connected to ground; the "ground" (or reference) terminals of the amplifier input and output are also connected to ground.

The reader should be clear on two points here. First, although often no power supply connections are shown connected to the op-amp triangle, they must in fact be connected. They are shown only as dashed lines in the drawing. In general, both positive $V+$ and negative $V-$ supply voltages are used (equal in magnitude), and the zero potential or *ground* of the supply is connected to the operational amplifier circuit in some way. In this circuit, it is to the $+$ input of the op amp.

NOTE: This ground might *not* be truly connected to *earth* however; the amplifier is then said to be *floating* relative to true ground.

Second, the op amp along with resistors and wires is placed in a box, and the whole now becomes the inverting amplifier—or simply amplifier—with which we subsequently work. It has a pair of input posts and a pair of output posts as shown in Figure A6–2a.

Notice that the voltage into the amplifier is v_{in}, while the voltage into the operational amplifier *itself* is v_d. The voltage out of either is the same v_{out}. The arrows drawn by these voltages in Figure A6–2a show the sense of positive polarity (arrowhead near more positive point). If the voltage is reversed in any case, the value is negative.

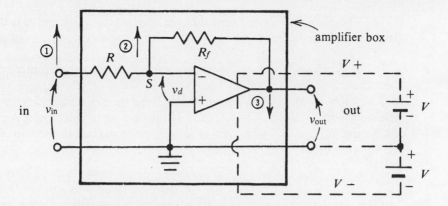

(a) Connection of Two Resistors to an Op Amp to Make an Inverting Amplifier

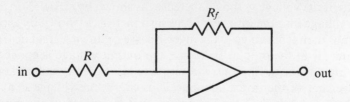

(b) Current Path and Voltages with the Ideal Op Amp

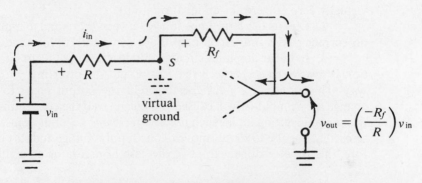

(c) Very Simplified Representation

FIGURE A6-2. *Inverting Amplifier Constructed from an Operational Amplifier Gain Block*

There are now three points that are central to a quick and easy derivation of amplifier behavior using op-amp design analysis:

1. The magnitude of the output voltage of the op amp must be less than the supply voltage value. For example, if the supply voltages used are ±15 V, there is *no way* the output voltage can be more than 15 V above or below ground. (Refer to Chapter A5.) If the op amp is *functioning properly*, the output voltage of the op amp is directly proportional to the voltage into the *op-amp input*. Then from Equation A6–1 we have

$$v_d = \frac{v_{out}}{A_{vo}}$$

But if v_{out} is limited to 15 V and A_{vo} is 150,000, for example, then v_d must be less than 15 V/150,000 = 0.1 mV = 100 μV. If A_{vo} were arbitrarily large, as for an ideal op amp, the voltage v_d would be vanishingly small; even so, v_d is a small voltage. Thus we have the rule: If a linear operational amplifier circuit is functioning, the voltage difference between the − and + inputs is virtually zero (*is* zero for an ideal op amp).

2. Due to the large impedance between the − and + inputs, virtually no current passes into an op-amp input (zero current for an ideal op amp).

3. In linear amplifier circuits—that is, not digital circuits—a connection is always made between the output and the inverting − input in some way. This is *negative feedback,* wherein the output tends to oppose the change at the input (which caused the output). (If the connection were made to the noninverting input, such *positive feedback* generally causes the output to oscillate or else to simply move to one supply voltage and stay there. Therefore, this is never done, except in the case of oscillator or digital circuits.)

With these points in mind, we next consider the circuit in Figure A6–2a. First, let's try to get a qualitative understanding of what happens. Notice that there is a connection between the output and the − op-amp input. Thus, if the voltage v_2 should increase [as shown by arrow (1) in the drawing], the voltage into the inverting input also increases [shown by arrow (2)]. The output then tends to go in the inverse sense or down a great deal as shown by arrow (3) at the output. However, the output voltage is connected back to the input through R_f. Thus, the output tends to greatly counteract the upward movement of the inverting input. This causes the voltage v_d at the − input to be much less than the voltage v_{in} that is applied to the amplifier input. Consequently, the output voltage is much less than $A_{vo} \times v_{in}$. (However, v_{out} is always equal to $A_{vo} \times v_d$.) We can see qualitatively that the negative feedback effect is less if R_f is made larger; therefore we expect a larger amplifier gain if larger R_f is used.

Next we consider a quantitative analysis that is exact if an ideal op amp is used and quite accurate for many real op-amp situations. Because the voltage v_d between the − and + inputs is so small and the + input *is* connected to ground, the − input is always "virtually at ground." Indeed, the − input is referred to as a *virtual ground* in the circuit. It is labeled as point S and is often called the *summing point*. We see why this term is useful later in the situation of the *summing amplifier*.

Regard the input voltage v_{in} as a battery as shown in Figure A6–2b. A current then flows through R toward the $-$ input of the op amp, but it does *not* flow into the op amp because of its high input resistance (for example, for the 741 there are 2 megohms to the $+$ terminal and thus to ground). It therefore flows through R_f toward the output, which should be at a negative voltage anyway. Now the current flowing from v_{in} through R is completely predictable since one end is at voltage v_{in} and the other is virtually at ground. We have a voltage v_{in} across the resistance R, and the current i_{in} through it (from the battery) is

$$i_{in} = \frac{v_{in}}{R} \qquad \text{(A6–2)}$$

This same current flows through the feedback resistor R_f so the voltage across it is clearly

$$v_{R_f} = i_{in} R_f = v_{in}\left(\frac{R_f}{R}\right) \qquad \text{(A6–3)}$$

But the end of R_f connected to the $-$ input is virtually at ground and is the more positive as drawn in Figure A6–2b because the current is flowing *in* at that end. The negative end of R_f is connected to v_{out}. Then the output voltage is negative and just equal to the voltage across R_f as calculated in Equation A6–3. We have

$$v_{out} = -v_{R_f} = -v_{in}\left(\frac{R_f}{R}\right) \qquad \text{(A6–4)}$$

The minus sign in this equation reflects the fact that v_{out} will be negative when the input is positive (or it will be positive when the input is negative). It is an inverting amplifier. Finally the ratio of the output voltage v_{out} to the input voltage v_{in} is the voltage amplification of the amplifier. Dividing both sides of Equation A6–4 by v_{in} gives

$$\frac{v_{out}}{v_{in}} = Av = -\frac{R_f}{R} \qquad \text{(A6–5)}$$

Thus the voltage gain of an inverting amplifier using an ideal op amp is simply the ratio of the feedback resistance to the value of the input resistor.

This gain is quite different from the voltage gain of the op amp itself, which is A_{vo}. A_{vo} is called the *open-loop gain* of the op amp since it is the gain without feedback or with an *open* in the feedback loop ($R_f =$ infinity).

The *input impedance* of the inverting amplifier is examined next and is very easy to obtain. In Chapter A5 we examined the concept of amplifier input impedance; quite clearly it is that an amplifier presents some impedance (resistance) R_{inA} to a voltage v_{in} connected to its input. Thus, a current i_{in} flows into the amplifier input that must be given by $i_{in} = v_{in}/R_{inA}$. This expression can be turned around. If the current that flows into an amplifier input as a consequence of a certain applied voltage is known, we can quickly solve for R_{inA}. In our amplifier the current in was argued to be $i_{in} = v_{in}/R$. Then

$$R_{inA} = \frac{v_{in}}{i_{in}} = \frac{v_{in}}{v_{in}/R} = R \qquad (A6-6)$$

Therefore, the input impedance to this amplifier is simply R.

Actually, this result is obvious. Note that the end S of resistor R (connection to the $-$ input of op amp) acts as though it is connected *virtually* to ground and the other end is connected to the voltage in. But the "bottom end" of voltage v_{in} is connected to ground, too, so it is simply connected across a resistance R, and this resistor must then be the input impedance presented to the outside world by the input of the inverting amplifier circuit.

Unfortunately, this resistance for practical amplifiers cannot be terribly large, and although the operational amplifier itself may have quite an ideal input resistance, the *constructed* inverting amplifier does *not*. The reader may ask: Why not simply use a large value for R; for example, 1 megohm? Suppose the desired gain is 50. Then the feedback resistor R_f must be $A_v R_f = 50 \times 1$ megohm. The 50-megohm resistor is larger than any standard resistor and could not be easily obtained with high accuracy. Also, high humidity conditions cause leakage of current over the resistor surface or mounting board that changes its value in an unknown and variable way. Finally, R and R_f are then of the order of R_{in} for the op amp itself, and the ideal op-amp analysis we have used for voltage gain fails. Not all of the current i_{in} in Figure A6-2b flows through R_f; some flows into the $-$ input of the op amp.

The *output impedance* of an amplifier constructed from a high-gain amplifier through use of negative feedback can be shown to be very low. In general, the output impedance R_{outA} of a feedback amplifier based on an op amp is on the order of $R_{out}(A_v/A_{vo})$, where R_{out} is the corresponding impedance of the op amp itself. If the open-loop gain of the op amp is very large, the output impedance of the constructed amplifier approaches zero even though the output impedance of the op amp itself is quite finite (recall that it is 75 ohms for the 741). Thus, the op amp with feedback approaches the ideal in its output behavior. But a warning is needed: The current that small integrated circuit op amps can deliver is typically limited to a few milliamperes (10 to 20).

Finally a comment should be made about the highly simplified op-amp amplifier representation that is sometimes encountered. Figure A6-2c shows this approach where even the ground line is omitted, as well as $-$ input designation. Of course, the ground connections must really be there, and the in and out voltages are assumed to be relative to ground.

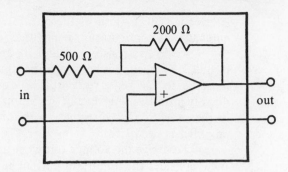

FIGURE A6–3. *Operational Am-plifier Circuit*

Example: Consider the operational amplifier circuit pictured in Figure A6–3. Find the *black-box equivalent amplifier* (general amplifier model of Chapter A5) for this circuit.

Solution: The voltage gain A_v for this circuit is $A_v = -2000\ \Omega/\ 500\ \Omega = -4$. The output impedance is virtually zero. The input impedance is just the 500 Ω of that resistance R. We therefore obtain the black-box equivalent or model shown in Figure A6–4. Notice we have a minus sign beside the magnitude of the output generator to indicate that the polarity of v_{out} is inverted from v_{in}.

Noninverting Amplifier

The fact that the output of the inverting amplifier is reversed in polarity from the input can be inconvenient; also the low input impedance of that amplifier

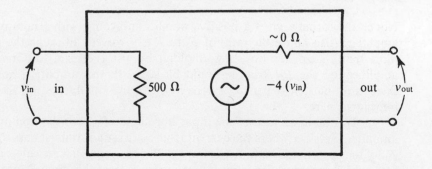

FIGURE A6–4. *Black-Box Model*

is less than ideal. Both of these features are remedied in the *noninverting amplifier;* its configuration is pictured in Figure A6–5a.

Again two resistors, R and R_f, are involved and again notice that the feedback connection is between the output and the inverting (or –) input. This must be so for negative feedback. However, the input voltage v_{in} comes directly into the noninverting (or +) input. This causes the output to change in the same voltage direction as the input voltage so that a noninverting amplifier is produced.

To derive the voltage out when an ideal (or at least "good") op amp is used, consider the important current path from the op-amp output through R_f and R to ground. (The fact that the op amp also sends current to R_L does not matter unless the current capability of the op-amp output is exceeded.) If v_{in} is positive, we expect the output to also go positive so that the current will flow in the direction shown for i in Figure A6–5b. Because of the high impedance of the op-amp input, none of the current flows into the – input. The output voltage appears across the series R and R_f combination, so that the current i is given by

$$i = \frac{v_{out}}{R + R_f} \qquad (A6\text{–}7)$$

The voltage at point S relative to ground is just the current i times the resistance R. But the voltage difference between point S (the – input) and the amplifier input (the + input) is virtually zero if the amplifier is functioning properly. Therefore, the input voltage v_{in} and the voltage at S are virtually the same relative to ground. Then

$$v_{in} = v_S = iR = \left(\frac{v_{out}}{R + R_f}\right) R \qquad (A6\text{–}8)$$

We solve Equation A6–8 for the ratio of v_{out}/v_{in} to obtain the voltage gain of the amplifier; that is,

$$\frac{v_{out}}{v_{in}} = A_v = \frac{R + R_f}{R} = 1 + \frac{R_f}{R} \qquad (A6\text{–}9)$$

Notice the formula gives a positive number in accord with a noninverting amplifier. Also notice the ratio of R_f to R is involved, although the gain is more than that of the inverting amplifier by just 1. Again, to obtain high amplification the R_f/R ratio should be large. In this amplifier, however, there is no particular penalty for having R quite small. It is *not* the input impedance here.

To obtain an idea of the input impedance R_{inA} for the noninverting amplifier, consider where the current from v_{in} must go. It must pass through R_{in} of the operational amplifier toward S. But R_{in} itself is a large value, and we are assured the amplifier input impedance is at least this large. More subtle is the fact that S is at almost the same voltage as v_{in}. Therefore, the input current has very little inclination to travel through R_{in} to S. The value of the

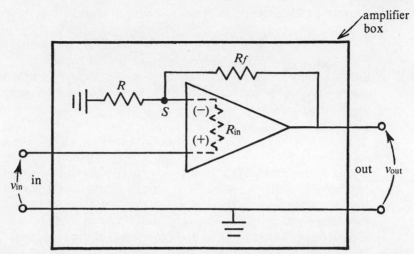

(a) Two Resistors Connected to an Op Amp to Produce a Noninverting Amplifier

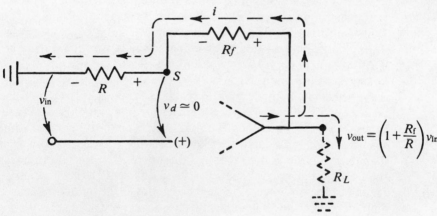

(b) Important Current Path and Voltages

FIGURE A6–5. *Noninverting Amplifier Based on an Operational Amplifier*

input current through R_{in} is obtained by realizing that the voltage across it is v_d and then solving for this input current from the equation, $v_d = i_{in}R_{in}$. Now the output voltage is *always* more than v_d by the factor of the op-amp open-loop gain. So $v_d = v_{out}/A_{vo}$. Next remember $v_{out} = A_v v_{in}$, where A_v is the gain of the amplifier, so that

$$v_d = \left(\frac{A_v}{A_{vo}}\right) v_{in} \qquad\qquad \text{(A6–10)}$$

The current through R_{in} is then

$$i_{in} = \frac{v_d}{R_{in}} = \left(\frac{A_v}{A_{vo}}\right)\left(\frac{v_{in}}{R_{in}}\right) \tag{A6-11}$$

Finally we solve for the ratio of v_{in}/i_{in} from Equation A6-11, because *this is the effective resistance* R_{inA} presented by the overall amplifier to the input voltage. We see

$$\frac{v_{in}}{i_{in}} = R_{inA} = \left(\frac{A_{vo}}{A_v}\right) R_{in} \tag{A6-12}$$

The result for R_{inA} from Equation A6-12 can be an *extremely* large number (for example, $R_{in} = 2$ megohms, $A_{vo} = 200{,}000$, and $A_v = 100$ for the 741 op amp). Actually, the resistance from the $+$ input as well as the $-$ input to ground in the operational amplifier itself is likely to be less. Also, the capacitance between the input and ground will present an impedance that can be lower than this at higher frequencies. Capacitance effects must always be watched at higher frequencies. There will be capacitance between structures in the op amp and between circuit structures on the circuit board. Finally, leakage of current along the surface of the circuit board or the IC socket (for example, through moisture) can easily limit the input resistance of the amplifier to something less than 500 megohms.

The resistance from the $+$ input terminal to ground within the op amp is called the *common-mode input impedance* R_{icm+}; there is a similar resistance from the $-$ input terminal to ground, R_{icm-}. The parallel resistance of these two common-mode input resistances can be measured (in principle) by connecting the $+$ and $-$ inputs together (or in common) and measuring the ac resistance to ground, R_{icm}. Typically this is on the order of 100 times larger than the *differential* input resistance R_{in}, but it is very seldom specified by manufacturers. In a noninverting amplifier, R_{icm+} appears in parallel with the resistance given by Equation A6-12 and is often the determining factor for the input resistance of the amplifier, R_{inA}. The output impedance of the amplifier is very low due to negative feedback, just as in the inverting amplifier case.

Voltage-Follower Amplifier

If the feedback resistance R_f is made equal to zero—that is, a short circuit or wire—in Figure A6-5, the *amplifier* shown in Figure A6-6a results. The voltage gain and input impedance for this amplifier are still given by Equation A6-9 and Equation A6-12, respectively. But since $R_f = 0$, the voltage gain is just unity from Equation A6-9 and the input impedance should be extremely large.

The output voltage is just the same as the input voltage; it *follows* the input wherever it goes (but between the values of the supply voltages). There

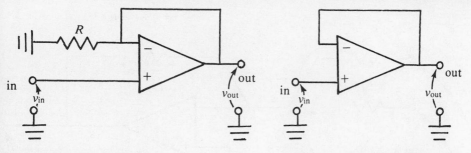

(a) Resistance R_f Equals Zero   **(b) Common Voltage-Follower Circuit**

FIGURE A6–6. *Voltage-Follower Amplifier Constructed from an Operational Amplifier*

is no voltage gain, but the amplifier is *not* useless. It may amplify power a great deal, as discussed in Chapter A5. The very large input impedance and small output impedance of this amplifier are its great virtues. However, the current that can be delivered by the op amp should again be kept in mind, as was mentioned earlier.

In fact, the resistance R can be made infinite, and the voltage would again be seen from Equation A6–9 to be unity. Omitting R entirely is the same as making it infinite. Therefore, the usual op-amp voltage-follower circuit used is shown in Figure A6–6b. Simply connect a wire from the output to the − input, and use the + input as the amplifier input.

Summing Amplifier

We next consider the first circuit for which the operational amplifier can be used to perform a mathematical operation: *the summing amplifier*. We want to arrange an amplifier that will produce as output a voltage that is the sum of several input voltages. Thus, if 2.1 V, 3.6 V, and −1.6 V are put to the amplifier inputs, the output voltage will be (2.1 + 3.6 − 1.6) V = 4.1 V. We would then have an electronic adding machine, where a voltage proportional to a number (the *analog* of a number) is input, and a voltage proportional to the result is output. This is the first requirement for an analog computer, but is not the most common application in this world of cheap digital computers. The summing amplifier is useful in solving various instrumentation problems in science and industry. We may simply want a signal that is the literal sum of two signals that are available to the user.

The circuit used for a summing amplifier is a simple extension of the inverting amplifier, and its analysis is simple if the analysis of the inverting amplifier has been well understood. A circuit is illustrated in Figure A6–7. Notice that three resistors (there could be more) are shown connected to the

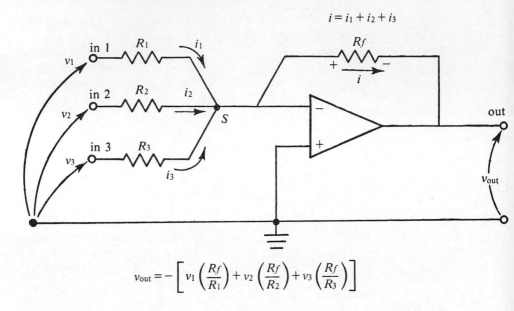

$$v_{out} = -\left[v_1 \left(\frac{R_f}{R_1}\right) + v_2 \left(\frac{R_f}{R_2}\right) + v_3 \left(\frac{R_f}{R_3}\right) \right]$$

FIGURE A6–7. *Summing Amplifier Constructed from an Operational Amplifier*

summing point S, the inverting input of the op amp. These resistors are each rather like the R resistor of the simple inverting amplifier. Voltages v_1, v_2, and v_3 may be independently connected between each input and ground as illustrated. But the point S remains virtually at ground for the same reasons as argued earlier. Then, the current through each *input resistor* is determined by the input voltage effectively appearing across it. We have

$$i_1 = \frac{v_1}{R_1} \quad i_2 = \frac{v_2}{R_2} \quad i_3 = \frac{v_3}{R_3} \qquad \textbf{(A6–13)}$$

These currents merge at the summing point S and flow through R_f to the op-amp output. (Here we see reason for the term summing point.) They do *not* flow into the op-amp − input because of its high impedance.

Now the voltage out is just the voltage across the feedback resistor R_f because the end at the S point is virtually at ground and the other end is connected to the output. We see that

$$v_{out} = v_{Rf} = -iR_f = -(i_1 + i_2 + i_3)R_f \qquad \textbf{(A6–14)}$$

Finally inserting the currents from Equation A6–13, we have

$$v_{out} = -\left[v_1 \left(\frac{R_f}{R_1}\right) + v_2 \left(\frac{R_f}{R_2}\right) + v_3 \left(\frac{R_f}{R_3}\right) \right] \qquad \textbf{(A6–15)}$$

Now suppose $R_1 = R_2 = R_3 = R_f$ in Equation A6–15. Then

$$v_{out} = -(v_1 + v_2 + v_3)$$

and the output is just the sum of the input voltages (the sum is inverted, however) and we have the desired summing amplifier.

However, the more elaborate expression of Equation A6–15 shows a nice possibility. It is clearly possible to take a *weighted sum* of the input voltages by using different values for R_1, R_2, and R_3. For example, if $R_f/R_1 = 2$, $R_f/R_2 = 7$, and $R_f/R_3 = 4$, the output is $-(4v_1 + 7v_2 + 4v_3)$.

Difference Amplifier

We considered the behavior of a difference or differential amplifier in Chapter A5. It is really an *analog subtractor* because it subtracts the voltage at the inverting input from the noninverting input in determining the output. The operational amplifier itself is a difference amplifier, and we might think there is then no need for any special design work to produce a difference amplifier. Actually, the need exists because the operational amplifier cannot be used "naked": Its gain is too high.

The trick is to combine inverting and noninverting amplifier designs in one package. As the first effort, consider the design shown in Figure A6–8a. If the v_{in-} input is grounded, the output is just $+(1 + R_f/R)v_{in+}$ because we clearly have the simple noninverting amplifier. If v_{in+} is grounded, the output is $-(R_f/R)v_{in+}$ since we merely have an inverting amplifier. If voltages are present at both inputs simultaneously, it is reasonable (though not really proven by these statements) that the voltage out is the sum of these two voltages. The proof is left as an exercise. Then

$$v_{out} = + \left(1 + \frac{R_f}{R}\right) v_{in+} - \left(\frac{R_f}{R}\right) v_{in-} \qquad \textbf{(A6–16)}$$

If $R_f/R \gg 1$ we have (approximately) a difference amplifier; that is,

$$v_{out} = \frac{R_f}{R} \left(v_{in+} - v_{in-}\right)$$

The common-mode rejection by this approach will not be extremely good due to the approximation used. Also, the input impedances presented to v_{in+} and v_{in-} are *very* different. The problem is that the gain from the noninverting amplifier is more than that from the inverting amplifier. This situation could be remedied by putting a voltage divider between v_{in+} and the + input of the op amp (see Figure A6–8b). Simply reduce the voltage from v_{in+} by a factor so that this factor times $(1 + R_f/R)$ is the same as R_f/R. The voltage divider factor is $R_2/(R_1 + R_2)$ so we want

$$\frac{R_2}{R_1 + R_2} \left(1 + \frac{R_f}{R}\right) = \frac{R_f}{R} \qquad \textbf{(A6–17)}$$

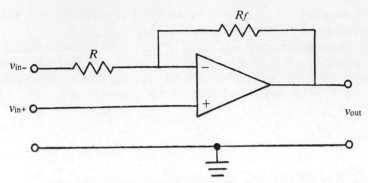

(a) Attempt at Difference Amplifier

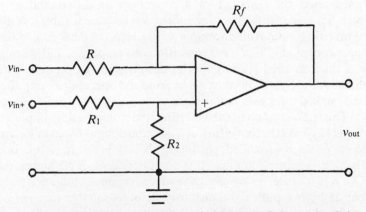

(b) Voltage Divider in Noninverting Input to Balance the Gain

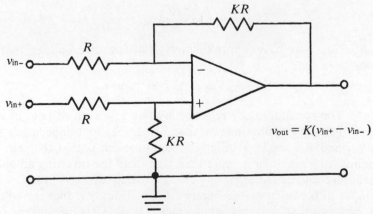

(c) Difference Amplifier with Balanced Gain K at Each Input, but Unbalanced Input Impedances

FIGURE A6-8. *Difference or Differential Amplifier*

Move this factor to the right side of the equation as follows

$$\left(1 + \frac{R_f}{R}\right) = \frac{R_f}{R}\left(1 + \frac{R_1}{R_2}\right)$$

We can solve for the ratio R_1/R_2 in this expression (or simply notice the solution by inspection). We find

$$\frac{R_f}{R} = \frac{R_2}{R_1} \tag{A6-18}$$

as the requirement on the resistance ratio of the voltage divider. In particular, one possibility is to set $R_1 = R$ and $R_2 = R_f$. Let $K = R_f/R$. From Equation A6-14 we then have

$$v_{out} = \frac{R_f}{R}\,(v_{in+} - v_{in-}) = K(v_{in+} - v_{in-}) \tag{A6-19}$$

This situation is pictured in Figure A6-8c. We can show (with some work) that the common-mode rejection ratio of the resulting amplifier is the same as that of the operational amplifier itself, provided the resistors are exactly matched.

Rather than having to select resistors so carefully, a simple approach is to use a potentiometer for the voltage divider in the noninverting input. The proper setting of this potentiometer can be done experimentally by applying a signal to both inputs at once—that is, in common, or common mode—and adjusting the potentiometer for a *minimum* signal at the output. Figure A6-9 shows the amplifier and experimental arrangement. Since the potentiometer permits optimizing the common-mode rejection ratio (CMRR) for the differential amplifier, it is given the label *CMRR adjustment* in the figure. The amplifier is shown connected to a common-mode input signal to adjust the CMRR potentiometer.

The amplifier pictured in Figure A6-8c does have the disadvantage of different input impedances relative to ground at the two inputs. The input impedance at v_{in-} is just R (like an inverting amplifier), while that at v_{in+} is $(R + KR)$ because these two resistors are simply in series to ground and no current flows into the op-amp + input. It is possible to work with other resistances for R_1, R_2 in the voltage divider network of Figure A6-8b. Choose $R_1/R_2 = R/R_f$, and also $R_1 + R_2 = R$. These are two simultaneous equations that satisfy both the balanced-gain and equal input-impedance requirements. It is left as a problem to show that R_1 and R_2 must satisfy

$$R_1 = \frac{R^2}{(R + R_f)} \qquad R_2 = \frac{RR_f}{(R + R_f)}$$

The difference gain of the amplifier in Figure A6-8b with these values for R_1 and R_2 will still be R_f/R. However, the *simplest solution* is to use a potentiometer—CMRR *pot*—with resistance R, as shown in Figure A6-9. Then, the v_{in+} input impedance is clearly R, just as it is for v_{in-}.

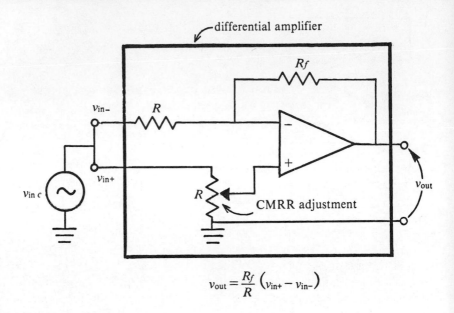

$$v_{out} = \frac{R_f}{R}\left(v_{in+} - v_{in-}\right)$$

FIGURE A6–9. *Difference Amplifier with CMRR Adjustment*

Instrumentation Amplifier

The difference amplifier of Figure A6–9 still falls short of the ideal in that it does not have a very high input impedance. This situation can be remedied by using a pair of voltage followers ahead of the two inputs as shown in Figure A6–10. These followers are often called *buffer amplifiers* since they act as an intermediary to present a desirable high impedance to the outside world. If the op amps used are all low offset voltage, low drift, very high gain, and wide bandwidth (in short, excellent) units, the resulting amplifier is often called an *instrumentation amplifier* because it is desirable for use in various instruments.

Current-to-Voltage Converter

Suppose we want to measure current very accurately using a voltmeter (for example, to construct an ammeter from a DVM). The simple approach is to place a resistance in the current-carrying line and measure the voltage across the resistance. Unfortunately, a finite voltage then clearly develops across the resistance, and hence the ammeter; the ammeter is not ideal since it has this resistance.

A nice approach can be thought of that is a simple alteration of the inverting amplifier. Simply remove the *input resistor R* in Figure A6–2a to

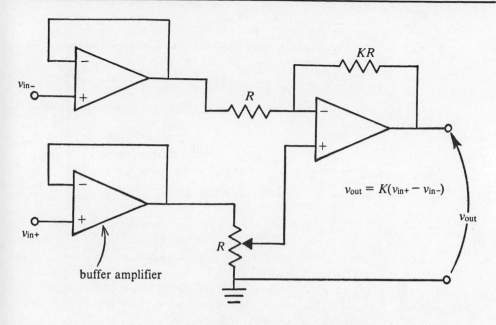

FIGURE A6–10. *High Input-Impedance Difference Amplifier*

obtain the circuit shown in Figure A6–11. Then, whatever current i that flows in toward S will flow through R_f by arguments that should now be familiar. A voltage develops across R_f that becomes the amount of voltage that the output is below ground. Thus, the output voltage is directly proportional to the current in and is given by

$$v_{out} = -iR_f \qquad \textbf{(A6–20)}$$

A voltmeter connected across the output can then be calibrated in terms of the input current. If R_f is a precision resistor, the current-to-voltage conversion that is affected here is very accurate.

A nice feature of this approach is that the voltage that develops between the ammeter leads (1) and (2) in Figure A6–11 is very small. This voltage is simply the v_d between the op-amp inputs that must in fact be there to produce v_{out} at the output. But $v_{out} = A_{vo}v_d$ so this voltage is $v_d = v_{out}/A_{vo}$. Because of the large value of A_{vo}, v_d is a very small voltage and the ammeter approaches the ideal of causing a small voltage drop when inserted in a circuit.

> **Example:** Suppose we have a voltmeter that reads 1 V full scale and we wish to construct an ammeter that reads 10 microamperes full scale. Find R_f and also the voltage that appears between the microammeter leads if a 741 op amp is used.

Solution: The voltmeter will be connected across the output terminals of the circuit in Figure A6–12. We want 1 V out when 10 microamperes flow through R_f. Then,

$$1 \text{ V} = (10^{-5} \text{ A})R_f \text{ or } R_f = 10^{+5} \text{ } \Omega$$

For this current in, the voltage between the microammeter leads will be

$$v_d = \frac{1 \text{ V}}{A_{vo}} = \frac{1 \text{ V}}{200,000} = 5 \text{ } \mu\text{V}$$

for a typical 741. The circuit is shown in Figure A6–12.

One application of this circuit involves measuring the short-circuit current of photovoltaic cells (solar cells). A silicon photovoltaic cell produces an open-circuit output voltage of about 0.6 V when in bright light. As mentioned in Chapter A3, the short-circuit current from a photovoltaic cell is accurately proportional to the light intensity falling on it and can be used to monitor light intensity. However, when an ammeter is used to measure the short-circuit current, the voltage across it must be much less than 0.6 V. The op-amp–based current-to-voltage converter fits this requirement very well, as we see from the preceding example.

NOTE: There is one practical problem and warning with respect to the use of the op-amp microammeter of Figure A6–12 in a general electrical circuit. In fact, this problem often occurs in using electronic instruments and was discussed briefly in Chapter A2. We will examine the problem in more detail as an aside here.

If the leads of the op amp are inserted into a general circuit that is at some point *truly grounded to earth,* the op-amp circuit itself must

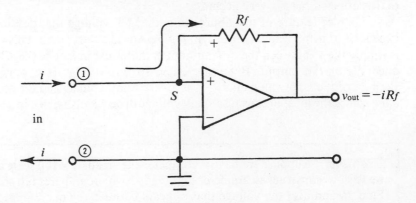

FIGURE A6–11. *Current-to-Voltage Converter*

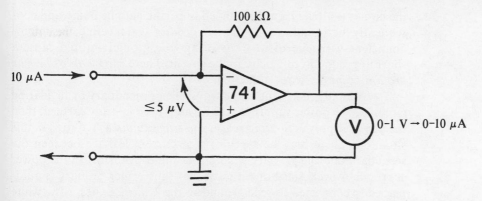

FIGURE A6–12. *Microammeter Using 1-V Voltmeter*

have a *floating ground*. Indeed (as we have mentioned earlier), the term *common* rather than ground is preferred here, since the ground of the V± supply is then not really "earthed," but merely is a common point used in the power supply and the op-amp design.

Figure A6–13 illustrates the problem. Suppose we wish to measure the current through the resistor R_3; therefore we open the circuit at that point and insert our electronic microammeter. However,

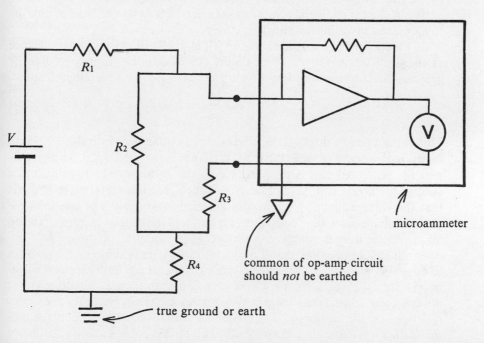

FIGURE A6–13. *Circuit Illustrating the Need for a Floating Ground or Common*

the circuit is already truly grounded or earthed at one point, and consequently both ends of R_3 are *off ground*. Connecting the micro-ammeter—with one of its leads being true ground—would cause a short to ground at this place in the circuit. There can be *only one true ground point* (or wire) in a circuit.

Actually, no point in the transformer secondary or regulating circuit of the power supply for the op amp need be truly earthed; then the power supply is *floating relative to true ground* as required in this situation. There may be a problem of current leakage between the secondary and the primary windings of the transformer in the power supply, however, since one lead of the transformer primary is automatically connected to true ground in the United States. (The white wire of the 110-V line is connected to earth.) Sometimes the simplest solution for a true floating power supply is to use batteries for the op-amp power.

Voltage-to-Current Converter (Constant Current Source)

There are times when we want to produce a well-defined and controlled current. This current could be controlled by a voltage input that is itself constant or varying as the situation may require. The voltage-to-current converter performs this function and is quite easy to understand on the basis of how the fundamental inverting amplifier operates.

We simply put the *load* through which the current should pass in place of the feedback resistor, R_f (see Figure A6–14). Since point S is virtually ground, the current i that flows from the battery V_s is determined to be

$$i = \frac{V_s}{R} \qquad \text{(A6–21)}$$

This current passes through the load (virtually none goes into the $-$ op-amp input) independent of what the load resistance is (within limits). Thus, a current i is generated that is proportional to the input voltage V_s only, and a *voltage-to-current converter* has been designed. The limit referred to above is that the voltage that appears across the load must always be less than the supply voltage since this load voltage is actually the output voltage of the op amp, and the output voltage cannot exceed the supply voltage used.

It should be noted that if only a current meter is at hand, it is possible to construct a voltmeter with this circuit; simply use the ammeter as the load in this circuit. In fact, this method is very similar to the way a voltmeter has always been constructed from a d'Arsonval meter. R becomes the *series resistance* of the voltmeter. The difference is that the resistance of the ammeter does not matter in this approach. This circuit could be used to calibrate an ammeter (as the load) with the aid of an accurate V_s and R.

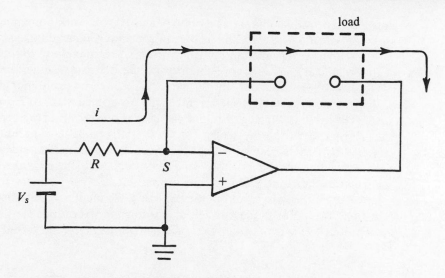

FIGURE A6–14. *Voltage-to-Current Converter*

More important is the fact that if V_s is constant in Figure A6–14 and Equation A6–21, the current i is also constant. Therefore, we have designed a circuit that sends a *constant current* through a load, no matter what its resistance is. This circuit is the opposite of an ideal battery, which supplies a *constant voltage* across a load, regardless of its resistance.

Logarithm Function Block

There are a number of situations where the laboratory signal runs over a large range of amplitude, and we want to take the logarithm of the signal voltage in order to display the relative variations at low levels as well as high. For example, the ear is responsive to a wide range of sound intensity. To obtain the *reverberation time* in a room involves measuring the time for the sound after a noise burst (for example, a pistol shot) to decay by a factor of 1,000,000 or 60 decibels. This is a large change that could not possibly be read from a meter with a single range and would be difficult to measure by switching ranges on a multirange meter.

Another application would be to linearize a voltage that is either exponential or follows a power law; this can be done by using the property of logarithms. Thus, an exponential (in time) signal sent to a logarithm converter and then to a stip-chart recorder can be expected to generate a straight line on the recorder's ordinary graph paper. Finally, the fact that $\log AB = \log A + \log B$ and also $\log A^n = n \log A$ permits us to perform multiplications, square roots, and so on, of voltage signals with op-amp–based *logarithm function blocks*. This is certainly a powerful capability.

The basic log function block or *log amplifier* makes use of the exponential characteristic of the semiconductor diode as given in Equation A4–1 of Chapter A4. The diode is simply placed in the inverting amplifier in place of the feedback resistor, as shown in Figure A6–15.

The current flowing through the diode is determined by the input voltage v_{in} and resistor R to be $i = v_{in}/R$ (think voltage-to-current converter). This current flows through the diode and a modest and decidedly nonlinear voltage develops across it. The output v_{out} is the negative of this voltage since the point S is at virtual ground.

To find the voltage across the diode, we use the theoretical diode law Equation A4–1. For diode voltage V_D greater than about 0.12 V for germanium and 0.25 V for silicon, the exponential term dominates. We then have

$$i \simeq i_R e^{|e|V_D/nkT} \qquad (A6\text{–}22)$$

Here a genuine "fudge factor," n, has been introduced to more closely approximate the experimental situation for silicon as opposed to germanium. The n is approximately 1 for germanium diodes and 2 for silicon. Reverse diode leakage current is represented by i_R.

We solve for the voltage across the diode V_D (and thus get at the amplifier output voltage) by taking the logarithm of Equation A6–20. This gives

$$\log \frac{i}{i_R} = \left(\frac{|e|V_D}{nkT}\right) \log e \qquad (A6\text{–}23)$$

Solving for V_D (at room temperature and inserting $\log_{10} e$, Boltzmann's constant k, and the charge of the electron e) gives

$$V_D = 0.059\, n \left(\log \frac{i}{i_R}\right) V \qquad (A6\text{–}24)$$

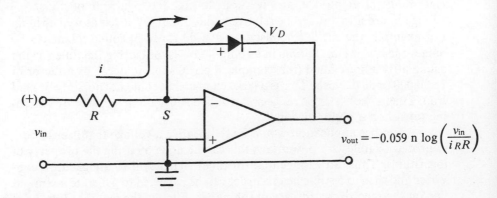

FIGURE A6–15. *Logarithm Function Block*

Now i_R is a constant, (of order 10^{-8} amperes for silicon) and $i = v_{in}/R$. Also $v_{out} = -V_D$ so that

$$v_{out} = -0.059 \text{ n log } \frac{v_{in}}{Ri_R} \text{ V} \qquad \text{(in volts)}$$

$$= -0.059 \text{ n log } v_{in} + 0.059 \text{ n log } i_R R$$

$$= -0.059 \text{ n log } v_{in} + \text{constant} \qquad \text{(A6-25)}$$

Thus, the output is proportional to log v_{in} and of the order of a few tenths of a volt. The voltage can be increased by use of an amplifier following this circuit.

This circuit can operate over 5 orders of magnitude (factor of 10^5) change in the input voltage. Notice it will only work for positive input voltage (true of the logarithm function anyway). However, it is sensitive to temperature due to T in Equation A6-22 and is sensitive to offset errors for small input voltages. Commercial units are available that involve more elaborate design to give more input range and temperature tolerance.

Antilogarithm Function Block

To do the inverse of the logarithm, or the antilogarithm, simply interchange the diode and the resistor in Figure A6-15 (see Figure A6-16). Then the current that flows through the diode is obtained from the fact that its cathode is virtually at ground. The current is given (for V_D greater than 0.25 V) by Equation A6-22, where the voltage across the diode is the input voltage v_{in}. To the base 10 we have

$$\frac{i}{i_R} = 10^{(|e| \log e/nkT)v_{in}} = 10^{Kv_{in}} \qquad \text{(A6-26)}$$

where K is a constant. This current flows through the feedback resistor R_f so that

$$v_{out} = -i_R R_f 10^{Kv_{in}} \qquad \text{(A6-27)}$$

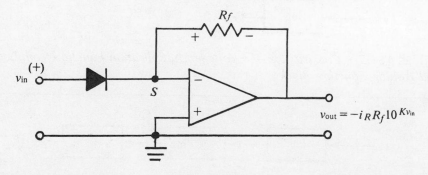

FIGURE A6-16. *Antilogarithm Function Block*

Multipliers and Square Root Functions

We now briefly examine how two voltages may be multiplied together and how the square root of a voltage may be taken using the op-amp–based function blocks. These are basic operations for an analog computer, but may be desirable in a laboratory situation as well.

Let us represent the summing amplifier of Figure A6–7 and the log and antilog amplifiers by boxes so marked. Now using the properties of logarithms

$$\log AB = \log A + \log B \qquad \text{(A6–28)}$$

and

$$\text{antilog } (\log AB) = AB = \text{antilog } (\log A + \log B) \qquad \text{(A6–29)}$$

Thus, we may take the antilog of the sum of the logs of A and of B to obtain the product of A and B (see Figure A6–17).

As a second example of what can be done, consider taking the square root of a voltage. We use

$$\log A^{1/2} = 1/2 \log A \qquad \text{(A6–30)}$$

$$A^{1/2} = \text{antilog } (1/2 \log A) \qquad \text{(A6–31)}$$

Multiplication by $1/2$ can be performed by an amplifier with voltage gain of $1/2$ (for example, $R_f/R = 1/2$ in Figure A6–2). The block diagram of the circuit is shown in Figure A6–18.

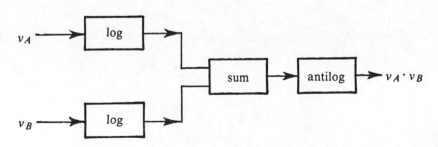

FIGURE A6–17. *Construction of a Voltage Multiplication Function from Log, Sum, and Antilog Function Blocks*

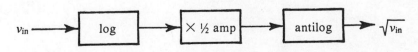

FIGURE A6–18. *Construction of the Square Root Function*

Integrating Function Block

It is quite easy to construct an op-amp–based circuit that produces an output in time that is an integral with respect to time of the input voltage; that is, an *integrating function block*.

We simply take the inverting amplifier and replace the feedback resistor with a capacitor (see Figure A6–19). The current that flows from v_{in} through R is determined again only by v_{in} and R. This current *accumulates* on the capacitor and the capacitor charges, so the voltage across the capacitor changes. The voltage across the capacitor (which becomes the output voltage) is proportional to the charge q_c that has accumulated on the capacitor, and this is simply the integral of the input current. By Ohm's Law:

$$i = \frac{v_{in}(t)}{R} \tag{A6–32}$$

Also

$$i = \frac{dq}{dt} = \frac{dq_c}{dt}$$

so that

$$\frac{dq_c}{dt} = \frac{v_{in}(t)}{R} \tag{A6–33}$$

Then we solve for q_c by doing the integral of Equation A6–33.

$$\int_0^t \left(\frac{dq_c}{dt}\right) dt = \int_0^t \left(\frac{v_{in}(t)}{R}\right) dt \tag{A6–34}$$

Thus

$$q_c(t) - \overset{0}{\cancel{q_c(0)}} = \frac{1}{R} \int_0^t v_{in}(t)\, dt \tag{A6–35}$$

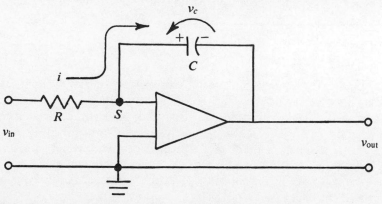

FIGURE A6–19. *Integrating Amplifier or Function Block*

To simplify matters we *assume* the capacitor was discharged at $t = 0$. Next

$$v_{\text{out}} = -v_c = -\frac{q_c}{C}$$

so that

$$v_{\text{out}} = -\frac{1}{RC} \int_0^t (v_{\text{in}}t) \, dt \qquad \text{(A6–36)}$$

Thus, the output voltage is proportional to the integral of the input voltage, with a proportionality constant of $(1/RC)$. Also, the output voltage is inverted.

Example: We wish to obtain a voltage that increases linearly in time with a high accuracy.

Solution: Simply connect a battery V to the input of an integrating amplifier. Then

$$v_{\text{out}} = \frac{-1}{RC} \int_0^t V dt = \left(\frac{-V}{RC}\right) t \qquad \text{(A6–37)}$$

For example, if $V = 0.5$ V, $R = 100$ kilohms, and $C = 10$ microfarads, we have

$$v_{\text{out}} = \left(\frac{-0.5 \text{ V}}{10^5 \times 10^{-5} \text{s}}\right) t = (-0.5 \text{ V/s})t$$

The circuit is shown in Figure A6–20a, and the output voltage behavior is shown in Figure A6–20b. The switch S is assumed to be held closed until it is opened at time $t = 0$; consequently the output voltage is held to virtual ground (or zero volts) until the switch is opened. After the switch is opened, the output voltage grows steadily more negative.

Notice in the example just discussed that if the switch connected across the capacitor is closed every T seconds, a sawtooth generator with period T is formed. (The switch can be a field-effect transistor to make a completely electronic circuit.) Thus, we have a sweep generator for an oscilloscope.

If a square wave that is symmetric in voltage and time such as in Figure A1–12b is applied to the input, the reader should be able to reason that a "triangle wave form" is produced at the output of the integration circuit

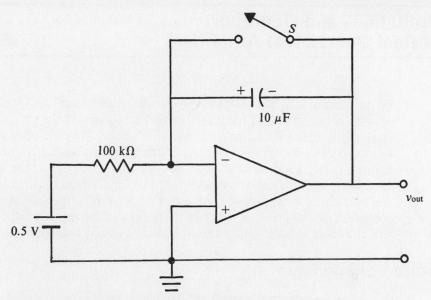

(a) Integrating Circuit with Switch S Closed until $t = 0$

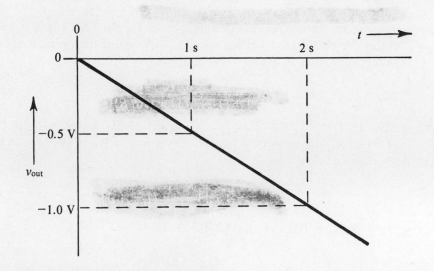

(b) Voltage Out of Integrating Circuit

FIGURE A6–20. *Circuit to Produce Voltage That Changes Linearly in Time*

Limitations and Operation
of Real Operational Amplifiers

Up to this point in the chapter, the circuit behavior and the formulas to describe it have assumed ideal operational amplifiers. If the op amp were ideal, the formulas would be generally quite simple. They are often referred to as *classical op-amp formulas*. Although modern operational amplifiers are remarkably good in most respects, they only approximate the ideal op amp. In critical applications, it is important to understand the limitations of real operational amplifiers and to attempt to minimize their effects as much as possible. The remainder of the chapter speaks to these rather practical matters, including actual op-amp connections and circuit construction.

Finite Voltage Gain

The classical op-amp formulas that have been derived thus far assume an ideal op amp with infinite open-loop gain. In fact, IC operational amplifiers typically have an open-loop gain of perhaps 200,000. To what extent are the closed-loop—that is, op amp with feedback—formulas in error?

For the basic inverting amplifier of Figure A6–2a it is possible to derive the closed-loop voltage gain A_v in terms of the op-amp open-loop gain A_{vo}, R_f, and R. It is

$$A_v = \frac{-R_f/R}{1 + (1/A_{vo})\,[1 + (R_f/R)]} \qquad \text{(A6–38)}$$

Now $R_f/R = A_{vI}$, the ideal op-amp gain formula. Since the term $(1/A_{vo})$ $[1 + (R_f/R)]$ is a small quantity, we may use the relation $(1 + x)^{-1} \cong (1 - x)$ for small x. Then

$$A_v \approx -A_{vI}\left[1 - \frac{1}{A_{vo}}(1 + A_{vI})\right] \qquad \text{(A6–39)}$$

Suppose $A_{vI} = 100$ and $A_{vo} = 200{,}000$. Then

$$A_v = -A_{vI}\left(1 - \frac{1}{2000}\right)$$

and the classical formula is in error by one part in 2000 or 0.05%.

Finite Bandwidth

The open-loop gain of the op amp does not remain at the high value of 200,000 to particularly high frequencies. For the 741 op amp, at about 10

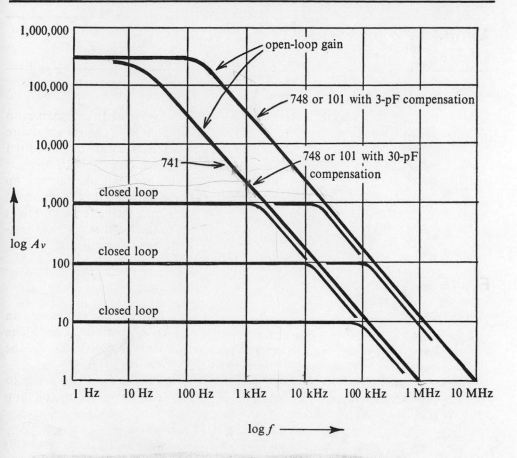

FIGURE A6–21. *Frequency Response for Op-Amps Models 741, 748, and 101*

hertz the gain begins falling at a rate of a factor of 10 for every factor of 10 increase in frequency. Figure A6–21 illustrates gain versus frequency or *frequency response* for the 741 and 748 operational amplifiers. The 101 model op amp behaves similarly to the 748.

The closed-loop gain for the op amp can only hold constant for frequencies up to where the open-loop gain of the op amp falls to the closed-loop value. Then the gain of the op amp with feedback falls, too. Notice the curves labeled *closed loop* in Figure A6–21. Thus, for the 741 op amp the gain is *flat* for a gain of 1,000 up to about 1 kilohertz; flat for a gain of 100 up to about 10 kilohertz; flat for a gain of 10 up to about 100 kilohertz; although not shown, it is flat for unit gain to almost 1 megahertz. There is a moral about amplifiers here that holds for any type of amplifier design, not only with op amps: The product of the gain times the bandwidth is constant for a given amplifier. Notice that this *gain-bandwidth product* (GBP) is about 10^6 for the 741 op amp. Also notice that the 748 (and the 101 op amp) has a larger gain-bandwidth product of about 10^7. However an external *compensation capacitor* must be connected between the appropriate pins of this type of op amp to prevent oscillations. Three picofarads should be used for a gain of 100 or more; increasing capacity must be used for amplifiers with lower closed-loop gain. Thus, 30 picofarads must be used for a unity-gain amplifier; then its performance is about the same as for the 741.

Unwanted op-amp instability and oscillations occur because of positive feedback. Although we have been careful to connect the feedback in a negative fashion for all of the designs presented thus far, the phase of the signal passing through the op amp becomes increasingly shifted at higher frequencies (due to internal capacitances). For example, significant phase shifts begin at about 100 kilohertz for the 748 and 101 devices. This means that the signal fed back to the input can reinforce the signal already there at high frequencies, and this reinforcement can produce an oscillator. The compensation capacitor reduces the gain at high frequencies so that the level of the signal fed back is insufficient to sustain oscillations.

The 741 is called an *internally compensated* operational amplifier, because no fuss with an external capacitor is required. The more recent (introduced in 1976) CA3140 op amp from RCA is also internally compensated and has a bandwidth about the same as the 748 (the GBP is quoted as 4.5 megahertz). The CA3140 is a combination MOSFET-bipolar op amp that has an ultra low input bias current; this device and property are in the section on input bias current. Other op amps with *very* wide bandwidth have been introduced. Thus, in 1979 Signetics announced the NE5539 op amp with a GBP of 1200 megahertz (1.2 gigahertz). (They have advertised the NE5539 with the catchy phrase, "dc to daylight"; what does this imply?)

An output (pulse-response) limitation related to the gain-bandwidth product is the *slew rate* of an operational amplifier. Figure A6-22 tells the story. Suppose a *square pulse* is applied to a 741 op amp connected as a voltage follower. Although the voltage of the input pulse rises and falls very rapidly, the voltage of the output pulse from the amplifier responds to the pulse *edges* at a very definite rate. The output voltage moves along a slant line at the rate of 0.5 volts/microsecond; this rate is called the *slew rate* of the op amp. Generally, an op amp with a larger GBP also has a faster slew rate. The fact that the 741 is of limited application in digital and computer circuits becomes evident. Computer circuits often use pulses on the order of 5 V in amplitude and 1 microsecond in duration. The 741 cannot be used to follow or produce a pulse with these *high-speed* characteristics. Other op amps have been designed to be high-speed devices. An example is the LM118/218/318 from National Semiconductor; its GBP is 15 megahertz, and its slew rate is 70 volts/microseconds. The slew rate of the NE5539 mentioned above is 600 volts/microsecond, a thousand times faster than the 741.

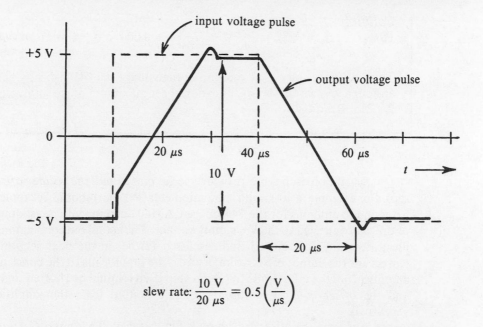

$$\text{slew rate:} \quad \frac{10\ V}{20\ \mu s} = 0.5 \left(\frac{V}{\mu s}\right)$$

FIGURE A6–22. *Pulse-Response Limitation (Slew Rate) for a 741 Op Amp Connected as a Voltage Follower*

Input Offset Voltage

As mentioned in Chapter A5, real dc amplifiers have a voltage at the output even though none is present at the input. The amplifier behaves as though a small battery—called the *input offset voltage* v_{io}—is inserted at the amplifier input. The voltage that appears at the output (when the input leads are shorted) is the *closed-loop* amplifier gain times the input offset voltage.

For the 741, 748, and 101 bipolar transistor op amps, the input offset voltage is of the order of 1 millivolt. Field-effect–transistor (FET) op amps usually have a larger op-amp offset, although the CA3140 has only 2-millivolts typical v_{io}.

Example: An inverting amplifier with a gain of −50 has been constructed from a 741 op amp. When the input to the amplifier is shorted to ground, the output reads +0.2 V.

1.   What is the input offset voltage?
2.   Is it necessary to live with this rather large error?

Solution:
1.
$$v_{io} = \frac{v_{\text{out}}}{A_v} = \frac{+0.2 \text{ V}}{-50} = -0.004 \text{ V} = -4 \text{ mV}$$

This voltage is somewhat more than the voltage the 741 typically has, although it is within the specification sheet maximum of ±6 millivolts.
2. No. Read on.

Several op-amp types provide special pins to *null the voltage offset* to zero. For example, a 10-kilohm potentiometer (10K pot) should be connected between the null pins for the 741 or the CA3140 op amp, with the sliding tap of the pot connected to the V− supply voltage. The actual pin connections are illustrated in Figure A6–23 and discussed further in the next section. To correct for the output offset voltage error, the input leads to the constructed amplifier (*not* the input leads to the op amp itself) should be shorted together and the *offset null pot* adjusted until the output from the amplifier is very small.

Although the offset can be nulled in this way, the *input offset voltage drift* causes the output to drift away from zero when the temperature changes. The 741, 748, and 101 op amps typically drift about 10 microvolts per centigrade degree. A special precision op amp, the 725, has a v_{io} drift of only 0.5 microvolts/centigrade degrees. (It costs about 10 times the 741 price.) The OP−7 op amp from Precision Monolithics, Inc. has a similar offset drift specification, but also has an *input bias current* that is an order of magnitude smaller than the 725 and 741. Later we find that this current can be an important parameter.

Op-Amp Connections

Figure A6–23a illustrates pin connections for the 741, 748, 101, and 3140 op amps. The numbers shown are the pin numbers to the 8-lead metal can as well as the 8-lead mini-DIP IC packages (these packages are pictured later in Figure A6–28). Note that this group of widely used op amps may all be connected in the same fashion; they are basically pin interchangeable. Pins 2 and 3 are the inverting and noninverting inputs, respectively, while pin 6 is the op amp output.

As we have mentioned, the 101 and 748 op amps each require a phase compensation capacitor. Notice the placement of the compensation capacitor C_1 between pins 1 and 8 in the circuit of Figure A6–23a. Since the 741 and 3140 are internally compensated, Figure A6–23b reveals that pin 8 is not used on these op amps.

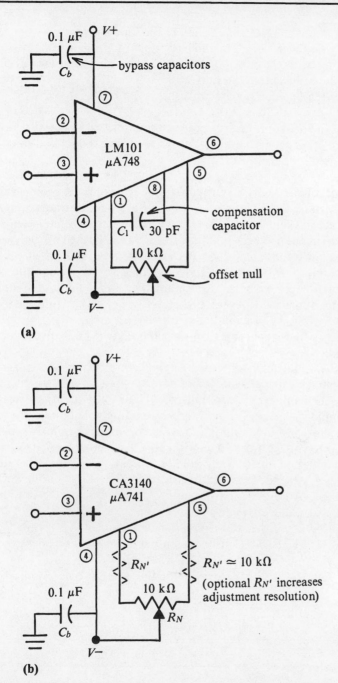

FIGURE A6–23. *Pin Connections, Including Compensation and Offset Null, for Popular Op-Amp ICs*

The null pot connections for any of the four op amps may be seen to be the same from Figures A6–23a and b. Optional additional resistors R_N' are shown in series with the null pot R_N in Figure A6–23b; these permit increased resolution in setting the null.

Notice the *bypass* capacitors C_b shown connected to the V+ and V− power-supply terminals (pins 7 and 4, respectively) in Figures A6–23a and b. These capacitors are connected in order to suppress unwanted oscillations, especially for op amps with a high gain-bandwidth product and in circuits with high closed-loop gain. Rather like the oscillation problem requiring a compensation capacitor, the root cause of the problem is positive feedback of high-frequency signals from output to input. This time the problem comes about because of feedback from the op-amp output stages through the power-supply connections and back to the input stages through the supply connections. At least one pair of bypass capacitors should be used on each printed circuit board. In troublesome cases they should be connected directly between the supply pins for the IC and ground. Low inductance capacitors should be used—for example, disc-ceramic or tantalum types—because inductive impedance increases at higher frequencies. The purpose of the bypass capacitors is to provide a *short* or bypass to ground for high frequencies. Long wires to the capacitors should be avoided since even a straight length of wire possesses inductance.

While on the topic of power-supply connections, let us examine briefly the voltage capabilities of these popular op amps. As we have indicated earlier, the output voltage cannot exceed the power-supply voltage from which an amplifier operates. But if the power-supply voltages V+ and V− should exceed certain limits for a particular op amp, the op amp may be destroyed due to voltage breakdown within it. On the otherhand, if the supply voltages are too small, the op amp will not function properly. Generally the supply voltages V+ and V− should be nearly equal in magnitude and well regulated. Table A6–1 gives power-supply limitations for the popular op amps that we have already mentioned.

It will be noted that the μA741C has a smaller upper-voltage limit than the μA741. The μA741C differs from the μA741 in that it has generally *relaxed specifications* compared to the μA741, and μA741C is designated the *commercial* temperature range device for the op-amp type. Similarly, the

TABLE A6–1. *Power-Supply Limitations for Popular Op Amp IC's*

Op Amp	Power-Supply Limitation
μA741, μA748, LM101	$3\ V \leq |V\pm| \leq 22\ V$
CA3140B	$2\ V \leq |V\pm| \leq 22\ V$
CA3140	$2\ V \leq |V\pm| \leq 18\ V$
μA741C, μA748C, LM301	$3\ V \leq |V\pm| \leq 18\ V$

TABLE A6–2. *Operating Temperatures for Popular Op Amp IC's*

Op Amp	Operating Temperatures
μA741, μA748, LM101, CA3140, CA3140B	−55°C to +125°C (military range)
μA741C, μA748C, LM301	0°C to +70°C (commercial range)

LM301 is the commercial version of the LM101; that is, the LM301 has relaxed specifications (and a lower price) relative to the LM101. The temperature ranges for satisfactory operation of these op amps is given in Table A6–2. The μA741 and LM101 are called *military temperature range* devices, while the μA741C and LM301 are called *commercial temperature range* devices.

Input Bias Current

Any of the electronic active discrete devices—bipolar transistor, field-effect transistor (FET), vacuum tube, or metal-oxide-silicon field-effect transistor (MOSFET)—require some current (that is, *bias current*) flowing into the controlling input of the device (base, gate, or grid) in normal operation. Relatively speaking, the bipolar transistor requires much more bias current than the others; this is a shortcoming of the ordinary (bipolar) transistor. The FET and especially the MOSFET (transistors) are the most recent and have a high input impedance rather like the venerable vacuum tube. The MOSFET significantly exceeds most vacuum tubes. The principles of operation of these devices are described in Chapter A8.

The 741, 748, and 101 are examples of bipolar-transistor integrated-circuit op amps. For operation they require a bias current on the order of 0.1 microamperes = 100 nanoamperes = 10^{-7} amperes *into each input*. There must be a dc path into the + input and the − input that supplies this current. Thus, Figure A6–24a illustrates an amplifier that will *not* work because the capacitor blocks any dc path into the + input. The input voltage connected to the noninverting amplifier must supply this bias current to the + input (see Figure A6–2b). However, if the voltage source connected to the op amp has a high output impedance, there can be a severe and literally upsetting voltage drop across its output impedance due to the bias current.

A case in point is the pH meter that is a common fixture in a chemistry department. The pH electrode, which determines acidity of a solution, consists of glass and reference electrodes that can produce up to 1-V emf, but has an output impedance (because the current must flow through glass) of about

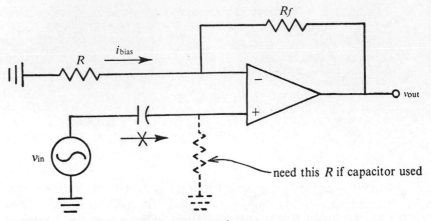

(a) Op Amp Circuit That Will *Not* Function Because No Bias
Current Can Flow into the + Input

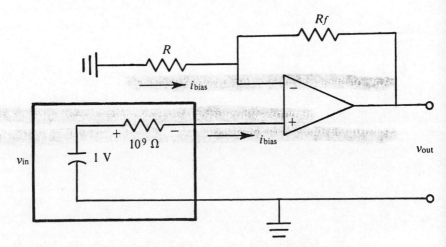

(b) Effect of Bias Current in a High Output Impedance Voltage Source

FIGURE A6–24. *Bias-Current Problems*

10^9 ohms. See the situation illustrated in Figure A6–24b. If the op amp is a
741, the bias current is about 10^{-7} amperes so that a voltage drop of 10^{-7}
amperes $\times 10^9$ ohms = 100 V would occur across the output impedance of
the source. The op amp would *not* function. Even if the input current were
reduced to 1 nanoampere, the voltage drop would be 1 V across the output
impedance, and a 100% error would occur in the voltage actually reaching the
+ input of the op amp.

In the recent past, special *electrometer* vacuum tube triodes were required to work at the extremely low bias currents required by such items as pH electrodes. However, MOSFETS and the CA3140 MOSFET-input op amp have opened a new era. The bias current required by the CA3140 is about 10 picoamperes = 10^{-11} amperes. The voltage drop across the 10^9-Ω impedance of the pH electrode is then 10^9 ohms $\times 10^{-11}$ amperes = 0.01 V— much better. Furthermore, the input impedance of the CA3140 is about 10^{12} ohms (compare to 10^6 ohms for the 741).

There is one worry about MOSFET devices however: They may be ruined by static electricity. RCA claims the CA3140 has protected inputs that require no special handling procedures. However, in seasons or regions of low humidity, it is generally recommended that a person be grounded to discharge static electricity before handling MOSFET devices. These devices are generally quite safe after connection in a circuit. Other manufacturers are now also producing MOSFET-bipolar–transistor op amps, as well as FET-bipolar–transistor op amps. We will shortly look at the Op–15/16/17, which is an FET-bipolar type. Standard FET transistors are not subject to static damage; therefore, this op-amp type is not either. However, FET-bipolar op amps often do not have such extremely low input bias currents as the MOSFET-input type.

When working with op amps in situations where small voltages— millivolts or less—are being measured, it is important that the same impedance to ground be present from each op-amp input. This is so that the voltage drop from the input bias currents through these resistances is the same at each input and also so that temperature problems are minimized. The bias-current changes significantly with temperature and if the currents flow through different resistors to the + and − inputs, they will experience a temperature-dependent dc offset voltage from this effect.

Figure A6–25 illustrates how a recommended resistance R_b should be placed in the two important op-amp amplifier configurations in order to minimize voltage offset from the bias currents, i_b. The resistor R_b should be placed between the + op-amp input and ground for the inverting amplifier (see Figure A6–25a), while it should be placed between the + op-amp input and the v_{in} terminal in the noninverting amplifier (see Figure A6–25b). The resistor R_b is simply the parallel equivalent resistance of R and R_f. This is indicated in the figure with the common notation $R \| R_f$. The resistance R_b does *not* affect the classical gain formula for either amplifier, provided the op amp has high open-loop gain.

The fact that R_b should equal $R \| R_f$ can be argued as follows. In either amplifier, we desire the output to be precisely zero ($v_{out} = 0$) when the input is grounded ($v_{in} = 0$). In fact, the two amplifier circuits are then identical, with identical bias-current paths for each (see Figures A6–25a and b). Now, the output voltage v_{out} can only be zero if the voltages at the − and + op-amp inputs are precisely equal (assuming no input offset voltage, of course). But the − op-amp signal input will be *below* ground due to the

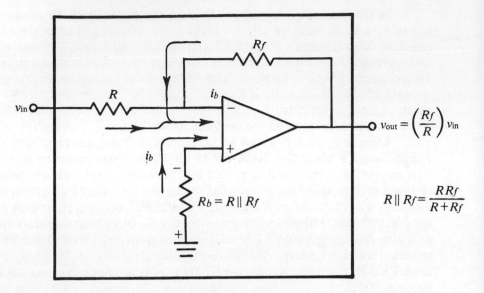

(a) Op-Amp Inverting Amplifier with Recommended R_b

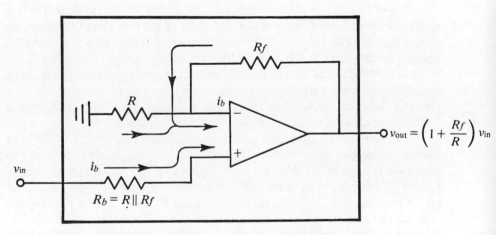

(b) Op-Amp Noninverting Amplifier with Recommended R_b

FIGURE A6–25.   *Op-Amp Amplifiers, Showing Recommended Bias-Current–Drop Correcting Resistors (R_b), and Bias-Current Flow Paths*

voltage drop of i_b flowing from zero volts (from ground and from $v_{out} = 0$) through the *parallel* resistors R and R_f to the $-$ op-amp input. We desire the $+$ op-amp input to be below ground by just the same amount, and this will be true *if* the bias current into it flows through a resistor $R_b = R \| R_f$.

It is true that this argument assumes the bias currents into the two op-amp inputs to be identical. Unfortunately, there generally is a difference, called the *bias-current offset*. For the 741 it is on the order of 20 nanoamperes, which is 20% of the bias current. This could be corrected for by adjusting R_b; then better temperature stability could be expected. However, generally R_b is simply selected as we have discussed, and the voltage offset adjustment is used to balance the amplifier output to null.

The input bias current does change with the temperature of the op amp. Particularly if bias-current correction resistor R_b is *not* used, this bias-current drift causes an offset voltage drift that is as troublesome as the op-amp (inherent) offset voltage drift. Therefore, the *input bias-current drift* specification is normally listed on the manufacturer's specification sheets. Of course, a device that simply has a very small bias current generally causes fewer problems in regard to this effect. The bias voltages across the resistors to the + and − op-amp inputs are necessarily smaller in the first place and, therefore, can change by at most a smaller amount in the second place. The input bias-current drift for the 741 is about −1 nanoampere/centigrade degrees.

Example: Assume a 741 op amp has been especially selected so that its input offset voltage at 20°C is extremely small. However, its input bias current is typical (it must exist for op-amp operation). This op amp is connected to make an inverting amplifier as shown in Figure A6–26; note that the recommended R_b of Figure A6–25a is absent.

1. What output voltage is expected when the input is shorted to ground? What is the equivalent input offset voltage?
2. What output voltage may be expected if the ambient temperature changes to 30°C?

Assume the following typical specifications for the 741:

input bias current = 100 nanoamperes

input bias-current drift = −1 nanoampere/centigrade degrees

input offset-voltage drift = ±10 microvolts/centigrade degrees

Solution:
1. This problem is easy provided the proper viewpoint is taken. A bias current must flow into the − input of the op amp. Now if the op amp has very high gain A_{vo}, negative feedback requires that the summing point S is virtually at zero volts (virtually at ground). This means that the potential at the two ends of the 10-kilohm resistor is the same, and no current flows through it. (This is like the case of the balanced bridge.) The bias current therefore *must* flow through the R_f resistor.

Then

$$v_{out} = +i_b R_f = 100 \text{ nA} \times 100 \text{ k}\Omega$$
$$= 10^{-7} \text{ A} \times 10^{+5} \text{ }\Omega = 0.01 \text{ V}$$

This is equivalent to an input offset voltage of

$$\frac{v_{out}}{A_v} = \frac{0.01 \text{ V}}{10} = 1 \text{ mV}$$

Note that this is comparable to the *inherent* input offset-voltage value for a typical 741 (that is, for a 741 that is not offset nulled).

2. When the temperature changes from 20°C to 30°C, the bias current i_b changes by

$$\Delta i_b = (-1 \text{ nA}/\text{C}°)(10 \text{ C}°) = -10 \text{ nA} \text{ (or } -10\%)$$

Then

$$\Delta v_{out} = \Delta i_b R_f = (-10 \text{ nA})(100 \text{ k}\Omega) = -1 \text{ mV} \text{ (or } -10\%)$$

The output voltage also changes due to the inherent input offset-voltage drift; that is,

$$\Delta v_{out} = A_v \Delta v_{io} = (10)(10 \text{ }\mu\text{V}/\text{C}°)(10 \text{ C}°) = \pm 1.0 \text{ mV}$$

We use ($\pm$) here because the drift may be upward for one 741, and downward for another. In the worst case (Murphy's Law!), the output drifts $-1 \text{ mV} - 1 \text{ mV} = -2 \text{ mV}$. This voltage change adds to the voltage output value from part 1, leaving the output voltage at -1.0 mV.

Comments: In part 1, note that the output offset voltage could be calculated by assuming that the bias current actually flows through the R (10 kΩ) resistor and multiplying the voltage drop across R by the voltage gain of the *amplifier* to get the output voltage. This somewhat intuitive approach will be discussed as a problem in the problem/exercise set for this chapter.

In part 2, notice that the influence of input current drift is equal to that of offset voltage drift. However, placement of the proper R_b in the circuit would greatly reduce the bias-current drift problem, so that the remaining drift would represent 100 μV referred to the input (10 μV/C° $\times$ 10 C°). Suppose for example that a thermocouple voltage were being amplified. Then 100 μV drift would correspond to an actual signal change for about 2 to 3 C° change in sensor temperature. It should be clear that a 741 would not permit high precision thermocouple amplification. An op amp with better offset-voltage drift specifications should be selected (for example, a 725 or even better, an OP–07).

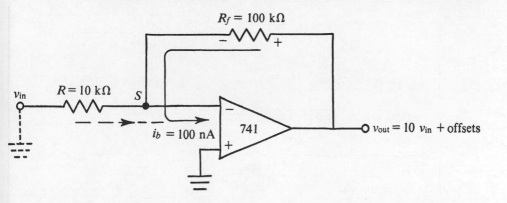

FIGURE A6-26. *Example Inverting Amplifier Circuit without Recommended R_b*

Output Capabilities of an Op Amp

Most common IC operational amplifiers cannot dissipate much heat and are not capable of supplying more than 5 to 20 milliamperes. If the voltage of the op amp reaches a value such that the limiting current is being delivered to the load resistor R_L, it will simply go no higher. The output voltage will therefore clip at a value

$$v_{out,max} = i_{out,max} R_L \qquad\qquad \text{(A6-40)}$$

Example: For the 741 op amp, the maximum output voltage for a load resistance of 200 ohms is listed as 5 V. What maximum current can be supplied by it to a load?

Solution: The maximum current is 5 V/0.2 kΩ = 25 mA. In fact, this current is listed as the output short-circuit current for the amplifier.

NOTE: To obtain accurate amplifier operation with some margin of safety, a smaller maximum output current should be assumed.

An operational amplifier can be readily helped along to supply more current by means of a transistor connected to its output. A transistor is basically a current-amplifying device, where the amplified current, I_C—that is, *collector current*—is more than the base current I_B by some factor beta or h_{fe}, which typically is 30 to 200. Negative feedback must be connected from the *overall* output to − input (see Figure A6-27). In this way the load current

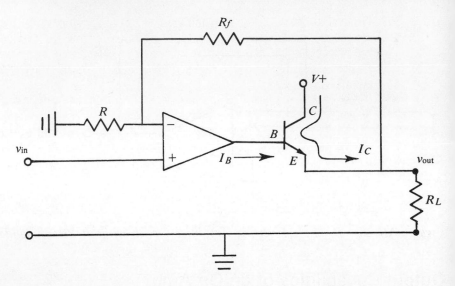

FIGURE A6-27. *"Outboard" Transistor to Increase Current Capabilities of the Op Amp by the Beta Factor of the Transistor*

can be β times as much as the current capabilities of the op amp. The op amp supplies the base current and the transistor multiplies it by the factor beta.

Selecting an Op Amp

In many rather standard applications without especially stringent requirements, the old standby—the general-purpose 741—is sufficient. However, the preceding discussion of op-amp realities shows that the 741 is only an approximation of the ideal op amp. A better approximation may be required if the 741 does not meet certain requirements. Perhaps a wider bandwidth, faster slew rate, higher input impedance, lower bias current, lower offset-voltage drift, lower power-supply drain, or higher output-current capability are needed.

In general, the op-amp designer can improve certain specifications, but only at the expense of others. Consequently, each manufacturer typically offers a spectrum of op-amp devices; there are also interesting variations among manufacturers. Table A6-3 presents a dozen specifications for five categories of op amps. (Even so, some specifications of possible interest were omitted, for example, bias-current offset and its drift, power-supply rejection ratio, large-signal bandwidth, and short-circuit output current.) The categories presented are:

1. *General purpose*—generally a balance of good specifications.
2. *Precision*—particularly outstanding *input specifications,* such as high input impedance, low offset voltage and offset-voltage drift, low bias current and bias-current drift, high common-mode rejection ratio (CMRR). These specifications typically come at the expense of bandwidth and slew rate. Therefore, these op amps are particularly appropriate for very low voltage input signals at dc to low frequencies.
3. *High speed*—especially wide bandwidth and fast slew rate, but often at the expense of the input characteristics mentioned under the "Precision" category; particularly appropriate for high-frequency (and pulse) input signals at higher voltage levels.
4. *Micropower*—very low power-supply current and/or power voltage are required. Some operate well from a single voltage supply; well suited to battery operation, although other specifications may be only fair.
5. *Power out*—capable of rather high output currents or high output voltages. Several of these devices have 741-like characteristics in other respects since they use a 741 to drive more "robust" output transistors on the chip.

The devices presented in Table A6–3 are not necessarily the best available within each category, but they are representative of devices that were available in 1980. In general, the devices are from the commercial-temperature-range offerings; for example, μAXXX*C*, LM*3*XX, LF*3*XX, LHXXXX*C*. Premium devices—literally handpicked—are often available with better specifications, but the prices are often premium also ($30 to $70 each). These devices often have additional suffix designations and are not presented in the table. The LF356A, LF357A (which are selected LF356 and LF357 parts) and the OP–07 are modest exceptions. The OP–07 is available with both tighter specifications (OP–07A) and more relaxed specifications (OP–07E, OP–07C, and OP–07D).

It is interesting to contrast properties of the devices, both between categories and within them. Note also the *comment* column at the far right of the table. For example, the FET and MOSFET input-stage devices have very outstanding input impedance (10^6 megohms $= 10^{12}$ ohms) and very low bias current, but do not compare with the precision devices in terms of offset-voltage drift. However, the input bias current for an FET-input device does increase rapidly with temperature: a factor of two for every 10 C° temperature increase. This bias-current drift represents an exponential behavior, and the bias-current values in the table are for temperatures near room temperature.

Although the precision devices indeed have very low drift of input bias current and offset voltage, notice that they are "turtles" relative to the "jackrabbit" high-speed devices. Actually, as all-around high-performance devices, the rather recent (about 1977) LF357A and OP–17 are quite impressive. They are both placed in the high-speed category. The OP–17C was priced at about $10 when it was introduced.

TABLE A6–3. *Typical (Not Guaranteed) Specifications for Operational Amplifiers in Five Categories*

	Minimum-Maximum Supply Voltage (V)	Compensation Required	Open-Loop Gain (dB)	Supply Current ($v_{out} = 0$) (mA)	$A_{vo} = 1$ Bandwidth (MHz)
General Purpose					
μA741C	±3 to ±18	no	110	2	1
μA748C	±3 to ±22	yes	110	2	4
LF356A	±5 to ±18	no	105	2	4.5
LM301	±3 to ±18	yes	110	3	1
CA3140	±2 to ±22	no	100	4	4.5
Precision					
μA725	±3 to ±22	yes	130	3	2
LH0044C	±2 to ±20	yes	140	1	0.4
LM308	±3 to ±18	yes	110	0.3	1
OP-07	±3 to ±22	no	115	4	0.6
High Speed					
LF357A	±5 to ±18	no	105	2	20
LH0032C	±5 to ±18	yes	70	18	70
LM318	±5 to ±20	yes	110	5	15
OP-17C	to ±18	no	110	7	26
Micropower					
LH0001AC	±5 to ±20	yes	95	0.06	1
OP-20	±1.5 to ±15	no	110	0.03	0.1
Power Out					
μA759C	to ±18	no	95	12	1
μA791C	to ±18	yes	100	25	1
LH0021C	±5 to ±18	yes	100	3	1
LH0061C	to ±18	yes	95	10	5

The manufacturer of the original part may be recognized by the prefix used:
μA = Fairchild Semiconductor;   OP- = Precision Monolithics, Inc. (PMI);
LM, LF, LH = National Semiconductor;   CA = RCA

Op-Amp Packages (Circuit Construction Comments)

Many of the monolithic integrated circuits first available (circa 1962) were in the standard TO–5, 8-lead, round *metal can* package shown in Figure

Slew Rate $(V/\mu s)$	Bias Current (nA)	Bias-Current Drift (nA/C°)	Input Offset Voltage (mV)	Input Offset-Voltage Drift $(\mu V/C^\circ)$	Diff. Input Resistance $(M\Omega)$	CMRR (dB)	Comment
0.5	80	1	2	15	2	90	
0.5	120	1	1	6	1	90	
12	0.03	0.003	1	1	10^6	100	FET input
0.5	70	0.4	2	15	2	90	
9	0.008	0.001	5	8	10^6	90	MOSFET input
0.3	40	0.25	0.2	0.6	1.5	115	
0.06	10	0.1	12	0.2	8	140	
0.3	1.5	—	0.3	1	40	110	
0.2	±2	0.008	0.03	0.3	60	120	
50	0.03	0.003	1	1	10^6	100	FET input
500	0.025	0.002	5	25	10^6	60	FET input
70	150	0.5	4	—	3	100	
65	0.1	0.01	0.7	4	10^6	96	FET input
0.25	20	0.3	2	3	—	90	
0.02	13	0.02	0.08	1	—	110	
							Maximum I_{out}
0.5	50	—	1	—	1.5	100	0.5 A
5	80	1	2	—	1	>70	1.0 A
3	150	1	3	5	1	90	1.0 A
70	200	—	3	5	1	80	0.5 A

A6–28a. Notice the *tab* identifies pin number 8. Digital integrated circuits required more input and output pins so that the 14-pin and also 16-pin *dual-in-line-pin* (DIP) package soon appeared as shown in Figure A6–28b. The pins are spaced 0.1 inch apart in each row. An identifying U-shaped indentation and usually a dot to identify pin number 1 are found at one end. The widespread use of the DIP pin spacing soon gave rise to the *Mini-DIP* 8-pin package suitable for op amps (see Figure A6–28c).

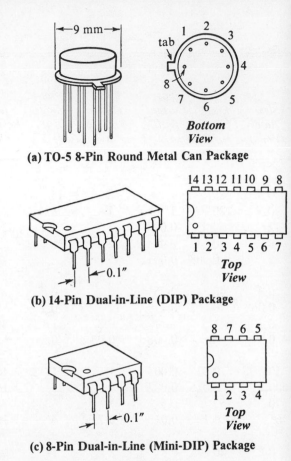

(a) TO-5 8-Pin Round Metal Can Package

(b) 14-Pin Dual-in-Line (DIP) Package

(c) 8-Pin Dual-in-Line (Mini-DIP) Package

FIGURE A6–28. *Common Integrated-Circuit Packages*

NOTE: In a convention that dates back to vacuum tubes, the pin order for the package goes in the clockwise direction when the package is viewed from the *bottom*.

These devices may be soldered into printed circuit boards using appropriate soldering irons (for example, 15-watt irons), but it is a project to remove them for testing. Generally, the solder must be almost completely removed by some means; for example, a suction bulb or *solder wick*. Therefore, sockets are convenient for troubleshooting, although often they are as expensive as the IC. Perforated epoxy/fiberglass boards—perf-boards— with holes prepunched on a rectangular grid with 0.1-inch spacing are commonly available and are convenient for mounting DIP sockets and components for prototype or small-quantity designs. *Wire wrapping* has become popular in small-quantity digital circuitry and is also useful for analog circuitry. In this technique, socket pins and posts for holding components are nominally 2-centimeters long with square cross section. Number 28-30—

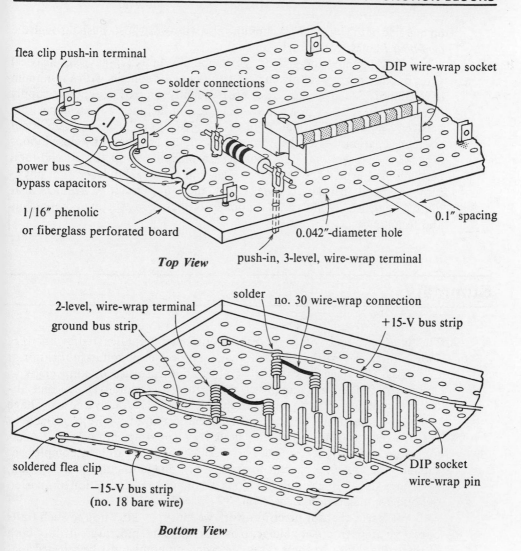

Top View

Bottom View

FIGURE A6-29. *Circuit Board Construction Using Perforated Board, Push-Through Terminals for Mounting Components, and Solder as well as Wire-Wrap Connection Techniques*

gauge, silver-plated, wire-wrapping wire with Kynar insulation is wrapped perhaps 7 times around a post using a wire-wrapping tool. This gives a surprisingly secure, gas-tight, electrical contact. However, this very small wire is only suitable for currents less than about 50 milliamperes. Number 22-gauge wire is suitable for electronic work where greater currents are involved (up to 500 milliamperes) but is generally not wire wrapped; it is soldered to *solder-tail sockets* or to *flea clips* that hold various components on one side of the board. Flea clips and also wire-wrap posts push through the *perf-board* holes with a friction fit.

Power supply and ground wires should be hefty (20-gauge or heavier) wires or bars to carry supply current to circuit components with a minimum of resistance and inductance. They are frequently referred to as power-supply *bus strips*. It is good practice to place low-inductance *bypass* capacitors between V+/V− and ground right on the board to reduce the possibility of circuit oscillations. Also, the ground lines should not form any closed loops because such a *ground loop* provides an inductive loop for ground-loop oscillations. Further, the output of high-gain circuits should be kept physically separated (perhaps shielded) from the input circuit to avoid oscillations. Figure A6−29 illustrates a number of these construction components and techniques.

Summary

The interior circuit of a modern operational amplifier represents very sophisticated electronic design; yet modern processes permit its fabrication at low cost. The scientist can with comparative ease use op-amp chips to design the fundamental amplifier types: inverting, noninverting, and difference amplifiers. High-quality dc amplifiers with accurately known voltage gains are quite straightforward. (Precision dc amplifiers were difficult to design a generation ago; the actual design of an op-amp chip still is.) In addition, a veritable arsenal of signal processing functions can be accomplished: summing of voltages, current-to-voltage or voltage-to-current conversion, logarithm and antilogarithm functions of voltages, multiplication or division of voltages, integration, and so on.

It is true that for precision work we must pay attention to such traits of real op amps as offset voltage, bias current, and temperature drift of both of these quantities. In some cases, precision op amps must be selected that minimize these problems. Also, work at high frequencies or with very short pulses requires selection of particular op amps. Finally, we must either select a special op amp or help an op amp with external transistors if a significant current level or power is required from the op amp. Virtually, the only area of scientific analog electronics that is difficult to solve with the op amp at the present time is one that requires high voltages (perhaps hundreds of volts) at high frequencies (more than 10 megahertz). However, it is probable that in the near future op amps that incorporate VMOS FETs (discussed briefly in Chapter A8) as their output stages will move into even this last stronghold of discrete transistor and vacuum tube electronics.

This chapter has been designed to give the scientist a *working knowledge* of how to solve a variety of laboratory electronics problems through use of the operational amplifier, but it cannot claim to be comprehensive. For more op amp details and applications, the reader is referred to the *IC OP-AMP Cookbook* by Walter Jung, or the *Transducer Interfacing Handbook* by Sheingold from Analog Devices, as well as other texts given in the Reference section.

REVIEW EXERCISES

1. (a)   What is an IC?
    (b)   What is an op amp?
2. Give typical values for the following aspects of the 741 op amp:
    (a)   input resistance, between + and − terminals
    (b)   open-loop voltage gain
    (c)   output resistance
    (d)   maximum power supply voltage
3. Name 4 qualities for an ideal operational amplifier.
4. Make a drawing of the circuit for each of the following using an operational amplifier and other circuit elements are needed (no values need be included):
    (a)   voltage follower   (d)   integrating function block
    (b)   logarithmic amplifier   (e)   noninverting amplifier
    (c)   inverting amplifier
5. Suppose you construct 10 amplifiers from op amps: Each amplifier is to have an accurate voltage gain of 20. However, the open-loop gain of the op amps used varies by ±20%. Does this cause a problem? Explain briefly.
6. The circuit drawn in Diagram A6–1 is intended to be a non-inverting amplifier with a gain of 10. Find two circuit errors.

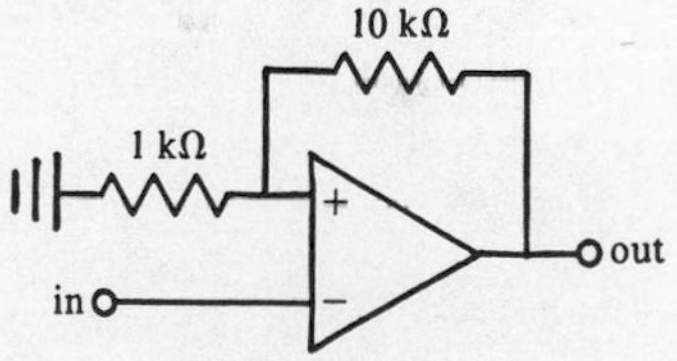

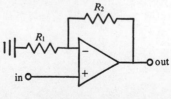

DIAGRAM A6–1.

7. The circuit shown in Diagram A6–2 can be changed to a voltage follower simply by (choose one): A. shorting R_2, B. removing R_2, C. shorting R_1, D. removing R_1. NOTE: More than one answer is correct.

DIAGRAM A6–2.

8. Rank the following amplifiers from largest to smallest in terms of input impedance and briefly justify your ranking:
    (a)   inverting amplifier, gain of 100   (c)   noninverting amplifier,
    (b)   voltage follower   gain of 100

9. Name 3 factors that may limit the input impedance of the voltage follower in practice.

10. Both the operational amplifier (generally) and the difference amplifier have inverting and noninverting inputs. What then distinguishes the two amplifier types?

11. (a) How many op amps are commonly used in an instrumentation amplifier? What is the principle purpose of each?

    (b) What is the important performance difference between an instrumentation amplifier and a difference amplifier constructed from one op amp?

12. What is the origin of the term *operational* in operational amplifier? Comment on its double meaning in the valid sentence: An operational amplifier is used in an operational amplifier to integrate a function.

    NOTE· Because of this problem, the term *function block* is substituted for the latter meaning in this book.

13. (a) An integrating function block can perform the integral of a function $F(x)$. For the actual circuit, what must the quantity x be?

    NOTE: x has dimensions.

    (b) What is the nature of the function F itself for the circuit; for example, what are its dimensions?

    (c) What is the nature of the output from the function block; for example, what are its dimensions?

14. (a) What is the principal problem of a simple log or antilog circuit constructed from only a diode, a resistor, and an op amp?

    (b) What is likely to be the cost-effective solution if a log or antilog circuit is desired?

15. Which of the following statements is *not* true about real operational amplifiers?

    (a) They can amplify an input signal of zero frequency, but not infinite frequency.

    (b) They require an input bias current.

    (c) They produce zero output voltage when the input is shorted.

    (d) They require connections to some power supply.

16. (a) What is typically required to be connected to an uncompensated op amp that is not required for an internally compensated op amp?

    (b) What advantage can an uncompensated op amp have, however?

17. (a) What is meant by nulling an op-amp amplifier circuit?

    (b) How is it done?

    (c) Why is this of little concern if the circuit is to amplify ac signals?

18. (a) Why is there a need for bypass capacitors on an op-amp circuit board? Where are they placed?

    (b) What type of capacitor should be selected?

19. What is the particular problem when using a bipolar op-amp circuit with a transducer that has a very high output impedance?

20. (a) What is the operating temperature range for military-range op amps as well as for commercial-range units?

(b) Select the military-range op amps from the following list of popular types: μA741, LM301, μA741C, LM101.

21. Name the two input properties of an op amp that can present significant drift problems when the op-amp temperature changes.

22. (a) What is the principle advantage of an op amp that uses MOSFETs or FETS for its input stage?

(b) However, very few FET-input op amps are classified as precision op amps. What is their principal failing?

23. When is the slew rate of an op amp of particular concern?

24. A 741 op-amp circuit is used to amplify the output from a thermocouple before reading with a DVM. The circuit is placed in a room to monitor room temperature. Explain why the circuit will not perform satisfactorily (unless the op-amp circuit is nulled before each reading).

25. (a) An op amp and a voltmeter can be used to make an excellent ammeter. Draw the op-amp circuit involved.

(b) What feature of the op amp permits the resulting ammeter to approach the ideal?

26. (a) Diagram a circuit constructed from an op amp that becomes a constant current source. Describe what determines the current.

(b) What is the upper limit for the current value if typical low-power operational amplifiers are used?

27. A 741 op amp is to be used in a circuit that should output up to 5 V to a 50-Ω load.

(a) Why will the 741 need assistance?

(b) What can be done to provide this assistance?

28. Name 5 principal categories of operational amplifiers. Give an example application, in general terms, for each category.

29. (a) What does DIP stand for; to what does the phrase refer?

(b) What is the direction of increasing pin numbers for TO–5 and DIP IC packages when viewed from the *bottom:* clockwise or counterclockwise?

(c) Why is 0.1-inch-spacing perforated board convenient for contemporary circuit boards?

(d) What wiring technique avoids soldering and is suitable for permanent circuits?

(e) What are bus strips (also called rails) on a circuit board?

PROBLEMS

1. Draw the op-amp design for an inverting amplifier with an input impedance of 5 kΩ and a voltage gain of 20.

2. Design a noninverting amplifier with a voltage gain of 10. The smallest resistor used is to be 1 kΩ.

3. Design a noninverting amplifier with a voltage gain of 20. With no exterior load on the amplifier, the output current from the op amp is to be 1 mA at 10-V output.

4. Assume an ideal op amp is used in the circuit pictured in Diagram A6–3.
   (a) What is the reading of the voltmeter V? Justify your answer.
   (b) What is the reading of ammeter I? Justify your answer.

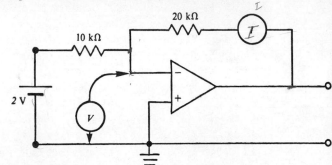

DIAGRAM
A6–3.

5. Consider the op-amp circuit shown in Diagram A6–4.
   (a) If B is grounded and A is used as the amplifier input, what is the voltage gain (including sign) and input impedance of the amplifier?
   (b) If A is grounded and B is used as the amplifier input, what is the voltage gain (including sign) of the ampli-

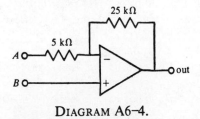

DIAGRAM A6–4.

   fier? Comment on the order of magnitude of its input impedance.

6. (a) Can an amplifier (noninverting) be constructed with gain $+1/2$ from a single op amp? Explain.
   (b) Design a circuit that provides a gain of $+1/2$ constructed from two op amps.
   (c) Discuss what factors limit how small the resistors may be in this circuit.
   (d) Design a circuit that has high input resistance and provides a gain of $+1/2$. 3 op amps may be used.

7. Consider the expanded interior model for only the op-amp inputs, as shown in Diagram A6–5.
   (a) Suppose the two inputs are connected together, and the resistance between the inputs and ground is measured. What is obtained from the

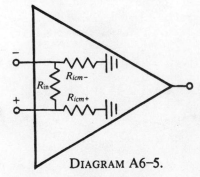

DIAGRAM A6–5.

model for this common-mode input resistance R_{icm}?

(b) Diagram a voltage follower constructed with this op-amp model. Show that R_{icm+} represents a direct shunt to ground at the follower input. (The effective resistance presented by R_{in} remains as argued in the chapter, and R_{icm-} is of no consequence here.)

(c) Assume that a voltage follower is constructed with a 741. Assume R_{in} and A_{vo} are typical and the $R_{icm+} = 100\ R_{in}$. Find the expected input impedance of the voltage-follower amplifier.

NOTE: Actually, this should be called the ac input impedance because the input bias current affects the dc value.

8. Consider the derivation of the voltage gain for the noninverting amplifier assuming finite open-loop gain, A_{vo}.

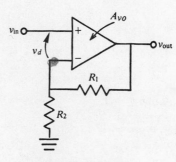

DIAGRAM A6–6.

(a) Justify that the following expression holds for the quantities shown in Diagram A6–6:

$$v_d = v_{in} - v_{out}\left(\frac{R_2}{R_1 + R_2}\right) = \frac{v_{out}}{A_{vo}}$$

(b) First let $A_{vo} \rightarrow \infty$ in this expression and quickly deduce the classical expression for the voltage gain of the noninverting amplifier.

(c) Let A_{vo} remain finite. Solve for v_{out}/v_{in}.

NOTE: This is the expression corresponding to Equation A6–38, but for the noninverting amplifier.

9. Consider the amplifier shown in Diagram A6–7.

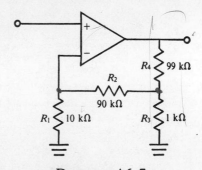

DIAGRAM A6–7.

(a) Is this an inverting or a noninverting amplifier?

(b) Show that the voltage gain of the amplifier is approximately 1000.

NOTE: Consider R_4/R_3 and R_2/R_1 to be successive voltage dividers.

(c) What is the advantage of this connection over the 2-resistor connection in obtaining an amplifier with very high gain?

10. The circuit shown in Diagram A6–8 represents a precision-adjustable voltage source of high stability.

    (a) Why is the voltage across the load R_L adjustable? What are the minimum and maximum values?

    (b) Why is the voltage across R_L expected to be insensitive to changes in this load resistance? However, roughly, what maximum current may be drawn by the load?

    (c) Why is a mercury (Hg) battery desirable?

    (d) Why is a multiturn pot desirable for the potentiometer in the circuit?

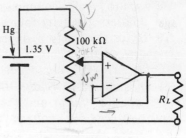

DIAGRAM A6–8.

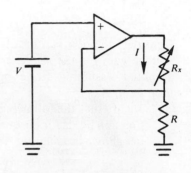

DIAGRAM A6–9.

11. Consider Diagram A6–9. Show that even though R_x varies, this circuit maintains a constant current $I = V/R$ through R_x.

12. Consider Diagram A6–10. We wish to design a box that receives a variable dc voltage V_1 at one input, and a 0.1 V_{p-p} ac voltage at the second input. The box is to output the ac voltage at 4 V_{p-p}, and this ac signal is to be superposed on a dc voltage that is 5 times V_1. See the diagram. The input impedance of the ac input should be 1 kΩ. Draw the amplifier design, including component values required. Justify your design briefly.

    NOTE: The output behavior here is similar to the dc offset adjustment available on many function generators.

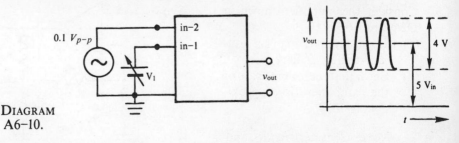

DIAGRAM A6–10.

13. Draw an amplifier design for which the output voltage v_{out} is related to three input voltages v_1, v_2, v_3 by

$$v_{out} = -(v_1 + 2v_2 + 3v_3)$$

The smallest input impedance (for any of the 3 input voltages) is to be 1 kΩ.

A232

14. We want to justify the input voltage relation given by Equation A6–16 for the "attempt at a difference amplifier" in Figure A6–8a. Our objective is to find v_{out} in terms of v_{in-} and v_{in+}. Use the notation of the drawing as shown in Diagram A6–11.

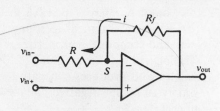

DIAGRAM A6–11.

(a) What can be said about the voltage of S compared to v_{in+}?

(b) Solve for the current i in terms of v_{out} and v_{in-}.

(c) Also find a relationship between current i and v_{in+}, v_{in-}.

(d) Solve now for v_{out} in terms of the two input voltages and compare with Equation A6–14.

15. We wish to use an op amp and a 5-V voltmeter to construct a milliammeter with a 10-mA full-scale reading. Draw the circuit design.

16. (a) Consider the circuit shown in Diagram A6–12, where V_{in} and R are fixed. Show that the circuit may be considered to be a resistance-to-voltage converter. What is the proportionality constant between V_{out} and R_x?

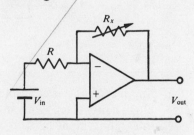

DIAGRAM A6–12.

(b) What could be the utility of this circuit in connection with a resistance-type transducer?

17. What is the voltage reading of the voltmeter V in the op-amp circuit pictured in Diagram A6–13?

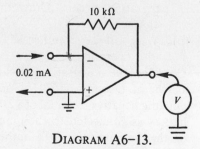

DIAGRAM A6–13.

18. (a) Consider the circuit shown in Diagram A6–14. The output voltage can be expected to be not very far from (choose

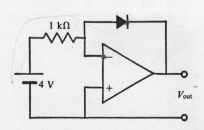

DIAGRAM A6–14.

A233

one): A. +0.6 V, B. −0.6 V, C. +4.6 V, D. −3.4 V

(b) Give an argument to support your answer in (a) using only simple circuit and component properties.

19. The logarithm function block of Figure A6–15 operates only with positive input voltage and produces a negative voltage out. How could it be changed quite simply to accept negative voltage in and produce positive voltage out? Justify briefly.

20. (a) Draw a block diagram of a circuit to divide a voltage v_A by a voltage v_B. Briefly justify its action.

(b) Draw a block diagram of a circuit to perform the square of an input voltage. Briefly justify its action.

21. Consider the circuit pictured in Diagram A6–15. Write an expression for the output voltage, v_{out}. Justify your result.

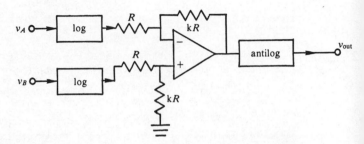

DIAGRAM
A6–15.

22. (a) Suppose a short is connected across the capacitor in an integrating function block constructed from an op amp. Is the voltage source connected to the integration input liable to damage? Explain.

(b) Find the input impedance of an op-amp integrating function block.

23. (a) Suppose a unipolar square wave (see Figure A7–1a) is input to an integrating circuit. Draw the output from the integrator, justifying its character briefly.

(b) Why will the circuit cease functioning at some time after the circuit is put into operation?

24. Consider the integrating circuit shown in Diagram A6–16. Suppose the negative terminal of a 2-V battery is connected to the input of the amplifier (and the other terminal to ground). Draw a graph of the output voltage as a function of time and justify your graph briefly.

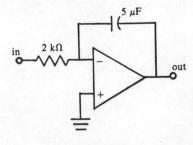

DIAGRAM A6–16.

25. (a) Consider the above integrating circuit. Suppose the input signal is given by $v_{in} = 2$ V sin (ωt), where the frequency is 1 kHz. What expression for

v_{out} is expected (theoretically)? What is the phase of the output compared to the input? What is the amplitude of the output? Can a typical real op amp accommodate this amplitude?

(b) Suppose the resistor and capacitor are interchanged in the circuit. Answer the questions of part (a) for the new circuit.

26. Suppose a 741 op amp is operated in the circuit shown in Diagram A6–17. Over what frequency range can the amplifier be expected to operate with flat response?

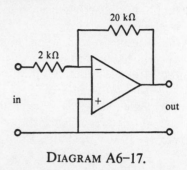

DIAGRAM A6–17.

27. (a) Suppose an amplifier with a voltage gain of 2000 is constructed from a 741 op amp. What bandwidth may be expected for the amplifier? Obtain the answer two ways: working from Figure A6–19, and using the quoted GBP for the 741.

(b) Suppose the amplifier is constructed instead with a 748 op amp using a 3-pF compensation capacitor. What is the approximate upper-frequency limit for satisfactory operation of this amplifier?

28. (a) A student constructs an op-amp amplifier with a gain of 60. With the input shorted the output voltage reads 0.015 V. What is the input offset voltage for the op amp used?

(b) The op amp has a drift of the input offset of 7 μV/C°. If the amplifier temperature is increased by 10 C°, what output would be expected with the input shorted? Give two possible values.

29. Consider the amplifier shown in Diagram A6–18.

(a) Is this an ac or a dc amplifier? Why?

(b) Give a possible reason for putting C_1 in the amplifier.

(c) Suppose $R_2/R_1 = 10$. There is probably no point in arranging an offset null for the amplifier. Why?

(d) Suppose $R_2/R_1 = 1000$. In this case there may be good reason to arrange an offset null for the amplifier. Why?

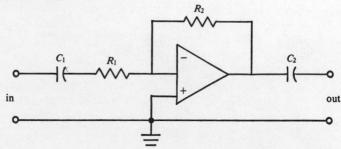

DIAGRAM A6–18.

A235

30. The 741, 308, 318, and 3104 are four op-amp types that are widely available and inexpensive. Give the typical values of the following parameters for the respective devices. Circle the "winner" in each case.
    (a) differential input resistance
    (b) input bias current
    (c) input offset-voltage drift
    (d) slew rate

31. Suggest an op-amp type that would be appropriate for use as an amplifier in each of the following tasks. Justify your choice briefly in each case.
    (a) Voltage pulses of 5-μsec duration and 0.1-V amplitude need to be amplified to 2-V amplitude.
    (b) Essentially dc signals on the order of 100 μV are to be amplified to 10 mV. The ambient temperature changes by ±5 C° during its use.
    (c) A 10-mV$_{p-p}$ 500-Hz signal from a source with 1-kΩ output impedance is to be amplified to 1.0 V$_{p-p}$.
    (d) A 10-mV$_{p-p}$ 200-kHz signal from a source with 1-kΩ output impedance is to be amplified to 1.0 V$_{p-p}$.
    (e) A 10-mV$_{dc}$ signal from a voltage source with 50-MΩ output impedance needs to be amplified to 1.0 V.
    (f) A 100-mV$_{dc}$ signal from a voltage source with 1-kΩ output impedance needs to be amplified to 2.0 V. The circuit is to operate from 4 penlight batteries to permit portable field operation.

32. (a) A 741 op amp is to be operated from a pair of small 8.4-V nickel-cadmium transistor radio batteries. They have a rated capacity of 0.1 ampere-hour. Approximately how long can the circuit be expected to operate before the batteries require recharging?
    NOTE: Assume the load to the circuit is high impedance.
    (b) Suppose an OP–20 is substituted for the 741 in the circuit. Find the operational duration.

33. Consider Diagram A6–19. This exercise deduces the output voltage error due to input bias current, if there is no compensating resistor connection between the + op-amp input and ground. The approach differs from that followed in the text example. Again it is assumed that A_{vo} is large, and that no input offset voltage exists, but the bias current i_b into each op-amp input is finite.

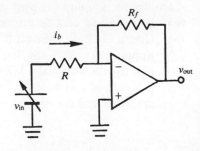

DIAGRAM A6–19.

    (a) Assume a small voltage v_{in} at the amplifier input is adjusted until v_{out} is precisely zero. Justify that the only current flowing is in R, and that it must consist of the bias current i_b.
    (b) Justify that $v_{in} = i_b R$ (the voltage drop across R).

(c) Suppose v_{in} is reduced to zero; then the amplifier input is shorted to ground. Argue that the amplifier output should be $v_{out} = +(R_f/R)v_{in}$, where v_{in} is the value obtained above. This is an output voltage error. What is its value in reference to the input?

(d) Show that $v_{out} = i_b R_f$, in agreement with the text example.

CHAPTER
A7

Waveform-Shaping Circuits

The square-wave voltage waveform is that rather curious situation where the voltage changes rapidly from a low voltage level to a higher voltage, remains there for a time $T/2$, and then suddenly switches back again where it remains for a time $T/2$ before repeating the process. This situation is the symmetrical square wave (see Figure A7-1a). In the asymmetrical case, the time intervals for low and high are different (see Figure A7-1b). If the time that the voltage is low is much longer than the time that it is high, we think more of a sequence of *pulses* (see Figure A7-1c).

For *ideal* square waves and pulses the transitions between the low and high levels would be instantaneous; this feature is indicated in Figure A7-1 by the dashed vertical lines. However, real square waves and pulses have a finite *rise time* and *fall time* for these transitions. Furthermore, Figure A7-1a illustrates that a square wave may essentially be a changing dc voltage, or *unipolar* in terms of voltage, or the square wave may be true ac and therefore *symmetrical* in terms of voltage. In general, when a square wave or other waveform is not symmetrical in voltage, it is said to have an *offset*. A function generator often possesses an offset control for the waveform output.

There are a number of situations in analog electronics where these waveforms that are either high or low are of interest, although today the *"high" or "low"*—or *ON or OFF* or 1 or 0— situation is generally considered to be digital electronics. This latter field has expanded tremendously in the past twenty years and indeed, we devote *Digital and Microprocessor Electronics for Scientific Application* to the topic. Nevertheless, pulse waveforms are also useful in instruments that are primarily analog and therefore require some consideration.

Comparator

The *comparator* is a circuit that compares two input voltages V and V_r. We think of V_r as a *reference voltage;* hence the r. If $V>V_r$, the output voltage goes to a high voltage, while if $V<V_r$, the output voltage goes to a low voltage.

One use for a comparator is as a null detector in a Wheatstone bridge, replacing a galvanometer that has long been used to detect equality of voltage on the two sides of the bridge; that is, the comparator can be connected between points A and B of Figure A2–4 and the comparator output connected to a light bulb as a balance indicator. Actually, the comparator would not detect balance as does the galvanometer but rather the *state* of being on one side or the other of balance. The light bulb would indicate this state for small changes in R_3 near balance, and the balance point is thus accurately selected.

The reader may have realized already that a high-gain difference amplifier performs the job of a comparator. Because an operational amplifier is a high-gain difference amplifier, it is often used for the task. Figure A7–2a illustrates an op-amp comparator circuit in which the input voltage is compared to a fixed voltage V_r. In Figure A7–2b we see the output swings from V_- to V_+ when the input signal exceeds the reference voltage by a few microvolts. The output swings back to V_- when the input signal again falls below the reference level. Thus, we refer to the circuit as a *voltage level detector.* The term *threshold* is often used for the input level (V_r) at which the output switches. If we want the output to swing in the opposite sense from that shown in Figure A7–2b, we merely interchange the V_{in} and V_r connections to the op amp.

The simple circuit of Figure A7–2a has essentially the two power-supply voltages as the two possible output voltage levels (for example, $+12$ V and -12 V). Different levels might be desirable, such as $+5$ V for the high level and 0 V for the low level. A slightly clever use of diodes does the job, as shown in Figure A7–3a. Here the diode D_1 conducts when the op-amp output swings negative; this diode will not permit the voltage at its cathode to become more negative than about 0.6 V (for silicon) relative to its anode, which is at ground (see Figure A7–3b). (Almost -12 V then develops across the 1-kilohm resistor.) However, diode D_1 does *not* object to v_{out} being positive. We say diode D_1 *clips* the output near ground.

It is diode D_2 that conducts when the output swings above the voltage of the D_2 cathode, which is connected to a $+5$-V supply. The output thus cannot move more than about 0.6 V above the 5-V level (diode D_2 clips the output near the 5-V level). The 1-kilohm resistor protects the op amp by limit-

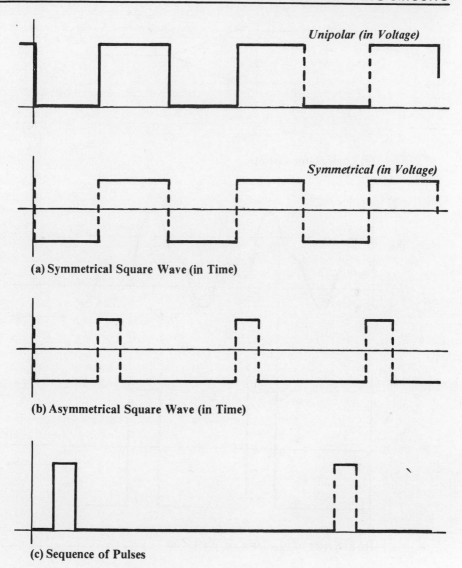

Unipolar (in Voltage)

Symmetrical (in Voltage)

(a) Symmetrical Square Wave (in Time)

(b) Asymmetrical Square Wave (in Time)

(c) Sequence of Pulses

FIGURE A7–1. *Various Square-Wave and Pulse Forms*

ing the current flowing from the op-amp output in these two situations; the actual op-amp output itself *still* swings between V_- and V_+, and the difference between the output voltage and V_- or V_+ is absorbed across the 1-kilohm resistor. (Actually, most modern op amps self-limit the output current to protect themselves, but this resistor plays safe.) Also notice in Figure A7–3a that an adjustable reference level is made possible by the *level set potentiometer*. This is simply a voltage divider that can send an adjustable V_r to the − input.

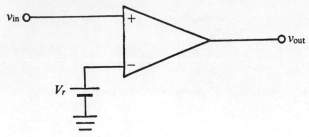

(a) Comparator Circuit

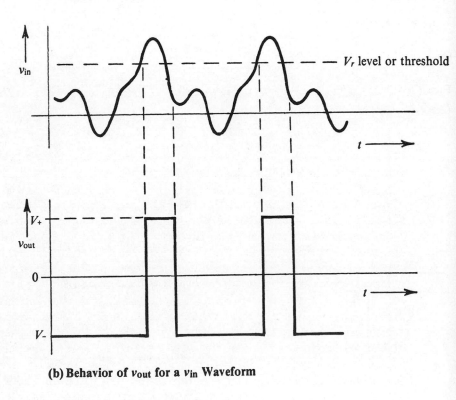

(b) Behavior of v_{out} for a v_{in} Waveform

FIGURE A7–2. *Operations of a Comparator*

Schmitt Trigger

A close relative of the comparator is the *Schmitt trigger* circuit, named after the biophysicist who invented it in the 1930s. In fact, the only difference is the presence of *hysteresis* in the switching level or threshold; that is, the level at which the output switches from low to high is different from the level at which

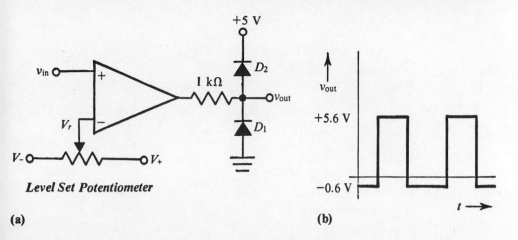

(a)

Level Set Potentiometer

(b)

FIGURE A7–3. *Diodes Used with a Comparator to Clip Op-Amp Output to Desired Low and High Voltages*

the output switches from high to low. This little quirk is very useful in working with noisy signals, as illustrated by Figure A7–4.

Figure A7–4a shows a situation where a noisy signal is input to a single-threshold comparator; Figure A7–4b shows the same situation for a Schmitt trigger. This signal situation is common in the life sciences. For example, the pulse may be an EKG voltage generated in the body during a heartbeat. The noise represents static or high-frequency fluctuations super-posed on the more slowly varying true or pure signal. It is the intention of our level-detecting circuit to detect only when the main peak of the pure signal occurs (for example, for one heartbeat) and output one pulse for this. Un-fortunately, the little noise spikes generate spurious additional short pulses before and after the main pulse (see Figure A7–4a). By having separate thresholds for the upward and downward transitions, the spurious pulses are eliminated in Figure A7–4b. Notice the trick is to have these two detecting levels spaced more widely than the peak-peak noise signal. In addition, the signal may have a secondary true peak that should *not* be counted (Figure A7–4a). As shown in Figure A7–4b, the thresholds must be set above this peak (for example, so that single true heartbeats are detected).

To obtain the hysteresis behavior, two resistors should be added to the comparator or op amp in a sense that gives positive feedback; that is, between the op-amp output and the + op-amp input (see Figure A7–5a). The − input should be used for the signal input. Notice the output goes negative rather than positive when the level is exceeded in this case, as mentioned earlier. The clever scheme uses a voltage divider connected between the output voltage and the reference voltage. The divider output is connected to the noninvert-ing or + input. Thus, the example in Figure A7–5 has the junction of the 1-kilohm and 9-kilohm resistors connected to the + input.

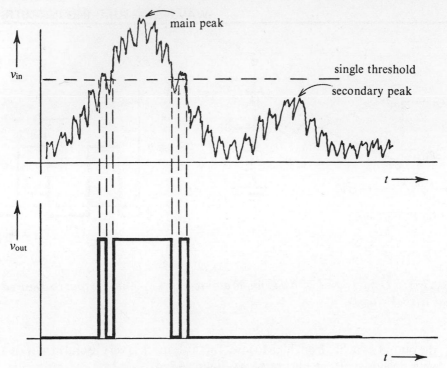

(a) v_{in} **and** v_{out} **for a Single-Threshold Comparator**

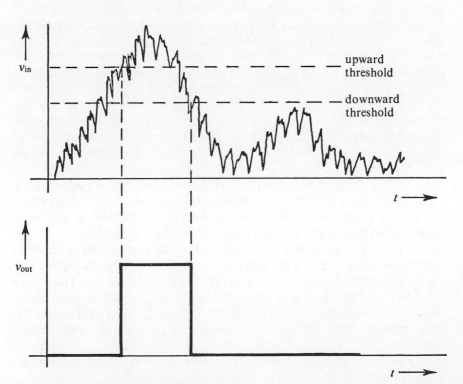

(b) v_{in} **and** v_{out} **for a Schmitt Trigger or a Comparator with Hysteresis**

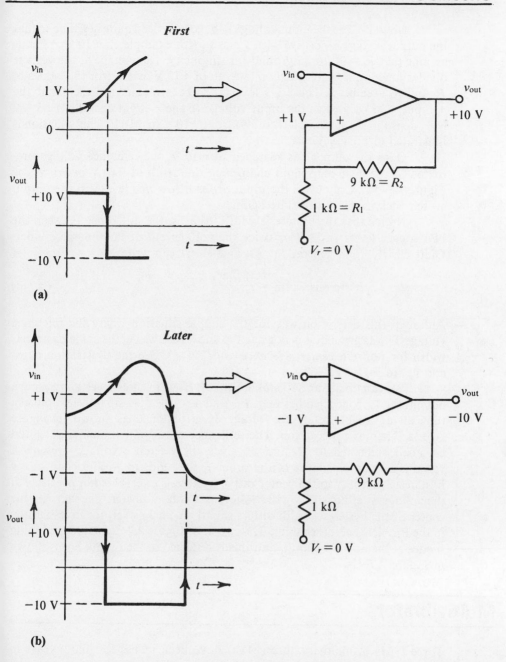

FIGURE A7–5. *A Voltage Divider from the Output That Produces Two Thresholds Symmetrically Placed about a Reference Voltage of Zero, or Ground*

FIGURE A7–4. *Response of a Comparator as well as a Schmitt Trigger to a Noisy Input Signal*

A245

Now suppose the input voltage had recently been quite negative so that the output voltage is positive with value V_+ (for example, at $+10$ V).* Let us assume that $V_r = 0$ V or at ground for simplicity. The voltage at the voltage divider junction is quite clearly one tenth of $+10$ V or 1 V (for the values of R_1 and R_2 used here). This $+1$-V level (and not zero volts) is presented to the $+$ input, and only when the input voltage to the $-$ input exceeds the $+1$-V level does the output switch (rapidly) from $+10$ V to -10 V. This situation is illustrated in Figure A7–5a.

Once the output has switched to -10 V, the reference voltage presented to the $-$ op-amp input changes to one tenth of -10 V or -1 V (see Figure A7–5b). Only when the input drops below *this* level will the output switch back to the $+10$ V state again.

Notice that the hysteresis width—that is, the difference between the two trigger levels—is 2 V or twice the voltage out of the voltage divider. Quite clearly, for a general R_1, R_2, and V_+ we can write

$$\text{hysteresis width} = \frac{2R_1 V+}{R_1 + R_2} \tag{A7-1}$$

Although this derivation was for the simple situation where the reference voltage V_r was ground, it is not hard to show that we get the same hysteresis width for nonzero *center reference voltages* V_r. See the illustration of v_{in} and v_{out} in Figure A7–6b.

We can obtain an adjustable Schmitt trigger center-level V_r by using a potentiometer connected between $V+$ and $V-$ (the op-amp power supplies); thus an adjustable reference voltage V_r is obtained as shown in Figure A7–6a. There is a precaution. The resistance of the potentiometer R should be small compared to R_1 and R_2 since the reference voltage presents a variable output impedance of the order R that adds to R_1 and changes the hysteresis width. Also the center of the hysteresis interval is not precisely at the voltage V_r established by the V_r-level set potentiometer. The fact that the center of the hysteresis width differs slightly from V_r is left for investigation in the Problems of this chapter. The circuit of Figure A7–6a includes clipping diodes at the op-amp output, and this is reflected in the output levels shown in Figure A7–6b.

Multivibrators

Three types of multivibrators (MVs) have been in use for many years in electronics—monostable, bistable, and astable MVs. They were first designed

---

*In general, the upper limit V_+ for the op-amp output can be expected to be near the voltage $V+$ that is used for the $+$ power connection to the op amp. Similarly, the lower limit V_- can be expected to be close to the $V-$ power-supply value. We will assume $|V-| = |V+|$ here.

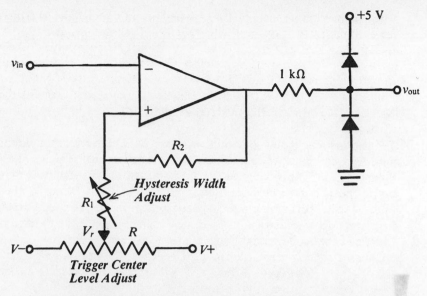

(a) Schmitt Trigger with Adjustable Level and Hysteresis and Output Clipped to Near 0 V, +5 V

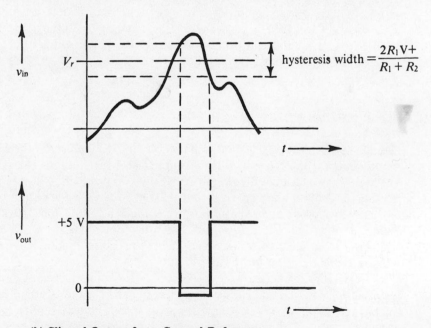

$$\text{hysteresis width} = \frac{2R_1 V+}{R_1 + R_2}$$

(b) Clipped Output for a General Reference Level and Hysteresis Width

FIGURE A7–6.   *General-Purpose Schmitt Trigger from an Op Amp*

with vacuum tubes, later with transistors, and now are available in integrated circuits. All multivibrators deal with pulses or rectangular waveforms.

Monostable (One-Shot) Multivibrator

The *monostable* (one-shot) *multivibrator* (MMV) receives a pulse as input and, as a consequence, immediately generates an output pulse of a certain time duration that is *independent* of the length of the input pulse. Only one output pulse is generated for each input *trigger pulse*. Typically, the trigger pulse is a negative-going pulse; the output pulse begins at the time of the negative slope of the trigger square wave. The output pulse duration is controlled by the *RC* (charging) time constant of a resistance and a capacitance connected somewhere in the circuit. Generally, the output pulse length is of the order of *RC*. Figures A7–7a and b illustrate the typical situation.

There is a similarity between the Schmitt trigger and the monostable multivibrator in that one pulse out is produced for each pulse in. However, the pulse duration of the Schmitt trigger changes with the duration of the incoming pulse, while that for the MMV does *not*. Thus, one common use of the MMV is to take pulses of various lengths and "change" them to only one length. The MMV is generally operated between some positive supply voltage and ground. The low of the output pulse is also near ground and the high near the positive supply voltage.

Bistable Multivibrator or Flip-Flop

While the monostable had only one stable or "resting" state, the bistable multivibrator (BMV) has two. Its output remains low until a trigger pulse is received, at which time the output abruptly switches high; the output then remains high until another trigger pulse is received, and the output quickly switches to a low voltage. The output "flips" high and later "flops" back low—hence its alternate name *flip-flop*. Typically (but not always) the output changes on the negative-going edge of the trigger pulse. Figures A7–8a and b illustrate this situation for the BMV.

The flip-flop action is often also called *toggle* action because it reminds us of a toggle switch that can be flipped or toggled back and forth. This type of bistable flip-flop with a single input has been used in digital counting circuits since the 1920s and is often called a *toggle flip-flop* or *T-type FF;* its input is conventionally labeled *T,* while its output is labeled *Q.*

The reader should be able to justify that if a sequence of pulses with period *T* is fed to a bistable input, the output is a symmetrical (in time) square

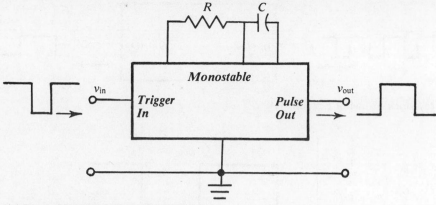

(a) Block Model of Monostable MV

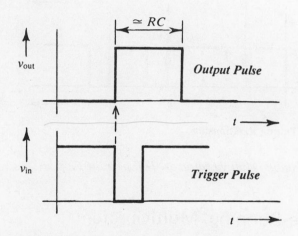

(b) Pulse Timing Relationship

FIGURE A7–7.   *Monostable (One-Shot) Multivibrator*

wave with period $2T$. This bistable output could be fed to a second bistable input, and its output would be a still lower frequency or longer period square wave of $4T = 2^2 T$. Feeding this to a third bistable gives a square wave of $8T = 2^3 T$. In general, we can easily produce a square wave with period precisely $2^n T$ if a pulse train of period T is available. Figure A7–9 illustrates the bistable chain and pulses at each stage. Indeed, the system counts in binary the number of pulses that have occurred at the input. Much more can be said of counting circuits, and *Digital and Microprocessor Electronics for Scientific Application* devotes an entire chapter to the subject. Here, only a brief exposure is given.

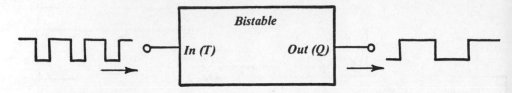

(a) Block Model of Bistable MV

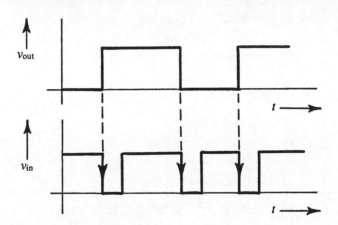

(b) Pulse and State Timing Relationship

FIGURE A7-8.   *Bistable Multivibrator or T-Type Flip-Flop*

Astable (Free-Running) Multivibrator

The *astable* (free-running) *multivibrator* (AMV) is simply a square-wave generator that generates an output square wave similar to those in Figure A7-1 but uses no input. Since it runs by itself, the AMV is an oscillator.

Suppose we take two monostables and connect the output of the first to the input of the second and then connect the output of the second back into the first. The result is a self-contained pulse scheme that will perpetuate itself. (Rather like two children poking each other. The first pokes the second, but then the second pokes the first, but then....) Figure A7-10 illustrates an astable multivibrator constructed from two monostable vibrators.

555 Timer Integrated Circuit

In 1973 Signetics introduced the *555 timer integrated circuit* that has proven to be an extremely versatile device. It can be used for everything from washing dishes (timing the washing cycle) to making a siren. Basically, the 555

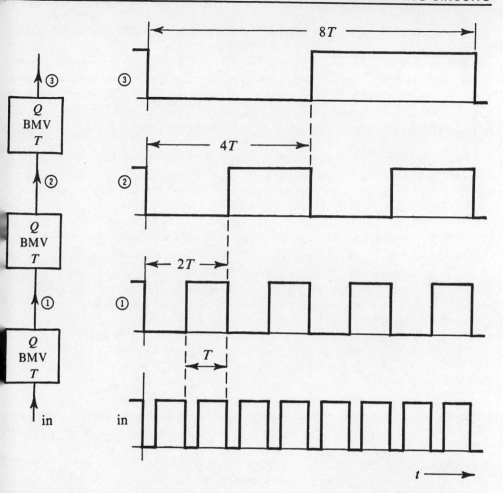

FIGURE A7–9. *Pulses in a String of Bistable Multivibrators or Flip-Flops*

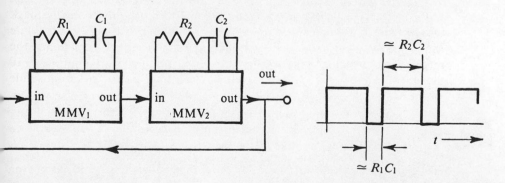

FIGURE A7–10. *Astable Multivibrator Constructed from 2 Monostable Multivibrators*

timer consists of a pair of comparators, a flip-flop, and a (transistor) switch. The pins of the IC may be connected in various ways to achieve various functions. However, the fundamental connection is the one that produces a monostable MV; as such the 555 produces a pulse of duration determined by a capacitor and a resistor connected to the device pins. The pulse duration or time interval is changeable by using an adjustable R (or C), and thus the 555 becomes a timer in the sense of an egg timer.

Figure A7–11 illustrates the important function blocks inside the 555 timer IC. The two comparators should be readily noted, as well as the switch in the lower left corner. However, the flip-flop block near the center is *not* the toggle-type flip-flop noted earlier. The bistable flip-flop within the 555 IC is called a set-reset or *RS flip-flop*. This flip-flop type has two input leads; one is labeled R for *reset* while the other is labeled S for *set*. The action of an RS flip-flop is really quite simple. If a sufficiently high voltage pulse is applied to the S input, the output Q is *set* to the high voltage state. Another pulse to the S input will *not* cause the output to toggle back to a low voltage in this flip-flop type; rather a positive pulse to the R input *resets* the output to a low voltage state. The second flip-flop output $\overline{Q}$ simply does the opposite of Q (the bar over the Q indicates inverted behavior).

Note that 8 pin connections extend from the timer. The 555 timer is available in the 8-pin mini-DIP package as well as the 8-pin round TO–5 metal can. The pin numbers for either of these 8-pin packages are given in Figure A7–11. Moreover, a dual timer is available in the 14-pin DIP package as the 556 timer; this IC simply contains two 555 timers.

Let us now examine the function of the circuit within the 555 package as it is diagrammed in Figure A7–11. Notice that three 5-kilohm resistors are connected between $V+$ and ground, and the two comparators are connected at the $1/3$ $V+$ and $2/3$ $V+$ voltages along this 3-resistance divider. The *lower comparator* can set the flip-flop output Q to a high voltage; the *upper comparator* can reset the flip-flop output Q to ground. Voltage transitions to initiate these actions are shown in Figure A7–11 as arrows; thus the figure shows that a low-to-high arrow to the $+$ input of the upper comparator, called the *threshold input* (pin 6), resets the RS flip-flop. Actually, this reset happens as soon as the voltage into the $+$ input of the upper comparator exceeds the $2/3$ $V+$ that enters the $-$ input of this comparator. Similarly, when the voltage into the *trigger input* (pin 2) or $-$ input of the lower comparator moves below $1/3$ $V+$, the RS flip-flop is set to high and the output moves to $V+$.

A negative pulse on the reset input (pin 4) can pull Q low, also resetting the flip-flop and output to low. When the output is low, the $\overline{Q}$ output is high and the switch S connects the *discharge* (pin 7) to ground. Note the rule given in the figure that a low voltage opens switch S. When a 555 timer reset is desired, the voltage into the reset pin should move momentarily from near $V+$ to near ground; for example, momentarily shorting pin 4 to ground produces a reset.

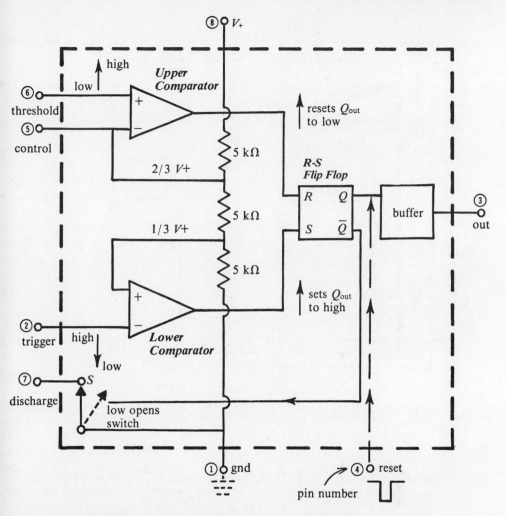

FIGURE A7–11. *Block Diagram of Interior of 555 Timer IC*

555 Multivibrators

In operation as a *monostable* MV, a capacitor C and resistor R are connected between ground and $V+$ (see Figure A7–12). The threshold of the upper comparator (pin 6) and the discharge (pin 7) are both connected to the junction between R and C. The resting state has the output low and discharge switch closed. The capacitor C is then shorted to ground through the switch. When an input pulse on the trigger input (pin 2) goes below $1/3\ V+$, the lower comparator goes high and sets the flip-flop. The switch S opens, and the 555

A253

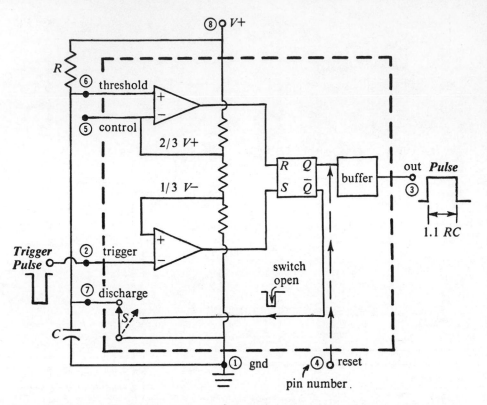

FIGURE A7-12. *Multivibrator Circuit with Monostable Connection*

out (pin 3) also goes high. Thus, the pulse begins. Current flows through R, capacitor C charges, and its voltage grows toward $V+$. However, when the voltage on C reaches 2/3 $V+$, the threshold lead to the upper comparator rises above the threshold level for this comparator and the comparator resets the flip-flop to low output. The switch S closes, discharging the capacitor, and the 555 timer output simultaneously goes low, thus ending the pulse. The timer is now back to its resting state.

The pulse duration is determined by the timer required for the capacitor C to charge through R to 2/3 of the supply voltage. Thus

$$V_C = (2/3)V+ = (V+)(1 - e^{-t_p/RC})$$

identifies the time duration of the pulse, t_p. Solving for t_p we have

$$t_p = RC \ln 3 = 1.1 \ RC \qquad (A7-2)$$

Thus, the formula for the duration of the pulse in the monostable mode is:

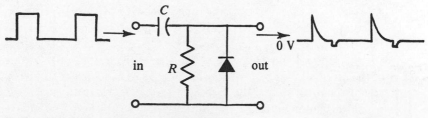

(a) Simple (Approximate) Differentiator ($RC \ll T$)

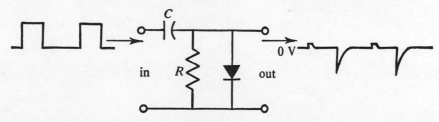

(b) Diode Placed to Clip Negative Spikes

(c) Diode Placed to Clip Positive Spikes

FIGURE A7–13. *High-Pass Filter or Simple Differentiator Used to Produce Spike Pulses from Long Pulses*

Pulse length = 1.1 RC (R is in ohms and C is in farads for t_p in seconds). However, there is one unfortunate behavior characteristic of the 555 monostable: The input pulse must be shorter than the output pulse; otherwise the output stays high until the input returns high.

Especially if the trigger pulses are output from a Schmitt trigger, the pulses may be of variable duration and exceed the length of the monostable output pulse. The solution is to shorten up the trigger pulses to *spikes* with the assistance of the *simple differentiating circuit*. If we connect a capacitor in series with a resistor to form a high-pass filter (see Figure A7–13a), we can show that the output is approximately the derivative of the input voltage. In the illustration, the square wave first charges the capacitor in one sense, and the surge of current that flows produces a voltage spike across the output resistor. A time T later, the input voltage returns low and the capacitor discharges through R, producing a voltage spike in the opposite direction. Of course, the situation is simply an RC charging-discharging circuit. Exponential spikes of duration $\cong RC$ form across the resistance, and the sharpness is just determined by the RC time. Making either R or C small produces sharp pulses.

It may be that the negative spikes are not desirable or are even injurious to the electronic device that receives the spike pulses. They may be mostly clipped off (to about 0.6 V) by using diodes as shown in Figure A7–13b. Reverse the diode to clip in the other sense, as shown in Figure A7–13c. Actually, spikes going negative from $V+$ (or at least from some value above $1/3$ $V+$) are required to trigger the 555 timer. The circuit of Figure A7–13c will do the job provided the cathode end of the diode/resistor combination is connected to $V+$. This raises the resting or quiescent level out of the differentiator to $V+$. Figure A7–14 shows such a circuit with values of R and C chosen so that the spike duration is less than 10 microseconds. This should accommodate nearly any situation since the manufacturer recommends that the minimum output pulse duration of the 555 timer be 10 microseconds. It is important to realize that the amplitude of the differentiator's output spikes will be the same as the amplitude of the pulses input to the

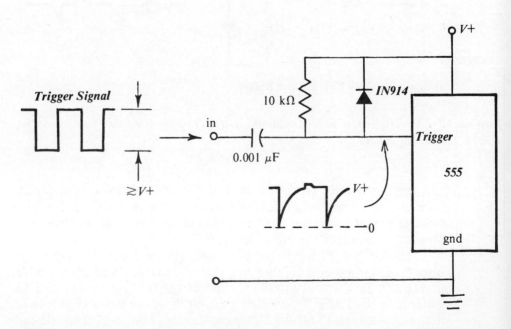

FIGURE A7–14. *Simple Differentiator Used to Produce Short Input Trigger Pulses to the 555 Timer*

differentiator. To achieve triggering, this means the pulse amplitude should equal $V+$, as shown in Figure A7–14.

The 555 *astable* multivibrator connection is shown in Figure A7–15. Here both the upper threshold and lower trigger comparator leads are connected to the "top" of capacitor C. The discharge switch connects to the junction between two resistors R_A and R_B, which are in series with capacitor C. Thus, if switch S is open, the capacitor charges through R_A and R_B toward $V+$. But if S is closed, the capacitor discharges through R_B toward ground.

Suppose S is closed (discharge shorted to ground). Then any charge on C will leak off through R_B to ground, with time constant R_BC. However, when the voltage across capacitor C gets down to $1/3$ $V+$, the lower comparator sets the flip-flop; this causes the output to go high and also opens the discharge switch. Now capacitor C charges through R_A and R_B toward $V+$ with time constant $(R_A + R_B)C$. However, when the voltage on C reaches $2/3$ $V+$, the upper comparator resets the flip-flop to low. Simultaneously the output goes low, the discharge switch closes so that C begins discharging again, and the cycle repeats. We have examined here the behavior of one cycle or period of the square wave.

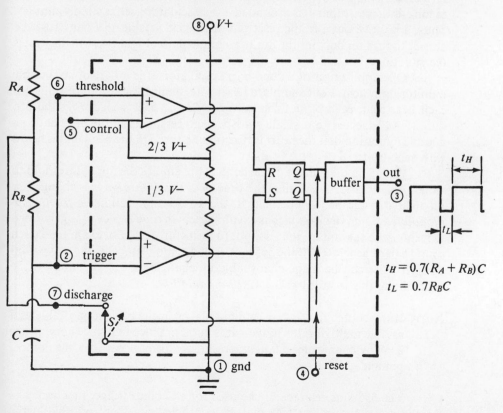

FIGURE A7–15. *555 Multivibrator Circuit with Astable Connection*

A257

Note that since C charges through $(R_A + R_B)$ but discharges through R_B, the time constants for the output to be high and low are different. Thus, an asymmetric (in time) square wave is produced. The time for the output to be high t_H is given by

$$t_H = 0.7(R_A + R_B)C \qquad \text{(A7-3)}$$

while the time to be low t_L is given by

$$t_L = 0.7R_B C \qquad \text{(A7-4)}$$

The times t_H and t_L are illustrated at the output in Figure A7–15. The period of the square wave is given by

$$T = t_H + t_L = (1.4R_B + 0.7R_A)C = 1/f \qquad \text{(A7-5)}$$

Manufacturers' specification sheets also show useful graphs of frequency versus resistance and capacitance that may be used to determine quickly the R and C required for a desired frequency.

It is possible to produce a *gated oscillator* or *tone-burst oscillator* from the 555 astable MV quite easily; that is, we can cause the oscillator to turn on for awhile and then off again. The 555 oscillator output will go low for as long as the reset (pin 4) is grounded—the oscillator itself is simply shut off. Thus, a positive pulse to the reset pin of the 555 astable MV will cause the output to turn on only for the duration of the pulse. Figure A7–16 illustrates the situation.

One application of a tone-burst oscillator is as a part of an audible monitoring system. For example, a heart-rate monitor can produce a pulse at each heartbeat; each pulse turns on or *gates* the 555 oscillator. If the 555 output is connected to a small loudspeaker, personnel in the area have an audible indication that the heart is functioning through the beep that is heard with each beat.

Changing the voltage of the control pin adjusts the upper threshold to values other than $2/3 \, V+$; thus the time t_H of the square wave is changed or modulated if the 555 is operated in the astable connection. A *frequency-modulated square wave,* which is asymmetrical in time however, is generated in response to the voltage that is input to the control pin. For example, a siren sound can be generated. If the 555 is operated in monostable mode, the period of each pulse can be made changeable by changing a voltage input to the control pin; this is called *pulse width modulation.*

NOTE: If the control pin is not being used—as in the basic monostable and astable multivibrator usage—it is good practice to reduce noise problems by connecting a 0.01-microfarad capacitor between the control pin and ground.

The 555 timer can readily be used for a Schmitt trigger function. The threshold and the trigger pins may be connected together and used as the

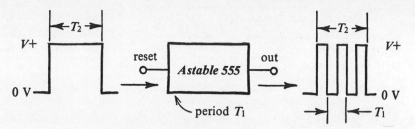

FIGURE A7–16. *555 Used as a Tone-Burst Oscillator*

device input; no additional resistors or capacitors need be connected, simply the power-supply voltage. Then the output of the timer moves high as soon as the input voltage exceeds 2/3 $V+$; the output moves low when the input falls below 1/3 $V+$. Notice that a Schmitt trigger with hysteresis width (for noise rejection) equal to 1/3 $V+$ is obtained. The two triggering levels can be adjusted—although not independently—by adjusting the voltage to the control input of the 555 timer.

   For more information on these uses and many other 555 applications, the interested reader is referred to the books that are devoted to the 555; *IC Timer Cookbook* by W. Jung is a good representative.

Capabilities of the 555

The 555 can operate from supply voltage or $V+$ as low as 4.5 V and as high as 18 V. The output pulse height corresponds to the supply voltage used. The pulse width is quite stable against temperature variations: only 0.005% change per Celsius degree change. It is also stable against power-supply variations: only 0.1% change in pulse length per volt change in $V+$. The output is capable of supplying (as well as sinking) a substantial current: up to 200 milliamperes through an output impedance of about 20 ohms. This current is quite adequate to operate small light bulbs, LEDs, relays, and other small devices.

   The shortest pulse width recommended for the 555 has already been mentioned: 10 microseconds. The longest pulse width is determined by the maximum desirable values for R and for C. Various small currents into the 555 limit R to about 10 megohms, and leakage current in capacitors of large size limits C to perhaps 10 microfarads, so that the maximum reliable pulse length is on the order of 100 seconds. If R and C are precisely known, inaccuracies in the 555 timer itself cause pulse duration precision of about 1 to 2%. Very long pulses are possible with various new types of IC timers. Thus, the LM322 has a wider range of pulse duration, while the Exar 2240 uses digital techniques to provide programmable pulse width of hours or days. The manufacturers' specification sheets should be consulted for limitations and recommendations for usage of these various devices.

A259

Some Multivibrator Applications

Sequence Timing Control

Many situations in the laboratory as well as industry require that a sequence of operations or processes be controlled. Perhaps first a valve is to be opened for a certain interval to permit fluid to flow into a vessel. Then a mixing motor is to be operated for a certain time. After opening a drain valve for a time to permit emptying, the whole process is to be repeated some time later. The time-intervals for these processes should be individually adjustable, and a device to control the order and timing of the operations is called a *sequencer*.

Perhaps the simplest way to sequence processes in this manner is to use several monostable MVs in cascade. See Figure A7–17, where some "process A" and then "process B" are controlled. In this connection of monostable MVs, each stage quite literally becomes a timer, as its output is assumed to turn a process on during the time it is at the "high" voltage, and turn the process off while it is at the "low" voltage. As the output of a certain timer moves low to conclude a process, it triggers the next monostable timer into operation. This operation assumes negative pulse triggering as illustrated in Figure A7–7 (recall the 555 timer is triggered on a negative pulse). It is rather like a chain of dominoes with adjustable fall times. The entire sequence could be triggered by some initiating pulse (for example, from a push button) each time it is required. On the other hand it may automatically recycle, either by connecting the output from the last monostable MV to the input of the first, or by using the output from an astable MV to operate the first monostable. The latter technique is shown in Figure A7–17.

The various time intervals are set by adjustment of the RC time constant for corresponding monostable MVs, of course; this is illustrated by the adjustable resistors (potentiometers) in Figure A7–17a. The time interval of the overall recycling is controlled by the RC time constant(s) of the astable MV, and in fact operation similar to the 555 astable MV mode is assumed in the figure. Notice the *cause-effect* timing diagram of the three outputs in Figure A7–17b.

The output from a 555 monostable MV can control a process directly if it requires less than 200 milliamperes and less than 18 V_{dc}. However, in many cases the output will rather control an electromagnetic relay or a solid-state relay (see Chapters A3 and A8, respectively), which in turn switches the rather large ac current to a device such as an electric motor or a solenoid valve. Therefore, relays are parenthetically suggested as typical immediate destinations for the monostable MVs in Figure A7–17a. Note that if 555 timers are used for the monostable stages, a differentiating circuit such as shown in Figure A7–14 is required at each trigger input. Otherwise the low period from the previous monostable MV prevents the next monostable MV from completing its pulse.

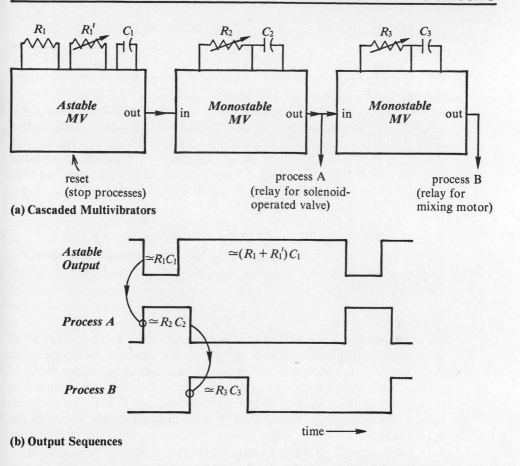

FIGURE A7–17. *Multivibrators Used to Obtain a Self-Cycling Sequencer*

Frequency-to-Voltage Converter or Ratemeter

There are a number of situations where a scientist or engineer wants to measure the frequency or rate at which something is occurring. We might want to monitor the heart rate of an animal, or the level of radioactivity, or the speed of a turning wheel. It is true that there are *digital* frequency meters that permit very precise measurement of the frequency (or the related period) of a repetitive electrical signal. However, there are circumstances where a voltage or *analog* indication of a rate is desired. We may want a quick visual indication of the rate through use of the needle of a meter, especially if it is somewhat rapidly changing; or we may want to monitor the rate over a period of time by recording it on a strip-chart recorder (these recorders typically accept a voltage as input). Also, this analog frequency meter that we are about to describe can be quite inexpensive and simple to construct and use.

The technique we describe here requires that each event in the repetitive process to be measured causes a voltage pulse of a definite length or duration and amplitude. Note that this suggests utilization of a monostable MV as a pulse-shaping device. As a specific example, assume a heartbeat ratemeter. Each beat could produce an electrical pulse of 0.25 seconds duration. If a pulse stream of this character is input to a *very* low-pass filter, the dc voltage out of the filter is proportional to the frequency of the pulses. This results from the fact that the voltage out of the low-pass filter is the "dc part" (or time average) of the input pulse signal. A similar behavior was presented for the *L*-section low-pass filter in Figure A4–17.

We will justify this output-voltage versus input-frequency relationship. If a voltage $v(t)$ is varying in an arbitrary way during a time T, the average (or dc part) of the voltage during that time is just the *area* under the corresponding $v(t)$ curve, divided by the time T (see Figure A7–18a). Mathematically,

$$v_{ave} = T^{-1} \int_0^T v(t)\,dt$$

To calculate the average voltage of our train of pulses, let each pulse be of amplitude V_p and time duration T_d (see Figure A7–18b). Let the frequency of the peaks be f; then there are f pulses per second. In a time T there will be fT, each with a v area of V_pT_d. The total area under the pulse curve in time T is the number of pulses multiplied by the area of each, or fTV_pT_d. To calculate the average voltage v_{ave} during time T, we finally divide by T and obtain $v_{ave} = fV_pT_d$.

For example, if the pulse amplitude is 5 V and pulse duration is 0.25 seconds, we have $v_{ave} = 1.25f\,\text{Hz}^{-1}$ V. Then if the pulse frequency is 1 hertz, its average voltage is 1.25 V, while if the pulse frequency is 2 hertz, its average voltage is 2.5 V. This proportionality holds up to a maximum frequency of 4 Hz, for which the pulses abut each other, and the average voltage is clearly just the pulse amplitude voltage itself.

Figure A7–18c illustrates this example pulse-form input to a low-pass filter that is followed by a buffer amplifier and analog voltmeter. The time constant of the RC filter should be selected to be about 6 times longer than the *period* of the *lowest* frequency expected. Thus, the filter illustrated in Figure A7–18c will produce a reasonably well-filtered dc output that is proportional to frequency from about 0.3 hertz (or a 3-second period) to the upper limit of 4 hertz. The filter output is buffered with a voltage follower to isolate the high impedances of the filter from disturbance by the voltmeter load. Finally, a potentiometer is used as an amplitude adjustment. It permits adjustment of the meter to a convenient scale such as one volt per hertz. This adjustment is generally done during an initial calibration of the meter using an input pulse stream of known frequency from a function generator.

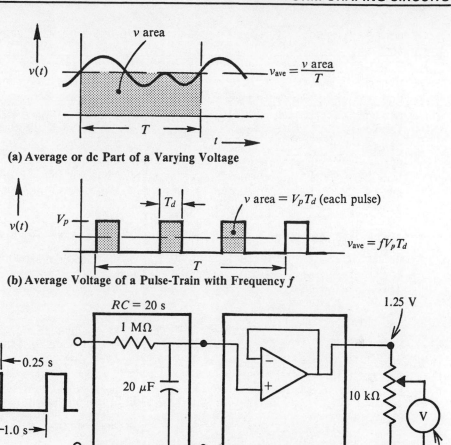

(a) **Average or dc Part of a Varying Voltage**

(b) **Average Voltage of a Pulse-Train with Frequency** f

(c) **Example Frequency Meter Using an Input Pulse-Train with Fixed 5-V Amplitude and 0.25 Second Duration Pulses (1.0-Hz Frequency)**

FIGURE A7–18. *Basic Functions in an Analog Frequency Meter or Ratemeter*

General Ratemeter Instrument

This example illustrates the application of many of the circuit types and principles, discussed in this and earlier chapters, to obtain a functional instrument. A block diagram of the example ratemeter instrument is presented in Figure A7–19, together with a representation of the signal as it passes through the instrument stages and is processed.

Block A of the instrument is the transducer, which senses the repetitive aspect of the experimental object. For example, it may be a photoresistor that senses darkening due to the spokes of a wheel as they pass or of the finger-

A263

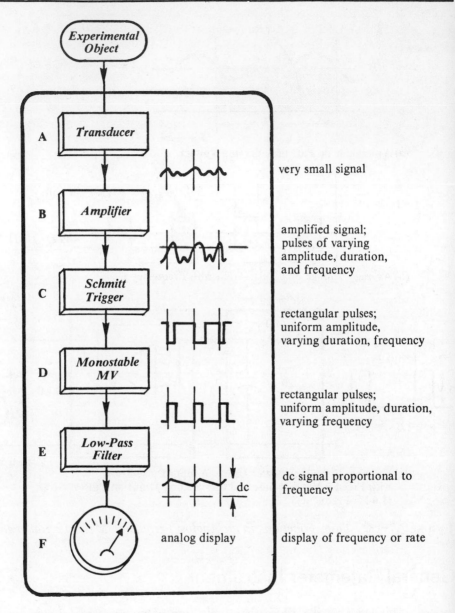

FIGURE A7-19. *A Ratemeter Instrument Constructed from Signal Processing Blocks*

tip each time blood moves into the capillaries. The photoresistor may be in a voltage divider circuit with capacitive coupling at the output to block the dc level but pass the voltage pulses. Note there is actually an ac signal from the repetitive process.

The ac signal from the transducer is generally quite small and must be processed next by an amplifier stage with voltage gain. The amplifier is shown as block B in the figure. However, the output from the amplifier will typically be pulses which vary somewhat in shape, amplitude, and duration. Also low-level noise pulses may be present in the signal. Therefore, the next signal processing step is block C—a Schmitt trigger that is set to discriminate against small spurious pulses and noise and produces rectangular output pulses of definite amplitude.

However, the Schmitt trigger output pulses may vary in duration, due to variations in the input pulse shape and its relationship to the threshold. Recall that the low-pass filter rate meter requires pulses of uniform duration as well as amplitude. Therefore, the Schmitt trigger output is presented to block D, a monostable multivibrator stage, which outputs a single uniform pulse for each input pulse.

Next the pulse train, which is now uniform in all respects but frequency, is presented to the low-pass filter in block E. The slowly varying dc voltage output from this stage is finally presented to an analog display such as a d'Arsonval meter. This meter may be marked with a convenient scale such as heartbeats per minute. Alternatively, a strip-chart recorder may be connected to obtain a convenient permanent record of the frequency versus time for many minutes, hours, or even days.

REVIEW EXERCISES

1. (a) A comparator box has 3 input/output connections. Tell what each is for.
   (b) Give another name for comparator.
2. A comparator constructed from an op amp uses which of the following: A. negative feedback, B. no feedback, C. positive feedback.
3. Suppose an op amp is used as a comparator and operates from power-supply voltages of ± 9 V. The comparator output is taken directly from the op-amp output. Someone asserts that a DVM connected to the comparator output will read any of a range of voltages between -9 V and $+9$ V while the comparator is being used. Criticize the statement.
4. (a) Consider the comparator circuit shown in Diagram A7–1. The output voltage will be close to (choose one): A. -12 V, B. -6 V, C. 0 V, D. $+6$ V, E. $+12$ V.
   (b) Which diode is forward biased and conducting: A. D_1, B. D_2, C. both, D. neither.
   (c) Repeat question (a) if the 1-V battery is reversed.
   (d) Repeat question (b) if the 1-V battery is reversed.

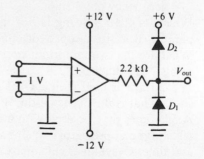

DIAGRAM A7–1.

5. What is the purpose of each diode in the above comparator circuit?
6. (a) What is the important difference between a comparator and a Schmitt trigger in terms of their behavior? What is the characteristic term used for the Schmitt-trigger behavior?
   (b) What feature of input signals often dictates use of a Schmitt trigger rather than a comparator?
7. A Schmitt trigger constructed from an op amp uses which of the following: A. negative feedback, B. no feedback, C. positive feedback.
8. The purpose of the voltage divider in the feedback circuit of the op-amp-based Schmitt trigger is to (choose one of the following): A. reduce the input signal before entering the op-amp input, B. clip the output signal at the ground, C. protect the op-amp output circuitry, D. produce two thresholds to the op-amp comparator.
9. A Schmitt trigger constructed from a single op amp has an inverting character. Explain this statement.
10. Consider the Schmitt-trigger circuit pictured in Diagram A7–2.
   (a) Which resistors are primarily responsible for the hysteresis of the trigger circuit?
   (b) Which resistors are primarily responsible for the average triggering level?

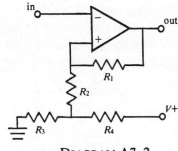

DIAGRAM A7–2.

11. Select a multivibrator type for each of the following tasks.
   (a) A pulse-output oscillator is needed.
   (b) A certain long-duration pulse out is required for each short-duration pulse in.
   (c) The frequency of a pulse train should be divided by 4 to obtain a lower-frequency pulse train.
12. Which of the following is *not* inside a 555 timer integrated circuit? A. comparator, B. resistor-capacitor combination, C. flip-flop, D. transistor switch.
13. What are the two important multivibrator types that may readily be obtained using a 555 timer IC?
14. A 555 timer is used with a 1-kΩ resistor and a 1-μF capacitor to make a one-shot. What is the expected duration of the output pulse?
15. A 555 timer may be used with a capacitor and two identical resistors to make which type of oscillator? A. sine wave, B. asymmetrical square wave in voltage and time, C. symmetrical square wave in voltage and time.
16. What are the two important threshold voltage levels inside the 555 timer IC (in terms of the supply voltage used)?
17. Why is a simple RC differentiating circuit sometimes required when using the 555 timer?

18. (a) Draw a simple *RC* differentiating circuit.
    (b) Describe in qualitative terms why two short pulses occur at the *RC*-circuit output in response to a single long pulse input.
    (c) What determines the duration of these short pulses?
19. (a) What is a sequencer?
    (b) Describe how a sequencer may readily be constructed from multivibrators.
20. Suppose the signal pictured in Diagram A7–3 is input to a good low-pass filter. What is the dc voltage expected from the filter?

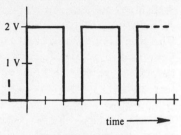

DIAGRAM A7–3.

21. (a) What is the difference between the output of the frequency information from a ratemeter as compared to a digital frequency counter?
    (b) Why is a Schmitt trigger often required in a ratemeter instrument?
    (c) Why is a monostable MV almost always required in a ratemeter instrument?

PROBLEMS

1. An op amp is operated from ±6-V supplies to form a comparator circuit as shown in Diagram A7–4. Give the output voltage for the following input voltage V_{in}:

    (a) −2 V   (d) +1 V
    (b) −1 V   (e) +2 V
    (c)   0 V

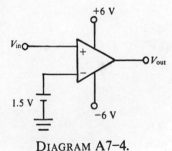

DIAGRAM A7–4.

2. The op amp in the circuit shown in Diagram A7–5 is to serve as a voltage level detector relative to a reference level of −9 V. Describe why the circuit will *not* work. Suggest a change so that it may function properly.

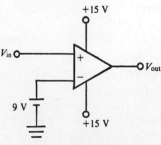

DIAGRAM A7–5.

A267

3. Design a comparator that produces a high voltage out equal to +6 V when the input voltage is greater than +3 V and a low voltage out of −6 V when the input voltage is less than +3 V. The comparator is to be constructed from an op amp that is operated from ±12 V power-supply voltages. Two designs may be developed.

    (a) Do a rather simple design that uses only diodes and appropriate batteries along with the op amp and ±12-V power supply.

        NOTE: Assume self-current-limiting by the op amp.

    (b) Diagram a design that requires no batteries; diode and resistors are to be used (along with the op amp and ±12-V power supply). Arrange to have about 20-mA current drain from the ±12-V supplies and to have the op-amp output current limited to 2 mA.

4. Suppose we want a comparator that switches its output from 0 V to +5 V in 0.5 μsec. Discuss why the 741 op amp could *not* do the job. Suggest an op amp that might and justify your choice.

5. Consider the Schmitt trigger shown in Diagram A7-6. Assume the output switches between +10 and −10 V. The reference voltage is +3 V as shown. Find the two switching levels and also evaluate the hysteresis width for the unit. Show that it agrees with the formula in the text. Is the center of the two levels at 3 V?

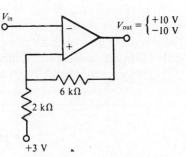

DIAGRAM A7-6.

6. Block-diagram a circuit that performs as a square-wave oscillator. It should have a precisely symmetrical square-wave output in terms of time, with some frequency *f*. Use two devices from the multivibrator family.

7 Assume that in response to a certain negative input pulse, a process *A* is to be turned on for one of three possible time periods: 1 second, 2 seconds, or 3 seconds. These time periods are to be switch selectable by an operator. At the conclusion of process *A*, there is to be a 5-second delay, after which process *B* is turned on for 10 seconds. Diagram a design that assumes a block model and timing relationships such as those shown in Figure A7-7 for the monostable MVs used.

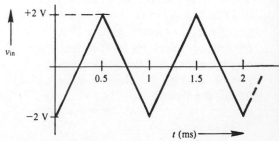

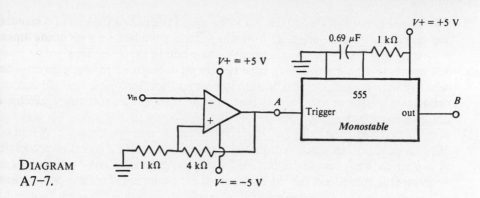

DIAGRAM
A7-7.

8. (a) A symmetrical triangle-wave voltage that is 4 V_{p-p} with 1-kHz frequency is illustrated in Diagram A7-7. Suppose this voltage is input as v_{in} to the circuit shown. Draw with some accuracy the time graphs of the voltages v_A and v_B appearing at points A and B in the circuit.

(b) What problem (perhaps unanticipated) occurs with the signal at B if the capacitor for the 555 timer is made less than about 0.5 μF in this application?

9. We have a design problem where pressing push button PB1 should cause a 6-V_{dc} motor to begin running. Subsequently, pressing push button PB2 causes the motor to stop. A design based on the 555 timer IC is shown in Diagram A7-8.

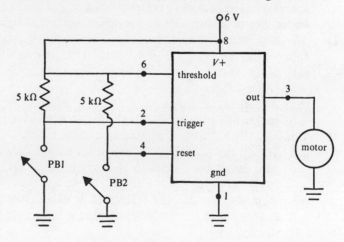

DIAGRAM
A7-8.

(a) Justify that a negative pulse to ground is input to the particular 555 input when a push button is pressed. (The trigger and reset inputs have high resistance.) Which push-button type should be used, NO or NC?

(b) Draw the circuit, filling in the interior model for the 555 timer. Justify that the circuit will perform the desired function. What current limitation is placed on the motor?

(c) Suppose the threshold input is to be used rather than the reset (threshold and trigger have very high input impedance, similar to an op amp). Illustrate and justify briefly the push-button circuit then required.

10. We want a small lamp in a rat's cage to turn on in response to the rat pressing a sensitive snap-action switch. The light is to turn on for 2 seconds. Assume that we conveniently have at hand lamps that operate from 6 V at 100 mA. Develop a design using a 555 timer.

11. Assume that a certain timing sequence is required for three processes A, B, and C. When a push button is pressed, process A is turned on for 2 seconds; process B is also immediately turned on, but for 5 seconds. At the termination of process B, process C is turned on for 20 seconds. Use 555 timers, and a 1-MΩ timing resistor in each case. (Low leakage tantalum electrolytic capacitors are assumed.) It is not necessary to draw in the interior functions in the 555 timers, but connections to their input/output pins should be shown and the pins labeled. Note that one differentiating circuit is required. Explain why.

12. A 555 timer is used with a 1-μF capacitor and two 1-kΩ resistors to make an oscillator. The power supply voltage is 6 V.
   (a) What is the frequency of the output signal?
   (b) Make a moderately accurate graph of the output signal as a function of time.

13. Research demonstrates that rats can generate and sense ultrasonic sounds. We want a 30-kHz tone of 2-second duration to be produced near a rat's cage in response to the rat pressing a sensitive snap-action switch. Assume an ultrasonic sound transducer that operates from a signal level of 6 V_{p-p} and has an input impedance of 200 Ω. Develop a design using 555 timers.

14. The *duty cycle* of an asymmetrical square wave (in time) is usually defined as the ratio of the time that the signal is high to the overall period of the wave.
   (a) Show that for the 555 timer, the duty cycle is given by $(R_A + R_B)/(R_A + 2R_B)$.
   (b) Argue that the duty cycle may be adjusted between 50% and 100%. Characterize the ratio R_A/R_B for these two extremes, respectively.

15. Consider the 555 timer operated in astable mode.
   (a) Justify the statement (actually somewhat careless) that reducing R_A to zero causes the output to be a symmetrical square wave in terms of time (50% duty cycle).
   (b) Demonstrate that the statement is careless because, if $R_A = 0$, the discharge switch (a transistor) within the 555 would be destroyed. What would destroy it?
   NOTE: The minimum value for R_A shown on the manufacturer's graph is 1-kΩ.

16. (a) The bias current into the threshold input of the 555 timer is specified as typically 0.1 μA (with a maximum of 0.25 μA). Assume that a typical 555 device is used in conjunction with a 6-V supply to make a long-pulse monostable. Show that if the timing resistor R exceeds 20 MΩ, the pulse cannot terminate.

NOTE: Thus the bias current limits the use of very large timing resistors. The LM322 monostable typically has a 0.3-nA bias current.

(b)   One electrolytic capacitor family is specified to have a minimum leakage resistance given by $R = 50/C$ ΩF, where C is in farads. This resistance appears in parallel with the ideal capacitor. For example, if $C = 10$ μF then $R = 5$ MΩ. Note that large capacity implies smaller resistance and more leakage current. Assume that a 1-MΩ timing resistor is used with a 555 timer as a monostable. Show that if the timing capacitor C exceeds 25 μF for this type of electrolytic family, the pulse cannot terminate.

NOTE: Selected standard electrolytic capacitors can have a factor-of-10-lower leakage current and therefore higher leakage resistance than this example; selected tantalum electrolytics can be a factor of 100 better.

17.   Rectangular pulses with 12-V amplitude and 2-msec duration are input to a low-pass filter that is part of a ratemeter.

(a)   What is the maximum operating frequency for this ratemeter, and what is the voltage out of the filter at this frequency?

(b)   If the frequency of the pulses is 50 Hz, what is the dc voltage out of the filter?

18.   (a)   What is the disadvantage of making the time constant of the low-pass filter in a ratemeter very long; for example, 10 minutes?

(b)   What problem exists if the time constant of the filter is made short; for example, equal to the period of the incoming pulse train?

CHAPTER
A8

Discrete Electronic Devices

We now begin the study of *discrete active devices;* that is, basic single electronic elements such as a vacuum triode, bipolar transistor, or field-effect transistor that can be used in a circuit to increase the power level of a voltage signal. Note that the additional power does not come from the device itself, but rather from the power supply.

The low price of IC operational amplifiers has revolutionized much of analog electronics, almost to the point of wondering why bother with transistors or tubes (discrete devices) at all? We do in fact scale down their consideration greatly in this book; a brief overview is given, however, to better understand the limitations and requirements of integrated circuits, as well as to permit some understanding of older circuitry when it is encountered. Also, in some situations a transistor is quite simple to apply and is all that is required. For example, when simple current amplification is required, the bipolar transistor is a convenient device. If electronic switching of rather high current or high voltage is required, transistors—or in ac circuits, the SCR perhaps aided by a transistor—are very useful devices. This book develops a proficiency in transistor circuits to this level of application; it does *not* consider the broad field of transistor amplifier design.

General Amplifier Model

General Electronic Current-Controlling Element

The various electronic devices that are used in amplifier circuits to cause the circuits to do their "magic" of increasing power level all operate on one principle: They control the current passing through them in response to a low-power input voltage/current. A simple analogy is the water flowing through a garden hose (see Figure A8–1). By squeezing on the sides of the hose, we can control the stream of water through the hose. If we use pliers or some clamp with mechanical advantage, it is possible to control a powerful stream of water passing through the hose. The water pressure comes from an external pump, of course.

A vacuum tube or transistor behaves like such an element; it controls the current that a battery or power supply attempts to force through it. In fact, the British use the descriptive term *valve* rather than vacuum tube. Only a small voltage or current input (like the pliers force) is needed to effect the control.

Figure A8–2 illustrates a general active or current-controlling device with a control input lead to which voltage V_{in} is applied and two main current-carrying wires that carry the current to be controlled I_T. (T may represent transistor or tube here.) Note that three basic connections are involved. The most important parameter characterizing an active device is its *mutual transconductance* g_m. The mutual transconductance is simply the ratio of the *current change produced* to the *input voltage change* that caused it. Let ΔI_T be this change in device current, while ΔV_{in} is this change in control input voltage V_{in}. We may write

$$g_m = \frac{\Delta I_T}{\Delta V_{in}} \qquad\qquad \text{(A8–1)}$$

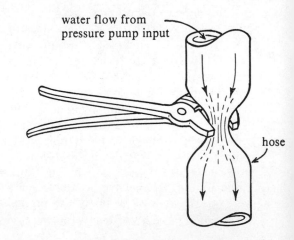

water flow from
pressure pump input

hose

FIGURE A8–1. *Analogy of an Active Electronic Device*

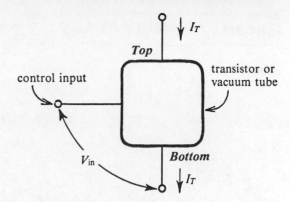

FIGURE A8–2. *General Elec-tronic Active Device*

Notice that the dimensions of this quantity are amperes/volts = 1/ohms, or reciprocal ohms. The reciprocal of resistance is called *conductance,* and the unit for conductance has long been called the *mho.* Transconductance for transistors and tubes is typically given in millimhos or micromhos.

General Discrete Amplifiers

An amplifier is constructed by use of a resistor and power supply as shown in Figure A8–3. The dc voltage supply causes a current I_T to flow through R_L, which is in series with the transistor (or tube). The bias voltage at (or current into) the control lead establishes the value of this current. A voltage then develops across R_L and also across the transistor. V_b is usually chosen so that about half the supply voltage appears across R_L and half across the transistor; this is the *steady or operating situation.*

When an ac voltage is applied to the input (shown as v_{in} in Figure A8–3), it passes through the *coupling capacitor* C_{in} to the control lead for the transistor; consequently, the transistor permits more or less current to flow through it. A variation in I_T—that is, ΔI_T—occurs that is proportional to v_{in}. From Equation A8–1 the variation is given by

$$\Delta I_T = g_m v_{in} \tag{A8–2}$$

This varying current through R_L causes a variation in the voltage across R_L in the amount

$$\Delta V_{R_L} = \Delta I_T R_L = g_m v_{in} R_L \tag{A8–3}$$

But the voltage at the top of R_L is fixed at the supply voltage, V_{supply} (relative to ground). Therefore, the voltage at point T (bottom end of R_L and top of transistor/tube) must *vary* by the amount given in Equation A8–3. We see shortly that this voltage becomes the ac voltage out of the amplifier.

A graph of V_T relative to ground (the voltage across the transistor/ tube) and of v_{in} are shown in Figure A8–4. Notice that there is an ac voltage

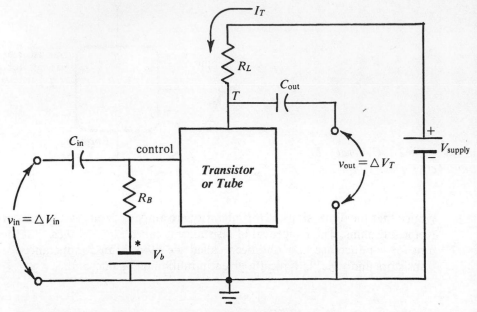

*(+) if bipolar transistor; (−) if junction FET or tube

FIGURE A8-3. *General Discrete Component Amplifier*

superposed or added to a large dc voltage. Hopefully, the ac voltage is a larger replica of the input voltage. A *blocking capacitor* C_{out} is connected between point T and the amplifier output as shown in Figure A8-3. This blocks the dc component of the voltage at T, but passes the ac to the output. The amount of the output voltage (peak-peak) is noted in Figure A8-4.

Note that V_T swings *down* while v_{in} swings *up*. This is because in the typical configuration of the tube or transistor, the current through the transistor/tube (as well as R_L) increases when $V_{control}$ increases. Then the increasing current through R_L causes an increasing voltage across the resistor R_L and a decreasing voltage across the transistor. Consequently, there is a *180° phase reversal* between the input and output signals.

We have the ac voltage out of the amplifier from Equation A8-3. It is

$$v_{out} = -(g_m R_L)v_{in}$$

In this relation for v_{out}, a minus sign has been inserted to take into account the 180° phase reversal or inversion of the output voltage relative to the input voltage. Then

$$A_v = \frac{v_{out}}{v_{in}} = -g_m R_L \qquad (A8-4)$$

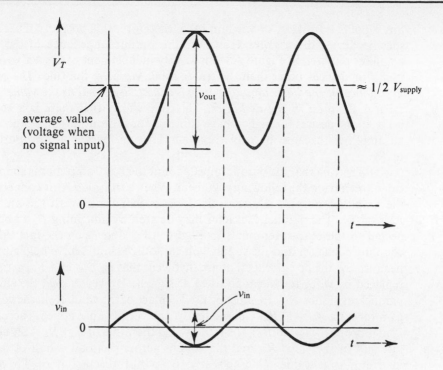

FIGURE A8–4. *Graph of Active Device Voltage and Input Voltage for a Typical Amplifier*

The ratio of the output voltage to the input voltage of an amplifier is called the *voltage amplification* or the *voltage gain A_v* of the amplifier, as discussed in general terms in Chapter A5. We therefore have the following general rule: *The amplification of a basic amplifier is simply the transconductance of the device times the load resistance used.*

Because of various small effects that are present in real discrete devices, this rule is only a good approximation to the voltage gain. Nevertheless, it is quite sufficient for many scientific purposes and certainly for the purposes of this book. The rule applies equally well to the operation of an important class of amplifier constructed from one of the various types of field-effect transistors, a bipolar transistor, or a pentode tube; the rule holds less accurately if a triode tube is used as the active device. The general mode of operation for these various active devices is presented in the following sections. Specific basic amplifier designs are also briefly illustrated and discussed.

We know from Chapter A5 that the input and output impedances of an amplifier are very important amplifier properties, and they will be discussed here. The input impedance of the basic amplifier shown in Figure A8–3 depends largely upon whether the active device is a field-effect transistor, bipolar transistor, or vacuum tube; therefore, this property must await specific device discussions. However, the output impedance of the basic amplifier pictured in Figure A8–3 is largely independent of the active device used, for devices other than the triode tube. We have the rule: *The output impedance of the basic amplifier type is essentially equal to the value of the resistor R_L used in the amplifier.* This rule shows that there is a conflict between the desires for high voltage gain and for low output impedance from an amplifier, because both of these amplifier properties are proportional to R_L.

The rule that the output impedance of the basic amplifier is simply R_L can be seen from the following argument. When a *true load* $R_{L'}$ is connected to the amplifier output, it effectively appears in parallel with the amplifier resistor R_L. The parallel character may be seen by imagining $R_{L'}$ to be connected to the output terminals in Figure A8–3 and using the fact that the coupling capacitor and the supply voltage source should have negligible impedance for the ac currents that are involved; that is, C_{out} and V_{supply} may be replaced by wires for the analysis of ac signals. However, then the effective parallel resistance $R_L \| R_{L'}$ must be used in place of the value R_L in the voltage-gain formula $A_v = g_m R_L$. Consequently, the voltage that appears across the load is proportional to $R_L \| R_{L'}$. If $R_L = R_{L'}$, the value of $R_L \| R_{L'}$ is reduced to just half of the value R_L, and the voltage across the load is half of the unloaded output value. Consequently, from our discussion of Thevenin's Theorem in Chapter A1, we see that the output impedance of the amplifier must be R_L.

NOTE: The term *basic* amplifier has been used for the circuit configuration shown in Figure A8–3. The important feature of this configuration is that the *bottom* lead of the active device pictured in Figure A8–2 is shown connected to *ground* in Figure A8–3. Notice that the bottom lead is the reference lead for the voltage V_{in} as it is presented to the control input. The formal term for this basic amplifier type is *grounded-X amplifier,* where X is the name for the bottom lead of the specific active device used. We shall see that X is *cathode* for vacuum tube, *source* for field-effect transistor, and *emitter* for bipolar transistor.

Vacuum Tubes

Vacuum Triode

The first electronic amplifying device, the *vacuum triode,* was invented by Lee De Forest in 1906. Although now used very seldom in new designs, it remains the easiest current-controlling element to understand. A wire spiral is introduced between the cathode and plate of the diode in Figure A4–3a to produce the *triode*. Figure A8–5a shows the triode structure, while Figure A8–5b gives the conventional schematic symbol.

Plenty of space is afforded by the wire of the grid for electrons to pass readily through it to the plate. Indeed, if the grid is connected directly to the cathode, the current through the device as a function of the *plate voltage* connected between the plate and the cathode shows just the same behavior as that for the vacuum diode. If the grid is made negative relative to the cathode, however, the current flowing through the tube can be greatly reduced because the electrons tend to be repelled back toward the cathode. Figure A8–5c shows the electron behavior in a graphic way. (Note that the filament connection is omitted from the drawing; this omission is conventional.) Thus, the grid becomes the current-controlling input so essential for an amplifying device. For further discussion of the triode, see the first supplement to this chapter.

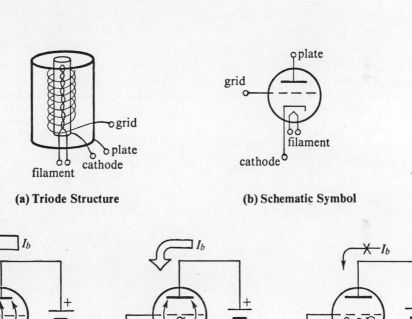

(a) **Triode Structure**

(b) **Schematic Symbol**

No Bias, Large Current

Negative Bias, Reduced Current

Large Bias, Current Cut Off

(c) **Diagram of Basic Vacuum Triode Electron Action**

FIGURE A8–5. *Vacuum Triode*

Vacuum Tetrode and Pentode

Because of the capacitance between the control-grid and the plate structures, the triode is generally not well suited to radio-frequency amplifier applications; therefore, a *screen grid* was early introduced between the control grid and the plate. Then 4 important structures exist in this tube, and it is called a *tetrode*. However, the electrical characteristic for the tetrode has a problem that tends to produce unwanted oscillations. Therefore, still an additional grid structure was introduced between the screen grid and the plate; the resulting tube is called a *pentode*. Although vacuum tubes have been largely superseded by transistors, the pentode has continued to be used in high-frequency applications that involve large amounts of power. Only recently has there appeared a type of field-effect transistor that threatens to displace the pentode in this area. Indeed, the electrical characteristics and circuitry for the FET and the pentode are very similar, although only the FET is discussed in some detail in this book. Notice that the cathode-ray tube is, in fact, a special-purpose vacuum tube.

Field-Effect Transistors and Amplifiers

The simplest transistor type to understand is the *field-effect transistor* (FET). Although it became widely available in the mid-1960s, some years after the bipolar transistor, it had actually been proposed much earlier; however, semiconductor fabrication techniques had not been adequate at that time. The FET combines many of the best features of the vacuum tube and the transistor. It has a voltage-controlled input with a high effective resistance like the vacuum tube; on the other hand it is compact and lacks the vacuum tube's heat-producing and power-hungry filament (the bipolar transistor also has no filament).

N-Channel Junction FET

The schematic construction of the *N-channel junction field-effect transistor* is shown in Figure A8–6a. We can think of taking a bar of N-type semiconductor—which has a modest number of electrons as charge carriers—and constructing a region of P-type semiconductor on its side. Recall from Chapter A4 that a P-type semiconductor has holes that behave like plus charges as the majority charge carrier. The body of P-type material in contact with the body of N-type material constitutes a PN junction; hence the name junction FET, or JFET. Recall also from Chapter A4 that a junction of P- and N-type semiconductors such as we now have constitutes a diode

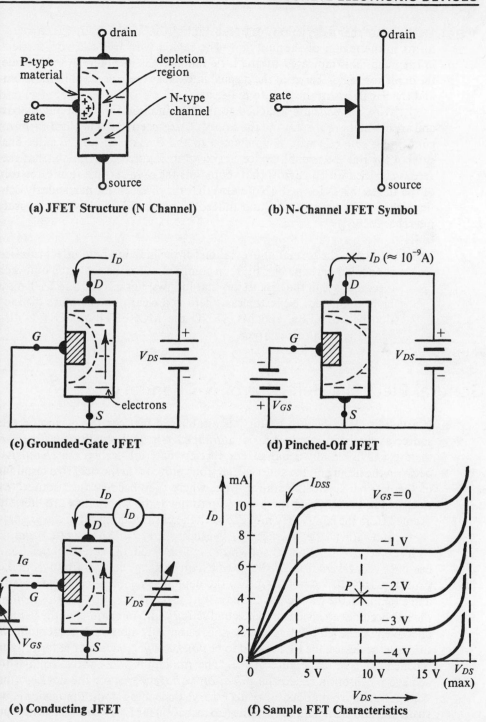

(a) JFET Structure (N Channel)

(b) N-Channel JFET Symbol

(c) Grounded-Gate JFET

(d) Pinched-Off JFET

(e) Conducting JFET

(f) Sample FET Characteristics

FIGURE A8–6. *Junction Field-Effect Transistor (JFET) for the N-Channel Case*

A281

junction and that a depletion zone (substantially lacking any charge carriers) forms in the region of the junction. The region with free electron carriers in the material is indicated by the little minus signs in Figure A8–6a, while the depletion region between the dashed lines lacks the − carriers in the N bar and the + carriers in the P-gate material.

Wires or *leads* are attached to the top and bottom of the N-type bar and are called the *drain* (*D*) and the *source* (*S*), respectively. The third current-controlling *gate* (*G*) wire is connected to the P material on the side. The symbol for this 3-terminal device is shown in Figure A8–6b; note that the gate is signified with an arrow that represents the easy-current-flow direction of the diode that is formed. (Note also that the drain is not particularly distinguishable from the source, and indeed on some JFETs they can be used interchangeably.)

NOTE: Although the formal abbreviation for the junction field-effect transistor should perhaps be JFET, in common usage the J is often omitted. Accordingly, in the discussion that follows, both JFET and FET may be encountered. Nevertheless, there is a clear nomenclature distinction between FET and MOSFET; the MOSFET-type FET is discussed later in this chapter.

General Electrical Behavior of N-Channel JFET

If a voltage V_{DS} (the V_{DS} battery) is established between the drain and the source as shown in Figure A8–6c, a *drain current* I_D flows quite easily since there exists essentially a bar of conducting material—called the *channel*—between the drain and the source. Electrons move from the negative terminal of the V_{DS} battery to the source wire, where they become the "source" of electrons in the bar, and then move up to the drain, where they are literally drained from the bar as they move toward the positive terminal of the battery.

If a rather large voltage V_{GS} is established to make the gate *negative* with respect to the source as shown in Figure A8–6d, the gate-channel diode becomes very *reverse biased*. Then only a tiny leakage current flows from the gate (typically 10^{-9} A = 1 nA), but the depletion region is enlarged greatly and extends all the way across the bar. With no carriers existing in this region, the bar becomes an insulator. The conducting width or channel of the bar has effectively been pinched to zero, and essentially no drain current flows through the device; the FET is said to be *pinched off*. Notice the analogy to the pinched-off hose of Figure A8–1. The minimum gate-source voltage to achieve pinch-off is called the *pinch-off voltage* $V_{GS,\text{off}}$ for the device. This voltage varies from about −2 V to −15 V, depending upon the device construction, and is even quite variable (up to ±50%) for FETs with the same type number from a given manufacturer.

Electrical Characteristics of N-Channel JFET

To study the characteristics of an FET in conditions between the *conducting-hard* and the *cutoff* situations, a circuit to establish variable gate-source and drain-source voltages and to measure the resulting drain current is constructed as shown in Figure A8–6e. First suppose the gate-source voltage V_{GS} is set to zero (basically the gate is shorted to the source as in Figure A8–6c) and the drain-source voltage V_{DS} is slowly increased from zero. Observing the drain-current meter, we find that at first I_D increases quite linearly with increasing V_{DS} (just as current increases with the voltage across a resistor) until V_{DS} approaches the value of the pinch-off voltage for the unit. The I_D behavior is plotted in Figure A8–6f as the $V_{GS} = 0$ line that rises at an angle from the origin. Notice that the current I_D is plotted versus the drain-source voltage V_{DS} across the device.

When the drain-source voltage increases further, however, something rather surprising happens: The drain current levels off and remains virtually constant with increasing V_{DS}. The reason is a voltage drop (IR drop) along the resistive N-channel material. If the gate is at ground potential (relative to source) and the channel region near the top of the bar is at a voltage V_{DS}, the gate is negative relative to the channel by about this voltage. Thus, the gate-channel diode junction is *reverse biased* by the amount V_{DS}, and a large depletion zone is produced that tends to pinch off the channel. However, the current does not stop because the IR drop would then vanish and the channel would open again; instead, a narrow channel forms that becomes longer with increased V_{DS} so that the current flow remains practically constant.

Notice for the example FET of Figure A8–6f that for $V_{GS} = 0$ the drain current levels off at 10 milliamperes when the drain-source voltage is greater than about 4 V. This current value is called the *saturation current* I_{DSS} for the particular FET and is the maximum current that the device will pass. If the gate-source voltage V_{GS} is put equal to -1 V, the current increases more slowly from zero due to the smaller channel and levels off at a lower current of about 7 milliamperes (again when the drain-source voltage V_{DS} exceeds about 4 V). Similar behavior is seen for other V_{GS} voltages until finally, when $V_{GS} = -4$ V, the channel is pinched off and no current flows through the device. In normal amplifier operation the FET is operated in the region of the graph where the current curves are almost horizontal; that is, I_{DS} is independent of V_{DS}.

JFET Operating Limitations

An important practical limitation of any transistor is illustrated in the FET characteristic curves of Figure A8–6f. Notice that the current increases sharply as the drain-source voltage approaches $V_{DS,\max}$. This large current can quickly destroy the transistor, and the FET must be operated with V_{DS} less than this value. The particular FET type will therefore have a maximum safe operating V_{DS} specified by the manufacturer. In addition, the device should not dissipate power above a certain maximum, specified by the manufacturer as the *maximum device dissipation*. If this limit is ignored, the FET will quickly overheat and become ruined. The power dissipated in the FET is simply *the current through the FET times the voltage across it,* or $I_D V_{DS}$. Small FETs have typically been capable of only 1/2- to 1-watt dissipation and a maximum of 30 V to 50 V for the drain-source voltage.

However, recently high-power and high-voltage types have become available (for example, up to 600-V V_{DS} and 100-watts dissipation). These devices are actually a particular type of FET called the MOSFET, which is introduced later in this chapter. The high-power/high-voltage type of MOSFET is constructed with a *vertical* geometry over an area of semiconductor chip; hence, it is often called VMOS. Since the drain current is dispersed over greater area than in the *planer* technology of conventional transistors, greater current and power is possible.

N-Channel JFET in an Amplifier

Figure A8–7a shows a basic *grounded-source amplifier*. This circuit uses a separate *bias battery* V_{GG}, as well as a *supply battery* V_{DD}. The V_{GG} bias voltage is usually chosen to set the current flowing through the FET to a value such that the voltage across R_L ($V_{R_L} = I_D R_L$) is about half of the supply voltage V_{DD}. This bias rule is in accord with typical amplifier practice discussed in connection with Figure A5–6, and again with Figure A8–4. Then about half the supply voltage also appears across the FET as V_{DS}. Notice that the bias-battery voltage is arranged so that the gate of the N-channel FET is made *negative* relative to the source because we require the FET's gate-channel diode to be reverse biased. The operation of this amplifier now follows the general discussion given for Figure A8–3 and Figure A8–4.

The basic amplifier pictured in Figure A8–7a has some typical values written in for resistors, voltages, and capacitors. We discuss the amplifier by answering a number of questions using the illustrated circuit values and by assuming that the FET used has the characteristics shown in Figure A8–6f.

Example: Working from Figure A8–6f and Figure A8–7a:

1. What is the gate-source bias for the amplifier?
2. What is the drain current I_D, the voltage across R_L, and the V_{DS} voltage for the FET?
3. What power is dissipated in the FET?
4. Find the *operating point* for the FET on its characteristic graph.

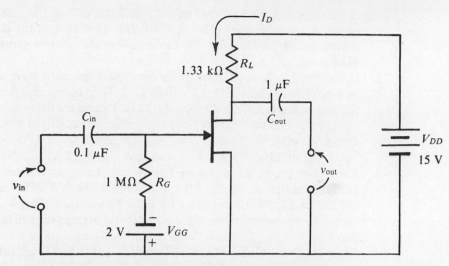

(a) Grounded-Source JFET Amplifier Using a Bias Battery
As Well As Supply Battery

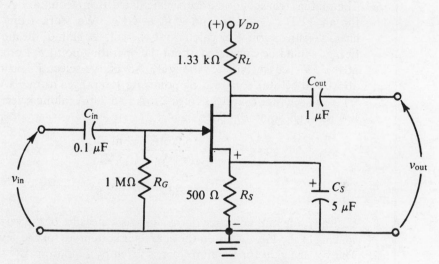

(b) Self-Biased, Grounded-Source JFET Amplifier

FIGURE A8–7. *JFET Grounded-Source Amplifier*

5. What is the mutual transconductance for the FET?
6. Calculate the expected voltage gain for this amplifier. If 0.05 V peak-peak is applied to the input, what voltage is expected at the output?

Solution:
1. The gate-source voltage is established by the bias battery V_{GG}. Be-

cause there is a gate current of only perhaps 10^{-9} A, the voltage across R_G is very small (10^{-9} A $\times 10^6$ $\Omega = 10^{-3}$ V), and the gate-source voltage is virtually the same as the V_{GG} battery voltage, namely -2 V.

2. If $V_{GS} = -2$ V, from Figure A8–6f we expect the drain current to be 4 mA (assuming V_{DS} is more than 4 V). Then the voltage across the R_L resistor is $I_D R_L = 4$ mA $\times 1.33$ kΩ. To find the drain-source voltage V_{DS}, we realize that the supply voltage equals the voltage across R_L plus the drain-source voltage across the FET: $V_{DD} = V_{R_L} + V_{DS}$ or 15 V = 5.3 V $+ V_{DS}$ so that $V_{DS} = 9.7$ V.

3. The power dissipated in the FET is the voltage across it times the current through it: $V_{DS}I_D = 9.7$ V $\times 4$ mA $= 39$ mW. The heat-dissipation capabilities of the FET must be greater than this, but should be no problem here since even low-power units can manage 500 mW.

4. Since $V_{DS} = 9.3$ V and $V_{GS} = -2$ V (and $I_D = 4$ mA), the operating point can be plotted on the graph of Figure A8–6f as being at point P.

5. The mutual transconductance is calculated from Equation A8–1; for an FET $\Delta I_T = \Delta I_D$ and $\Delta V_{in} = \Delta V_{GS}$. We work from the characteristic graph. For calculating the voltage gain of the amplifier, g_m should be calculated about the operating point P. Looking at the FET characteristic in Figure A8–6f, we select V_{GS} curves above and below the operating point. As V_{GS} ranges from -3 V to -1 V, we see that I_D ranges from 2 mA to 6.7 mA (along a vertical line through point P). Then

$$g_m = \frac{\Delta I_D}{\Delta V_{GS}} = \frac{(6.7 \text{ mA} - 2 \text{ mA})}{(-1 \text{ V}) - (-3 \text{ V})}$$

$$= \frac{4.7 \text{ mA}}{2 \text{ V}} = 2.3 \times 10^{-3} \text{ mhos}$$

Basically, the mutual transconductance is a measure of the vertical spacing of the V_{GS} curves on the characteristic curves for the device.

6. The voltage gain for the amplifier is given by Equation A8–4.

$$A_v = -g_m R_L = -2.3 \times 10^{-3} \text{ mhos} \times 1.33 \text{ k}\Omega = -3.0$$

If an input signal of 0.05 V peak-peak is applied to the input, we expect an output signal of

$$V_{out} = A_v v_{in} = 3 \times 0.05 \text{ V} = 0.15 \text{ V}_{p-p}$$

A few comments about the behavior of this amplifier are in order. Notice that the accuracy of the voltage-gain calculation relies on an accurate knowledge of g_m. Often, this is not accurately known for FETs "merely picked from the drawer"; this is a significant advantage of the op-amp design approach, where the gain is known as accurately as the circuit resistance values are known. However, the FET circuit can be expected to operate to high radio frequencies (perhaps 100 megahertz) that cannot generally be expected from op amps.

Notice, too, that the voltage gain is really rather low. This gain could be improved in either of two ways. First, an FET with a higher transconductance could be used; values to 1.5×10^{-2} mhos are quite common. Second, a larger R_L value could be used, but there is a penalty. As we saw in the general amplifier discussion earlier, the output impedance of the amplifier is essentially equal to R_L; it is usually desirable that this value not be too high.

Self-Biased JFET Amplifier

Next we examine the *self-biased amplifier* of Figure A8–7b. It is a nuisance to need two batteries or power supplies as shown in Figure A8–7a. The essential requirement in biasing the FET here is that the gate be somewhat negative relative to the source. This is usually accomplished by connecting the one end of resistance R_G to ground and introducing a resistance R_S between the source and ground as shown in Figure A8–7b. The current I_D flowing through R_S causes the source to be positive relative to ground as shown in the figure. However, the gate is nearly at ground (very little leakage current flows through the gate and through R_G to ground). Thus, the gate is negative relative to the source as required. The value of R_S is chosen by the fact that $V_{RS} = I_D R_S$ equals the gate-bias voltage V_{GS}.

The capacitor C_S smooths out the ac voltage that tends to develop across R_S when amplifying an ac voltage (we want a dc voltage across R_S). The resulting amplifier is called a *grounded-source amplifier,* even though the source is *not* at dc ground (as it is in Figure A8–7a). However, it *is* at ac ground if a large capacitor C_S is used because the small reactance of the capacitor effectively shorts ac currents to ground.

The input impedance of the FET amplifier is quite evident from Figure A8–7a. The resistance presented to the input voltage is just R_G (here 1 megohm) because the parallel resistance through the back-biased gate-source FET diode junction is very high. We might think that the input impedance could be made very high just by choosing a very large value for R_G or even leaving it out completely, but this is not true; a path must be provided for the leakage current through the gate-source diode. Typically, 10 megohms is the maximum recommended value.

P-Channel JFET

The FET type pictured in Figure A8–6 and discussed thus far has a channel for carrier flow constructed of N-type material. The complementary possibility is to use P-type material for the channel and a region of N-type material on the side as the gate, as shown in Figure A8–8a. The resulting device is called a *P-channel FET*. The easy-current-flow direction for the gate-channel diode junction is now *out* of the gate, and the arrow drawn on the gate of the N-channel symbol reflects this (see Figure A8–8b). When used, the gate-source diode must always be reverse biased, so the gate must be made positive relative to the source for the P-channel type; then the drain is made negative. The consequence is that the polarities of the supply voltage must be *reversed* for the P-channel JFET as compared to the N-channel JFET; otherwise, the circuit design considerations are identical, and the representative form for the grounded-source-type amplifier is shown in Figure A8–8c.

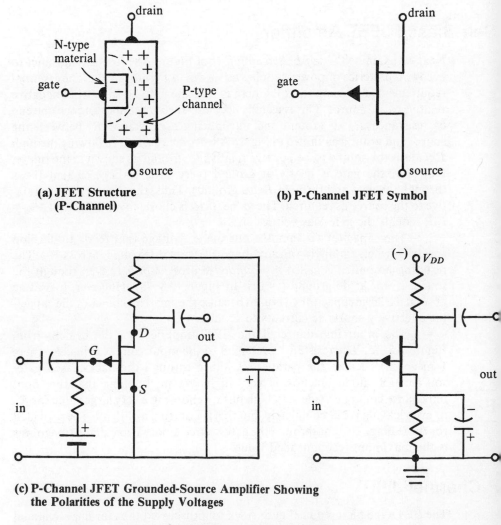

(a) **JFET Structure (P-Channel)**

(b) **P-Channel JFET Symbol**

(c) **P-Channel JFET Grounded-Source Amplifier Showing the Polarities of the Supply Voltages**

FIGURE A8–8. *P-Channel JFET and Circuit Polarities*

It should be emphasized that the gate is made quite positive relative to the source in order to pinch off the P-channel JFET, while we saw that the N-channel JFET requires a quite negative gate-to-source voltage. This complementary behavior can be useful in logic or switching circuits.

Metal-Oxide-Silicon FET (MOSFET)

While the input current is very small for the JFET amplifier (only the gate-channel-diode reverse-bias leakage), it is made astonishingly small for the *metal-oxide-silicon field-effect transistor* or MOSFET. The scheme is basically to put a layer of electrical insulation—typically silicon dioxide—between the metal gate plate and the silicon channel. The order of materials here is the reason for the name of this device. Of course the insulation restricts the current through the gate to very small values, typically 10^{-14} amperes.

Two different structures exist for MOSFETs, giving the depletion type and the enhancement type. The operation of the *depletion-type MOSFET* is very similar to the JFET: A negative gate-source voltage is required to pinch off the current through the N-channel version, while a positive V_{GS} is required for the complementary P-channel version. The symbols for these two versions are shown in Figure A8–9a. Notice that the gate is drawn as not electrically connected to the drain-to-source channel because it is insulated from it.

The *enhancement-type MOSFET* actually has a physical break in the channel so that no current flows through the device unless its gate is properly biased with respect to the source. To obtain device current, the gate must be positively biased relative to the source for the N-channel version, while the gate must be negatively biased relative to the source for the complementary P-channel version. The circuit symbols for the enhancement-type MOSFET are shown in Figure A8–9b; notice the breaks in each symbol's line joining the drain to the source that indicate the channel construction. For a more detailed discussion of the construction and mode of operation for MOSFETs, see the second supplement to this chapter.

Bipolar Transistors and Amplifiers

The invention of the transistor in 1948 at Bell Telephone Laboratories has revolutionized electronics. Its chief advantages relative to the vacuum tube are: (1) a much smaller size, (2) no heat-producing and power-consuming filament, and (3) a long, useful life. In a vacuum tube—similar to a light bulb—the filament eventually burns out; also the cathode loses its electron-emitting capability.

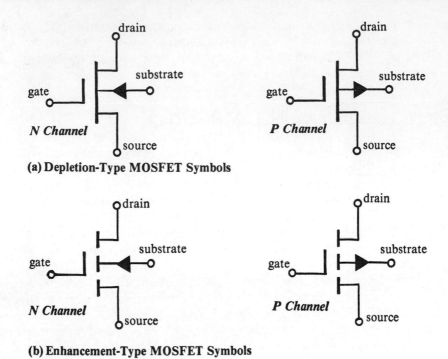

(a) Depletion-Type MOSFET Symbols

(b) Enhancement-Type MOSFET Symbols

FIGURE A8–9.　*MOSFET Symbols*

NPN Bipolar Transistor

The basic construction of an *NPN bipolar transistor* is quite simple: A *thin* layer of P-type material is sandwiched between two blocks of N-type material as shown in Figure A8–10a. Wires are connected to the three elements and are referred to as *collector* (*C*) (of electrons, like the plate), *base (B)*, and *emitter (E)* (of electrons, like the cathode). The base is the input control element. However, in normal operation the base is somewhat positive relative to the emitter, whereas the grid was negative relative to the cathode and the gate was negative relative to the source in the JFET.

Because there are two PN junctions in the NPN transistor, the transistor consists of two diodes with their anodes inherently connected together, as modeled in Figure A8–10b. This diode structure is important to the operation of the bipolar transistor. Note, however, that merely connecting two diodes together will *not* make a transistor; as is shown in the next section, a *thin* base (the P material here) is needed. The circuit symbol for the NPN transistor is given in Figure A8–10c. The arrow is in the slant line corresponding to the emitter and points in the easy-current-flow direction of the base-emitter diode.

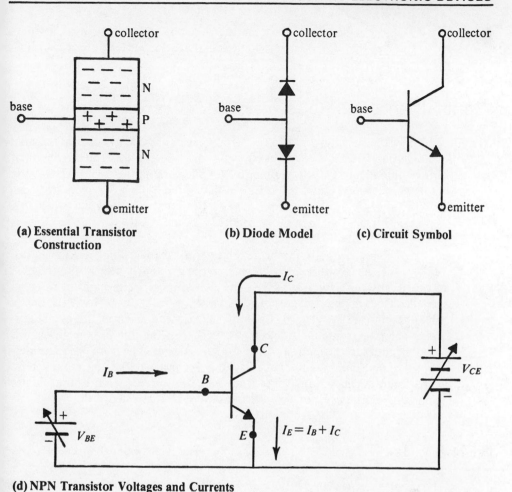

(a) Essential Transistor Construction

(b) Diode Model

(c) Circuit Symbol

(d) NPN Transistor Voltages and Currents

FIGURE A8–10. *NPN Bipolar Transistor*

NOTE: A very useful and simple test for a good or bad bipolar transistor is to make ohmmeter connections between the various pairs of transistor leads and observe the resistance. Thus, between the base and emitter, the ohmmeter should register a low resistance if the base is made positive relative to the emitter, but a very high resistance if the reverse connections are made. (For example, the Simpson VOM uses the red lead as positive for ohmmeter use; *not* all VOMs use this convention, however.) A bad transistor often exhibits a low resistance in both senses (a shorted junction) or a high resistance in both senses (an open junction). If either of these conditions is present, the transistor is certainly defective. A similar test can be made between the base and collector junctions. Between the collector and the emitter, the ohm-meter should register a high resistance for either polarity of connection.

General Electrical Behavior of NPN Transistor

Consider the operation of the transistor when connected to a pair of variable voltage supplies V_{BE} and V_{CE} as shown in Figure A8–10d. The directions of conventional current I_C flowing into the collector and the current I_B flowing into the base are shown. First notice that if the battery V_{BE} were *not* connected, essentially *no* current I_C would flow through the transistor. This situation is clear from the diode model in Figure A8–10b. The *C-B* diode is reverse biased and blocks the attempted current flow from V_{CE}.

The battery V_{BE} is connected in the forward-bias sense across the *B-E* diode. Then electrons begin to flow from the emitter (N block) into the base block as shown in Figure A8–11. The electrons can be thought of as being repelled from the negative terminal of the V_{BE} bias battery. However, only a small fraction of the electrons go out the base lead and constitute base current. The largest fraction of electrons zips across the *thin* base region and is quickly under the attraction of the large positive voltage from V_{CE}. The electrons are then collected by the collector and constitute the collector current. (The following paragraph gives a more rigorous description of the bipolar transistor mechanism for those readers who are interested.)

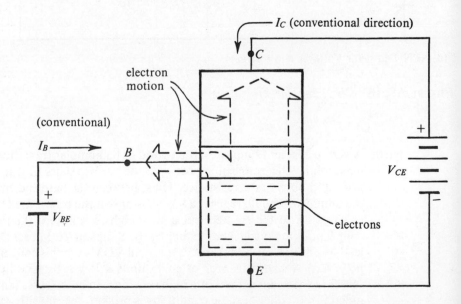

FIGURE A8–11. *Representation of Electron Currents in an NPN Transistor*

The forward bias imposed by the V_{BE} battery on the base-emitter diode junction reduces this particular junction barrier. Electrons then diffuse across the junction from the emitter block into the base block. However, the base block is made very thin and is also lightly doped so that there is little recombination of the electrons with the holes in the P-type base, which would draw carriers from the base lead. (Further, the light doping in the P-type base implies that few holes exist here to flow toward the *B-E* junction to give base current.) The electrons thus diffuse through the base block over to the base-collector diode junction. This junction is *reverse biased* by the rather large V_{CE} battery. But the large electric field existing in the depletion zone at this junction has the proper direction to push the electrons into the N-type collector block. Here they move to the positive collector terminal. Thus, the main current flow is between the collector and the emitter of the transistor and consists of electrons in the NPN transistor. Some holes are involved in the P region, however, so the device uses both types or poles of carriers; hence the term *bipolar* transistor.

Electrical Characteristics of NPN Transistor

The ratio of electrons moving through the transistor to those going out the base lead is quite constant since it depends primarily on geometrical construction. This ratio of I_C/I_B is called the *beta (β) or forward-current transfer ratio* h_{fe} of the transistor; values of 50 to 150 are quite common. That is,

$$\beta = h_{fe} = \frac{I_C}{I_B} \qquad (A8-5)$$

The electrical characteristics of the transistor can be represented on two graphs, considered the input characteristic and the output characteristic. The *input* or *base characteristics* are a plot of base current I_B versus the applied base-emitter voltage V_{BE}. It is simply a diode-like curve, but with a smaller current for a given V_{BE} than may be expected for a simple diode (because most of the current goes to the collector rather than to the base). See Figure A8-12a. Figure A8-12b is a plot of collector current versus applied collector-emitter voltage V_{CE}; this plot is called the *collector characteristics* or *output characteristics* of the transistor.

The collector characteristics show that the current flowing through the transistor is indeed determined almost entirely by the base current (which is initiated by V_{BE}). *Curves of constant base current* are drawn and for the transistor pictured $I_C \simeq 100\, I_B$ for all but quite small values of V_{CE}; that is, the β for this transistor is 100. Notice that the collector-emitter voltage has little effect on the collector current (except in the *saturation region;* if V_{CE} is very small, there is not much current flow).

The transistor is quite clearly a current amplifier in regard to the collector current compared to base (input) current. However, the base current

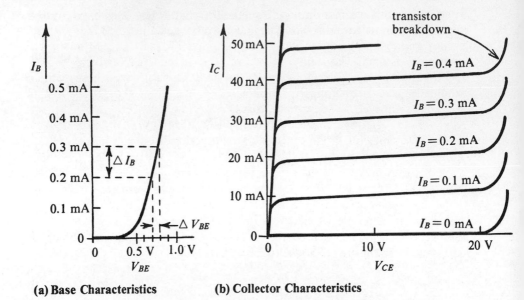

(a) Base Characteristics   **(b) Collector Characteristics**

FIGURE A8-12.   *Voltage-Current Behavior of the Bipolar Transistor*

is always caused by a base-emitter voltage. A small variation in V_{BE} causes a modest change in base current I_B, which in turn "causes" a large change (β times more) in collector current. Thus, the transistor follows the model of a voltage controlling a current that was shown in Figure A8-2.

To calculate its transconductance from Equation A8-1, we need

$$g_m = \frac{\Delta I_C}{\Delta V_{BE}} \tag{A8-6}$$

because $V_{in} = V_{BE}$ and $I_T = I_C$ in the case of the transistor. But ΔV_{BE} causes a certain change ΔI_B in the base current (see Figure A8-12a). We can write

$$\frac{\Delta V_{BE}}{\Delta I_B} \equiv r_{BE} \tag{A8-7}$$

where this ratio of voltage to current has dimensions of resistance and may be called the *ac input resistance* of the transistor. Further, the change caused in I_C due to a change in I_B is related through the β of the transistor (or h_{fe}). That is,

$$\Delta I_C = \beta \Delta I_B \tag{A8-8}$$

Then

$$\Delta I_C = \beta \Delta I_B = \frac{\beta \Delta V_{BE}}{r_{BE}} = \frac{\beta}{r_{BE}} \Delta V_{BE} \tag{A8-9}$$

A294

Substituting this expression for ΔI_C into Equation A8–6 then gives an expression for transistor transconductance:

$$g_m = \frac{\beta}{r_{BE}} \qquad (A8\text{--}10)$$

The value for r_{BE} depends on the value of base current because it is the reciprocal of the slope of the input characteristic curve (which is exponential). However, as an *order-of-magnitude value,* we can assume that $r_{BE} \simeq 1000\ \Omega$ for low-power transistors. In fact, this is the situation diagrammed in Figure A8–12a, where the I_B current increases by 0.1 mA (from 0.2 mA to 0.3 mA) as the V_{BE} voltage increases by 0.1 V (from 0.7 V to 0.8 V) so that $r_{BE} = 0.1$ mA/ 0.1 V = 1 kΩ.

Example: What is the transconductance of the transistor with characteristics given in Figure A8–12 if operated with a collector current of 25 mA?

Solution: The base current for a collector current of 25 mA is 0.25 mA for this transistor. This is the point about which ΔV_{BE} and ΔI_{BE} equal 0.1 V and 0.1 mA, respectively. Then $r_{BE} = 1$ kΩ as argued above. Next the transconductance is calculated from

$$g_m = \frac{\beta}{r_{BE}} = \frac{100}{1000\Omega} = 0.1 \text{ mhos} = 100{,}000\ \mu\text{mhos}$$

since we saw earlier that $\beta = I_C/I_B = 100$ for this transistor.

NOTE: The interested reader may refer to Problem 26 at the end of this chapter for a useful theoretical relation for g_m and r_{BE} for a transistor.

Basic Grounded-Emitter Amplifier

A *grounded-emitter amplifier* that uses a simple base-bias scheme is shown in Figure A8–13. As mentioned in the general amplifier case earlier, the transistor should be biased so that a continuous idle current I_C flows through the transistor even if no input signal is present. The R_B resistor supplies a base current I_R to the transistor input so that a proportional collector current I_C is flowing. In selecting the value of R_B, the idea is to adjust the idle-current value of I_C through the transistor so that $V_{R_L} \simeq 1/2 V_{CC}$, where V_{R_L} is the voltage across resistor R_L. But $V_{R_L} = I_C R_L$, and if V_{CC} and R_L are given (or assumed), the value of I_C is determined as $I_C = V_{CC}/2R_L$. Next, the base current I_B must be less than this value by the factor β of the transistor. However, I_B is established by choosing the proper R_B. In Figure A8–14 we see that

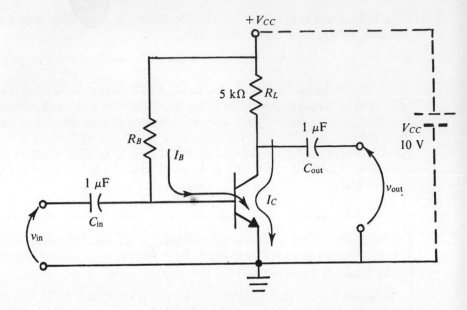

FIGURE A8–13. *Grounded-Emitter Amplifier Using Simple Base-Bias Current Scheme*

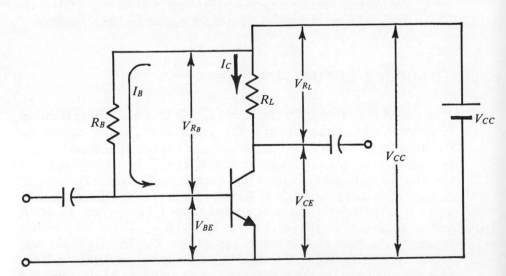

FIGURE A8–14. *Voltages Involved in Establishing the Base-Bias Resistor R_B*

$V_{CC} = V_{R_B} + V_{BE} = I_B R_B + V_{BE} \simeq I_B R_B + 0.6$ V. Usually V_{CC} is much larger than 0.6 V so that we have $V_{CC} \simeq I_B R_B$. Then

$$R_B = \frac{V_{CC}}{I_B} = \frac{V_{CC}}{I_C/\beta}$$

determines the bias resistor R_B.

Example: Suppose $V_{CC} = 10$ V and $R_L = 5$ kΩ for a transistor amplifier as shown in Figure A8–13. Assume the β of the transistor is 100. Find R_B. Also estimate the voltage amplification.

Solution: For normal operation we assume

$$V_{R_L} = \frac{V_{CC}}{2} = \frac{10 \text{ V}}{2} = 5 \text{ V}$$

Then

$$I_C = \frac{V_{R_L}}{R_L} = \frac{5 \text{ V}}{5 \text{ k}\Omega} = 1 \text{ mA}$$

Next

$$I_B = \frac{I_C}{\beta} = \frac{1 \text{ mA}}{100} = 0.01 \text{ mA}$$

Finally

$$R_B = \frac{10 \text{ V}}{0.01 \text{ mA}} = 1,000 \text{ k}\Omega = 1 \text{ M}\Omega$$

The voltage amplification is given by

$$A_v = g_m R_L$$

Here $R_L = 5$ kΩ. Further

$$g_m = \frac{\beta}{r_{BE}} \simeq \frac{100}{1,000 \ \Omega} = 0.1 \text{ mhos}$$

Then

$$A_v = 0.1 \text{ mhos} \times 5,000 \ \Omega = 500$$

(Here the rule-of-thumb estimate was used for r_{BE}.)

Input and Output Impedance of Grounded-Emitter Amplifier

The input impedance of the grounded-emitter amplifier of Figure A8–13 is generally determined by the ac resistance appearing between the base and emitter of the transistor. This is simply the r_{BE} resistance that has already been discussed and is typically on the order of 1 kilohm. This value is indeed low compared to what is often desired and comes about because the input is across a *forward-biased* diode junction. The JFET presents a much higher input impedance ($\sim 10^7$ ohms) because its controlling input is across a reverse-biased diode, while the MOSFET presents an extremely high input impedance ($\sim 10^{14}$ ohms) because its input is to an insulating layer.

As we mentioned earlier in the discussion of the general basic amplifier, the output impedance of the amplifier is generally close to the value of the R_L resistor used in the design. Although this resistor may be made small to obtain a low output impedance, notice that the voltage amplification is proportional to R_L so that a price of lower amplification is paid.

Transistor as a Switch

In digital circuits we are interested in yes/no, on/off, or open/closed switch situations. Also we are sometimes in need of an electronic switch. A transistor can be used as a voltage-controlled switch. Consider the circuit shown in Figure A8–15a. If the in lead is connected to ground as in Figure A8–15b, no base bias is present and no base current I_B flows. Then I_C is zero as well and the transistor behaves like an open switch. In spite of V_{CC}, no current flows through the load R_L. The out voltage must be at V_{CC} because no voltage drop exists across R_L either. Although the input voltage is zero (low), the output voltage is high (at V_{CC}). The input and output are seen to be opposites.

On the other hand, suppose the in lead is connected to V_{CC} as shown in Figure A8–15c. Also, assume $R_B = R_L$. Then a base current I_B flows that is given by

$$I_B = \frac{V_{R_B}}{R_B} \simeq \frac{V_{CC}}{R_L} \qquad \text{(A8–11)}$$

Next a collector current *tries* to flow that is β times as much as this base current. Actually, the maximum possible collector current is also the value of Equation A8–11. It is limited by the fact that the supply voltage must equal the voltage across the load resistor plus the voltage across the transistor (see Figure A8–14); that is,

$$V_{CC} = V_{R_L} + V_{CE} = I_C R_L + V_{CE} \qquad \text{(A8–12)}$$

V_{CC} is fixed and the minimum that V_{CE} can be is zero; then maximum collector current possible is $I_C = V_{CC}/R_L$. The result is that the voltage appearing across the transistor goes virtually to zero (as does the out voltage). The current flowing through R_L is not limited by the transistor at all; it behaves like a closed switch. Also notice that the output voltage is again the opposite of the input voltage: Although the input is connected to a high voltage (V_{CC}), the output voltage is low (nearly zero).

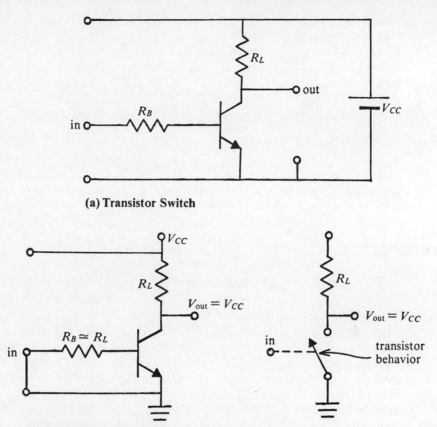

(a) Transistor Switch

(b) Transistor Switch Open because Input Voltage
Is Zero (or Unconnected)

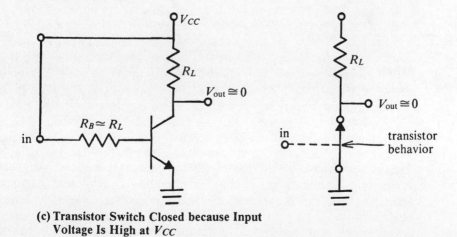

(c) Transistor Switch Closed because Input
Voltage Is High at V_{CC}

FIGURE A8–15.   *Transistor as a Switch*

The transistor switch is controlled by applying a suitable voltage to the input. Zero volts should be applied to open the switch, and a high voltage should be applied to close the switch. The load resistance R_L can be any resistive element; for example, a light bulb, relay coil, dc motor, and the like.

Graphical View of Transistor Amplifier and Switch

It can help to clarify transistor circuit operation to use a graphical representation on the collector characteristics. Equation A8–12 contains two variables: I_C and V_{CE}. Suppose we solve for I_C in terms of V_{CE} and the other constant quantities V_{CC} and R_L. Then

$$I_C = \left(\frac{-1}{R_L}\right) V_{CE} + \frac{V_{CC}}{R_L} \qquad \text{(A8–13)}$$

This is an equation of form $y = mx + b$ and therefore clearly represents a straight-line form if I_C is plotted versus V_{CE}. The slope of the line is $(-1/R_L)$ and the I_C intercept is V_{CC}/R_L. The variables are just the same as those for the collector characteristic, and we can plot the line on such a graph for the specific transistor used. Figure A8–16 illustrates the situation for a numerical example. The line plotted, as well as the collector characteristics, is for the circuit with transistor as diagrammed at the left in the figure. It should be noted that $I_C = 0$ in Equation A8–12 or Equation A8–13 implies $V_{CC} = V_{CE}$; this determines the V_{CE} intercept as V_{CC}. The line is called the *load line*. It really represents the requirement imposed by Kirchhoff's Voltage Law on the resistor R_L in series with the transistor; that is, by Equation A8–12. The state of transistor current and voltage *must* fall somewhere along this line. If the base current I_B is now given, a unique state is determined by the intersection of the given required base-current curve with the load line. For example, in Figure A8–16 if the base current is known to be 0.2 milliamperes, the operating point must be at the little circle pictured. Then I_C is about 10 milliamperes and V_{CE} is about 5 V. Furthermore, the voltage V_{RL} across the R_L must be 10 V since $V_{CE} + V_{RL} = 15$ V. This V_{CE} and V_{RL} relationship to V_{CC} is diagrammed below the V_{CE} axis in Figure A8–16.

To use this transistor as a switch, the base current should either be zero, or more than 0.3 milliamperes. If $I_B = 0$, V_{CE} and also the output voltage is 15 V. If I_B is 0.3 milliamperes *or more,* all these I_B curves come down nearly vertically at about 0.5 V for V_{CE}. Then $V_{CE} = V_{\text{out}} \simeq 0.5$ V and the transistor is conducting hard at about 14 milliamperes. The transistor switch is closed and the output voltage is the *transistor saturation voltage* of about 0.5 V.

Finally, the operation of the transistor as an amplifier can also be appreciated from this graph. Suppose an input voltage causes I_B to vary between 0.1 milliamperes and 0.2 milliamperes. Then $V_{CE} = V_{\text{out}}$ can be seen

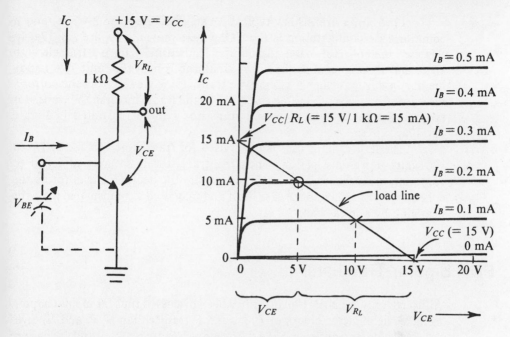

FIGURE A8–16. *Load Line on Collector Characteristics for a Transistor*

to vary between 10 V and 5 V, giving a peak-peak voltage of 5 V. But the input voltage that causes the 0.1-milliampere base-current variation is certainly considerably less than 1 V since the diode curve rises so steeply. It is of the order $V_{in} = \triangle V_{BE} = 0.1$ mA $\times$ 1,000 Ω = 0.1 V. Then the voltage amplification is about 5 V/0.1 V = 50.

Some Practical Transistor Considerations

Transistors are specified by a certain type number usually prefixed by 2N; for example, 2N708 (a switching transistor), 2N3055 (a power transistor), and 2N2222 (small general-purpose transistor). They are rated according to maximum current I_C, maximum collector-emitter voltage V_{CE}, and range of β or h_{fe}. The maximum-allowed V_{CE} is determined by the collector-emitter voltage for which the current begins to increase excessively; this *transistor breakdown* situation is evident in Figure A8–12b for V_{CE} greater than about 20 V. Unfortunately, the β value can vary by 50% or more between transistors of even the same type from the same manufacturer. (Vacuum tubes are much more uniform.) Another important rating is the *maximum device dissipation*. The heating in a transistor is determined by the product of voltage and current: $P = V_{CE}I_C$. If a transistor overheats, it can be ruined quickly. (Tubes are more forgiving.)

Low-power transistors typically can dissipate 1 or 2 watts, and a common case configuration is the TO–5 case shown in Figure A8–17a. In this case the collector, base, and emitter leads usually form a triangle with *C, B,* and *E* designated as shown. A small tab is near the emitter. A handy memory aid is that when a TO–5-type transistor is viewed from the *bottom,* the wires lead out in the same direction as the leads drawn in the transistor symbol. See the bottom view and transistor symbol illustrated in Figure A8–17a.

The larger TO–3 case is often used for transistors capable of 10- to 150-watts power dissipation. Then the transistor is securely attached to aluminum heat fins (a heat sink) to dissipate the heat. One lead (often the collector) is connected to the case itself and may need to be insulated from the heat sink by a mica spacer.

PNP Bipolar Transistor

Although only the NPN transistor has been discussed thus far in this chapter, using semiconductor blocks of P, N, and P (rather than N, P, and N) gives the *PNP bipolar transistor.* Then the diode senses are reversed and the battery polarities must be reversed; that is, the collector as well as the base must be made negative relative to the emitter. Otherwise, the operation of the transistor is similar to the NPN transistor (see Figure A8–18).

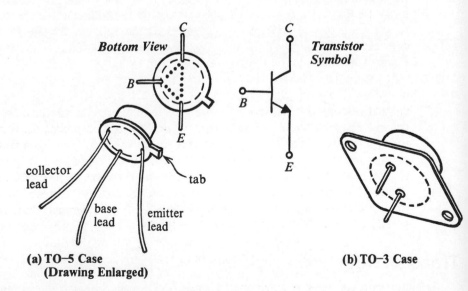

FIGURE A8–17. *Two Common Transistor Cases*

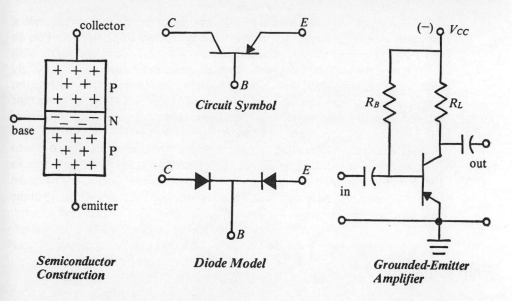

FIGURE A8–18. *PNP Bipolar Transistor*

Below the figure, labels read: *Semiconductor Construction*, *Circuit Symbol*, *Diode Model*, *Grounded-Emitter Amplifier*

Transistor Biasing

For pedagogical reasons, a simple base-bias scheme was used in discussing the bipolar-transistor grounded-emitter amplifier (for example, the circuit of Figure A8–13). In fact, we often encounter a more elaborate circuit because the transistor's β or h_{fe} typically varies greatly. As has been mentioned, β varies between devices with the same type number. Further, the β for a transistor increases significantly with temperature; it increases about 1% for each degree Celsius for silicon transistors and much more for germanium types. This is the reason germanium is now seldom used.

To largely overcome the problem of β variation, the better and more elaborate transistor bias circuit uses a voltage divider to establish the base current, along with a negative-feedback resistor between the emitter and ground. Problem 13 of the Problems for this chapter illustrates the form of the typical better-bias circuit; the interested reader may investigate this circuit further via that problem. Also, Figure A8–35b in the second supplement to this chapter shows a MOSFET in a better-bias circuit. The MOSFET circuit illustrated in the latter figure has the same structure and is used because the transconductance (or drain characteristic) for FETs generally varies greatly between unselected devices as well.

Transistor Current Amplifier/Switch Application

Suppose we want to construct a water-level sensing device that sounds a 120-V_{ac} buzzer (or activates some 120-V_{ac} device) when the level reaches a certain point. We propose to use a pair of wire probes and the fact that when water surrounds the probes, the resistance between them is 100 kilohms or less due to the conductivity of the water.

Assume we have available an electromagnetic relay with a coil resistance of 2 kilohms and that the coil requires 10 milliamperes to operate the relay. (Recall from Chapter A3 that the coil is a small electromagnet that attracts a small iron armature and thereby closes a pair of switch contacts if the coil current exceeds the pull-in current for the device.) The voltage that must appear across the coil to operate it is then 20 V minimum. We assume a 25-V_{dc} supply is available; this voltage provides a 25% operating margin for the coil.

A circuit to accomplish the task is shown in Figure A8–19. Notice first that current amplification is necessary. When 25 V is placed across the probes and the probes are in water, a current of only $25\,V/100\,k\Omega = 0.25\,mA$ flows, which is much less than the 10 milliamperes required to operate the relay (and, of course, very much less than that required to operate a large lamp, motor, or other power-consuming device). Therefore the water probe is connected in series with the base-emitter junction of a transistor so that the water resistance effectively becomes R_B of Figure A8–15a. The transistor becomes a current-controlled switch placed in series with the coil in the 25-V circuit. When water is present around the probes, we desire the transistor switch to close and a coil current of at least 10 milliamperes to flow through the coil and transistor (as transistor collector current I_C).

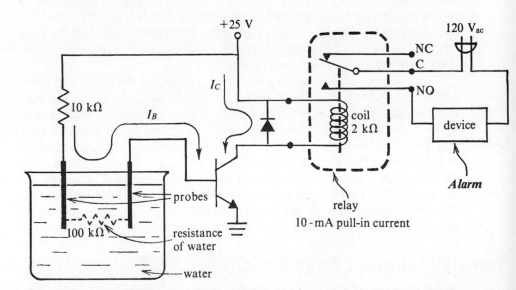

FIGURE A8–19. *Transistor Used to Drive a Relay-Controlled 120-V_{ac} Device*

A 10-kilohm protective resistor has been placed in series with the water probe in the base circuit to protect the transistor from direct connection of the base to 25 V in the event that the probes become accidently shorted. If water is present we calculate the base current from $V_{CC} = I_B R_B + V_{BE}$ or 25 V = I_B (10 kΩ + 100 kΩ) + 0.6 V. Then $I_B \simeq 0.23$ mA. The collector current and therefore coil current is proportional to this by $I_C = \beta I_B$. We desire $I_C > 10$ mA; then $\beta I_B > 10$ mA, or $\beta > 10$ mA/0.23 mA = 43. The transistor chosen should have a β (forward-current transfer ratio h_{fe}) of at least 43 to multiply the base current up to the 10 milliamperes required to operate the relay. (A larger β does no harm since the transistor is simply driven further into saturation.) Furthermore, the transistor must have a maximum collector-emitter voltage rating $V_{CE,max}$ of more than 25 V because when the transistor is not conducting, it acts as an open switch. The 25-V supply voltage will then appear across the transistor from collector-to-emitter. A transistor with β or $h_{fe} = 75$ or more and $V_{CE,max}$ of 35 V or more would be a safe selection. The $I_{C,max}$ specification for the transistor should be no problem since almost any contemporary transistor is capable of 100 milliamperes or more. Power is no problem either since V_{CE} is low when I_C is high, and vice versa.

Notice that the 120-V_{ac} circuit makes no electrical connection to the probe circuit, as the insulation between the armature and coil should be quite good. This electrical isolation of 120-V circuits from controlling electronics is often desirable. A final practical element is placed in this circuit. Notice the diode, placed with anode to collector and cathode to power supply. This diode arrangement protects the transistor from the large voltage that may be induced in the coil of the relay when the current through it is stopped suddenly by the opening of the transistor switch (recall inductive emf and Equation A1–41). A voltage transient can be produced that swings well above the supply voltage of 25 V and consequently exceeds the $V_{CE,max}$ rating of the transistor. The diode becomes forward biased during such an excursion and clips off the voltage spike in a manner similar to that discussed in Figure A7–13 for the differentiating circuit.

Darlington Connection

The *Darlington connection,* which sounds like the name of a movie, is actually a rather simple and useful connection of two transistors. The transistors are connected so that the emitter current of the first transistor passes into the base of the second (see Figure A8–20). Then the base current I_{B1} into transistor 1 is amplified by the factor β of that transistor before it enters the base of transistor 2 as its base current I_{B2}. The collector current for transistor 2 is in turn greater than its base current by the factor of its β_2, so that the resulting device current is a factor $\beta_1 \times \beta_2$ greater than its input current. We can regard the transistor pair as a *super beta* transistor, and indeed such

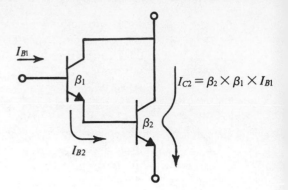

FIGURE A8-20. *Darlington Connection of Two Transistors*

devices are available in a single 3-terminal transistor package called Darlington transistors with a β on the order of $10^2 \times 10^2 = 10^4$. Notice that a Darlington transistor pair used in the water-sensing circuit of Figure A8-19 would increase the sensitivity greatly; the water resistance could be as high as 10 megohms and still give satisfactory operation.

Emitter Follower or Grounded-Collector Amplifier

The problem of low input impedance and generally high output impedance for the grounded-emitter amplifier was discussed earlier. The *grounded-collector amplifier* greatly improves on both of these ills, although at the price of providing only unity gain (actually slightly less than unity). The load resistor R_L is connected between the emitter and ground as shown in Figure A8-21 and the collector is connected to the positive power supply (for an NPN transistor). Although the collector is not at dc ground, it is in fact at ac ground if the power supply is of good quality and has a low impedance to ground. The name of the amplifier follows from this fact.

It is not difficult to see that if the input voltage goes up by a certain amount, the emitter voltage will increase by nearly as much. This is because the base-emitter voltage is basically that for a forward-biased diode, and the base-emitter voltage changes very little even though the current passing through the transistor changes a great deal. Therefore, the emitter voltage will quite faithfully follow the input voltage up and down, and the amplifier output will follow suit because it is connected (through a dc blocking capacitor) to the emitter; hence the grounded-collector amplifier's other name, *emitter follower*.

Because the emitter follows the base quite closely, there is a greatly reduced tendency for current to flow into the r_{BE} resistance that effectively appears between the base and emitter of the transistor. It is possible to show that the input impedance R_{in} of this amplifier is greater than merely r_{BE}; it is usually given to a good approximation as $R_{in} = r_{BE} + \beta R_L$. In addition,

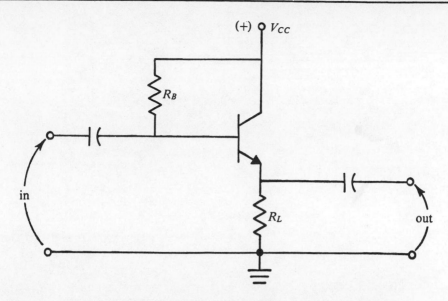

FIGURE A8–21. *Basic Emitter Follower or Grounded-Collector Amplifier*

the output impedance R_{out} is generally much less than R_L; it can be shown to be approximately given by $R_{out} \simeq [R_L \| (1/g_m)]$. Here g_m is the transconductance of the transistor, and its reciprocal has dimensions of ohms. For example, if $g_m = 0.1$ mho, $(1/g_m) = 10\ \Omega$. This value is generally much less than R_L so that the parallel resistance of R_L with $(1/g_m)$ is nearly just that of $(1/g_m)$, or 10 ohms. This is the typical output impedance of a low-power bipolar transistor emitter follower.

We can construct a follower amplifier with a triode, pentode, JFET, or MOSFET as well. They are termed *cathode follower* or *source follower* as the case may be. In all cases, the output impedance can be expected to be given by $R_{out} \simeq (1/g_m)$.

To obtain an amplifier with high input impedance, high voltage gain, and low output impedance, we can construct a multistage or cascaded amplifier with emitter followers as input and output stages in order to obtain desirable input/output impedances. In between may be placed one or more grounded-emitter stages to obtain the necessary gain.

Basic Differential Amplifier

Figure A8–22 illustrates a *basic differential amplifier* constructed from bipolar transistors. The amplifier essentially consists of two grounded-emitter–type amplifiers with the output taken between the two collectors. An input passes into the base lead of each transistor. Suppose each input changes

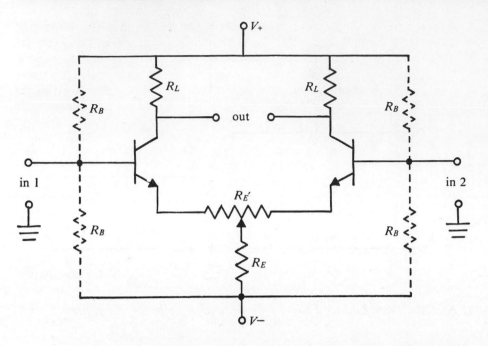

FIGURE A8–22. *Basic Differential Amplifier Constructed from Bipolar Transistors*

positive by the same amount. Then we expect the collector of each transistor to move negative by the same amount (though the amount is different from the input voltage) because of the symmetry of the circuit. The output voltage is really the *difference* between the two collector voltages, and it is clear that for perfectly matched resistors and transistors, the difference will be zero for the input case stated. Actually, this input case represents a common-mode input, and since the output is zero, we clearly have the common-mode rejection desired of a difference amplifier. The R_E' potentiometer serves to help balance the circuit against small mismatches in resistors or transistors.

If one input changes positive while the other changes negative, however, the collectors of the two transistors change in opposite senses by some amplified amount, and the output signal is then very substantial. Indeed, it is possible to show that the difference-voltage gain is approximately $g_m R_L$, where g_m is the transconductance of either transistor and R_L is the load resistance. To obtain further voltage gain, several difference amplifiers may be cascaded together. This is generally the method of choice to obtain high-gain dc amplifiers, and the examination of a dc oscilloscope or op-amp schematic invariably reveals several cascaded differential amplifiers. For example, to obtain very high input impedance in the RCA 3140 op amp, the first stage consists of a pair of MOSFETs.

When designing a differential amplifier, the base-bias current would generally be supplied by resistors such as those labeled R_B in Figure A8–22.

These resistors then appear in parallel with the effective input impedance of the transistor amplifier. In order to permit the largest possible input impedance, these resistors are *omitted* in virtually all operational amplifiers; therefore they are shown as dashed components in Figure A8–22. Consequently, the bias current required by the transistors must be supplied by the signal source connected to the op amp. This is precisely the warning made in Chapter A6 with regard to input bias current for op amps.

Other Semiconductor Devices

Phototransistor

The photodiode was discussed in Chapter A3. An interesting variant on this theme is the *phototransistor*. Such transistors are fabricated in a transparent case so that light may fall on the reverse-biased collector-base junction. Transistor action then essentially multiplies the photocurrent in the base region (which is generated by the light), and a device more sensitive than a simple photodiode results. The base lead may not be available from some phototransistors, so that they look rather like diodes. If the base lead is available, it is *not* used for the phototransistor application.

Figure A8–23 illustrates the symbol for a phototransistor and also the use of a phototransistor to operate a sensitive relay directly. Thus, if the incident light intensity is above 5 milliwatts/centimeter^2, the TIL81 photo-

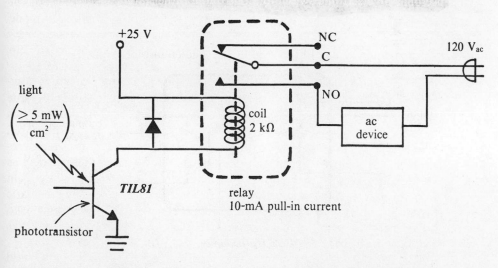

FIGURE A8–23. *Phototransistor Used in a Simple Relay Control Circuit*

transistor passes some 20 milliamperes for a V_{CE} greater than 3 V. The relay assumed for Figure A8–19 could then be operated by this phototransistor and is employed again in Figure A8–23.

Optocoupler

The optically coupled isolator or *optocoupler* is a useful, rather recent device for providing electrical isolation between systems operating with different voltages, different grounds, and so forth. It typically consists of an infrared *light-emitting diode* (LED) placed in a light-tight, electrically insulating package near a phototransistor. If a current is passed through the LED, light from the diode falls on the phototransistor, and current will pass through the transistor if a voltage exists across the transistor. The output current I_C through the transistor is approximately directly proportional to the input current I_f through the LED. If no current passes through the input LED, the output transistor behaves like an open switch. Figure A8–24 illustrates the essential construction and electrical characteristics for the 4N26 opto-coupler. Optocoupler types also exist that have a Darlington transistor output stage; this output increases the dc current transfer ratio, as well as the maximum output capability. Thus, the 4N33 Darlington-transistor–type optocoupler has a current transfer ratio of 500 and a maximum current capability of 60 milliamperes. This may be contrasted with the corresponding respective values of 20 and 3.5 milliamperes that are listed for the 4N26 type in Figure A8–24.

Silicon-Controlled Rectifier (SCR)

The *silicon-controlled rectifier* or SCR is a semiconductor device that is very useful as an electronic switch for controlling rather large ac currents (on the

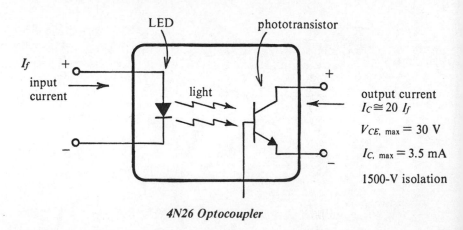

4N26 Optocoupler

FIGURE A8–24. *An Optically Coupled Isolator*

order of amperes) to motors, light bulbs, electric heaters, and so on. It is a 4-layer PNPN device, with 3 leads attached called anode, gate, and cathode as shown in Figure A8–25a. The schematic symbol for an SCR is shown in Figure A8–25b. We see that there is a gate terminal added to the cathode of the familiar diode symbol. The diode arrow points in the possible easy-flow direction for current through the SCR.

The characteristic for the SCR is presented in Figure A8–26. For the purpose of this book, it is not necessary to justify this characteristic in detail in terms of the 4-layer semiconductor structure of the SCR, although some features can be understood in terms of elementary diode behavior. Rather, we consider the action of the SCR as presented by the experimental characteristic and discuss in general terms how it is commonly exploited.

Of course, the term anode implies that the terminal so named is normally connected to a voltage source in a manner to make it positive relative to the cathode. However, as we examine the possible current path from anode to cathode, we note a PN, an NP, and a PN junction; these are connected in series. The NP junction is *reverse biased* when the anode is connected positive.

Assume first that the gate is left unconnected or is negative relative to the cathode. Then, when a positive voltage is applied from anode to cathode, only a small *forward-leakage current* I_{FX} flows through the SCR until the anode is made very positive relative to the cathode. Examining the characteristic in Figure A8–26, we see that the SCR current finally begins to flow substantially when the voltage across the SCR exceeds the *breakover voltage*. This situation is represented by the SCR characteristic curve labeled $I_G = 0$ since no gate current I_G is flowing into the gate in this case. Of course, we expect that at some voltage the reverse-breakdown capabilities of the

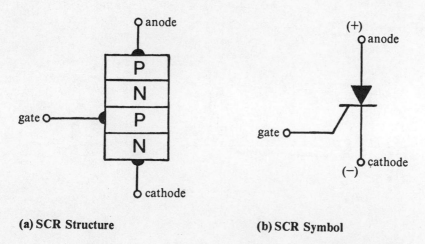

(a) SCR Structure   (b) SCR Symbol

FIGURE A8–25. *Structure and Symbol for the Silicon-Controlled Rectifier* blocking diode will be exceeded and current will flow. It is interesting that "once the dam is broken," so to speak, current flows easily through the device, with only a small voltage drop of about 1 V across the SCR (from anode to cathode). The SCR has changed from an open-switch mode to a mode much like a forward-biased diode or a closed switch.

Also notice in Figure A8–26 that very little *reverse-leakage current* I_{RX} flows when the anode is made negative relative to the cathode. This can be expected from the fact that the PN junctions in the SCR are reverse biased in this case (the other two junctions are forward biased). However, if the reverse voltage is made sufficiently large, reverse diode breakdown will occurs for the blocking junctions. This is just the same as the typical reverse breakdown shown for diodes in Figure A4–7. The voltage for reverse break-down is about the same as the SCR's forward-breakover voltage (for $I_G = 0$). As was true for normal diodes discussed in Chapter A4, the reverse-break-down situation can ruin the diode through VI—voltage $\times$ current—heating if the current is allowed to become large. The SCR is *not* similarly ruined in the forward-direction breakover case since $V_{anode-cathode}$ quickly drops to about 1 V (the VI product is then small). Typical SCRs can pass a current of 1 to 15 amperes in the forward direction without harm, depending on the SCR rating and whether proper heat sinking has been employed.

Generally an SCR is operated with the anode-cathode voltage always *less* than some *maximum forward-blocking voltage V_{FM}* and also less than some *maximum reverse-blocking voltage V_{RM}* in the reverse sense. For example, the V_{RM}, V_{FM} values for the 2N2322, 2N2323, 2N2324, 2N2325, and 2N2326 SCR devices are, respectively, 25 V, 50 V, 100 V, 150 V, and 200 V.

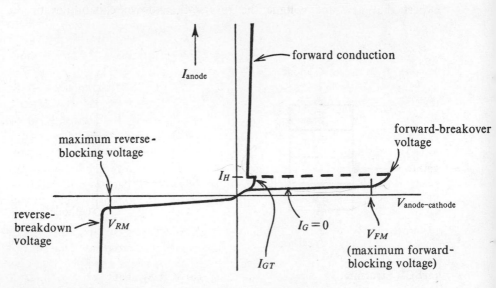

FIGURE A8–26.　*Silicon-Controlled Rectifier Characteristic*

These SCRs can have an average on-state current of 1.0 amperes if their TO−5-style case is maintained at less than 85°C. The 2N1842/3/4/5/6/7/8/9/2N1850 SCRs have a blocking voltage ranging from 25 V for the 2N1842 to 500 V for the 2N1850. This family can handle the rather substantial current of 16 amperes. A 2N184X SCR must be bolted to a heat sink to achieve this current, and the threaded stud is in fact the anode.

However, when a gate current is supplied to the SCR, the forward-breakover voltage (but not the reverse-breakdown voltage) is reduced in proportion to the gate current. If a gate current greater than some *gate-trigger current* I_{GT} is supplied to the gate, the device goes into the breakover or conduction state for a *small* positive anode-cathode voltage on the order of 1 to 2 V. The gate must be brought positive by only about 1 V relative to the cathode to cause the gate-trigger current I_{GT} to flow. Notice that this voltage forward biases the bottom PN junction and, therefore, gate current flows into the SCR. For the low-power 2N232X family of SCRs, I_{GT} is less than 0.1 milliamperes. For the rather high-power 2N184X family, I_{GT} is typically less than 15 milliamperes, although 80 milliamperes is the guaranteed maximum required.

Once in the conducting state, the SCR remains so even after the gate current/voltage is removed. The SCR remains in the "on" state until the anode voltage is reduced so that the anode current falls below a small *holding current* I_H (typically a few milliamperes). The SCR will certainly be turned off if the anode is actually made negative relative to the cathode. However, a negative voltage to the SCR gate will *not* turn off the SCR. The gate-trigger current I_{GT} to turn on an SCR must be supplied for some minimum time, ranging from about 1 microsecond for 1-ampere SCRs, to about 20 microseconds for 15- to 50-ampere SCRs. The turn-on time for an SCR is on the order of 1 microsecond, while the turn-off time after reverse bias is about 20 microseconds.

In order to experiment with an SCR, a simple circuit can be constructed with an SCR, a light bulb, and a switch. The circuit is illustrated in Figure A8−27a and shows how an SCR can electronically control the current through the bulb. Assume first that 120 V_{dc} is applied to the series circuit. We require the blocking voltage capability V_{FM}, V_{RM} for the SCR to be greater than 120 V for these experiments. Then the light bulb remains dark as long as the gate to the SCR is connected to its cathode or is left open-circuited. The SCR behaves like an open switch. However, if the gate is brought positive by about 1 V relative to the cathode, gate current will flow that exceeds I_{GT} (provided the voltage source to the gate is capable of this small current of a few milliamperes). The SCR is triggered into the "on" condition, and the light bulb lights as current flows. The current continues to flow even if the gate voltage (and hence gate current) is removed. Thus, only a brief gate-current pulse is required to turn on the light permanently. This fact is indicated by the pulse form to the gate in Figure A8−27a. Of course, if the switch S is opened, the current to the light is interrupted and the light

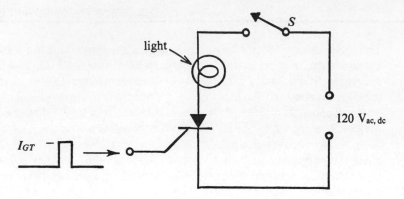

(a) Simple Control of a Light Bulb

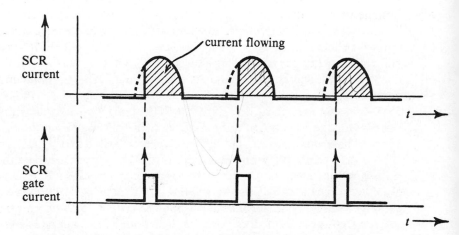

(b) Current Flowing in Nearly Full Half-Cycles

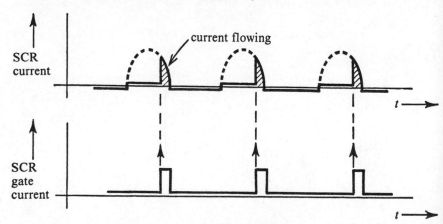

(c) Current Flowing for Small Portions of Each Cycle

FIGURE A8–27. *Control of Current (Especially ac Current) with an SCR*

A314

bulb goes dark. It then remains dark after the switch is closed until another current pulse is input to the SCR gate. Another way to extinguish the bulb is to reduce the voltage to the SCR/bulb to zero or even negative. Then the bulb remains dark after the voltage is increased to 120 V_{dc} again.

Suppose on the other hand that 120 V_{ac} is connected to the light bulb and SCR series circuit in Figure A8–27a. Even if switch S is closed, the light remains dark until a gate-trigger current I_{GT} is supplied to the SCR. If this gate current is supplied *continuously* to the SCR, the light bulb glows since current flows each half-cycle that the SCR is positively biased. Half-rectified current (such as shown in Figure A4–9c) flows through the bulb, as the SCR behaves very much like a simple semiconductor diode. However, if the gate current is removed from the SCR, the light bulb extinguishes as soon as the supply voltage swings negative. The SCR current stops flowing and the SCR reverts to the "off" state. Therefore, the SCR behaves rather like an electrically controlled switch or relay in this application. The SCR can be a convenient solid-state switch for ac currents.

The SCR can be used to control the light bulb brightness in the ac case of Figure A8–27a by repetitively sending the current pulse I_{GT} to the SCR gate. One pulse is sent to the gate during each cycle of the 120 V_{ac}, as illustrated in Figure A8–27b and Figure A8–27c. By adjusting the timing of the gate pulses so that they occur early in the cycle (see Figure A8–27b), the light bulb shines quite brightly (at only half of its normal power since only half-wave current is flowing). However, if the gate pulse is applied late in each half-cycle (see Figure A8–27c), the current flowing through the bulb is reduced to only a fraction and the bulb shines dimly. Typically, this timing is adjusted through the use of an RC timing circuit with an adjustable R. (Such an RC circuit is illustrated later in conjunction with a similar triac circuit in Figure A8–29.)

Triac and Diac

The *triac* (or TRIAC) semiconductor device performs like two SCRs in parallel and oriented in opposite directions. The symbol for the triac is shown in Figure A8–28a. When sufficient current I_{GT} is supplied to the gate of a triac, it is triggered into conduction and conducts current in *either* direction through the device. This bidirectional current capability can be seen from its characteristic shown in Figure A8–28b. Therefore, it is well suited to use as an electrical switch in ac circuits. By proper timing of the gate-current pulses, the SCR current can be adjusted from full-wave ac (in contrast to the half-wave rectified case of Figure A8–27b) to small current or no current.

As example applications, triacs are commonly used in light-dimmer circuits and as motor-speed controls for universal ac/dc electric motors. The timing of the trigger current is made adjustable during each half-cycle through use of an RC circuit with adjustable R. If the triac is turned on later in the

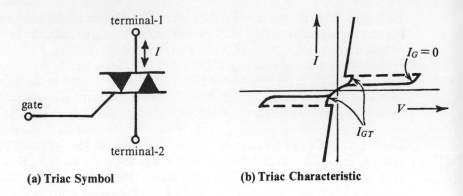

(a) Triac Symbol　　　　　(b) Triac Characteristic

FIGURE A8-28. *Triac Semiconductor Switch*

half-cycle, the light becomes dimmer due to the reduced *duty cycle*. In the case of the motor, it runs more slowly with a reduced duty cycle. The schematic of a simple circuit to achieve a light dimmer with a triac is shown in Figure A8-29.

The circuit of Figure A8-29 uses still another device with a breakover characteristic called a *diac* or bilateral trigger. This device breaks over in *either* direction at a voltage of about 20 V to 35 V, depending on the type. It is like a triac without a gate, and its symbol in Figure A8-29 corresponds to this fact. A diac is generally placed in a triac circuit such as this to buffer the *RC* phase-shift (or timing) network from the SCR gate until the firing point

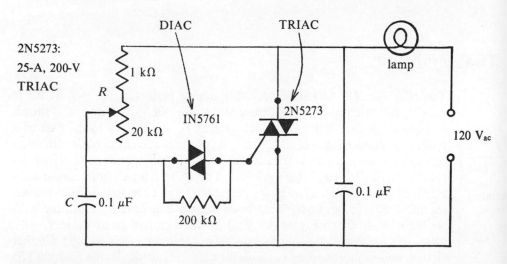

FIGURE A8-29. *Triac in a Light-Dimmer Control Circuit (Courtesy of Texas Instruments)*

is reached. Alternatively, it *is* possible to use a high-voltage transistor or FET follower between the *RC* circuit and the triac gate to provide the isolation desired.

In the vacuum tube era, a triode with a mercury vapor within the envelope served a switching function very similar to that of the modern-day SCR. This tube is called a *thyratron*. In a similar manner, an SCR or a triac solid-state device is referred to as a *thyristor*.

Solid-State Relay

In recent years, *solid-state relays* have been gaining wide usage in place of electromechanical relays. They have no moving parts, nor do they have the contact points that become pitted and inoperative after perhaps 10^5 or 10^6 operations in conventional relays. The typical solid-state relay represents a wedding between the optocoupler and a triac; Figure A8–30 illustrates its essential structure. If a certain minimum current is applied to the control input, the LED causes a photodetector in the device to trigger the triac, and an ac-capable switch effectively closes between the load output lines. As shown in Figure A8–30, the output lines should be connected in series with the ac device to be controlled, and the device will then be turned on for as long as current is supplied to the control input. The device indeed functions in nearly the same way as a relay; however, it will *not* switch a dc load, while a conventional relay can, of course. The triac is replaced with a power transistor in devices intended for dc loads.

A typical solid-state relay might operate with 15 milliamperes at 2 V to its input and control up to 10 amperes at 140 V_{ac}. Thus, a 0.03-watt input can control 1400 watts, with a life expectancy of 10^8 operations. These devices are very useful in electronic control of high-power devices; for example, when a microcomputer must control an electric motor.

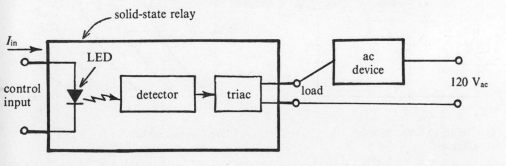

FIGURE A8–30. *Solid-State Relay*

Supplement to Chapter:
Triode Characteristics and Basic Circuit

The essential construction, circuit symbol, and current-controlling action of the triode were given in the chapter.

There are three variables involved in the electrical characterization of the triode: the *plate current* I_b flowing from plate to cathode (conventional-current sense); the *plate-to-cathode voltage* V_b; and the controlling *grid-to-cathode voltage* V_c. A circuit to obtain the relationship between these variables is shown in Figure A8–31a, and a typical *plate-characteristics* graph is shown in Figure A8–31b. Notice that curves of constant grid voltage V_c are drawn. The curve for $V_c = 0$ is indeed like that for a diode, while making the grid more negative at a given plate voltage V_b does decrease the plate current I_b.

Figure A8–32 shows a basic *triode grounded-cathode amplifier* that uses a *bias battery* V_{CC} as well as *supply battery* V_{BB}. The V_{CC} bias is usually chosen such that the voltage across R_L ($V_{R_L} = I_b R_L$) is about half the supply voltage V_{BB}. Then about half of V_{BB} also appears across the tube.

It is inconvenient to use two batteries or supply voltages. The essential requirement in biasing the tube is that the grid be somewhat negative relative to the cathode; this is usually accomplished by connecting the resistance R_g to ground and introducing a resistance R_K between the cathode and ground as shown in Figure A8–33. Now the current I_b flowing through R_K causes the cathode to be positive relative to ground, as shown in the figure. However,

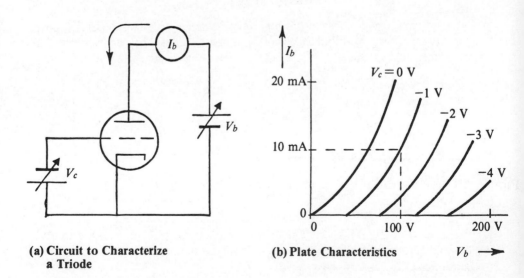

(a) Circuit to Characterize a Triode

(b) Plate Characteristics

FIGURE A8–31. *Characteristics of a Typical Triode*

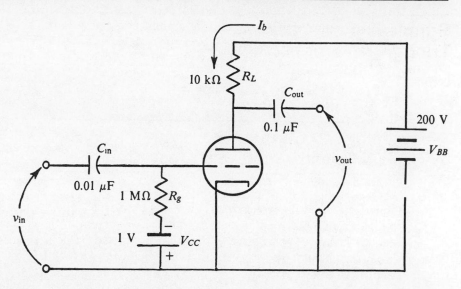

FIGURE A8–32. *Triode Grounded-Cathode Amplifier Using Two Batteries or Supply Voltages*

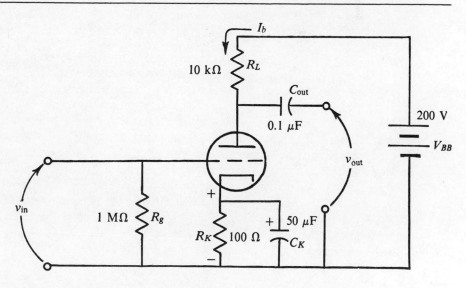

FIGURE A8–33. *Self-Biased, Grounded-Cathode Triode Amplifier*

the grid is nearly at ground because very little current flows to the grid and through R_g to ground. Thus the grid is negative relative to the cathode as required.

The capacitor C_K smooths out the ac that tends to develop across R_K when amplifying an ac voltage; we want a dc voltage across R_K, or else

A319

negative feedback will decrease the amplification obtained. The resulting amplifier is called a *self-biased, grounded-cathode amplifier*. The cathode is not at ac ground (as it is in Figure A8–32), but it *is* at dc ground if the large capacitor C_K effectively shorts ac currents to ground.

Supplement to Chapter:
MOSFET Construction and Operation

Some of the general properties of the metal-oxide-silicon field-effect transistor (MOSFET), as well as circuit symbols, were given in the chapter. The central feature of this device is the fact that the gate structure is insulated from the channel; hence, the name *insulated-gate FET* or IGFET is also applied to these devices.

N-Channel Depletion-Type MOSFET

Two different schemes exist for constructing MOSFETs that result in the enhancement type and the depletion type. The *depletion type* operates rather similarly to the JFET and is discussed first. Figure A8–34a shows the essential features of the construction. For the N-channel version, drain, channel, and source regions are all constructed of N-type material, produced on a base or *substrate* of P-type material. Metal contacts are made to these three regions (as well as to the substrate), but a layer of insulation is established between the gate metal plate and the N-type semiconductor channel. Now suppose the gate is made negative relative to the source as shown. The negative gate plate attracts holes into the channel region near the plate. This configuration partially *depletes* the channel of some of the N-type carriers that conduct electricity between the drain and the source; hence the name *depletion* for this MOSFET type. The size of the channel is effectively reduced, and the device operation is very similar to that for the N-channel JFET. Its characteristic is therefore also similar to that drawn in Figure A8–6f.

However, the gate can also be made positive relative to the source without harm to the MOSFET (this *cannot* be done for the N-channel JFET since the gate diode becomes forward biased). The channel now is actually enlarged or *enhanced* into the P-material substrate, and more current will flow through the FET. Thus I_D versus V_{DS} curves exist also for positive V_{GS} values, and these simply occur in regular fashion *above* the negative V_{GS} curves. Figure A8–34b shows the characteristic curves for the N-channel depletion-type MOSFET.

The substrate P-type material must be *reverse biased* relative to the N-type channel so that it behaves like an inert base material. A connection

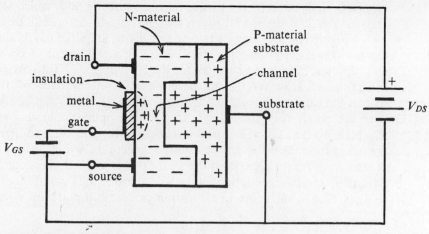

(a) Construction Scheme

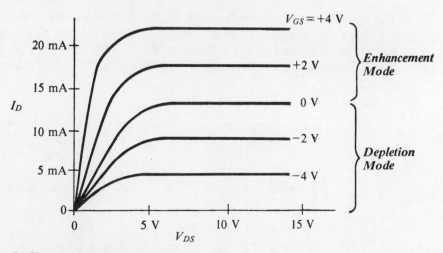

(b) Characteristic Curves

FIGURE A8–34. *N-Channel Depletion-Type MOSFET Construction and Characteristics*

exists to the substrate material that is often internally connected to the source lead inside the transistor package; if it does extend separately out of the package, the substrate lead is simply connected to the source lead or perhaps to ground.

The circuit symbol for the N-channel depletion-type MOSFET was shown in Figure A8–9a. Notice that the gate is drawn as quite separate from the channel to emphasize its insulated aspect. Note also that the N-channel version is designated by the arrow on the substrate lead, which shows the easy-current-flow direction through the substrate-to-channel diode junction.

Figure A8–35a shows a typical self-biased amplifier configuration for the N-channel depletion-type MOSFET. The arrangement of components and supply voltage is the same as for the N-channel JFET discussed earlier in Chapter A8. However, the gate need not be biased negatively relative to the source, but can even be biased positively. Thus R_S and C_S can be eliminated from the circuit of Figure A8–35a to give an amplifier operating with zero V_{GS} bias. To bias the gate positive relative to the source, a voltage divider operating from the $+V_{DD}$ power supply is generally used, as is illustrated by R_1 and R_2 in Figure A8–35b. If the R_S resistor is retained, this circuit has the advantage of accommodating FETs with considerable variation in characteristics; that is, variations in saturation current and pinch-off voltage.

N-Channel Enhancement-Type MOSFET

The essential construction features of the N-channel *enhancement-type* MOSFET are shown in Figure A8–36a. Notice that two separate N-channel regions are produced in the volume of P-type substrate, with *no* N-type material connecting the two; rather there is P-type substrate material be-

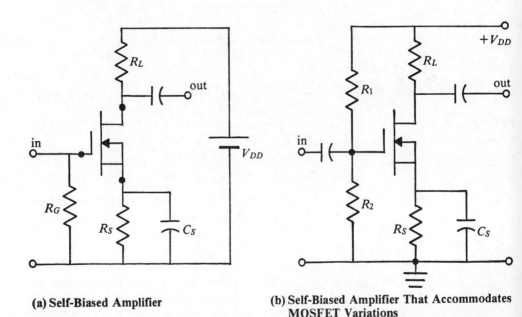

(a) Self-Biased Amplifier

(b) Self-Biased Amplifier That Accommodates MOSFET Variations

FIGURE A8–35. *N-Channel Depletion-Type MOSFET Grounded-Source Amplifier Circuits*

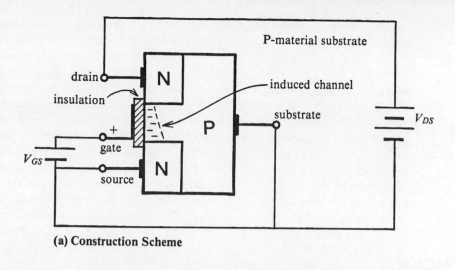

(a) Construction Scheme

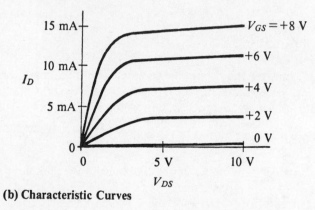

(b) Characteristic Curves

FIGURE A8–36. *N-Channel Enhancement-Type MOSFET Construction and Characteristics*

tween the two regions. These regions become the drain and source when metallic connections are attached. Insulating material is placed over the area between the drain and source regions, and a metal plate for the gate is placed on top of this, as shown in Figure A8–36a.

The NPN regions give two diode junctions rather like the bipolar transistor. Then if only a voltage V_{DS} is connected between the drain and the source, no current will flow because of the back-biased drain-substrate diode. However, if the gate is made *positive* relative to the source by some V_{GS}, (−) carriers (which are minority carriers in the P substrate) are attracted out of the substrate bulk to the region under the gate plate. Then an N-channel bridge is induced between the drain and source so that essentially a piece of

N-type material now exists between the drain and source leads and current will flow under the push of V_{DS}.

A large positive V_{DS} will cause a large channel and a large drain current will flow. The resulting characteristics are shown in Figure A8–36b. Notice that when $V_{GS} = 0$ there is only a tiny leakage current through the device; the MOSFET is turned off very much like the bipolar transistor is under similar circumstances. This behavior makes the enhancement-type MOSFET convenient for use as a switch in on/off or digital circuits. Indeed, it is very commonly used in microprocessors and other large-scale digital integrated circuits. The term *enhancement* comes from the fact that a channel is enhanced into existence in this type of MOSFET. The circuit symbol for this device graphically shows the break between the drain and the source (see Figure A8–9b).

An amplifier for the N-channel enhancement-type MOSFET must have the gate biased positively relative to the source, and a circuit such as that in Figure A8–35b is typically used.

P-Channel MOSFETs

We have examined the N-channel version of both the depletion and enhancement types of MOSFETs. Clearly the substrate could be made of P-type material rather than N type, and the channel should then be P type. This construction change produces a *complementary* or P-channel form of each MOSFET type, and the circuit symbols are shown on the right side of Figure A8–9.

The story is now very much like that for the complementary forms of the JFET and the bipolar transistors: All applied voltages should have reversed polarity. Thus if a P-channel MOSFET is used, the drain supply voltage V_{DD} in Figure A8–35 must supply negative voltage to the drain; turn the battery V_{DD} around in the figure. Also, the P-channel enhancement-type MOSFET requires the gate to be negative relative to the source in order to turn it on; that is, give drain-current flow.

REVIEW EXERCISES

1. (a) What is the difference between a vacuum diode and a vacuum triode?
   (b) Briefly, how does a vacuum triode control current?
2. (a) What is generally controlled by a discrete electronic device?
   (b) Give the definition of transconductance, both in words and as a mathematical relation.
   (c) What are the dimensions of transconductance?
3. (a) Diagram the (pedagogical) structure of an N-channel JFET. Label the three leads attached.

(b) Draw the corresponding JFET symbol. What aspect of the symbol indicates the N-channel character?

(c) What is the channel in the device?

(d) Why does a large negative gate-source voltage pinch off the current through an N-channel JFET?

(e) What is meant by the saturation current for a JFET? Sketch the typical FET characteristic; label the axes and the curves and point out the saturation current on it.

4. Name two safe operating limits specified by manufacturers for JFETs.

5. What is the reason for the interest in the new VMOS devices?

6. (a) What is meant by the bias or biasing in an amplifier?

   (b) How is a JFET amplifier typically self-biased?

7. (a) What determines the output impedance of a grounded-source amplifier?

   (b) What determines the input impedance of a self-biased grounded-source amplifier?

   (c) What determines the voltage gain of a grounded-source amplifier?

8. (a) Diagram the construction and the symbol for the P-channel JFET.

   (b) What determines the arrow direction for the gate in the P-channel JFET?

   (c) Briefly characterize the difference in the electrical usage of the P-channel JFET from the N-channel device.

9. (a) What do the letters in MOSFET stand for?

   (b) Which MOSFET type has an electrical behavior or characteristic very similar to the corresponding (N-channel or P-channel) JFET?

   (c) What distinguishes the other MOSFET type physically and electrically?

10. (a) Select the NPN transistor from the symbols shown in Diagram A8–1.

    (b) Select the N-channel FET from the symbols shown in Diagram A8–1.

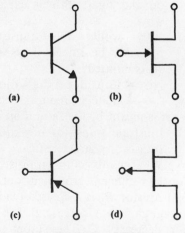

DIAGRAM A8–1.

11. (a) Diagram the (pedagogical) construction of an NPN transistor along with the schematic symbol; label the three connections for both.

    (b) Draw a diode equivalent for the NPN transistor.

    (c) Why is the collector current much larger than the emitter current in a normally operating transistor?

(d)   Why can an NPN transistor not be constructed by soldering the anode leads of two diodes together?

12.   What is the forward-current transfer ratio of a bipolar transistor? Give the definition both in words and as a formula.

13.   (a)   Why are two graphs required to show the electrical characteristics of a bipolar transistor?
           NOTE: Only one was required for the FET or the vacuum tube.

      (b)   What determines the ac input resistance r_{BE} for a transistor? Answer with reference to an appropriate graph.

      (c)   Draw a collector characteristic for some typical transistor, and show how the β for the transistor may be determined from it.

      (d)   Relate the transconductance of a transistor to the above quantities.

14.   (a)   What determines the input impedance of the grounded-emitter amplifier?
      (b)   What determines the output impedance of the grounded-emitter amplifier?
      (c)   What determines the voltage gain of the grounded-emitter amplifier?
      (d)   What penalty is paid for reducing the output impedance of a grounded-emitter amplifier?

15.   The transistor with SPDT switch S controls the light bulb in the circuit shown in Diagram A8–2.

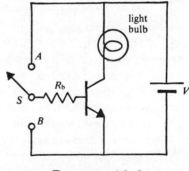

DIAGRAM A8–2.

      (a)   What setting of the switch turns off the light? Explain why briefly.

      (b)   What setting of the switch turns on the light? Briefly explain why.

      (c)   Why would the transistor probably be ruined if resistor R_b is omitted?
           NOTE: Consider the diode model of the transistor.

16.   What is meant by the saturation region for a bipolar transistor?

17.   (a)   Illustrate transistor breakdown behavior in a sketch of an appropriate transistor characteristic.

      (b)   What manufacturer transistor rating is related to this behavior?

18.   Consider either a grounded-source or grounded-emitter amplifier. When the load resistor R_L is increased (choose one): A. The output impedance and the voltage gain both increase. B. The output impedance increases, while the voltage gain decreases. C. The output impedance decreases, while the voltage gain increases. D. The output impedance and voltage gain both decrease.

19.   In which of the following is the input element—grid, gate, or base—biased positive with respect to the grounded element—cathode, source, or collector? A. triode, B. N-channel FET, C. NPN transistor.

20.   Discuss why the input impedance of an FET amplifier is much greater than that

of a bipolar transistor amplifier. Invoke the construction of each device in your discussion.

21. (a) What is the universal voltage-gain formula for a grounded–source/emitter/cathode amplifier constructed from an FET/transistor/pentode?

(b) Explain why it is difficult to construct an amplifier from a single transistor or tube with an accurately predictable voltage gain.

22. It is useful to have a constant-current source to obtain the conventional characteristic for (choose one): A. FET, B. triode, C. (bipolar) transistor, D. MOSFET.

23. When the temperature of a bipolar transistor increases, its h_{fe} (choose one): A. decreases, B. remains almost constant, C. increases.

24. (a) Diagram the (pedagogical) construction of a PNP transistor. Draw the corresponding PNP transistor symbol and diode model.

(b) What should be the polarity of the base relative to the emitter to forward bias the PNP transistor?

25. What basic property of the bipolar transistor may be exploited when the current in a situation is not sufficient to operate a relay?

26. Suppose very large current amplification is required. Diagram a simple transistor circuit that provides it and give its name.

27. (a) Diagram a transistor amplifier that affords low output impedance and relatively high input impedance.

(b) Give two names for this amplifier and justify each briefly.

28. (a) Diagram the basic amplifier type that is used for the input of an op amp (and in dc amplifiers generally).

(b) What is missing from this amplifier when used for an op-amp input? What is consequently required of the circuitry connected to the op-amp inputs?

(c) Argue why this amplifier type has high common-mode rejection.

29. What is the advantage of a phototransistor over a photodiode?

30. (a) Diagram an optocoupler. What is its purpose?

(b) Discuss qualitatively why the output current might be expected to be proportional to the input current.

31. (a) What does SCR stand for?

(b) Diagram the symbol for an SCR and label its leads.

(c) What is the utility of the SCR?

32. (a) Diagram the symbol for a triac.

(b) What is the advantage of a triac over an SCR?

33. (a) Diagram the components of a solid-state relay that utilizes a triac.

(b) Why can't this relay type be used with dc loads?

(c) Name two advantages of a solid-state relay over a conventional relay.

(d) A conventional relay provides good electrical isolation between its input and output. How does a solid-state relay accomplish a similar desirable characteristic?

PROBLEMS

1. (a) Suppose that an ohmmeter is alternately connected in the two connections A and B as shown in Diagram A8–3 to a "good" N-channel FET. The + terminal of each ohmmeter connection is shown. Tell whether the ohmmeter reads a small resistance or a large resistance in each case.

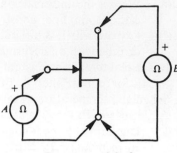

DIAGRAM A8–3.

   (b) Suppose the + terminal is reversed in each connection. Tell the ohmmeter readings.

2. (a) The saturation current for a certain FET is 20 mA, and its pinch-off voltage is −6 V. $V_{DS,max}$ for the device is 30 V. Sketch the characteristic for this FET, making the *approximation* that the curves of constant gate voltage are equally spaced.

   (b) Calculate the transconductance of the FET in this approximation.

   (c) If the FET is used in a grounded-source amplifier with a load resistance of 10 kΩ, what voltage gain is expected?

   (d) If the FET is used in a source-follower circuit, what output impedance is expected?

3. Assume I_{DSS} for the JFET in the circuit pictured in Diagram A8–4 is 6 mA, and the pinch-off voltage is very small. What is the voltage V_{out} (relative to ground)?

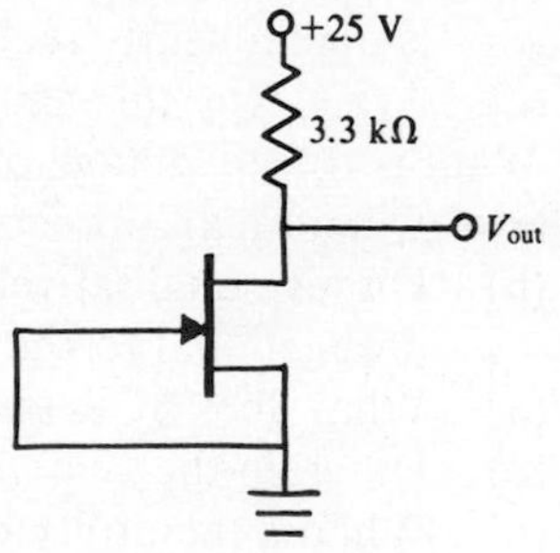

   DIAGRAM A8–4.

4. (a) Consider the circuit shown in Diagram A8–5. Someone claims the ammeter I reads 20 mA. Explain why this is impossible if all other features are correct as drawn.

   (b) What input impedance is expected for this amplifier?

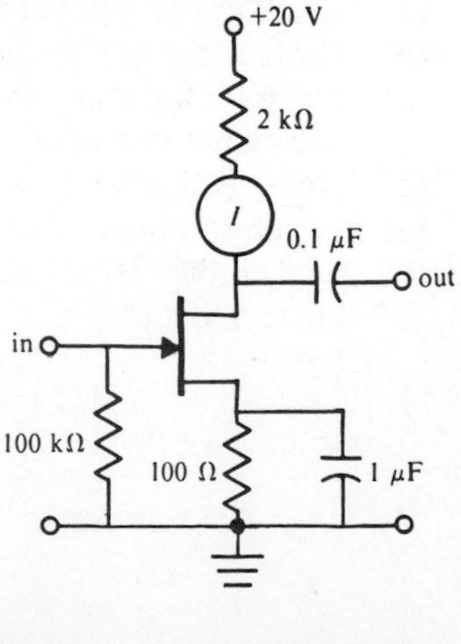

   DIAGRAM A8–5.

(c) What output impedance is expected for this amplifier?

(d) If the transconductance of the FET is 10 mmhos (10^{-2} mhos), what voltage gain is expected for the amplifier?

5. (a) Suppose a JFET is operated with its drain-source voltage at less than 50% of its pinch-off voltage. Argue from its characteristic that between the drain and source, it functions like an Ohm's Law resistor whose resistance can be changed by changing the gate-source voltage V_{GS}.

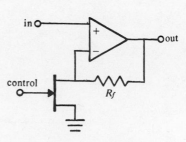

DIAGRAM A8–6.

(b) Argue that the circuit pictured in Diagram A8–6 will function as an adjustable gain amplifier where the control input changes the gain in response to a negative voltage. Suppose the control input is grounded. Is the gain a minimum or a maximum? Why?

6. Suppose an ohmmeter is connected respectively in the three connections shown in Diagram A8–7 to a "good" transistor. Tell whether the ohmmeter reads a small resistance or a very large resistance in each case. Note that the + terminal of the ohmmeter is indicated for each connection.

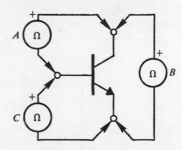

DIAGRAM A8–7.

7. (a) Sketch the appearance of a typical base characteristic for a bipolar silicon transistor. Include reasonable numbers of the horizontal and vertical axes.

(b) Illustrate how the resistance r_{BE} is determined from this characteristic.

(c) Sketch a collector characteristic for a transistor with a beta of 40. Use five I_B values, in increments of 50 μamps. Assume that the maximum V_{CE} allowed for the device is 40 V.

8. (a) Consider the transistor circuit illustrated in Diagram A8–8. If $V_{out} = 5$ V, what is the approximate h_{fe} of the transistor?

(b) What power is dissipated in the transistor?

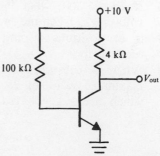

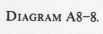

DIAGRAM A8–8.

A329

9. The silicon transistor in the circuit shown in Diagram A8–9 has a β of 40. What are the readings expected for the voltmeters V_1 and V_2 and milliammeter I?

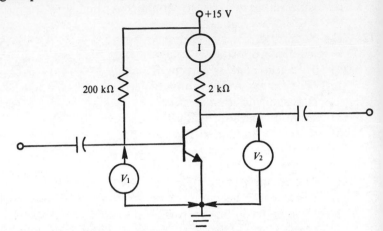

DIAGRAM
A8–9.

10. Suppose a silicon transistor with an h_{fe} of 50 is used in each of the circuits (a) and (b) shown in Diagrams A8–10a and b. Find the voltage V_{out} relative to ground in each case.

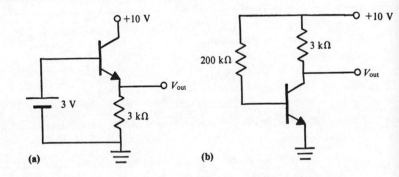

DIAGRAM
A8–10.　(a)　　　　　(b)

11. A silicon transistor with a beta of 50 is used in the circuit shown in Diagram A8–11.
   (a) If $R_b = 5$ kΩ, what is the voltage V_{out} when the switch is at positions A and B, respectively?
   (b) What is the approximate maximum value of R_b for which the V_{out} voltages re-

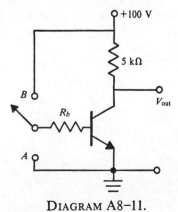

DIAGRAM A8–11.

main the same as in part (a) when the switch is operated?

(c) What minimum ratings for collector current and collector-emitter voltage capability are required for the transistor used?

12. The transistor in the amplifier pictured in Diagram A8–12 has $r_{BE} = 1200\ \Omega$ and $h_{fe} = 80$.

(a) Find the collector current and collector-emitter voltage.

(b) What is the approximate largest peak-peak output voltage without distortion from this amplifier?

(c) What is the voltage gain for this amplifier?

(d) Select C_1 and C_2 to have reactive impedances of 10% of the input impedance and output impedance, respectively, of the amplifier at a frequency of 500 Hz.

(e) Discuss the reasons for the rule used in part (d); for example, why would we *not* want the reactance to be 10 times the input or output impedance?

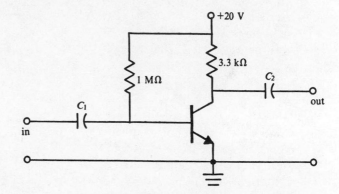

DIAGRAM
A8–12.

13. Consider a silicon transistor in the better-bias circuit shown in Diagram A8–13.

(a) Assume the base current to be very small (due to the large β of the transistor). Deduce the voltage relative to ground at points A, B, and C, respectively.

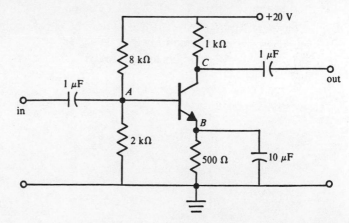

DIAGRAM
A8–13.

NOTE: At A consider a voltage divider; at B consider the base-emitter characteristic for a silicon transistor; at C use Ohm's Law and the currents flowing.

(b) Suppose β increases by 25%. Discuss why none of the voltages in part (a) change. Thus, the circuit is desirable if the circuit experiences temperature variations. Explain this statement.

(c) Why is it evident that the amplifier pictured must be an ac amplifier?

14. (a) Justify the following statement about transistors in terms of their characteristics: The drain current for a given JFET cannot exceed a certain value, but the collector current for a bipolar transistor can be increased to any value (in principle).

(b) In practice, can the current through a bipolar transistor be made arbitrarily large? Why?

15. Consider the FET circuit shown in Diagram A8–14. Justify that this circuit is approximately a constant-current source to R_L, with current I_{DSS}. However, R_L must be less than V/I_{DSS}; explain why.

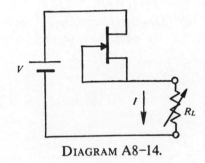

DIAGRAM A8–14.

16. Consider the bipolar transistor circuit shown in Diagram A8–15. Justify that this is approximately a constant-current source to R_L, with current $I = \beta V/R_b$ (if $V \gg$ 0.6 V). However R_L must be less than R_L/B; explain why.

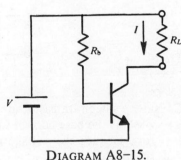

DIAGRAM A8–15.

17. Consider Diagram A8–16. The switching versus input character of JFET and bipolar transistors is contrasted.

(a) Suppose both inputs are grounded. What can be said about the two output voltages?

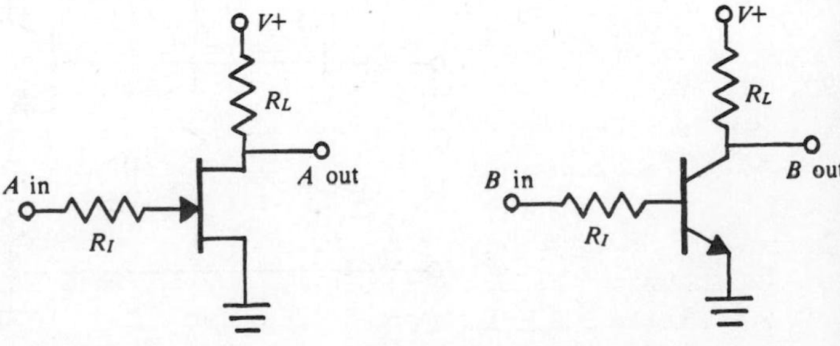

DIAGRAM A8–16.

(b) Does the answer to part (a) depend on the value of R_I in either case?

(c) Suppose B in is connected to $V+$. What can be said about B out? Does it depend upon the value of R_I?

(d) A in should *not* be connected to $V+$. Why?

(e) What voltage should be connected to A in so that the A-out voltage equals $V+$?

18. Consider the emitter-follower amplifier shown in Diagram A8-17. The transistor has an h_{fe} of 120 and r_{BE} of 800 Ω.

(a) What should be the value of R_B so that the emitter voltage is 5 V relative to ground?

(b) What then is the maximum undistorted peak-peak voltage that may be output (or input) for the amplifier?

(c) What is the expected input impedance and output impedance of the amplifier?

(d) Select C_1 and C_2 to have 10% of these respective impedances at 1 kHz.

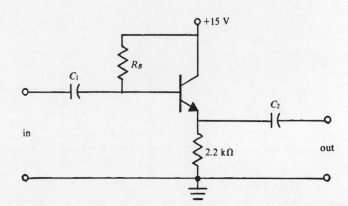

DIAGRAM
A8-17.

19. (a) Suppose the voltage supply used with the basic differential amplifier of Figure A8-22 is not stable, but fluctuates. Argue that this should have no effect on the output from a good differential amplifier.

NOTE: This favorable property is called good *supply voltage rejection*.

(b) Suppose the temperature changes so that the beta of the two transistors change in the differential amplifier. Although this changes the current through each transistor, argue that no effect is expected at the output from a good differential amplifier.

NOTE: This is a favorable temperature drift characteristic.

20. (a) It is quite clear that the grounded-emitter amplifier pictured in Figure A8-13 is not a dc amplifier. Why?

(b) Discuss how the differential amplifier pictured in Figure A8-22 avoids the need for each of the two offending elements in part (a).

21. (a) Consider the ac device operated in the circuit with a phototransistor in Figure A8-23. Is the ac device turned on when it is dark or when it is bright at the T1L81 transistor? Explain why.

(b) Describe a simple change in the circuit to obtain the opposite behavior from (a).

22. Consider Diagram A8–18. We wish to count objects as they pass a certain point and have at hand an electromechanical counter that increments once for each 240-mA pulse of current through its 100-Ω coil. Thus, a 24-V pulse to the coil is required for each count. Assume that the objects interrupt a light beam and that the resistance R_p of a photoresistor increases from 1 kΩ to 100 kΩ when the light beam is blocked. A circuit to operate the counter is illustrated.

(a) Assume the transistor beta is very large. Discuss how the circuit achieves the counting.

NOTE: Use an emitter follower argument.

(b) Assume that the transistor β is 100. Prove that the maximum current to the counter is only about 150 mA. Thus, the circuit will not operate.

(c) What transistor connection could be used to obtain a super-beta transistor for application here?

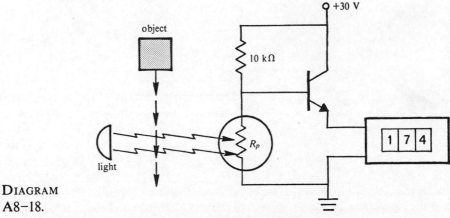

DIAGRAM
A8–18.

23. By opening or closing the proper switches in the circuit shown in Diagram A8–19, we may obtain 500 W, 250 W, or 0 W from the electric resistance heater. What switch settings are required for each of the three heating conditions? Explain how the circuit operates in terms of the SCR and triac behavior. Assume $I_{GT} = 10$ mA for both the SCR and the triac.

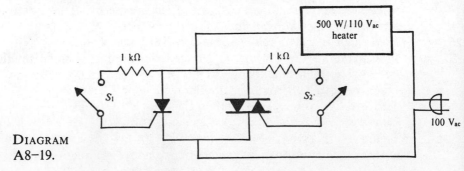

DIAGRAM
A8–19.

24. The intrusion alarm shown in Diagram A8–20 is constructed from an SCR and an automobile horn that operates from 12 V at 1.5 A. A snap-action switch S_1 is positioned against a door so that the switch is depressed until the door opens.

    (a) Justify that the horn sounds when the door opens for a properly selected SCR. Will it stop sounding if the door is quickly closed again? What is the utility of switch S_2?

    (b) What forward-blocking-voltage, on-state-current, and trigger-current characteristics are required for the SCR in this circuit?

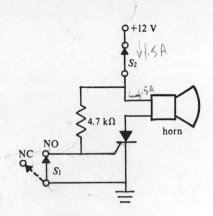

DIAGRAM A8–20.

25. A flashing circuit is desired for a conventional 100-W, 110-V_{ac} lamp with a 2-prong plug. The lamp plugs into the box that we design, and the box in turn plugs into a "mains" 110-V_{ac} socket with a 2-prong plug. The lamp is to be on for 4 seconds and off for 2 seconds in each cycle. Assume that a solid-state relay is available with a control-input requirement of 3 mA at 2 V; its triac output can switch 3 A at 125 V_{ac}. Also, a small 9-V_{dc}-encapsulated power supply is available to be incorporated in the box.

    (a) Develop a design using a 555 timer. The solid-state relay and also the power supply may be incorporated as blocks in the diagram. Design 100% over-drive current to the solid-state relay input (LED). Note that the knee of the LED diode characteristic is about 2 V.

    (b) An SCR could be considered in place of the solid-state relay in this design. However, the bulb will not shine at the 100-W brightness. Why? Why would a triac permit full brightness of the bulb during its on-time?

    (c) Use of an SCR or triac presents one point to be watched, however. The power supply output must be floating relative to ground. Explain why with the help of a sketch of an SCR design.

26. Consider a theoretical relation for g_m and r_{BE} for a transistor.

    (a) The voltage applied to the base-emitter diode in a transistor initiates a diode current that in fact almost entirely passes out the collector. For significant current levels in a transistor, we expect

$$I_c = I_{RE} \frac{|e| V_{BE}}{kT}$$

    Show how this relation was properly adapted from Equation A4–1.

(b)   The transconductance for a transistor may be written as a derivative:

$$g_m = \frac{dI_c}{dV_{BE}}$$

Argue that this relation is properly adapted from Equation A8–1.

(c)   Show the transconductance for a silicon transistor may be expected to be

$$g_m = \frac{e}{kT} I_c$$

At room temperature (300°K) show that the transconductance is given by the relation

$$g_m = (39 \text{ V}^{-1})I_c$$

(d)   Justify that

$$r_{BE} = \frac{h_{fe}}{(39 \text{ V}^{-1})I_c}$$

(e)   In practice, an inherent base-emitter resistance δ due to the ohmic resistance of the transistor must be added to this r_{BE} value. It may vary from a few ohms in a transistor designed for large currents to several hundred ohms for a small transistor. Why would we expect it to be more for a physically smaller transistor?

(f)   Note that then

$$g_m = \frac{h_{fe}}{(h_{fe}/39 I_c) + \delta}$$

Suppose a small transistor has an h_{fe} of 100 and a base-emitter resistance δ = 200 Ω. Find both r_{BE} and g_m at the respective collector currents of 1 mA and 20 mA.

(g)   If δ is small, the voltage gain of a common emitter amplifier is simply 39 times the number of volts across the load resistor. Justify this statement.

Manufacturers' Specifications

µA7800 Series
3-Terminal Positive Voltage Regulators
Fairchild Linear Integrated Circuits

GENERAL DESCRIPTION — The µA7800 series of monolithic 3-Terminal Positive Voltage Regulators is constructed using the Fairchild Planar* epitaxial process. These regulators employ internal current limiting, thermal shutdown and safe area compensation, making them essentially indestructible. If adequate heat sinking is provided, they can deliver over 1 A output current. They are intended as fixed voltage regulators in a wide range of applications including local (on card) regulation for elimination of distribution problems associated with single point regulation. In addition to use as fixed voltage regulators, these devices can be used with external components to obtain adjustable output voltages and currents.

- OUTPUT CURRENT IN EXCESS OF 1 A
- NO EXTERNAL COMPONENTS
- INTERNAL THERMAL OVERLOAD PROTECTION
- INTERNAL SHORT CIRCUIT CURRENT LIMITING
- OUTPUT TRANSISTOR SAFE AREA COMPENSATION
- AVAILABLE IN THE TO-220 AND THE TO-3 PACKAGE
- OUTPUT VOLTAGES OF 5, 6, 8, 8.5, 12, 15, 18, AND 24 V

ABSOLUTE MAXIMUM RATINGS

Input Voltage (5 V through 18 V)		35 V
(24 V)		40 V
Internal Power Dissipation		Internally Limited
Storage Temperature Range		−65°C to +150°C
Operating Junction Temperature Range	µA7800	−55°C to +150°C
	µA7800C	0°C to +150°C
Lead Temperature (Soldering, 60 s time limit) TO-3 Package		300°C
(Soldering, 10 s time limit) TO-220 Package		230°C

CONNECTION DIAGRAMS
TO-220 PACKAGE
(TOP VIEW)
PACKAGE OUTLINE GH
PACKAGE CODE U

- OUTPUT
- COMMON
- INPUT
2
3
1

ORDER INFORMATION

OUTPUT VOLTAGE	TYPE	PART NO.
5 V	µA7805C	µA7805UC
6 V	µA7806C	µA7806UC
8 V	µA7808C	µA7808UC
8.5 V	µA7885C	µA7885UC
12 V	µA7812C	µA7812UC
15 V	µA7815C	µA7815UC
18 V	µA7818C	µA7818UC
24 V	µA7824C	µA7824UC

TO-3 PACKAGE
(TOP VIEW)
PACKAGE OUTLINE GJ
PACKAGE CODE K

COMMON (3) — OUTPUT
2
1
INPUT

ORDER INFORMATION

OUTPUT VOLTAGE	TYPE	PART NO.
5 V	µA7805	µA7805KM
6 V	µA7806	µA7806KM
8 V	µA7808	µA7808KM
8.5 V	µA7885	µA7885KM
12 V	µA7812	µA7812KM
15 V	µA7815	µA7815KM
18 V	µA7818	µA7818KM
24 V	µA7824	µA7824KM
5 V	µA7805C	µA7805KC
6 V	µA7806C	µA7806KC
8 V	µA7808C	µA7808KC
8.5 V	µA7885	µA7885KC
12 V	µA7812C	µA7812KC
15 V	µA7815C	µA7815KC
18 V	µA7818C	µA7818KC
24 V	µA7824C	µA7824KC

EQUIVALENT CIRCUIT

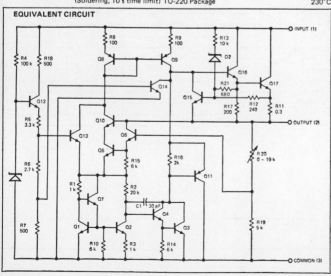

Reprinted with permission of Fairchild Camera & Instrument Corp.; Mountain View, California.

*Planar is a patented Fairchild process.

µA7805

ELECTRICAL CHARACTERISTICS

(V_{IN} = 10 V, I_{OUT} = 500 mA, −55°C ≤ T_J ≤ 150°C, C_{IN} = 0.33 µF, C_{OUT} = 0.1 µF, unless otherwise specified)

PARAMETER	CONDITIONS		MIN	TYP	MAX	UNITS
Output Voltage	T_J = 25°C		4.8	5.0	5.2	V
Line Regulation	T_J = 25°C	7 V ≤ V_{IN} ≤ 25 V		3	50	mV
		8 V ≤ V_{IN} ≤ 12 V		1	25	mV
Load Regulation	T_J = 25°C	5 mA ≤ I_{OUT} ≤ 1.5 A		15	50	mV
		250 mA ≤ I_{OUT} ≤ .750 mA		5	25	mV
Output Voltage	8.0 V ≤ V_{IN} ≤ 20 V 5 mA ≤ I_{OUT} ≤ 1.0 A P ≤ 15 W		4.65		5.35	V
Quiescent Current	T_J = 25°C			4.2	6.0	mA
Quiescent Current Change	with line	8 V ≤ V_{IN} ≤ 25 V			0.8	mA
	with load	5 mA ≤ I_{OUT} ≤ 1.0 A			0.5	mA
Output Noise Voltage	T_A = 25°C, 10 Hz ≤ f ≤ 100 kHz			40		µV
Ripple Rejection	f = 120 Hz, 8 V ≤ V_{IN} ≤ 18 V		68	78		dB
Dropout Voltage	I_{OUT} = 1.0 A, T_J = 25°C			2.0		V
Output Resistance	f = 1 kHz			17		mΩ
Short Circuit Current	T_J = 25°C			750		mA
Peak Output Current	T_J = 25°C			2.2		A
Average Temperature Coefficient of Output Voltage	I_{OUT} = 5 mA, 0°C ≤ T_J ≤ 150°C			−1.1		mV/°C

µA7805C

ELECTRICAL CHARACTERISTICS

(V_{IN} = 10 V, I_{OUT} = 500 mA, 0°C ≤ T_J ≤ 125°C, C_{IN} = 0.33 µF, C_{OUT} = 0.1 µF unless otherwise specified)

PARAMETER	CONDITIONS		MIN	TYP	MAX	UNITS
Output Voltage	T_J = 25°C		4.8	5.0	5.2	V
Line Regulation	T_J = 25°C	7 V ≤ V_{IN} ≤ 25 V		3	100	mV
		8 V ≤ V_{IN} ≤ 25 V		1	50	mV
Load Regulation	T_J = 25°C	5 mA ≤ I_{OUT} ≤ 1.5 A		15	100	mV
		250 mA ≤ I_{OUT} ≤ 750 mA		5	50	mV
Output Voltage	7 V ≤ V_{IN} ≤ 20 V 5 mA ≤ I_{OUT} ≤ 1.0 A P ≤ 15 W		4.75		5.25	V
Quiescent Current	T_J = 25°C			4.2	8.0	mA
Quiescent Current Change	with line	7 V ≤ V_{IN} ≤ 25 V			1.3	mA
	with load	5 mA ≤ I_{OUT} ≤ 1.0 A			0.5	mA
Output Noise Voltage	T_A = 25°C, 10 Hz ≤ f ≤ 100 kHz			40		µV
Ripple Rejection	f = 120 Hz, 8 V ≤ V_{IN} ≤ 18 V		62	78		dB
Dropout Voltage	I_{OUT} = 1.0 A, T_J = 25°C			2.0		V
Output Resistance	f = 1 kHz			17		mΩ
Short Circuit Current	T_J = 25°C			750		mA
Peak Output Current	T_J = 25°C			2.2		A
Average Temperature Coefficient of Output Voltage	I_{OUT} = 5 mA, 0°C ≤ T_J ≤ 125°C			−1.1		mV/°C

Reprinted with permission of Fairchild Camera & Instrument Corp.; Mountain View, California.

*Planar is a patented Fairchild process.

µA741
Frequency-Compensated Operational Amplifier
Fairchild Linear Integrated Circuits

GENERAL DESCRIPTION – The µA741 is a high performance monolithic Operational Amplifier constructed using the Fairchild Planar* epitaxial process. It is intended for a wide range of analog applications. High common mode voltage range and absence of "latch-up" tendencies make the µA741 ideal for use as a voltage follower. The high gain and wide range of operating voltage provides superior performance in integrator, summing amplifier, and general feedback applications.

- **NO FREQUENCY COMPENSATION REQUIRED**
- **SHORT CIRCUIT PROTECTION**
- **OFFSET VOLTAGE NULL CAPABILITY**
- **LARGE COMMON-MODE AND DIFFERENTIAL VOLTAGE RANGES**
- **LOW POWER CONSUMPTION**
- **NO LATCH UP**

ABSOLUTE MAXIMUM RATINGS

Supply Voltage		Storage Temperature Range	
Military (741)	±22 V	Metal Can, DIP, and Flatpak	−65°C to +150°C
Commercial (741C)	±18 V	Mini DIP	−55°C to +125°C
Internal Power Dissipation (Note 1)		Operating Temperature Range	
Metal Can	500 mW	Military (741)	−55°C to +125°C
DIP	670 mW	Commercial (741C)	0°C to +70°C
Mini DIP	310 mW	Lead Temperature (Soldering)	
Flatpak	570 mW	Metal Can, DIP, and Flatpak (60 seconds)	300°C
Differential Input Voltage	±30 V	Mini DIP (10 seconds)	260°C
Input Voltage (Note 2)	±15 V	Output Short Circuit Duration (Note 3)	Indefinite

EQUIVALENT CIRCUIT

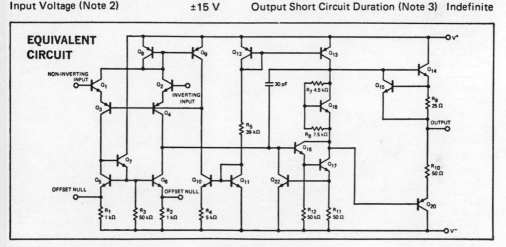

CONNECTION DIAGRAMS

8-LEAD MINI DIP
(TOP VIEW)
PACKAGE OUTLINE 9T

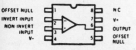

ORDER INFORMATION

TYPE	PART NO.
741C	741TC

8-LEAD METAL CAN
(TOP VIEW)
PACKAGE OUTLINE 5B

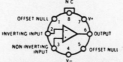

Note: Pin 4 connected to case

ORDER INFORMATION

TYPE	PART NO.
741	741HM
741C	741HC

14-LEAD DIP
(TOP VIEW)
PACKAGE OUTLINE 6A

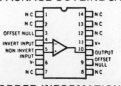

ORDER INFORMATION

TYPE	PART NO.
741	741DM
741C	741DC

A339

741C

ELECTRICAL CHARACTERISTICS ($V_S = \pm15$ V, $T_A = 25°C$ unless otherwise specified)

PARAMETERS (see definitions)	CONDITIONS	MIN.	TYP.	MAX.	UNIT
Input Offset Voltage	$R_S \leqslant 10$ kΩ		2.0	6.0	mV
Input Offset Current			20	200	nA
Input Bias Current			80	500	nA
Input Resistance		0.3	2.0		MΩ
Input Capacitance			1.4		pF
Offset Voltage Adjustment Range			±15		mV
Input Voltage Range		±12	±13		V
Common Mode Rejection Ratio	$R_S \leqslant 10$ kΩ	70	90		dB
Supply Voltage Rejection Ratio	$R_S \leqslant 10$ kΩ		30	150	μV/V
Large Signal Voltage Gain	$R_L \geqslant 2$ kΩ, $V_{OUT} = \pm10$ V	20,000	200,000		
Output Voltage Swing	$R_L \geqslant 10$ kΩ	±12	±14		V
	$R_L \geqslant 2$ kΩ	±10	±13		V
Output Resistance			75		Ω
Output Short Circuit Current			25		mA
Supply Current			1.7	2.8	mA
Power Consumption			50	85	mW
Transient Response (Unity Gain) — Risetime	$V_{IN} = 20$ mV, $R_L = 2$ kΩ, $C_L \leqslant 100$ pF		0.3		μs
Transient Response (Unity Gain) — Overshoot			5.0		%
Slew Rate	$R_L \geqslant 2$ kΩ		0.5		V/μs

The following specifications apply for $0°C \leqslant T_A \leqslant +70°C$:

Input Offset Voltage				7.5	mV
Input Offset Current				300	nA
Input Bias Current				800	nA
Large Signal Voltage Gain	$R_L \geqslant 2$ kΩ, $V_{OUT} = \pm10$ V	15,000			
Output Voltage Swing	$R_L \geqslant 2$ kΩ	±10	±13		V

TYPICAL PERFORMANCE CURVES FOR 741C

OUTPUT VOLTAGE SWING AS A FUNCTION OF SUPPLY VOLTAGE

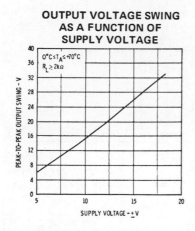

INPUT COMMON MODE VOLTAGE RANGE AS A FUNCTION OF SUPPLY VOLTAGE

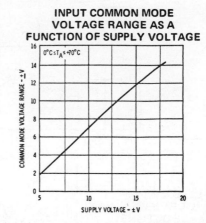

NOTES:
1. Rating applies to ambient temperatures up to 70°C. Above 70°C ambient derate linearly at 6.3 mW/°C for the Metal Can, 8.3 mW/°C for the DIP, 5.6 mW/°C for the Mini DIP and 7.1 mW/°C for the Flatpak.
2. For supply voltages less than ±15 V, the absolute maximum input voltage is equal to the supply voltage.
3. Short circuit may be to ground or either supply. Rating applies to +125°C case temperature or 75°C ambient temperature.

TYPICAL PERFORMANCE CURVES FOR 741C

INPUT BIAS CURRENT AS A FUNCTION OF AMBIENT TEMPERATURE

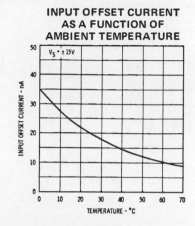

INPUT OFFSET CURRENT AS A FUNCTION OF AMBIENT TEMPERATURE

POWER CONSUMPTION AS A FUNCTION OF SUPPLY VOLTAGE

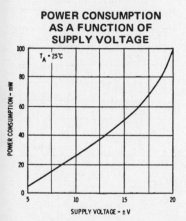

OPEN LOOP VOLTAGE GAIN AS A FUNCTION OF FREQUENCY

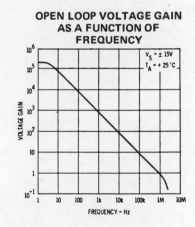

OPEN LOOP PHASE RESPONSE AS A FUNCTION OF FREQUENCY

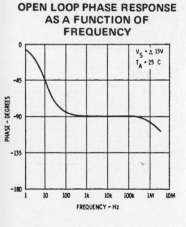

INPUT RESISTANCE AND INPUT CAPACITANCE AS A FUNCTION OF FREQUENCY

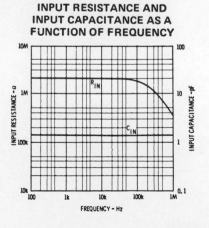

OUTPUT VOLTAGE SWING
AS A FUNCTION OF
LOAD RESISTANCE

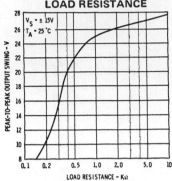

OUTPUT VOLTAGE SWING
AS A FUNCTION OF
FREQUENCY

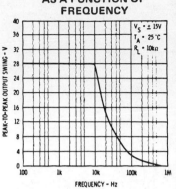

INPUT NOISE VOLTAGE
AS A FUNCTION OF
FREQUENCY

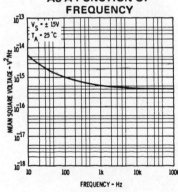

TRANSIENT RESPONSE

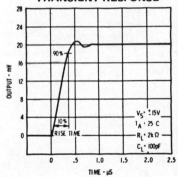

VOLTAGE OFFSET
NULL CIRCUIT

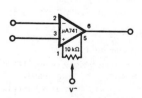

VOLTAGE FOLLOWER
LARGE-SIGNAL PULSE RESPONSE

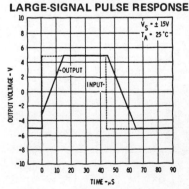

CA3140B, CA3140A, CA3140 Types
Linear Integrated Circuits
Monolithic Silicon
RCA, Solid State Division

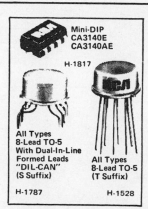

Mini-DIP
CA3140E
CA3140AE

H-1817

All Types
8-Lead TO-5
With Dual-In-Line
Formed Leads
"DIL-CAN"
(S Suffix)

All Types
8-Lead TO-5
(T Suffix)

H-1787   H-1528

BiMOS Operational Amplifiers
With MOS/FET Input, Bipolar Output

Features:

- MOS/FET Input Stage
   (a) Very high input impedance (Z_{IN}) — 1.5 TΩ typ.
   (b) Very low input current (I_I) — 10 pA typ. at ± 15 V
   (c) Low input-offset voltage (V_{IO}) — to 2 mV max.
   (d) Wide common-mode input-voltage range (V_{ICR}) — can be swung 0.5 volt below negative supply-voltage rail
   (e) Output swing complements input common-mode range
   (f) Rugged input stage — bipolar diode protected
- Directly replaces industry type 741 in most applications

The CA3140B, CA3140A, and CA3140 are integrated-circuit operational amplifiers that combine the advantages of high-voltage PMOS transistors with high-voltage bipolar transistors on a single monolithic chip. Because of this unique combination of technologies, this device can now provide designers, for the first time, with the special performance features of the CA3130 COS/MOS operational amplifiers and the versatility of the 741 series of industry-standard operational amplifiers.

The CA3140, CA3140A, and CA3140 BiMOS operational amplifiers feature gate-protected MOS/FET (PMOS) transistors in the input circuit to provide very-high-input impedance, very-low-input current, and high-speed performance. The CA3140B operates at supply voltages from 4 to 44 volts; the CA3140A and CA3140 from 4 to 36 volts (either single or dual supply). These operational amplifiers are internally phase-compensated to achieve stable operation in unity-gain follower operation, and, additionally, have access terminals for a supplementary external capacitor if additional frequency roll-off is desired. Terminals are also provided for use in applications requiring input offset-voltage nulling.

The use of PMOS field-effect transistors in the input stage results in common-mode input-voltage capability down to 0.5 volt below the negative-supply terminal, an important attribute for single-supply applications. The output stage uses bipolar transistors and includes built-in protection against damage from load-terminal short-circuiting to either supply-rail or to ground.

The CA3140 Series has the same 8-lead terminal pin-out used for the "741" and other

- Includes numerous industry operational amplifier categories such as general-purpose, FET input, wideband (high slew rate)
- Operation from 4-to-44 volts Single or Dual supplies
- Internally compensated
- Characterized for ± 15-volt operation and for TTL supply systems with operation down to 4 volts
- Wide bandwidth — 4.5 MHz unity gain at ± 15 V or 30 V; 3.7 MHz at 5 V
- High voltage-follower slew rate — 9 V/μs
- Fast settling time — 1.4 μs typ. to 10 mV with a 10-V_{p-p} signal
- Output swings to within 0.2 volt of negative supply
- Strobable output stage

Applications:

- Ground-referenced single-supply amplifiers in automobile and portable instrumentation
- Sample and hold amplifiers
- Long-duration timers/multivibrators (microseconds—minutes—hours)
- Photocurrent instrumentation
- Peak detectors   ■ Active filters
- Comparators
- Interface in 5 V TTL systems & other low-supply voltage systems
- All standard operational amplifier applications
- Function generators   ■ Tone controls
- Power supplies   ■ Portable instruments
- Intrusion alarm systems

industry-standard operational amplifiers. They are supplied in either the standard 8-lead TO-5 style package (T suffix), or in the 8-lead dual-in-line formed-lead TO-5 style package "DIL-CAN" (S suffix). The CA3140 is available in chip form (H suffix). The CA3140A and CA3140 are also available in an 8-lead dual-in-line plastic package (Mini-DIP-E suffix). The CA3140B is intended for operation at supply voltages ranging from 4 to 44 volts, for applications requiring premium-grade specifications and with electrical limits established for operations over the range from $-55°C$ to $+125°C$. The CA3140A and CA3140 are for operation at supply voltages up to 36 volts (±18 volts). The CA3140 ages up to 36 volts (±18 volts). All types can be operated safely over the temperature range from $-55°C$ to $+125°C$.

TYPICAL ELECTRICAL CHARACTERISTICS

CHARACTERISTIC	TEST CONDITIONS $V^+ = +15$ V $V^- = -15$ V $T_A = 25°C$	CA3140B (T,S)	CA3140A (T,S,E)	CA3140 (T,S,E)	UNITS
Input Offset Voltage Adjustment Resistor	Typ. Value of Resistor Between Term. 4 and 5 or 4 and 1 to Adjust Max. V_{IO}	43	18	4.7	$k\Omega$
Input Resistance R_1		1.5	1.5	1.5	$T\Omega$
Input Capacitance C_I		4	4	4	pF
Output Resistance R_O		60	60	60	Ω
Equivalent Wideband Input Noise Voltage e_n (See Fig. 39)	BW = 140 kHz $R_S = 1$ MΩ	48	48	48	μV
Equivalent Input Noise Voltage e_n (See Fig.10)	f = 1 kHz $R_S =$	40	40	40	$nV/\sqrt{Hz}$
	f = 10 kHz 100 Ω	12	12	12	
Short-Circuit Current to Opposite Supply Source $I_{OM}{}^+$		40	40	40	mA
Sink $I_{OM}{}^-$		18	18	18	mA
Gain-Bandwidth Product, (See Figs. 5 & 18) f_T		4.5	4.5	4.5	MHz
Slew Rate, (See Fig.6) SR		9	9	9	$V/\mu s$
Sink Current From Terminal 8 To Terminal 4 to Swing Output Low		220	220	220	μA
Transient Response: Rise Time	$R_L = 2$ kΩ $C_L = 100$ pF	0.08	0.08	0.08	μs
Overshoot (See Fig. 37) t_r		10	10	10	%
Settling Time at 10 V_{p-p}, (See Fig.17) t_s	1 mV	$R_L = 2$ kΩ $C_L = 100$ pF Voltage Follower	4.5	4.5	4.5	μs
	10 mV		1.4	1.4	1.4	

Printed in USA/3-77

Supersedes issue dated 5-76

ELECTRICAL CHARACTERISTICS FOR EQUIPMENT DESIGN

At V^+ = 15 V, V^- = 15 V, T_A = 25°C Unless Otherwise Specified

CHARACTERISTIC	LIMITS									UNITS
	CA3140B			CA3140A			CA3140			
	Min.	Typ.	Max.	Min.	Typ.	Max.	Min.	Typ.	Max.	
Input Offset Voltage, $\lvert V_{IO} \rvert$	–	0.8	2	–	2	5	–	5	15	mV
Input Offset Current, $\lvert I_{IO} \rvert$	–	0.5	10	–	0.5	20	–	0.5	30	pA
Input Current, I_I	–	10	30	–	10	40	–	10	50	pA
Large-Signal Voltage Gain, A_{OL} ● (See Figs. 4,18)	50 k	100 k	–	20 k	100 k	–	20 k	100 k	–	V/V
	94	100	–	86	100	–	86	100	··	dB
Common-Mode Rejection Ratio, CMRR (See Fig.9)	–	20	50	–	32	320	--	32	320	μV/V
	86	94	–	70	90	–	70	90	–	dB
Common-Mode Input-Voltage Range, V_{ICR} (See Fig.20)	–15	–15.5 to +12.5	12	–15	–15.5 to +12.5	12	–15	–15.5 to +12.5	11	V
Power-Supply Rejection Ratio, PSRR $\overline{\Delta V_{IO}/\Delta V}$ (See Fig.11)	–	32	100	–	100	150	–	100	150	μV/V
	80	90	–	76	80	–	76	80	–	dB
Max. Output Voltage ■ (See Figs.13,20) V_{OM}^+	+12	13	–	+12	13	–	+12	13	–	V
V_{OM}^-	–14	–14.4	–	–14	–14.4	–	–14	–14.4	–	
Supply Current, I^+ (See Fig.7)	–	4	6	–	4	6	–	4	6	mA
Device Dissipation, P_D	–	120	180	–	120	180	–	120	180	mW
Input Current, I_I ▲ (See Fig.19)	–	10	30	–	10	–	–	10	–	nA
Input Offset Voltage $\lvert V_{IO} \rvert$ ▲	–	1.3	3	–	3	–	–	10	–	mV
Input Offset Voltage Temp. Drift, $\Delta V_{IO}/\Delta T$	–	5	–	–	6	–	–	8	–	μV/°C
Large-Signal Voltage Gain, A_{OL} ▲ (See Figs.4,18)	20 k	100 k	–	–	100 k	–	–	100 k	–	V/V
	86	100	–	–	100	–	–	100	–	dB
Max. Output Voltage, ★ V_{OM}^+	+19	+19.5	–	–	–	–	–	–	–	V
V_{OM}^-	–21	–21.4	–	–	–	–	–	–	–	
Large-Signal Voltage Gain, A_{OL} ♦★	20 k	50 k	–	–	–	–	–	–	–	V/V
	86	94	–	–	–	–	–	–	–	dB

● At V_O = 26V_{p-p}, +12V, –14V and R_L = 2 kΩ.   ■ At R_L = 2 kΩ.

▲ At T_A = –55°C to +125°C, V^+ = 15 V, V^- = 15 V, V_O = 26V_{p-p}, R_L = 2 kΩ.

♦ At V_O = +19 V, –21 V, and R_L = 2 kΩ.   ★ At V^+ = 22 V, V^- = 22 V.

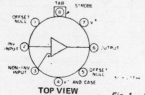
TOP VIEW
S and T Suffixes

Fig. 1 – Functional diagrams of the CA3140 series.

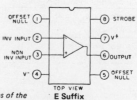
TOP VIEW
E Suffix

MAXIMUM RATINGS, *Absolute-Maximum Values:*

	CA3140, CA3140A	CA3140B
DC SUPPLY VOLTAGE (BETWEEN V+ AND V− TERMINALS)	36 V	44 V
DIFFERENTIAL-MODE INPUT VOLTAGE	±8 V	±8 V
COMMON-MODE DC INPUT VOLTAGE	$(V^+ +8 V)$ to $(V^- -0.5 V)$	
INPUT-TERMINAL CURRENT		1 mA

DEVICE DISSIPATION:
WITHOUT HEAT SINK —
UP TO 55°C . . . . 630 mW
ABOVE 55°C . . . . Derate linearly 6.67 mW/°C
WITH HEAT SINK —
Up to 55°C . . . . 1 W
Above 55°C . . . . Derate linearly 16.7 mW/°C
TEMPERATURE RANGE:
OPERATING (ALL TYPES) . . . . −55 to + 125°C
STORAGE (ALL TYPES) . . . . −65 to +150°C
OUTPUT SHORT-CIRCUIT DURATION* . . . . INDEFINITE
LEAD TEMPERATURE (DURING SOLDERING):
AT DISTANCE 1/16 ± 1/32 INCH (1.59 ± 0.79 MM)
FROM CASE FOR 10 SECONDS MAX. . . . . +265°C

* Short circuit may be applied to ground or to either supply.

TYPICAL ELECTRICAL CHARACTERISTICS FOR DESIGN GUIDANCE
At $V^+ = 5$ V, $V^- = 0$ V, $T_A = 25°C$

CHARACTERISTIC		CA3140B (T,S)	CA3140A (T,S,E)	CA3140 (T,S,E)	UNITS
Input Offset Voltage	$|V_{IO}|$	0.8	2	5	mV
Input Offset Current	$|I_{IO}|$	0.1	0.1	0.1	pA
Input Current	I_I	2	2	2	pA
Input Resistance		1	1	1	TΩ
Large-Signal Voltage Gain	A_{OL}	100 k	100 k	100 k	V/V
(See Figs. 4,18)		100	100	100	dB
Common-Mode Rejection Ratio,	CMRR	20	32	32	μV/V
		94	90	90	dB
Common-Mode Input-Voltage Range	V_{ICR}	−0.5	−0.5	−0.5	V
(See Fig.20)		2.6	2.6	2.6	
Power-Supply Rejection Ratio	$\Delta V_{IO}/\Delta V^+$	32	100	100	μV/V
		90	80	80	dB
Maximum Output Voltage	V_{OM}^+	3	3	3	V
(See Figs.13,20)	V_{OM}^-	0.13	0.13	0.13	
Maximum Output Current: Source	I_{OM}^+	10	10	10	mA
Sink	I_{OM}^-	1	1	1	
Slew Rate (See Fig.6)		7	7	7	V/μs
Gain-Bandwidth Product (See Fig.5)	f_T	3.7	3.7	3.7	MHz
Supply Current (See Fig.7)	I^+	1.6	1.6	1.6	mA
Device Dissipation	P_D	8	8	8	mW
Sink Current from Term. 8 to Term. 4 to Swing Output Low		200	200	200	μA

Timer 555
Linear Integrated Circuits
Signetics

DESCRIPTION

The NE/SE 555 monolithic timing circuit is a highly stable controller capable of producing accurate time delays, or oscillation. Additional terminals are provided for triggering or resetting if desired. In the time delay mode of operation, the time is precisely controlled by one external resistor and capacitor. For a stable operation as an oscillator, the free running frequency and the duty cycle are both accurately controlled with two external resistors and one capacitor. The circuit may be triggered and reset on falling waveforms, and the output structure can source or sink up to 200mA or drive TTL circuits.

- TIMING FROM MICROSECONDS THROUGH HOURS
- OPERATES IN BOTH ASTABLE AND MONOSTABLE MODES
- ADJUSTABLE DUTY CYCLE
- HIGH CURRENT OUTPUT CAN SOURCE OR SINK 200mA
- OUTPUT CAN DRIVE TTL
- TEMPERATURE STABILITY OF 0.005% PER °C
- NORMALLY ON AND NORMALLY OFF OUTPUT

APPLICATIONS

PRECISION TIMING
PULSE GENERATION
SEQUENTIAL TIMING
TIME DELAY GENERATION
PULSE WIDTH MODULATION
PULSE POSITION MODULATION
MISSING PULSE DETECTOR

PIN CONFIGURATIONS (Top View)

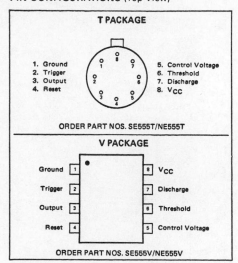

T PACKAGE

1. Ground
2. Trigger
3. Output
4. Reset
5. Control Voltage
6. Threshold
7. Discharge
8. V_{CC}

ORDER PART NOS. SE555T/NE555T

V PACKAGE

Ground — 1
Trigger — 2
Output — 3
Reset — 4
8 — V_{CC}
7 — Discharge
6 — Threshold
5 — Control Voltage

ORDER PART NOS. SE555V/NE555V

ABSOLUTE MAXIMUM RATINGS

Supply Voltage	+18V
Power Dissipation	600 mW
Operating Temperature Range	
NE555	0°C to +70°C
SE555	−55°C to +125°C
Storage Temperature Range	−65°C to +150°C
Lead Temperature (Soldering, 60 seconds)	+300°C

BLOCK DIAGRAM

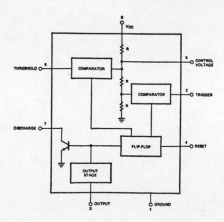

ELECTRICAL CHARACTERISTICS $T_A = 25°C$, $V_{CC} = +5V$ to $+15$ unless otherwise specified

PARAMETER	TEST CONDITIONS	SE 555			NE 555			UNITS
		MIN	TYP	MAX	MIN	TYP	MAX	
Supply Voltage		4.5		18	4.5		16	V
Supply Current	V_{CC} = 5V R_L = ∞		3	5		3	6	mA
	V_{CC} = 15V R_L = ∞		10	12		10	15	mA
	Low State, Note 1							
Timing Error (Monostable)	R_A, R_B = 1KΩ to 100KΩ							
Initial Accuracy	C = 0.1 µF Note 2		0.5	2		1		%
Drift with Temperature			30	100		50		ppm/°C
Drift with Supply Voltage			0.05	0.2		0.1		%/Volt
Threshold Voltage			2/3			2/3		X V_{CC}
Trigger Voltage	V_{CC} = 15V	4.8	5	5.2		5		V
Timing Error (Astable)	V_{CC} = 5V	1.45	1.67	1.9		1.67		V
Trigger Current			0.5			0.5		µA
Reset Voltage		0.4	0.7	1.0	0.4	0.7	1.0	V
Reset Current			0.1			0.1		mA
Threshold Current	Note 3		0.1	.25		0.1	.25	µA
Control Voltage Level	V_{CC} = 15V	9.6	10	10.4	9.0	10	11	V
	V_{CC} = 5V	2.9	3.33	3.8	2.6	3.33	4	V
Output Voltage (low)	V_{CC} = 15V							
	I_{SINK} = 10mA		0.1	0.15		0.1	.25	V
	I_{SINK} = 50mA		0.4	0.5		0.4	.75	V
	I_{SINK} = 100mA		2.0	2.2		2.0	2.5	V
	I_{SINK} = 200mA		2.5			2.5		
	V_{CC} = 5V							
	I_{SINK} = 8mA		0.1	0.25				V
	I_{SINK} = 5mA					.25	.35	
Output Voltage Drop (low)								
	I_{SOURCE} = 200mA		12.5			12.5		
	V_{CC} = 15V							
	I_{SOURCE} = 100mA							
	V_{CC} = 15V	13.0	13.3		12.75	13.3		V
	V_{CC} = 5V	3.0	3.3		2.75	3.3		V
Rise Time of Output			100			100		nsec
Fall Time of Output			100			100		nsec

NOTES
1. Supply Current when output high typically 1mA less.
2. Tested at V_{CC} = 5V and V_{CC} = 15V
3. This will determine the maximum value of R_A + R_B. For 15V operation, the max total R = 20 megohm.

EQUIVALENT CIRCUIT (Shown for One Side Only)

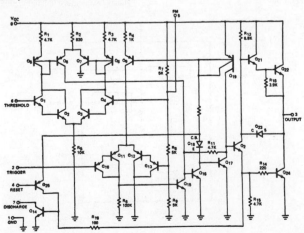

TYPICAL CHARACTERISTICS

MINIMUM PULSE WIDTH
REQUIRED FOR TRIGGERING

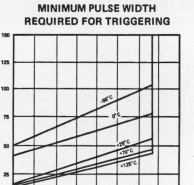

SUPPLY CURRENT
vs SUPPLY VOLTAGE

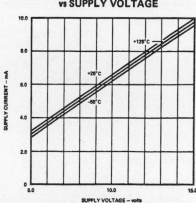

LOW OUTPUT VOLTAGE
vs OUTPUT SINK CURRENT

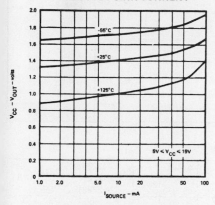

HIGH OUTPUT VOLTAGE
vs OUTPUT
SOURCE CURRENT

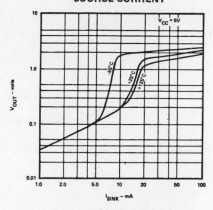

LOW OUTPUT VOLTAGE
vs OUTPUT SINK CURRENT

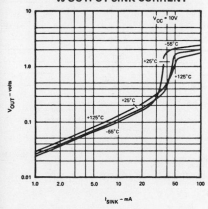

LOW OUTPUT VOLTAGE
vs OUTPUT SINK CURRENT

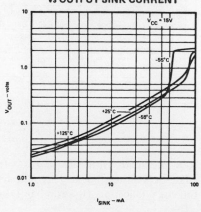

A349

Types 2N2217 thru 2N2222, 2N2218A, 2N2219A, 2N2221A, 2N2222A
NPN Silicon Transistors

DESIGNED FOR HIGH-SPEED, MEDIUM-POWER SWITCHING AND GENERAL PURPOSE AMPLIFIER APPLICATIONS

- h_{FE} ... Guaranteed from 100 μA to 500 mA
- High f_T at 20 V, 20 mA ... 300 MHz (2N2219A, 2N2222A)
  250 MHz (all others)
- 2N2218, 2N2221 for Complementary Use with 2N2904, 2N2906
- 2N2219, 2N2222 for Complementary Use with 2N2905, 2N2906

*mechanical data

Device types 2N2217, 2N2218, 2N2218A, 2N2219, and 2N2219A are in JEDEC TO-5 packages.
Device types 2N2220, 2N2221, 2N2221A, 2N2222, and 2N2222A are in JEDEC TO-18 packages.

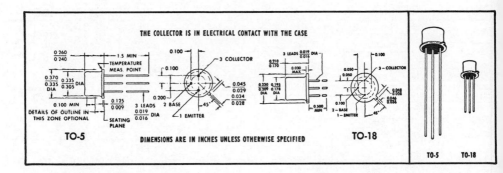

*absolute maximum ratings at 25°C free-air temperature (unless otherwise noted)

	2N2217 2N2218 2N2219	2N2218A 2N2219A	2N2220 2N2221 2N2222	2N2221A 2N2222A	UNIT
Collector-Base Voltage	60	75	60	75	V
Collector-Emitter Voltage (See Note 1)	30	40	30	40	V
Emitter-Base Voltage	5	6	5	6	V
Continuous Collector Current	0.8	0.8	0.8	0.8	A
Continuous Device Dissipation at (or below) 25°C Free-Air Temperature (See Notes 2 and 3)	0.8	0.8	0.5	0.5	W
Continuous Device Dissipation at (or below) 25°C Case Temperature (See Notes 4 and 5)	3	3	1.8	1.8	W
Operating Collector Junction Temperature Range	−65 to 175				°C
Storage Temperature Range	−65 to 200				°C
Lead Temperature 1/16 Inch from Case for 10 Seconds	230				°C

NOTES: 1. These values apply between 0 and 500 mA collector current when the base-emitter diode is open-circuited.
2. Derate 2N2217, 2N2218, 2N2218A, 2N2219, and 2N2219A linearly to 175°C free-air temperature at the rate of 5.33 mW/°C.
3. Derate 2N2220, 2N2221, 2N2221A, 2N2222, and 2N2222A linearly to 175°C free-air temperature at the rate of 3.33 mW/°C.
4. Derate 2N2217, 2N2218, 2N2218A, 2N2219, and 2N2219A linearly to 175°C case temperature at the rate of 20.0 mW/°C.
5. Derate 2N2220, 2N2221, 2N2221A, 2N2222, and 2N2222A linearly to 175°C case temperature at the rate of 12.0 mW/°C.

USES CHIP N2

Reprinted with permission of Texas Instruments, Dallas, Texas.
*JEDEC registered data. This data sheet contains all applicable registered data in effect at the time of publication. (Bulletin No. DL-S7311916, March 1973)

2N2217 THRU 2N2222

*electrical characteristics at 25°C free-air temperature (unless otherwise noted)

PARAMETER		TEST CONDITIONS	TO-5 → 2N2217 TO-18 → 2N2220		TO-5 → 2N2218 TO-18 → 2N2221		TO-5 → 2N2219 TO-18 → 2N2222		UNIT
			MIN	MAX	MIN	MAX	MIN	MAX	
$V_{(BR)CBO}$	Collector-Base Breakdown Voltage	$I_C = 10\,\mu A$, $I_E = 0$	60		60		60		V
$V_{(BR)CEO}$	Collector-Emitter Breakdown Voltage	$I_C = 10\,mA$, $I_B = 0$, See Note 6	30		30		30		V
$V_{(BR)EBO}$	Emitter-Base Breakdown Voltage	$I_E = 10\,\mu A$, $I_C = 0$	5		5		5		V
I_{CBO}	Collector Cutoff Current	$V_{CB} = 50\,V$, $I_E = 0$		10		10		10	nA
		$V_{CB} = 50\,V$, $I_E = 0$, $T_A = 150°C$		10		10		10	μA
I_{EBO}	Emitter Cutoff Current	$V_{EB} = 3\,V$, $I_C = 0$		10		10		10	nA
h_{FE}	Static Forward Current Transfer Ratio	$V_{CE} = 10\,V$, $I_C = 100\,\mu A$			20		35		
		$V_{CE} = 10\,V$, $I_C = 1\,mA$	12		25		50		
		$V_{CE} = 10\,V$, $I_C = 10\,mA$	17		35		75		
		$V_{CE} = 10\,V$, $I_C = 150\,mA$ See Note 6	20	60	40	120	100	300	
		$V_{CE} = 10\,V$, $I_C = 500\,mA$	20				30		
		$V_{CE} = 1\,V$, $I_C = 150\,mA$	10		20		50		
V_{BE}	Base-Emitter Voltage	$I_B = 15\,mA$, $I_C = 150\,mA$ See Note 6		1.3		1.3		1.3	V
		$I_B = 50\,mA$, $I_C = 500\,mA$		2.6		2.6		2.6	
$V_{CE(sat)}$	Collector-Emitter Saturation Voltage	$I_B = 15\,mA$, $I_C = 150\,mA$ See Note 6		0.4		0.4		0.4	V
		$I_B = 50\,mA$, $I_C = 500\,mA$		1.6		1.6		1.6	
$|h_{fe}|$	Small-Signal Common-Emitter Forward Current Transfer Ratio	$V_{CE} = 20\,V$, $I_C = 20\,mA$, $f = 100\,MHz$	2.5		2.5		2.5		
f_T	Transition Frequency	$V_{CE} = 20\,V$, $I_C = 20\,mA$, See Note 7	250		250		250		MHz
C_{obo}	Common-Base Open-Circuit Output Capacitance	$V_{CB} = 10\,V$, $I_E = 0$, $f = 1\,MHz$	8		8		8		pF
$h_{ie(real)}$	Real Part of Small-Signal Common-Emitter Input Impedance	$V_{CE} = 20\,V$, $I_C = 20\,mA$, $f = 300\,MHz$	60		60		60		Ω

NOTES: 6. These parameters must be measured using pulse techniques. $t_w = 300\,\mu s$, duty cycle ≤ 2%.
7. To obtain f_T, the $|h_{fe}|$ response with frequency is extrapolated at the rate of −6 dB per octave from f = 100 MHz to the frequency at which $|h_{fe}| = 1$.

switching characteristics at 25°C free-air temperature

PARAMETER		TEST CONDITIONS†	TYP	UNIT
t_d	Delay Time	$V_{CC} = 30\,V$, $I_C = 150\,mA$, $I_{B(1)} = 15\,mA$,	5	ns
t_r	Rise Time	$V_{BE(off)} = -0.5\,V$, See Figure 1	15	ns
t_s	Storage Time	$V_{CC} = 30\,V$, $I_C = 150\,mA$, $I_{B(1)} = 15\,mA$,	190	ns
t_f	Fall Time	$I_{B(2)} = -15\,mA$, See Figure 2	23	ns

†Voltage and current values shown are nominal; exact values vary slightly with transistor parameters.

*JEDEC registered data

Bibliography

It can be helpful to read about a topic when it is presented in a manner different from the student's own textbook. The presentation may be more elementary or more sophisticated. Furthermore, the reader may wish to study a topic in more depth, particularly if a certain project is being developed. Therefore, a short list of references follows. The first nine references are general texts on electronics for scientists and are listed in chronological order. Brief comments are included with each to help in choosing a reference. The last four references focus on topics emphasized in this book.

Malmstadt, H.V., C.G. Enke, and E.C. Toren. 1963. *Electronics for Scientists*. New York: W.A. Benjamin.
Text is one of the first books to recognize a different approach is needed for scientists. It has tube and transistor emphasis, but was among first to stress operational amplifiers. A later version of this book is *Electronic Measurements for Scientists* by H.V. Malmstadt, C.G. Enke, and S.R. Crouch. 1974. Menlo Park, Calif.: W.A. Benjamin. It is almost "encyclopedic," but a good reference. The latest version is Malmstadt, H.V., C.G. Enke, and E.C. Toren. 1981. *Electronics and Instrumentation for Scientists*. Menlo Park, Calif.: Benjamin/Cummings.
Suprynowicz, V.A. 1966. *Introduction to Electronics for Students of Biology, Chemistry, and Medicine*. Reading, Mass.: Addison-Wesley.
Stresses general principles of operation for many kinds of electronic circuits, but with tube emphasis.
Brophy, J. 1966, 1972, 1977. *Basic Electronics for Scientists*. New York: McGraw-Hill.
Good selection of material; intermediate level, with transistor emphasis.
Diefenderfer, A.J. 1972. *Principles of Electronic Instrumentation*. Philadelphia: Saunders.
Closer to the level of this book; includes digital electronics. The second edition, 1979, moved to intermediate level. Substantial transistor work.
Vassos, B., and G. Ewing. 1972. *Analog and Digital Electronics for Scientists*. New York: Wiley.
Emphasizes the operational amplifier. Uses complex impedance approach for ac circuits.
Anderson, L., and W. Beeman. 1973. *Electronic Circuits and Modern Electronics*. New York: Holt, Rinehart and Winston
Intended for scientists, but at a moderately sophisticated level; all solid-state.

Simpson, R. 1974. *Introductory Electronics for Scientists and Engineers.* Boston: Allyn and Bacon.

Good selection of material for intermediate analog electronics course; includes digital topics.

Jones, B. 1974. *Circuit Electronics for Scientists.* Reading, Mass.: Addison-Wesley.

Quite a lot of network theory in an attempt to avoid obsolescence; also moderately sophisticated.

Weber, L., and D. McLean. 1975. *Electrical Measurement Systems for Biological and Physical Scientists.* Reading, Mass.: Addison-Wesley.

Good presentation of many topics in laboratory electronics at a very basic level; especially intended for biological scientists.

Brown, Burr. 1971. J.G. Graeme, G.E. Tobey, L.P. Huelsman, eds. *Operational Amplifiers, Design, and Applications.* New York: McGraw-Hill.

Written by a pioneering manufacturer in the field. This book is quite comprehensive and sophisticated, but may have answers when others do not.

Jung, W. 1974. *IC Op-Amp Cookbook.* Indianapolis, Ind.: Sams.

A "Sam's paperback" that is a compendium of operational amplifier techniques. Also discusses characteristics of actual important op-amp devices available.

Jung, W. 1977. *IC Timer Cookbook.* Indianapolis, Ind.: Sams.

This is another paperback; good discussion of characteristics and compendium of uses for this widely used linear integrated-circuit type (especially the 555 timer).

Sheingold, D.H., ed. 1980. "Analog Devices." *Transducer Interfacing Handbook.* Norwood, Mass.: Analog Devices, Inc.

Written by an important manufacturer of analog integrated circuits. Readable discussion of transducers and instrumentation for them. Half of the book discusses a cross section of applications.

Answers to Problems

The answers to odd-numbered problems, except for diagrams and lengthy discussions, are provided. In the case of derivations or discussion answers, only brief summary answers are given.

Chapter A1
1. $0.011 \ \Omega$
5. (a) for $47 \ \Omega$, 146 mA; for 47 kΩ, 4.6 mA; (b) for 47 Ω, 6.8 V; for 47 kΩ, 217 V
7. (b) 0.545 kΩ; (c) 11 mA; (d) for 1 kΩ, 6 mA; for 2 kΩ, 3 mA; for 3 kΩ, 2 mA
9. for 10 kΩ, 0.4 mA; for 5 kΩ, 0.695 mA; for 2 kΩ, 0.26 mA; for 3 kΩ, 0.174 mA
11. 3.36 V
13. 565 cm^2
15. plot $v = 20 \ \text{V}(1 - e^{-t/1.55 \ \text{ms}})$
17. (a) 0 V; (b) 5 V; (c) 10 V; (d) 3.54 V; (e) 0.01 Hz; (f) 100 s
21. (a) 818 turns; (b) 273 turns
23. (a.1) 0.532 mA; (a.2) 5.32 V; (a.3) 8.46 V; (a.4) 0.532; (a.5) $-57.8°$; (a.6) 2.83 mW; (b) 1.59 kHz
25. (a) $P_{max} = V^2/R$; (b) $P = V^2R/(R^2 + X_c^2)$; at f_o have $P = V^2/2R$
27. (a) $R = 500 \ \Omega$; $C = 0.32 \ \mu$F; (b) $-45°$
29. $I_1 = -2/19$ A; $I_3 = 12/19$ A; $I_4 = 10/19$ A
31. (a) $V_{Th} = 2.28$ V; $R_{Th} = 2.72 \ \Omega$; then $I = 0.103$ A; (b) $V_{Th} = 2.5$ V; $R_{Th} = 0.75 \ \Omega$; then $I = 0.526$ A
33. $I_1 = 2/19$ A; $I_3 = 12/19$ A; $I_4 = 10/19$ A
35. $I_N = V/R$; $R_N = R$

37. $V_{out} = V_{in}/[1 + (X_c/R)^2] = V_{in}/[1 + (f_o/f)^2]$; for $f_o/f \gg 1$: $V_{out} = f^2(V_{in}/f_o^2)$

Chapter A2
1. (a) $R_{sh} = 1.002 \ \Omega$; (b) 0.1 V
3. $\pm 0.55°$
5. (a) 1.5 kΩ; (b) 1.5 kΩ
7. $R_x = V/(10^{-3} \ \text{A}) = V(10^3 \ \text{A}^{-1}) = V(\text{k}\Omega/\text{V})$
9. 3% (worst case)
13. $\Delta V/V$ is a small fraction, requiring a high precision detector.
15. Scope alternately triggers on two different positive slope points of the waveform at a given level.
17. (a) 1/11; (b) 0.235 V_{p-p}; (c) 94.1 Ω
19. (a) 0.063; (b) 0.25
21. $V_{fo}/V_{pass} = 0.707 = V_2/V_1$; dB ratio $= 20 \log (0.707) = -3$ dB

Chapter A3
1. 210 Ω
3. (a) 1.08 V; 0.0 V; 0.95 V; (b) B; neither; A
5. (a) 5 mV; (b) 75 mV
7. (a) A is in extension; B is in compression;

(b) $\triangle R_A \cong -\triangle R_B$ when the bar is bent. Therefore, the strain gauge pair may be put in a half-active bridge in order to double the bridge output in accordance with Problem 12(b) of Chapter A2.

(c) Support hinged plate with strain gauged bar on opposite side from hinge. Place gauges in half-active bridge and use bridge output voltages as indication of weight placed on plate.

11. (a) Ferromagnetic material placed within a coil increases its inductance; fractional insertion causes a fractional increase in inductance.

(b) Measure its inductance. However, an ac-measuring circuit is required to measure this ac parameter.

13. (a) Maximum single cell output voltage of about 0.6 V is less than voltage required across relay coil.

(b) Connect 9 cells in series.

(c) Cells must supply required current at the coil voltage; however, current capability is proportional to cell area.

Chapter A4

1. 0.575 A

   (a) same graph as diagram A4–8a;

   (b) 10 V_{dc} voltage graph

5. 4.3 V_{rms}

9. (a) 10.8 V; (b) 0.02 V

13. (a) 3 mA in 1 kΩ; 1 mA in 6 kΩ; 2 mA in diode

   (b) 3 mA in 1 kΩ and in 6 kΩ, 0 mA in diode

   (c) As current through R_L increases, current through zener diode must decrease. But minimum zener current is zero, as obtained with $R_L = 2$ kΩ. Zener diode effectively becomes an open circuit for smaller R_L values.

Chapter A5

1. 4.0 V_{rms}

5. (b) 8.9 V_{p-p}

7. 56%

9. $v_{out}/v_{in} = [R_{in}^2/(R_{in} + R_{out})^2]A_v^3$

11. (a) for dc: 6 V; for ac: 0 V; (b) for each: 6 V_{rms}, provided the ac frequency is within the bandwidth of each.

13. (a) 1.0 V_{rms}; 10 V_{rms}; (b) 0.0793 V_{rms}; 0.793 V_{rms}; (c) 10 kΩ in amplifier 1 and 200 pF in amplifier 2; (d) 79 kHz

15. $V_1 = +0.5$ V; $V_2 = -0.5$ V; $V_3 = +1.0$ V

17. -6.0 V

19. 0.1 V_{p-p}

21. (a) plot: for $f < f$ and $f > f_2$: $A_v = 0$; for $f_1 < f < f_2$: $A_v = 1$; (b) 1.8 μV_{rms}; (c) 1.8 μV_{rms}

23. 8.5 mV_{rms} noise output; 56 μV_{rms} signal input

Chapter A6

1. $R_f = 100$ kΩ and $R = 5$ kΩ in Figure A6–2a.

3. $R_f = 9$ kΩ and $R = 1$ kΩ in Figure A6–5a.

5. (a) -5; 5 kΩ; (b) $+6$; many megohms

7. (a) $R_{icm+} \| R_{icm-}$; (c) 199.9 MΩ (for $R_{in} = 2$ MΩ, $A_{vo} = 200,000$)

9. (a) noninverting

   (b) $v_{in} \cong [10 \text{ k}\Omega/(10 \text{ k}\Omega + 1000 \text{ k}\Omega)]$
   $[1 \text{ k}\Omega/(1 \text{ k}\Omega + 99 \text{ k}\Omega]v_{out}$
   $= v_{out}/1000$; then $v_{in}/v_{out} = A_v = 1000$

   (c) Neither very large nor very small resistors are required.

11. Because $v_d \cong V$, voltage V appears across R; then current through R is equal to $I = V/R$. But current I flows through R_x, since there is negligible current into $-$ input of op amp.

13. $R_1 = 3$ kΩ; $R_2 = 1.5$ kΩ; $R_3 = 1$ kΩ; $R_f = 3$ kΩ in Figure A6–7.

15. $R_f = 500$ Ω in Figure A6–11, with voltmeter at output.

17. 0.2 V

19. Turn diode in Figure A6–15 around.

21. $v_{out} = (v_B/v_A)^k$

23. (a) Descending "staircase form" with slanting descenders between horizontal steps. (b) v_{out} remains at $V-$ after reaching this level.

25. (a) $v_{out} = +0.032$ V $\cos(\omega t)$; v_{out} leads v_{in} by 90°; 0.032 V; yes
    (b) $v_{out} = -125$ V $\cos(\omega t)$; v_{out} lags v_{in} by 90°; 125 V; no

27. (a) 500 Hz; (b) 5000 Hz

29. (a) ac amplifier because of C_1 and C_2; (b) block dc offset in input signal; (c) small dc offset in op-amp output is blocked by C_2; (d) possible large dc offset at output limits output amplitude due to possible clipping at $V+$ or $V-$.

31. (a) high speed category (e.g., 318); (b) precision category (e.g., OP–07); (c) general purpose (e.g., 741); (d) high speed category (e.g., LH0032C); (e) FET input (e.g., CA3140); (f) micropower (e.g., OP–20)

Chapter A7

1. (a) -6 V; (b) -6 V; (c) -6 V; (d) -6 V; (e) $+6$ V

3. (a) Use $V_r = 3$ V in Figure A7–2a; have output as in Figure A7–3a, but diode D_2 is connected to $+6$-V battery, and diode D_1 is connected to -6-V battery (rather than ground). Also omit 1 kΩ = resistor in Figure A7–3a. (b) Use voltage divider of 9-kΩ and 3-kΩ resistors in series between $V+ = +12$ V and ground to establish $V_r = 3$ V. (One mA flows in this circuit.) Use a 3-resistor voltage divider with two 300-Ω resistors and one 600-Ω resistor connected between $+12$ V and -12 V to establish ± 6 V clipping voltages in place of batteries in part a. (Twenty mA flows in this circuit.) Use 3-kΩ current limit resistor in op-amp circuit.

5. Upper level = 4.75 V; lower level = -0.25 V; then hysteresis = 5 V; Center = 2.25 V, not 3 V.

7. Three cascaded monostable MVs. First monostable uses $C = 1.0$ μF and switch selectable $R = 1$ MΩ, 2 MΩ, 3 MΩ; second "delay" monostable uses $R = 5$ MΩ and $C = 1.0$ μF; third monostable uses $R = 5$ MΩ and $C = 2.0$ μF.

9. (a) 5 kΩ "pulls" 555 input high to $+6$ V due to voltage divider action between 5 kΩ and high resistance of input. When (NO) push button is pressed, input is grounded and negative pulse is generated.
    (b) Pushing PB1 causes RS flip-flop to set to high volts and motor to start; pressing PB2 causes 555 to reset to low volts output and motor stops. Motor must require less than 200 mA.
    (c) Connect threshold input through 5 kΩ to ground and also through (NO) PB2 to $+6$ V. Positive pulse to upper comparator resets RS flip-flop and stops motor.

11. Three 555 timer devices in separate monostable circuits as in Figure A7–12 are required. $R = 1$ MΩ in all three, but $C = 1.8$ μF for process A monostable; $C = 4.5$ μF for process B monostable; $C = 18$ μF for process C monostable. A single push-button circuit like that for PB1 in Diagram A7–8 feeds both process A and B monostable trigger inputs. Process B monostable triggers process C monostable through a differentiating circuit as shown in Figure A7–14; this is required because the low voltage state from the process B monostable would otherwise prevent termination of the process C pulse.

13. Use the monostable 555 timer circuit of Problem 10. Output of this monostable connects to reset of a second 555 timer that is connected as an astable MV as in Figure A7–15. Let $R_A = 1$ kΩ; $R_B = 10$ kΩ; $C = 0.0023$ μF in this astable circuit. Operate both 555 timers from $V+ = 6$ V, and

connect output of the astable to the second transducer.

15. (b) When transistor switch S in Figure A7–15 closes, it acts as direct short between $V+$ and ground. High current flow would destroy the transistor.

17. (a) 500 Hz, 12 V; (b) 1.2 V

Chapter A8

1. (a) small resistance for A, small resistance for B; (b) large resistance for A, small resistance for B

3. 7 V

5. (a) For $V_{DS} < V_{pinch-off}$, I_D is proportional to V_{DS} with proportionality constant depending on V_{GS}. Then FET exhibits resistance R_{DS} between drain and source that is controlled by V_{GS}. When V_{GS} is zero, R_{DS} is a minimum.

   (b) The circuit is of the same form as the noninverting amplifier of Figure A6–5a, with R_{DS} of FET replacing resistor R. Then $A_v = (1 + R_f/R_{DS})$ is adjustable. When V_{GS} is zero, R_{DS} in minimum and voltage gain A_v is maximum.

9. $V_1 \cong 0.7$ V; $V_2 = 9$ V; $I = 3$ mA

11. (a) 100 V; $\cong 0$ V; (b) 250 kΩ; (c) $I_{Cmax} > 20$ mA; $V_{CEmax} > 100$ V

13. (a) 4.0 V; 3.3 V; 13.4 V

    (b) Since V_C does not depend on the transistor β, the operating point does not shift with changing transistor temperatures or different transistors.

    (c) The dc blocking capacitors are at the input and output.

15. I through R_L equals I_D of the FET. But $V_{GS} = 0$ here, so that $I_D = I_{DSS}$. Since I_{DSS} is approximately constant (for $V_{DS} > V_{pinch-off}$), the load current is constant. However, $V \geq V_{RL} = I_{DSS}R_L$. Then $R_L \leq V/I_{DSS}$.

17. (a) $V_{A out} = (V+) - I_{DSS}R_L < V+$; $V_{B out} = V+$; (b) no; (c) $V_{B out} = (V+) - I_C R_L < V+$; yes; (d) would forward bias the gate-channel diode; (e) negative voltage equal to pinch-off voltage

19. (a) By symmetry, $\triangle V$ of the two output terminals must be the same. Since $V_{out} = V_{left} - V_{right}$, V_{out} experiences change $\triangle V_{out} = \triangle V - \triangle V = 0$; (b) If transistors are matched, the symmetry again requires $\triangle V$ of the two output terminals must be the same. Again as in part a, $\triangle V_{out} = 0$.

21. (a) Turned on when it is bright; transistor passes current that pulls in the armature and closes the NO contact; (b) Make connection to NO switch contact rather than NC.

23. Switches S_1 and S_2 open for 0 W; only switch S_1 closed for 250 W; switch S_2 closed for 500 W. For switch S_1 closed, the SCR conducts when the instantaneous ac voltage exceeds about 10 V; however, negative half cycles are blocked by the SCR. For switch S_2 closed, the triac conducts for most of the half cycle for both positive and negative swings and 500 W is attained.

25. (a) Power the 9-V_{dc} supply from the 110 V_{ac} plug input; also connect box receptacle in series with solid-state relay output and to 110 V_{ac} input. Connect V+ and ground of 555 timer to 9-V_{dc} supply +, − outputs. Use $C = 10$ μF, $R_A = R_B = 285$ kΩ in astable connection for the 555 timer. Connect 555 timer output through 1 kΩ resistor to the solid-state relay control input (this limits input current to about 6 mA). (b) SCR permits only half-wave current flow, while triac permits full-wave current flow. (c) One terminal of the power-supply output must be connected to one of the ac lines in this approach. A short may occur if the supply output is not floating.

Digital and
Microprocessor Electronics
for Scientific Application

CHAPTER D1

Digital Logic Elements

DIGITAL

Computers are known even to the layperson as logical "beasts" that make decisions in the process of performing their tasks. The study of logic with propositional variables dates to Aristotle in the 4th century B.C. The *syllogism* or deductive reasoning of his logic involved the basic form: *If A is true AND B is true, then T is true*. This propositional relationship is called the *logical AND*. For example: *If* (the key in the ignition is on) *AND* (the transmission is in park), *then* (the car will start). The *propositional variables*—or simply propositions—are indicated by parentheses in this statement.

Each proposition can have only a yes/no or true/false condition. Only two states are possible. During the 1940s John von Neumann realized that electrical circuits with only two states—that is, on or off— are particularly reliable and easy to design. He pointed out that binary numbers involve only two states and, as a result of his suggestion, binary numbers (implemented by two-state electronic circuits) became the common medium of numerical computation in digital computers.

Chapter D1 examines both the fundamental logic propositions and the important electrical circuits that implement logical decisions, ultimately permitting very powerful and useful digital electronic computation and decision processing. The elements of switching circuits and Boolean algebra are introduced, and rather practical properties of contemporary digital electronic building blocks—that is, integrated-circuit logic—are presented. It is desirable that the student gain familiarity and intuition through experimentation with these devices; the information provided in Chapter D1 permits the student to begin some laboratory work early on in the course.

NOTE: A brief review of binary numbers is given at the end of this chapter.

Basic Logic Gates

Logical AND

All the possibilities for a propositional expression can be set forth in a *truth table*. The truth table for the logical AND given in terms of true and false is shown in Table D1-1. All possible states of *A* and *B* are shown on the left side, and the states of the conclusion *T* are shown on the right. To save time and effort, and also to relate to binary numbers, Table D1-2 shows the logical AND truth table in terms of *logical zero* (0), which represents false, and *logical one* (1), which represents true.

A self-taught English mathematician, George Boole (died 1864), developed an algebra for two-state variables. In this algebra the logical AND operation between two variables is represented by the dot. Thus in the statement

If *A* AND *B* (are true), THEN *T* (is true)

AND can be represented by the *dot operator* and *then* by an *equal sign*, resulting in the equation

$$A \cdot B = T \qquad \text{(D1-1)}$$

Examining the logical zero/one truth table of Table D1-1 shows the dot operator for the AND to be a reasonable notation because of its use in ordinary algebra (indeed, only one times one equals one), but the dot is *not* multiplication of course; it represents the *AND operation* between the two variables to either side of it.

It is useful to consider a simple electrical circuit that can implement the logical AND. Consider two switches labeled *A* and *B* that are connected in series with, for example, a 5-V battery (see Figure D1-1). A 5-V light bulb or a voltmeter is connected to the output of the circuit. Our convention will be that if proposition *A* is true, we will close the switch named *A*, otherwise we will open it. The procedure for switch *B* is similar. The output of the logical operation is indicated by the light bulb (the *indicator*); if the conclusion is true, the light bulb will be lit, but if not true the light bulb will be dark. Alternatively, the output conclusion *T* can be indicated by the voltmeter. If the conclusion is true, the voltmeter will read near 5 V or a high voltage. If the output is near 0 V or low voltage, the conclusion is false. Indeed, these output

A	B	T
false	false	false
false	true	false
true	false	false
true	true	true

TABLE D1–1. *Truth Table for the Logical AND Using True, False*

A	B	T
0	0	0
0	1	0
1	0	0
1	1	1

TABLE D1–2. *Truth Table for the Logical AND Using Logic 0, 1*

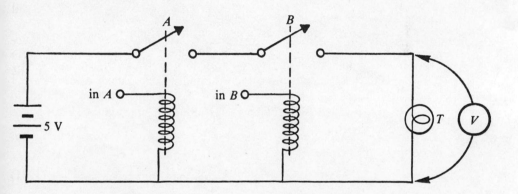

FIGURE D1–1. *Simple Electrical Implementation of the Logical AND*

conclusions are commonly simplified to *high* and *low,* synonymous with true and false, respectively.

It is quite clear that since the switches are connected in series, the output will be high only if both switches are closed. The circuit quite obviously implements the logical AND. The circuit can be made more automatic by using electrical switches or relays for *A* and *B*. In particular, it would be desirable to have relays with characteristics such that the switch closes for input (coil) voltage of more than 4 V, for example, or the switch opens for input voltage of less than 1 V (or, of course, for no connection). With the use of relays, both the input variables and the output variable are established or indicated by the same high and low voltages. The relay coils are drawn in Figure D1–1 with inputs indicated *in A* and *in B*.

Logical Inclusive OR

Suppose that a house has two doors. It is possible to enter the house easily without keys if either door is unlocked. That is: *If* (door *A* is unlocked) *OR* (door *B* is unlocked) *then* (I can enter the house). Again the propositions have been enclosed in parentheses, and each can have only true/false answers. The situation here of course is that if either input variable is true, or certainly if both are true, the conclusion "I can enter the house" is true.

This propositional expression is called the *logical inclusive OR,* and its general form is

If *A* OR *B* (is/are true), THEN *T* (is true)

A truth table may again be used to consider all possibilities for the input variables and the output variable (see Table D1–3). The inclusive-OR operation is indicated in Boolean algebra by the *plus operator.* We write

$$A + B = T \qquad\qquad \textbf{(D1–2)}$$

Looking at the truth table using logical zero/one (see Table D1–4), this notation is reasonable from ordinary arithmetic except for the last entry, $1 + 1 = 1$. Of course, the logical plus is *not* the arithmetic plus.

To implement the inclusive OR in a simple electrical fashion, merely connect two switches (or relays) in parallel as shown in Figure D1–2. The same conventions should be followed as stated earlier. Clearly if either switch *A* or switch *B* is closed (or certainly if both), the indicator bulb will light or the output voltage will be high. Using relays, if either input voltage is high, the output voltage is high.

A	B	T
false	false	false
false	true	true
true	false	true
true	true	true

TABLE D1–3. *Truth Table for the Logical Inclusive OR Using True, False*

A	B	T
0	0	0
0	1	1
1	0	1
1	1	1

TABLE D1–4. *Truth Table for the Logical Inclusive OR Using Logic 1, 0*

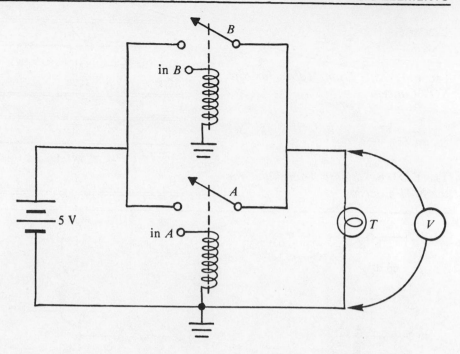

FIGURE D1–2. *Simple Electrical Implementation of the Logical Inclusive OR*

Logical NOT

Certainly an important part of logical statements in ordinary speech (even of a three-year-old child!) is the *NOT* concept. "No, I am NOT (going to do it)." Of course, it simply means the opposite situation, or the *inverted* state, or the *complement* of the given state. The general form of the *logical NOT* is

$$\text{NOT } A, \text{ or NOT } T$$

In Boolean algebra the *NOT operation* is indicated by a *line over the variable:* $\overline{A}$. The truth table for NOT is very simple and brief (see Table D1–5). The truth table for NOT can also be presented in binary form (see Table D1–6).

To implement the NOT electrically, we could use a relay with a single-pole-double-throw (SPDT) switch. Let the *common* of the switch be the NOT output and the *normally open* post be connected to high V, while *normally closed* is connected to ground (see Figure D1–3a). The variable-state input should be the usual high or low voltage to the relay coil.

However, with some knowledge of discrete electronics, the inverting properties of the common emitter amplifier immediately come to mind. In Figure D1–3b we see that the input is simply sent to a transistor switch and

D5

TABLE D1-5. *Truth Table for the NOT Concept*

A	$\overline{A}$
true	false
false	true

TABLE D1-6. *Binary Truth Table for the NOT Concept*

A	$\overline{A}$
1	0
0	1

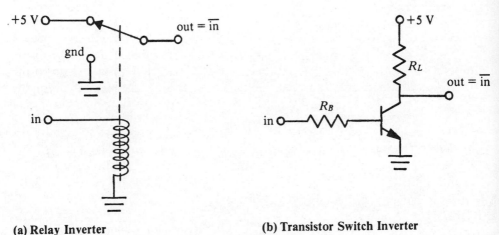

(a) Relay Inverter

(b) Transistor Switch Inverter

FIGURE D1-3. *Simple Electrical/Electronic Implementation of the NOT Concept*

R_B versus R_L is adjusted so that the transistor goes into saturation, giving a low output if the input is connected to high (for example, +5 V). Notice, however, that the low output voltage is NOT zero because of the saturation voltage of perhaps 0.4 V across the transistor. If the input is connected to ground, the transistor is not biased on at all and the output is high. Notice that leaving the input unconnected gives the same output as if the input were grounded or low. Because the output is inverted from the input, we refer to the device as an *inverter*.

Exclusive OR

All logical operations required in digital electronics and computer design can be implemented using only the three basic concepts (and circuits) of the logical AND, OR, and NOT. It is quite remarkable that the complex machine

A	B	T
0	0	0
0	1	1
1	0	1
1	1	0

TABLE D1-7. *Truth Table for the Exclusive OR Concept*

we call a digital computer can be constructed from only these elements. Indeed, the Mark I, the first electrical—but not electronic—computer was constructed at Harvard (beginning in 1939) using relays! The project was initiated by a physicist, Howard Aiken, who needed numerical solutions to nonlinear differential equations.

Therefore, the concept of the *exclusive OR* that we consider next is not in the fundamental rank, but nevertheless is introduced here to clarify the OR notion. Suppose someone says, "Either Dick OR Jane will go to the store." It is commonly accepted that the intended meaning is: One or the other, but *not both* will go. This is the notion of the exclusive OR.

The truth table for the exclusive OR is given in Table D1-7. The Boolean algebra symbol for the exclusive OR is the *plus within a circle:*

$$A \oplus B = T \tag{D1-3}$$

More Complex Logical Statements

More elaborate logical schemes can readily be written in Boolean algebra and represented by simple switches. For example: If either [(the temperature is too high) AND (smoke is detected)] OR [a circuit overload exists] THEN [trip the main circuit breaker]. This statement involves three propositions or variables, and parentheses and brackets have been used to indicate the variables relating to each *dyadic operator;* that is, each operator is defined to operate only on two variables.

This statement may be written in Boolean algebra as

$$(A \cdot B) + C = T \tag{D1-4}$$

where letters representing the propositions are used:
A = The temperature is too high
B = Smoke is detected
C = A circuit overload exists

Note that the position of parentheses is important. Thus the statement

$$A \cdot (B + C) = T \tag{D1-5}$$

is quite a different logical proposition than Equation D1-4, as can be seen by writing out the truth tables for the two situations or by considering the simple switch network needed to implement both. Figures D1–4a and b illustrate the switch implementation for each Boolean expression above. It is quite clear that the outputs will be different. We can build up any Boolean algebra statement in terms of switches and thus obtain an electrical implementation of the compound logical statement.

We can readily verify that some expressions do not require parentheses. Thus consider the *multiple AND*:

$$(A \cdot B) \cdot C = A \cdot (B \cdot C) = B \cdot (A \cdot C) = A \cdot B \cdot C \qquad \textbf{(D1–6)}$$

Perhaps the easiest justification follows from a simple switch implementation. No matter the parentheses groupings, the switch network will simply be three switches in series. Similarly, the *multiple OR* requires no parentheses:

$$(A + B) + C = A + (B + C) = B + (A + C) = A + B + C \qquad \textbf{(D1–7)}$$

The switch implementation would here be three switches in parallel for any case.

Standard Symbols for Gates

In recent years the U.S. military-standard symbols for electronic circuits that implement the various logical notions have gained wide acceptance. Logical

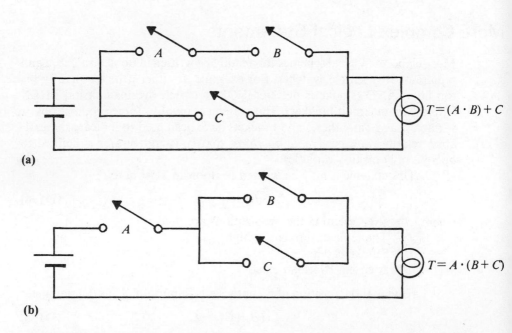

(a)

(b)

FIGURE D1–4. *Simple Switch Electrical Implementation of Two Compound Logic Expressions*

circuits are implemented using *boxes*—integrated circuits—with electrical inputs and outputs and interconnecting wires from various outputs to other inputs in order to implement various complex logical requirements (much like the simple switch drawing of Figure D1-4). It is convenient to have special box shapes to represent the various basic logic operations or circuits.

The symbol for the logical AND is a D-shaped element with the inputs on the straight side (see Figure D1-5a). Note the extensions used if many inputs lead into a gate. The symbol for the logical inclusive OR is an arrow-head-shaped symbol, with the inputs opposite the point and the output lead from the point, as shown in Figure D1-5b. The symbol for the exclusive OR is shown in Figure D1-5c. An extra curve is added to the input side of the OR

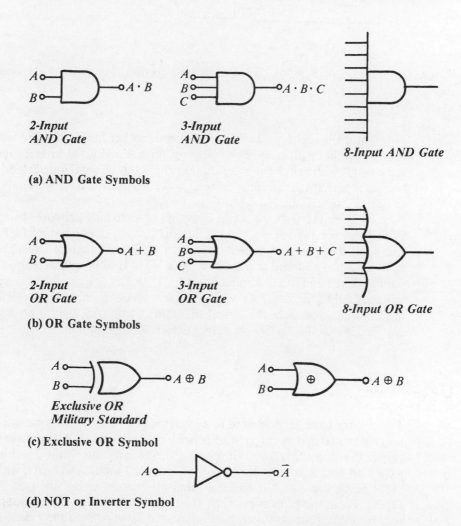

(a) AND Gate Symbols

(b) OR Gate Symbols

(c) Exclusive OR Symbol

(d) NOT or Inverter Symbol

FIGURE D1-5. *Standard Logic Symbols (Military Standard 806C)*

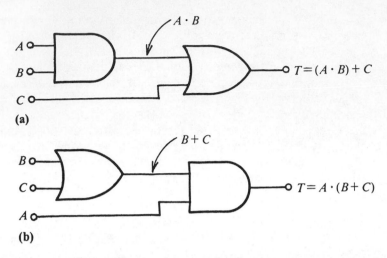

FIGURE D1–6. *Logic Symbol Circuit Drawing for Implementing Two Boolean Expressions*

symbol for the military standard. However, another frequently seen usage is the OR symbol with an encircled plus within it. Finally, the inverter symbol is a triangle with a circle (bubble) at the output as shown in Figure D1–5d. The bubble is perhaps the essential feature, as we see shortly; it is commonly used to indicate inversion.

Figure D1–6 shows circuit drawings or *switching networks* using this symbolism for the two compound logical circuits drawn earlier in Figure D1–4. Each network represents a certain Boolean function. Unless stated otherwise, it is assumed that each variable input is to be connected to a high voltage if true and to a low voltage if false. Typically, these are the two supply voltages, and indeed supply voltages must be connected to the electronic devices that implement the logical operations; however, the supply voltage connections to the devices are rarely drawn in the diagram.

Gates

The circuits have been referred to as *gates* several times, and some explanation for this term is in order. Imagine we have an information or *data* line that carries the data either 0 or 1 (low or high). We can control whether this data passes on past a point in the circuit by using a 2-input AND gate, with one input being the data line and the other an *enable/inhibit* line (see Figure D1–7). From the properties of the AND gate, we can see that the data will pass on to the output (*the output follows the input*) only if the enable line is 1 or high so that the gate is enabled; otherwise, the output is low irrespective

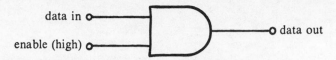

FIGURE D1-7. *AND Function as an Enabling "Gate"*

of the data line. The circuit acts like a gate that can be opened or closed in terms of permitting data to pass through it.

NAND Gate

If an AND gate is followed by an inverter as in Figure D1–8a, the output is NOT (A AND B) or $\overline{A \cdot B}$. The overall unit is a NOTTED-AND or simply *NAND gate.* Figure D1–8b shows the common symbolic abbreviation wherein the triangle is left off and *only the circle* remains to indicate the inversion at the output. The truth table is readily written out by adding an additional column to the AND table as shown in Figure D1–8b. We see that: *The output is low only if both inputs are high.* It is quite possible to have a multiple-input NAND gate as shown in Figure D1–8c, along with its lengthier truth table. There we see that: *Only if all inputs are high will the output be low.* The truth table should contain all possible combinations of the input-variable values. Examination of Figure D1–8c shows an easy recipe for assuring that no combinations are left out: Simply count in binary to set down the possible states. For n inputs there are 2^n possible combinations (for example, 8 combinations for a 3-input case) obtained in this way. A brief review of binary numbers supplements this chapter.

NOR Gate

If an OR gate is followed by an inverter as in Figure D1–9a, the output is NOT (A OR B) or $\overline{A + B}$. The combination is a NOTTED-OR or simply *NOR gate.* Figure D1–9b shows the common symbolic abbreviation, as well as the truth table for this device. We see that: *The output is low if either input is high.* Figure D1–9c shows a 3-input NOR gate along with its truth table. For a multiple-input NOR, we can see that: *The output is low if any one or more of the inputs is high.*

Inverter from a NAND or a NOR

Suppose input A of the 2-input NAND in Figure D1–8b is connected permanently high and only the other input may change states as shown in Figure D1–10a. Then the truth table of Figure D1–8b is restricted to the sub-

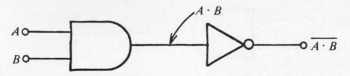

(a) NOTTED-AND or NAND Function

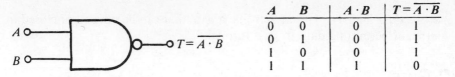

A	B	A · B	T = $\overline{A \cdot B}$
0	0	0	1
0	1	0	1
1	0	0	1
1	1	1	0

(b) 2-Input NAND Gate Symbol and NAND Truth Table

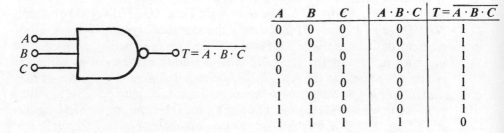

A	B	C	A · B · C	T = $\overline{A \cdot B \cdot C}$
0	0	0	0	1
0	0	1	0	1
0	1	0	0	1
0	1	1	0	1
1	0	0	0	1
1	0	1	0	1
1	1	0	0	1
1	1	1	1	0

(c) 3-Input NAND Gate and Its Truth Table

FIGURE D1–8. *NAND Gate*

set with $A = 1$. Looking across at the output column we see that: *The output is just the opposite of input B;* therefore, it functions as an *inverter.* At times we encounter the NAND symbol with only a single input line drawn. This implies an inverter, indeed, perhaps a NAND gate implemented as an inverter. (In fact, we see shortly that if an input is left unconnected in the TTL system, the input behaves as though connected high.)

In Figure D1–10b we follow a NAND gate with an inverter. It should be clear that the two inversion operations cancel each other, giving a network that behaves like an AND gate. Since an inverter can be readily produced from a NAND gate, we see that NANDs can be used to implement the NAND, inverter, and AND functions.

In Figure D1–11a we assume that one input of a NOR gate is connected permanently low. Then the truth table of Figure D1–9b is restricted to the top half where $A = 0$, and we see that: *The output performs the inverse of the input.* Thus, a NOR can easily be used to implement an inverter also. Furthermore, two NORs may be used to obtain an OR gate as shown in Figure D1–11b. The inversion operations cancel.

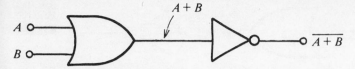

(a) NOTTED-OR or NOR Function

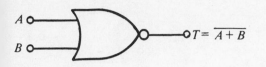

A	B	A + B	$T = \overline{A + B}$
0	0	0	1
0	1	1	0
1	0	1	0
1	1	1	0

(b) NOR Gate Symbol and NOR Truth Table

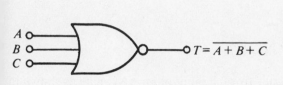

A	B	C	A + B + C	$T = \overline{A \cdot B \cdot C}$
0	0	0	0	1
0	0	1	1	0
0	1	0	1	0
0	1	1	1	0
1	0	0	1	0
1	0	1	1	0
1	1	0	1	0
1	1	1	1	0

(c) 3-Input NOR Gate and Its Truth Table

FIGURE D1–9. *NOR Gate*

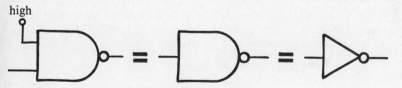

(a) NAND with One Input Tied High

(b) NAND Inverter on NAND Output Gives AND

FIGURE D1–10. *Making an Inverter and an AND from NAND Gates*

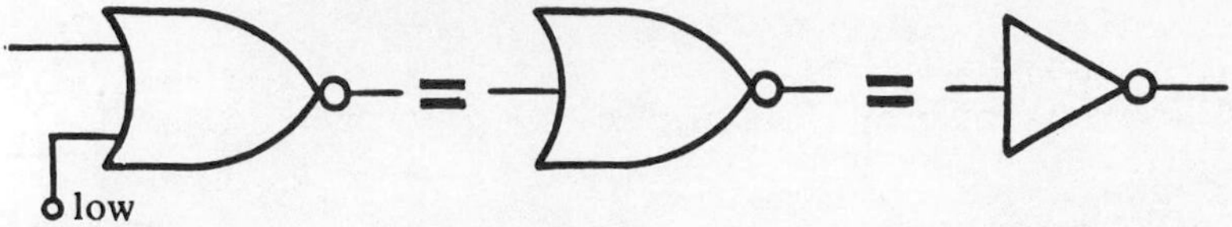

(a) NOR with One Input Tied Low

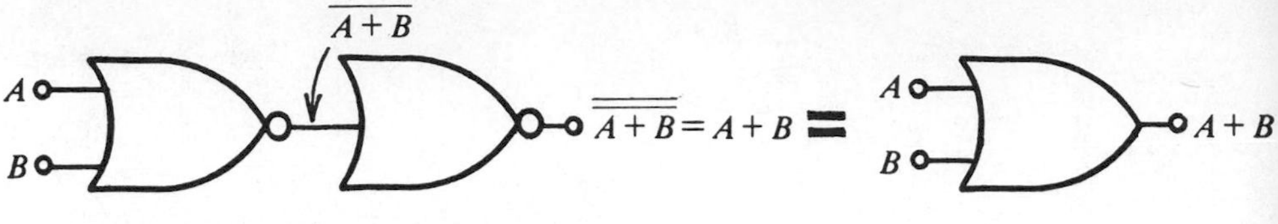

(b) NOR Inverter on NOR Output Gives OR

FIGURE D1–11   *Making an Inverter and an OR from NOR Gates*

Negated-Input AND (the NOR)

Consider connecting an inverter to each input of an AND gate as shown in Figure D1–12a. This situation again can be compactly represented by showing only the inverter circles, as shown in Figure D1–12b. In Boolean algebra it is clear that if the inputs are variables A and B, the function that is implemented here—that is, the output—is

$$\overline{A} \cdot \overline{B} = T \tag{D1-8}$$

Because of the inverters at the inputs to the AND, we can readily see that: *Only if both inputs A AND B are low will the output be high.* On the other hand, it is quite clear that this statement is the same as saying: *If either input A OR B is high, the output is low.* Notice that the second statement is the operating principle of the NOR gate; therefore we have argued the equivalence of the negated-input AND gate to the NOR gate as diagrammed in Figure D1–12c. In Boolean algebra we would write

$$\overline{A} \cdot \overline{B} = \overline{A + B} \tag{D1-9}$$

and this is one of the two *De Morgan's theorems* that are named after an English logician of the nineteenth century. As an exercise the student is asked to formally verify this theorem by a truth table.

If we invert both sides of Equation D1–9, the double inversion cancels on the right side, giving

$$\overline{\overline{A} \cdot \overline{B}} = A + B \tag{D1-10}$$

Alternatively, in working with the gate diagram, if both gates in Figure D1–12c are fed into inverters, a new pair of equivalent gate networks must

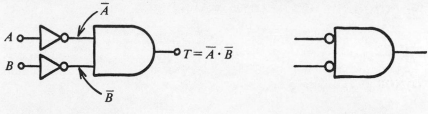

(a) Negated-Input AND

(b) Circle Abbreviation

(c) Equivalence of Negated-Input AND and the NOR

(d) Equivalence of Negated Input/Output AND and the OR

FIGURE D1-12. *De Morgan's Theorem: The Negated-Input AND*

result. But the two inverters (two circles) on the NOR gate cancel, and the result is drawn in Figure D1-12d: *An AND gate with inverters at all inputs as well as the output behaves the same as an OR gate.*

It should now be clear that if only NAND gates are available, it is possible to construct an OR gate by using two NANDs as inverters at the input to one NAND. Then, of course, a NOR could also be readily obtained by feeding the output into a NAND as inverter. Therefore, it is possible to implement all the logic functions using only NAND gates; indeed, it is possible to construct any digital computer using only NAND gates! (Initially, because of the nature of construction, the TTL integrated-circuit system had only NANDs available; no inverters, ORs, and such.)

Sometimes a digital logic situation exists where: *The output should go high when both inputs are low.* De Morgan's theorem as we have just deduced it tells us that a NOR gate does the job, and indeed a NOR gate can be purchased and wired into the circuit. However, to make clear the situation that two lows are being responded to, designers often draw the gate as a negated-input AND, as shown in the left of Figure D1-12c.

Negated-Input OR (the NAND)

Consider connecting an inverter to each input of an OR gate as shown in Figure D1–13a. The compact symbolic representation is drawn in Figure D1–13b. It should be clear that the Boolean algebra expression for the overall operation is

$$\overline{A} + \overline{B} = T \qquad\qquad \text{(D1-11)}$$

In this case, because of the inverters connected ahead of the OR: *If either A OR B is low, the output is high.* Again, to most people this is clearly equivalent to saying: *Only if both A AND B are high will the output be low.* But the latter statement is simply the logical NAND statement given earlier. Therefore the gate equivalence of Figure D1–13c must be true. In Boolean algebra terms

$$\overline{A} + \overline{B} = \overline{A \cdot B} \qquad\qquad \text{(D1-12)}$$

and this is the second of De Morgan's theorems (one may say the second form of De Morgan's theorem since we see shortly that the two statements are related to each other).

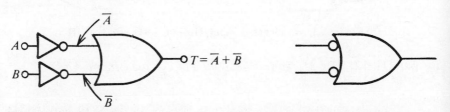

(a) Negated-Input OR   **(b) Circle Abbreviation**

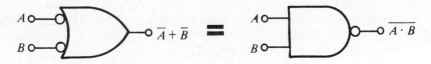

(c) Equivalence of Negated-Input OR and the NAND

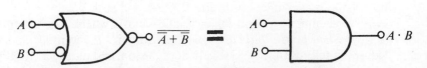

(d) Equivalence of Negated Input/Output OR and the AND

FIGURE D1–13. *De Morgan's Theorem: The Negated-Input OR*

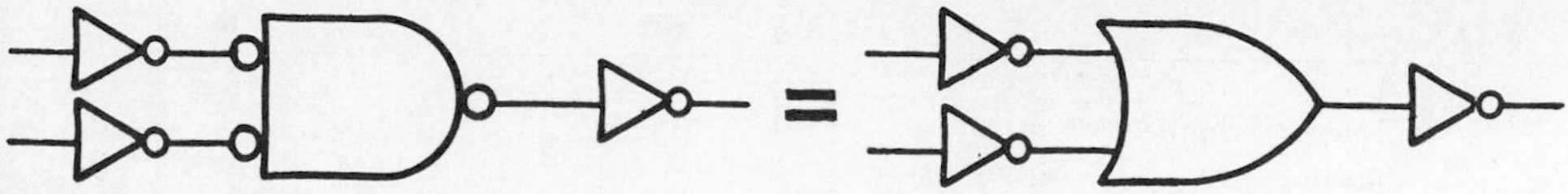

FIGURE D1–14. *Attaching Inverters to Inputs and Outputs of Figure D1–12d to Obtain Figure D1–13d Equivalence*

It is possible to feed both gates of Figure D1–13c into inverters to obtain another equivalence shown in Figure D1–13d. Clearly the inverter on the NAND is then canceled to give the AND on the right side. We see that this is a complementary situation to the equivalence drawn in Figure D1–12d: *If inverters are placed at all inputs as well as at the output of an OR, the whole behaves like an AND.* Actually, we can quickly see that this form follows from the logic-gate equivalence of Figure D1–12d; simply connect inverters to all inputs and the output of that diagram. This situation is drawn in Figure D1–14. The double circles on the AND in Figure D1–14 cancel, and the result of Figure D1–13d is obtained.

Because inverters are readily constructed from NOR gates, notice that it is also possible to produce all the required logic elements using only NOR gates as well. Indeed, the NOR gate is the fundamental gate in the RTL system, which is now outmoded.

Positive and Negative Logic

The usual convention in implementing electronic logic is to consider that a *true* or *logic 1* corresponds to a high voltage (for example, 5 V) and that *false* or *logic 0* corresponds to a low voltage (for example, 0 V). However, this correspondence is clearly only conventional and is referred to as *positive logic.* The alternative is certainly also possible: Low = true or 1, high = false or 0. It is instructive to consider a certain gate and examine how it behaves according to the two conventions.

Consider a positive-logic OR gate. Its behavior in terms of voltage is definite and is shown in Figure D1–15a. Figure D1–15b then shows the interpretation of both inputs and outputs in the positive-logic scheme, while Figure D1–15c shows the interpretation in terms of negative logic. The negative-logic truth table is seen to be that for an AND gate. Therefore, a positive-logic OR gate performs as a negative-logic AND gate.

This statement is actually reasonable from Figure D1–12d, although the gate picture *can be confusing,* and the truth table argument is the clearest justification. A diagram of the situation in terms of symbols is given in Figure D1–15d. If inverters are connected to the inputs and outputs of a positive-logic AND gate, the resulting unit will certainly behave as a nega-

A	B	T
low	low	low
low	high	high
high	low	high
high	high	high

A	B	T
0	0	0
0	1	1
1	0	1
1	1	1

A	B	T
1	1	1
1	0	0
0	1	0
0	0	0

(a) Voltage Levels for the "Usual" OR Gate

(b) Positive Logic; Is an OR

(c) Negative Logic; Is an AND

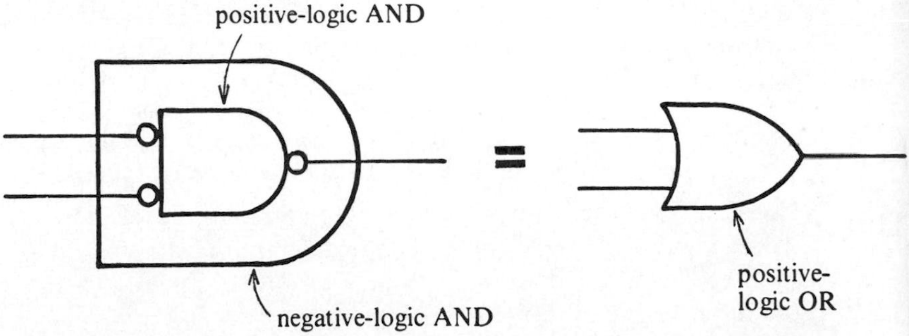

positive-logic AND

negative-logic AND

positive-logic OR

(d) Positive/Negative Logic Equivalence Using One of De Morgan's Theorems

FIGURE D1-15. *Illustrating Positive-Logic OR Is Negative-Logic AND*

tive-logic AND gate; that is, only if both inputs are low will the output be low. But by Figure D1-12d, the negated input-and-output AND gate is the same as a positive-logic OR gate. Therefore the assertion is proven.

Similarly, it can be shown that a positive-logic AND gate is a negative-logic OR gate. In the early days of IC logic elements, the units were often described as "positive-logic AND/negative-logic OR," but only the positive-logic descriptor is now usually given.

Gate Constructions

There now exist quite a number of circuit techniques for accomplishing logic gates. Several of these were first constructed from discrete elements on circuit cards; they later evolved into integrated-circuit form. An *integrated circuit* or IC is a small solid-state device that combines or integrates transistors and resistors together on one small *chip* of semiconductor. Complete, functional electronic circuits are fabricated with the same materials and processes used in the manufacture of the epitaxial planar transistor.

NOTE: The terms *epitaxial* and *planar* refer to the structure of this transistor type. A thin layer of single-crystal silicon is grown from a vapor onto a silicon crystal wafer; this is called epitaxial growth. The transistor structure is subsequently developed by diffusion of impurities into selected areas of the plane. In the case of integrated circuits, many transistors, resistors, and diodes are formed simultaneously in the epitaxial layer. The wafer foundation is called the *substrate*.

The electrical characteristics of only two IC logic families—that is, TTL and CMOS—are considered in some detail here. Some mention of names and important characteristics is made with regard to the other families; however, TTL and CMOS account for perhaps 95% of *discrete logic* usage in instruments and minicomputers.

Diode Logic (DL)

An early and simple improvement over electrical relays for logic implementation involved the lowly diode. There remain situations where the diode may be the simplest means to solve a problem; thus we should certainly be aware of this approach. Logic gates based principally on diode elements are referred to as *diode logic,* or simply DL.

Consider three diodes with their anodes connected together to a resistor that in turn is connected to +5 V or some other positive voltage (see Figure D1–16a). This common-anode connection becomes the output, and the cathodes become inputs *A, B,* and *C.* To assert a logic 0, the given input is grounded as in Figure D1–16b, while to assert a logic 1, the input is connected to high (to the positive supply).

Notice that if any input is connected low, that diode conducts and the output is pulled to about +0.6 V or a low; the output becomes the diode drop voltage. Any other diode inputs that are connected high (for example, input *A* in Figure D1–16b) do not tend to pull the output up because those diodes are reverse biased. An unconnected input (for example, input *B*) has no effect, of course, and acts as though it were connected high (*acts high*). Only if all inputs are connected high will the output be high. Therefore this diode circuit functions as a 3-input AND gate. We do need to agree that an output voltage *near* ground (perhaps 1 V or less) suffices to be considered low or logic 0.

Notice no significant current flows into an input when it is made high; however, any wire or electrical element that makes an input low must *absorb current* in asserting an effective short to ground. An element connected to an input must therefore *sink current* without developing an appreciable voltage drop across itself. If a voltage drop does occur across the input element when it asserts a low, this drop is added to the diode drop and the output voltage

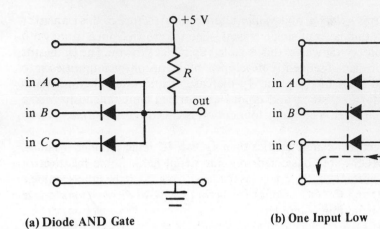

(a) Diode AND Gate

(b) One Input Low

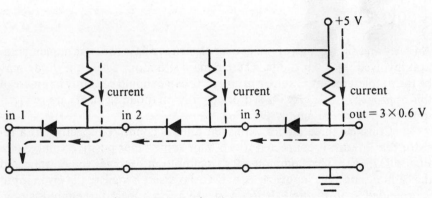

(c) Cascaded Diode-Logic AND Gates Showing Increase in
    Low Voltage Level

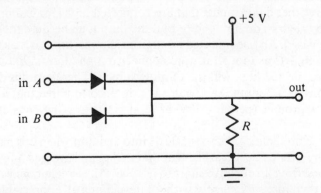

(d) Diode OR Gate

FIGURE D1-16. *Diode-Logic Gates*

will be that much higher. It may then move above the region we agree to call low.

Indeed, this situation represents a significant shortcoming of the simple diode-logic gate. In complex systems, the output of one gate often becomes the input for another, and so on. The situation is diagrammed in Figure D1–16c, where we see the output-low voltage becomes degraded to about 1.8 V (which is more than our assumed 1-V upper limit for the low state).

If diodes are connected with cathodes together to a resistor R that in turn is connected to ground, a diode OR gate develops (see Figure D1–16d). If any input is connected to the supply voltage, that diode conducts and the output goes *near* the supply voltage (it is less by the diode drop). Again we might agree that 4 V to 5 V is regarded as high. In this case an unconnected input *acts low*. Also, any device that is connected to an input must supply or *source* a current in asserting a high, but must *sink* very little current if asserting a low (because that diode is then reverse biased). Therefore, this type of diode logic is called *current sourcing*. Again, as in the case of the diode AND gate, there is a cascading problem.

Resistor-Transistor Logic (RTL)

An early solution to the problem of logic-level degradation when gates are cascaded made use of transistors connected in parallel to a collector resistor that in turn connected to the positive supply. This use of transistors and a resistor is called *resistor-transistor logic* or RTL (see Figure D1–17). Fairchild marketed an IC form of this logic in 1961; it was the first commercial IC logic system. RTL logic operates with a 3.5-V supply voltage. (The transistors could not operate at significantly higher voltages because of voltage breakdown.)

If all the inputs are connected either low (to ground) or unconnected, the transistors are unbiased or off. They all therefore behave like open switches, and the out voltage will be pulled high through the 640-ohm resistor (see Figure D1–17). But, if any input is connected high, that transistor will be biased into saturation (notice R_B is actually less than R_L). The transistor turns on and behaves like a closed switch; the output is then pulled low to the collector-emitter saturation voltage (perhaps 0.4 V). If several inputs are high, there will be several parallel switches connected to ground, and the output will certainly be low. We clearly have a 3-input NOR gate. The NOR was the building block of the RTL family.

The past tense is used because RTL logic was superseded, first by DTL (diode-transistor logic) and then by TTL (transistor-transistor logic). The switching speed of RTL was an important fault. The output of a gate always finds some capacitance connected between it and ground as diagrammed in Figure D1–18a. This is due to the diode-junction capacitances of

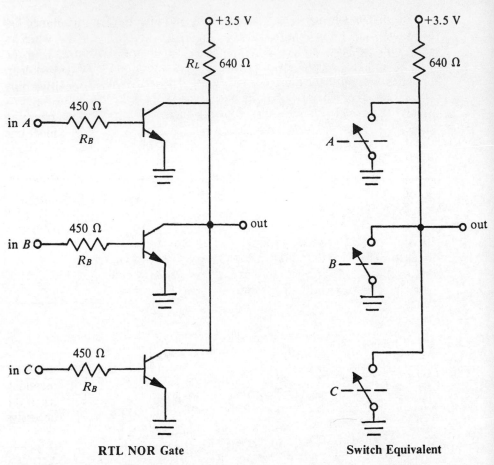

RTL NOR Gate   **Switch Equivalent**

FIGURE D1–17. *Switch Equivalent of a Resistor-Transistor-Logic (RTL) NOR Gate*

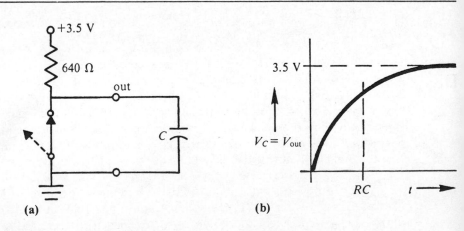

(a)   (b)

FIGURE D1–18. *RTL Capacitive Loading Illustration*

the gates to which the output is connected and also to the capacitance between connecting wires (of the order of 20 to 100 picofarads). Now, when an RTL output asserts a low, a low-resistance switch is connected from the capacitance to ground and the capacitor can discharge quickly—no problem. However, when the output then goes high, the output moves positive only as the capacitor charges through the 640-ohm resistance toward 3.5 V— that is, toward the high output level (see Figure D1-18b). This charging occurs exponentially with time constant RC and can be slow in the time frame of a computer.

Example: Suppose an RTL NOR gate is connected to a capacitance of 50 picofarads. What is the time constant of the low-to-high transition?

Solution: $R = 640 \ \Omega$ and $C = 50 \times 10^{-12} \ F$

so $RC = 640 \times 50 \times 10^{-12} \ sec = 3.2 \times 10^{-8} \ sec = 32 \ nsec$

Indeed, the *propagation delay* of a gate is an important merit indicator; this is the time interval between the time when an input changes levels and when the output finally changes to its appropriate level. For the RTL system the guaranteed maximum delay is 80 nanoseconds (80×10^{-9} seconds). This delay is a long time for modern computers; the supercomputers of the 1980s can perform several whole instructions involving many successive logical decisions in this time.

Associated with this speed is the *toggle rate*—that is, the fastest possible operating rate—of RTL bistable flip-flops. For example, this rate determines the maximum counting frequency of a frequency counter constructed with flip-flops from the family. Although flip-flops and counters are discussed in the next chapter, it should be noted here that the maximum toggle rate of RTL flip-flops is only about 2 megahertz.

Diode-Transistor Logic (DTL)

Diode-transistor logic or DTL also eliminaied the DL gate problem of level degradation by incorporating a transistor. However, the DTL system has the same problem with slow rise times on capacitive loads as the RTL gate, and neither system is used in new design.

Transistor-Transistor Logic (TTL)

Transistor-transistor logic or TTL corrects the capacitive load problem by connecting two transistor switches in series at the output; they are arranged so that one switch is always closed (to either a high or a low) while the other is open. TTL logic existed in a discrete form also, but Sylvania was the first to use a *multiple-emitter* transistor for the input and thus design a specifically integrated-circuit form in 1963 called its "SUHL" line.

However, a TTL system introduced by Texas Instruments rapidly became the industry standard and was subsequently manufactured by almost all other major IC companies. (This curious "second-sourcing" arrangement is actually encouraged by a company so that its parts will be regarded as widely available and competitively priced.) The large-volume production of TTL soon caused its price to drop below that of RTL and DTL, and TTL became the dominant logic family in the 1970s.

The plateau price is about $.15 for a TTL *quad 2-input NAND gate*— that is, an IC with 4 NAND gates in it, each with 2 inputs. It costs considerably more to purchase a socket into which to plug the IC! Indeed, because of this cost, ICs are often soldered directly to a printed-circuit board, although replacement of a defective unit is tedious (14 pins or more to unsolder at once). If it wasn't defective before removal, the IC may well be after!

Texas Instruments numbered their TTL *commercial line* beginning at SN7400 for the quad NAND gate. This line is usable over the temperature range 0°C to +70°C. The *military line* is numbered SN5400 and up and operates over the temperature range −55°C to +125°C. Other companies use the same numbers but usually use different prefix letters. Also, suffix letters typically indicate various package forms; for example, plastic case, ceramic case, dual-in-line plug, and flat package.

The power requirement of the standard 7400 line is about 10 milliwatts per gate (40 milliwatts for a quad NAND gate IC), and the propagation-delay time is about 10 nanoseconds. There is a trade-off between these two features in that one can be lowered but the other must be raised; therefore, various 7400 series have appeared that feature special power/propagation delay characteristics. These are designated by an appropriate letter after 74. Thus we have

74XX	Standard series	(10 nsec, 10 mW)
74LXX	Low-power series	(33 nsec, 1 mW)
74HXX	High-speed series	(6 nsec, 22 mW)
74SXX	Schottky (high-speed) series	(3 nsec, 19 mW)
74LSXX	Low-power Schottky series	(9 nsec, 2 mW)

In parentheses after each series have been placed the typical propagation-delay time and power dissipation for that series. Notice, for example, that the low-power version uses only one-tenth the power of the standard series, but at a cost of three times the delay time. The XX stands for various digits that distinguish the logic elements available; thus, the 7404 (or 74H04 or 74LS04, and so forth) is a *hex-inverter* IC—that is, 6 inverters in one IC package— while the 7432 is a *quad 2-input OR gate*.

Both Schottky series use high-speed *Schottky diodes*—that is, diodes constructed from a metal-semiconductor junction—placed in the circuit in a manner that prevents the transistors from going into saturation. Transistors that are saturated take a rather long time to clear stored charge out of the base region in the process of turning off. Saturation thus slows down the switching speed and increases the propagation-delay time of conventional transistors. Notice the very favorable speed/power combination of the low-power Schottky (74LSXX) series; they accordingly gained widespread use in the late 1970s, although at some price premium.

TTL logic operates with a +5-V power supply voltage and is compatible with DTL logic. The supply voltage must be quite well regulated; the minimum and maximum voltages recommended are 4.75 V and 5.25 V. Given the power dissipation of the IC, we can calculate the supply current requirements and, of course, this is important for power supply design or selection. Thus the 7400 NAND IC, with a power dissipation of 40 milliwatts, is expected to use 0.04 W/5 V = 8 mA supply current. More complex gates and flip-flop ICs require some 25 milliamperes per package. The absolute maximum supply voltage for TTL devices is on the order of 7 V; should the voltage rise above this level for a board of ICs, we can expect that many will quickly be permanently damaged.

The great majority of IC logic circuits are packaged in dual-in-line-pin packages (DIP) using 14 pins or 16 pins for the less complex devices. Most TTL packages use pin 14 (or 16 if a 16-pin package) for +5 V and pin 1 for ground. The pin spacing in a line of pins is 0.1 inch. Pin 1 is usually designated with a dot on top of the package; the pin order is clockwise as viewed from the *bottom* of the package, a convention dating back to vacuum tubes.

The circuit of the basic TTL NAND gate is drawn in Figure D1–19a. There are three stages: the *multiple-emitter transistor* input stage, the *phase-splitter* stage, and the *totem pole transistors* output stage. As the user of a logic family connects together the inputs and outputs of these logic boxes, the behavior of the inputs and outputs is of concern and deserves understanding. This is further true because we make connections or *interface* to the electrical world outside the IC through the inputs and outputs of these devices. Therefore, the electrical properties of the input stage and output stage should be understood; the remaining details of electrical circuitry in this section may be regarded as optional material for the student.

To understand the operation of the input stage, it suffices to use a rather simple diode model for transistor Q_1. This diode model is drawn in Figures D1–19b and c. However, 3 diodes are involved because, in addition to the collector-base diode, there are 2 base-emitter diodes. For a 3-input NAND there are 3 emitter diodes, and so on.

NOTE: The multiple-emitter transistor is used instead of simply a number of diodes because it gives faster switching time.

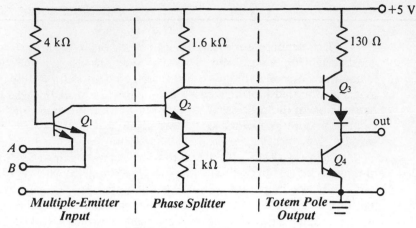

(a) Circuit Equivalent of TTL Integrated-Circuit NAND

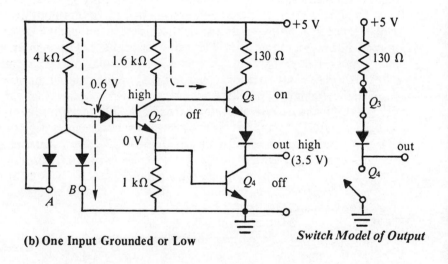

(b) One Input Grounded or Low

Switch Model of Output

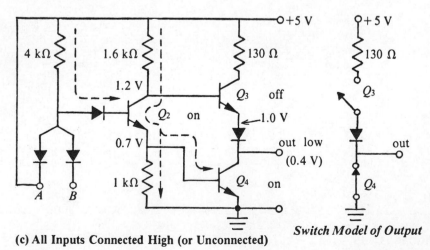

(c) All Inputs Connected High (or Unconnected)

Switch Model of Output

First suppose one (or more) input is connected to ground as shown in Figure D1–19b; that diode is then forward biased and conducts current. The diode drop across the diode is small and transistor Q_2 does not receive a significant base-bias voltage or current. Then transistor Q_2 is off, no current flows through it, and no voltage appears across the 1-kilohm resistor. Consequently, transistor Q_4 receives no base bias, is also off, and acts like an open switch. However, the 1.6-kilohm resistor is effectively connected to the base of Q_3 and Q_3 is biased into saturation; that is, it is turned on and acts like a closed switch (see the switch picture to the right in Figure D1–19b). Clearly the output will be high if either or both inputs are low.

On the other hand, suppose both inputs are connected high (or left unconnected) as shown in Figure D1–19c; no current flows through the input diodes in either situation, but now transistor Q_2 is biased on by current flowing through the 4-kilohm resistor to its base. Transistor Q_2 acts like a closed switch and base current flows to the bottom totem pole transistor Q_4, turning it on. However, the base voltage to Q_3 now drops to perhaps 1.2 V due to the current flowing through the 1.6-kilohm resistor. The base-emitter voltage of this top totem pole transistor becomes less than 0.5 V and the transistor turns off (acts like an open switch). The output is then pulled low due to the closed bottom and open top switches, as shown to the right in Figure D1–19c. Actually the voltage does not go all the way to zero due to the saturation voltage across Q_4 (it is not a perfect switch). We see that only if all inputs are high (or unconnected) will the output be low. Therefore the circuit is a positive-logic NAND gate.

Input/Output Considerations for TTL

Notice that when a low is asserted at an input, a reasonably decent short circuit must be provided to ground, and approximately $5\,\text{V}/4\,\text{k}\Omega = 1.25\,\text{mA}$ is expected to flow through this short. If a resistance is used to connect an input to ground, a voltage of about $1.25\,\text{mA} \times R$ will develop across it. Should this voltage become too large, the Q_2 transistor may be turned on rather than off. Thus we have the *TTL input-level requirement: A low input must be asserted at less than 0.8 V while sinking 1.6 milliamperes. For the high level, it is required that the input be greater than 2.0 V.* Because the input becomes a reverse-biased diode, a small leakage current of at most 50 microamperes must be supplied or sourced for this high input level. These input-voltage levels for guaranteed gate operation are pictured in Figure D1–20a. Notice that the output from a TTL gate is not determined if an input voltage

FIGURE D1–19. *TTL NAND-Gate Construction and Operation*

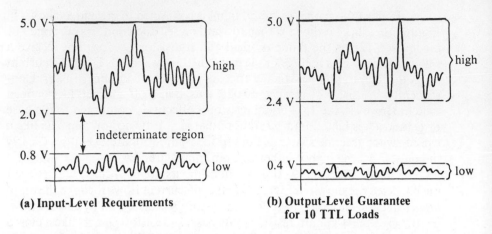

(a) Input-Level Requirements

(b) Output-Level Guarantee
for 10 TTL Loads

FIGURE D1–20. *TTL Input/Output Level Definitions and Guarantees*

is in the range from 0.8 V to 2.0 V; therefore, an input to a TTL gate should not be maintained in this *indeterminate region.*

Clearly the TTL outputs should meet these input requirements with some margin of safety. The most difficult requirement is the low. Indeed, the TTL-system manufacturers guarantee for the standard 7400 series that the output-low voltage will be less than 0.4 V for currents up to 16 milliamperes flowing into the output (through the saturated transistor Q_4, which is attempting to behave like a proper closed switch to ground). This *output-level guarantee* is pictured in Figure D1–20b. Notice that there is a margin of safety of 0.4 V on both the high and low levels in the TTL series. Thus, if a noise spike of 0.4 V should occur on an output level, no movement into the indeterminate region of the input characteristic would occur. TTL is said to have a 0.4-V *noise margin.*

NOTE: The rapidly switching voltage levels and attendant current fluctuations on the +5-V and ground power-supply wires leading to the ICs introduce noise on the outputs from the gates. It is desirable to *bypass* noise to ground with low-inductance capacitors (for example, 0.1-microfarad ceramic-disc types) that are connected between +5 V and ground. These capacitors must be located on the board among the ICs, perhaps one capacitor for every 2 to 4 ICs.

Notice that the output low is guaranteed to be well within input specifications while sinking 10 times as much current as should be required from one TTL input. Ten TTL *input loads* may be connected to a TTL output and a quite satisfactory performance can still be expected. Thus the *fanout* for a standard TTL output is said to be 10 standard TTL inputs. This fanout capability is illustrated in Figure D1–21.

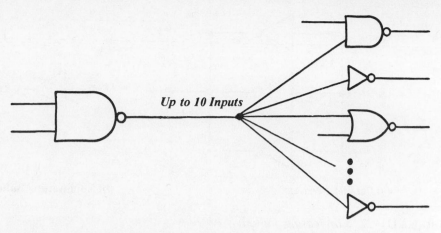

FIGURE D1–21. *Illustrating the Literal "Fanout" Capability of the TTL Logic Line*

The different 7400 types have different input loads, however. Listed in Table D1–8 are the high-level and low-level current characteristics for the different types. Each family type has outputs that have a fanout of 10 input loads of its own family (except 74L and 74LS have fanouts of 20). Thus a 74XX gate that can sink 16 milliamperes can drive nearly 100 74LXX inputs. However, a 74LXX output is only guaranteed to sink 20×0.18 mA, or about 2 standard TTL inputs!

It is possible to obtain more output drive by connecting gates in parallel. Thus 3 inverters from a hex-inverter IC can be connected as in Figure D1–22a to obtain 30-load-units capability. The inverters should be from the same IC chip to assure uniform load sharing. *Buffer* ICs with 30-load fanout

TABLE D1–8. *Input Load and Output Drive Capability for Guaranteed Logic-Level Performance for the TTL Family*

	Input Load		Ouput Drive	
	Max High-Level Input Current (μA)	Max Low-Level Input Current (mA)	Max High-Level Output Current (μA)	Max Low-Level Output (Sink) Current (mA)
74XX	40	−1.6	400	−16
74LXX	10	−0.18	200	− 3.6
74HXX	50	−2	500	−20
74SXX	50	−2	1,000	−20
74LSXX	20	−0.4	400	− 8

Note: A few 74L inputs require 20 μA and −0.8 mA, respectively.

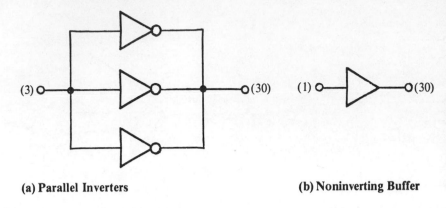

(a) Parallel Inverters   (b) Noninverting Buffer

FIGURE D1–22. *Increasing Fanout*

are available in NAND gates, NOR gates, inverters, and noninverters. The noninverting buffer is drawn with no circle as in Figure D1–22b.

Open-Collector and 3-State Outputs

There are situations when it is desirable to connect several gate outputs directly together to one wire or line; we will see this is the case with computer memory-data lines. For example, if several NAND gate outputs are connected together as in Figure D1–23a, we might hope that: *If any one of the outputs goes low, the line will go low.* This is a negative-logic OR function, and the attempted approach is called a (negative-logic) *wired OR* of the outputs.

Actually, we cannot do this with TTL because of the totem pole output-transistor switches. Recall that they operate in such a way that one switch is always closed. TTL always *actively asserts* either a high or a low. Then if two outputs S and T are connected together and attempt to assert different levels, they will "fight." Figure D1–23b shows the switch picture for this situation. We can see that a short would occur through the two closed switches (transistors) that could burn them out. (Fortunately the 130-ohm resistor is there to limit the current.)

The first TTL solution to this problem was to leave out the top totem pole transistor Q_3. Thus, only the bottom transistor switch Q_4 is connected to the output as shown in Figure D1–23c. Because the collector of this transistor is not connected to anything but the output wire (it's dangling), it is called an *open-collector* output. Now suppose a number of open-collector output gates are connected together to form a wired OR as shown in Figure D1–23d. If any output goes low, that switch closes and connects the line to ground so that the line goes low. If several close that is fine; there is no fighting because no output asserts a high. If it is desirable for the output line to

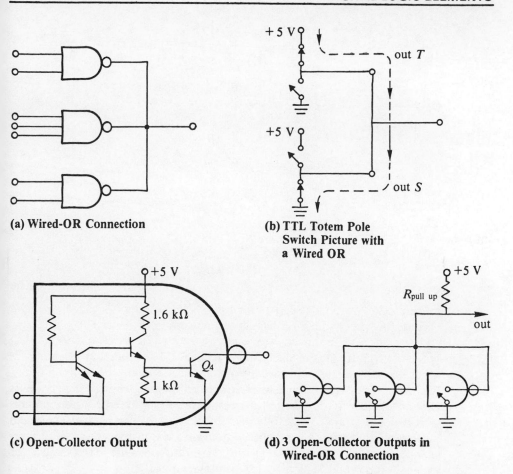

(a) Wired-OR Connection

(b) TTL Totem Pole Switch Picture with a Wired OR

(c) Open-Collector Output

(d) 3 Open-Collector Outputs in Wired-OR Connection

FIGURE D1–23.   *Wired-OR and Open-Collector Outputs*

truly go high, a *pull-up resistor* must be connected between the line and +5 V as shown in Figure D1–23d.

Notice that if a gate with open-collector output is connected only to an indicator light bulb (with no pull-up resistor) it *cannot* light the bulb because it acts only as a switch to ground. However, it *will work* without a pull-up resistor when connected into another TTL gate (though there can be noise problems). The latter behavior results from the fact that when an open-collector gate indicates a high by disconnecting the output, the TTL input to which it is connected acts high, as any disconnected TTL input will do. Of course, the open-collector output does properly assert a low, so the next TTL gate will perform correctly.

Unfortunately, the open-collector output scheme does not actively assert a high and will suffer the same speed slowdown from capacitive loading as RTL and DTL. Therefore, in about 1972 a rather obvious solution was

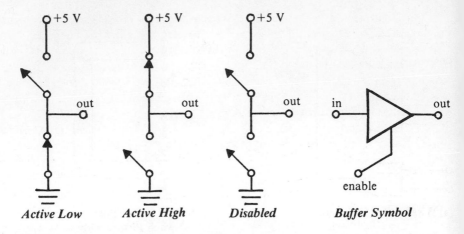

FIGURE D1–24. *Illustrating Tri-State® Outputs*

introduced by National Semiconductor. This device type is called *Tri-State* because the gates and buffers have three output states: active high, active low, and disabled or high impedance. (Other manufacturers use the term *3-state* because Tri-State® is registered by National.) These units have an *enable* input line that causes *both* totem pole transistor switches to be open simultaneously unless the chip is enabled. If both are open the output line is dangling, of course. A number of these outputs can be connected together, provided it is arranged that only one output is enabled at a time. The active pull-up or pull-down on the enabled output rapidly charges or discharges capacitances as required for high-speed operation. Figure D1–24 illustrates the three states and the Tri-State® buffer symbol.

CMOS Logic

A family introduced by RCA in about 1971 and gaining rapidly in many applications is the CMOS or *complementary metal-oxide-semiconductor* CD4000 family. These units decreased in price to nearly the 7400 prices by the mid-1970s. They make use of the fact that MOS field-effect transistors—MOSFETs—require a very small input current. Further, they can be manufactured in complementary N-channel and P-channel types (just as NPN and PNP bipolar transistors are complementary to each other). Because they are complementary, they require opposite input voltages to turn them on. Then it is possible to connect the same input line to two complementary transistors and turn one on and the other off. This is just what is desired for a totem pole output.

Now follows a short phenomenological discussion of the MOSFET along with a switch model that is useful in understanding and applying CMOS logic devices. Figure D1–25a shows the N-channel (enhancement-type) MOSFET action. The term *metal-oxide-semiconductor* arises from the tri-layer construction of this important transistor type. A *metal* plate called the *gate,* placed on the side of a bar of *semiconductor* controls the current flowing between the ends of the bar, which are called the *source* and the *drain.* These construction features are diagrammed rather schematically with dashed lines on the accepted symbol for a MOSFET to the left in Figure D1–25a. The symbol design loosely follows the construction of the device. The current path through the bar is called the *channel* and presents a resistance to current flow that is controlled by the relative voltage between the gate and the channel/source. Between the metal gate and the semiconductor channel is placed a layer of highly insulating semiconductor *oxide.* Thus no current flows to the gate structure (unless the oxide layer becomes damaged by excessive gate-channel voltage). The symbols for the N-channel and P-channel MOSFETs are shown to the left in Figure D1–25, and the separate gate structure denoting its insulation from the bar may be seen. The *substrate* arrow indicates the MOSFET channel type; the drain, gate, and source connections are evident.

The *enhancement-type* MOSFET, which is the type used in logic circuits, permits essentially no current flow through it if the gate is at the same voltage as the source; for example, if the gate is connected to the source. The FET then acts like an open switch. If the gate is made *positive* relative to the source for the N-channel type, the channel opens and electrons may flow rather easily from the source to the drain (this is the origin of the source/drain names). The conventional current flow is thus from drain to source. On the other hand, the polarities for the P-channel type are just the reverse (see Figure D1–25b): When the gate is made *negative* relative to the source, conventional current flows from the source to the drain. The FET then behaves like a closed switch between the drain and the source. Note that a switch model with various relative voltage polarities for the two MOSFET types is shown on the right in Figure D1–25. A drain-source resistance R_{DS} that is due to the resistance of the channel is also drawn in the switch model. For our purposes we will regard R_{DS} as a constant, although the resistance actually depends on the gate-source voltage and drain-source voltage.

The diagram of a CMOS inverter is shown in Figure D1–26a. Notice that it is simply constructed from a pair of complementary MOSFETs connected in series, with the gates connected together as the input. The transistors constitute a totem pole output rather like TTL. The switch equivalent is shown to the right in Figure D1–26a, where it is assumed that the in connection is grounded or low. Then the N-channel bottom transistor gate is connected to its source so that it is an open switch or off. The top P-channel transistor gate is significantly negative with respect to its source so that it is a closed switch or on. Consequently the output is connected (through a channel resistance R_{DS} of nominally 400 ohms) to the $V+$ supply voltage and the output will be high. Changing the in connection to $V+$ or high reverses the switch situation, resulting in an inverter.

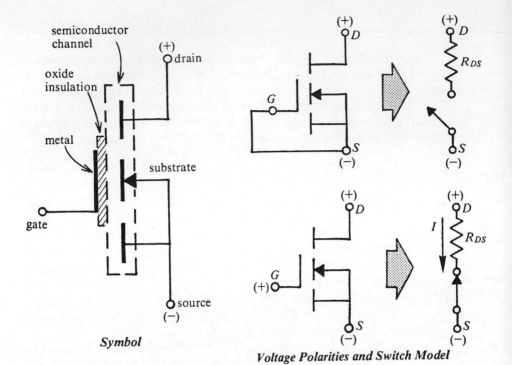

semiconductor channel

oxide insulation

metal

gate

substrate

Symbol

Voltage Polarities and Switch Model

(a) N-Channel (Enhancement-Type) MOSFET Action

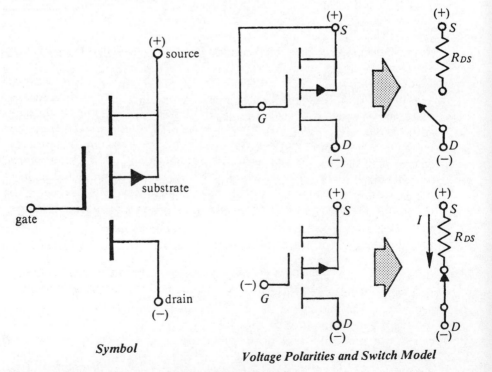

gate

substrate

Symbol

Voltage Polarities and Switch Model

(b) P-Channel (Enhancement-Type) MOSFET Action

An arrangement of series/parallel MOSFET switches produces a 2-input NAND gate as shown in Figure D1–26b. The switch arrangement for one input low and the other high is illustrated, and it is seen that the output is connected to $V+$ or high. Notice that only if both inputs are high will the bottom series switches both be closed (and the top parallel switches open) so that the output is low. Clearly we have a NAND.

Input/Output Considerations for CMOS

Several features of CMOS logic may be understood from further examination of the simple CMOS inverter circuit. First, when a CMOS output stands high or low, it is essentially at the $V+$ voltage or ground, respectively, provided it is connected to a high impedance load. This behavior is quite different from TTL where the voltage drop across one or two diode junctions occurs between the output and either supply voltage. Further, if current is sourced (by a high output) or sunk (by a low output), the output voltage may be calculated to a first approximation as different from the supply voltage or ground to the extent of the IR drop across the 400-ohm R_{DS}.

Second, because the gate (input) to a MOSFET presents a very high impedance of some 10^{12} ohms to external circuitry (due to the oxide layer), very little current is required by a CMOS-logic input in either the high or low state. Rather, the input metal-gate structure represents a capacitance of some 5 to 10 picofarads.

NOTE: The term *gate* here refers to the MOSFET *terminal* of Figure D1–25.

Third, unless the logic-gate output is connected to a low-resistance load, no power supply current flows from $V+$ into the device when it is standing in a certain state. The reason is that at least one switch is open in the series path from $V+$ to ground. Current flows only for a brief period during the switching of states and the charging of gate input capacitances. Therefore, the CMOS logic family is ideal for low-current-drain, low-switching-speed applications. Battery-operated digital wristwatches and remote data acquisition systems are examples. However, at switching rates of 1 megahertz, the power requirement approaches that of TTL (for gates actually operating at that rate).

Example: A resistance of 4,000 ohms is connected between a CMOS-inverter output and the supply voltage. What output voltage may be

FIGURE D1–25. *Symbols and Switch-Resistor Model for Enhancement-Type MOSFETs*

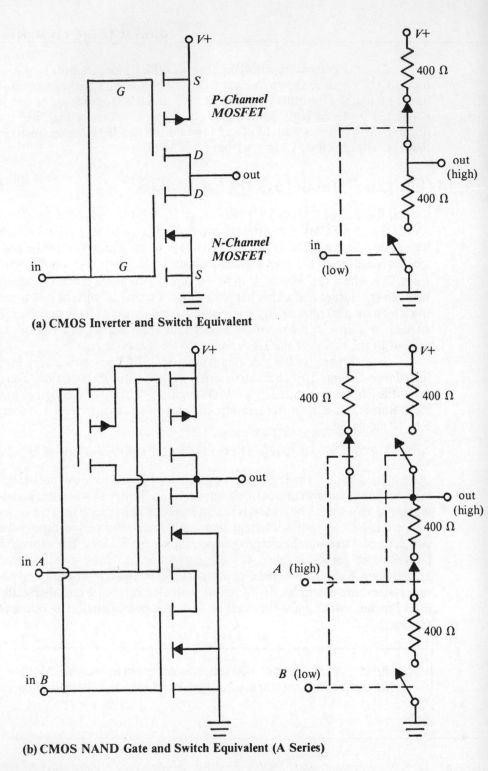

(a) CMOS Inverter and Switch Equivalent

(b) CMOS NAND Gate and Switch Equivalent (A Series)

FIGURE D1-26. *CMOS Construction and Switch Equivalents*

expected for the high and low states, respectively, if a +5-V supply is used?

Solution: The resistance model for this problem is shown in Figure D1–27a for the high-output case. Notice that no current flows through the 4-kilohm resistor; therefore, the high-output voltage V_{high} equals 5 V.

The current flow path for the low-output case is shown in Figure D1–27b. Now the output voltage is more than 0 V by the voltage drop across the 400-ohm R_{DS} of the bottom FET switch. Indeed, voltage-divider action occurs, and the output voltage V_{low} may be quickly calculated to be $V_{low} = 5 \text{ V} \times 400/(400 + 4{,}000) = 0.45 \text{ V}$.

NOTE: The input to a typical TTL gate may be modeled as essentially a 4-kilohm resistor connected to +5 V (see Figure D1–19). Then this calculation shows that V_{high} and V_{low} into the TTL input would fall within the allowed high/low input range for a *typical* TTL gate, and satisfactory logic operation would be expected. However, the worst-case TTL input requires 1.6-milliampere sinking current. This current would flow through the 400 ohms and result in 1.6 mA $\times$ 0.4 kΩ = 0.64 V for a low. Should R_{DS} happen to be more than 400 ohms, the low could move above the accepted low of a TTL input. Thus, it is normally *not* recommended to connect a standard CMOS output to a standard TTL input. Interfacing CMOS and TTL is discussed more formally shortly.

CMOS gates can operate over a large range of supply voltages and thus give significant versatility. The earlier *A series* (for example, designated CD4000A, CD4011A, and so forth) can operate from 3 V to 15 V and has low- and high-input ranges of 20% of the supply voltage. Thus, if a 10-V supply is used, low = 0 V to 2 V and high = 8 V to 10 V, resulting in a noise margin of 2 V and good noise immunity for difficult applications (such as in an automobile engine compartment). The propagation-delay time depends on the power supply voltage used, as well as on the amount of capacitance connected to the output; this capacitance must be charged or discharged through R_{DS} of the MOSFET switches. When an A-series gate output is connected to 15 picofarads (2-gate inputs), the propagation-delay time is on the order of 45 nanoseconds for a 5-V supply and 25 nanoseconds for a 10-V supply. Notice that these switching speeds compare to 74LXX speeds (the slowest of the TTL family). To achieve faster switching speeds, a higher supply voltage should be selected; for example, 10 V.

Beginning about 1975 a new *buffered* series of CMOS logic became available that became standardized as the *B series*. This series is sometimes

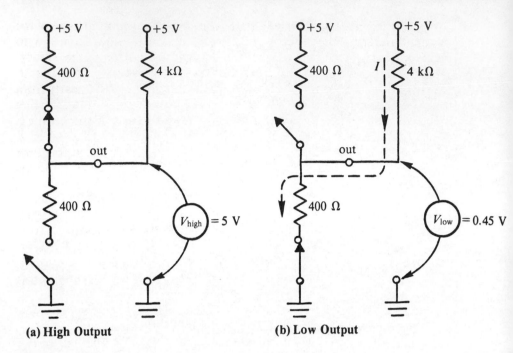

FIGURE D1–27. *Example: Effect of Resistive Load on Output Levels of a CMOS Inverter*

termed the *high-voltage* series in that it has a maximum $V+$ or V_{DD} supply rating of at least 18 V. Perhaps more important is the fact that a pair of inverters as shown in Figure D1–26a are placed after the output of a gate such as that shown in Figure D1–26b, and act as a buffer to the output. The actual gate output then comes from the last inverter (which amounts to the midpoint connection between just *two* series switches), and the output resistance then has the advantage of being independent of the logic conditions of the gate. This resistance will be about 400 ohms to $V+$ if the output is high, or 400 ohms to ground if the output is low. In contrast, the A-series-style output of the NAND gate in Figure D1–26b will be 400 ohms to $V+$ if just one upper switch is closed, but 200 ohms if both (parallel) upper switches are closed for a high output. For a low output, the output resistance is 800 ohms to ground. (Why?)

An additional benefit of the B series is the fact that the overall voltage gain from input to output is increased with the additional stages. This increased gain causes the division between high and low levels for the input voltages to occur very sharply at half the $V+$ supply voltage (typically within 5%). Thus the low region and the high region are, respectively, about 45% of the supply voltage, and a noise margin of this size can be expected. The B-series standard margin, however, is taken to be 30% of $V+$.

The increased gain of the B series also causes the transition time of the output waveform (for example, time for the output to move from low to high) to be very rapid even though the input signal may change rather slowly. The output changes states in some 75 nanoseconds (assuming a 50-picofarad load) even when the input represents a *ramp voltage* changing linearly from low to high in 1 millisecond. However, in any logic family slowly changing inputs are best *squared up* first with a Schmitt trigger device; this procedure is discussed in Chapter D5. The propagation delay of the B series may be up to double that of the A series due to the additional stages, although this time varies with the manufacturer. Generally, the B series is regarded to be the first choice for new designs.

Unused inputs to CMOS must be connected low or high, or else charge may accumulate on the very high input impedance gate and cause erratic behavior. CMOS outputs cannot be wire-ORed because they have a totem pole output (like TTL). Three-state output devices also exist in CMOS. The effect of temperature on CMOS is less pronounced than on TTL; indeed, the less expensive commercial line is usable over the range $-40°C$ to $85°C$ (compared with $0°C$ to $+75°C$ for TTL).

When CMOS is operated from a +5-V power supply, the interface with TTL can be relatively simple. The output from CMOS can drive 2 low-power TTL (74LXX) input loads or 1 low-power-Schottky TTL (74LSXX) input load. Notice that sinking the TTL input current through 400 ohms to ground to assert the low input is the problem. CMOS buffer ICs exist (for example, CA4049 and CA4050) that drive 2 regular TTL load inputs. On the other hand, when a TTL output must operate into a CMOS input, the 2.4 V-minimum guaranteed high out of the TTL is a problem; for example, it is below the 0.7×5 V = 3.5 V safe minimum high into the B-series CMOS. The solution is to connect a 2.2-kilohm pull-up resistor between the TTL output and +5 V.

Various manufacturers produce the CMOS family with various prefixes. Thus Fairchild calls theirs F4XXX, Motorola uses MC14XXX, while National Semiconductor uses the original (RCA) CD4XXX designation. National further introduced a CMOS line with the same pin-outs and logic functions as the TTL 7400 series; this line is numbered the 74CXX line and satisfies the B-series specifications for voltage and buffering.

Other Logic Families

In 1961 General Electric introduced an *emitter-coupled logic* (ECL) that was later expanded and improved by Motorola. This family relies on the higher frequency capabilities of the common-base transistor amplifier and is similar to the transistor difference amplifier in construction. It has very high speed: typically 2-nanosecond propagation delays. However, it operates from a negative power supply—and consequently is *not compatible* with TTL or DTL—and requires more power. (However ECL-to-TTL and TTL-to-ECL converter ICs exist.) ECL is used in applications requiring the highest speed, although the Schottky series 74SXX now performs nearly as fast.

In about 1972 Phillips and IBM in Europe invented a fast, low-power logic type that makes use of complementary bipolar transistors; it is usually called *integrated-injection logic* (IIL or I^2L). Rather like CMOS, using the two transistor types eliminates the need for resistors in the chip, and a significant savings in power as well as chip area results. No basic logic devices are readily available for consumers as of this writing, however. IIL is primarily being used in special-function, large-scale integration, such as wristwatches, some microprocessors, and the like.

Small-Scale, Medium-Scale, and Large-Scale Integration

There is an interesting story relating to how the many resistors and transistors (and a few capacitors but no inductors!) can be produced on a small chip of semiconductor only a few millimeters square. There is not the time or space to relate it here, but the interested reader is referred to the special September 1977 *Scientific American* "theme issue" on microelectronics. (The principal story of this issue is the microcomputer.)

It has been observed that the number of components on the most advanced integrated circuits has doubled every year since 1959. The era from 1959 to 1966 is called the SSI—*small-scale integration*—era when up to 74 components or up to 10 gates could be put on a chip. The MSI—*medium-scale integration*—maximum-capability era extended from about 1966 to 1969, when 1,000 components or 10 to 100 gates could be placed on a chip. During this period more elaborate combinations of logic functions became available. LSI—*large-scale integration*—has followed since that time; in 1971 the microcomputer on a chip became possible when 4,000 components could be put in an IC (also making 1,000-bit memory ICs a reality). LSI chips are defined to incorporate the equivalent of 100 to 1,000 gates.

The first LSI circuits were made with P-channel MOSFET devices—called PMOS—because they were the easiest to make. However, PMOS circuits are also the slowest, and N-channel or NMOS circuits represented the next improvement. Most of the classic microprocessors use NMOS technology, although several are available that use I^2L and CMOS. Rather power-hungry bipolar LSI is used for high operating speed in some applications.

In 1978 what is usually called the VLSI—*very-large-scale integration*—era dawned with the commercial production of single chips containing more than 50,000 devices or over 1,000 gate equivalents. The first VLSI device was the 64,000-bit memory IC. The 1980s began with the availability of microprocessors—computers on a chip—such as the Motorola 68000, which in fact consists of some 68,000 transistors; the 68000 possesses the capability of a very sophisticated minicomputer of 1970. LSI and VLSI devices portend a remarkable decade. Nevertheless, SSI and MSI devices will continue to be useful and important building blocks for scientists and engineers. Indeed, the number of MSI and LSI devices has grown so dramatically that remaining aware of the many rather complex functions that may be purchased in IC form is a task in itself.

Supplement to Chapter:
Binary Numbers and Other Number Systems

Presumably because we were born with 10 fingers, humans have developed the convention of counting in groups of 10 or base 10. 10 symbols represent the 10 whole numbers from 0 through 9. If we add 1 to 9, a *carry* is generated to the 10's place, which keeps count of the number of groups of 10. Of course, when 9 (the top symbol possible) is exceeded in the 10's place, a carry is generated into the 100's place, which indicates the number of groups of 100. Thus the number 5467_{10} means 5 thousands plus 4 hundreds plus 6 tens plus 7 units or

$$(3210) \leftarrow \text{place}$$
$$\dot{.}\,\dot{.}\,\dot{.}\,\dot{.}$$
$$5467_{10} = (5 \times 10^3) + (4 \times 10^2) + (6 \times 10^1) + (7 \times 10^0)$$

This then is the *decimal system,* in which we count *base 10.*

If 8 symbols are used (0, 1, 2, 3, 4, 5, 6, 7), we have the *octal* or *base-8* number system. A carry out of the units place occurs when counting past 7 (because symbol 8 does not exist in this system). Then the number 67_8 means a carry out of the units place has occurred 6 times, and the number is 6 eights plus 7 units. The number 167_8 means a carry has occurred once out of the eights place as well, signifying 8 eights, so that we have in decimal

$$(1 \times 8 \times 8) + (6 \times 8) + 7 = (1 \times 8^2) + (6 \times 8) + 7$$

For the larger number 5467_8 we have

$$(3210) \leftarrow \text{place}$$
$$\dot{.}\,\dot{.}\,\dot{.}\,\dot{.}$$
$$5467_8 = (5 \times 8^3) + (4 \times 8^2) + (6 \times 8^1) + (7 \times 8^0)$$

The similarity to the decimal number is quite obvious; simply use the new base 8 (rather than 10), with an exponent according to the *place* of the digit. Notice that the least significant digit is used with *zero* exponent.

The smallest possible number of symbols with which to indicate numbers is two (for example, 0 and 1); therefore, the use of only two numerical symbols is called the *binary system* or *base 2.* Now $0 + 1 = 1$, but $1 + 1 = 10$

(zero, carry 1) because a carry must already be generated out of the least significant digit; that is, single symbols for numbers greater than 1 do not exist. Consider then counting sheep as they jump over the fence, but using binary. We have

000	0	**Example:** $11 \leftarrow$ carry
$+1$		011
001	1	$+1$
$+1$		100
010	2	
$+1$		
011	3	
$+1$		
100	4	
$+1$		
101	5	
$+1$		
110	6	
$+1$		
111	7	

The digits in a binary number are called *bits*. Notice that a 3-bit number can represent 8 states or numbers along the real-number line. Again it can be argued that a number such as 110101 can be converted to decimal by

$(543210) \leftarrow$ place

$$110101 = (1 \times 2^5) + (1 \times 2^4) + (0 \times 2^3) + (1 \times 2^2) + (0 \times 2^1) + (1 \times 2^0)$$
$$= (1 \times 32) + (1 \times 16) + (0 \times 8) + (1 \times 4) + (0 \times 2) + (1 \times 1)$$
$$= 53_{10}$$

The largest 8-bit binary number is 11111111_2. The easiest way to evaluate its decimal equivalent is to realize that the number that is larger by one unit is 100000000. This number is $(1 \times 2^8) + (0 \times 2^7) + \ldots + (0 \times 2^0) = 256$, so that $11111111_2 = 256 - 1 = 255$. Similarly, the largest 16-bit binary number is $2^{16} - 1 = (2^8 \times 2^8) - 1 = 256^2 - 1 = 65,535$.

Although it is rather a chore to convert binary numbers to base 10 or decimal, it is quite easy to convert binary numbers to any base that is a power of 2. Thus 3 bits can represent 8 states, and there is a carry out of a 3-bit number group every time there is a carry out of an octal digit. It is therefore possible to partition off a binary number into groups of three, and each group will correspond to an octal digit. For example

$$101110011 = 101, 110, 011 = 563_8$$

since $101 = 5$, $110 = 6$, and $011 = 3$.

Alternatively, it is possible to partition the number into 4-bit groups. Four bits can represent 16 states or base 16 (see Table D1–9); however, deci-

	Binary-Hexadecimal		
Binary-Octal			
0111	7	1111	F	(15)
0110	6	1110	E	(14)
0101	5	1101	D	(13)
0100	4	1100	C	(12)
0011	3	1011	B	(11)
0010	2	1010	A	(10)
0001	1	1001	9	
0000	0	1000	8	

TABLE D1–9. *Octal and Hexa-decimal to Binary Correspondence*

mal symbols exist only up to 9 and new symbols for 10 through 15 must be invented. The letters A through F have been conventionally used. A number written in *base 16* is termed a *hexadecimal number.* Thus the number

$$1101001111001001_2 = 1101, 0011, 1100, 1001$$
$$= D3C9_{16}$$

since $1101 = D$, $0011 = 3$, $1100 = C$, and $1001 = 9$. A hexadecimal number can be converted to decimal along the same lines as the earlier conversions. Thus

$$D3C9 = (D \times 16^3) + (3 \times 16^2) + (C \times 16^1) + (9 \times 16^0)$$
$$= (13 \times 16^3) + (3 \times 16^2) + (12 \times 16^1) + (9 \times 16^0)$$
$$= 54217_{10}$$

It is frequently faster to convert a binary number to decimal by first converting it to octal or hexadecimal and from there to decimal.

There are several schemes for converting from decimal to some other base. Perhaps the most obvious and therefore easily remembered method is to calculate the number of times the number contains (base)^n for successively smaller values of n. Thus 367_{10} contains $16^2 = 256$ one time with a remainder of 111; 111 contains 16^1 six times with a remainder of $15 = F$. Then $367_{10} = 16F_{16}$.

On the other hand, converting to base 8 or octal, we have that 367_{10} contains $8^2 = 64$ five times with a remainder of 47; 47 contains 8^1 five times with a remainder of 7. Then $367_{10} = 557_8$.

An alternative approach is to divide successively by the base number. The remainders become the digits of the number in the desired base, beginning with the least significant. The whole part of the quotient becomes the dividend for the next division. Thus $367/8 = 45$ with remainder 7 (for the 8^0 digit); then $45/8 = 5$ with remainder 5 (for the 8^0 digit); 5 is not divisible by 8^1 and becomes the most significant digit. Thus $367^{10} = 557_8$ again.

REVIEW EXERCISES

1. Why should digital electronic circuits be expected to be more reliable than analog electronic circuits?
2. What is meant by the terms logic 0 and logic 1?
3. (a) Write out the truth table for the logical AND function with two input variables; use logic 0 and logic 1 in the table.
   (b) Draw an electrical circuit that implements a 2-input logical AND function through the use of switches.
   (c) What rules apply to manipulating the switches and interpreting the output?
   (d) What is the utility of using electrical relays rather than simple switches in the circuit of part (b)?
4. (a) Suppose a 2-input AND function is implemented with a pair of electromagnetic relays. Diagram the circuit.
   (b) Write out a truth table for this circuit; use the words *high* and *low* as its elements.
5. (a) Draw an electrical circuit that implements a 2-input logical inclusive-OR function through the use of switches.
   (b) Write out a truth table for this logical system using logic 0 and logic 1 as the table elements.
6. (a) Write the Boolean algebra expression for the logical AND between two variables A and B.
   (b) Write the Boolean algebra expression for the logical inclusive OR between two variables A and B.
   (c) How is the opposite state of a logical variable indicated in Boolean algebra?
7. (a) State in words the difference between the inclusive-OR concept and the exclusive-OR concept.
   (b) How may the truth table for the inclusive OR be changed to the truth table for the exclusive OR?
8. Draw the commonly used symbol for each logic element:
   (a) 3-input AND
   (b) 6-input (inclusive) OR
   (c) inverter
   (d) 2-input exclusive OR
9. Five inverters are connected in series. What is the function of the circuit; that is, how is the output related to the input?
10. Diagram a circuit that gates data from some input line to some output line; that is, the data may either be passed or be blocked by the circuit.
11. What type of logic gate is implied by each of the following statements:
    (a) If either input is high, the output is high.
    (b) Only if both inputs are high will the output be low.
    (c) If either input is high, the output is low.
    (d) Only if both inputs are high will the output be high.
12. (a) Diagram a 2-input NAND function that is constructed from an AND gate and an inverter.

(b) Draw the single-gate symbol for the NAND function.

(c) Diagram a 2-input NOR function that is constructed from an OR gate and an inverter.

(d) Draw the single-gate symbol for the NOR function.

13. Describe in one or two sentences what is meant by positive and negative logic.

14. (a) "Only if both inputs are high will the output be low." This statement corresponds to what type of positive-logic gate?

(b) Reword the function given in part (a) to an equivalent statement that is presented in terms of the opposite states at the input and output.

(c) What negative-logic gate does the reworded statement in (b) correspond to? Justify your answer.

(d) Write the Boolean algebra form for the equivalence of part (a) and part (b) above.

(e) What name is associated with this equivalence statement?

15. (a) "If either input is high, the output will be low." This statement corresponds to what type of positive-logic gate?

(b) Reword the function given in part (a) to an equivalent statement that is presented in terms of opposite conditions at the input and output.

(c) What negative-logic gate does the reworded statement in (b) correspond to? Justify your answer.

(d) Write the Boolean algebra form for the equivalence of part (a) and part (b) above.

16. (a) What basic logic function is obtained by inverting both inputs to a 2-input AND gate, as well as inverting its output?

(b) What basic logic function is obtained by inverting both inputs to a 2-input OR gate, as well as inverting its output?

(c) Explain why knowing the answer to part (a) permits the answer to part (b) to be quickly proven.

17. (a) Show with gate diagrams how the OR, AND, and NOT functions can each be constructed using only NAND gates.

(b) Repeat (a), but use only NOR gates instead of NAND gates.

18. (a) Diagram how a 2-input AND gate can be constructed from 2 diodes and a resistor. Briefly explain how it achieves the AND function.

(b) Must a device connected to the gate input of part (a) be capable of sourcing or of sinking current? Explain.

(c) Diagram how a 2-input OR gate can be constructed from 2 diodes and a resistor. Must a device connected to a gate input be capable of sourcing or of sinking current here?

19. What behavior severely limits the application of diode logic to complex digital logic systems?

20. (a) What feature of RTL and DTL gate construction tends to limit rapid switching action?

(b) Is the switching slow for a low-to-high or a high-to-low transition of the gate output? Explain why one case is slow while the other is fast.

21. What is meant by the propagation delay time of a gate?

22. (a) What do the letters designate in each of the following 7400-series device types: A. 74LXX, B. 74HXX, C. 74SXX, D. 74CXX, E. 74LSXX.

  (b) How are the military temperature range TTL devices distinguished from the commercial temperature range devices?

  (c) Write the temperature ranges respectively for the military and commercial device lines.

23. (a) What is the advantage of 74HXX devices over 74XX devices? What is the disadvantage?

  (b) What is the advantage of 74LXX over 74XX? What is the disadvantage?

  (c) What is the advantage of 74LSXX over 74XX? Is there a disadvantage in terms of power or speed?

24. What does the term Schottky come from with respect to the 74SXX and 74LSXX families?

25. What is the supply voltage for the TTL family of logic ICs?

26. (a) Name the three principle sections of a TTL NAND gate.

  (b) What feature greatly improves the switching speed when TTL is used in circuits as opposed to either RTL or DTL?

27. (a) What rather curious transistor construction is used in the input section of a TTL NAND gate?

  (b) The input section of a TTL NAND gate corresponds to a diode-logic gate. What logic function does this section of the gate perform?

  (c) Does a TTL gate input require current sinking or current sourcing?

  (d) Explain your answer to part (b) in terms of the operation of the DL logic equivalent of the input section.

28. (a) What are the input voltage-level requirements for a TTL gate?

  (b) What are the input-current requirements for a 74XX gate and also for a 74LSXX gate?

  (c) What are the output voltage-level guarantees for a TTL gate?

  (d) What are the output-current capabilities for a 74XX gate and also for a 74LSXX gate?

29. (a) Explain why we say the TTL family has a 4-V noise margin.

  (b) Why is a large noise margin desirable?

30. (a) What is meant by the fanout of a logic family?

  (b) What is the utility of a buffer device in a logic family?

31. (a) Explain why the output of two regular TTL gate outputs should not be connected together. What harm may be done?

  (b) Explain why two open-collector TTL gate outputs may be connected together; that is, why no harm is possible to the gates.

32. (a) The output of a 3-state device may be high, low, or off. Explain.

  (b) What utility do both 3-state and open-collector gates have?

  (c) What is the advantage of the 3-state type over the open-collector type in part (b)?

33. (a) Why are complementary forms of MOSFETs useful for the totem pole output of a CMOS gate?

(b)　Why do CMOS logic devices require essentially no current while they are not switching?

(c)　Explain why CMOS logic devices lose their low-power advantage at high switching frequencies.

34.　Select between TTL and CMOS for answers to the following questions.

(a)　Which family is superior in terms of flexible power supply voltage requirements?

(b)　Which family is superior in terms of switching speed?

(c)　Which family is superior in terms of noise margin?

35.　(a)　What is the difference in general construction between the A series and the B series of 4000-type CMOS devices?

(b)　Name three advantages of the B series relative to the A series.

36.　What do the acronyms TTL, DTL, ECL, RL, DL, IIL, and CMOS stand for?

37.　(a)　How many transistors are incorporated on a quad 2-input NAND gate chip?

(b)　How many components (resistors, diodes, transistors) are incorporated in the chip of part (a)?

(c)　What do SSI, MSI, LSI, and VLSI stand for, respectively?

(d)　Characterize each designation in (c) in terms of the number of transistors or the number of equivalent gates.

PROBLEMS

1.　Read the supplement to this chapter: "Binary Numbers and Other Number Systems." Then answer the following questions.

(a)　How many digit symbols exist in each of the following number systems: binary, decimal, octal, and hexadecimal?

(b)　Almost everyone has in fact used a number system that employs only *one* symbol: "1." How are 6 sheep represented in this system (assume we are counting sheep)? Discuss the rule for addition of numbers in this system; also discuss the "compactness" of this number system.

(c)　Convert the decimal numbers 28, 100, and 341 to binary, respectively.

(d)　Convert the binary numbers 1101, 10101010, and 001100 to decimal.

(e)　Write the successive binary numbers for the following successive decimal numbers: 17, 18, 19, 20.

(f)　Convert the binary numbers of part (d) to octal numbers.

(g)　Convert the binary numbers of part (d) to hexadecimal numbers.

2.　(a)　Two single-pole-single-throw (SPST) switches A and B are to cause a 5-V light bulb to turn on only if both switches are closed. Draw a circuit using these switches that accomplishes this task.

(b)　Show how a single-pole-double-throw (SPDT) switch may be connected to a +5-V source and to ground in order to output high and low voltage levels as the switch is flipped between its two states.

   (c)   Diagram how two SPDT switches may be used in conjunction with an appropriate logic gate to accomplish the function in part (a). Assume the gate uses 5 V and 0 V for its logic levels.

3.   Suppose the voltages v_A and v_B as graphed in Diagram D1–1 are input to the respective inputs of the following 2-input gates. Draw a time graph of the gate output in each case.

   (a)   AND

   (b)   OR

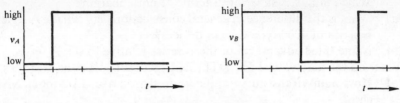

DIAGRAM D1–1.

4.   Consider the switching network shown in Diagram D1–2 that allows current to flow from a to b. Deduce the Boolean algebra expression for the condition that the circuit conducts current.

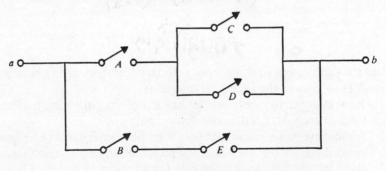

DIAGRAM D1–2.

5.   How many rows are in the truth table for a 6-input AND gate?

6.   Draw a 3-input AND circuit constructed from a group of 2-input NAND gates.

7.   (a)   Consider a 3-input NAND gate for which 1 input is permanently high. Prove with the aid of a truth table that the output functions as a 2-input NAND gate in terms of the remaining 2 inputs.

   (b)   What is the NAND-gate function if instead 1 input of the 3 is permanently connected low?

8.   The logic statement "A or B and C-- can be interpreted in two ways. Show the two interpretations as corresponding gate circuits. State each gate circuit output in an unambiguous Boolean algebra form.

9.   (a)   Make a truth table for the negated-input OR gate and also for the NAND gate. The following headings should be used. Compare the outputs; what Boolean algebra theorem is proven here?

A	B	$\overline{A}$	$\overline{B}$	$\overline{A} + \overline{B}$	$A \cdot B$	$\overline{A \cdot B}$

(b)   Design and complete a similar truth table for a negated-input AND and for a NOR. What Boolean algebra theorem is proven?

10. (a) Draw a gate diagram for the logical statement: T is the result of A or the result of not-B and C.

     (b) Write down the Boolean expression that follows directly from the statement in (a).

     (c) Write out the truth table for this logical system.

11. The control panel for a certain project has 2 switches, A and B, and 2 lights that indicate whether or not conditions C and D are true. Assume that an alarm is to sound if switch A is on and light C is off, or is to sound if switches A and B are both on while light D is on.

     (a) Write the Boolean function directly from this statement that describes the state of the alarm in terms of the states A, B, C, and D.

     (b) Draw a gate circuit that implements the stated alarm function.

12. Consider a committee with 3 members that each vote yes or no on a proposal. Each is provided with a switch that he or she should flip to output a high for a yes vote and a low for a no vote. Design a logic gate network that causes a light bulb to light when the majority vote yes.

13. A square-wave v_A with a period of 2 seconds as illustrated in Diagram D1-3 is input to 1 terminal of a 2-input exclusive-OR gate. Assume that the other terminal B of this gate is held low for the time interval (in seconds) $0 \leq t < 7$, and then held high for the time interval $7 \leq t < 14$. Draw time graphs of v_A, v_B, and the gate output for $0 \leq t < 14$. Comment on a use of

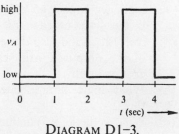

DIAGRAM D1-3.

the exclusive-OR gate that follows from this example.

14. A control panel has 3 switches A, B, and C. Design a logic circuit for which the output is high if 1 and only 1 of the 3 switches is on.

15. (a) Consider the circuit pictured in Diagram D1-4. Suppose E is logic 0. What is the relation of A', B', and C' to their input counterparts A, B, and C?

     (b) Repeat part (a) for the case that E is logic 1.

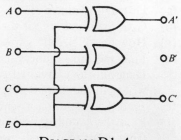

DIAGRAM D1-4.

D49

16. Consider the diode-logic circuit shown in Diagram D1–5. Silicon diodes are used.

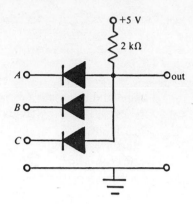

DIAGRAM D1–5.

(a) Suppose C is brought low by connecting it to ground. A and B are connected to +5 V (high). What is the output voltage?

(b) Suppose A and B are left unconnected, but C is connected to ground. What is the output voltage?

(c) Suppose A and B are left unconnected, but C is connected through a 500-ohm resistor to ground to bring it low. What is the output voltage?

17. (a) Consider the circuit pictured in Diagram D1–6. Suppose A is connected to ground, B is left unconnected, and C is connected to +3.5 V. What is the state of each of the transistors and also the state of the output? Justify each answer briefly.

(b) What logic family gate is this?

(c) What is the logic function of this gate?

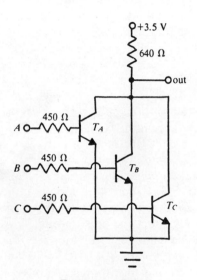

DIAGRAM D1–6.

18. Look up the 7400 NAND-gate specifications in a TTL manual from one of the many manufacturers of the 7400 series. (Example manufacturers are Texas Instruments, Fairchild Semiconductor, Motorola, National Semiconductor, and Signetics.) Answer the following questions.

(a) How many pins does the DIP version have?

(b) Give pin numbers for the +5-V supply and ground pins.

(c) How many NAND gates are on one chip?

(d) Find the pin numbers for the inputs and outputs of the respective gates. Diagram the individual gates in a vertical column (inputs at the left) and write pin numbers beside appropriate pins.

(e) Find the output short-circuit current range given.

(f) Find the stated typical turn-off delay (time for 1-to-0 output transition) from input to output; also find the turn-on delay.

19. (a) Suppose the 2 outputs from a pair of open-collector 2-input NAND gates are connected together. What is the logic function of the resulting device?

    (b) Explain why two "regular" 2-input NAND gates could not be used in part (a).

20. A certain logic board uses 16 74XX gates and 8 74LSXX gates. What supply current is the board expected to require?

21. (a) Use Table D1–8 to deduce the fanout of the 74XX family, and also of the 74LSXX family.

    (b) Suppose a 7400 gate output is connected to N 74LSXX gate inputs. What is the maximum number that N should be?

22. A 3-input NAND gate is to be used as an inverter in a circuit. (It is used because it is a "leftover" gate in a triple 3-input NAND chip.) Diagram three different ways that the input leads may be connected.

23. (a) A switch S, as illustrated in Diagram D1–7, is connected to the input of an inverter, while a sensitive 5-V light bulb L (requiring only 1 mA to light) is connected to the inverter output. Assuming a normal TTL (7404) inverter, what is the condition of the light when S is open and when S is closed?

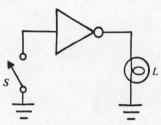

DIAGRAM D1–7.

    (b) Justify in terms of TTL input operation that the simple SPST switch connected to ground will cause the light to turn on and off in part (a).

    (c) Suppose the inverter in Diagram D1–7 is changed to an open-collector type (for example, 7405). Explain why the switch will *not* operate the light now. NOTE: No pull-up resistor is used.

    (d) Consider the circuit of Diagram D1–8, where the inverter A is an open-collector type, and inverter B is a normal TTL type. Justify that opening and closing switch S causes the light L to turn on and off, respectively. Explain why the open-collector output causes the input of TTL inverter B to function properly without a pull-up resistor.

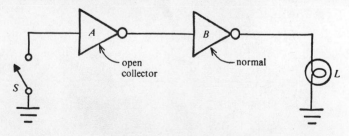

open collector   normal L

DIAGRAM D1–8.

24. Suppose the signals shown in Diagram D1–9a are input to the 74L01 open-collector NAND-gate circuit shown in Diagram D1–9b. The L series has a

typical propagation delay of 30 nanoseconds (nsec). Sketch with some accuracy a time graph of the output signal. Briefly justify the various transitions in your sketch.

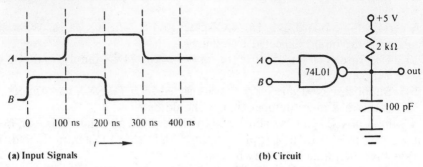

(a) Input Signals   **(b) Circuit**

DIAGRAM D1–9.

25. (a) Suppose that 1 input of a TTL NAND gate is connected to ground and the other is connected high as shown in Figure D1–19b. Assume the diode model for the multiple-emitter input transistor, and that it is a silicon device. Find the current passing through the grounded input wire and compare with the maximum low-level input current given for the 74XX unit in Table D1–8.

    (b) Suppose the input of the NAND gate is connected through a resistor R to ground (rather than directly to ground). What is the largest value for R that can be used and still have the input voltage remain within the maximum allowed for a low or logic 0?

26. A resistor R is connected between the output and ground of a TTL NAND gate. One input of the NAND gate is low. Consequently the output should be high because transistor Q_3 is on (saturated) and transistor Q_4 is off as shown in Figure D1–19b. Assume transistor Q_3 and the diode in the output stage each have a 0.6-V drop across them, regardless of the current passing through them. What is the smallest value permitted for R that still finds the output voltage of the NAND within the output-high specification for TTL?

27. The output of an open-collector NAND gate is connected through a 1-kilohm resistor to +5 V. This output is further connected into a circuit that has a capacitance of 50 picofarads to ground. Suppose both inputs are high and one is subsequently brought low. How much time delay will there be before the output rises into the TTL output-high specification region? Assume for simplicity that the output voltage begins at 0 V and neglect propagation delay within the gate.

28. Suppose the output of a TTL NAND gate is shorted to ground when the state of the inputs is such that the output should be high. Let us assume that transistor Q_3 (Figure D1–19) remains on and saturated; then we may assume that a 0.6-V drop exists across the Q_3 transistor as well as across the diode in the output stage. Calculate the short-circuit output current and compare with the range of short-circuit current given in a manufacturer's manual for a 7400 NAND gate.

29. A 1,000-ohm resistor is connected between the output and ground for a CMOS inverter (or from the output of a B-series CMOS gate). Approximately what output voltage is expected when the output is high and low, respectively? Assume the CMOS device is operated from a 5-V power supply.

30. (a) Assume that a 250-picofarad capacitance exists between the output and ground of a CMOS inverter (or a buffered-output CMOS gate). If the gate output makes a high-to-low transition, sketch with moderate accuracy the waveform at the gate output. Assume the gate is operated from a 5-V supply and that the output model of Figure D1-26a is valid.

   (b) The R_{DS} channel resistances modeled as 400 ohms in Figure D1-26a are appropriate for a CMOS 4000 output when the chip is operated from a 5-V supply. However, when a 4000 series chip is operated from 8 V or more, R_{DS} declines to about 200 ohms. Discuss why CMOS performance therefore improves when supply voltages higher than 8 V are used.

CHAPTER
D2

Gate Circuits

This chapter considers the use of logic gates to accomplish a number of functions that are useful in experimentation aided by electronics, within digital instruments, and in computer-based applications. Some facility with Boolean algebra is useful to the general scientist or engineer in this work and the chapter begins with this topic. A number of basic features relating to Boolean algebra were introduced when appropriate in Chapter D1; they are brought together here, along with some additional features. The treatment is quite informal and not exhaustive.

lements of Boolean Algebra

Boolean algebra is an area of mathematics that had its origins in the attempt to express logical reasoning in a mathematical form. It has become prominent through its usefulness as a mathematical foundation for switching functions and logic design. In the spirit of generalized algebra, Boolean algebra may be formally defined by means of a set of axioms. In fact, these axioms usually include the associative and distributive properties.

A rather pragmatic approach is used here that accepts proof of theorems or laws through the use of truth tables or switching diagrams. For our purposes, Boolean algebra is based on a set B of just two distinct elements;

the elements are arbitrarily taken to be 0 and 1. Two *binary operations* for combining elements of B to obtain other elements of B are defined. They are the *AND operation* ($\cdot$) and the *OR operation* (+). The term *binary* refers to the fact that these operations are defined to operate on just two elements. Further, a *unary operation,* the complement (‾), is defined: $\overline{1} = 0$ and $\overline{0} = 1$. Clearly, this is the *NOT concept* in logic. Variables such as $A, B, C, \ldots$ are used to express axioms and theorems in Boolean algebra. A variable may represent different elements of the set B at different times—that is, 0 or 1—but it may only be one value at a given instant.

We assume the + operation is defined for $A + B$ in terms of the truth table for the logical OR. Further, the dot operation is defined for $A \cdot B$ in terms of the truth table for the logical AND (refer to Tables D1–1 and D1–2). Finally, both operations are assumed to be *commutative:* $A + B = B + A$ and $A \cdot B = B \cdot A$. This assumption is consistent with the switch equivalent because the order of switch placement in the series or the parallel placement is not consequential.

On the basis of the above assumptions or axioms, a number of *theorems* may be proved. First, Boolean algebra is *associative*; that is, we may verify with truth tables that

$$A + (B + C) = (A + B) + C \tag{D2–1}$$

so that we write $A + B + C$. Also

$$A \cdot (B \cdot C) = (A \cdot B) \cdot C \tag{D2–2}$$

so that we write $A \cdot B \cdot C$. Indeed, similar to conventional algebra we often omit the dot operator and simply write ABC for this triple AND.

Second, Boolean algebra is *distributive*. In the problem section the reader is asked to verify that

$$A \cdot (B + C) = (A \cdot B) + (A \cdot C) \tag{D2–3}$$

which has a familiar appearance from ordinary algebra, of course.

There are a number of *one-variable identities* worthy of reflection:

1. $\overline{\overline{A}} = A$ 6. $A + 0 = A$
2. $A \cdot 0 = 0$ 7. $A + 1 = 1$
3. $A \cdot 1 = A$ 8. $A + A = A$
4. $A \cdot A = A$ 9. $A + \overline{A} = 1$
5. $A \cdot \overline{A} = 0$

Some appear the same as in ordinary algebra, but others do not (for example, cases 4, 7, and 8). The reader should prove each one.

For economy in writing, a precedence for operations is assumed whereby the AND or dot takes precedence over the OR or +. Thus Equation D2–3 may be written as $A \cdot (B + C) = A \cdot B + A \cdot C$ and the parentheses for grouping *on the right* may be omitted without loss of meaning. As a second economy, the dot operator for the AND is often omitted; thus $AB = A \cdot B$. (A similar convention is used for multiplication in ordinary algebra, of course.) Consequently, Equation D2–3 may be written $A(B+C) = AB + AC$.

There are quite a number of theorems involving expressions of several variables. An interesting pair have received the name *absorption theorems:*

$$A + (A \cdot B) = A \qquad\qquad \text{(D2–4)}$$

$$A \cdot (A + B) = A \qquad\qquad \text{(D2–5)}$$

In both cases the name clearly derives from the way B is made to disappear. Equation D2–4 may be justified mentally by considering the consequence of first $A = 0$ and then $A = 1$. When $A = 0$ we have

$$0 + (0 \cdot B) = 0 + 0 = 0 = A$$

(applying a one-variable identity). When $A = 1$ we have similarly

$$1 + (1 \cdot B) = 1 = A$$

so that indeed only A ever matters. The second form in Equation D2–5 is quickly proved by using the distributive property and then applying a one-variable identity along with Equation D2–4:

$$A \cdot (A + B) = A \cdot A + A \cdot B = A + A \cdot B = A$$

Other identities can be deduced, but the many possibilities are not listed here. However, as an example

$$
\begin{aligned}
(A + B) \cdot (A + C) &= A \cdot (A + C) + B \cdot (A + C) \\
&= A \cdot A + A \cdot C + B \cdot A + B \cdot C \\
&= (A + A \cdot C) + A \cdot B + B \cdot C \\
&= (A + A \cdot B) + B \cdot C \\
&= A + B \cdot C \qquad\qquad \text{(D2–6)}
\end{aligned}
$$

Here, the distributive property and the absorption theorem were put to use. (Also, to avoid some parentheses the convention that dot takes precedence over $+$ is used.) Another identity that is useful (and left to the problems to verify) is the following:

$$A + \overline{A}B = A + B \qquad\qquad \text{(D2–7)}$$

The two forms of *De Morgan's theorems* may be generalized to more variables; thus $\overline{A \cdot B} = \overline{A} + \overline{B}$ may be generalized to

$$\overline{A \cdot B \cdot C \cdots} = \overline{A} + \overline{B} + \overline{C} + \cdots \qquad\qquad \text{(D2–8)}$$

That is, a NAND gate with n inputs is equivalent to an n-input OR gate with all inputs inverted. Similarly $\overline{A + B} = \overline{A} \cdot \overline{B}$ may be generalized to

$$\overline{A + B + C \cdots} = \overline{A} \cdot \overline{B} \cdot \overline{C} \cdots \qquad\qquad \text{(D2–9)}$$

Thus an n-input NOR gate is equivalent to an n-input AND gate with all inputs inverted.

De Morgan's theorems along with the simpler identities already mentioned can be used to manipulate and *reduce* Boolean algebra expressions.

Example: Consider $\overline{\overline{A} \cdot (B + (\overline{C} \cdot D))}$

Solution: Applying De Morgan's theorem (Equation D2–8) we have

$$\overline{\overline{A} \cdot (B + (\overline{C} \cdot D))} = \overline{\overline{A}} + \overline{(B + (\overline{C} \cdot D))}$$

But $\overline{\overline{A}} = A$ and applying Equation D2–9, followed by applying Equation D2–8, we have

$$\overline{B + (\overline{C} \cdot D)} = \overline{B} \cdot (\overline{\overline{C} \cdot D}) = \overline{B} \cdot (\overline{\overline{C}} + \overline{D})$$

Using the distributive law we finally have

$$\overline{\overline{A} \cdot (B + (\overline{C} \cdot D))} = A + \overline{B} \cdot C + \overline{B} \cdot \overline{D} \qquad \textbf{(D2–10)}$$

$$A + \overline{B}\,(C + \overline{D})$$

Standard Forms

The reduction process above finally resulted in a *sum-of-products* form. The form of Equation D2–10 is nearly that of one of the two so-called standard forms. The other standard form is a *product-of-sums* form. It is always possible to manipulate a Boolean function of n variables to a sum of products of the n variables. Every product is to contain all n variables. Boole showed that *if, and only if, two functions reduce to the same standard form—that is, reduce to the same nonzero terms—are they the same function.*

Perhaps the best mode of discussion is through an example. This example is also important in that it illustrates another of Boole's discoveries; that is, *it is always possible to obtain a sum-of-products Boolean function for any given relationship between variables as presented in a truth table.* Consider a function F described by the truth table in Figure D2–1. It is a function of three variables, and has five 1's or true's for the outcome. We construct the Boolean function from the truth table by using the following approach. First note $F = 1$ at the top of the table when A, B, and C are all 0 or $\overline{A}\,\overline{B}\,\overline{C}$ is 1. Also $F = 1$ when $A = B = 0$ and $C = 1$; that is, $\overline{A}\,\overline{B}C$ is 1. We can continue down the table and write the occurrences of $F = 1$ in terms of necessary conditions on A, B, C, as done to the right of the table. Finally, F is 1 for *any* of these occurrences, so the logical OR is involved. We may write

$$F = \overline{A}\ \overline{B}\ \overline{C} + \overline{A}\ \overline{B}\ C + A\ \overline{B}\ \overline{C} + A\ \overline{B}\ C + A\ B\ C \qquad \textbf{(D2–11)}$$

and this is the one standard form for this logical function.

A	B	C	F
0	0	0	$1 \leftarrow \overline{A}\,\overline{B}\,\overline{C}$
0	0	1	$1 \leftarrow \overline{A}\,\overline{B}\,C$
0	1	0	0
0	1	1	0
1	0	0	$1 \leftarrow A\,\overline{B}\,\overline{C}$
1	0	1	$1 \leftarrow A\,\overline{B}\,C$
1	1	0	0
1	1	1	$1 \leftarrow A\,B\,C$

(a) Truth Table for Some 3-Variable Boolean Function

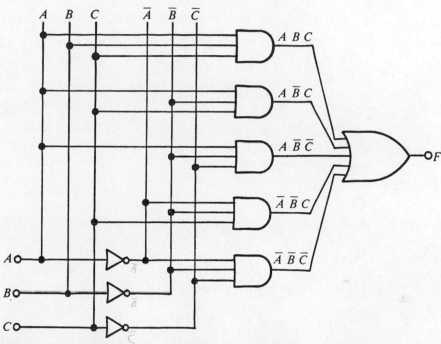

(b) Direct Gate Implementation of Minterm Form of the Boolean Function of (a)

FIGURE D2-1. *An Example Truth Table and Gate Implementation of Its Minterm or Sum-of-Products Statement*

Note each term involves all three variables. The individual products are called *minterms* and the sum of minterms gives the standard sum-of-products form. The function F may be implemented directly from this expression using five 3-input AND gates, one 5-input OR gate, and three inverters. The logic diagram is illustrated in Figure D2-1b. However, this is *not* the minimum gate system possible for this function, as we see shortly.

Next we deduce the product-of-sums standard form. This can be done by noting the states of A, B, C in Figure D2-1a for which the function is 0.

First we see that $F = 0$ for $A = 0$, $B = 1$, $C = 0$; in other words for $\overline{A}\,B\,\overline{C} = 1$. There are two other occurrences of $F = 0$; $\overline{A}\,B\,C = 1$ and $A\,B\,\overline{C} = 1$. For all three of these, $F = 0$ or $\overline{F} = 1$. Thus we may write

$$\overline{F} = \overline{A}\,B\,\overline{C} + \overline{A}\,B\,C + A\,B\,\overline{C} \qquad \text{(D2-12)}$$

Of course, the terms involved are just those *not* used in our earlier function, Equation D2–11.

Now each product term can be rewritten using De Morgan's theorem (Equation D2–8) to obtain

$$\overline{F} = \overline{(A + \overline{B} + C)} + \overline{(A + \overline{B} + \overline{C})} + \overline{\overline{A} + \overline{B} + \overline{C}} \qquad \text{(D2-13)}$$

Applying De Morgan's theorem again to these quantities on the right gives

$$\overline{F} = \overline{(A + \overline{B} + C) \cdot (A + \overline{B} + \overline{C}) \cdot (\overline{A} + \overline{B} + C)} \qquad \text{(D2-14)}$$

Inverting both sides of Equation D2–13 finally gives

$$F = (A + \overline{B} + C) \cdot (A + \overline{B} + \overline{C}) \cdot (\overline{A} + \overline{B} + C) \qquad \text{(D2-15)}$$

Notice that this expression involves a product of sums of three variables each. The individual sum quantities—for example, $(A + \overline{B} + C)$—are called *maxterms,* and Equation D2–15 is sometimes called the *maxterm form*. It is the other standard or *canonical* form for a multivariable logic function, and it is always possible to manipulate a Boolean function into this form as well. Notice that Equation D2–11 and Equation D2–15 must represent the *same* function.

To implement Equation D2–15 in terms of gates involves three 3-input OR gates and one 3-input AND gate, as well as three inverters. The circuit for the direct implementation of the maxterm form is shown in Figure D2–2. This logic network must perform the same function as that in Figure D2–1b. Notice that the maxterm form involves fewer gates than the minterm form if there are fewer 0's than 1's in the truth table. But if there are fewer 1's, the minterm form is more gate efficient.

NOTE: Diagrams for complex logic circuits such as that illustrated in Figure D2–1 often involve many crossing lines. These lines are only electrically connected if a bold dot is drawn at the junction. This convention for logic diagrams is now also becoming the preferred convention for analog electronic circuit drawings. (Past electrical circuit drawing practice required a "skip-over" U-shape in one of the wires at the crossing of two wires.)

Gate Reduction

For reasons of economy and simplicity, we are usually interested in a gate network that will implement a given logic function with the minimum number of gates. There exist a number of techniques for minimizing the number of

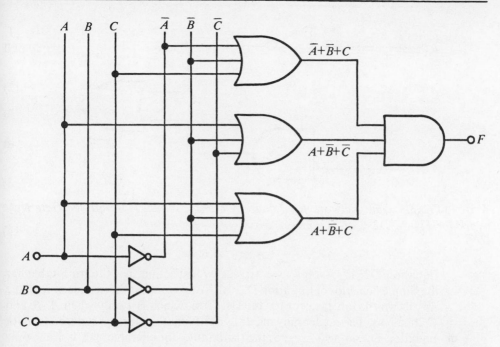

FIGURE D2–2. *Logic-Gate Implementation of Maxterm or Product-of-Sums Form of Figure D2–1a*

gates required. These include the Karnaugh map method, the Quine-McCluskey method, and the iterative consensus method. For more details on these approaches, the reader is referred to the texts by Lee (1978) and Dietmeyer (1978). However, for most scientific applications, the price of IC gates and size of the gate networks involved do not warrant substantial efforts at gate reduction. Typically, a few minutes work with Boolean algebra manipulations obtains satisfactory reductions.

It should be pointed out that the standard forms typically do *not* give minimum gate networks. Thus consider Equation D2–11, which represents the truth table of Figure D2–1a. Some Boolean algebra reduction of terms can be done quite easily:

$$F = \overline{A}\,\overline{B}\,\overline{C} + \overline{A}\,\overline{B}\,C + A\,\overline{B}\,\overline{C} + A\,\overline{B}\,C + A\,B\,C$$
$$= \overline{A}\,\overline{B}(\overline{C} + C) + A\,\overline{B}(\overline{C} + C) + A\,B\,C \quad \text{(using distributive law)}$$
$$= \overline{A}\,\overline{B} + A\,\overline{B} + A\,B\,C \quad \text{(using } \overline{C} + C = 1)$$
$$= (\overline{A} + A)\overline{B} + A\,B\,C = \overline{B} + A\,B\,C \quad \text{(D2–16)}$$
$$= \overline{B} + B(AC) = \overline{B} + AC \quad \text{(using identity of Equation D2–7)} \quad \text{(D2–17)}$$

Thus the truth table of Figure D2–1a can be implemented by the simple gate network of Figure D2–3, which is constructed from the reduced form of

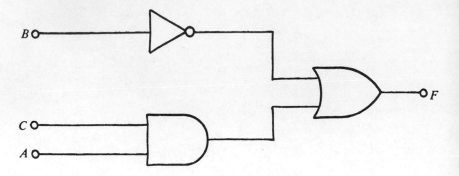

FIGURE D2–3. *Gate Network for Equation D2–17, Which Is Simplified Gate Network for Figure D2–1 or D2–2*

Equation D2–17. Actually we can see by inspection that the truth table has the simple behavior of Equation D2–16. Notice *F* is just the inverse of *B* all the way down the table except for the last term, which is 1 only when *A, B,* and *C* are all 1's. The reader may mentally verify that the further reduced form of Equation D2–17 also satisfies the truth table; for example, *AC* is 1 one time other than the last entry, but so is $\overline{B}$ in that case.

Gate Applications

Exclusive OR (X-OR)

The truth table for the exclusive OR is given in Table D1–7. It should be quite clear that the minterm or sum-of-products Boolean expression for this table is

$$A \oplus B = \overline{A} \cdot B + A \cdot \overline{B} \qquad \text{(D2–18)}$$

This is the standard form for the *exclusive OR* (X-OR); any network that implements the X-OR should be reducible to this form. The direct gate implementation of Equation D2–18 is shown in Figure D2–4a.

On the other hand, the maxterm or product-of-sums expression for the X-OR is obtained from

$$\overline{A \oplus B} = \overline{A} \cdot \overline{B} + A \cdot B$$
$$= \overline{(A + B)} + \overline{(\overline{A} + \overline{B})}$$
$$= \overline{(A + B) \cdot (\overline{A} + \overline{B})} \qquad \text{(D2–19)}$$

so

$$A \oplus B = (A + B) \cdot (\overline{A} + \overline{B}) \qquad \text{(D2–20)}$$

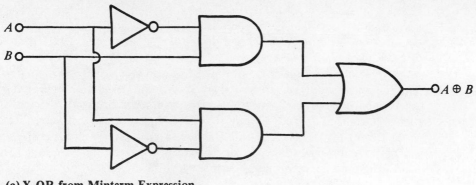

(a) X-OR from Minterm Expression

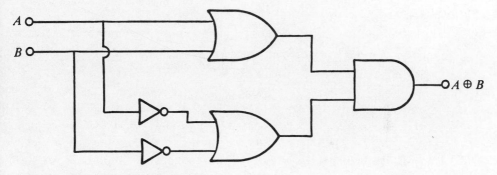

(b) X-OR from Maxterm Expression

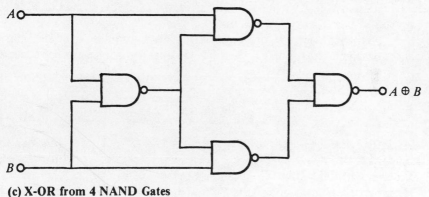

(c) X-OR from 4 NAND Gates

FIGURE D2–4. *Three Implementations of the Exclusive OR*

The direct gate network from Equation D2–20 is shown in Figure D2–4b. However, a nicely symmetrical circuit using all NANDs can be used to implement the X-OR. This circuit is shown in Figure D2–4c. Verification of its X-OR behavior is left as a problem.

In these days of MSI and LSI, it is no surprise that we can purchase a number of X-ORs in one integrated circuit. The 7486 contains 4 exclusive-OR circuits (the 7400 quad NAND SSI device can be interconnected to produce just 1 X-OR).

One of the applications of the X-OR is in a *parity generating circuit*. This is a rather simple but commonly used technique to catch a single binary-digit or bit error when a multibit binary number is transmitted from one digital machine to another. (*Bit* means binary digit and is in fact a contraction of the two words.) Transmission difficulties such as random noise can cause one or more bits to be changed from their correct value. One technique to detect the fact that an error has occurred is to transmit an additional bit called the *parity bit*. Thus if the data are 7-bit numbers, an eighth bit is transmitted in the most significant position (the left-most bit) such that the total number of bits in the number is even. This rule for the parity bit is called *even parity*. The transmitting apparatus thus requires a *parity-generator* box that receives the actual data bits as input and produces a 1 as output if the number of bits in the data is odd; this output becomes the parity bit. The box may also be called an *odd-parity detector*.

Suppose the number of bits in the data word were only 2: Observe that an X-OR gate can serve as the odd-parity detector. Furthermore, X-OR gates can be cascaded to detect the odd condition for a greater number of bits. This situation is illustrated for 4 bits in Figure D2–5 and may be quickly justified in a manner that may be applied to more bits. Suppose the number is partitioned into two groups of bits. The overall number is odd only if one group OR the other group is odd, but not both. Thus if each group of bits is input to a parity detector box (of that size), the 2 outputs should be X-ORed to give the overall parity of the number.

At the receiving end of a parity checker is required. For the even-parity convention mentioned, this checker should indicate that an error has occurred

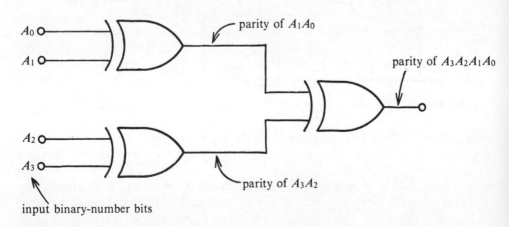

FIGURE D2–5. *Illustrating a 4-Bit Odd-Parity Detector*

A_0	B_0	Sum	Carry
0	0	0	0
0	1	1	0
1	0	1	0
1	1	0	1

TABLE D2-1. *Truth Table for the Addition of 2 Binary Digits*

if the total bit group (including parity) is odd, so that again an odd-parity detector is required. Of course, just which bit is in error would not be indicated and a retransmission of the data would be needed. It is necessary to only point out that more sophisticated techniques involving *Hamming codes* are used to provide self-correcting capability. Also, a parity convention opposite to that which we have discussed is clearly possible; this is called *odd-parity* convention. Parity generator/checker MSI chips exist in TTL (74180 is 8-bit, 74LS280 is 9-bit) and CMOS (CD40101B is 9-bit).

A second application of the X-OR is in *implementing binary addition*. Certainly a driving force behind the development of the digital computer was the desire for automatic computing machines. It is interesting to find the rather straightforward switching circuitry or logic circuits that accomplish arithmetic.

The procedure for the addition of 2 multidigit binary numbers is very similar to that which we learn for multidigit decimal numbers. Fundamental to the process is the addition of 2 *single* binary digits, A_0 and B_0. Indeed, in the binary numbers supplement to Chapter D1, the rule is indicated in connection with a discussion of simply counting in binary. It may be conveniently presented in a truth table (see Table D2-1). This table actually represents 2 Boolean functions on A and B, namely *sum* and *carry* or S and C, respectively. Notice that $S = A \oplus B$ while $C = A \cdot B$. Therefore, a switching circuit to accomplish the desired addition merely requires an X-OR gate and an AND gate, and this circuit is shown in Figure D2-6a. It is called a *half adder* because this circuit becomes half of a more useful circuit as we see shortly.

The addition of 2 multidigit binary numbers A and B involves the addition of 2 bits in a given place or column, plus the carry bit from the previous place as shown in the following example:

```
                1    1    1                  ← carry-in bits, C
        A →   0    0    1    1    0
        B →   0    1    0    1    1
 sum of A, B →  1    0    0    0    1
                          ↑
                          └──────────── typical column
```

Thus an *interior addition* for a multidigit number in fact requires the addition of 3 bits (A_i, B_i, C_i), and for this situation a box with 3 input wires is required. The truth table for the addition of 3 bits is given in Table D2-2.

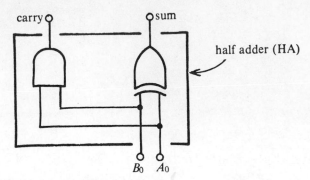

(a) Construction of a Half Adder from Logic Gates

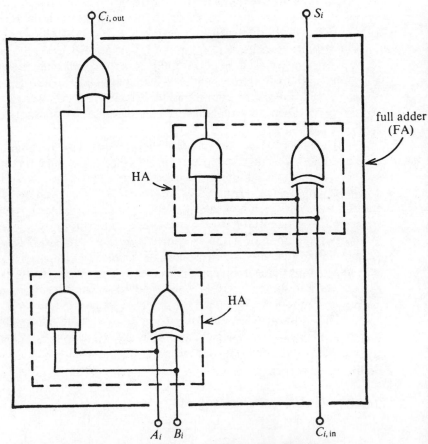

(b) Construction of a Full Adder from a Pair of Half Adders and an OR

FIGURE D2-6. *Logic Circuits to Produce Basic Binary Addition*

A	B	C	Sum	Carry
0	0	0	0	0
0	0	1	1	0
0	1	0	1	0
0	1	1	0	1
1	0	0	1	0
1	0	1	0	1
1	1	0	0	1
1	1	1	1	1

TABLE D2–2. *Truth Table for Addition of 3 Bits*

Gate networks may be designed using the truth-table-to-network approach already discussed. However, the circuit to generate the sum S_i can be quickly deduced. Notice S_i is 1 whenever the number of 1's in A_i, B_i, C_i is odd. Therefore, a 3-input parity detector forms the sum and may be constructed from a pair of X-OR gates. Such gates exist within a pair of half adders. Further, it is left as an exercise in the problem section to show that an OR of the carry bits from the interconnected half adders will properly generate the carry bit. The desired *full adder* constructed from a pair of half adders and an OR gate is shown in Figure D2–6b.

Finally, to perform the simultaneous or *parallel* addition of all the digits in 2 multibit binary numbers, a number of full adders are used side by side. Each adds the pair of digits in the given place, plus the carry-in from the previous place.

Figure D2–7 illustrates how a half adder and 2 full adders may be used to accomplish the addition of two 3-bit numbers. Suppose $A = 101$ and $B = 011$. Then the least significant bit of A is $A_0 = 1$. The next least significant bit of A is $A_1 = 0$ in this example, and the most significant bit of A is $A_2 = 1$. The input levels for the digits of the 2 binary numbers are thus input to the circuitry, and the various digits of the sum appear as S_0 (least significant) up to S_2 and C (carry out) or S_3.

Clearly more full adders could readily be appended to the left so that the adder could accommodate numbers of any size desired. Actually, 4 full adders are available in the 7483 MSI circuit to provide a *4-bit binary full adder*. The 7483 device has carry in and carry out so that 8-, 12-, 16-bit adders and higher can be readily built up. A similar CMOS device is available as the CD4008A.

Equality Detector

A close cousin of the X-OR is a circuit that produces a true or 1 as output if the two input bits are the same; that is, if they are both 0's or both 1's. Thus

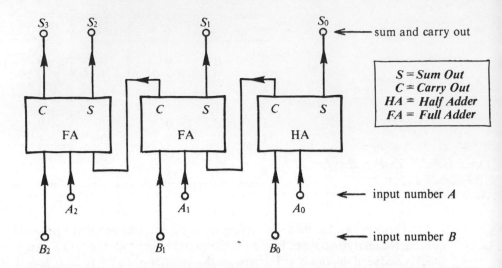

FIGURE D2-7. *Use of Half and Full Adders to Add Multidigit Binary Numbers*

the output indicates equality of the two input bits, and the circuit is termed an *equality detector* or coincidence circuit.

Figure D2-8a gives the truth table for this logic function. Clearly the output is just the inverse or complement of the X-OR. Therefore the negated-output exclusive OR (sometimes called the exclusive NOR) performs the task, as shown in Figure D2-8b. An inverter may be attached to any circuit output in Figure D2-4 to obtain an equality-detector gate network. The minterm Boolean algebra expression has already been written down in Equation D2-19.

Certainly an important operation in the instruction set of any computer is the comparison of two numbers. Such a comparison is usually at the heart of the decision-making process (for example, in doing a branch or in looping). We therefore consider the design of a circuit that compares two multidigit binary numbers A and B and has one output that is true if $A = B$ and a second that is true if $A > B$; the outputs are so labeled.

Before examining the circuit design, we will review the logical process we use to compare $A = 476$ with $B = 471$ to decide if $A > B$ or if $A = B$. We begin with the most significant digits ($A_2 = 4$ and $B_2 = 4$) and compare them. If $A_2 > B_2$ then certainly $A > B$. But if $A_2 = B_2$, as is true in this case, we go to the next most significant digits ($A_1 = 7$ and $B_1 = 7$) for a comparison. If $A_1 > B_1$ then $A > B$, but if $A_1 = B_1$, as is true in this case, we finally examine the least significant bits ($A_0 = 6$ and $B_0 = 1$). Here $A_0 \neq B_0$ so the numbers are *not* equal, but $A_0 > B_0$ so $A > B$.

The gate design for a 3-bit equality and relative magnitude detector in Figure D2-9b follows the same progression. Three 2-bit equality detectors are used; these are exclusive NOR gates, but they are diagrammed as boxes

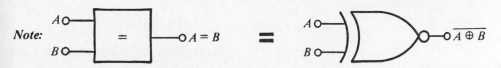

A	B	T
0	0	1
0	1	0
1	0	0
1	1	1

FIGURE D2–8. *Equality Detector*   **(a) Equality Detector**   **(b) Equality Detector**
                                         Truth Table   **Gate**

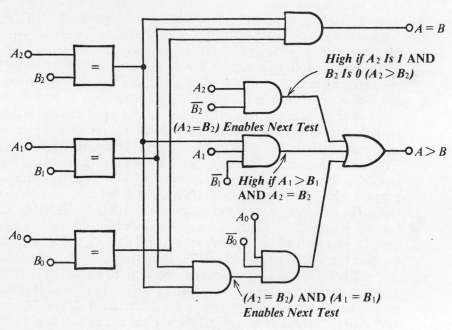

(a) Box Diagram of 2-Bit Equality Detector

High if A_2 Is 1 AND B_2 Is 0 $(A_2 > B_2)$

$(A_2 = B_2)$ *Enables Next Test*

High if $A_1 > B_1$ AND $A_2 = B_2$

$(A_2 = B_2)$ *AND* $(A_1 = B_1)$
Enables Next Test

(b) Gate Design for 3-Bit Equality and Relative Magnitude Detector

FIGURE D2–9. *Equality and Relative Magnitude Detector for Two 3-Bit Numbers*

with equal signs in order to emphasize their function (see the definition in Figure D2–9a). The corresponding bits of the two numbers A and B to be compared are fed to the 3 equality detectors at the left in Figure D2–9b. A_2 and B_2 are the most significant bits, while A_0 and B_0 are the least significant.

D69

The 3 outputs from the 3 equality detectors are sent to a 3-input AND; certainly if

$$(A_2 = B_2) \cdot (A_1 = B_1) \cdot (A_0 = B_0)$$

we have $A = B$.

But if $A_2 = 1$ while $B_2 = 0$ (that is, $A_2 \cdot \overline{B_2}$ is true), then $A_2 > B_2$ and $A > B$. Thus this true may be fed to an OR.

Should $A_2 = B_2$ (so $A_2 \cdot \overline{B_2}$ is false), the output of this equality is used to enable a comparison of the next most significant bits; that is, the $A_2 = B_2$ true line connects to a 3-input AND, along with A_1 and $\overline{B_1}$. Then the output of this gate will be high if

$$(A_2 = B_2) \text{ AND } (A_1 = 1) \text{ AND } (B_1 = 0)$$

However, then $A > B$ and the true passes through the OR to produce $A > B$ true.

Finally, if $A_2 = B_2$ and $A_1 = B_1$, a comparison of A_0 with B_0 is enabled in the bottom gate.

It is left as a problem for the student to design an additional output: a $B > A$ output. Actually MSI circuits are available in the TTL series (the 7485), as well as in the CMOS series (the 4063), which compare two 4-bit numbers to produce all 3 outputs. Furthermore, the MSI ICs have the capability of being cascaded with other units of the same type so that, for example, two 8-bit numbers can be compared using 2 ICs.

A single MSI chip (the 74181) exists that can perform any of the arithmetic functions and logic functions discussed thus far with respect to 4-bit binary numbers. Several chips may be cascaded to handle larger numbers. In response to the state of 4 function-select pins on the chip, the 74181 chip may be used to add two numbers, subtract them, make a magnitude comparison, perform a bit-by-bit logical OR, NAND, X-OR on the two numbers, and more! The chip performs many of the computations fundamental to computing and is called an *arithmetic-logic unit*. Indeed it may be used in that capacity as a part of the *central processing unit* (CPU) of a computer; we examine the function of a CPU in Chapter D7.

The 74181 chip can certainly be used in the design of logic circuits that must accomplish various computations, perhaps very rapidly. However, for situations involving elaborate computations, the designer should now consider using a "computer on a chip," namely, the *microprocessor*. The design problem then becomes one of program design. Furthermore, if a general-logic design problem becomes large (involving many ICs), the use of a microprocessor often becomes the most effective solution in terms of cost and effort. In a very real sense, the microprocessor represents programmable general-purpose logic that replaces dedicated logic circuitry.

Binary Decoder

Another gate application is in the design of a decoder. For example, computers (and calculators) work with binary numbers, which we might think of as *coded* numbers. To quickly comprehend the number we should like the number *decoded* to decimal form. One scheme is to have a string of light bulbs that are numbered with conventional symbols; that is, 1, 2, 3, ... When a multibit binary number goes into the black box *decoder,* just one corresponding output line goes high and lights the bulb with the correct number; for example, the 3-bit binary number 011 into the box causes the number 3 output line to go high (and then causes the number 3 light to go bright).

We next consider a specific example of a decoder that accepts 3-bit binary numbers in and selects one of 8 lines out. Indeed, such a decoder is often called a *3-line to 1-of-8-line decoder,* or simply a *1-of-8 decoder.* Figure D2–10a lists the eight possible 3-bit binary numbers, along with the decimal equivalents. The least significant bit is labeled *A,* next is *B,* and most significant *C.* The idea is to notice, for example, that only if *C* is low AND *B* is high AND *A* is high is the intended output line number 3. That is, $\overline{C} \cdot B \cdot A$ should cause line 3 to go high. Clearly a 3-input AND is required with $\overline{C}$, *B,* and *A* as its inputs, and line 3 becomes its output. A minterm approach can be used. A partial drawing of the gate circuit to accomplish the decoding appears in Figure D2–10b. The reader should be able to fill in the required remaining 5 AND gates and connections.

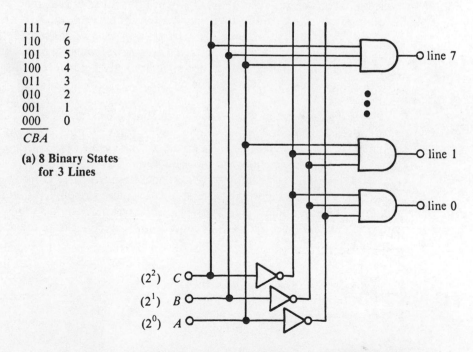

111	7
110	6
101	5
100	4
011	3
010	2
001	1
000	0
CBA	

**(a) 8 Binary States
for 3 Lines**

(b) Partial Circuit for 3-Line to 1-of-8-Line Decoder

FIGURE D2–10. *3-Bit Binary Decoder*

Notice that 2 lines (2-bit binary numbers) can designate one of 4 lines. Indeed, the 74155 and 74156 ICs are dual 2-line to 1-of-4-line decoders (the 155 has totem pole outputs and the 156 has open-collector outputs). On the other hand, 4 lines (4-bit binary numbers) can designate one of 16 lines. The 74154 IC is a 4-line to 1-of-16-line decoder (and can also be used as a demultiplexer, which is discussed next). The CMOS family includes the 4555, which is a dual 1-of-4-line decoder (that is, two separate decoders) and the 4514 1-of-16-line decoder. Again these CMOS decoders may be used as data demultiplexers.

Data Demultiplexer (DEMUX) or Data Distributor

It is often desirable to route data from one line down one of several lines. For example, data from a computer's memory typically needs to be sent along different paths depending on the circumstances. The simple electrical requirement is a single-pole multiposition (multithrow) switch as shown in Figure D2–11a. The switch position should be electrically controllable. Such a device that passes information from one line down one of several lines is called a *demultiplexer* (DEMUX). Perhaps a more easily remembered term is *data distributor* because data may be distributed between various lines under a control input; however, this term is only occasionally used. If only logic voltage levels are involved, it is a *digital demultiplexer;* if any of a range of voltages must be passed along, the device is called an *analog demultiplexer.* (The ordinary multiposition switch is an analog multiplexer as well as demultiplexer.)

A digital demultiplexer can be implemented by using a decoder (already discussed) along with a number of 2-input enabling AND gates (see Figure D2–11b). The data line is sent to each AND gate, along with one line from the decoder. In response to the *n*-bit binary selection code (here $n = 3$), one of 2^n lines (here one of $2^3 = 8$ lines) goes high from the decoder output and enables the particular gate so that the data passes through it to that output line. The other lines will all remain low. Notice that a data demultiplexer or distributor may be used as a decoder simply by connecting the data line permanently high.

Data Multiplexer (MUX) or Data Selector

The telephone company may take a number of telephone conversations and manipulate them so that they all travel down one wire. This technique is called *multiplexing the signals* and involves going from several wires to one

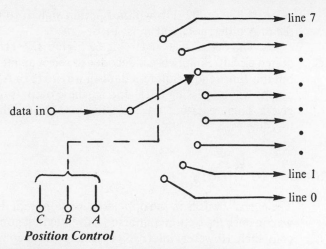

(a) Switch Equivalent of a 1-Line to 1-of-8-Line Demultiplexer or Data Distributor

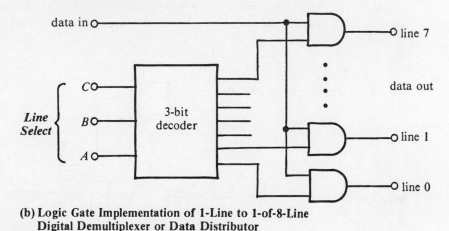

(b) Logic Gate Implementation of 1-Line to 1-of-8-Line Digital Demultiplexer or Data Distributor

FIGURE D2–11. *Illustrating the Digital Demultiplexer or Data Distributor*

wire. In our simpler digital application we do not send the data from several wires down one wire simultaneously, but rather select from just one of several data-in lines and pass the data down a single line out. For example, if data goes from one of 8 lines to 1 line, the device required is a *1-of-8-line to 1-line multiplexer* (MUX); it goes in the opposite sense from the demultiplexer (hence the name for that circuit). A more descriptive term for this logic function is *data selector*; this term is used, for example, in the Texas Instruments TTL Data Book.

The simple electrical multiplexer is again the switch of Figure D2–11a, because it can pass electrical signals in either direction. However, the logic gates of Figure D2–11b will *not* permit signals to pass backwards through them. A different circuit must be designed.

The demultiplexer circuit of Figure D2–11b is not far from the required circuit. Simply use a decoder to select an individual AND gate again, but this time send a different data-in wire to each AND gate. Only one AND output will be passing data, and all these outputs may be ORed together to give a single data-out line. See Figure D2–12, which illustrates an 8-line-to-1-line case.

Encoder to Binary

The *encoder* works in the opposite direction from the decoder. For example, we can push the button numbered 3 to enter that number into a calculator or a computer. However, internally calculators and computers work with binary numbers and the number must be converted or encoded (presumably it is a "code" to us) to binary form. In operation, pressing the key causes a certain single line to go high, and this line into the encoder box must cause a certain combination of out lines to go high (which represents the number in binary code).

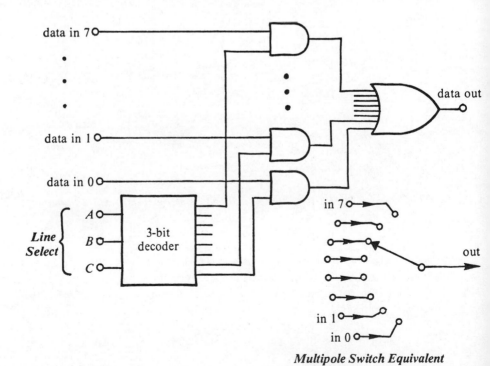

Multipole Switch Equivalent

FIGURE D2–12. *Diagram for an 8-Line-to-1-Line Multiplexer*

Consider for example a situation with 8 input lines (an 8-key keyboard) that can then be encoded to a 3-bit binary number. If key 3 is pressed or line 3 high, the *C, B, A* output lines should be low, high, high or 011, respectively.

Examine Figure D2–10a for the octal-to-binary correspondence. Notice line *A* (sometimes called the 2^0 line) must go high if line 1 OR line 3 OR line 5 OR line 7 is high (due to one of those 4 buttons being pressed). This statement clearly involves a 4-input logical OR. One 4-input OR is required for each binary output line. The required circuitry is drawn for the OR to line *A* in Figure D2–13. Next, Line $B(2^1)$ should go high if in-line 2 OR 3 OR 6 OR 7 is high, and so on. The reader should fill in the remaining required connections. Notice that if no octal line is high, the output is 000. Thus in theory key 0 need not be connected to the encoder. (Actually, all 8 keys *would* need to be connected to an octal calculator to signal that *some* key has been pressed.)

CMOS Analog Switches and Multiplexers

When a MOSFET is on, it is approximately a resistor between the drain and source; therefore the current through a MOSFET is quite proportional to the voltage across it—that is, the drain-source voltage—especially when the

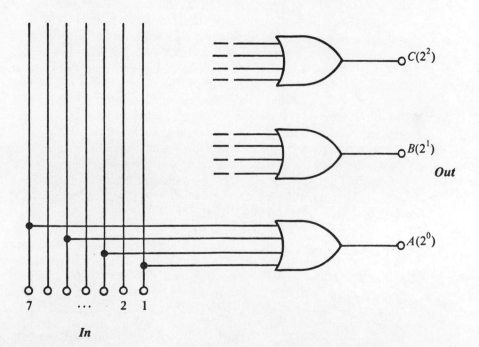

FIGURE D2–13. *Octal-to-Binary Encoder (Connections Only Partially Completed)*

voltage approaches zero. (Note that the series-diode character of a bipolar transistor prevents a similar behavior for it.) Consequently, a solid-state switch for *analog* signals can be constructed that behaves very much like an electrically controlled ordinary switch. To obtain rather uniform resistance, a pair of complementary MOSFETs are connected in parallel. The source of the P-channel device is connected to the drain of the N-channel device as shown in Figure D2–14a. Both devices are turned on or off simultaneously by a control voltage $V_{control}$ into the gates. The gate for the N-channel unit should be near the $V+$ supply voltage or high, while the gate for the P-channel unit should be near the $V-$ supply voltage or low in order to turn the FETs on and close the switch. (The opposite gate voltages are needed to turn the FETs off or open the switch.) Therefore an inverter is required between the control and the P-channel gate and is included in the particular IC.

The switch/resistor model for the device is shown in Figure D2–14b. Current may pass in either direction through this switch just as for an ordinary switch; thus the device is often called a *bilateral switch*. Both signal pins are labeled in/out, and the standard device symbol shown in Figure D2–14c emphasizes the bilateral nature, with triangles pointed in both directions. However, the in/out voltages must be within the range between the power supply values used of $V+$ and $V-$. If $V-$ is ground, then the input voltage cannot be negative; however, use of negative $V-$ gives a quite constant on resistance that is desirable. The on resistance is on the order of a few hundred ohms and varies on the order of 15% as the input voltage varies. The off resistance is very high, with a leakage current of 10 picoamperes (10^{-11} amperes) typically. It is a good open switch!

The 4016A is a *quad bilateral switch* with 4 switches like that shown in Figure D2–15a in one IC. Additional MOSFETs in a somewhat more elaborate connection are used in the 4066B to give lower, more constant on resistance (about 125 ohms) and less dependence on the threshold of the control input signal. These devices can be used in many ways as useful electronic analog switches. For example, if one end of each switch is connected in common, an electronic single-pole–4-throw switch is produced (provided only 1 switch is turned on at a time). This switch gives the essence of an analog-voltage multiplexer/demultiplexer as indicated by the switch equivalents in Figure D2–11a and Figure D2–12. Notice that the direction arrows go *both* ways for this CMOS device. Also, the device can be used with digital in/out signals as well as analog.

Actually, 8 MOSFET bidirectional switches, along with a decoder to provide switch selection, exist in one chip as the 4051 8-channel analog multiplexer/demultiplexer. This device has $V+$ or V_{DD} and $V-$ or V_{EE} power supply connections as well as a V_{SS} (normally ground) connection. Then, logic-level voltages (for example, $+5$ V and 0 V) may be used to input the binary selected-channel number, while the analog voltages (in/out voltages) passing through the switch may range from V_{DD} to V_{EE} ($+5$ V to -5 V if these V_{DD} and V_{EE} supply voltages are used). Figure D2–14d illustrates the functional parts of

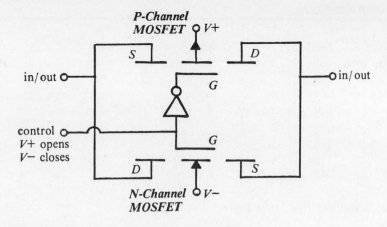

(a) Analog or Bilateral Switch Constructed from MOSFETs

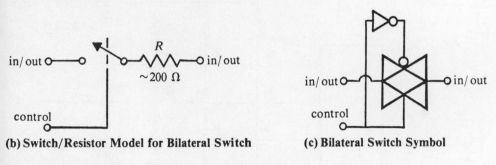

(b) Switch/Resistor Model for Bilateral Switch

(c) Bilateral Switch Symbol

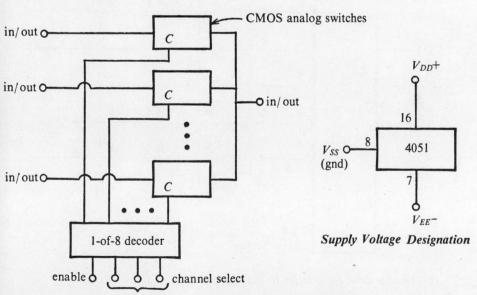

(d) Functional Diagram for 4051 8-Channel Analog MUX/DEMUX

Supply Voltage Designation

FIGURE D2–14. *CMOS Analog Switching*

Input	Output			
CBA	T	U	V	W
000	0	0	0	1
001	0	1	0	0
010	0	0	1	1
011	1	1	0	0
100	0	0	1	1
101	1	1	1	1
110	0	0	0	0
111	1	0	0	0

(a) A Multifunction Truth Table

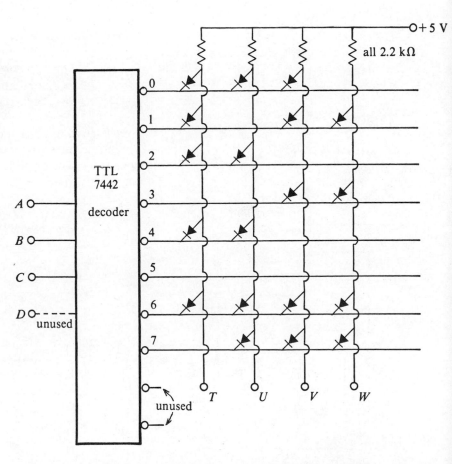

(b) Decoder with Diode Logic to Implement a Truth Table or ROM

FIGURE D2–15. *Truth Table by a Constructed ROM*

the 4051, as well as the power supply voltage designation. As we see in the digital instrumentation chapter, Chapter D6, this device is very useful for a data acquisition system.

ROM: Implementation of a Multioutput Truth Table

Consider the case where a truth table possesses 4 output functions on the basis of 3 input variables. This situation is illustrated in Figure D2–15a. We have 4 output wires labeled T, U, V, W and these states depend on inputs C, B, A. Thus, when all inputs are low, only line W should be high; when only A is high, only line U is high; when only line B is high, lines V and W should both be high, and so on. This truth table could represent a control function on 4 devices; these devices (T, U, V, W) are on or off in various combinations as time passes. It is then assumed here that the inputs count up in binary as time passes (the next chapter discusses how to accomplish this).

To accomplish this truth table behavior with logic gates, each output column could be generated with a set of logic gates deduced from minterm arguments as shown in Figure D2–1. An alternative approach is to use a decoder in conjunction with logic gates. In fact, simple diode logic can be conveniently used as shown in Figure D2–15b. Here a TTL 3-line to 1-of-8-line decoder with *negative-logic* outputs is used. (This decoder is illustrated as constructed from a 7442 decoder, which in fact decodes the first 10 binary states to one of 10 outputs; the 7442 chip is a BCD-to-decimal decoder, discussed in the next chapter.) Then only decoder-output-line 0 goes low for inputs C, B, A = 000; only output-line 1 goes low for C, B, A = 001, and so on. Each T, U, V, W output line is connected through a pull-up resistance of 2.2 kilohms to +5 V and therefore normally stands high (at +5 V). Notice that a grid of wires results from the decoder output lines and T, U, V, W output lines. These crossing wires are *not* connected except that a diode connection is made in this grid wherever a 0 appears in the output truth table. This connection implements a negative-logic OR. Thus for the output line T, diodes connected to decoder outputs 0, 1, 2, 4, and 6 will conduct and pull T low for the corresponding binary inputs CBA. T is low if 0 OR 1 OR 2 OR 4 OR 6 is low (otherwise T is high), and the truth table for the T output is implemented. A similar argument justifies the operation of outputs U, V, W.

An alternative view of the device constructed in Figure D2–15b is that the output lines T, U, V, W represent 4 digits of a binary number. The various binary numbers presented as outputs from the device are then 0001, 0100, 0011, ... as the CBA inputs count through successive binary values 000, 001, 010, ... We may think of the 4-bit binary numbers as being stored in the device, perhaps in 8 successive boxes that are numbered. The device represents a *memory* for eight 4-bit binary numbers. The 4-bit number contained in a particular memory box is obtained on the 4 output lines $TUVW$ after the binary number of the desired memory box is input on lines CBA. For example, setting $CBA = 010$ results in $TUVW = 0011$. The numbers are not easily changed (different diode connections are required) so that new numbers are not easily *written into* this memory. However, a number in any one of the boxes is easily *read out* from the memory. Therefore, the device may be called a *read-only-memory* or ROM.

Large-scale integration has made possible the production of very large ROMs in a single IC. The placement of the particular diode pattern to obtain a given truth table is done at the time of manufacture in a *masking process*.

NOTE: A *mask* is a photographic negative that performs rather like a stencil; several masks are used in the manufacture of an integrated circuit to define or to interconnect the various transistors, diodes, and resistors.

However, this means of obtaining a ROM is only economical if several thousand ROMs with the given contents are desired. As the 1980s commence, the largest ROMs available contain 65,536 bits (called 64K). These ROMs are generally organized to be 8,192 (called 8K) boxes or memory locations, each containing 8 bits. Thus 13 lines go into a decoder to select a particular memory location (analogous to the 3 lines CBA in Figure D2–15), and there are 8 output wires that carry respective 8-bit numbers out (analogous to the 4 lines $TUVW$ in Figure D2–15). Such a memory is said to be organized 8K×8.

MSI and LSI also permit a general-purpose type of ROM where the contents may be established or *programmed* in the unit *after* the time of manufacture. Such a device is called a *programmable read-only-memory* or PROM. In one approach, diodes are placed at all of the line intersections in an IC circuit corresponding to Figure D2–15b. Thus the ROM is initially programmed with all 0's. However, a small fuse is placed at each diode and in series with it. By properly selecting lines and applying certain overvoltages to the IC, a large current flows in a selected diode and burns that fuse. This amounts to removing that diode from the lattice and programming in a 1. Special PROM programming instruments exist for this purpose (often computer controlled). Clearly, a PROM can only be programmed once.

Examples of bipolar (TTL) PROMs are the 74188 (organized 32 locations by 8 bits each), the 74S387 (organized 256 by 4 bits), and the 74S572 (organized 1,024 by 4 bits or 1K×4). The 74188 costs about $2 at this writing and is clearly a very cost-effective way to implement a truth table with up to 5 input variables and up to 8 outputs. Designing a gate array for this sort of truth table can quickly become more expensive both in time and ICs!

REVIEW EXERCISES

1. State two absorption theorems of Boolean algebra.
2. What is a minterm and what is a maxterm?
3. What is the utility of the standard forms or canonical forms to the study of logic?
4. (a) What is the utility of a parity bit in data transmission?
   (b) What is meant by odd-parity or by even-parity convention in data transmission?
5. (a) Write the truth table for the exclusive OR of two input variables.
   (b) Present the minterm or sum-of-products Boolean algebra expression that follows from the table of part (a). Justify the expression briefly.
6. Consider a circuit that accepts two binary bits as input and produces the sum and carry as outputs. Show a design for this circuit and justify briefly how it functions.
7. What is the difference between a binary half adder and a binary full adder?
8. (a) What is an equality detector for two input lines? What does it do?
   (b) How is an equality detector related to an exclusive-OR gate?
9. Suppose A and B are each 4-bit binary numbers. Show the design of a circuit that detects the condition $A = B$.
10 What is the function performed by a decoder? Explain with reference to a 2-line to 1-of-4-line decoder.
11 (a) Describe the difference between data multiplexer and data demultiplexer. Illustrate the concept of each of the devices with the aid of arrows on single-pole–multiposition switches.
   (b) Associate the terms data distributor and data selector with the two devices of part (a).
12. What is the function performed by a binary encoder? Explain with reference to a device that produces 2-bit code as output.
13. (a) Draw the standard symbol for a bilateral switch.
   (b) What is the function of a bilateral switch? How does the symbol tend to show this function?
14. (a) Explain the difference between a digital multiplexer and an analog multiplexer.
   (b) Can a digital multiplexer chip function as a demultiplexer as well?
   (c) Can a CMOS analog multiplexer chip function as a demultiplexer as well?
15. (a) What does the acronym ROM stand for?
   (b) A certain ROM is 64×8. What does this mean? How many output lines does the ROM have? How many input lines are required for this ROM?
   (c) What is the difference between a ROM and PROM?
   (d) Describe how the 64×8 ROM of part (b) can be used to implement 8 different truth tables simultaneously, each with 6 input variables. (Each truth table is assumed to have 1 output.)
16. What is meant by mask programming a ROM?
17. Suppose the CBA input lines to the ROM of Figure D2–15 are at 100, respectively. What are the respective values of the output lines $TUVW$? Justify these

respective values in terms of the diode placement and circuit action.

18. (a) What does the acronym PROM stand for?

    (b) Describe in general terms how the output functions of a PROM are established.

PROBLEMS

1. Consider the implementation of the exclusive-OR function that uses only 4 NAND gates as illustrated in Figure D2–4c.

    (a) Draw the logic diagram for Figure D2–4c, including direct Boolean algebra expressions for the output function of each NAND gate in the circuit.

    (b) Reduce the direct Boolean algebra expression obtained for the circuit output in part (a) to the standard minterm form characteristic of the exclusive-OR function.

2. (a) Verify with a truth table that the associative law $A + (B + C) = (A + B) + C$ holds for Boolean algebra. Use a truth table with the following readings:

A B C	$B + C$	$A + (B + C)$	$A + B$	$(A + B) + C$

    (b) Verify with a truth table that the associative law $A \cdot (B \cdot C) = (A \cdot B) \cdot C$ holds for Boolean algebra. Use a truth table form similar to that given in (a); merely substitute the dot operator for the plus operator.

3. Verify with a truth table that Boolean algebra is distributive with respect to the dot operation on the plus operation:

$$A \cdot (B + C) = (A \cdot B) + (A \cdot C)$$

Use a truth table with the following headings:

A B C	$(B + C)$	$A \cdot (B + C)$	$A \cdot B$	$A \cdot C$	$(A \cdot B) + (A \cdot C)$

4. Use truth tables to show that De Morgan's theorem is valid for three variables.

5. (a) Show that $A + \overline{A}B = A + B$ using either a truth table or by Boolean algebra manipulation.

   (b) Consider the expression

   $$\overline{A}\overline{B}\overline{C} + \overline{A}\overline{B}C + \overline{A}B\overline{C} + \overline{A}BC + AB\overline{C} + ABC$$

   Show that this expression reduces to merely $\overline{A \cdot \overline{B}}$.

   (c) Draw the gate implementation of the original statement in (b) as well as that for the reduced statement. How many gates are saved by use of the reduced form?

6. (a) Consider the Boolean algebra expression

   $$T = (A + B)(\overline{B} + A)$$

   Draw a gate circuit that follows directly from this statement.

   (b) Suppose A is high and B is low. Put the logic levels 0, 1 into the gate diagram of part (a) at all outputs.

   (c) Reduce the Boolean algebra expression of part (a) as much as possible. Check the reduced expression for agreement with the single truth table entry used in part (b).

7. Reduce the expressions shown.
   (a) $\overline{A} \cdot ((B \cdot C) + B) \cdot \overline{A}$
   (b) $\overline{A}\,\overline{B} + (A + \overline{B})$
   (c) $(A + AB) + \overline{A}B$
   (d) $(\overline{A} + \overline{B})(A \cdot \overline{B})$
   (e) $[(AB + A\overline{B}) + AB] + \overline{A}B$

8. (a) Consider the circuit pictured in Diagram D2–1. Find the direct Boolean function for the output in terms of the A, B inputs.

   (b) Reduce the above Boolean algebra statement to the simplest possible equivalent.

   (c) Test your result in (b) by assuming $A = 1$, $B = 0$, and working through the gate network to find its output for this case.

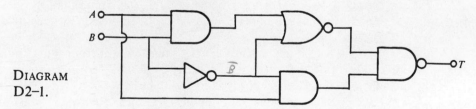

DIAGRAM
D2–1.

9. Use De Morgan's relationship to show that $\overline{A \cdot (B + C)} = \overline{A} + (\overline{B} \cdot \overline{C})$.

10. (a) Show that $\overline{ABCD} = \overline{A} + \overline{B} + \overline{C} + \overline{D}$ by repeated use of a De Morgan's theorem as stated in terms of two variables (and proven in Chapter D1).

    (b) Show that $\overline{A + B + C + D} = \overline{A} \cdot \overline{B} \cdot \overline{C} \cdot \overline{D}$ by repeated use of a De Morgan's theorem as stated in terms of two variables (and proven in Chapter D1).

11. (a) Write the sum-of-products or minterm Boolean algebra expression for the truth table. Also draw a direct gate implementation of this logical statement.

    (b) Find the product-of-sums or maxterm Boolean algebra expression for the truth table shown.

A	B	C	T
0	0	0	0
0	0	1	1
0	1	0	0
0	1	1	1
1	0	0	1
1	0	1	0
1	1	0	0
1	1	1	0

12. Show how an odd-parity detecting circuit for a 16-bit-input binary number can be constructed from a pair of 8-bit-input odd-parity detector circuits and a quad-NAND-gate chip. The 8-bit parity detector circuits may be represented as boxes.

13. (a) Consider the full-adder circuit pictured in Figure D2–6b. Write down the Boolean algebra expression that follows directly from the gate connections used to obtain the carry-out bit.

    (b) Working from a truth table for the carry-out bit that is obtained from the sum of three binary digits A, B, C, write out the minterm Boolean algebra expression for carry-out in terms A, B, C. Reduce this Boolean expression to correspond to the form obtained in part (a), thus validating the carry-out circuit.

14. Add the following binary numbers as indicated:
    (a) $111011 + 101110$
    (b) $01011 + 110$
    (c) $010101 + 01101$

15. Draw the circuit for a binary adding machine that accepts two 6-bit numbers A, B as input. Use boxes as required to represent half adders and full adders.

16. (a) A certain control panel has three switches. Show a circuit that produces as output a 2-bit binary number equal to the number of switches turned on.

    (b) A certain control panel has 6 switches. Design a circuit that produces as output a 3-bit binary number equal to the total number of switches that are turned on.

17. *Binary subtractor.* Consider the problem of subtracting A from B to obtain the difference D: $B - A = D$. In general, D may be obtained by inverting each bit in the binary number A (including leading 0's) to obtain $\overline{A}$ and forming the sum: $D = B + \overline{A} + 1$. Any carry-out from the most significant bits of the sum should be discarded.

    (a) Verify the above rule for one case: Let $B = 9_{10} = 1001$ and $A = 3_{10} = 0011$. Show that application of the rule gives the binary equivalent of 6_{10}.

    (b) We see that a binary subtractor may be constructed from inverters and adders. Draw the design of a 4-bit subtractor that accepts 4-bit numbers for B and A as input.

    (c) Design a 4-bit machine that can perform either $B - A$ or $B + A$ on the respective A and B 4-bit inputs in response to an add/subtract control. The control input line should be low to cause addition and high to cause subtraction.

18. Design the addition of a *B greater than A* output to the 3-bit equality and relative magnitude detector of Figure D2–9. Draw the logic-gate system.

19. Draw the complete gate circuit for a 2-line to 1-of-4-line decoder. Include a justification of the circuit.

20. A binary decoder with 6 input lines is to be constructed. What is the minimum number of AND gates required to produce the decoder if all the possible states are to be decoded? How many inputs are required in each AND gate?

21. Draw the complete gate circuit for a 3-line to 1-of-8-line decoder.

22. A binary decoder with 16 output lines is to be constructed from a pair of decoders that each has 4 outputs and a 2-bit binary input. Design a circuit by adding gates and output lines to the diagram shown in Diagram D2–2. Label the output lines 0 through 15. Describe in general terms how the circuit operates.

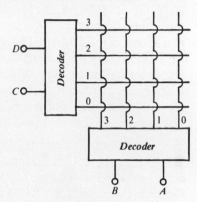

DIAGRAM D2–2.

NOTE: One output line should result from each of the 16 "intersections" of the decoder outputs.

23. Draw a circuit that routes the data from 1 input data line down 1 of 4 lines. Use a box to represent the decoder involved. What is the name of the overall circuit?

24. Draw a circuit that selects the data from 1 of 4 input data lines and routes this data down the single output line. Use a box to represent the decoder involved. What is the name of the overall circuit?

25. Show how a 3-line to 1-of-8 decoder can be constructed from an 8-output data distributor or demultiplexer.

26. Draw the complete gate circuit for a binary encoder with a 2-bit output. Include a justification of the circuit.

27. (a) Consider a 32-to-1 multiplexer. How many data input lines and data output lines are involved? How many line-select input lines are required?

(b) Draw a circuit for a 32-to-1 multiplexer that is constructed from 8-to-1 and 4-to-1 multiplexer packages. Boxes with appropriate data lines and line-select input lines may be used to represent these packages. Identify clearly the function of each line-select into the overall circuit by labelling them, $A, B, C, \ldots$, where A is the least significant (or right-most) bit of the line-select binary input numbers.

28. A *priority encoder* is a useful device for some applications, including computer circuitry. For example, 4 lines enter the priority encoder—labelled 1 to 4—and 4 lines also pass out of the device with the same labels. If several input lines are high, only the output for the highest-numbered input should go high. For

example, if input lines 1 and 3 are high, only output line 3 goes high. Design a 4-line priority encoder from gates and justify its operation. Write a Boolean expression for each output.

29. The position of a push-rod is measured with the aid of 8 sensors that are placed along a fixed cylinder as shown in Diagram D2-3. A sensor outputs a high if no adjacent rod is detected. Thus the outputs are high from sensors 1 and 2, while the outputs are low for the remaining sensors for the rod position shown in the diagram. Design a position encoder that accepts the sensor lines as input and produces a binary number as output; the latter number tells the rod position. For example, if sensors 1 through 5 are high while the remainder are low, the encoder should output 101_2. A box representing an 8-line-to-3-line encoder may be incorporated in the design.

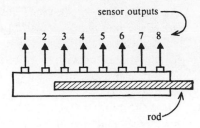

DIAGRAM D2-3.

30. Suppose one of the outputs ($T, U, V,$ or W) from the ROM circuit of Figure D2-15 is to drive 10 TTL inputs. What problem may arise? (Assume silicon diodes are used in the matrix.)

31. Diagram the circuit for a ROM constructed from a decoder and diodes that implements the truth table. Assume that a 7442 decoder is used.

Input	Output					
BA	U	V	W	X	Y	Z
00	0	0	1	0	1	0
01	1	1	1	0	0	0
10	0	1	1	1	0	0
11	1	1	0	0	0	0

32. Diode logic may be used to construct a decoder. Thus consider a 3-line to 1-of-8-line decoder with 3 input lines CBA and 8 output lines 0 through 7 as shown in Diagram D2-4. A matrix of 6 horizontal wires ($A, \overline{A}, B, \overline{B}, C, \overline{C}$) and 8 vertical output wires (0 through 7) is diagrammed. Note the 2.2-kΩ pull-up resistor on each output line. Draw the complete circuit, inserting diodes as required at wire intersections.

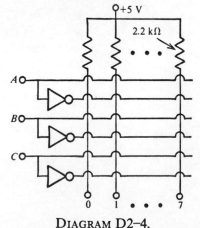

DIAGRAM D2-4.

33. Two regions of a house are individually electrically heated, and a thermostat is placed in each that produces a logic 1 when heat is required. However, the electricity pricing structure is such that only one region of heating should be on at any given time (otherwise the rates increase by a factor of 5).

    (a) Design a gate circuit that does not permit region B to be heated if region A requires heat. Thus region A has priority.

    (b) Design a gate circuit that does not permit the heat to be turned on to one region if the heat is already on in the other region. Neither region should get priority in this circuit.

34. The 74LS139 is a dual 1-of-4 decoder (it may also be used as a pair of demultiplexers through use of the enable input to each decoder). The 74LS139 outputs are active low. One catalog description states: "Each decoder in the 74LS139 can be used as a function generator providing all four minterms of two variables." Explain what this statement means.

CHAPTER
D3

Basic Flip-Flops and Registers

The *flip-flop* (FF) circuit or bistable multivibrator (BMV) has been an important element of scientific digital circuitry for many decades. Eccles and Jordan in England constructed the first flip-flop from two vacuum tubes in 1919; in the 1950s a pair of transistors replaced the vacuum tubes in the classic flip-flop. With these elements it has been possible to construct counting circuitry (for example, radioactivity scalers or Geiger counters), as well as storage circuits for numbers.

However, since the advent of IC logic gates, it has become common to construct various kinds of flip-flops from gates and indeed to make available in IC form networks of flip-flops as counters and registers. ICs containing thousands of flip-flop equivalents are now the most common data-storage (or memory) devices in computers.

An alternate title for this chapter might be *Sequential Networks* because the value of flip-flops and associated circuitry outputs depends on the past history of the inputs as well as the current values of the inputs. In other words, the particular sequence of inputs matters.

asic Flip-Flops

'S Flip-Flop

The simplest logic-gate flip-flop, the *RS flip-flop*, can be constructed from a pair of NAND gates as shown in Figure D3–1. Simply cross-couple the

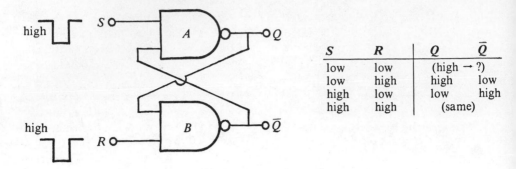

S	R	Q	$\overline{Q}$
low	low	(high → ?)	
low	high	high	low
high	low	low	high
high	high	(same)	

FIGURE D3-1. *RS Flip-Flop from NAND Gates and Its State Table*

NAND outputs to inputs, and use one input on each NAND as the flip-flop inputs labeled S (for set) and R (for reset). The Q output from the FF is the output of the same NAND that has the S input. The other output is labeled $\overline{Q}$ because it is normally in the opposite state from Q, as we shall see. This flip-flop gets its name from the RS labels conventionally used for its inputs.

In the NAND-gate version of the RS flip-flop, the two inputs are normally high (we often say *stand high*). Therefore R and S should be assumed high throughout the following discussion unless explicitly stated otherwise. It is first argued that this flip-flop network can exist indefinitely (as long as the power isn't removed) in either of two stable states. The argument assumes an initial state and then shows that this state is self-consistent.

First assume S and R are high, but that Q is low. Since Q connects into one (bottom) NAND B input, there is one low into this NAND and its output $\overline{Q}$ must be high. However, the $\overline{Q}$ output connects to one input of NAND A and both its inputs are then high, causing its output to be low. This state of Q is consistent with our initial assumption, and the network can certainly remain in this state. Notice that Q and $\overline{Q}$ are indeed in opposite states (low and high, respectively).

However, the circuit is clearly symmetrical about a horizontal line. Therefore, if $\overline{Q}$ were initially assumed low, a self-consistent state can also be argued (with Q being high). Thus there are two stable states for the RS flip-flop; it is indeed a *bistable* circuit.

We next examine how the RS flip-flop responds to manipulation of its inputs R and S. Suppose that the flip-flop is in the state Q = low, $\overline{Q}$ = high (also, R and S are high). If the Q output is taken to represent the (binary) state of the FF, we may say that the FF is at 0 (zero) for Q = low. Now let the S (set) input be brought low for a moment. Remember that a NAND gate can be characterized as: *Any input low implies the output is high.* Then while S is low, one of the inputs to the (top) NAND A is low and the output Q will go high (or to a 1). This Q output is connected to one NAND B input and, because R is standing high, both inputs to B are high; the output $\overline{Q}$ of NAND

B will then go low. But the low out of $\overline{Q}$ feeds to one input of NAND A, and the NAND A output then is certainly high. Indeed Q will remain high or 1 even after the S input returns high because the one input from $\overline{Q}$ is low. Therefore the state of Q *flips* from 0 to 1 in response to a negative pulse at the S input. We say the FF has been *set* to a 1.

Thus, a momentary low or negative pulse to the S input sets the Q output to high or 1 if it was originally low or 0. It is left to the reader to justify that if the FF were already 1—that is, if Q were high—it would remain that way. No change would occur.

On the other hand, the symmetry of the circuit implies that if a negative pulse is applied to the R (reset) input, the output $\overline{Q}$ of that NAND gate must go high and remain there. (This behavior, of course, can be argued in a way completely analogous to the argument for the S input just presented.) Again Q will do the opposite of $\overline{Q}$ and go low or to 0, and we say that the FF has been *reset* to 0; it *flops* back to 0. If the FF were already 0, it would remain there.

These consequences of applying pulses to the S and R inputs are shown in Figure D3–1 as the last three entries in a kind of truth table for the flip-flop called the *state table* or *characteristic table*. The table represents the state of the FF *after* a manipulation of the FF according to the S, R entries. Of course, if S and R remain high, no manipulation of the inputs has been made, and the bistable outputs remain unchanged. This situation is shown as the last table entry, and is justified in the first stability argument above. It is precisely this property that permits the circuit to be used as a memory.

The first entry of the table represents bringing both S and R low simultaneously. In fact, this shows a troublesome behavior of the *RS* FF. As long as both inputs are low, both NAND outputs Q and $\overline{Q}$ are high (they are *not* opposite during this time). Then, if the inputs are both brought high again, the *last* input to go high will determine the state of the FF. For example, if S goes high last, it is equivalent to setting the FF to 1. If both inputs are brought high "simultaneously," there will in fact always be some tiny difference in the NAND speeds (even in the length of wires used), and it is not possible to predict the final state of the FF outputs. Thus the consequence is indeterminate, and the first entry of the state table shows a question mark final result.

The *RS* flip-flop responds to low input pulses, and this behavior can perhaps be better represented using negated-input OR gates rather than NAND gates in the circuit drawing. This usage, of course, is clearly possible from the De Morgan theorem gate equivalence of Figure D1–13c. Figure D3–2 illustrates this equivalence.

It is also quite possible to construct an *RS* flip-flop from NOR gates. Figure D3–3 shows the circuit along with a state table. In this case both inputs normally stand low, and the FF is set to 1 by a positive pulse (a momentary high) on the S input. A positive pulse to the R input resets the FF to 0. Note, however, that the Q output is from the gate to which the R input is connected (different from the NAND gate case). It is left as an exercise to justify the behavior of the NOR-gate *RS* FF.

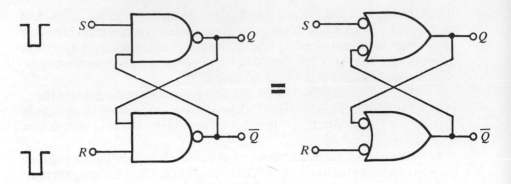

FIGURE D3–2. *Equivalent Circuits for the NAND RS Flip-Flop*

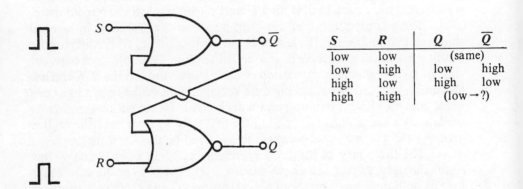

S	R	Q	$\overline{Q}$
low	low	(same)	
low	high	low	high
high	low	high	low
high	high	(low → ?)	

FIGURE D3–3. *RS Flip-Flop from NOR Gates and Its State Table*

   The instant that the flip-flop outputs change states relative to the time that the input levels change is important for all flip-flops. Notice that for the *RS* FF, the outputs change at the same instant (except for a small propagation delay) as the inputs first change levels from their normal (standing) states. Thus the NAND-type *RS* FF goes to a 1 as soon as the *S* input goes low and does not wait for *S* to return high.

Digital Data-Storage Registers

   It should be clear that the *RS* flip-flop can be used as a storage or memory element for a binary digit or bit. The memory element can be set to a 1 or reset to a 0 by appropriate pulses on the input lines. To store an *n*-bit (*n*-digit) binary number would require *n* flip-flops. For example, the 5-bit number 10110 requires 5 *RS* flip-flops. Each FF would be designated for one of the bit values and could be set to that value by its inputs. The FFs would be pictured and usually drawn side by side just as the digits are. Only the Q output from each is used to represent the state or value of that bit (although the inverted or complement outputs $\overline{Q}$ can be useful, too). Such a device that stores a multibit binary number is called a *digital data-storage register* or simply *register*.

Clocked or Gated *RS* Flip-Flop

The data-input-line levels to register flip-flops (in a computer, for example) typically change in time according to various activities in the computer. We usually want the register FFs to respond to the data input lines only at certain times and to ignore the other data. This can be done with the aid of *enabling gates* that pass the R and S levels through to the FF inputs only when the enabling input —called the *clock input*—is high (see Figure D3–4).

NAND gates are used as the enabling gates and, as long as the clock input is low, the NAND outputs will stand high as required for the S^* and R^* inputs of the *basic RS* FF. However, when the clock input goes high, the levels at S and R are passed on (inverted) to S^* and R^*, respectively. If S and R are both 0 or low, the S^* and R^* inputs remain high and no change in Q or $\overline{Q}$ results (by the state table for the RS FF). This situation is told in the state table of Figure D3–4 by writing that the state of the FF after the nth clock pulse (Q_{n+1}) is the same as its state before the clock pulse (Q_n) if both inputs are 0 or low.

However, if R is 1 or high and S is 0 or low, a negative pulse develops on the R^* input (which is the same in duration as the clock pulse) and clearly the FF is reset to $Q = 0$. Therefore $Q_{n+1} = 0$ in the state table; the state of Q_n does not matter. We can similarly argue that $S = 1$ and $R = 0$ will set Q to 1.

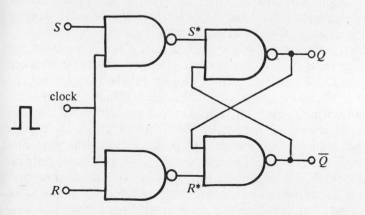

S	R	Q_{n+1}
0	0	Q_n
0	1	0
1	0	1
1	1	?

FIGURE D3–4. *Clocked RS Flip-Flop and Its State Table*

Unfortunately, if both inputs are high or 1 (which amounts to an attempt to set the FF to both 0 and 1 simultaneously), the state of the flip-flop after the pulse is unknown. Both R^* and S^* go low simultaneously and high again simultaneously; however, one input will be delayed a tiny bit in going high, and the FF will come up in a corresponding state. This behavior is typically repeatable for the given circuit and FF, but we cannot predict it. Therefore, the Q_{n+1} entry for $S = R = 1$ is indeterminate or a ?, just as in the corresponding RS case. This indeterminacy can be a problem.

Notice that the FF changes states (Q_n changes to Q_{n+1}) as soon as the clock goes high because the status of R and S is then passed along; that is, the FF changes on the *rising edge* of the clock pulse. This behavior is shown in Figure D3–5 at instants a and e. However, if R and S are changed during the clock pulse, the output will change immediately (if it changes at all), just as for the basic RS flip-flop. At times it can be a problem to assure that R and S are not changing while the clock is high. In Figure D3–5 notice that during the time interval from c to d, there are variations in S and R during the clock pulse that cause output changes.

NOTE: As a diagram aid, the polarity of the clock input pulse that initiates flip-flop activity is drawn at the clock input in Figure D3–4. The positive pulse shown indicates that the clock input should stand low except when the flip-flop is to be activated. Similar pulse forms are often diagrammed for other flip-flops in this book.

D Flip-Flop or Data Latch

The problem that an indeterminate state exists for the clocked RS FF when both inputs are high can be readily remedied. Simply connect an inverter between the S and R inputs and let the data information come in only to the S input. This S input will now be called the D input (see Figure D3–6). (Although the designation D is said to originate from the term *delay,* it seems more reasonable to think *data,* as we shall see.)

Now the S and R inputs of the clocked RS FF in Figure D3–6 can never be both high (or both low, either). Clearly the state table for the clocked RS FF of Figure D3–4 has been restricted to the middle two entries. The resulting D *flip-flop* (consider it named for the single data input) is a very convenient means of storing a binary bit; only one input line is involved, and this memory unit is only sensitive to the data-in when the clock is high. During this time the data value *latches* into the unit and is saved. Hence the term *data latch* is commonly used for this FF, and *D-type flip-flop* is commonly reserved for a more elaborate edge-triggered type that is discussed shortly.

It is important to notice that the data-latch output changes to the value of D as soon as the clock goes high (the clock stands low). If the value of D (its logic level) changes during the clock pulse, the output follows suit; then

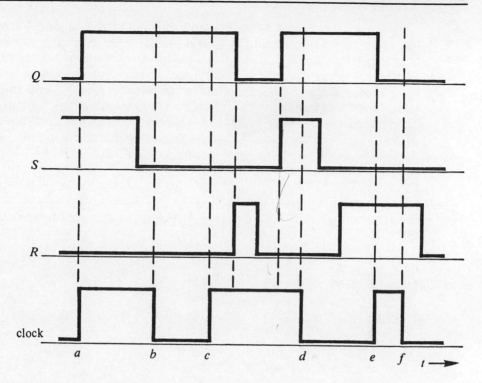

FIGURE D3–5. *Q Behavior for a Clocked RS Flip-Flop for some R, S, and Clock Combinations*

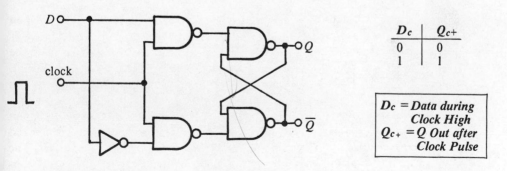

D_c	Q_{c+}
0	0
1	1

D_c = *Data during Clock High*
Q_{c+} = *Q Out after Clock Pulse*

FIGURE D3–6. *D Flip-Flop or Data Latch and Its State Table*

whatever value is at *D* just before the clock goes low is saved in the latch. The resulting state table for the data latch is very simple and is presented in Figure D3–6. Notice that the condition of the *D* line just before the clock input moves from high to low is designated by D_c, while the state of *Q* after the clock pulse moves low is designated by Q_{c+}.

D95

Four data-latch FFs are available in one IC as the *quad-latch* 7475 in the TTL family and the 4042 in CMOS. This device amounts to a 4-bit IC read/write memory and is commonly used to store (4-bit) BCD numbers in digital frequency counters, voltmeters, and the like. These applications are discussed in Chapter D6. Dual 4-bit latches are also available as the 74100 and 74116 in TTL and the 4508 in CMOS. They are dual in the sense that two clock lines enter the chip, one for each set of 4 data latches. An 8-bit latch IC also exists as the 74LS373 (TTL). Manufacturers often use the terms *strobe, store,* or *enable* for clock input lines to these devices.

Edge-Triggered and Master-Slave Flip-Flops

Edge-Triggered *D*-Type Flip-Flop

The data latch has the problem that it responds to changes in the *D* input while the clock is high. This problem is eliminated in the *edge-triggered D-type flip-flop*. The gate circuit is more elaborate and is given in Figure D3–7a. An examination of the gate operation is not provided here, but is left

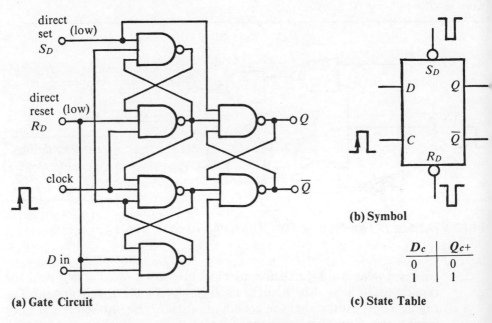

(a) Gate Circuit

(b) Symbol

(c) State Table

D_c	Q_{c+}
0	0
1	1

FIGURE D3–7. *Edge-Triggered D-Type Flip-Flop*

as an optional exercise. It should be quite clear that this circuit was *not* commonly used before ICs made it possible to put such complex circuits into inexpensive little packages (many transistors would be involved).

As with the earlier clocked FFs, the clock stands low. The value of the *D* input just as the clock makes the low-to-high transition—that is, on the positive-going edge—is passed immediately to the output; changes in *D* after this time, or significantly before, do not matter. The fact that *output transitions occur on the rising edge* of the clock pulse is often indicated or emphasized by drawing a *rising arrow* on that edge (see Figure D3-7a and b).

Actually, the *D* level must often be established or *set up* a short time before the rising edge and maintained or held a brief time after. For the common 7474 (dual *D* FF) the set-up time should be 20 nanoseconds (though 5 nanoseconds will typically work) and the hold time should be 5 nanoseconds.

The *D* FF of Figure D3-7a also has *direct-set* and *direct-reset* (or direct-clear) inputs. These inputs should stand high. A momentary low on the direct-set immediately or "directly" sets *Q* to 1, while a low on direct-reset immediately resets *Q* to 0. The value of *D* and the fact that the clock is low do not matter.

It is necessary to have a symbol for this rather elaborate circuit. A rectangle is used as shown in Figure D3-7b. The data (*D*), clock (*C*), *Q*, and $\overline{Q}$ outputs are there indicated. The direct-set (S_D) and direct-reset (R_D) inputs are indicated along with little circles. These circles indicate the inverted logic used; a low is required in each case. Note that if an *R* or *S* input of a TTL type is left unconnected (not recommended because of possible noise problems), the FF will *not* get set or reset, and this is desirable.

The state table for the edge-triggered *D*-type flip-flop is presented in Figure D3-7c. Although this table appears the same as the table for the data latch given in Figure D3-6, D_c here represents the state of the *D* line immediately before the rising edge of the clock pulse. Q_{c+} represents the state of the *Q* output immediately after the rising edge of the clock pulse.

Groups of edge-triggered *D*-type FFs have been commonly used as data registers in applications of digital electronics and computers to laboratory instrumentation and control. In particular, binary data as presented in an experiment must often be picked up at a certain instant and preserved for transmission into a computer at a somewhat later time (see Figure D3-8a). Therefore, quad (74175) and hex (74174) *D*-type FF ICs are available to make up such registers; that is, 4 and 6 FFs are available in the respective IC packages. Corresponding ICs in CMOS are the 4175 and 4174, which even use the same pins for given functions. In the TTL family, the 74LS374 octal *D*-type FF contains 8 positive-edge-triggered FFs, which is a very convenient size for microcomputer applications.

Furthermore, it is often the case that just one set of lines carries data into the computer. As a result, if several registers contain information that may be alternately desired on the *same* lines into the computer, the outputs should be connected in parallel (see Figure D3–8b). However, TTL outputs would fight in such a wired-OR connection. One solution is to use open-collector buffers *after* the *D*-type FFs. The open-collector outputs can then be connected together. This approach is used in interfacing to the PDP-8/E and PDP-11 data lines or data bus.

NOTE: A group of lines carrying simultaneous signals is called a *bus*.

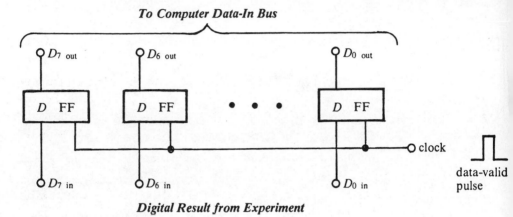

Digital Result from Experiment

(a) An 8-Bit Data Register

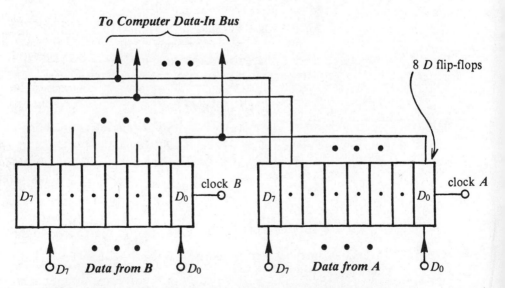

(b) Parallel Data Registers, Requiring Open-Collector or Tri-State Outputs

FIGURE D3–8. *Registers Constructed from D-Type Flip-Flops*

A more contemporary approach is to have Tri-State outputs as the D-FF Q outputs. Thus, National Semiconductor's DM8551 is a Tri-State quad D flip-flop, and the 74LS374 octal D FF is also 3-state.

In fact, if the data bus of the computer is *bidirectional*—that is, carries data out of the computer as well as in—the registers connected to the bus must be open collector or Tri-State, even if only one register is connected to the lines. This is the typical situation. All *output* connections to the PDP-8/E "omnibus" and PDP-11 "unibus" must be open collector, and virtually all microprocessors work with a 3-state data bus.

JK Master-Slave Flip-Flop

A versatile FF type with no indeterminate states and a pair of control inputs, called J and K, exists. It is called the *JK master-slave FF* because of the convention of using control input names and the fact that this device is basically made up of two clocked RS FFs, with the output FF being the *slave* to the input *master* FF.

The gate diagram for the JK FF is shown in Figure D3–9a. Before examining the operation of this FF in some detail as an important example, it is helpful to present its rules of operation as summarized in the state table of Figure D3–9c:

a. If J and K are both low before and during a clock pulse, *no change* in the output occurs after the clock pulse; $Q_{n+1} = Q_n$.

b. If $J = 0$, $K = 1$ before and during a clock pulse, the FF Q always goes to 0 at the falling edge of the clock pulse. (If Q is already 0, it remains 0.)

c. If $J = 1$, $K = 0$ before and during a clock pulse, the FF Q always goes to 1 at the falling edge of the clock pulse. (If Q is already 1, it remains 1.)

d. If $J = 1$, $K = 1$ before and during a clock pulse, the FF Q changes to the opposite of its state before the clock pulse; that is, $Q_{n+1} = \overline{Q}_n$. This change occurs at the falling edge of the clock pulse.

Entries a, b, and c are much like the clocked RS FF. In entry a, no change occurs in output even though a clock pulse occurs. This behavior gives increased versatility to the JK FF over the conventional D-type flip-flop, since the latter always copies the state of D to the Q output at each clock pulse. (However, some modern D FFs have an enable for clock input so that clock pulses do not always cause the FF to change states in response to the D input.)

Entries b and c are also like the corresponding state-table entries for the clocked RS FF. Note that J is like S and K is like R. We can arrange to set the FF to 1 or clear the FF to 0 after a clock pulse.

Entry d causes *toggle action* of the FF. If both J and K are high, for successive input clock pulses, Q flips to state high and then flops back to

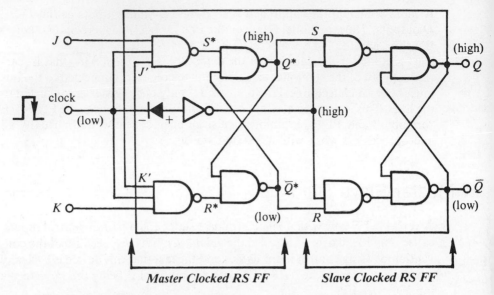

(a) *JK* Master-Slave Flip-Flop Constructed from Gates and One Diode

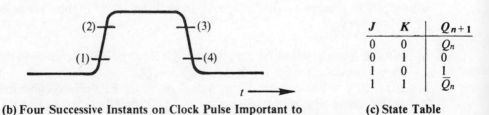

(b) Four Successive Instants on Clock Pulse Important to Master/Slave Operation

J	K	Q_{n+1}
0	0	Q_n
0	1	0
1	0	1
1	1	$\overline{Q_n}$

(c) State Table

FIGURE D3–9.   *JK Master-Slave Flip-Flop*

state low. (This is the important action of the historical two-tube or two-transistor toggle-input bistable as used to construct binary counters. The term *flip-flop* originated from this action.)

NOTE: All *changes at the output* occur on the *negative-going transition* of the clock pulse. This fact is indicated by putting a *downward arrow* on that edge of the pulse in Figure D3–9a and Figure D3–10.

We next examine the behavior of the gates that make up the *JK* flip-flop. In particular, the first and last entries of the state table are justified (the other entries are left as problems). As illustrated in Figure D3–9a, the *JK* FF is constructed from two clocked *RS* FFs. The *master* clocked *RS* FF

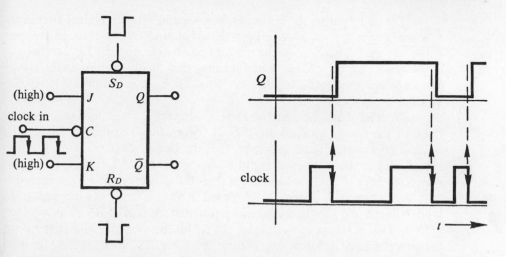

FIGURE D3-10. *JK Flip-Flop Basic Symbol and Output Behavior in Toggle Mode (J, K Both High)*

uses 3-input NANDs for its enabling gates, while the *slave* uses ordinary 2-input NANDs. The clock is normally low, and the enabling gates of the master disconnect the master *RS* FF from the *J*, *K* inputs. Then the inputs to the master *RS* FF (labeled *R** and *S** in Figure D3-9a) stand high as they should.

The inverter between the clock input and the clock of the slave FF causes the clock input of the slave to stand high while the actual *JK* clock in is low. Thus the *R, S* inputs of the slave FF are normally enabled to the $\overline{Q}$, *Q* of the *JK* FF and simply reflect the same levels that exist on the master. This situation is illustrated in Figure D3-9a by assuming *Q** of the master FF as high; then *Q* of the slave is high also.

Now suppose that a positive-going clock pulse occurs. There are four distinct events in the FF as indicated by Figure D3-9b:

1. At point (1) the inverted clock to the slave has already fallen enough so that the enabling gates isolate the slave *RS* FF from the master. The 0.7-V drop across the diode causes the early response of these gates. After this point any change in the master *RS* FF will *not* be passed to the slave.
2. At point (2) the clock to the master has entered high and the *J*, *K* inputs are enabled into the master *RS* FF. (Two *J*, *K* combinations are examined shortly.)
3. At point (3) the clock to the master passes down out of high and the master *RS* FF becomes isolated from the influence of *J* and *K*.
4. At point (4) the slave *RS* FF is again enabled to the master and will change to reflect the master if the master has changed.

Let us return to the state between (2) and (3) and assume first that J, K are low for case (a) above. Then the input NANDs remain high at their outputs so that R^* and S^* of the master remain high. In this case, no change in the master FF occurs, and when the master is finally enabled to the slave at time (4), no change in $Q, \overline{Q}$ results. This argument justifies the $J = K = 0$ state-table entry in Figure D3-9c.

Next let us assume that $J = K = 1$ during the clock pulse. Then we may think of the master clocked RS FF as "completely enabled" because the clock is high, too. Notice, however, that the output Q of the slave is connected back to the "reset-like" input K' of the master, and the output of $\overline{Q}$ is connected back to the "set-like" input J' of the master. If Q and Q^* are high as drawn for example purposes in Figure D3-9a, a high goes to the reset-like input (while a low goes to the set-like input) and the master RS FF is reset to $Q^* = 0$. That is, notice a low develops at R^* for the master RS FF that resets the master FF; S^* remains high. Thus the master RS FF changes states immediately at time (2). However, the slave FF (which is the output of the overall JK FF) does *not* change until time (4)—on the trailing edge of the clock pulse—because it is disconnected from the master until then.

The justification for the other state-table entries is left to the reader. However, we can see that the master behaves like a clocked RS FF in those cases (which it basically is).

NOTE: A word of caution about J,K input manipulation that is seldom emphasized in the manufacturers' manuals: If J and K change while the clock is high, the FF can behave other than might be expected. Basically, the master responds to some variations of J and K while the clock is high; therefore the JK inputs should be maintained without change during the clock pulse.

Figure D3-10 shows the box-type symbol for a JK FF and also the behavior of the Q output for a possible clock input waveform. J and K are shown connected high, so that toggle action results. Notice the instants that Q changes in relation to the falling edge of the clock waveform; a propagation delay has been drawn in the figure. This delay is on the order of 20 nanoseconds for regular TTL-series JK FFs and 45 nanoseconds to 150 nanoseconds for CMOS (for 15-V and 5-V supply voltages, respectively). The clock pulse must have a minimum width (about 20 nanoseconds for TTL, 60 nanoseconds for CMOS) and should have fast rise and fall times even though of long duration (less than 1 microsecond for TTL and 5 microseconds for CMOS).

The JK flip-flop shown in Figure D3-10 possesses direct-set (or preset) and direct-reset (or clear) inputs that each respond to a low level; this active-low behavior is indicated by circles at these inputs. It is left as an exercise to extend the design of Figure D3-9a to include direct-set and direct-reset

TABLE D3–1. *Maximum Input Clock Frequency for Common Family Types of Flip-Flops*

Family		Typical Maximum Frequency (MHz)	Guaranteed Minimum Frequency (MHz)
TTL	74XX	20	15
	74LXX	3	2
	74HXX	50	40
	74SXX	125	80
	74LSXX	45	30
CMOS	CD4XXX	5	3
ECL		140	125

inputs. The 7476 *dual JK* master-slave FF is a 16-pin IC that contains two flip-flops, each with direct-set and direct-reset as diagrammed in Figure D3–10. The 7473 dual *JK* master-slave FF lacks the direct-set inputs and is in a 14-pin package.

Of interest for flip-flops is the maximum-input clock frequency for which they will toggle. These frequencies are given for the common family types in Table D3–1.

Edge-Triggered *JK* Flip-Flops

The fact that the *JK* master-slave flip-flop is sensitive to changes in *J* and *K* while the clock is high can lead to problems. Therefore, *negative-edge-triggered JK* FFs, such as the 74H102 and 74S113, exist. In these units the *J, K* inputs may change while the clock is high; only the value just before the negative transition matters (minimum set-up time of 13 nanoseconds and 6 nanoseconds, respectively), and the outputs then change on this same falling-edge transition, just as for the normal *JK* master-slave FF.

Positive-edge-triggered JK FFs, such as the 7470, also exist. The state of *J, K* just at the positive-going edge matters, and the *output also changes* at this time. Therefore, these units are much like edge-triggered *D*-type flip-flops, except that these FFs have *JK* control inputs and corresponding state table. The various edge-triggered *JK* FFs available do *not* use a master-slave FF configuration in their construction.

To distinguish flip-flop clock behavior, the terms *level-triggered* or *pulse-triggered* are often used for the 7473/7476 type of clock action where *J, K* can influence the FF master while the clock is high. As just mentioned, edge-triggered is used for the often preferred type that responds only at a rising or a falling transition.

NOTE: The trigger arrow drawn on the clock pulse does *not* tell whether a flip-flop is edge triggered or pulse triggered; the arrow simply indicates when changes in the flip-flop output occur.

As of this writing, all low-powered Schottky (74LSXXX) family *JK* flip-flops are *not* of the master-slave type and *are* edge triggered. Thus, the standard 7473 is a pulse-triggered master-slave *JK* FF, while the 74LS73 is a negative-edge-triggered *JK* FF (not master-slave). Both FFs have the same *JK* state-table behavior, and both change output states only at the falling edge of the clock pulse. However, the *J* and *K* inputs in general should *not* change while the pulse is high for the 7473, while they *may* change for the 74LS73. The *Texas Instruments TTL Data Book* specifies that the *J, K* inputs to the 74LS73 should be held steady for a 20-nanosecond interval before the falling edge of the clock pulse.

Most CMOS flip-flops are positive-edge triggered, and the $Q/\overline{Q}$ outputs change immediately on this rising edge (as mentioned above). The 4027 is a dual *JK* flip-flop (two separate flip-flops) rather like the 7476. However, the direct-set/reset inputs on these CMOS units are active high and should stand low; moreover, they may not be left unconnected.

Clock Inputs from Switches

There are a number of applications where we want to clock a *JK* FF from an ordinary switch. For example, suppose each time a push button is pressed, a high is output from the switch circuit to the *JK* FF clock input and, when released, the switch output returns low. Assume that the FF is designed for toggle operation (*J, K* both high) so that for each push on the button, we expect the *Q* output to change states. Thus, if *Q* controls a lamp, the lamp should turn on when the button is pressed once and turn off when the button is pressed again. The left of Figure D3–11a shows a simple SPST (single-pole–single-throw) normally open push-button switch arranged to input a high into the *JK* FF when the button is pressed. Unfortunately, this circuit will *not* work properly for most mechanical switches due to the fact that the switch contact "bounces" as it closes and again as it opens. Thus, within perhaps a millisecond after pressing the switch, an unknown number of pulses are output by the switch circuit to the *JK* clock input, and the *JK* FF toggles a corresponding number of times. A switch-output waveform and *JK* FF response are illustrated to the right in Figure D3–11a. Indeed, in this case the lamp would *not* be on after releasing the push button; it turned on very briefly as the button was pushed and again when it was released.

Figure D3–11b illustrates how a *clean* single pulse can be produced by a mechanical switch circuit, although an SPDT (single-pole–double-throw) switch is required along with an *RS* flip-flop. An SPDT push button

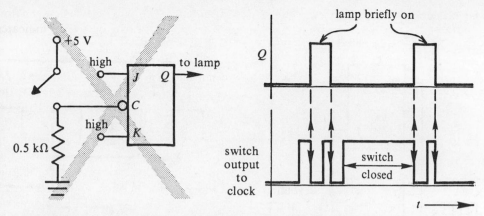

(a) A Clocking Circuit That Does Not Work Due to Bounce Problem with the Switch

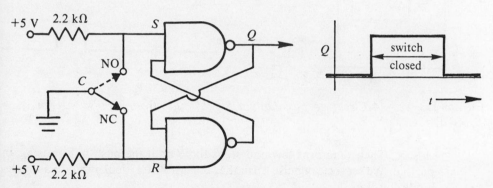

(b) Use of an *RS* Flip-Flop with an SPDT Switch to Produce Bounce-Free Clock Pulse

FIGURE D3–11. *"Bounce" Problem When Using Regular Switches to Produce Clock Pulses and Its Elimination with the Aid of an RS Flip-Flop*

with *normally open* (NO) and *normally closed* (NC) contacts is shown connected to a NAND-gate *RS* FF. The common *C* of the switch is grounded, while the *S* and *R* inputs are pulled up to +5 V with 2.2-kilohm pull-up resistors (these are optional but desirable). Then the *R* input stands low because the NC contact is low; the FF is normally reset. When the push button is pressed, the NC contact opens and a few low impulses go into *R* before finally staying high. However, the FF is already reset, and more reset pulses cause no change in *Q*. When the NO contact is finally grounded, the first low *spike* into *S* sets the FF *Q* output to 1. Subsequent spikes during bouncing have no effect, and a single low-to-high transition of the *RS* FF output occurs. When the push button is finally released, no change in the *RS* FF *Q* occurs (both *R* and *S* are high) until the first negative spike of the NC contact

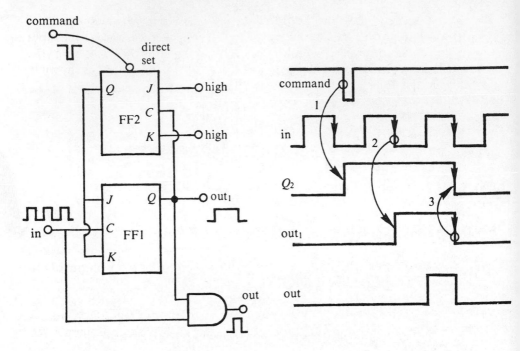

FIGURE D3–12. *A Circuit to Pass Only a Single Pulse from a Pulse Stream*

closure. Then Q returns low and stays there until the push button is again pressed. We see a clean pulse form that is suitable for clock input to a toggle-mode flip-flop.

Single-Pulse-Only Gate

As an example of the utility of the control inputs of the JK flip-flop type, we next consider how to design a box that on command allows only one pulse of a stream of pulses to pass through it. This circuit could be called a single-pulse-only gate. A pair of JK FFs may be used as shown in Figure D3–12. The pulse stream is input to the flip-flop labeled FF1, while the command to admit a pulse is required to be a brief negative pulse to the set of FF2. The command pulse causes the FF2 output Q_2 to go high; this is shown in the waveform diagram of Figure D3–12 by a cause/effect relationship arrow labeled 1. The Q_2 high into J, K of FF1 enables this FF to toggle to a high on the next falling edge of the input clock pulse stream, as shown by arrow 2 in Figure D3–12. However, the next clock pulse toggles Q_1 low, and this input to FF2 toggles Q_2 low, as shown by arrow 3. Consequently, both J and K of FF1 move low and disable this FF from further toggle action until another command pulse is received. Only a single pulse is produced from FF1.

A circuit presented later in the book uses the fact that the output of Q_1 or out$_1$ is a single pulse with duration just equal to the *period* of the input pulse stream. If a pulse with duration actually equal to the duration of the incoming pulses is desired, an AND can be used to produce out as shown in Figure D3–12.

REVIEW EXERCISES

1. (a) Diagram an *RS* flip-flop constructed from NAND gates.
    (b) What are the normal or resting states for the *R,S* inputs?
    (c) Describe how the output can be set to a 1 or reset to a 0 as may be desired.
    (d) What problem arises from bringing both the *R* and *S* inputs low simultaneously?
    (e) At what instant relative to the input pulse to *S* or to *R* does the output of the flip-flop change states?
2. What is a register in digital electronics?
3. (a) Diagram a clocked *RS* flip-flop that is constructed from NAND gates.
    (b) What is the advantage of the clocked *RS* flip-flop over the simple *RS* flip-flop?
    (c) Should the clock input stand low or high? Explain why.
    (d) Write the state table or characteristic table for the clocked *RS* flip-flop.
    (e) To set the clocked *RS* flip-flop to $Q = 1$, what should the levels of *R* and *S* be?
    (f) When do the outputs of this flip-flop type change relative to the timing of the clock pulse?
    (g) Is it possible for the outputs of a clocked *RS* flip-flop to change if the *R* and *S* levels change while the clock is high?
    (h) What is the subsequent flip-flop state if both *R* and *S* are at logic 1 and a clock pulse occurs?
4. (a) Diagram a *D* flip-flop or data latch.
    (b) Describe why this flip-flop type is particularly suitable as a 1-bit memory. What are the advantages of the data latch over the clocked *RS* flip-flop?
    (c) When does the output of a data latch change states relative to the clock input transitions?
    (d) What happens at the flip-flop output if the *D* input changes while the clock input is high?
5. (a) What is the advantage of the edge-triggered *D*-type flip-flop over the data latch?
    (b) When does the output of the edge-triggered *D*-type flip-flop change relative to the timing of the clock pulse?
    (c) What is meant by the "set-up time" of an edge-triggered flip-flop?
    (d) Explain the function of the direct-set and direct-reset inputs that are typically available.

6. Diagram a 4-bit data register or memory constructed from D-type flip-flops. Label the data-in and data-out lines, as well as the strobe or clock input.

7. (a) Draw a gate diagram for a master-slave JK flip-flop. Identify two RS flip-flops in the diagram by drawing a dotted rectangle around each. Identify the master and the slave clocked RS flip-flops in the diagram by drawing dashed rectangles around them.

   (b) Write the state table for the master-slave JK flip-flop.

   (c) What is meant by the toggle action of a JK flip-flop?

   (d) Should the clock to this flip-flop type be normally low or normally high?

   (e) At what time does the Q output change relative to the clock pulse timing for this flip-flop?

   (f) Do the states of the JK inputs matter for the master-slave JK flip-flop during the time that the clock is high?

8. Suppose J is high and K is low for a JK flip-flop when a clock pulse occurs for the device.

   (a) If Q was high before the clock pulse, what will be its state after the clock pulse?

   (b) If Q was low before the clock pulse, what will be its state after the clock pulse?

9. Provided the J and K inputs to the JK flip-flop are not both at logic 1, they function rather like the R and S inputs to a clocked RS flip-flop. Justify this statement. Does J correspond to R or to S?

10. (a) Consider Diagram 3–1 for the 7473-type JK flip-flop. What is the significance of the small circle at the direct-reset input?

    (b) What is the significance of the small circle at the clock input?

    (c) How is the function referred to in (b) sometimes indicated in the clock pulse waveform?

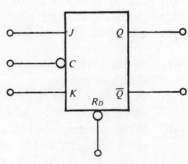

DIAGRAM D3–1.

11. (a) Explain the difference between a pulse- or level-triggered JK flip-flop and an edge-triggered JK flip-flop.

    (b) What are the two general types of edge-triggered JK flip-flops available? How do they differ in function?

    (c) Are most CMOS family flip-flops pulse-triggered or edge-triggered types?

12. (a) Explain what is meant by switch bounce and why it presents a problem for clock pulses generated by a switch for a toggle-mode flip-flop.

    (b) Diagram a circuit that uses an SPDT switch to generate bounce-free pulses.

PROBLEMS

1. Consider an *RS* flip-flop that is constructed from a pair of NAND gates. Assume that the Q output is high and that a negative "set" pulse is input to the set input of the flip-flop. Give an argument to justify the fact that the flip-flop does not change its output state.

2. Consider the *RS* flip-flop constructed from NOR gates.
   (a) Justify that the flip-flop is bistable (that is, has two stable states) if the R and S inputs are both low.
   (b) Justify that this flip-flop responds to a positive pulse to an input, causing the output from the *other* NOR gate to go high. Thus justify the location of R and S relative to Q and $\overline{Q}$ on the gates for this *RS* flip-flop type.

3. Consider the circuit constructed from an AND gate and an OR gate as pictured in Diagram D3–2.

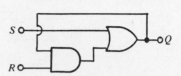

   (a) Assume S is low and R is high; show that Q output is bistable.
   (b) Justify that the circuit is a form of *RS* flip-flop. What are the rules for setting and resetting the flip-flop?

   DIAGRAM D3–2.

4. Design a clocked *RS* flip-flop that uses NOR gates for the *RS* flip-flop section.

5. Design a clocked *RS* flip-flop that includes direct-set and direct-reset inputs. A momentary low to either of these inputs should respectively set or reset the flip-flop outputs irrespective of the state of the clock input.

6. Draw the following waveforms as shown in Diagram D3–3 and also the waveform for the Q output from a clocked *RS* flip-flop that receives these R, S, and clock waveforms. Q is initially low.

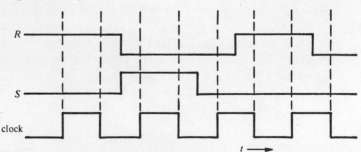

DIAGRAM D3–3.

7. (a) Draw the circuit for a clocked *RS* flip-flop. Find the states of the two outputs while R, S, and the clock are all high.
   (b) Comment on the state of the output when the clock input subsequently returns low.

8. Design a data latch that includes direct-set and direct-clear inputs. Thus, a momentary low applied to the direct-set input causes the Q to immediately be set to logic 1. Similarly, a momentary low to the direct-reset input immediately resets Q to logic 0.

9. Give an argument that justifies the state of Q after a clock pulse to a JK master-slave flip-flop if $J = 1$ and $K = 0$ during the clock pulse. Include two possible initial situations: $Q = 1$ and $\overline{Q} = 0$, as well as $Q = 0$ and $\overline{Q} = 1$. This argument justifies the $J, K = 1, 0$ entry in the state table for the JK master-slave flip-flop.

10. The illustrated waveforms for J, K, and the clock as shown in Diagram D3–4 are input to a JK master-slave flip-flop. Plot the output waveform of Q as a solid line and the clock waveform as a dashed line on a time graph. Assume a direct-reset had occurred before the first clock pulse; thereafter the direct-set and direct-clear are held inactive.

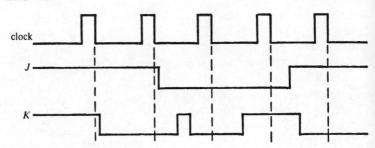

DIAGRAM
D3–4.

11. Design a JK master-slave flip-flop that includes direct-set and direct-reset or clear capability.

12. (a) Suppose $Q = 1$ for a JK master-slave flip-flop. Justify from the circuit construction and action that the state of J during a clock pulse does not matter; that is, J may move high or low even during the pulse with no effect on the subsequent state of the flip-flop outputs.

   (b) Again assume $Q = 1$ for the JK master-slave flip-flop. Justify the fact that if K is high or moves high at any time during the clock pulse, the Q output will move to logic 0 after the clock pulse.

13. A reset pulse followed by a train of clock pulses as diagrammed in Diagram D3–5 are input to a TTL master-slave JK flip-flop.

   (a) Diagram the reset, clock, and Q waveforms for the JK flip-flop connected as shown in Diagram D3–5a.

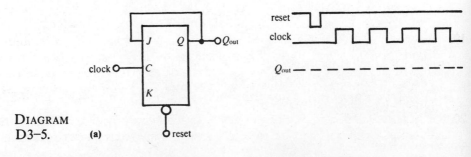

DIAGRAM
D3–5.   (a)

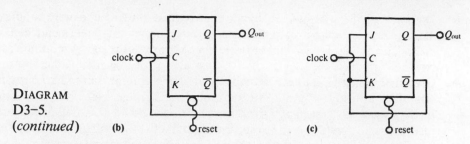

DIAGRAM
D3–5.
(*continued*) **(b)**

(b) Repeat question (a) for the circuit shown in Diagram D3–5b.
(c) Repeat question (a) for the circuit shown in Diagram D3–5c.

14. The state table for what may be called an AB flip-flop is shown here. Show how this flip-flop can be designed using a JK flip-flop and any other logic required.

A	B	Q_{n+1}
0	0	$\overline{Q}_n$
1	0	Q_n
0	1	0
1	1	1

15. Suppose a connection is made between the $\overline{Q}$ output and the D input of an edge-triggered D-type flip-flop. Show that a toggle-mode (or T-type) flip-flop results for the Q output behavior with respect to the clock input.

16. Suppose a line labeled D is connected to the J input of a JK edge-triggered flip-flop. Further, the D line is inverted and connected to the K input. Show that an edge-triggered D-type flip-flop results.

17. Switch bounce is seldom a problem if the switch is used in a simple pulse generator circuit (like that in Figure D3–11a, for example) to the S or R inputs of an RS flip-flop, or to the clock input of a clocked RS flip-flop or of a data latch (D-type flip-flop). Explain why this is true.

18. (a) The clock circuit for the JK flip-flop shown in Figure D3–11a uses a normally open push button so that the clock input stands low. However, the 500-ohm resistor to ground that is shown is at the upper limit of resistance that is permissible for a normal TTL input; explain why this is true. A small value for this *pull-down* resistor is desirable. However, what problems may arise if the resistance is chosen quite small (for example, 10 ohms)?

(b) A much larger resistor (a *pull-up* resistor) could be used in conjunction with a normally closed push button. Draw this more desirable switch circuit for TTL inputs. What limits choosing the pull-up resistor very large or indeed, eliminating it altogether in the TTL case?

19. A room has 1 light and 4 push-button switches. Design a circuit that permits the light to be turned on or off simply by pressing any one of the switches. Assume a solid-state relay is available that operates from a logic-level input to switch the ac current to the light. Show the switch circuitry used. How many wires must be extended to each switch?

20. A burglar alarm is to be arranged that detects the breaking of 4 windows. A thin aluminum strip is placed across each window pane in a manner so that opening

or breaking the window will break the particular strip. If a strip should be broken, we want the alarm to sound even if the strip were quickly mended; also a light indicator (1 of 4) will light to tell which window is broken. A reset should be provided to turn the alarm off. Assume an alarm and light indicators that operate from a TTL output are available; diagram a design for this alarm system.

21. The logic levels of 4 lines are to be monitored on respective indicator lights. These logic levels are changing rather rapidly, and a "hold" circuit is desired so that the indicators will hold the state of the 4 lines at the instant that a push button is depressed. As soon as the button is released, the indicators should continue showing changing logic levels that are then present. Show a circuit design. Assume sensitive indicator lights that operate from TTL outputs are available; however, show the push-button circuit used.

22. Two processes called *fill* and *mix* are controlled by respective logic-level inputs; when a process input is high, the given process runs. Three push-button switches are to be used, called *start-fill, stop-fill,* and *stop-mix*. When start-fill is momentarily pressed, the fill process begins but the mix process should be stopped if it is not already stopped. Pressing stop-fill causes the fill process to stop and the mix process to begin running. Pressing stop-mix causes the mix process to stop and also stops the fill process if it is not already stopped. Design a circuit that accomplishes the above process control function. Show the actual switch circuits in the design; discuss whether bounce-free circuits are required.

23. (a) A simple indicator of minimum overnight temperature is desired. Assume 3 bimetallic switches are available that close when the temperature falls below 10°C, 5°C, and 0°C, respectively. Design an instrument with 3 light indicators; each indicator lights if the ambient temperature falls below the temperature label of that light. A reset button should be provided so that the instrument can be "rearmed" after reading it on the following day. Assume that sensitive logic-level indicator lights are available.

(b) Suppose 20 bimetallic switches are available in increments of 1°C. Diagram how an instrument with an analog-like readout could be constructed; that is, a row of lights could replace the familiar column of mercury of a conventional thermometer. Those lights should be lit that correspond to the mercury column.

CHAPTER
D4

Flip-Flop Circuits

There are many situations where the scientist or engineer wants to count events: the number of nuclear particles passing through a volume; the number of times a rat drinks water; the number of times a machine produces a part; the passing of seconds or minutes, and so forth. The numerical value needs to be shown on a display of some sort, or input to a control computer. Further, it may be that something is to happen *after* a specified number of events: The nuclear counter stops counting; a signal is given to an operator; a bin is refilled, and so on. In addition to these direct applications, counters are often important constituents within such digital instruments as voltmeters. Thus, an alternative title to this chapter could be *Counters, Displays, and Shift Registers.*

Counting circuits have been constructed from toggle-mode flip-flops since the vacuum tube flip-flop was invented by Eccles and Jordan. Since 1965 it has been particularly straightforward to design and construct them from modern IC flip-flop types. With the advent of LSI (large-scale integration), it is possible to purchase complete general-purpose counting circuits within single integrated-circuit packages. However, some understanding of digital counter design is desirable for selecting and using these units. There are a number of counter-circuit types and techniques that are useful for the scientist to know, and we examine them along with techniques for displaying digits. The chapter concludes with a related useful circuit, the shift register.

Counters

A *counter,* then, is a circuit that counts the number of input pulses. Toggle-mode or *T*-type flip-flops are connected together to make a digital counter. The *JK* FF has a toggle mode, as well as useful control possibilities, and is a very common building block for the many kinds of counters constructed from ICs. We begin with the most elementary counter type and progress to sophisticated and versatile types. In the process a rather elaborate nomenclature develops: What is a BCD presettable synchronous up/down counter?

Asynchronous Binary Up Counter

Suppose the Q output from a *JK* FF (of the type that toggles on a high-to-low clock) is connected to the clock input of a next FF. Such interconnections can be made in a string of *JK* FFs, as shown in Figure D4–1a. The *JK* inputs are connected high (or left unconnected) for the toggle mode. A sequence of pulses is input to the clock of the first flip-flop, FF-A. Of course, these pulses should have high and low voltages appropriate to the logic high/low for the logic family being used. In particular, the rise and fall times should be rapid. Assume that on every *negative transition* of the input pulse, output A of the first FF changes state. The waveforms involved are diagrammed in Figure D4–1b, where we see pulses develop at A at just half the frequency of the input pulse train. However, the output A is fed to the clock input of FF-B and the output of B must similarly toggle (change state) on every negative transition of A. Thus the frequency out of FF-B is half that of its input, and so on down the line of FFs. If the FFs are all first reset to low or 0 by a common negative *clear pulse,* the sequence of states is as shown in Figure D4–1b.

Notice that *after* 1 input pulse, the respective states for D, C, B, and A are low, low, low, and high or 0, 0, 0, 1. After 5 pulses the $DCBA$ outputs are 0101, respectively, and after 9 pulses the outputs are 1001. Note that the input pulse numbers are written after each pulse has occurred (on the falling edge) along the bottom of the *pulses-in* waveform, and the states of the counters are labeled for the given time frame between the vertical dashed lines.

Figure D4–1c shows the successive states of the 4 FFs in terms of logic 0's and 1's, and we see that the system is simply counting up in binary. Indeed, if light bulb indicators are connected to the $DCBA$ outputs, the number of counts in binary is displayed on the indicators with the usual convention of bright = 1, dark = 0. The A output is the *least* significant digit or bit, and this first stage of the counter is drawn at the right so that the bit position

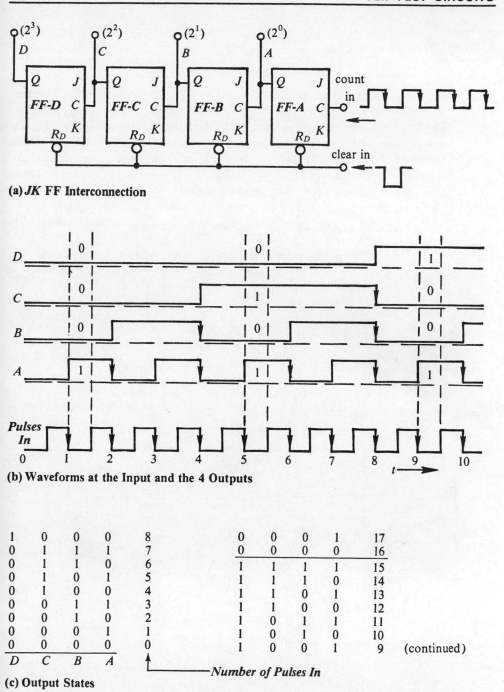

(a) *JK* **FF Interconnection**

(b) **Waveforms at the Input and the 4 Outputs**

1	0	0	0	8
0	1	1	1	7
0	1	1	0	6
0	1	0	1	5
0	1	0	0	4
0	0	1	1	3
0	0	1	0	2
0	0	0	1	1
0	0	0	0	0
D	*C*	*B*	*A*	

0	0	0	1	17
0	0	0	0	16
1	1	1	1	15
1	1	1	0	14
1	1	0	1	13
1	1	0	0	12
1	0	1	1	11
1	0	1	0	10
1	0	0	1	9

(continued)

Number of Pulses In

(c) Output States

FIGURE D4–1   *Asynchronous Binary Up Counter, Waveforms, and States*

is correct. (Otherwise, normal electronic practice puts signal inputs to the left in a schematic diagram.)

Notice that the highest count that these 4 FFs can accommodate is 1111 or 15_{10}. On the next pulse input, the counter "rolls over" to 0 again and continues counting, just like an automobile odometer that has reached 99,999.9 miles or kilometers. In all, the counter has $16_{10} = 2^4$ states (note the state zero must be included). Every additional FF *stage* added multiplies the number of states by 2. Thus an *n*-stage (or *n*-bit) counter has 2^n states. This, of course, corresponds to the fact that an *n*-bit binary number can represent 2^n values or states.

There is, however, a possible propagation-delay problem with this flip-flop counter design. For example, if TTL flip-flops are used, there is a delay of about 20 nanoseconds between the time of the negative clock transition and the time that the outputs settle to a new state. Suppose in Figure D4–1a that 7 pulses have been input so that the counter stands at 0111. On the negative transition of the 8th pulse, flip-flop A toggles to 0 about 20 nanoseconds later; but this negative transition into the clock of FF-B causes its output to go from 1 to 0 another 20 nanoseconds later. There is a ripple-like action down the string of FFs until FFs A, B, and C have finally all gone to 0 and FF-D goes from 0 to 1. A total delay of 4×20 nsec = 80 nsec is required for the counter to "settle down" to the new state. If 12 FFs were involved for a 12-bit counter, the worst delay would be 240 nanoseconds. This is a long time in the time frame of a computer because contemporary computers often complete a whole single instruction in this time. We consider how to remedy this problem shortly, but in non–time-critical applications this simple counter works quite nicely.

We have seen that this counter does not change all its output states precisely in synchronism. Furthermore, it counts in binary and obviously counts up. The counter is therefore termed an *asynchronous binary up counter*. The descriptive term *ripple-through* is often also used, rather than asynchronous.

To produce a counter that counts down rather than up (9, 8, 7, 6, ...), it can be shown that simply connecting the $\overline{Q}$ from the previous stage to the clock of the following stage (rather than Q) does the job. Verification is left as an exercise. The result is then an *asynchronous binary down counter*. We will see that down counters are useful in producing adjustable time intervals (like an egg timer running to zero). Note that the Qs are still used as the count indicator, however.

It is important to note that binary counters constructed from toggle flip-flops that toggle on the rising or low-to-high transition of the clock show just the opposite counting behavior to the above. To obtain an asynchronous *up* counter, the $\overline{Q}$ of a stage must be connected to the clock input of the next stage; to obtain an asynchronous *down* counter, the Q of a stage is connected to the clock input of the next stage. This rule must be followed for constructing asynchronous counters from the CMOS 4095 or 4027 *JK* FFs because they change states on the positive-going clock edge.

Medium-scale integration has made possible the 7493 TTL IC, which is a 4-stage or 4-bit asynchronous binary up counter constructed by cascading 4 *JK* FFs as discussed. The *Q*s from the stages are all available as outputs. The 74393 IC is a dual 7493 consisting of two separate 4-bit asynchronous up counters. Cascading them gives an 8-bit counter with 256 states. Toggling occurs on the negative edge.

LSI in CMOS gives the 4020 (14-stage), 4024 (7-stage), and 4040 (12-stage) asynchronous up counters. These also toggle on the negative transitions of the clock input. The 7-bit device has all *Q* outputs available from a 14-pin package, but not enough pins exist for them all on the 16-pin package used for the 12-bit and 14-bit devices. These large counters—in terms of top count—have prices on the order of only about $1.

Synchronous Counters

For critical high-speed applications we want all of the flip-flops to change state very precisely in synchronism with the falling edge of the clock. The only way to accomplish this is to feed the input clock pulses into *each* FF clock input simultaneously. Unfortunately, all the FFs would then be simply outputting the same square wave at half the input frequency.

To make the counter behave properly, we must inhibit the FFs from toggling too early by use of the *J, K* control inputs. The correct approach can be determined by noticing just when a given FF changes state. Consider, for example, the behavior of FF-C shown in Figure D4–1c. Notice that it changes state (either to a 1 or to a 0) only when all the earlier FFs (here FF-B and FF-A) are 1's or high. Similarly, FF-D toggles only when FF-C, FF-B, and FF-A are *all 1's*. Thus the solution is to AND together the *Q* outputs of all earlier FFs and put the output to *J, K* of a given stage. *J* and *K* will thus be low and inhibit toggling of the given stage until all earlier stages are high. Then *J* and *K* are brought high and the FF will toggle at the end of the next clock (or at the beginning of the next clock if it is of the other toggle type).

Figure D4–2 shows the circuit for 4 stages of a *synchronous binary up counter.* The waveforms from the stages still look like those of Figure D4–1b. Notice the method of cascading these units to make larger counters. The reader might also reason that 2-input ANDs could be used throughout in a cascaded scheme, but propagation delays could limit the high-frequency operation.

To produce a *synchronous binary down counter,* simply consider Figure D4–1c and the behavior of a single bit when counting down (8, 7, 6, 5, ...). Notice, for example, that bit *C* toggles only when all earlier bits are 0, when counting in this direction; but then all earlier $\overline{Q}$s will be 1. Simply con-

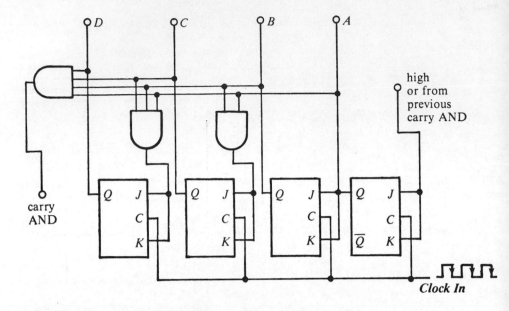

FIGURE D4–2. *Synchronous Binary Up Counter*

nect the AND inputs of Figure D4–2 to earlier $\overline{Q}$s rather than Qs to obtain a synchronous down counter.

It is sometimes useful to be able to switch the same counter between up-count mode and down-count mode in order to add counts or subtract counts at will. Clearly this could be accomplished if a single-pole–double-throw switch were used after each stage to select either Q (for up count) or $\overline{Q}$ (for down count) for the ANDs connected to the later stages. However, we would want to do everything with gates; indeed, single-pole–double-throw switches can be constructed from gates (recall the multiplexer).

As another approach we might think instead of enabling (with gate action) either the ANDed Qs from the earlier stages, *OR* enabling the ANDed $\overline{Q}$s into the *J, K* inputs of a given stage. One control input line with high for up count and low for down count selects the mode, and this line passes directly into each of the *up-count ANDs* to enable them (see Figure D4–3). This line is inverted before going to all the *down-count ANDs* so that they will be enabled for down count (low). The particular active AND output then passes through an OR to each *JK* input.

Presettable Counters

Using the direct-clear inputs to the FFs makes it easy to restart the counter from 0 at any time. However, we may want to start the counter from a count

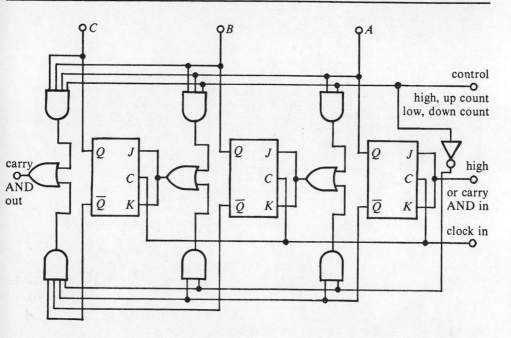

FIGURE D4-3.   *3-Bit Synchronous Up/Down Binary Counter*

other than 0. For example, the typical egg timer is set to 3 minutes (or whatever) and counts down to 0; when the mechanism detects 0, a buzzer goes off.

One technique uses the direct-set and direct-reset (or direct-clear) inputs on the FFs. First a reset pulse resets (clears) all FFs to 0. Next the desired stages are set to 1 by actuating the preset for just those FFs. It is desirable to be able to set up the particular binary number on switches or input lines and have a *load pulse* cause those FFs whose input lines are high to be preset to 1. Figure D4-4 illustrates a circuit for 3 FF stages that are to be preset to 101_2. The FFs themselves can be interconnected to count up or down, synchronously or asynchronously; these connections have been omitted from the drawing.

A more convenient arrangement than that given in Figure D4-4 uses gates such that only one *load-data* line is involved (no reset). Gating is arranged so that low on a given data-entry line causes that FF to reset, while high causes preset when a load-data (high) pulse occurs. The gating for this design improvement is left to a problem. In fact, the 74191 IC involves such gating and is a *4-bit synchronous presettable up/down counter*. We can now appreciate all the terms of this rather lengthy title; it is clearly a versatile unit. In addition to the load and up/down control inputs, it also has an enable (counting) input. A high on this input stops the counter. The 74193 TTL and 40193 CMOS ICs (with identical pin assignments) are also 4-bit counters of

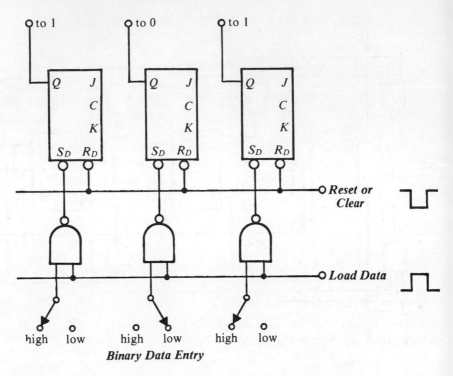

FIGURE D4-4. *Circuit that Presets a Counter (Preset to 101 Shown)*

this category, although separate clock inputs are used to obtain the up
count versus the down count. The decade version, 74192/4192, is discussed
at some length later.

Modulo-*n* or Count-by-*n* Counters

A *modulo-n counter* or *count-by-n counter* is a counter with *n* different
states. If *n* clock pulses are input to a modulo-*n* counter, the counter returns
to the given initial state. We will usually be concerned with a counter that
counts from 0 to $n-1$ in normal binary sequence (of code) and then begins
from 0 again. However, it is possible for a modulo-*n* counter to have *n* codes
for which the output code is different from normal binary; an example is the
creeping code of a *Johnson counter* of modulus 6:

000, 001, 011, 111, 110, 100, 000, 001, 011, ...

It was pointed out earlier that a counter with *N* FFs in the normal
cascaded connection has 2^N states. Therefore it is simple to produce a modulo-
2^N counter. For

modulo $n = 2$, 4 , 8 , 16 , 32 ... 2^N

we cascade

$$1 \quad 2 \quad 3 \quad 4 \quad 5 \dots N \text{ FFs}$$

To produce a modulo counter other than modulo 2^N from bistable FFs requires *feedback* to reset the counter to 0 prematurely. Furthermore, if the number n is greater than 2^N, but less than 2^{N+1}, we must use $N + 1$ flip-flops (so it would "naturally" count higher than n).

As one example we consider a synchronous modulo-3 counter, which may be constructed from 2 flip-flops (see Figure D4–5). Notice that the clock goes directly to every FF so it must be a synchronous counter. K is connected high or 1. Only the J is manipulated in this design, so that the J, K state table is restricted to $J, K = 1, 1$, which always gives a toggle to opposite state; or to $J, K = 0, 1$, which gives a 0 for Q after the clock pulse.

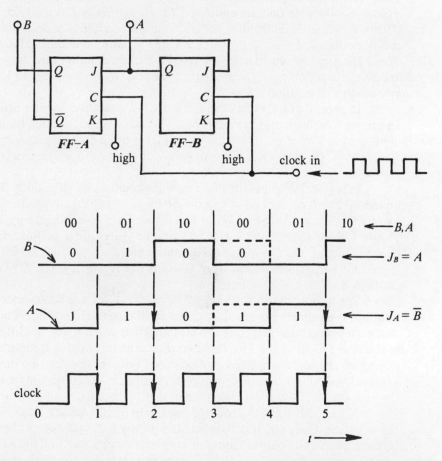

FIGURE D4–5. *Synchronous Modulo-3 Counter and Waveforms of the Clock, A and B*

D121

The waveforms or states of the FF Q outputs, as well as the clock, are drawn in Figure D4–5. To decide what the FF behavior will be on each clock negative-going edge, we have written into the waveform numbers telling the state of its J during the time interval up to the falling of the clock. J_A, K_A refer to the respective JK inputs of flip-flop A (FF-A), while J_B, K_B refer to the respective JK inputs of flip-flop B (FF-B). Thus, before the falling edge of clock pulse 1, we see $J_A, K_A = 1, 1$ so that A toggles from 0 to 1. However $J_B, K_B = 0, 1$ so that B remains at 0. The reader should follow along each waveform and justify its behavior in this way.

Notice the states of B, A go to 00, 01, 10, 00, 01, ... so that the counter counts 0, 1, 2, 0, 1, ... It is indeed a 3-state or modulo-3 counter. The counter is forced to follow the solid curves in Figure D4–5. The *normal behavior* (no feedback) is shown by dashed lines.

Designs exist for synchronous modulo counters for all small integers. Their derivation or justification is usually not obvious! One source of designs is a Motorola booklet entitled *TTL Design Ideas Using 54/75 Logic* (1970). Fairchild manufactures the 9305 variable-modulus counter that can count modulo 2, 4, 5, 6, 7, 8, 10, 12, 14, and 16 without additional logic. In *The TTL Applications Handbook* (1973), Fairchild shows how two 9305s and one gate package can give division by any odd number from 21 to 127 and any even number from 128 to 256.

In general at least one output line from a modulo-n counter produces an output waveform that has a frequency equal to the input clock frequency divided by n. Therefore, a modulo-n counter is often called a *divide-by-n* or $\div n$ counter. The frequency division behavior of modulo-n counters is often exploited.

It is possible to obtain some modulo counters by cascading. Thus a divide-by-2 ($\div 2$) counter input to a divide-by-3 ($\div 3$) obviously gives a divide-by-6 ($\div 6$). Also a divide-by-2 input to a divide-by-5 gives a divide-by-10 (see Figure D4–6). Indeed, the $\div 2$, $\div 5$ technique is used in a popular $\div 10$ or *decade counter*: the 7490. A $\div 6$ counter is useful to produce 10-hertz (or 0.1-second period) waveforms from 60-hertz line frequency. The 7492 device contains a $\div 2$ and a $\div 6$ counter.

We next consider a *general* way to construct a modulo-n counter, although the counter has one flaw that may at times be important. The technique simply involves detecting the bit pattern of count n and sending a low to the direct resets of the FFs. If the counter is an up counter, a complete decoding of the top count need *not* be done; only the 1's need be detected. Figure D4–7 illustrates an asynchronous modulo-5 counter implemented through the direct-reset (or clear) when $n = 101$ occurs.

Notice that when the counter counts up to 101, we are actually up to the 6th state. However, this state exists for only some tens of nanoseconds because the NAND output then quickly goes low and resets all the FFs. For many purposes (certainly to the eye), the 6th state did not exist. However, other TTL circuitry can detect this state; if so, it may not then be tolerable.

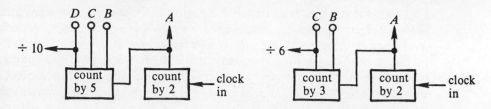

FIGURE D4–6. *Cascading Counters to Get Various Modulus Counters*

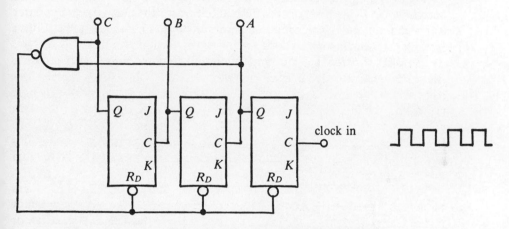

FIGURE D4–7. *Modulo-5 Counter by Direct-Reset Technique*

The above approach can be generalized to a *variable-modulus counter* using the direct-reset technique. The modulus n may be set in binary on switches, and that top count should then be detected and a reset generated. The detailed circuit is left as a problem.

Decade Counters
and the Binary-Coded-Decimal (BCD) Counter

Some of the earlier counters (for example, those found in early Geiger counter scalers) used a simple string of toggle FFs with a light indicator at each Q to give the number of counts in binary. Reading such a count, particularly for large numbers, is not immediately meaningful to people accustomed to decimal. It is also not particularly simple to construct a decoder that decodes from a large n-bit number to a multidigit decimal number.

The easiest approach is to cascade 10-state or *decade counters* (also called decimal or modulo-10 counters). Each counter should generate a *carry pulse* that increments the next higher counter when it has received 10 pulses in. In the process, it rolls over to begin at 0 again; this is the familiar mode of operation for an automobile odometer.

The basic task then is to construct a 10-state or modulo-10 counter from toggle flip-flops. From what has been indicated earlier, it is necessary to use 4 FFs (with outputs D, C, B, A) that would count to 16, but use interconnections that force the FFs to 0 after the 10th count. The rather natural approach is to let the FFs count normally in binary from 0 to 9. The resulting correspondence between 4-bit binary numbers and the 10 decimal digits is called *binary-coded-decimal* or BCD. The waveforms for the 4 FF outputs are shown in Figure D4–8a. The dashed line shows the normal operation of a 4-bit counter, while the solid line shows the desired 10-state mode. Figure D4–8b gives the binary bits or FF states corresponding to the 10 states; this is the *BCD code* for the 10 decimal symbols or digits. A counter that counts in this manner is called a *BCD counter*.

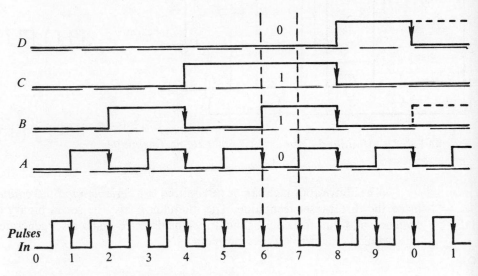

(a) Waveforms or States from BCD Counter

0	1	0	1	5
0	1	0	0	4
0	0	1	1	3
0	0	1	0	2
0	0	0	1	1
0	0	0	0	0
D	*C*	*B*	*A*	

0	0	0	1	(11)
0	0	0	0	(10)
1	0	0	1	9
1	0	0	0	8
0	1	1	1	7
0	1	1	0	6
D	*C*	*B*	*A*	

(b) Binary-Coded-Decimal States

FIGURE D4–8. *Waveforms and Codes for Binary-Coded-Decimal or BCD*

There are a number of ways to achieve BCD counters, and, as might be expected, the synchronous type is more elaborate than the asynchronous. Figures 4–9a and b show two designs using *JK* FFs plus AND gates.

Notice we can now connect a string of BCD counters together to obtain a multidigit decimal counter rather easily. Examination of Figure D4–8a shows the waveform of output *D* makes one negative transition after the 10th pulse (as the entire decade rolls over to 0). This carry-like pulse can be used as a clock into the next more significant digit BCD counter. The next counter will then increment once for every 10 pulses into the previous counter, as it should. Figure D4–10 shows a connection of BCD counters to make a multidigit counter in this way. The term *decade scaler* is also used for such a counting unit.

There are now four 1's place bits, four 10's place bits, four 100's place bits, and so on. These lines were connected to lights in early counters, and with a little practice we could quite quickly convert this mixture of binary and decimal numbers to decimal. Thus 0101, 1001, 0011 = 593_{10} (if the commas are omitted we should mentally perform the grouping).

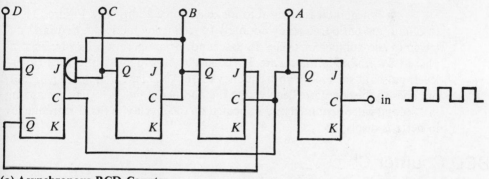

(a) Asynchronous BCD Counter

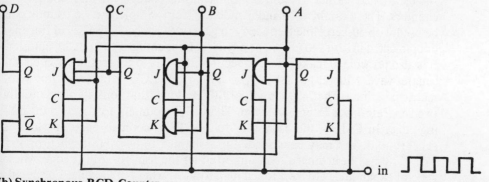

(b) Synchronous BCD Counter

FIGURE D4–9. *Two BCD Counter Designs*

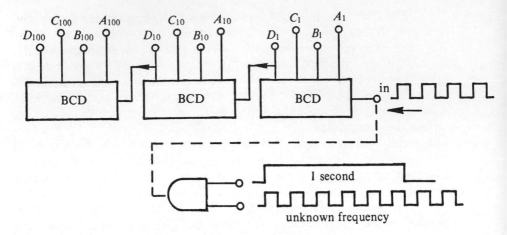

FIGURE D4-10. *Connection of BCD Counters to Give a 3-Decade Counter with Individual Digits in BCD Code (Simple Frequency Counter)*

At this point it is natural to make a simple addition in Figure D4–10 to obtain the basic frequency counter. In frequency mode, an f counter determines the number of cycles in 1 second. This operation can be accomplished by sending an accurate 1-second-duration pulse along with (logic-level) pulses at the unknown frequency to an AND gate; the AND gate output goes to the counter. Clearly, just the number of pulses (cycles) occurring in 1 second will be counted and indicated on the display so that the frequency in hertz is displayed.

BCD Counter Chips

BCD (decimal) counters exist in IC form. The 7490 is a basic unit of this type. As mentioned earlier it consists of separate count-by-2 and count-by-5 counters. These can be used independently (for example, the ÷ 5 counter can be used with 50-hertz line frequency to generate 0.1-second pulses in Europe) or connected in series to obtain an asynchronous count-by-10 (BCD) counter. It is also possible to make interconnections in a way to generate a symmetrical square-wave ÷ 10 output (the Q_D output from BCD counters is not symmetrical in time). The 74390 is a dual BCD counter that consists of essentially two separate 7490s in one package. These TTL counters advance on the falling edge. In CMOS, the 4518 is a dual BCD up counter, each of which is synchronous, and may be cascaded in a manner to be overall synchronous. The 4518 may be arranged to count on either the rising or falling edge. These general capabilities are mentioned here to show what is available. For details on how to use them, the reader should consult the data books available from the manufacturers.

LSI CMOS permits *one-package* counting systems. For example, the Intersil ICM7208 contains a 7-decade up counter in a 28-pin package. However, too many pins are required to bring all decades out simultaneously. Only one decade at a time is presented to the set of output lines, resulting in a *multiplexed output.* Three multiplex or MUX control input pins select the desired decade, which in fact is presented in 7-segment code over 7 wires. The 7-segment code is discussed shortly.

More versatile than the 7490 is the 74192 TTL or 40192 CMOS synchronous presettable up/down decade counter. It can be preset to any count and has one clock input that causes up counting, and a second clock input for down counting. The *positive* clock transition initiates a change of states on this device. Let us consider an application where we desire 1 pulse out for every n pulses in. The circuit can be "programmed" to accept a *multidigit* decimal number for the value of n. The value of n might be input from several 10-position *thumbwheel* switches; they should each produce a 4-line BCD output for the particular decimal position they are at. Then, if the number 47 is set up on the switches and pulses with a period of 0.1 second are input to the unit, an output pulse will occur every 47×0.1 sec $= 4.7$ sec. This response is accomplished by using several cascaded presettable down counters that are arranged to automatically reload their respective digits after *all* reach 0. Note that merely cascading two variable modulus down counters would *not* work: A modulo-4 down counter feeding a modulo-7 down counter would produce an output pulse for every $4 \times 7 = 28$ input pulses. We want $4 \times 10 + 7 = 47$.

Counters that can manage the trick we desire are said to be *cascadable counters,* and the 74192 is such a counter. When counting up, the 74192 outputs a negative *carry* during the low period of the 9th pulse. When the rising edge of the 10th pulse is received, the carry output goes high and this positive transition may be used to clock the next decade (see Figure D4-11a for the clock versus carry waveforms).

On the other hand, when counting down, the 74192 outputs a low on the *borrow* output during the low period after the pulse that caused the state 0 ($D, C, B, A = 0$) to be reached. On the next rising edge of the clock, the BCD counter goes to state 9 (from which it will continue to count down on successive clock pulses), and the borrow goes high; if the borrow is fed to the down count of a more significant decade, it will then count down one unit (see Figure D4-11b for the clock-versus-borrow waveforms). This is the mode we use for producing 1 pulse out for every n input pulses.

A negative-logic AND gate can be used to detect the simultaneous 0's of the decades and reload initial count data from the sets of BCD data lines into the counters (see Figure D4-11c). Thus, if two decades are used and the thumbwheel settings are at 47_{10}, the counters count 47, 46, 45, 44, 43, 42, 41, 40, 39, 38, ..., 02, 01, 00 pulse 47, 46, ... The 00 state is very brief because the load pulse immediately presets the counters to 47, and then the next positive-going clock causes the transition to state 46. Thus if N_{10} is set in the

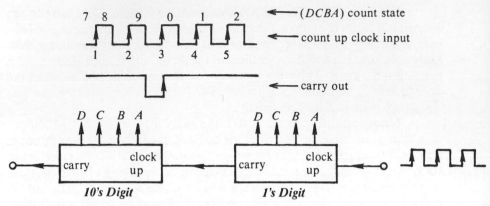

(a) Cascaded 74192s with Pulses to Clock-Up Input

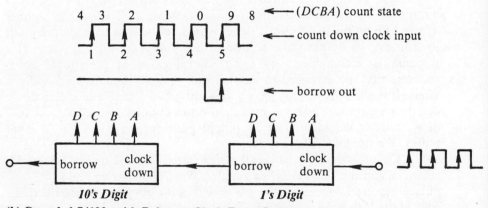

(b) Cascaded 74192s with Pulses to Clock-Down Input

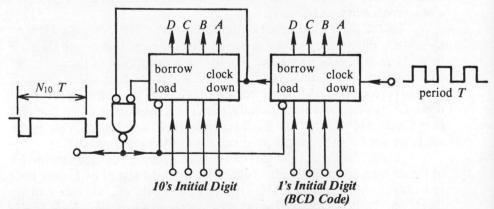

(c) Two Decimal Digit "Divide Frequency by N_{10}" or "Multiply Period by N_{10}" Circuit, Using Two 74192s in Down-Count Mode

FIGURE D4–11. *Uses for the 74192 Presettable Up/Down Decimal Counter*

preset inputs we have a modulo-N counter producing a pulse out for every N_{10} pulses in. This output pulse is basically the borrow output of the 7492, which is low only as long as the outputs are 0; because of the immediate reset, it is a very sharp pulse (perhaps 20 nanoseconds in duration).

Digital Displays

Neon Lamps

The need to decode mentally the BCD lights from a circuit like Figure D4–10 is a nuisance. However, it is not a difficult step to design a BCD-to-decimal decoder. This is a 4-line to 1-of-10-line decoder and is readily designed with AND gates (or even simply diodes) as discussed earlier. The simplest approach is to number a row of lamps or lights from 0 to 9 and connect them to corresponding lines from the decoder for a decade. Parallel rows of lamps with one bright digit from each row can then be quickly read to obtain the count in decimal. This was the approach commonly used from about 1940–1965 (using "twin" triode and later 2 transistor flip-flops—4 FFs for each decade—and diode decoding) with *neon lamps* as indicator lights.

In about 1965 the *Nixie tube* (Burroughs trademark) became quite common. This is basically a tube containing 10 neon-wire cathodes. Each wire is bent in the shape of a digit and glows if connected to ground while the anode is connected to approximately 200 V (through a current-limiting resistor of perhaps 10 kilohms). To cause the other digits to be dark, the remaining cathodes must be brought off ground to perhaps 30 V. Normal TTL IC outputs cannot withstand these high voltages. Thus the *7445 BCD-to-decimal decoder/driver* has special output transistors capable of withstanding 30 V. Furthermore, the outputs are negative logic (low when selected) in order to properly bring a Nixie cathode to ground (see Figure D4–12). The 7442 is a BCD-to-decimal decoder (not driver) with normal TTL outputs that can be used for normal decoding purposes (also with negative-logic outputs). Both units *decode completely*; that is, binary combinations for 10, 11, 12, and so on, give high at all outputs.

7-Segment Displays

Since about 1970 the *7-segment display* has become well known to everyone; it is the usual calculator display or digital watch display. These displays are available in incandescent, light-emitting diode (LED), liquid-crystal display (LCD), fluorescent, and other forms. In this case 7 bars or segments are lit up in such a way as to form each of the numerals (and also a few letters). A

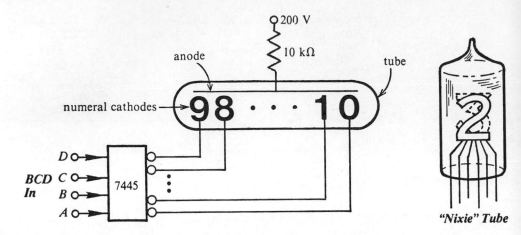

FIGURE D4–12. *BCD-to-Decimal Decoder/Driver (e.g., 7445) and Nixie Tube*

kind of "recoding" is required to select the proper segments to form the appropriate numeral for a given BCD code; therefore BCD-to-7-segment decoder/drivers exist in the TTL and CMOS families.

The *LED display* consists of a light-emitting diode for each segment bar. When a diode is forward biased so that current passes through the diode, light is given off as electrons make the energy level transition across the diode junction, and the given bar lights up. These diodes, of course, have a cathode and an anode each and have typical diode-like forward characteristics, with a knee at about 1.5 V for gallium-arsenide-phosphide (GaAsP) and about 2 V for gallium-phosphide (GaP) types. LED displays are available in two types: *common anode*—that is, all the anodes are connected together to one lead—or *common cathode*—that is, all the cathodes are connected together to one lead. The two types of diode connections are diagrammed in Figure D4–13. Also shown is the usual segment designation scheme (*a* through *g*).

In the case of the common-cathode LED display, the common cathode is connected to ground and the decoder/driver outputs must go high (positive-logic or active-high outputs) to light particular segments; they must also supply a significant current (5 milliamperes to 20 milliamperes) to each segment and hence must have *drive* capability. However, 5 V (for example, high from a decoder/driver output) should generally *not* be connected directly across a diode because of its knee characteristic (it is rather like connecting a 5-V battery to a 1.5-V or 2-V battery). A very large current may flow (depending on the 5-V source capacity), and burn out the diode. Current-limiting resistors are often required and can be calculated from $R = (5\,\text{V} - 2\,\text{V})/I$ where I is the desired segment current. Newer design decoder/drivers eliminate these resistors by having *programmed* current limiting through use of a single resistor at the chip; for example, the Fairchild 9660.

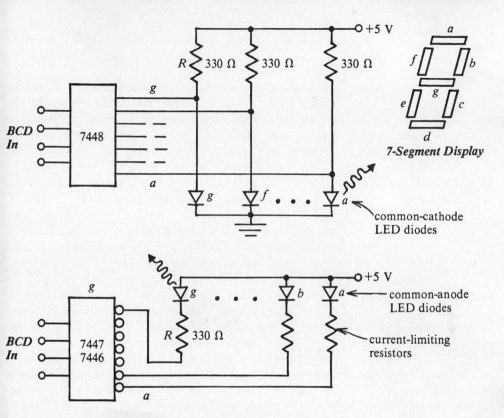

FIGURE D4–13. *Connections of 7-Segment Decoder/Drivers to LED Displays*

The 7448 is an example of a positive-logic BCD-to-7-segment decoder/driver. However, it can source only 2 milliamperes at 0.85 V and generally requires resistive pull-up help. This is diagrammed in Figure D4–13. A segment lights when a 7448 output goes high and current flows from +5 V through the 330-ohm resistor to the LED. However, when the 7448 output goes low, the current flows into the 7448 output (it sinks the current) and the LED goes dark. Notice that a current flows from the supply in either case, and in fact becomes a rather large current for multidigit displays: Consider 5 digits × 7 segments × 10 mA/segment = 0.35 A. Thus, battery-operated LED systems (for example, wristwatches) are generally arranged so that the LEDs are off unless a reading is desired.

Common-anode LED displays have the anodes connected to positive (for example, to +5 V) and the selected segment cathodes are brought low. Thus a decoder/driver with negative-logic or active-low outputs must be used. The 7446 and 7447 are examples of such devices; their outputs are capable of sinking up to 40 milliamperes each. Figure D4–13 illustrates the 7-segment display and typical connections to the 7446 or 7447 decoder/driver.

Incandescent 7-segment displays are among the brightest types and can be filtered to produce many colors. A tungsten filament (similar to a regular light bulb) is used for each line segment. They are prone to burn out, but improved types are capable of long life.

Liquid-crystal displays or LCDs are unique because they scatter rather than generate light; they have the lowest power requirements of any display. In an older type the applied voltage causes turbulence in the liquid-crystal material, making it reflective. The newer field-effect type uses the optical action on polarized light of properly oriented liquid crystals. A thin layer of transparent liquid-crystal (LC) material is placed between sheets of glass, and crossed polarizers are placed on the top and bottom glass surfaces. A reflecting surface is placed below the bottom polarizer. The LC layer is only some 10 microns thick. This "sandwich structure" is shown in Figure D4–14. Incident light on the structure is polarized by the top polarizer 1 and passes into the liquid crystal. The plane of polarization of the light is rotated 90° by the LC layer and the light then readily passes through polarizer 2 (because it is crossed relative to the first). The light is then reflected by the surface beneath polarizer 2 back through polarizer 2, through the crystal where the polarization is rotated 90° again, and finally passes back out through polarizer 1. An observer, therefore, sees the bright silver color of the reflector.

However, transparent metal films are deposited on the inner two glass surfaces. Because the liquid crystal is a good insulator, this construction is

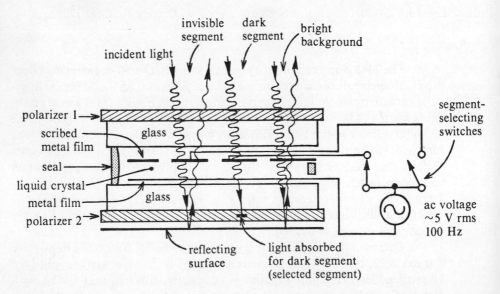

FIGURE D4–14. *Edge-View Diagram of a Liquid-Crystal Display (LCD) with One Dark Visible Segment Area and One Invisible*

like that of a parallel-plate capacitor. If a voltage is applied between the metal films, the resulting electric field in the LC destroys its light-polarization rotating property. The light passing through polarizer 1 is then absorbed by polarizer 2, and the crystal appears dark. By scribing electrically separate areas in the top metal film, it is possible to selectively apply voltage to segments, symbols, and so on, and make them appear dark when a voltage is applied to them.

However, the applied voltage should be ac between the two metal films; a dc voltage causes electrolysis between the films and short LCD life, so the two metal films must alternate in polarity. A symmetrical square wave, 3-V to 15-V ac at 30 to 100 hertz, is a typical requirement. Recent CMOS chips (CD4054, CD4055, MC14543) have been designed to provide the ac drive needed by LCDs. Only microampere currents are involved so the voltage source is not a great problem; CMOS can easily drive them, but an astable (oscillator) source is required. In the past, LCDs were subject to humidity, temperature, and slow-response problems. However, these problems have been largely solved, and LCDs have become common in wristwatches, calculators, and digital instrumentation. It is amusing that as recently as 1965 a science text stated, "While liquid crystals are uncommon and of no practical importance, they are of interest . . . ."

Single-Package Decade Chips

MSI technology has made possible single ICs that contain a 4-bit BCD counter, a 4-bit data latch, and a BCD-to-7-segment decoder/driver. The data latch serves as a small memory to latch the output from the counter and maintain a constant reading in the display while the counter is again counting. This device is discussed further in Chapter D6. The 74143 is an example of this technology. Indeed, the 7-segment-display drivers are current limited to 15 milliamperes so that just three 74143 chips and three common-anode LED display digits are all the parts required for a 3-digit counter. Furthermore, the BCD codes are available as well as the 7-segment codes; the BCD codes can thus be input to a computer system. The 4026 and 4033 are somewhat similar CMOS single-chip counting packages. Their segment drivers limit at about 3 milliamperes, making them usable with new low-powered LED displays.

Multiplexed Displays

When a counter and display contain many digits, a large number of interconnection lines between the counter and the display are involved in the approach discussed thus far. Thus a 6-digit, 7-segment display has 43 control wires plus power supply. By *multiplexing,* this interconnection can be reduced to 7 segment wires plus 6 separate power wires (one for each digit), or 13 wires. The technique involves scanning the digits. Each digit in turn is lit up briefly, but the rate is made high enough that no flicker is evident to the eye. In order to compensate for the dark period, each segment should receive more current than in the unmultiplexed case.

The corresponding segments from each display are connected together within the display module (all segment *a*s together, all *b*s together, and so forth). Seven wires lead from the module, one for each segment. In a common-anode display, lows are output to appropriate segments to form a numeral, and the anode of the given digit is brought high to light that digit. To work well, the display type should have a turn-on threshold; otherwise sneak paths can turn on unwanted digits. LEDs are well suited for multiplexed displays, while LCDs are difficult to multiplex (at least most contemporary types).

The outputs of each BCD counter are selected in turn by a data selector or multiplexer and presented to a BCD-to-7-segment decoder. The decoder in turn is connected to all the readout digits, but only the digit receiving anode power will light; the power is supplied in synchronism with the selected BCD counter stage. An oscillator through a modulo counter controls the scan rate (see Figure D4–15). Notice that only one decoder is needed in this technique—another saving.

This diagram involves the use of a number of logic and counting notions that have been discussed thus far. It is sufficiently complex that many wires and boxes must be left off the diagram; they have been indicated by dashes. Often a group of wires in complex systems is indicated by a single line with a slash through it and a nearby number that indicates the number of lines that have been abbreviated to the one line.

The ICM7208 CMOS 7-decade up counter mentioned earlier contains in a single 28-pin LSI package all of the elements indicated within the dashed box in Figure D4–15; that is, the oscillator, 7 BCD counters, multiplexer, and 7-segment decoder/LED driver. Thus, if a 7-digit multiplexed LED display module is also purchased, these two devices essentially require only interconnection in order to obtain a useful events counter (up to 10 megahertz). For battery operation, however, an LCD display is desirable, and LCDs do not multiplex easily. For this purpose the ICM7211 40-pin chip is available that converts a 7-segment multiplexed input to four 7-segment digits out (28 lines).

Shift Registers

Flip-flops can be cascaded in yet another manner to produce a useful device called a *shift register* (SR). A clock or shift input line to the register causes all bits to move over one place in response to each clock pulse. A data bit may be input at one end, called the *serial data input*. Thus, if a 6-bit register contains

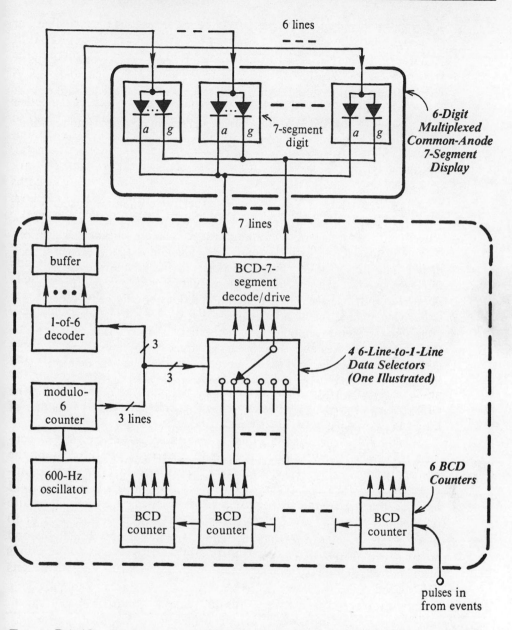

FIGURE D4–15. *Diagram of a 6-Digit Multiplexed-Display Decimal Events Counter*

101101 and the data-input bit is 0 at the left end, after the clock pulse it will
contain 010110. This register is called a *right-shift register* because the bits
each hop right one place in a clocking operation.

Shift Register Circuit Types

A shift register may be constructed from edge-triggered D-type flip-flops as shown in Figure D4–16a. All FFs receive the same clock line, and each D receives the Q output from the previous stage. On the rising edge of the clock pulse, the D input of a stage samples the D from the previous stage and passes this value to its own Q; thus the shifting operation occurs. Although the Q into a given D changes very, very soon *after* the rising edge, this has no consequence for an edge-triggered device. Propagation delay plus edge triggering permit the device to work. Data-latch or level-triggered D FFs would *not* work.

A shift register may also be constructed from JK FFs as shown in Figure D4–16b. Note that J and K are always opposite, so each JK FF always moves to the state of its J input when the clock makes its negative transition.

At times it is desirable to load all the bits into the shift register at once or *in parallel,* rather than sending each in from the end one after the other or *in series.* A shift register with this capability is called a *parallel-load* or *parallel-in* shift register. For n stages, n data lines should be presented (one to each stage), and the binary states of these lines are set up prior to a load pulse that transfers the multibit binary number into the register. If each FF in the register possesses direct-set and direct-reset capabilities, the gating for each stage may be arranged as in Figure D4–16c. The reader should be able to justify that the data is properly loaded into each stage.

Now if Qs from all stages are made available, the shift-register stage may be read at once; this is called *parallel-output* capability. If only the Q from the last stage is made available, then of course the bits can be obtained only one after the other and we have *serial-output* capability only.

A shift register may be made to shift left rather obviously by taking the Q from the stage to the right (rather than to the left) and feeding it into the given stage. A 4-bit *left-shift register* is diagrammed in Figure D4–16d. It is quite possible to design a shift register that shifts to the left or to the right, depending on the state of a *mode-control* input line. Simply arrange gating so that the stage behind or the stage ahead may be selected (in response to the mode-control line) to produce a right-shift or left-shift register. It is left as a problem to design this gating.

Shift registers are available in both the TTL and CMOS families with various bit sizes and capabilities. Thus the 7496 is a 4-bit parallel-in/parallel-out shift register (one direction only), while the 7495 is a left-shift/right-shift register with serial input and parallel (or serial) output. The newer 74194 is a 4-bit *universal-shift register* in a 16-pin package with all the features

FIGURE D4–16. *Shift Registers*

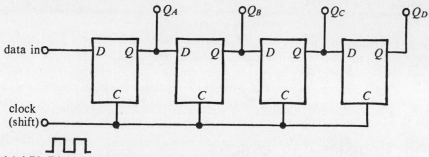

(a) 4-Bit Right-Shift Register from *D*-Type FFs

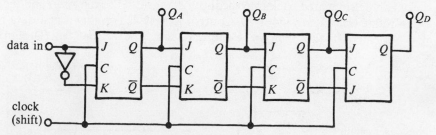

(b) 4-Bit Right-Shift Register from *JK* FFs

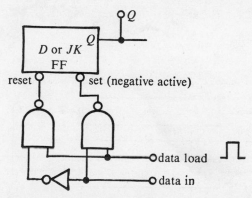

(c) Circuit for (Parallel) Data Entry to Each Stage

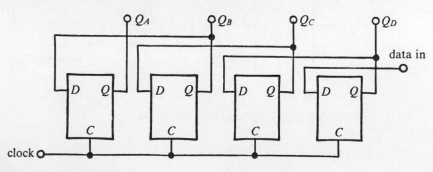

(d) 4-Bit Left-Shift Register

mentioned above; the 74198 is an 8-bit unit in a 24-pin package. Shift registers with many bits are available in CMOS (for example, the 32-bit 40100 and the 64-bit 4031). Very large shift registers are available in MOS (for example, the dual 200-bit 2511 or 1,024-bit 2512 Signetics ICs). Of course, these devices have only serial in/out; they are usually used as *solid-state rotating memories.*

Shift Register Applications

In the memory application, the shift register is arranged so that the output bit can be circulated back into the input stage rather than "lost," and the bits all rotate (see Figure D4–17a). Control is provided so that a new data bit may be entered at the input, or the output data may be recirculated. (Design of such

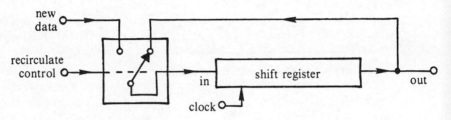

(a) Recirculating Shift Register

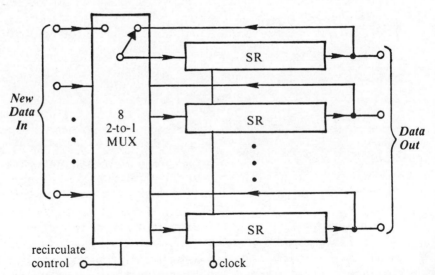

(b) Recirculating Shift Registers as Memory (FIFO)

FIGURE D4–17. *Shift Register Memories*

a control-circuit addition using gates is left to the problems.) Then if 8 shift registers are operated in parallel as shown in Figure D4–17b, the device becomes a *first-in–first-out memory,* FIFO, for 8-bit binary numbers. If only one shift register is used, it is a device for (serial) data storage that operates much like a magnetic disc. Indeed, the new *bubble magnetic-memory* device operates in this fashion—that is, like a recirculating shift register—with shifting of magnetic "bubbles" around paths within a thin film. The relatively small space (a 10-centimeters/side cube) to store 10^6 bits makes these devices very interesting for some computer applications.

Two more common shift register applications are mentioned here. First, essentially all computers possess an important register called the *accumulator* to which numbers may be added or other manipulations done. Various *shift-bits* or *rotate-bits* instructions are always available to manipulate the bits in this register and are clearly done with flip-flops in a shift register connection.

Another shift register application occurs in *serial data transmission.* Suppose 8-bit binary numbers are to be transmitted from one location to another. This may be accomplished by *parallel data transmission* over 8 parallel wires plus ground wire. A better approach for improved noise immunity is 8 pairs of twisted wires, one of each twisted pair being a ground wire. The least significant bit (LSB) appears on one pair, the next significant on another pair, and so forth.

Unfortunately, many wires are involved and parallel data transmission becomes expensive and cumbersome for long distances. Therefore, for distances greater than perhaps 10 meters, only a single pair of wires is generally used. The individual bits from a number must then be transmitted down the wire one after the other or in *serial.* Serial data transmission is usually done at a certain rate called the bit rate or *baud* that is agreed upon by the transmitter and the receiver. The familiar model 33 Teletype (registered trademark) communicates at 110 bits/second or 110 baud in a serial manner.

A shift register is useful in both the transmission and receiving process in serial communications. For transmission, the 8-bit number is generally loaded into a shift register by a parallel-load process. The shift register is then clocked at the specified bit rate, and the bit appearing at the shift register output is applied to the transmitting wire. When the bits appear at the receiver, they are clocked into a shift register and typically output from it in parallel mode when the complete number has been received. See Figure D4–18 for a diagram of the essential elements in the process.

This figure also illustrates a convention widely used to indicate the start of a transmission. The transmitting wire is maintained at logic 1 when no transmission is occurring. The transmitter transmits a single *start-bit* logic 0 to tell the receiver that a transmission is beginning. Immediately following, the 8 bits of the binary number or code (LSB first) are transmitted, followed by 2 *stop bits* that are 2 logic 1's. Notice that a total of 11 bits is

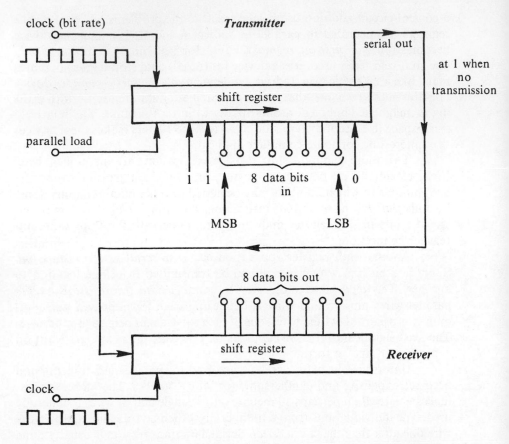

FIGURE D4-18. *Shift Registers for Transmission and Reception in Serial Data Communications*

transmitted for each bit group or *character*. If 10 characters are sent per second, the rate is 110 baud. Another bit group may then be transmitted immediately or after some arbitrary time interval. Because the time spacing between bit *group* transmissions is arbitrary, this approach is termed *asynchronous serial transmission*.

REVIEW EXERCISES

1. (a) Describe briefly what is meant by each word in the descriptive name: 3-bit asynchronous binary up counter.
   (b) Draw a circuit for a counter of the type named in (a) as constructed from typical TTL *JK* flip-flops. Include a clear capability.

(c) Explain why a counter constructed from TTL chips according to the circuit of (b) will probably function with the J,K inputs left unconnected. However, this is not considered good practice; explain why.

(d) The words *ripple-through* and *stage* could be substituted for certain words in the name of part (a); give the alternate name that uses these words.

2. (a) Why is the input clock presented in parallel to all of the flip-flop clock inputs in a synchronous counter?

(b) Describe the purpose of the gates that are used in addition to the JK flip-flops in a synchronous counter.

(c) Draw a circuit for a 3-bit synchronous binary up counter constructed from JK flip-flops.

(d) Draw a circuit for a 3-bit synchronous binary down counter constructed from JK flip-flops.

3. A computer may use a counter to input successive 16-bit binary numbers (for example, as memory addresses). Suppose the computer requires these numbers within a 200-nanosecond time interval after each clock pulse; describe the problem that results if an asynchronous counter were used to produce the binary numbers from the computer clock pulses. What type of counter is required here?

4. (a) Draw a circuit for a 3-stage asynchronous binary up counter as constructed from typical CMOS JK flip-flops (for example, 4027s or 4095s). What is the principal difference between this circuit and one constructed from TTL JK flip-flops such as the 7473 or 7476?·

(b) Can the counter be expected to operate if the J,K inputs to the CMOS flip-flops are left unconnected? Explain.

5. (a) What is the function or utility of a presettable counter?

(b) Diagram one stage of a design for a simple presettable counter that assumes clearing the stage before loading data.

6. (a) Describe what is meant by a modulo-5 counter

(b) What is meant by a BCD counter?

(c) Why are BCD counters useful for the construction of a laboratory scaler or counting instrument?

7. (a) Diagram a 3-decade counter that is constructed from BCD counter stages (these stages may be diagrammed as blocks). The output is then a mixture of binary and decimal; explain this statement.

(b) Explain how the counter achieves multidigit decimal counting.

8. Consider the two decimal digit modulo-N counter shown in Figure D4–11c. Suppose the digits are set up as 47_{10}. Describe the action of the 74192 presettable down counter that achieves 1 output pulse for every 47 input pulses. Explain carefully why an output pulse is not obtained for every $4 \times 7 = 28$ input pulses.

9. Describe the counting function of the 74192 synchronous presettable up/down decade counter that permits it to be cascadable.

10. (a) Explain why a BCD-to-decimal decoder chip is useful for the design of a decade counter or scaler that incorporates a numeric display.

(b) What is the difference between a BCD-to-decimal decoder chip and a BCD-to-decimal decoder/driver chip?

11. (a) Describe the similarity between a neon "glow" lamp or bulb and a Nixie (trademark) tube.
    (b) Why is it not possible for normal TTL logic to operate a Nixie tube directly?
12. Consider the LED-type 7-segment display.
    (a) Approximately what current is required to light a segment?
    (b) Tell why it is not permissible to connect 5 V directly to a segment.
    (c) What is the difference between a common-cathode display and a common-anode display? In each case, tell whether active-high or active-low decoder outputs are required.
13. Consider the liquid-crystal 7-segment display (LCD).
    (a) What is the function of the liquid crystal? Why does an LCD display appear more legible in bright light than in dim light?
    (b) Why is very little current required in the operation of an LCD display?
14. Describe what is meant by the term *multiplexed display*. What savings are possible through the use of a multiplexed display?
15. (a) Describe the general mode of operation of a shift register.
    (b) What is the difference between serial input and parallel input to a shift register?
    (c) Describe the utility of a shift register for serial data transmission.
    (d) Explain what is meant by a recirculating shift register.

PROBLEMS

1. The LSI CMOS 4020 asynchronous up counter is a 14-stage device. What is the top count attainable and also the number of states for this device?
2. Justify that connecting $\overline{Q}$ to the clock input of the next JK flip-flop in a multistage connection of such flip-flops produces a down counter. Develop a diagram of the Q and $\overline{Q}$ states as a function of time for a 3-stage counter and use it in your argument.
3. Design a 3-stage asynchronous up/down counter from JK flip-flops. This counter should have an up-count/down-count control that permits up counting when the control is high. Note that only 2-input gates are required in the design.
4. The up/down binary counter diagrammed in Figure D4-3 uses multiple-input AND gates where the number of inputs of an AND gate is related to the order of the associated stage; this scheme is sometimes called *parallel carry*. Design an up/down counter that only uses 2-input AND gates throughout; this scheme is sometimes called *series carry or ripple carry*. Describe how the maximum frequency of operation is limited in the latter design.
5. A building has a turnstile for incoming people and another turnstile for people leaving the building. Each turnstile produces a logic 1 pulse as output when a person passes through it. Design a 4-bit counter that shows the number of persons in the building at any time. This counter should have separate inputs for "count-up" pulses and for "count-down" pulses. Negative–edge-triggered JK

flip-flops may be assumed in the design (rather than pulse- or level-triggered types). The counter may be either synchronous or asynchronous.

6. The presettable counter diagrammed in Figure D4–4 requires a reset pulse prior to the load-data pulse. In this problem an improved preset scheme will be designed that requires only the load-data pulse. Direct-set (S_D) and direct-reset (R_D) are assumed that are active low, as is usual for the JK flip-flops of the counter.

(a) The inputs to the gate network for a given stage are called *data* and *load*. The data is to be loaded by the state logic 1 on the *load* line; data is to be positive logic. Write a truth table for the gating required to the S_D and R_D inputs, respectively:

Data	Load	S_D		Data	Load	R_D
0	0			0	0	
0	1			0	1	
1	0			1	0	
1	1			1	1	

(b) Write the Boolean algebra statement for the logic functions S_D and R_D, respectively, that follow from the truth tables of part (a).

(c) Deduce the logic-gate network required between the data and load inputs, and the S_D and R_D inputs of a flip-flop. Draw the circuit for a representative stage in the counter.

7. (a) Diagram a simple modulo-6 counter that exploits the direct-reset inputs of the flip-flop stages.

(b) What is the principal shortcoming with this simple design?

8. A count-by-3 counter is connected to a modulo-2 counter as shown in Diagram D4–1. Find the sequence of states for the A, B, C outputs. Show that the circuit is a modulo-6 counter (it has 6 states), but does not count in the normal binary sequence. Show that the output is a square wave with a frequency equal to 1/6 of the input frequency.

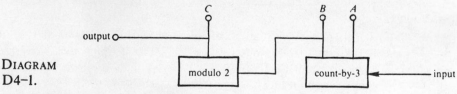

DIAGRAM
D4–1.

9. (a) Assume that a 60-Hz square wave is available (this might be derived from the 60-Hz power line frequency). Design a circuit from JK flip-flops that produces a 10-Hz square wave.

(b) Design a 0.1-second resolution 4-digit stopwatch; thus the readout of this stopwatch can be any value between 000.0 and 999.9 seconds. Two push buttons are on the device: (1) a reset push button that clears the readout, and (2) a start/stop push button that starts the counting process when it is pressed and stops the count when pressed again. Labeled boxes can be used for BCD counters and for BCD-to-7-segment decoder/drivers.

10. Suppose that the most significant bit from a modulo-5 counter that counts up in normal binary is input to a modulo-2 counter. Show that the output of the modulo-2 counter is a symmetrical square wave with frequency $f/10$, where f is the frequency of a pulse waveform that is input to the modulo-5 counter.

11. Diagram D4–2 illustrates an *attempt* to design a BCD counter; however, the dashed-line part of the circuit does not accomplish the goal.

    (a) First, plot Q_A, Q_B, Q_C, and Q_D as solid lines for the case of normal binary counting for the first 12 input pulses after a reset. Show by dashed lines in this plot how BCD counting deviates from binary counting. Also plot the function $Q_A \cdot Q_D$.

    (b) Argue that the clock input to FF-D does indeed produce the desired BCD counting behavior for Q_D.

    (c) Argue why the dashed-line circuit into FF-B *might* be expected to produce the desired BCD counting behavior for Q_B.

    (d) Explain why the dashed-line circuit in fact does *not* work reliably.
    NOTE: Consider the effect of propagation delays and the fact that J, K will change after the clock is high.

    (e) Think of a different connection to inhibit FF-B from toggling at the un-wanted time. (Only a single wire is required.)

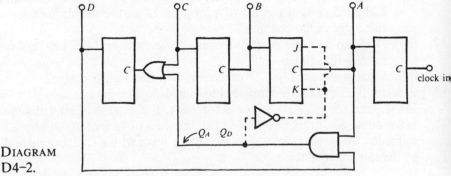

DIAGRAM
D4–2.

12. The logic diagram for a 7490 decade counter is shown. Outputs B, C, and D come from a count-by-5 counter, while in BD is the input to this counter.

    (a) To permit counting, $[R_{0(1)}$ OR $R_{0(2)}]$ AND $[R_{9(1)}$ OR $R_{9(2)}]$ must be low. Explain why in terms of circuit action (see Diagram D4–3).

    (b) To clear the counter to zero, $R_{0(1)}$ AND $R_{0(2)}$ must both be brought high. Explain why in terms of circuit action.

    (c) To obtain BCD counting, output A must be connected to in BD. Explain why.

    (d) What connection should be used to obtain as output a symmetrical square wave with a frequency that is $1/10$ the frequency of the input waveform. NOTE: Consider problem 10.

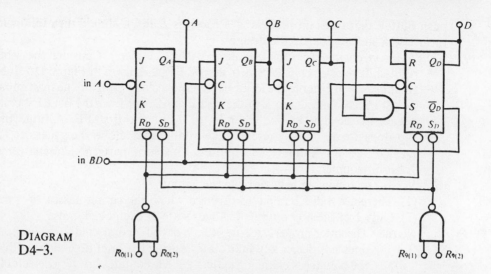

DIAGRAM
D4–3.

13. (a) Design an asynchronous binary up counter that counts from 0 up to 5 and then stops. A negative reset pulse to the counter permits it to repeat the cycle.

NOTE: A complete decoding of the top count is not necessary; refer, for example, to Figure D4–7.

(b) Design a circuit that permits 5 and only 5 pulses to pass through it after receiving a negative reset pulse that arms the circuit.

14. Design a variable-limit self-stopping 3-bit asynchronous binary up counter. The binary value of the state at which the counter stops is assumed to be present on 3 input lines to the device.

15. Design a 4-bit recirculating shift register. This circuit should possess 3 input lines: clock, recirculate-control, and new-data; and a single serial output line.

16. Describe why it is not possible to construct a shift register from data-latch flip-flops, even though this flip-flop type is clocked.

17. (a) Design a door lock based upon a shift register, suitable gates, a push-button SPDT switch, and a two-position SPDT switch. The bit pattern 10110010 must be loaded into the shift register before the lock opens. Assume an electromagnetic lock is available that opens in response to a TTL-high input. The bit pattern is to be entered by setting the switch to the proper successive bit values; each bit is entered by pressing the push button.

(b) Discuss how the lock code could readily be changed.

18. Three processes *A, B,* and *C* are to be operated in sequence by a controller that is to be designed in this problem. Each process is activated by a high level on its *control* line output from the controller; each process signals to the controller when it is complete by asserting a brief high level on its *process-complete* line into the controller. The controller therefore has 3 control output lines and 3 process-complete input lines. The controller has a *reset* push button that turns all processes off at any time when it is pressed; the controller also has a *start*

push button that turns on process A. Processes B and C should then follow in turn. Use a shift register in the design.

19. (a) *Johnson counter* (or ring counter, or shift counter). Consider the 4-bit right-shift register constructed from JK FFs as shown in Figure D4-16b. Suppose the inverter to the input FF is removed and Q_D from the right-most or last FF is connected to K of the first FF. Also $\overline{Q}_D$ from the last FF is connected to the data-in line (that is, to J) of the first FF. Assume the flip-flops are all initially reset. Make a table that shows the states of Q_A, Q_B, Q_C, Q_D for 8 input clock pulses. This state pattern characterizes a Johnson counter.

(b) Verify the following behavior for this circuit.

(1) There are 8 different states through which the circuit passes.

(2) Only 1 of the 4 Q outputs changes state at each clock pulse.

NOTE: The latter property assures that a decoder connected to the outputs does not detect any fake states during the brief time interval that the counter is changing states; these fake states are very detectable for a standard asynchronous counter (and may even be detected by a fast decoder to a synchronous counter).

(c) Design a decoder with 8 output lines for this Johnson counter. Only 1 of the 8 output lines should be high for each of the 8 states of the counter.

NOTE: Only 2-input AND gates are required.

CHAPTER
D5

Logic Family
Pulse Generation

The monostable multivibrator, astable multivibrator, Schmitt trigger, and voltage comparator were discussed in the first book in this series, *Analog Electronics for Scientific Application;* in particular the 555 timer was discussed for the multivibrator applications. These devices may also be used with digital logic ICs to produce appropriate pulses if the power supplies used are at the logic IC voltages. If a Schmitt trigger or comparator is constructed from op amps, the op-amp outputs must be clipped at 0 V and at +5 V with diodes to avoid damage to the logic IC inputs (some op amps have been designed to operate between 0 V and +5 V and then no clipping is needed).

In digital logic circuits there certainly are times when slowly varying or noisy signals must be *squared up* and the Schmitt trigger is desirable for this purpose. Furthermore, pulses of a duration different from those developed by the gates and flip-flops in a design may be needed; the monostable is useful here. Also, a square-wave oscillator may be needed to provide basic timing and, of course, the astable multivibrator is the solution. The 555 timer and op amp can provide these pulse forms, but not always at the speeds desired in logic-circuit applications. Thus, the 555 timer is recommended as an astable mutivibrator only up to 200 kilohertz. Further, the rise and fall times of a Schmitt trigger or voltage comparator constructed from an op amp are limited by the output voltage rate of change called the *slew rate* of the op amp; that is, the output will *not* change instantly, but at a rate of some volts/microsecond in response to a perfect step change at the op-amp input. This response is generally related to the gain-bandwidth product of the device; the higher the unity-gain frequency for the device, the faster its slew rate. It is reasonable that an amplifier having a top frequency of 1 megahertz would produce rather poorly defined 1-microsecond pulses.

For speed and voltage compatibility then, various pulse-generating circuits have been made available in the several logic families.

Voltage Comparator

The job of a *voltage comparator* is to produce a high voltage out for a positive voltage between its terminals, and a low voltage out for a corresponding negative voltage. Threshold detection is accomplished by putting a reference voltage to the − input and the signal on the other. This behavior of a voltage comparator was discussed in *Analog Electronics for Scientific Application.* If the − input is connected to ground, it is called a *zero-crossing detector.* The voltage comparator is essentially a medium-to-high-gain op amp designed for open-loop applications. However, a conventional op amp typically responds in some 10 microseconds to a step change at its input, which is slow for some applications as mentioned earlier.

Bob Widlar at Fairchild developed the μ710 monolithic IC comparator circa 1966 to answer this need. It uses a minimum of stages and an open-loop gain of about 1200 to achieve a response time of 40 nanoseconds. However, it operates with +12-V and −6-V supplies, which is inconvenient in TTL systems.

National introduced the LM111 (also 211 and 311, depending on temperature range) comparator in 1970 that can operate between a single +5-V supply and ground (see Figure D5−1a). The reference voltage, however, must then be *off* ground by 0.6 V or more; that is, the *common-mode range* does not include ground. For use as a true zero-crossing (voltage level) detector, it can be operated between +15 V and −15 V as shown in Figure D5−1b, although a resistance connected from the output to +5 V is necessary to clamp the output to +5 V for TTL use. Generally, the output should be connected through a resistor to some $V+$ in any case since the output is open collector. The output of the comparator then swings between $V+$ and nearly zero volts (or ground), even though a negative voltage is used for the $V−$ or low-potential connection (pin 4 of the LM311). The output can sink up to 50 milliamperes and switch voltages up to 40 V. Therefore it may operate lamps, relays, and the like. It has an open-loop voltage gain of 200,000 and a response time of 200 nanoseconds. There is also a *strobe* input; if the strobe terminal is connected to ground (for example, with a transistor as a switch), the output remains high regardless of the input (see Figure D5−1c). Thus, a TTL high to the base of the NPN transistor shown there turns on the transis-

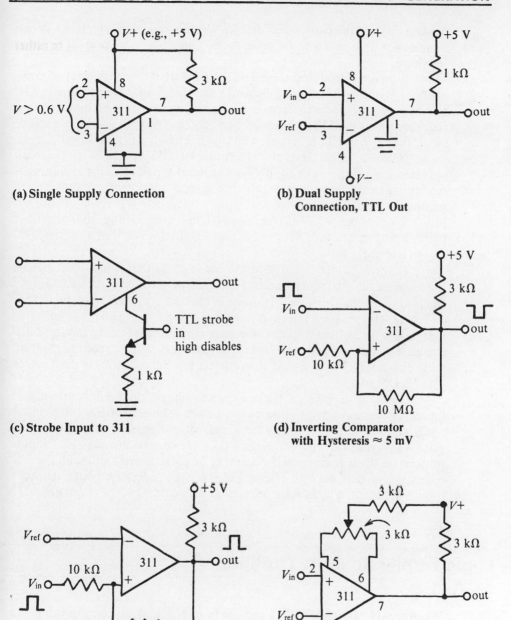

(a) Single Supply Connection

(b) Dual Supply Connection, TTL Out

(c) Strobe Input to 311

(d) Inverting Comparator with Hysteresis ≈ 5 mV

(e) Noninverting Comparator with Hysteresis ≈ 50 mV

(f) 311 with Offset Balance

FIGURE D5–1. *Various Connections with the LM111, 211, and 311 Comparators (Pin Numbers Given Are for the TO–5 Case.)*

tor and disables the comparator from responding to its inputs. If the strobe input is left unconnected, the comparator functions in its normal manner, of course.

Signetics introduced the NE521/NE522 dual comparator (two comparators in one package) using Schottky clamping diodes to give a very fast response time of 12 nanoseconds maximum, with the same input-current requirements as the 710. It operates between ±5-V supplies and has a strobe input; the 521 has a TTL output, while the 522 has an open-collector output.

National offers several comparators (LM339, LM2901) that can operate from a single +5-V supply (and ground) and have an input common-mode range that *includes* ground; that is, one input can be connected to ground as a reference voltage and proper operation will result. However, their response time of 1.3 microseconds is considerably slower than the other units already mentioned. They are actually quad devices; that is, 4 comparators in one package.

If the high-speed comparators are used to detect low-level signals (for example, signals from magnetic tape heads), operation in the linear region can lead to oscillation. Similarly, noise in the submillivolt range can produce switching. This problem can be avoided by arranging for perhaps 10-millivolt hysteresis with a positive feedback connection to the reference input, as discussed in connection with op amps in the *Analog Electronics* volume. Indeed, these comparators can be used to construct fast Schmitt trigger circuits (see Figures D5-1d and e).

Just as with op amps, the input offset voltage, input offset current, and input bias current are of importance. Offset voltage of a few millivolts is again typical. Similar to many op amps, offset balance connections often exist (see Figure D5-1f). The National LF311 comparator uses FET inputs to decrease the maximum bias current to 50 picoamperes, although the 0.1-microampere bias current of the LM311 is considerably better than the original 710 unit, which has a maximum bias current of 20 microamperes.

Logic Family Schmitt Triggers

When slowly varying signals are input to a logic gate, the output can make several transitions while the input is traversing the undefined region between low and high. For example, suppose a 60-hertz sinusoidal line signal is to be reduced to 10 hertz by sending it to a ÷6 flip-flop chain. Even if the signal is squared up using clipping diodes from an originally rather large signal (so that it appears on a scope to be a square wave with rather rapid rise and fall times), the output from the flip-flops will show erratic behavior.

There exist a number of TTL and MOS family ICs with *Schmitt trigger* inputs. The TTL units have a nominal 800-millivolt hysteresis; their

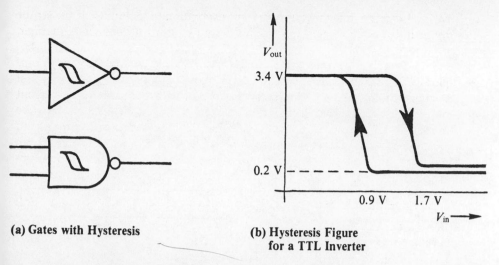

(a) Gates with Hysteresis

(b) Hysteresis Figure for a TTL Inverter

FIGURE D5–2. *Schmitt Trigger Input Gates*

positive-going threshold is typically 1.7 V, while the negative-going threshold is 0.9 V. These thresholds are *not* adjustable. Examples are the 7414 and the 4584 hex Schmitt trigger inverter ICs and the 74132 or 4093 devices, which contain four 2-input NAND gates with Schmitt trigger inputs to each.

Gates with Schmitt trigger inputs are commonly designated by a *hysteresis-loop* figure drawn within the symbol (see Figure D5–2a). This figure represents a plot of the output voltage as a function of the input voltage. Because of hysteresis it is a two-valued function (see Figure D5–2b).

For a larger hysteresis and also larger input-voltage range, the CMOS Schmitt trigger ICs (74C14, 4584, 4093) are useful. The supply voltage V_{CC} may range from 3 V to 15 V, and the typical hysteresis is 4/10 of the supply voltage. However, the thresholds again are *not* adjustable, and are typically at about 0.3 V_{CC} and 0.7 V_{CC}.

Logic Family Monostable Multivibrators

During the first few years of TTL ICs, there were no family monostables available. There were several techniques in common use then that may still be needed if the family monostables are not at hand, and one of these techniques is briefly mentioned here.

A pair of NAND gates with a resistor and capacitor forms a *mono-stable multivibrator* or MMV (see Figure D5–3). The input is to stand high. The resistor R between the input of gate 2 and ground pulls its input low so

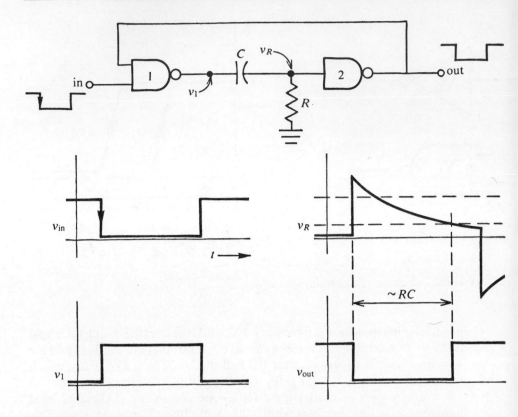

FIGURE D5–3. *Monostable Constructed from Two NANDs and an RC Filter*

that its output v_{out} is normally high. Then two highs to the input of gate 1 cause its output to be low. Consequently, there is normally no voltage across capacitor C; it is discharged. When a negative-going input pulse occurs, v_1 goes high and the capacitor C begins charging through R. This is the familiar high-pass filter or differentiating circuit. The voltage across R initially goes high, too, because the voltage across C cannot change instantaneously. Consequently, the output of gate 2 goes low immediately. As the capacitor charges, the voltage across R decreases exponentially until the voltage into gate 2 finally passes into the low region, and the output again goes high. Thus, a negative output pulse with duration of order RC is produced *if* the input pulse is longer than this value.

However, for versatility, temperature stability, and large pulse range, the IC monostables now available are much more desirable. The first and simplest is the *74121 single monostable*. The logic diagram for this device is given in Figure D5–4. Pin numbers for the IC are indicated in parentheses around the box. The actual monostable within the IC triggers on a positive-going transition at its input, as indicated in the figure. This transition can be

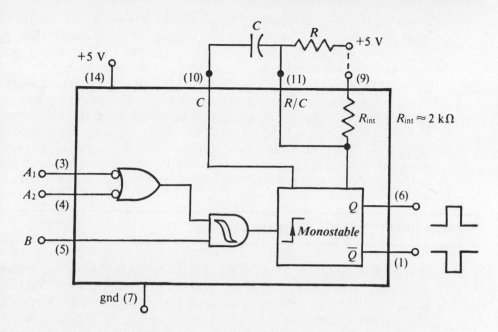

FIGURE D5–4. *Diagram of 74121 Monostable*

generated by manipulation of inputs A_1, A_2, and B according to the logic gates illustrated. Thus, if A_2 and B are held high, and A_1 makes a transition from high to low, a pulse is generated; in this way the monostable is negative-edge sensitive at the A_1 input. A_2 or B could be used as enabling inputs in that both must be high for pulses to be produced.

On the other hand, if A_1 OR A_2 are both held low and the B input makes a transition from low to high, a pulse is generated. Therefore, the B input is used if we desire to produce a pulse on the positive-going edge of a trigger pulse. Furthermore, the B input is a Schmitt trigger input with a nominal hysteresis of 0.2 V and operates with inputs having a rate of rise as slow as 1 V/second. The A inputs have no hysteresis, have a threshold of about 1.4 V, and should receive pulses with a rate of fall of 1 V/microsecond or faster.

Output pulse duration may be obtained in the range from 30 nanoseconds to 40 seconds by proper choice of R and C. The pulse duration is given by the formula

$$t \text{ pulse} = (\log_e 2)RC \tag{D5–1}$$

Values for R may range from 2 kilohms to 40 kilohms, while C can range from 10 picofarads to 10 microfarads. An internal resistance R_{int} of about 2 kilohms is available as illustrated in Figure D5–4. Then no external resistance is required, and pin 9 is connected to +5 V. If an external resistance is used, it is connected between pin 11 and +5 V as indicated, and pin 9 is not used. The input pulse to the 74121 monostable may be either longer or shorter than the output pulse (*not* true of the 555). If a second trigger pulse should occur during the time of an output pulse, it has no effect on the monostable.

There exists a *retriggerable monostable with clear*; for example, the 74122. The pulse from this monostable can be lengthened by applying another pulse to a trigger input during the time of an output pulse; it is *retriggered*. Furthermore, the output pulse can be terminated by applying a negative pulse to the clear input. The 74123 is similar to the 74122, but is a dual unit. Two monostables are available in one 16-pin DIP package in the case of the 74123, while the 74122 and 74121 are single monostables in 14-pin DIPs.

Some Monostable Applications

It is possible to obtain an *astable multivibrator* (AMV) from two mono-stables. In particular, the 555 timer cannot be used above about 200 kilo-hertz, while the TTL monostables can be used with periods as short as 30 nanoseconds so that astables with frequencies up to 10 megahertz can be constructed. Simply cross-connect two monostables as shown in Figure D5-5.

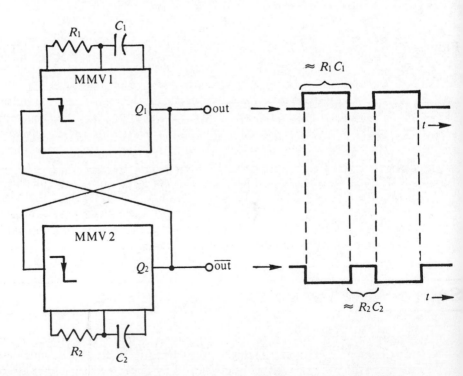

FIGURE D5-5. *Construction of Astable MV from Two Monostable MVs*

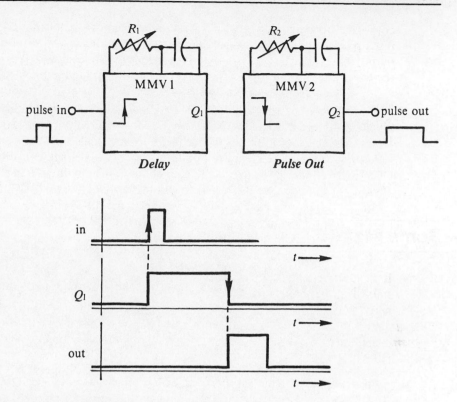

FIGURE D5–6. *Construction of a Delayed-Pulse Generator from Two MMVs*

Another design problem that can arise is how to obtain a pulse of a certain duration that is delayed by a certain amount from the occurrence of an input pulse. It may be desired that both the time delay and the output pulse duration be adjustable. This can be accomplished with two monostables that have adjustable durations; for example, through potentiometers as timing resistors (see Figure D5–6). Here MMV 1 triggers on the incoming pulse and produces a pulse of adjustable duration. The *trailing* edge of the MMV 1 pulse is used to trigger MMV 2, which then produces the delayed pulse. Notice that the pulse edge that causes triggering of each monostable is indicated by an upward or downward arrow on the monostable.

Square-Wave Oscillators

Digital circuitry often requires a square-wave signal for purposes of timing or clocking. This clock signal generally determines the rate at which events occur in the circuit and must be developed by some type of square-wave oscillator. It has been mentioned that the 555 timer is suitable for frequencies lower than 200 kilohertz. For high frequency requirements, an astable constructed from two monostable multivibrators can be used.

However, several integrated circuits have been developed that are convenient to use at higher frequencies. One such chip is the 74LS124/74S124 device, which contains two *voltage-controlled oscillators* or VCOs. The output frequency of each VCO is established by a single external component—either a capacitor or a crystal—in combination with two voltage-sensitive inputs; one input is for frequency range, while the other can be used to vary the output frequency to obtain VCO action. (Voltage-controlled oscillators are discussed further in the next chapter.) The output frequency of an oscillator can be selected from as low as 0.2 hertz to as high as 30 megahertz for the 'LS124, and as high as 85 megahertz for the 'S124.

For timing purposes, an oscillator with rather good frequency stability is often required. Oscillators that are based on a resistor-capacitor (*RC*) circuit or on an inductor-capacitor (*LC*) circuit can be stable to perhaps 1 part in 10^3. For better performance, the very stable resonant mechanical oscillation of a thin slab of quartz crystal is commonly exploited. Since quartz is piezoelectric, it is possible to couple this oscillation to electronic circuitry. *Quartz crystal oscillators* with a stability of 1 part of 10^6 are readily achieved. Crystals can be purchased that operate at a specific frequency from about 10 kilohertz to about 20 megahertz; use of an *overtone mode* permits crystals that operate up to about 200 megahertz. We have mentioned that the 74LS124/74S124 chip can be used with a quartz crystal. The ICM7209 is a CMOS clock generator chip from Intersil that operates up to 10 megahertz with a quartz crystal. Besides a buffered oscillator output, the ICM7209 has a ÷8 output. A third possibility will be mentioned: the 8224 clock generator and driver from Intel. This chip is crystal controlled and is intended for use with the 8080 microprocessor. It is widely available and may also be exploited as a TTL-compatible oscillator.

REVIEW EXERCISES

1. Describe the basic function or behavior of a comparator.
2. What is the principal reason for using an actual comparator device (such as the LM311) rather than a comparator based on an op amp?
3. (a) What is meant by the term *zero-crossing detector*?
   (b) What power supply arrangement is required in order to operate the LM311 as a true zero-crossing detector?
4. Why is a positive feedback connection desirable if a comparator is used to detect low-level or noisy signals?
5. What does the hysteresis-loop figure signify when drawn within a gate symbol?
6. (a) What determines the duration of the pulse from a 74121 monostable?
   (b) The shortest pulse width attainable is about: A. 40 nanoseconds, B. 40 microseconds, C. 40 milliseconds, D. 40 seconds.

(c) The largest pulse width attainable is about: A. 40 milliseconds, B. 40 seconds, C. 40 minutes, D. 40 hours.

7. Describe how the 74122 retriggerable monostable differs in its operating function from the 74121 monostable.

8. Describe in general terms how the 74123 dual monostable chip can be used to construct a square-wave oscillator.

9. (a) What is the "crystal" in a crystal-based oscillator?

   (b) Give typical frequency stabilities for an oscillator based on an RC time constant and on a crystal, respectively.

PROBLEMS

1. Describe how an LM311 can be used to produce a square wave with the same frequency as a given sine wave. Is the square wave unipolar or bipolar in voltage?

2. (a) Justify the fact that the circuit of Figure D5–1d is an inverting comparator, while the circuit of Figure D5–1e is a noninverting comparator.

   (b) Suppose V_{ref} in Figure D5–1d is connected to ground. Find the two threshold voltages for V_{in}.

3. (a) Suppose one terminal from the secondary of a transformer is connected to ground and the other terminal is connected to the clock input of a TTL decade counter such as the 7490. The secondary voltage is 3 V_{rms}. Describe why the TTL chip may be damaged.

   (b) To prevent the problem of part (a), a 1N914 diode is connected between the secondary terminal and the TTL input, and 500 Ω between input and ground. Justify that a half-wave rectified waveform develops at the TTL input.

   (c) However, the output of the counter can be expected to be erratic for the circuit of part (b). Explain why.

   (d) Describe how a 7414 chip can be used to correct the problem of part (c).

4. Refer to the 74121 input labels shown in Figure D5–4.

   (a) Suppose A_1 and B are high. The monostable will generate an output pulse if: A. A_2 goes low to high, B. A_2 goes high to low, C. neither, as it is inhibited.

   (b) Suppose A_1 is held low while B is high. The monostable will generate an output pulse if: A. A_2 goes low to high, B. A_2 goes high to low, C. neither, as it is inhibited.

   (c) Suppose A_1 is low while B is low. The monostable will generate a pulse if: A. B goes low to high, B. B goes high to low, C. neither, as it is inhibited.

   (d) Suppose A_2 is high while B is low. The monostable will generate an output pulse if: A. A_1 goes low to high, B. A_1 goes high to low, C. neither, as it is inhibited.

   (e) Which input(s) are Schmitt trigger types? A. A_1, B. A_2, C. B, D. none.

5. Design a circuit using the 74121 that produces an output pulse of 20-microsecond duration for each input pulse. The output pulse should begin as the input pulse moves from high to low. Use only a capacitor in addition to the 74121 chip.

6. Design a 50-kilohertz symmetrical square-wave oscillator that uses 74121 monostables. Only capacitors are to be used besides the monostables.

7. Design a circuit that converts a 100-hertz sinusoidal wave into a series of TTL-level positive pulses, one per cycle. Each pulse is to be 100 microseconds in duration. The sinusoidal wave is 20 V_{p-p}.

8. *Pulsed nuclear magnetic resonance* (PNMR) requires a two-pulse sequence for one type of measurement. The pulse generator for this sequence should produce two pulses, each of duration t_1. The second pulse should be delayed by a time t_2 from the beginning of the first pulse. The pulse pair should repeat in a time interval t_3. All three time intervals (t_1, t_2, and t_3) should be individually adjustable. Design a circuit based on 74121 monostables that accomplishes the task. Resistor and capacitor values need not be specified. Justify briefly the operation of the circuit.

NOTE: The waveform is a *repeating* two-pulse sequence.

CHAPTER
D6

Digital Instruments

This chapter deals with a number of basic digital instruments and elements useful in digital instrumentation. A common theme and justification for digital instrumentation is the high degree of accuracy made possible by presentation of a result in digital form, rather than as an analog needle position along a scale. In the past, precision measurements typically required some balancing technique in association with the turning of a dial for each digit. This is a slow process, and one certainly not applicable to high-speed measurements of transient signals or to automatic precision measurements.

igital Counting and Scaling Instruments

Perhaps one of the first laboratory instruments that gave a digital readout of a measured quantity was the frequency meter. Flip-flops connected in BCD mode made possible a multiple-digit indicating device in the 1930s. However, the vacuum tube version was bulky (about 1 meter^3), heavy (about 50 pounds or 20 kilos), and expensive (about \$3,000). The revolution in size and price that occurred first with transistors and then with integrated circuits in just ten short years from 1960 to 1970 is amazing. The size of a frequency meter now is about that of a textbook and the price approaches \$100.

Geiger Counter

Closely related to the frequency counter in terms of circuitry is the *Geiger counter with scaler*. It dates from the same era as the frequency counter and is a good first illustration. The Geiger counter detects nuclear particles or high-energy photons that pass through the active volume of a Geiger tube. It is, in fact, essentially an events counter. Figure D6–1 shows the basic elements of a Geiger counter/scaler. The typical Geiger tube consists of a metal cylinder as a cathode and a wire down the center as the anode. The space between is filled with a gas (often helium) and a voltage on the order of 1,000 V is applied between the electrodes. Note that a resistance R is in series with the tube. When an ionizing particle moves through the tube, the high voltage causes ion motion between electrodes, and ion collisions produce more ions so that *avalanche breakdown* occurs. The surge of current through the resistance R drops the voltage across the tube and tends to quench the current. Furthermore, a *quench gas* is typically mixed with the helium in the tube in order to absorb energy from the charge avalanche and stop it.

The negative voltage spike that occurs across the Geiger tube constitutes a pulse that may be detected and counted. To avoid counting noise fluctuations, a Schmitt trigger typically receives the pulses from the Geiger

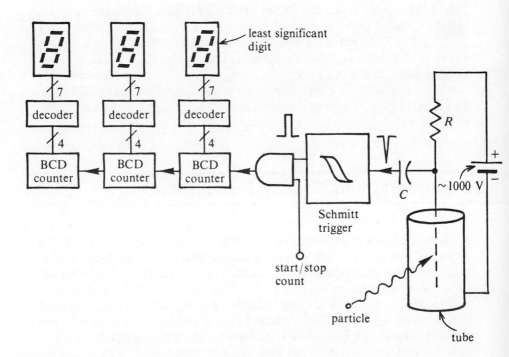

FIGURE D6–1. *Basic Geiger Tube with Scaler*

counter (through a blocking capacitor). The output from the Schmitt trigger is then passed to a counting or *scaling* circuit that counts the number of pulses and thus the particles that activate the Geiger tube. The counting is typically done for a specific period, and this count period can be determined by a start/ stop control as shown in Figure D6–1. During the time that this control is high, the BCD units count input pulses and the digital readout changes accordingly. This circuit is essentially that of Figure D4–10, along with the connection of decoders and display units as discussed at the end of Chapter D4. Notice the use of a slash through the single line leading from a BCD counter to a decoder. Again, this indicates that in fact several lines are depicted by the line; the 4 next to the slash tells that 4 lines (for the BCD code for one digit) are involved. The 7-segment display in turn receives 7 lines from a decoder, as indicated by that slash line for each display.

Frequency Meter

The basic *frequency meter* or counter has already been indicated in Figure D4–10 of Chapter D4. A count-enable input enables counting for a precise time interval—for example, for 1 second—and the counter then receives pulses at the unknown frequency for this time and counts them. The time period for which counting is enabled is often referred to as the *gate time* for the frequency counter. Notice that the AND gate of Figure D4–10 opens to pass through the pulses of unknown frequency during the gate-time interval. The display of Figure D4–10 counts rapidly during this period and, at the end of the period, displays the unknown frequency in hertz (if the counter had been cleared before counting). If the gate time is 1/1000 second, the display shows the frequency in kilohertz, and so on.

The original signal might have a rather arbitrary waveform that does not conform to logic levels. In this case, the waveform is amplified or attenuated first and then sent to a Schmitt trigger for reconstruction into neat logic-level pulses before presentation to the actual counter circuit (see Figure D6–2).

It is usually desirable that the frequency meter sample the unknown waveform rather continually and put each new measurement up on the display. The device then may be called an *automatically recycling frequency meter*. Early counters counted for 1 second (during which the display was changing), then stopped counting and held the display for some delay time so that it could be read, and finally cleared the counter and began counting again. But a more time-efficient scheme is to hold the display reading at the previous count while the next count is taking place; the delay period can then be shorter. This scheme requires use of a memory for each digit in order to hold constant the number being input to the decoder. The data latch is well suited to this purpose, using 4 latches for each BCD number.

Figure D6–2a illustrates a circuit design for an automatically recycling frequency meter with latched displays. Notice that a *crystal time base*—that is,

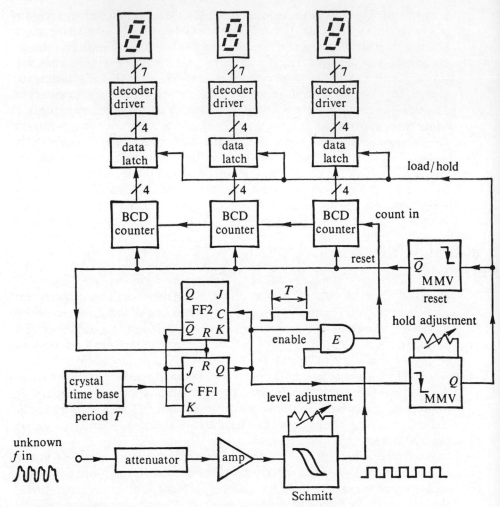

(a) Circuit Design

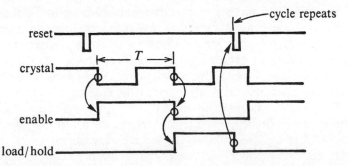

(b) Circuit Waveforms

FIGURE D6-2.   *Recycling Frequency Meter with Stable Display*

a crystal oscillator with some flip-flop divide chain—generates an accurate square wave with period T; typically, T may be selected as 10 seconds, 1 second, 0.1 second, 0.01 second, and so forth. FFs 1 and 2 constitute a *single-pulse-only* gate (see Chapter D3). If FFs 1 and 2 have been reset, they will produce a *single* enable pulse of duration T, which becomes the gate time for the frequency meter. This pulse enables the squared-up unknown frequency to the BCD counter chain in the meter, and the number of pulses occurring in T (for example, in 1 second) is counted (refer to Figure D6-2b for important circuit waveforms). The falling edge of the enable pulse triggers the load/hold monostable that clocks or loads the BCD numbers into corresponding latches; the displays change at this point. The falling edge of the load/hold pulse triggers a short reset-monostable pulse that clears the BCD counters and resets FF1 and FF2 so that the count cycle may be repeated. Notice that the load/hold MMV has an adjustable duration so that we can control how long the display *holds* the last measurement before it displays another one.

Period Meter

For low frequencies a *period meter* that measures the period of a waveform can produce many significant digits much more quickly than can a frequency meter. For example, a 10-second gate used with an unknown frequency of 9 hertz gives only 2 significant digits, but requires 10 seconds to accomplish with a frequency meter.

The circuit required is simply that of Figure D6-2a, except that the unknown frequency (from the Schmitt trigger output) is sent to the pair of FFs to generate the enable pulse with (unknown) period T (see Figure D6-3). Also, the crystal time base is set to some rather high frequency—let us assume 1 megahertz—and sent through the enabling AND gate E to the counter. Therefore the number of 1-microsecond pulses occurring in the period T of the pulse will be counted, and the display shows the period of the waveform in microseconds. For example, if the unknown signal is at 9 hertz, the display counts to 111,111 (representing the 111,111-microsecond period), giving a 6-significant-digit measurement in only 0.1 second.

Versatile frequency counters possess switch selection of either the frequency or the period measurement mode within the same instrument. Furthermore, it is often possible in period mode to select the average of 10, 100, 1,000, or 10,000 periods. Finally, it is usually possible to use the counter in a simple *events-counting mode*; then the basic circuitry within the counter corresponding to the scaler in Figure D6-1 is utilized.

Digital-to-Analog Conversion: The DAC

There are a number of situations where we want a box that produces a voltage or perhaps a current output that is proportional to some number presented to the input. Therefore, a conversion is made from the digital domain to the con-

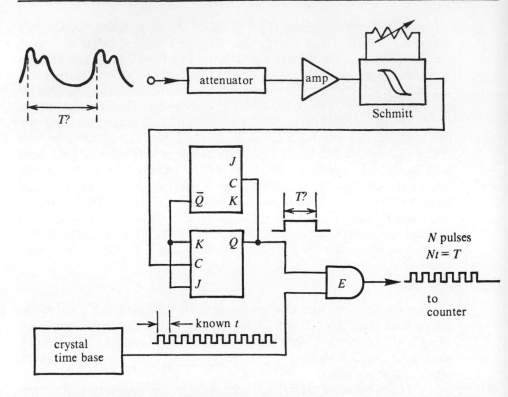

FIGURE D6–3. *Time-Base and Unknown-Period Connections for a Period Meter*

tinuous or analog domain of voltage or current; the device is called a *digital-to-analog converter,* D/A converter, or simply DAC. Typically the input numbers are in binary, and Figure D6–4a illustrates the situation.

Such devices are available from companies such as Analog Devices, Datel Systems Inc., Burr-Brown, and Teledyne Philbrick as compact *modules,* and recently as *monolithic*—that is, all on one chip—integrated circuits from some of these same manufacturers, as well as the large IC houses; for example, Motorola and National. Therefore, we can readily use them as building blocks in a design and the need to design a DAC is now rare. Nevertheless, it is useful and interesting to consider a basic scheme for construction of a DAC from an op amp.

Thus suppose the smallest increment of voltage out is to be 0.1 V as illustrated in Figure D6–4a. Notice that whenever the 2^0 bit is on, 0.1 V is added to the voltage out, while the 2^1 bit adds 0.2 V, the 2^2 adds 0.4 V, and so on. The number 0101 produces 0.4 V + 0.1 V = 0.5 V out. The essential notions involve the evaluation of a binary number as a weighted sum and the use of a summing amplifier to accomplish this feat. In general let $n_3 n_2 n_1 n_0$ be

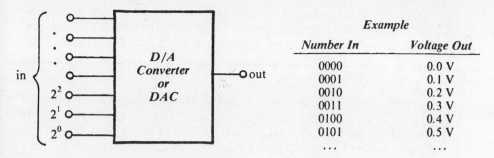

Example	
Number In	*Voltage Out*
0000	0.0 V
0001	0.1 V
0010	0.2 V
0011	0.3 V
0100	0.4 V
0101	0.5 V
...	...

(a) The D/A Converter Module and Operation

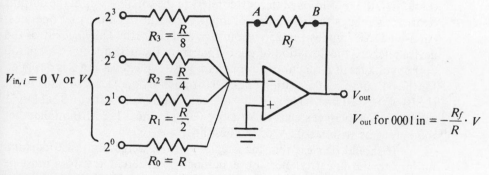

(b) Simple Implementation

FIGURE D6–4. *Digital-to-Analog (D/A) Converter Concept and a Simple Implementation*

a binary number so that n_i can only be 0 or 1 and represent the successive digits. The value of this number is given by

$$n_3n_2n_1n_0 = n_32^3 + n_22^2 + n_12^1 + n_02^0$$
$$= n_38 + n_24 + n_12 + n_01 \qquad \text{(D6–1)}$$

Thus, for the number 1011 we get the value $8 + 2 + 1$.

What is required is a summing amplifier where the input *weighting* resistors are in the ratio of the weights of the successive binary places, as illustrated in Figure D6–4b. The input voltages should be just 0 V or V (volts), depending on the state of the particular input bit.

Example: Suppose $R_f = 80$ k$\Omega/5$ while $R = 800$ kΩ. Then $R_0 = 800$ kΩ, $R_1 = 400$ kΩ, $R_2 = 200$ kΩ, $R_3 = 100$ kΩ, and so on. Let the input voltages operate as 0 V for binary 0 and 5 V for binary 1. The output voltage for 0001 input is $-(80\,k\Omega/5)5\,V/800\,k\Omega = -0.1\,V$; the output voltage for 0010 input is $-(80\,k\Omega/5)5\,V/400\,k\Omega = 0.2\,V$; the output voltage for 0011 input is $-0.1\,V - 0.2\,V = -0.3\,V$, and so on.

We notice that the output voltage is negative, but this voltage could be inverted by another op-amp stage. Also notice that if a current output rather than voltage output is desired, the output may be taken between B and A in Figure D6–4b. Then point A is virtually at ground, although not exactly at ground; the point B acts as a current *sink* for positive input voltages.

There are several performance characteristics of DACs that are of concern. First, the *resolution* of the device refers to the smallest step at the output; clearly this relates to the number of input bits with which the unit operates. An 8-bit DAC implies 1 in 256 resolution, and so forth. The *linearity* of the device refers to the deviation of the output from the best line fit to all of the output voltages as a function of input numbers. Typically a DAC is designed for the output to remain within one-half (or possibly one) least significant bit (LSB) of the best line. That is, if the full-scale output is 10 V for an 8-bit DAC, the theoretical perfect step is $10\,V/255 = 0.039\,V$ and $\pm 1/2$ LSB implies that the output be within 0.02 V of the best line.

It should be clear that the accuracy of the weighting resistors is important to the linearity. Because a number of different resistors must be accurately specified in the simple design of Figure D6–4b, this is usually *not* the technique of commercial choice. A common technique is to use an *R-2R ladder network* wherein there are only two resistor values: R and $2R$. This network is left to the problems for consideration.

The *accuracy* of a DAC converter refers to the precision with which the best fit line matches a specified case; in particular, whether the full-scale output differs by a certain percentage from a certain value (for example, 10 V). DACs typically operate with logic-level inputs (which are rather variable) and require a reference to achieve a specific accuracy. Some DACs actually possess this reference internally, and this type of DAC can be specified to have a certain inherent accuracy. However, often the full-scale value of a commercial DAC is adjustable by means of the amount of current (or perhaps voltage) that is input to some *reference input*. In those cases the accuracy of the device depends largely on the stability and accuracy of adjustment of this reference. Generally, the output of the DAC is directly proportional to the value of the reference input. At times this analog adjustability can be a desirable feature. The device is then called a *multiplying D/A converter* because the output depends on the product of the binary input number and the reference current (or voltage).

The *settling time* of a DAC is also an important characteristic. This is the time delay between establishment of an input number and the settling down of the output to within some amount (generally $\pm 1/2$ LSB) of the final output value. In general, a DAC with current-mode output settles more quickly than one with voltage output. The slew rate of the incorporated op amp is a determining factor in the latter case.

DAC ICs

To give some idea of real-world DACs, a few specific devices are mentioned here. The Motorola MC3408 is a low-cost DAC, available in a 16-pin plastic DIP package for about $3. A very similar part is the MC1408, also available as the SSS1408A from Precision Monolithics, Inc. (PMI). Direct replacement devices for the MC3408 are the DAC0808 from National Semiconductor and the AD559 from Analog Devices. They use a current-mode output $I_{out} \propto N_{in}$ that sinks current; however, this output can be changed to a (negative) voltage output by connecting a resistor between the output pin and ground. The output of the MC3408 is continuously sensitive to whatever binary number is presented to the chip's input lines, with an output settling time of 300 nanoseconds. It is specified to have a nonlinearity of 0.5%. (The MC1408, SSS1408A-8, and AD559 are specified to 0.19% nonlinearity, or 1/2 LSB.) The output current is proportional to a reference-input current; therefore the 1408-type DAC is, in fact, a multiplying DAC. The reference current must generally be trimmed to achieve a certain full-scale output. It can be supplied through a simple connection of a resistor to a fixed voltage. The MC3410 is a 10-bit DAC with 0.05% nonlinearity, but other operational features are similar to the MC3408/1408. These devices use standard supply voltages of +5 V and -15 V. As may be expected, the digital inputs are TTL and CMOS compatible.

The rather low-cost AD558JN was announced in 1980 for about $8 as a 16-pin plastic DIP IC from Analog Devices and provides interesting features to contrast with the MC3408. It is also an 8-bit DAC, with ±1/2-LSB specified relative accuracy. This device presents a voltage output and uses an internal voltage reference. Thus the output has a specified *absolute* accuracy of ±1-1/2 LSB, with a settling time of about 2 microseconds. No external components are required for its operation; a single supply voltage of 5 to 15 V is required. The full-scale output voltage can be selected to be 2.5 V or 10 V (the supply voltage must be more than 12 V for the latter). Furthermore, its digital input is latched, so that the binary input number may be changing at times other than the instant of clocking. This feature permits the AD558 to be connected directly to microprocessor data lines without the expense of an I/O port. (Microprocessor interfacing is discussed in the next chapters.)

Plotting or Graphing by Computer

An important application of DACs is in the generation of a picture on a scope or an *X-Y* plotter by a computer. Thus the PDP-8/E laboratory computer system (lab 8E) includes a pair of 10-bit DACs in the *VC 8-E point-plot display control* that may be operated by the computer. A 10-bit *D*-flip-flop data register (or data buffer) holds the number for each DAC and may be loaded with a binary number from the computer's accumulator by an appropriate output command in the computer's program (see Figure D6–5a). The analog voltage output from the *Y*-axis DAC is connected to the vertical input of the scope to control the vertical position of the spot on the cathode-ray tube or CRT. The *X*-axis DAC is connected to the horizontal input (*not* to external trigger) to control the horizontal position of the spot. The horizontal time-base control must then be set to disable the sweep sawtooth and enable the horizontal input jack to the horizontal deflection plates.

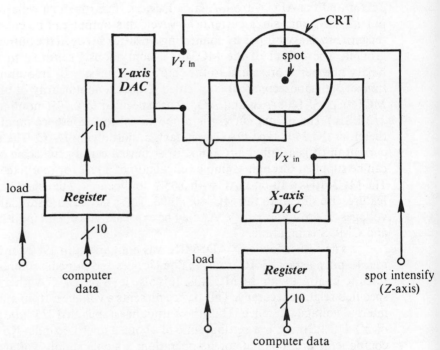

(a) Point-Plot Control to CRT

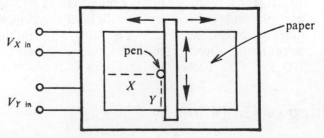

(b) Point-Plot Control to *X-Y* Plotter

FIGURE D6–5. *Use of DACs to Produce Graphic Output from Computers*

After a pair of numbers X, Y are output to the DACs by the computer, the CRT spot moves to corresponding coordinates on the scope face. A third *Z-axis* control from the computer to the intensity control grid of the CRT can then brighten or intensify the spot at the point. A succession of points can be output by the computer to the scope to produce a pattern of spots corresponding to a graph, characters, or whatever. In this way the computer "draws a picture" on the CRT. Alternatively, the DACs may input to an *X-Y* plotter that moves a pen in two dimensions over a sheet of paper (see Figure D6–5b). If the successive points are chosen close together, curves and graphs of high quality can be generated; thus the use of the term *point plot.*

When multiplying DACs are used, however, it is even possible to cause smooth straight-line segments to be drawn between points on a CRT or *X, Y* plotter. We then speak of *vector generation capability,* and this approach is often available on a *graphics display terminal.* Notice that in all of the CRT approaches discussed, the computer must continuously retrace the points or vectors because the image soon fades away. However, for complex displays of the type often generated on graphics displays, a *storage CRT* is often used. This special CRT type retains a bright picture for hours after the trace is produced only once, so the computer has more time to do other things. Indeed, *storage oscilloscopes* are often used in the laboratory to study rapid transient voltage waveforms that are produced only once or occasionally.

Voltage-to-Frequency Conversion: The VFC

There are a number of situations in which we desire a box that takes an analog voltage as input and produces a waveform with some frequency that is proportional to the input voltage. For example, one application is the production of electronic or computer-controlled music. Such a device is termed a *voltage-to-frequency converter,* V/F converter, or VFC. Since in fact an input voltage controls the frequency output by an oscillator, an alternate name for the VFC is *voltage-controlled oscillator* or VCO. VFCs are capable of good linearity— typically 0.002% to 0.05%—and excellent temperature stability. Just a few years ago, they were generally expensive, rack-mounted instruments; since about 1970, however, they have been available in compact *modules* about the size of a pack of cigarettes from the same manufacturers listed earlier for DACs. The 1980 price for these units is in the range of $30 to $50. Monolithic IC forms of the VFC are also beginning to appear; for example, the Raytheon RC4151 is a monolithic device that boasts 0.15% linearity and 100 parts per million/°C temperature stability at a 1980 price of $4. Therefore these devices become cost effective in more situations than previously possible. The RC4153 is a more recent device with tighter specifications; it has 0.01% linearity to a top frequency of 250 kilohertz.

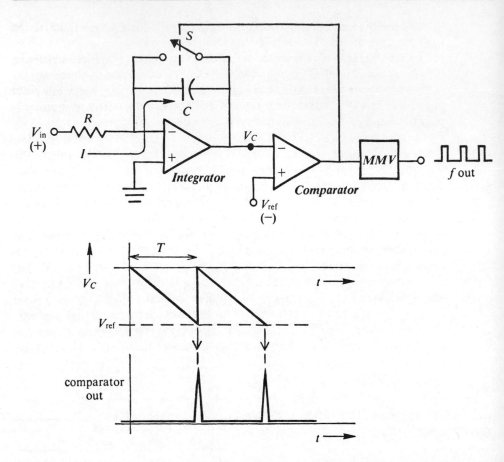

FIGURE D6–6. *Circuit and Operating Waveforms for a Simple Voltage-to-Frequency Converter Design*

It is useful to consider a simple VFC design as pictured in Figure D6–6. An op-amp integrating circuit is used to obtain a negative-going ramp at V_C in response to a dc V_{in}. The capacitor voltage at a time t is given by

$$V_C = \frac{-Q}{C} = \frac{-It}{C} = \frac{-V_{in}t}{RC} \qquad \text{(D6–2)}$$

When this voltage reaches V_{ref}, the comparator goes high and closes an electronic switch S (for example, a CMOS bilateral switch) that discharges the capacitor. The cycle then repeats. Pulses from the comparator therefore occur with a period T determined by $V_{ref} = V_C = V_{in}T/(RC)$, or a frequency

$$f = \frac{1}{T} = \frac{V_{in}}{V_{ref}RC} \qquad \text{(D6–3)}$$

We see that the frequency of the output-pulse waveform is proportional to the input voltage V_{in}.

The linearity of this circuit is limited at low voltage and frequencies by the leakage of C and at high frequencies by the discharge time of C through the electronic switch S. More sophisticated designs are usually used, but since both module VFCs and monolithic VFCs are quite inexpensive, it is unlikely that a contemporary scientist would build one.

The VFC modules available typically operate linearly from zero frequency to 10 kilohertz or to 100 kilohertz, depending on the price. The RC4151 operates to 100 kilohertz. For limited frequency range applications, the Signetics/National 566 voltage-controlled oscillator exists (in their linear IC line) for under $2. This unit can change frequency by a factor of 10 as the input voltage changes by 3 V (from the supply voltage V_{CC} to $V_{CC} - 3$ V). The output waveform is available both as square-wave and triangle shapes. The maximum operating frequency is about 1 megahertz, and the operating frequency range is selected by external R and C. A related device is the XR-205 monolithic (IC) waveform generator available since 1972 from EXAR. This device also has a 10-to-1 voltage-controlled frequency range and has 6 types of waveforms available; it is intended for inexpensive waveform generation.

As a final remark in this section, it should be mentioned that frequency-to-voltage converters also exist. Indeed, the RC4151 or RC4153 can also be operated in this mode. If the output is connected to a d'Arsonval meter, the result is an analog frequency meter.

Analog-to-Digital Conversion: The ADC

An important aspect of scientific experimentation is generally the measurement of some electrical quantity over a continuous range. As mentioned earlier, obtaining rapid high-precision measurement involves converting from the analog to the digital domain. If automatic computation and manipulation of the experimental data is to be accomplished by a minicomputer or microcomputer, this conversion is a necessity. Therefore, a box that accepts an analog electrical quantity (voltage or current) as input and produces a proportional number as output is very desirable. Such a device is called an *analog-to-digital converter,* A/D converter, or simply ADC. It is at the heart of the digital voltmeter or DVM, which has become commonplace in laboratories.

VFC-Based ADC

An obvious way to achieve an ADC is to connect together two devices that have already been discussed in this chapter: Connect the output of a VFC to a frequency meter (see Figure D6-7). For purposes of illustration, assume that

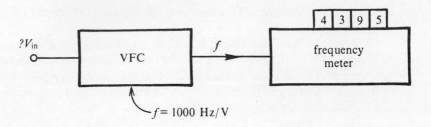

FIGURE D6-7. *Analog-to-Digital Conversion Using a VFC and Frequency Meter*

the VFC output is 1,000 hertz for 1-V input, 2,000 hertz for 2-V input, and so on. A frequency meter reading of 4,395 hertz clearly implies that the input voltage is 4.395 V.

The gate time required in the meter to achieve this count is 1 second. Therefore, the *A/D conversion time*—that is, the time required to obtain a voltage measurement—is 1 second for an accuracy of 1 part in 9,999 or 0.01%. A 0.1% measurement could be obtained with a 0.1-second gate time. This speed of conversion would be quite satisfactory for a DVM, which is read by humans, but is rather slow for high-speed applications. Nevertheless, if the voltage to be measured is at some distance from the readout (*remote data monitoring*), the VFC-based technique can be desirable because only one pair of wires need be used to communicate the pulse train from the VFC to the frequency counter. We may say that the VFC basically has serial output. Further, it is useful to notice that it is easy to isolate the VFC from the counter electrically, a procedure that may be necessary in some situations. An *optical isolator* can be used. These devices receive electrical pulses (from the VFC in this case) as input to an LED, and the light pulses from the LED are detected by an electrically separate photoresistor/transistor that regenerates the pulses again. These output pulses can be input to the counter.

Staircase-Ramp ADC

Another ADC technique (which often occurs to students after having studied the digital-to-analog converter and the comparator) is one in which the count outputs of a binary counter are connected to the input of a DAC; the counter proceeds to count up from zero due to an input pulse-train. The output of the DAC as a function of time is then a *staircase ramp* as pictured in Figure D6-8. The DAC output and the unknown voltage V_{in} are applied to a comparator. When the staircase voltage exceeds V_{in} slightly, the comparator causes the counter to stop counting so that the counter output tells the number of steps required to reach the unknown voltage. Suppose that the step size is 0.01 V and the counter reads 436 after stopping; the input voltage is then between 4.35 V and 4.36 V.

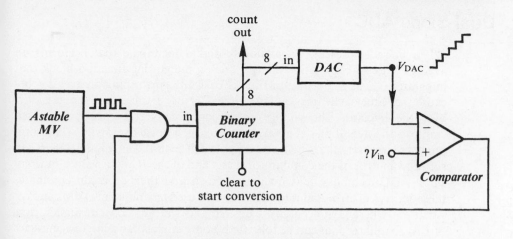

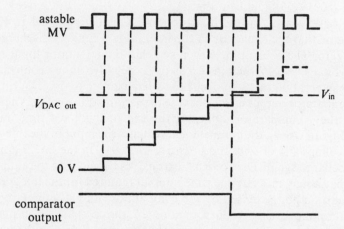

FIGURE D6–8. *Basic Operation of Staircase-Ramp ADC*

The resolution of the A/D process here is the same as that of the DAC, and the conversion time depends on the frequency of the oscillator, which is generally limited by the settling time of the DAC and speed of the comparator. Suppose a 100-kilohertz oscillator is used and 1,000 counts is chosen for full scale, giving 0.1% resolution. The largest conversion time would then require 10 milliseconds to complete; this speed is essentially the same as the VFC approach.

However, the staircase-ramp approach is sensitive to noise fluctuations in V_{in}. The value of V_{in} at the instant the staircase voltage reaches it determines the readout count; this is generally regarded as a disadvantage. For dc voltages that are fluctuating somewhat due to ac pickup or other noise sources, we prefer the fluctuations to be averaged out in the measuring process if possible.

Dual-Slope ADC

When noise is present, an analog-to-digital technique that performs an average is desirable. Notice that an analog integrating function block that integrates $v(t)$ as a function of time is basically performing an average, because the value of the integral after time T is just T times the average of $v(t)$ over the interval. The voltage-to-frequency converter already discussed employs an integrating circuit and is therefore a noise-averaging ADC component. However, the *single-slope* approach pictured in Figure D6–6 can suffer from drift of the comparator offset and of the R and C values. A *dual-slope* ADC technique that integrates down and then up again eliminates these sources of error and is the most widely used technique in DVMs and for situations where high accuracy is desired and a rather slow conversion time of 1 to 30 milliseconds can be tolerated. Some models can achieve accuracies better than 0.001% (5 significant digits).

The basic scheme of the dual-slope ADC is diagrammed in Figure D6–9. Assume that the capacitor in the integrator is initially discharged so that V_C is zero. The control logic then switches the integrator input to the unknown voltage V_{in}. V_C then proceeds to go negative as the control logic permits the integration of V_{in} to occur for a *fixed* length of time. During this time the comparator output is low because the + comparator input is negative relative to the − comparator input. At the end of this fixed time interval (time 1 in Figure D6–9), the control logic switches the input of the integrator to a fixed voltage V_{ref} of *opposite polarity, so that* C in the integrator proceeds to discharge again. The control also enables the clock to the counter at time 1 so that it may measure the time interval required for the integrator to return to zero output as sensed by the comparator. As V_C to the + input of the comparator moves slightly positive at time 2, the comparator output goes high and stops the counter with a count that is proportional to the time interval 1–2 in Figure D6–9. This time interval 1–2 will be proportional to the amount of voltage and charge acquired by the integrating capacitor while connected to V_{in}, and this charge is directly proportional to V_{in}. Notice the greater time interval 1–2′ involved for the higher V_{in} shown in Figure D6–9. Therefore, the count held by the counter after the measure interval is proportional to the input voltage.

Successive-Approximation ADC

When analog-to-digital conversion in a time less than 1 millisecond to a few microseconds is required, the *successive-approximation* ADC is the most widely used technique. This ADC type utilizes a fast DAC along with somewhat elaborate control logic; the circuit essentials are diagrammed in Figure D6–10. Basically, a control circuit manipulates the analog voltage out of a DAC until it matches the voltage to be measured V_{in}. Then the number input

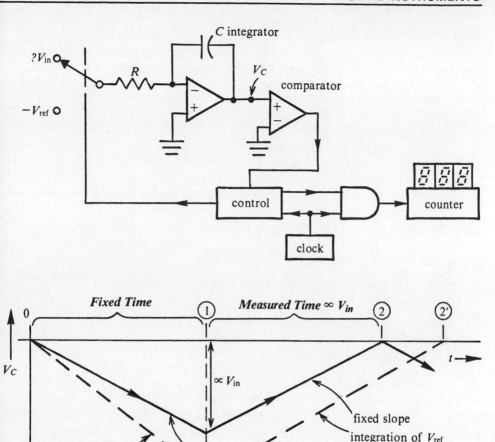

FIGURE D6–9. *Diagram of the Dual-Slope Analog-to-Digital Conversion Technique*

to the DAC tells the digital value of V_{in}. The control circuit may even be a microcomputer connected to the DAC; then the microcomputer performs the control process under direction of a program.

Let N be the number of bits with which the DAC in the circuit operates; this number determines the resolution of the device. N input lines to the DAC come from an N-bit register that is manipulated by the control logic. When an A/D conversion is initiated, the control logic first clears the register and then sets the most significant bit (MSB) to 1. Let us assume that $N = 8$ and call the MSB bit-7. Then the register is set first to 1000 0000, and the DAC produces a voltage V_{DAC} that is essentially half its full-scale value. The comparator then tests if the unknown input voltage V_{in} is greater than this value. If the answer is yes (comparator output high), the control logic leaves the

D175

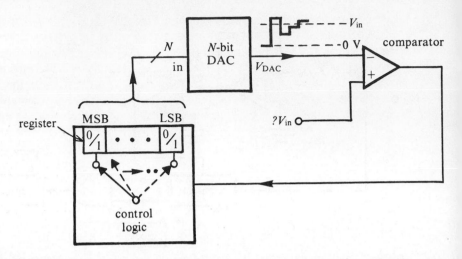

FIGURE D6–10. *Diagram of the Successive-Approximation Analog-to-Digital Conversion Technique*

MSB set to 1 and sets the next most significant bit (bit-6) to 1 so that 1100 0000 is input to the DAC. However, if the answer is no, the MSB is reset to 0 before bit-6 is set to 1, and 0100 0000 is input to the DAC. In either case the comparator again tests if the unknown V_{in} is greater than the new V_{DAC} value; if yes, bit-6 is left at 1, while if no, the bit is cleared before moving right to the next bit. This process continues down through the least significant bit (LSB). At this point the conversion is complete with the register containing the binary value of the input voltage, rather like in the staircase technique.

Suppose each comparison/register–manipulation/DAC settling time requires 2 microseconds; then the entire conversion to N bits requires just $N \times 2$ microseconds. This is much more rapid, for example, than the staircase approach where 2^N steps could be involved (worst case) to obtain the final conversion. If 2 microseconds is involved for each step, about $2^N \times 2$ microseconds is required for the conversion time of a staircase-based ADC. Consider a 10-bit ADC, which implies 0.1% resolution. The staircase approach could require $2^{10} \times 2$ μsec = 1048×2 μsec = 2 msec (worst case), while the successive-approximation technique requires 10×2 μsec = 20 μsec for every case.

Very-High-Speed ADC

The measurement of single, rapid transient voltage waveforms (for example, 100-microsecond duration and less) was possible only with an oscilloscope and camera until about 1970. Beginning about that time ADC instruments became available that could sample transient voltages as quickly as successive 0.1-microsecond points, for up to 1,000 points or 100 microseconds. To accomplish this blazing speed requires a number of comparators operating simultaneously or in parallel on an incoming voltage. This ADC type is often called a *parallel-encoder* ADC. For example, 32 comparators with thresholds set at intervals of 1/32 the total voltage span can accomplish a very rapid conversion to 5-bit accuracy. These devices must typically incorporate a memory to hold the measured values until they can be transferred to a printout, *X-Y* plotter, or a computer. Indeed, there are very few computers that can receive data at the rate of a number every 0.1 microsecond.

Large-scale integration now makes possible what seemed quite unreasonable a few years ago. A resistive voltage divider and 255 comparators are used in the TDC–1007 monolithic ADC produced by TRW (about $500 each in 1980). This device accomplishes conversion of an analog voltage to 8 bits in 33 nanoseconds, so that 30 million conversions can be done in 1 second (a 30-megahertz ADC rate)! Indeed, an ADC that uses parallel comparators is often called a *flash converter*.

Data Acquisition Systems

For a number of years laboratory computer systems have included an *analog multiplexer* in conjunction with a fast ADC under computer control. Thus the AM8–EA 8-channel analog MUX in the PDP–8/E lab system is equivalent to a single-pole–8-position switch that can pass an analog voltage from one of 8 input *channels* on to the ADC. Note that this multiplexer is more versatile than a digital multiplexer, which can only multiplex digital (2-state) signals. Chapter D2 discussed CMOS bilateral switches and the 4051 8-channel analog multiplexer. Figure D6–11a diagrams the situation. The computer can monitor 8 voltages essentially simultaneously by sending a channel code number to the MUX, thus moving the electronic switch to each channel, and subsequently performing an A/D conversion on that input. Note that each channel's analog signal must be scaled to the same dc voltage range for greatest accuracy. This must be done by suitable circuitry *before* the MUX. If the electrical parameter to be measured is not dc voltage, it must be transformed to such. The measuring of the various inputs is actually sequential, of course, but if the ADC is fast, there need be only a small delay between successive channel measurements. For example, the AD8–EA ADC used with the PDP–8/E system is a successive-approximation type with 10-bit accuracy and a conversion time of 20 microseconds. Generally, a number of parameters associated with an experiment may be monitored in this approach without the need for a separate ADC for each parameter. This approach has come to be called a *data acquisition system.*

The signal to be measured may in fact be changing during the conversion time of the ADC (for example, it may be changing during the 20-microsecond time of the AD8–EA above). This does not necessarily mean that a faster ADC must be purchased. A *sample-and-hold circuit* can be used that captures the signal value during a brief period—the *acquisition time*—and holds it constant for conversion by the ADC (see Figure D6–11b). Thus the AD8–EA ADC incorporates a sample-and-hold circuit with a 5-microsecond window. The time of the sampling can be controlled by a pulse from the computer or the experimental situation. If measurements along an entire waveform are desired, it is necessary that the waveform be periodic or else a repetitive transient so that the window may be stepped along the waveform on successive occurrences of the waveform. However, if the transient waveform occurs very seldom, this is a time-consuming process, and a fast ADC with memory such as that mentioned above becomes very desirable.

The sample-and-hold circuit consists essentially of an electronic switch and a *hold capacitor* C_H, as shown in Figure D6–11b. When the switch closes, the capacitor charges rapidly to the input voltage at that time (the time required for this charging is the acquisition time). The switch is then opened and the capacitor holds the voltage quite constant if the impedance

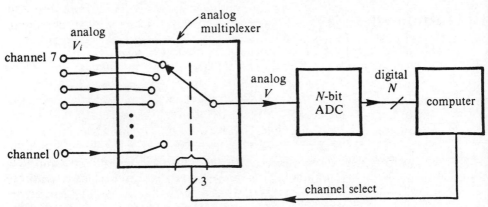

(a) 8-Channel Analog Multiplexer and ADC

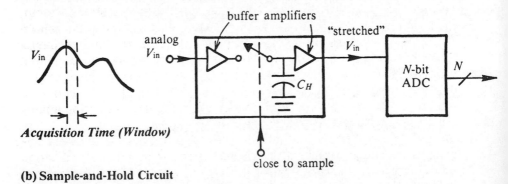

Acquisition Time (Window)

(b) Sample-and-Hold Circuit

FIGURE D6–11.   *Data Acquisition System*

across it is sufficiently large. There is always some decay, however, that is referred to as the *droop* of the sample-and-hold circuit.

The switches shown in Figures D6–11a and b cannot be mechanical switches for the submicrosecond speeds desired, of course. As mentioned, CMOS field-effect transistors serve quite nicely, with an *on* resistance on the order of 100 ohms and *off* leakage current of about 50 picoamperes. The CD4051B is an 8-channel CMOS analog multiplexer in a 16-pin package, while the CD4067B is a 16-channel analog multiplexer in a 24-pin package. The single switch for the sample-and-hold could be from a CD4066 quad bilateral switch.

Commercial *sample-and-hold amplifiers* exist in IC form. Examples are the SMP–11 (PMI), AD582 (Analog Devices), and LF398 (National Semiconductor). For example, the SMP–11 has an acquisition time of 3.5 microseconds (if a hold capacitor of 0.005-microfarad capacitance is used). This is the time for the output to move to within 0.1% of a 10-V *step* input signal. For small signal changes (on the order of 0.2 V), the acquisition time is about 800 nanoseconds for 0.1% accuracy. After the hold command is given to the device, a delay of 50 nanoseconds is required for the SMP–11 output to cease tracking the input signal. This delay is called the *aperture time* and should not be confused with the acquisition time. Note that it is very small, but the aperture time is *not* the actual window time that may be necessary to acquire the signal.

ADC Accuracy Specification

The *accuracy specification* or interpretation of maximum error for an ADC can be a confusing matter. In the first place, an ADC has an inherent *quantizing error* (as we have also seen for the DAC). For example, even a "perfect" ADC produces an output numerical value that is up to $\pm 1/2$ LSB in error. This situation is illustrated in Figure D6–12, where the digital output for a perfect ADC is presented. As a specific example, in this figure an ADC is assumed that outputs the code of 0 for 0-V input, the code of 1 for 0.1 V input, the code of 2 for 0.2-V input, and so on. The voltages here are the *center-value points* of the quantization intervals. Note the *steps* in the output characteristic. For example, the first step corresponds to the fact that for any input voltage in the (open) interval 0.05 V to 0.15 V, the *ideal* ADC produces the digit 1 as output. The ideal ADC always produces the nearest correct integer as output, and the *risers* between steps mark the boundaries on the analog input voltages that cause adjacent integers as output.

Now a real-world ADC does not have these risers at the precisely correct positions. For example, ADC behavior for an accuracy specification (more correctly, a maximum *error* specification) of $\pm 1/4$ LSB is diagrammed in Figure D6–12. A riser may occur anywhere in a *band* about the ideal position, with the maximum deviation being $\pm 1/4$ LSB. The possible region for

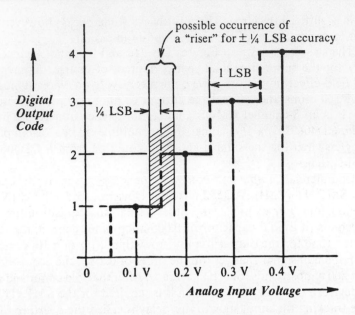

FIGURE D6–12. *Accuracy of an Analog-to-Digital Converter*

the occurrence of one riser is denoted by the crosshatching in the figure. In this example, it is possible for an input voltage as small as 0.125 V to produce a digital output of 2. On a different ADC with the same ±1/4 LSB specification, it is possible that the input voltage must slightly exceed 0.175 V to produce the output code of 2.

Notice that if the error specification is ±1/2 LSB, the riser from output code 1 to code 2 could in fact occur as early as 0.1 V or as late as 0.2 V. For this error specification then, a riser's range actually abuts the two center-value points.

In this discussion, it is assumed that the scale of the ADC output has been adjusted such that the center-value points on average are all correct. If this is not true, the specification is more correctly a *linearity specification,* or one of *relative accuracy.*

ADC ICs

From 1965 to 1975 ADCs were available only as modular converters, or else as hybrid converters. In the *modular* type, various passive components and transistors are interconnected and encapsulated in a small module the size of a cigarette pack and cost some hundreds of dollars. Precision wirewound resistors and other components are used, so that the modular type is very stable over temperature and time; actually, this type continues to be used in critical applications. In the hybrid type, several integrated-circuit chips are interconnected and packaged in one IC. This permits mixing and matching of chips for excellent performance levels at moderate prices (on the order of $50). These devices are generally quite self-contained (for example, precision reference, clock, and so forth) and easy to use.

In 1975 monolithic ADCs first appeared whereby a *single chip* in an IC accomplishes most—if not all—of the important functions. Only a few external resistors and capacitors need be connected to the IC pins. The devices introduced at that time also generally required an external voltage reference. One of the first single-chip ADCs available was the 8700-series monolithic CMOS ADC introduced by Teledyne in 8-bit, 10-bit, and 12-bit versions. This device includes parallel output lines, an initiate-conversion input line, and a data-valid output line. An incremental charge-balancing technique with noise-averaging and conversion-time characteristics similar to the dual-slope technique is employed. The device is sensitive to an input current and may be designed into a voltmeter mode very much like a d'Arsonval meter. Price is $10 to $20.

National Semiconductor has introduced the ADC0800 8-bit ADC, which is a low-cost monolithic device that uses the successive-approximation technique to achieve a 100-microsecond conversion time. Even more comprehensive is their ADC0816 *data acquisition system on a chip*. The ADC0816 includes an 8-bit ADC, 16-channel analog multiplexer, and latched channel-address inputs as well as latched data outputs. In fact, these latched lines permit rather direct connection of the chip to many microprocessors, as is discussed shortly. Again the successive-approximation technique is used to achieve a conversion time of 100 microseconds. Price is about $25.

Most ADC-chip manufacturers are very cognizant of the pervasive microprocessor and are introducing ICs that may be readily connected to microprocessors. An example is the ADC0801 *naked-8* 8-bit ADC chip from National Semiconductor; it is available in a 20-pin DIP package. The digital outputs are Tri-State latches that hold the code for input to a microprocessor data bus, but only present it at such time as requested by the microprocessor. This capability permits direct connection to virtually any microprocessor and saves the expense of an *interface* chip. In addition, the ADC0801 can work the *interrupt system* of the microprocessor for interrupt-driven I/O. (These microcomputer concepts are discussed in the coming chapters.)

Several manufacturers supply ADC chips especially designed for application in digital panel meters or in digital voltmeters (DVMs). *Digital panel meters* are modern digital display replacements for the familiar d'Arsonval (needle-type) meter. These are often placed in the *panel* of a system to monitor some voltage or current. They generally operate with a fixed input range and have compact size. The market for these devices is quite competitive, as they attempt to replace $30 analog meters.

Digital panel meters and DVMs continuously monitor the input voltage and convert to digital output about 5 times a second. The digital output from the ADC chip for this application is multiplexed for efficient connection to a multidigit display. Four lines output the BCD digits, and the digits are successively sent out on these lines in synchronization with a high on a corresponding digit strobe line (one line for each digit). A single BCD-to-7-segment decoder/driver can then be used to drive the multiplexed digital display, as discussed in Chapter D4. The rapid recycling causes the digits to appear continuously lit.

Representative digital-panel-meter (or DVM) chips are the Siliconix LD130, Teledyne 8750, and National ADC3501 devices. The LD130 is a 3-digit device (an output of 000 to 999, which corresponds to a 10-bit binary ADC resolution) and costs about $6. The 8750 and 3501 are *3-1/2-digit* devices; they output values from 0 to 1999. These devices have remarkable precision for their price. Further, BCD values can simplify (machine language) programming in computer applications. However, their continuous cycling of output without external control is not always convenient for use by a computer.

In this regard, the ADC3511 3-1/2-digit ADC from National Semiconductor is more appropriate. BCD digits are output on 4 lines, but the desired digit is selected *on demand* via 2 digit-select lines. The ADC3511 begins a conversion after receiving a *start-conversion* pulse on the input line with this name. After about 200 milliseconds (the conversion time), the ADC signals *conversion-complete* over the output line so named. This mode of operation is very appropriate for computer applications, as we see later on. Notice that the device has high accuracy—typically 1 count or ±0.05%—but at a price of a rather slow conversion time.

REVIEW EXERCISES

1. Briefly, what are the functions of the Geiger tube and the scaler in the so-called Geiger counter?
2. What determines the number of significant digits that appear in the display of a frequency counter?
3. (a) Describe in general terms the procedure used by a period meter to measure the period of a waveform.
   (b) In what circumstance can a period meter be more useful than a frequency meter?
4. Distinguish between how the time base is utilized in a frequency meter and in a period meter.
5. (a) What is the difference between resolution and accuracy in a D/A converter?
   (b) What is the name given to the speed of response of a D/A converter?
   (c) What is meant by a multiplying DAC?
   (d) Explain why a D/A converter with a reference input permits the DAC output to be calibrated.
6. Explain briefly how DACs permit a computer to draw pictures on an *X-Y* plotter.

7. Describe how an ADC can readily be constructed from a VFC and a frequency counter.

8. Select from the following ADC types those that best match the characteristic in each case listed below: A. VFC-based ADC, B. staircase-ramp ADC, C. dual-slope conversion ADC, D. successive-approximation ADC, E. flash-converter (parallel-conversion) ADC.

   (a) noise averaging (choose two)

   (b) lowest resolution (choose one)

   (c) 1-microsecond conversion time (choose one)

   (d) 50-microsecond conversion time (choose one)

   (e) 10-millisecond conversion time (choose three)

   (f) often capable of 0.01% accuracy and resolution (choose two)

   (g) commonly used in laboratory DVMs (choose one)

9. (a) Describe the general mode of operation for an ADC that is based on a staircase ramp.

   (b) Characterize this ADC in terms of conversion-time and noise-averaging characteristics.

   (c) What feature determines the resolution of this ADC type?

10. (a) Describe the activity associated with each slope in the dual-slope-type ADC.

    (b) Characterize this ADC in terms of conversion-time and noise-averaging characteristics.

    (c) What factors determine the resolution of this ADC type?

11. (a) Describe the general mode of operation for the successive-approximation ADC.

    (b) Characterize this ADC in terms of conversion-time and noise-averaging characteristics.

    (c) What feature determines the resolution of this ADC type?

12. (a) Describe the general mode of operation for the flash-converter or parallel-comparator converter.

    (b) Characterize this ADC in terms of conversion-time and noise-averaging characteristics.

    (c) What feature determines the resolution of this ADC type? Why is 10-bit resolution difficult to achieve with this approach?

13. (a) What are the basic elements of a data acquisition system?

    (b) What are the basic elements of a sample-and-hold circuit?

    (c) Describe the circumstance when a sample-and-hold circuit is desirable.

    (d) What are the acquisition time and droop, respectively, for a sample-and-hold circuit?

PROBLEMS

1. Diagram the construction of a crystal time base for use in a frequency counter. The time base uses a crystal square-wave oscillator and decade counter (for example, 7490 chips) to provide a switch-selectable frequency of 1 kHz, 100 Hz,

10 Hz, 1.0 Hz, and 0.1 Hz. Assume a 1-MHz crystal oscillator is used; use labeled boxes to represent the oscillator and decade counters.

2. (a) An ac signal with a frequency of 12.4968 kilohertz is input to a frequency meter. If the gate time of the frequency meter is 0.01 second, what digits are present in the display of the meter?

   (b) What gate time must be used to obtain all 6 significant digits of the given frequency in the display? Comment on the convenience or inconvenience of this measurement.

3. Describe the circuit changes required in the frequency meter or counter of Figure D6–2 in order to give the counter the option of an events-counting mode. To what terminal in Figure D6–2 should the event pulses be connected?

4. Many frequency counters label the display in units of kilohertz. These counters also often use a decimal point in the display that moves left or right as the gate time of the counter is changed. What is the position of the decimal point in the display if the gate time is selected to be 0.01 second and 10 seconds, respectively?

5. Some period meters include the facility to average 10 periods or 100 periods or 1,000 periods in the measurement of the period of a waveform. This is done by timing the duration of 10 cycles, 100 cycles or 1,000 cycles, respectively, and setting the decimal point properly in the display.

   (a) Discuss why it becomes inconvenient to average 1,000 cycles of a waveform if its frequency is below 1 kHz.

   (b) Discuss why more significant digits are obtained when averaging 1,000 periods than when measuring only 1 period, assuming that the time base is not changed.

   (c) Describe how the circuit of Figure D6–3 should be modified if we desire the "average" of 1,000 periods.

6. Consider a D/A converter that is based on binary-weighted resistors and a summing amplifier. Suppose a 10-bit D/A converter is constructed. If the smallest of the weighting resistors used is 1 kilohm, what is the resistance of the largest resistor?

7. Consider the D/A converter based on the summing amplifier as in Figure D6–4b. Explain why the DAC may be expected to have poor accuracy if the digital inputs are from TTL outputs.

8. (a) Suppose a *current-to-frequency converter* (IFC) is desired. Describe how the circuit of Figure D6–6 can be modified to obtain an IFC.

   (b) Find a mathematical expression that relates output frequency f to the input current I_{in} for this IFC.

9. Consider the basic VFC converter of Figure D6–6. The reference voltage employed is 5 V and the value of R is 10 kΩ. The VFC output frequency is to be 1.0 kHz for $V_{in} = 1.0$ V.

   (a) What value of C is required in the design?

   (b) An ADC instrument is constructed by connecting the VFC above to the input of a frequency counter that uses a gate time of 0.1 second. What is the voltage resolution of the ADC?

10. How many comparators are required in a flash converter that provides 6-bit resolution?

11. (a) Suppose an ac signal is input to an ADC that operates on an integration principle. Also suppose that the duration of the integral is an integer times the period of the ac signal; show that the ADC output will read zero.

 (b) The fixed-time integration in a dual-slope ADC is often chosen to be $N/60$ sec, where N is an integer. This procedure reduces 60-Hz line noise (interference) in the measurement of a dc signal. Explain this statement.

12. Assume that an ideal 3-bit DAC is used with an ideal comparator to construct a successive-approximation ADC. The output of the DAC is 0 V, 0.1 V, 0.2 V, 0.3 V... for respective inputs of 0, 1, 2, 3.... Assume each comparison takes 2 microseconds.

 (a) Make a graph of the DAC output versus time if the input voltage to the ADC is 0.19 V. What code is presented by the ADC at the end of conversion?

 (b) Make a graph of the DAC output versus time if the input voltage to the ADC is 0.021 V. What code is presented by the ADC at the end of conversion?

 (c) Make a careful graph of N_{out} versus V_{in} for the ADC and contrast with Figure D6–12. Show that this ADC possesses a 1/2 LSB offset.

13. (a) Draw the complete design for a flash converter with a 0.1-V resolution and a full-scale input voltage of 0.7 V. Let the output of the converter be in octal.

 (b) Extend the above design to have a binary output.

14. The voltage versus time during battery discharge is to be studied for nickel-cadmium batteries. Sixteen batteries are to be discharged to obtain an understanding of the variations between batteries; each is to be discharged for 24 hours. A computer will be used to acquire the data.

 (a) A single ADC could be used in an experiment that requires 16 days to perform. Describe how the experiment can be performed in 1 day without purchasing 16 ADCs. What equipment is required?

 (b) Is a sample-and-hold circuit required? Explain.

15. The binary-weighted resistor network of Figure D6–4b requires a wide range of precision resistors, while the R-2R ladder diagrammed in the R-2R resistance-ladder D/A converter shown here requires only 2 values of precision resistors. If only voltages of zero or V (volts) are input to the terminals A through D, the voltage appearing at output P is given by $V(N/2^n)$, where N is the binary number corresponding to the high/low states of the inputs D (MSB) through A (LSB), and n is the number of inputs. In this example $n = 4$, but the ladder may readily be extended to more inputs. This problem examines the behavior of the ladder network.

 (a) Assume all inputs A through D are grounded. Show that the resistance to ground of the network extending to the *left* of point II in Diagram D6–1 is simply $2R$. Also show that the resistance to ground of the network to the left of point III is $2R$. A similar property holds for point IV.

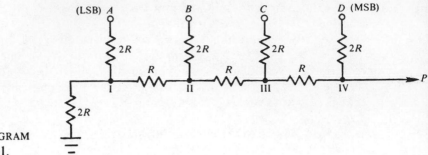

DIAGRAM
D6-1.

(b)   Suppose input D is connected to $V+$, while the other inputs are at ground. Show a voltage $V/2$ develops at point P, in agreement with the above rule.
NOTE: Consider the effective resistance to ground of the circuit to the left of point IV.

(c)   Suppose input A is connected to $V+$, while all the other inputs are at ground. Show that a voltage $V/16$ develops at a point P, in agreement with the above rule.
NOTE: Use Thevenin's theorem to show that the circuit to the left of point II is equivalent to a voltage $V/2$ connected through a resistance of $2R$ to point II. Then find a Thevenin replacement for the circuit to the left of point III and repeat for point IV.

(d)   Assume only input B is connected to $V+$, while all other inputs are at ground. Show that a voltage $V/8$ develops at point P.

(e)   Invoke the Superposition Theorem (see Problem 33 of Chapter A1 in *Analog Electronics for Scientific Application* by Barnaal) to justify the voltage that appears at P if any combination of inputs are connected high or low.

D
I
G
I
T
A
L

Microprocessor Fundamentals

Digital electronics has been useful in the laboratory as a means of obtaining and manipulating data with greater precision than is readily done with analog signals. Digital networks have also been useful in producing and controlling sequential events in a laboratory experiment or industrial process. However, the logic design for elaborate sequences can become quite complex; furthermore, the only way the control network can later be modified is by rewiring and circuit modification.

One of the principal attractions of computers in the laboratory is that a *program* is used to obtain computer actions that control, monitor, and obtain data from an experiment. Furthermore, powerful data-manipulation and decision-making capability is available. If the experimental procedure or sequence is to be changed, all that usually needs to be done (not always so trivial) is to change the programming, not necessarily any wiring. From one point of view, the microprocessor is a general-purpose, programmable, digital-logic array; it can be employed in diverse situations through the use of an appropriate control program and supporting electronics selected for a specific use. These advantages of the computer were available at an intermediate price in the minicomputer. Now, the power of the minicomputer of 1970 is available in the remarkably compact and low-priced microprocessor; its utility is clear and at least some of its applications are clear.

The laboratory microprocessor and microcomputing section of this book consists of four chapters; in these chapters, our study centers around one rather powerful 8-bit microprocessor, the Mos Technology/Commodore

6502, and some of the supporting digital ICs for it. By concentrating on one microprocessor, we hope to reduce confusion and to make effective use of the time and space available. The concepts learned here are quite readily applied to other microprocessors. The 6502 microprocessor is used in several important microcomputer systems, including the PET, Apple, OSI, and Atari machines.

The first chapter of the microcomputing section introduces fundamental concepts, terms, and methods for the operation and use of a microprocessor, thus providing a basis for early-on laboratory work. There is no substitute for actual hands-on experience with a microprocessor in order to develop an understanding of it. This chapter also provides a foundation upon which to build a more ornate structure in the following chapters. In a sense, a spiral approach to the subject of microcomputers is being followed here; thus, if time forces the issue, it is possible to stop after just this chapter and still have a basic understanding of what a microcomputer is and how it can be used.

The parts of a classical computer and how they function together are presented in the first major section of this chapter. We learn what a microprocessor is vis-à-vis a microcomputer. In the second major section we study a group of instructions sufficient to accomplish some tasks with a microcomputer. It is *not* assumed that the reader has studied programming previously, particularly the *machine language* that a computer actually uses and understands. The chapter concludes with a basic approach for connecting the microcomputer to the outside world—that is, *interfacing* to experiments or processes. The versatile LSI support ICs now available for use with microcomputers make interfacing much simpler, in terms of logic design, than it was just a few short years ago with minicomputers.

Basic Microcomputer Concepts

A computer is simply a machine that manipulates numbers or *data* while following a definite sequence of instructions or *program*. Almost every general-purpose computer can be described as having the same structure and, in basic terms, each is operated in the same manner. We want to consider this structure and operation and put the microprocessor in context.

Computer Word Size

As pointed out earlier, because of the simple and more reliable electronic circuits involved, essentially all contemporary digital computers operate using binary numbers. The individual binary digits in a binary number are called *bits*. The number of bits in a typical binary number that a computer manipulates is referred to as its *word size*. Minicomputers have typically worked with 12-bit and 16-bit words. The PDP–8/E is a 12-bit word minicomputer, while the PDP–11, the Nova by Data General, and the HP2100 by Hewlett Packard are 16-bit word minicomputers.

A number of years ago, IBM began using an 8-bit binary number in data transmission and this size number became known as the *byte*. Most classic microprocessors—first introduced in the years 1973–1976—operate with an 8-bit word. These include the Intel 8080, Motorola 6800, Fairchild F8, Mos Technology 6502, RCA 1802, Zilog Z80, and Signetics 2650 (in roughly chronological order). Notice that the word size for these microprocessors is then just 1 byte. Eight-bit numbers range from 0 to 255_{10}; this is not very large as numbers go, and *multiple-precision* operations—for example, 2 bytes or more—must often be resorted to. However, 1 part in 255 implies better than $1/2\%$ precision, and this is often reasonably good precision in a laboratory situation (witness 2% voltmeters).

At the beginning of the 1980s, VLSI technology spawned a number of 16-bit (word) microprocessors, including the Intel 8086, Zilog Z8000, and Motorola 68000. Available somewhat earlier were the PDP–11 minicomputer on 4 chips (the LSI–11), the Nova minicomputer in a chip (the micro-Nova), and the Texas Instruments 9900. (Actually, "only" the central processors of these minicomputers were reduced to a chip.) Sixteen-bit computers can perform basic operations on numbers ranging from 0 to $65{,}535_{10}$.

Computer Organization

Virtually all contemporary computers consist of three main aspects or sections. In Figure D7–1a these main aspects, diagrammed as the three larger blocks, are:

1. *Memory* from which program instructions or data are obtained and where results can later be stored;
2. *Input and output devices (I/O)* that permit instructions and data to be input to the computer and also results to be obtained from it;
3. *Central processing unit* (CPU) that determines the course of action of the computer and performs calculations.

These blocks of a computer are elaborated further in the following sections, and additional structures within the blocks are developed.

Computer Memory

It should be clear that the set of instructions that tells the computer what steps to perform—that is, the *program*—must be stored in some manner and be readily accessible to the computer as it performs these steps or *runs the*

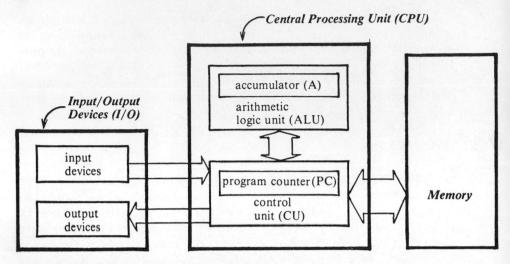

(a) Computer Principal Parts and Organization

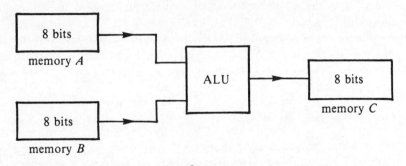

(b) A Three-Memory Address Instruction Computer

(c) A One-Memory Address Instruction Computer

FIGURE D7-1. *Basic Computer Organization and Operation*

program. The computer must therefore include an electronic *memory.* Furthermore, the computer typically receives data from some source (for example, a human, or an experiment apparatus) and performs various operations on it in the course of running the program. This data must be at least temporarily stored in some manner that is readily accessible to the computer. Again, an electronic memory is needed.

Most contemporary computers are of the *stored program type* as suggested by von Neumann during the early 1940s; that is, the instructions or program are placed in the same *memory store* as the data on which the program operates. Both the instructions and the data are simply binary numbers, and it is up to the programmer to be sure that the CPU does not accidentally begin using one type for the other, especially data for instructions.

I/O Devices

An I/O device is typically either an *input device* or an *output device*. An input device sends binary numbers *into* a computer; examples are a paper tape reader or a Teletype keyboard. An output device receives binary numbers as output *from* a computer; examples are a paper tape punch, Teletype printer, and cathode-ray tube or CRT. Input device and output device blocks are diagrammed within the larger I/O section block in Figure D7–1a. Note the arrows that indicate the direction of information flow to and from the central processing unit (CPU) of the computer. Magnetic tape and magnetic disc are examples of two-way I/O devices. They are usually used as adjunct memory for large amounts of data and program storage. When a computer interfaces to an experiment, the experiment becomes an input device, an output device, or both.

Central Processing Unit (CPU)

The central processing unit or CPU contains two important sub-blocks: the control unit or CU and the arithmetic-logic unit or ALU (see Figure D7–1a). The *control unit,* as its name implies, controls the operation of the computer. It is the boss or supervisor in that it decides where to go in memory to get the next instruction, what the instruction tells, and how it should be accomplished. In this process it operates as a switchboard in routing data to various destinations.

The *arithmetic-logic unit,* as its name implies, performs arithmetic operations such as add or subtract, and various logic operations such as AND, X-OR, or compare on two binary numbers. We can think of the ALU as the adding machine or perhaps calculator of the computer, and the ALU operates at the direction of the CU. A possible instruction for the control unit might be to use the ALU to add two 8-bit numbers together, which were obtained from two places or *addresses* in memory, and produce a sum that then should be stored in still a third address in memory. Figure D7–1b illustrates the situation (for 8-bit words such as those used by classic microcomputers). However, this general approach is *not* used in minicomputers and microcomputers because the instruction would be too large; the numbers specifying three memory addresses must be included in the instruction.

The most common approach in microcomputers is to operate always with just one number from memory and a second number in a register in the arithmetic-logic unit itself. This register is called the *accumulator* (abbreviated Acc or just A). Thus a typical operation would be to add the number from a certain place in memory to the number in the accumulator, with the result remaining in the accumulator. Another operation might be to store the number in the accumulator in some memory location; the number might remain in the accumulator or in some computers the accumulator might then be cleared (zeroed). The situation is diagrammed in Figure D7-1c. Only one memory location need be specified in the instruction in this approach, so it is referred to as *one-address* instruction. The accumulator is rather like the "result" register in an adding machine or calculator.

Microprocessor Chip and Microcomputer Board

Now that the general organization of a computer has been discussed—that is, Figure D7-1a—it is possible to tell what a microprocessor is. The classic *microprocessor* (8080, 6800, 6502, Z80, and so forth) is only the central processing unit (CPU) of a computer reduced to a thin integrated-circuit chip perhaps 0.5 centimeter square. This chip in turn is typically placed in a 1.5 centimeter × 5 centimeter plastic package with 40 pins that must make connection to memory or I/O devices. However, it is generally agreed that a machine should be called a computer only if it contains *all three* of the essential parts of a computer: CPU, memory, and I/O devices. Therefore, the focus of our study is a *micro-central processing unit* or, more simply, a microprocessor (μP). Although in fact the microprocessor integrated-circuit package encapsulates the silicon integrated-circuit chip, the entire package is often referred to as the *microprocessor chip*.

To be useful, the classic microprocessor must be connected to memory and possess I/O capability. In the spring of 1976, Mos Technology, Inc. introduced one of the first examples of the *computer on a board*. This single 21 centimeter × 27 centimeter printed circuit board contains the 6502 microprocessor, memory, a calculator-like keyboard for input, and a 6-digit (7 segments each) display for output. It may justly be called a *microcomputer* and has become a popular educational unit (in part because an expensive teleprinter or CRT is not required for its operation). The *microcomputer board* from Mos Technology, Inc., is called the KIM (for keyboard input monitor). Since 1977 rather similar microcomputer boards using the 6502 have been introduced by Synertec (the SYM) and Rockwell International (the AIM).

In 1977, devices called *single-chip microcomputers* began to appear. Examples are the Mostek 3870, Intel 8048, and Motorola 6802. The CPU, a modest amount of memory, and several dozen lines for input/output are typically incorporated in one IC. They are particularly suited to large-volume applications (the price is on the order of $5 each in quantities of 10,000).

Memory Organization

We can think of memory and its operation with the following analogy, which is timeworn but helpful: Imagine a column of pigeonholes such as were found in old desks. This is pictured in Figure D7–2. The pigeonholes or memory-storage locations are numbered, beginning at 0, 1, 2, ... These numbers are called *memory addresses M*. In each pigeonhole is one slip of paper with one number written on it. The number is referred to as the *contents of the memory location (M)*. These numbers constitute the data or the instructions for the CPU, depending on the situation. The numbers (M) are stored in binary form, and the 6502 microcomputer works with 8-bit memory word size, as is common for the classic microprocessors. Notice the number of bits on each slip of paper in Figure D7–2. As the microcomputer operates, we may think of the CPU as going to a certain memory location and reading the 8-bit number (M) from the slip of paper in that location M; this process is therefore called a *read-from-memory,* and the number in memory is *not* changed. Alternatively,

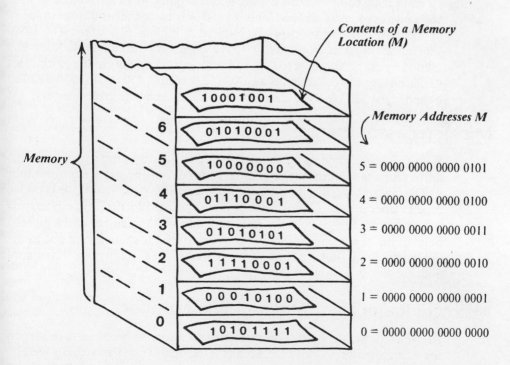

FIGURE D7–2. *Simple Pigeonhole Analogy of Computer Memory Organization*

the computer may write a completely different number on that slip of paper; or perhaps read the number, add one to it, erase the old number and write the new number $(M) + 1$ back on the slip. This process is called a *write-to-memory*.

The memory addresses M are also in binary, and the 6502 operates with 16-bit memory address numbers. The *bottom location* in memory is thus 0000 0000 0000 0000 = 0_{10}, while the *top location* is 1111 1111 1111 1111. Therefore the top memory address is $2^{16} - 1 = 65,535_{10}$; there are $2^{16} = 65,536_{10}$ possible memory locations. This range of memory locations is called the *address space* of the microprocessor. However, most microcomputer systems have only a portion of this capability actually connected to the CPU. For example, the KIM microcomputer board has only some 300+ memory locations physically supplied on the board, and the minimum SYM board has some 5100+ memory locations *populated*. It is, however, possible to purchase additional memory ICs and make more memory locations functional. Indeed, the fact that many memory locations are vacant is important for adding input/output devices to the 6502-based microcomputer, as we see shortly.

It is interesting to compare the memory address space of the classic microprocessor with that for the classic minicomputer, as that has been one measure of computer size in the past. The memory capacity of the PDP–8/E is 32,768 12-bit words (fewer bits than the 6502 capacity); the original Hewlett Packard 3000 computer was a large minicomputer when introduced in 1973 and had a capacity of 65,536 16-bit words (only twice the bit storage capacity of the classic microprocessors introduced a year or two later). The 1980-generation 16-bit microprocessors have a memory space on the order of 8 million bytes, comparable to that of the largest computers in the 1970s. This design change has occurred because memory costing $10,000 in 1970 could be obtained for $100 in 1980 through use of LSI semiconductor memory.

Microprocessor Program Counter

With this understanding of memory organization, we return to the control unit within the microprocessor in order to discuss an important register within it. This register is called the *program counter* or PC (see Figure D7–1a). This register does *not* count programs. It is manipulated by the logic circuitry of the control unit to contain the memory address (the number of the pigeonhole) of the next memory location to which the CPU should go to obtain the next instruction. Because 16 bits are required to specify any possible memory address, this is a 16-bit register.

Microcomputer Control Panel and Monitor

As we continue the discussion of microprocessors, it becomes necessary to use binary numbers often because this is the number system actually used by computers. However, it becomes tedious to write 16-bit and even 8-bit binary numbers. Decimal numbers are much more compact, but it is difficult to convert large binary numbers to decimal numbers mentally. It is much easier to convert binary numbers to octal numbers or to hexadecimal numbers (see supplement to Chapter D1). Eight-bit and 16-bit numbers break quite naturally into hexadecimal digits; therefore, *hex* is frequently used in writing the binary code and data used by such computers. In hexadecimal, the data in various memory locations for the 6502 can range from 00 to FF; 2-digit hex numbers are involved. Similarly, the memory addresses range from 0000 to FFFF and 4-digit hex numbers are required.

For many years the control panel for a computer indicated numbers such as memory address or memory data in binary form with rows of light bulbs. Each bulb could show a 1 or 0, of course, and as the numbers changed, we would see rows of blinking lights (still popular for public consumption in science fiction movies). However, most contemporary designs use more compact hex or octal readouts on digital displays instead. This technique is used on the KIM and SYM boards.

Furthermore, the traditional computer control panel had one or more rather long rows of switches to initially enter binary numbers into computer registers (such as the program counter), as well as into memory locations. The CPU was *not* actually running while these entries were made. Gating circuits permitted these switches to be connected to memory. Switches were flipped up or down to enter 1's or 0's, and a button pushed to cause the number to be entered. Now many minicomputers and microcomputers use a calculator-like keyboard instead to enter hex digits (this is done on the KIM and SYM). Furthermore, these keys do *not* have direct electrical connection to memory. Rather, the microcomputer must begin running a program called the *monitor program* as soon as it is turned on, or at least in response to a *reset* button. The microcomputer then monitors the keyboard and, in response to certain buttons and entered numbers, causes the display to show the contents of a desired memory location; or the monitor may cause new numbers to be placed in selected memory locations for us, in response to keys pressed on the keyboard. However, it is important to realize that when a number such as C5 is entered on the keyboard, the binary number 11000101 actually is put in memory.

Basic Microcomputer Operation

The general mode of operation for computers, including microcomputers, follows a rather simple pattern. First, the computer operator loads the program counter (PC) with the memory address of the first instruction that is to be performed. For purposes of discussion, let us assume that this first memory address is 0020_{16}; that is, $MA = 0020$.

NOTE: To clearly distinguish memory address numbers from memory content numbers, the designation MA is used here rather than the more compact M. It is also used as an abbreviation for the words *memory address*.

Then, upon receiving a GO or RUN command from the computer operator, the CPU requests or *fetches* from memory the number at MA 0020, which will always be interpreted by the CPU as an instruction. The CPU now does or *executes* what the instruction tells it to do. Meanwhile the CPU also changes the PC to the next higher memory address number; recall that the PC identifies the location from which the next instruction is to be fetched by the CPU. The computer, therefore, normally executes the instructions found in successive memory locations. The program-counter register behaves rather like an up counter as it progresses through the program, and this is the reason for its name. Notice that the typical computer is a *sequential machine,* basically accomplishing tasks one after the other in the order of the program in memory.

At this point we can say something about most of the wires or lines that must be within the broad arrow leading from the CPU to memory in Figure D7–1a. The CPU must communicate to the memory the address of the memory location from which, or to which, data should pass. This communication is done with 1 line for each bit, or 16 lines for the 16-bit memory address. Such a collection of lines is called a *bus,* and we speak of the *memory address bus* or *MA bus.* Furthermore, there must be 8 lines to carry the 8-bit binary data or instruction numbers between memory and the CPU (see Figure D7–3). This then is the *data bus* and must be a bidirectional bus (two-way street) because data can go from CPU to memory, as well as from memory to CPU. The MA bus is unidirectional; the CPU always tells the memory (not vice versa) which memory location data is to be read from or written to. Only 2 or 3 additional wires for control of orderly data transmission are needed besides the data bus and memory address bus. These *control lines* are described later.

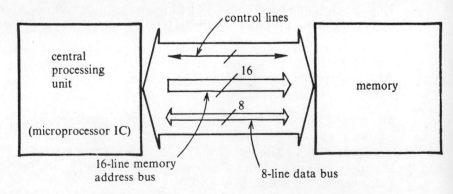

FIGURE D7–3. *Principal Buses for CPU-Memory Communications*

Essential Microcomputer Programming and Operation

From the discussion of the general mode of computer operation in the previous sections, it is clear that the computer program is crucial to the operation of a computer. We now investigate the nature and usage of some instructions that the 6502 microprocessor actually understands. That is, we examine some *machine instructions* and how a program can be written in *machine language* for the 6502 microprocessor. Only a group of the most important instructions are examined in this chapter, but these instructions permit us to write some first programs and accomplish some tasks with the microcomputer. They serve to illustrate how a microcomputer basically works and permit experimentation with a 6502-based microcomputer such as the KIM or SYM.

Four Basic Instruction Types: ADC, LDA, STA, and JMP

The CPU control unit only understands strings of bits or binary numbers that it receives from memory during a fetch. Thus, the instructions for the computer must be in the form of an *operation code,* abbreviated *OP code.* The computer itself does *not* understand algebraic equations or even plus or minus signs. In writing down and in reading a program for a computer, however, it is difficult to remember all the numeric codes for the many operations possible (70 to 150 for common microprocessors). Therefore, brief 3-letter *mnemonics* are usually used. A list of mnemonics, concise representations of each operation, and actual operation codes is very helpful and is often available as the *programmer's reference card.*

Important information of this sort is brought together for the 6502 in Figure D7–4. First, Figure D7–4a graphically illustrates all of the important registers in the CPU; that is, the 6502 chip. In particular, the 8-bit accumulator and 16-bit program counter already discussed are shown there. Next, Figure D7–4b presents the instruction summary; this is similar to that often found on a manufacturer's reference card. Figure D7–4b is referred to often in the discussion that follows and is simply termed the *reference card.* (Indeed, rather than referring to Figure D7–4b, the reader might have at hand an actual reference card from one of the manufacturers of the 6502.) Some abbreviations used in Figure D7–4b are explained in its caption, and additional information and abbreviations are presented in Figure D7–4c. It should be mentioned that not all of the *addressing modes* of the 6502 are presented on the card in Figure D7–4b. For pedagogical reasons, discussion in these chapters centers on those modes that are fundamental to the use of the 6502; indeed, several of the modes omitted were not available on earlier microprocessors (or minicomputers).

We begin our examination of the instructions available with the first (alphabetically) of the mnemonics.

1. ADC: *ADd memory to accumulator, with Carry.*

The letters for the mnemonic come from the phrase that describes its operation. The contents of a memory location are to be added to the accumulator, including any carry out from the previous operation. (As we see later on, it is often necessary to deal with numbers greater than 8 bits. A 16-bit number must thus be handled in two steps, and the carry from addition of the least significant bytes must be added to the addition of the most significant bytes.)

Notice that the reference card indicates the operation concisely by $A + M + C \rightarrow A$. More rigorously we might write $(A) + (M) + (C) \rightarrow (A)$ because it is the *contents* of some memory address M that will be added to the contents of the accumulator, with the result becoming the contents of the accumulator. The previous contents of the A are lost, but the contents of the memory location are not changed.

The question remains, just what memory location is involved? How is it specified to the CPU? There are a number of ways or modes in which it can be done for the ADC instruction. These are called the various *addressing modes* and are listed along the top of the card. Not all are available for the ADC instruction, however (unfortunately).

a. ADC# *add-immediate* mode. OP Code = 69

The # sign beside the mnemonic indicates that this mode is desired. The hex code is 69 as listed under the OP code column on the reference card. The number-of-bytes column (headed by #) tells us that 2 bytes of memory or 2 memory locations are involved. The first of the 2 contains the OP code, while "immediately" in the next location is the number that will be added to the accumulator. (Unfortunately, the # sign is used for two *different* purposes here.)

Example:

MA	Contents	Comments
0011	69	OP CODE TO ADD NEXT NUMBER TO ACCUM
12	04	THE NUMBER THAT GETS ADDED
13	--	THE NEXT INSTRUCTION

In this little example of how the instruction is placed in memory and operates, we quite arbitrarily assume that the OP Code 69_{16} is placed in the location with memory address 0011_{16} (MA 0011). Then the (arbitrary) 8-bit *addend number* 04_{16} is shown as placed in the immediate next address (MA 0012). Note that comments for the purpose of each code have been placed to the right in the *code sheet*. Now, as the CPU is executing the instruction, it first fetches the hex code 69 from memory. The microprocessor CPU has been constructed to know that 69 is the add-immediate instruction and requests from memory the number in the immediate next address (MA 0013). Upon receiving the number 04_{16} from memory, the CPU adds it to whatever is already in the accumulator and also proceeds to get the OP code for the next instruction from MA 0013. It does this because the program counter (PC) has been automatically adjusted by the CPU to 0013_{16} (to the next instruction). The CPU has recognized that 69 implies a 2-byte instruction.

b. ADC *add-absolute* mode. OP Code = 6D

The OP code column under the *Absolute* column gives the hex code as 6D. Under # we see that it is a 3-byte instruction. Three bytes are necessary because the instruction can specify "absolutely" any memory location as the

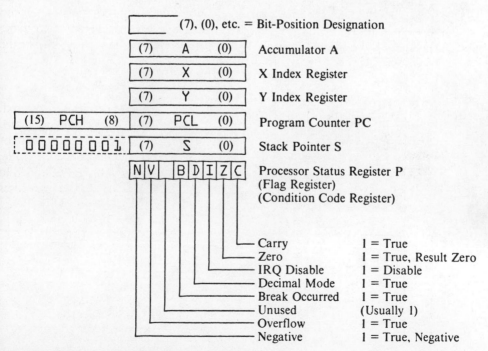

(a) **Register Model for the 6502 Microprocessor**

FIGURE D7–4.   *6502 Reference Card*

[handwritten margin annotations: "OVERFLOW" (pointing to the V column), "INDIR"]

Mnemonic	Operation	Immediate OP	Immediate N#	Absolute OP	Absolute N#	Zero Page OP	Zero Page N#	Accum OP	Accum N#	Implied OP	Implied N#	Relative OP	Relative N#	N	Z	C	I	D	V
ADC (1)	A+M+C→A	69	2 2	6D	4 3	65	3 2							*	*	*			*
AND (1)	A∧M→A	29	2 2	2D	4 3	25	3 2							*	*				
ASL (2)	C ←[7...0]← 0			0E	6 3	06	5 2	0A	2 1					*	*	*			
BCC (2)	BR ON C=0											90	2 2						
BCS (2)	BR ON C=1											B0	2 2						
BEQ (2)	BR ON Z=1											F0	2 2						
BIT (2)	A∧M			2C	4 3	24	3 2							M7*	*				M6
BMI (2)	BR ON N=1											30	2 2						
BNE (2)	BR ON Z=0											D0	2 2						
BPL (2)	BR ON N=0											10	2 2						
BRK	SOFT.INT.									00	7 1						1		
BVC (2)	BR ON V=0											50	2 2						
BVS (2)	BR ON V=1											70	2 2						
CLC	0→C									18	2 1					0			
CLD	0→D									D8	2 1							0	
CLI	0→I									58	2 1						0		
CLV	0→V									B8	2 1								0
CMP (1)	A−M	C9	2 2	CD	4 3	C5	3 2							*	*	*			
CPX	X−M	E0	2 2	EC	4 3	E4	3 2							*	*	*			
CPY	Y−M	C0	2 2	CC	4 3	C4	3 2							*	*	*			
DEC	M−1→M			CE	6 3	C6	5 2							*	*				
DEX	X−1→X									CA	2 1			*	*				
DEY	Y−1→Y									88	2 1			*	*				
EOR (1)	A⊻M→A	49	2 2	4D	4 3	45	3 2							*	*				
INC	M+1→M			EE	6 3	E6	5 2							*	*				
INX	X+1→X									E8	2 1			*	*				
INY	Y+1→Y									C8	2 1			*	*				

(b) Instruction summary; operation codes (OP), execution time as number of cycles (N), memory requirements as number of bytes (#), and condition codes that are modified in the

FIGURE D7-4 (*continued*). *6502 Reference Card*

Mnemonic	Operation	Immediate (OP n #)	Absolute (OP n #)	Zero Page (OP n #)	Accum (OP n #)	Implied (OP n #)	Processor Status (N V B D I Z C)
JSR	JUMP SUBR		20 / 3 / 6				
LDA (1)	M → A	A9 / 2 / 2	AD / 3 / 4	A5 / 2 / 3			* · · · · *
LDX (1)	M → X	A2 / 2 / 2	AE / 3 / 4	A6 / 2 / 3			* · · · · *
LDY (1)	M → Y	A0 / 2 / 2	AC / 3 / 4	A4 / 2 / 3			* · · · · *
LSR	0→[7···0]→C		4E / 3 / 6	46 / 2 / 5	4A / 1 / 2		0 · · · · * *
NOP	NO OPER					EA / 1 / 2	
ORA	A V M → A	09 / 2 / 2	0D / 3 / 4	05 / 2 / 3			* · · · · *
PHA	A→Ms S-1→S					48 / 1 / 3	
PHP	P→Ms S-1→S					08 / 1 / 3	
PLA	S+1→S Ms→A					68 / 1 / 4	* · · · · *
PLP	S+1→S Ms→P					28 / 1 / 4	(RESTORED)
ROL	[C][7···0]		2E / 3 / 6	26 / 2 / 5	2A / 1 / 2		* · · · · * *
ROR	[C][7···0]		6E / 3 / 6	66 / 2 / 5	6A / 1 / 2		* · · · · * *
RTI	RTRN INT					40 / 1 / 6	(RESTORED)
RTS	RTRN SUBR					60 / 1 / 6	
SBC (1)	A-M-C̄ → A	E9 / 2 / 2	ED / 3 / 4	E5 / 2 / 3			* * · · · * *
SEC	1 → C					38 / 1 / 2	· · · · · · 1
SED	1 → D					F8 / 1 / 2	(3)
SEI	1 → I					78 / 1 / 2	· · · · 1 ·
STA	A → M		8D / 3 / 4	85 / 2 / 3			
STX	X → M		8E / 3 / 4	86 / 2 / 3			
STY	Y → M		8C / 3 / 4	84 / 2 / 3			
TAX	A → X					AA / 1 / 2	* · · · · *
TAY	A → Y					A8 / 1 / 2	* · · · · *
TSX	S → X					BA / 1 / 2	* · · · · *
TXA	X → A					8A / 1 / 2	* · · · · *
TXS	X → S					9A / 1 / 2	
TYA	Y → A					98 / 1 / 2	* · · · · *

execution of an instruction. All instructions are included, with 7 addressing modes (6 addressing modes have been omitted).

Notes in Figure D7-4b
(1). Add 1 to "N" if page boundary is crossed.
(2). Add 1 to "N" if branch occurs to *same* page.
(3). NOT CARRY = Borrow

Abbreviations:

A   Accumulator

M   Contents of referenced memory address; strictly, (M)

M_7 Bit 7 (MSB) of memory

M_6 Bit 6 of memory

P   Processor status (condition code) register

S   Stack pointer register

M_s Memory per stack pointer

X   X-index register

Y   Y-index register

V   Logical OR

∀   Logical exclusive OR

∧   Logical AND

*   Modified condition code bit (other bits not changed)

Immediate: Immediate addressing. The operand is contained in the second byte of the instruction.

Absolute: Absolute addressing. The second byte of the instruction contains the 8 low-order bits of the referenced address and the third byte contains the high-order 8 bits.

Zero Page: Zero-Page addressing. The second byte contains the 8 low-order bits of the referenced address and the 8 high-order bits are zero.

Accumulator: Accumulator addressing. The instruction operates on the accumulator.

Implied: Implied addressing. The instruction operates on the register implied by the instruction.

Relative: Relative addressing. The destination address is obtained by adding the second byte of the instruction to the program counter contents. M + 2. Here, M is the 16-bit address of the Rel. Addr. mode OP code.

Indirect: Indirect addressing. (available only for JMP) The second and third bytes, respectively, contain the low- and high-order bytes of the address of some memory location M_1. The contents of M_1 give the low-order 8 bits of the destination address M_d. The high-order 8 bits for M_d are obtained from the next memory address $M_1 + 1$.

(c) Notes and Abbreviations

FIGURE D7-4 *(continued).*   *6502 Reference Card*

place from which a number is to be taken and added to A. Sixteen bits or 2 bytes are required for an arbitrary memory address (MA) specification, in addition to the 1 byte required for the OP code. The *low-order* byte of the MA is given next after the OP code; then the *high-order* byte is placed in the following memory location. This sequence is simply a convention, but it is important to remember it in 6502 usage.

Example:

MA	Contents	Comments
0014	6D	OP CODE FOR ADD-ABSOLUTE
15	03	LOW ORDER OF DESTINATION MA
16	21	HIGH ORDER OF DESTINATION MA
17	--	NEXT INSTRUCTION

Here, the computer will add the contents of memory location 2103_{16} to the accumulator. The program counter is automatically adjusted to 0017 (to the next instruction) when this instruction is received by the CPU because the CPU recognizes that 6D implies a 3-byte instruction.

Notice that the CPU must go to memory 4 times in all to execute the complete instruction:

1. To 14 to get 6D,
2. To 15 to get 03,
3. To 16 to get 21,
4. To 2103 to get the number stored at that location to add to A.

One machine cycle is required for each of these steps, and this is indicated under the N column on the reference card (notice 4 under N). The time for one machine cycle is determined by the frequency of the *clock* that cycles the microprocessor chip. On the KIM and the SYM boards, a 1-megahertz crystal-based clock is used so that a convenient 1 microsecond is required for each machine cycle. This *ADC-absolute* instruction thus requires an accurate 4 microseconds to complete.

The actual addition process must still take place, but the CPU overlaps the addition step with the fetch of OP code step (from MA 0017). Therefore, the instruction effectively requires 4 cycles to complete.

    c.   ADCz *add-from-zero-page* mode. OP Code = 65

NOTE: The appended z is a pedagogical convention used in this book to distinguish zero page mode from the absolute mode; however, the z is not used by the manufacturer.

This instruction saves one memory location (note # = 2) and one machine cycle (note N = 3) from the absolute mode; thus it executes faster and uses less memory, but at a price as we soon see.

Only 1 byte is available after the OP code to tell the computer what memory address is desired. The CPU automatically assumes this byte to be the low-order byte of the address and always appends zeros for the high-order byte of the MA.

Example:

MA	Contents	Comments
0017	65	OP CODE FOR ADD-PAGE-ZERO
18	34	GET NUMBER FROM 0034
19	--	NEXT INSTRUCTION

This instruction is therefore restricted in the range of destination addresses to those from 0000 to 00FF; these are the first 256_{10} locations in memory and are referred to as being on *page zero*.

The addresses from 0100 to 01FF are said to be on *page one* and immediately follow those on page zero; 0200 to 02FF are on page two, and so on. Memory may thus be conceived as divided into consecutive pages, each with 100_{16} or 256_{10} memory locations. Only the first two pages are of particular consequence for the 6502. On many minicomputers and 16-bit microprocessors, the page concept is very important to the addressing scheme.

Although there are other addressing modes available for the ADC instruction, they are deferred here to a later time. In fact, it is possible to accomplish most of the needs of scientific microprocessing with the three modes just discussed. Let us quickly review the differences between these three fundamental addressing modes:

1. *Immediate addressing* permits adding only the number immediately following the OP code in memory to the accumulator. This mode is clearly very restrictive; it is typically used to add some particular value to the accumulator.
2. *Absolute addressing* permits adding a number to the accumulator from (absolutely) anywhere in memory and is therefore very versatile. The 2 bytes following the OP code tell where the number is to come from.
3. *Zero-page addressing* permits adding a number from anywhere in the bottom 256 locations of memory (page zero) to the accumulator. It is quite restricted in terms of the destination addresses with which it may work, but it does use less memory and executes more rapidly than absolute mode.

For the next basic instruction, we consider the LDA instruction.

2. LDA: *LoaD Accumulator from memory.*

The operation is indicated concisely by $M \rightarrow A$. The 8-bit number from the memory address specified by the instruction is loaded into the accumulator and the previous contents of the A are lost; however, the memory location remains unchanged. This instruction is also available in several addressing modes, including the basic three types of immediate, absolute, and zero-page. Because there is much similarity with the examples just discussed, the discussion of each of these modes is brief. The schemes for specifying the particular memory location carry over for all of the *memory reference* instructions.

a.   LDA# *load A–immediate* mode. OP Code = A9

The number in the location immediately following the instruction is put into the A.

b.   LDA *load A–absolute* mode. OP Code = AD

The number at the address given by the next 2 bytes (low-order first) is put into the A. Thus, a number anywhere in memory can be loaded into the A.

c.   LDAz *load A–zero-page* mode. OP Code = A5

The number at the address on zero page, as told by the next byte, is put into the A.

Although the addressing modes to specify the referenced memory location are identical for the ADC and LDA instructions, notice that the actions obtained are different. The ADC instruction *adds to* whatever is already in the accumulator, while the LDA instruction *puts a new number into* the accumulator.

3.   STA: *STore the Accumulator in memory.*

The operation is indicated by $A \rightarrow M$ and is just the opposite of the LDA. The 8-bit number from the accumulator (whatever its present value) is stored or put into the memory location specified by the instruction. The contents of the A remain unchanged, but the previous contents of the memory location are lost. Again a number of modes are available, but there is *no* immediate mode because it would be rarely needed. We therefore consider two modes.

a.   STA *store A–absolute* mode. OP Code = 8D

The number in the accumulator is stored at the memory location given by the next 2 bytes (low-order first). Thus, the A can be stored anywhere in memory.

b.   STAz *store A–zero-page* mode. OP Code = 85

The number in the accumulator is stored on page zero at an address specified by the next byte.

4. JMP: *JuMP to a new address and commence doing instructions.*

This instruction causes the computer to always change the program counter to a new 16-bit memory address, rather than move to the normal next memory address for its instruction. Only two modes are available for this instruction—that is, absolute and indirect—and it is the only instruction that has the *plain* indirect mode, but its discussion is deferred.

a. JMP *jump-absolute* mode. OP Code = 4C

It is a 3-byte instruction, and the next 2 bytes after the OP code contain the absolute address to which the PC will be changed and therefore the address to which the computer will go to obtain its next instruction. The CPU then commences in the normal way to do succeeding instructions.

Example:

MA	Contents	Comments
0020	4C	OP CODE FOR JUMP-ABSOLUTE
2A	2F	LOW-ORDER OF DESTINATION MA
2B	00	HIGH-ORDER OF DESTINATION MA
2C	XX	THESE
2D	XX	CODES
2E	XX	ARE SKIPPED
2F	A9	NEXT OP CODE EXECUTED
30	00	CLEARS THE ACCUM

In this example the computer skips over the instruction(s) in the 3 locations 2C, 2D, and 2E; it does the instruction found in 2F (shown as *clear the accumulator* by LDA# 00). The arrow drawn in the example shows the program flow from OP code to OP code.

Example:

MA	Contents	Comments
0031	65	OP CODE FOR ADCz
32	36	FROM THIS ADDRESS (MA 0036)
33	4C	OP CODE FOR JUMP-ABSOLUTE
34	31	DESTINATION
35	00	OF JUMP
36	01	NUMBER THAT GETS ADDED TO ACCUM

In this example the computer runs in a tight loop, adding the number 01 (from location 36 on page zero) to the accumulator again and again. Indeed, the accumulator will soon "roll over" after exceeding FF_{16} and start again from zero; also the carry will be set. (The *carry* is discussed in some detail shortly.) The computer will be stuck in this loop because there is no instruction that can cause it to move on (for example, on to the code in 36). Only a reset (or power failure) can move the CPU from this endless loop.

At this time it should be pointed out that there is no *halt instruction,* as is commonly found on computers; this is true of several microprocessors. The processor must therefore always be doing something. There is a *reset* line on the 6502 that forces the CPU (in a manner described later) to abandon whatever it is doing and go to a specified location in memory and begin executing instructions there. In general, there must be a program already in memory at that place that permits the CPU to proceed in an orderly fashion. This may be the specific program for the task to which the microprocessor is dedicated. More generally, it can be a monitor program, as mentioned earlier, that can receive programs and commands from an I/O device such as a teleprinter or CRT keyboard, or a calculator-style keyboard. These commands include the possibility of examining and loading specific memory locations.

In experimenting with a microprocessor, it is typical to have such a monitor available in *read-only-memory* or ROM so that this program is not lost when power is turned off (more on ROMs and RAMs later). We may then load a program into memory through a keyboard or other input device with the help of the monitor program (which uses LDA from the device and STA instructions in the process). Then we run the program by indicating the starting address to the monitor and giving some GO command. The program then either runs perpetually or returns to the monitor by a *jump-absolute* instruction placed at the end point of the program. This jump is to some *entry point* in the monitor program and replaces the conventional halt. When the microprocessor is back running in the monitor, we can use it to examine memory locations or registers such as the accumulator (saved at memory locations) and check the performance of the program.

Before considering a small program, some further comment should be made about the *carry flag C.* This bit is part of the *processor status register P* that is considered more completely later. The *C flag* or *C bit* is simply a flip-flop or single-bit memory that is collected along with 6 other flip-flops to form another register in the 6502 microprocessor IC. The P register is drawn on the register model in Figure D7–4a; notice the box labeled C at its right end (LSB). The C bit is set to 1 when an overflow occurs during an addition to the accumulator; if no overflow occurs it is reset to zero. Thus consider the following addition:

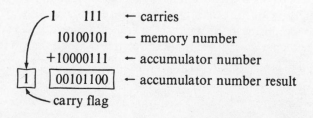

$$
\begin{array}{rl}
1 \quad 111 & \leftarrow \text{carries} \\
10100101 & \leftarrow \text{memory number} \\
+10000111 & \leftarrow \text{accumulator number} \\
\boxed{1}\ \ \boxed{00101100} & \leftarrow \text{accumulator number result} \\
\text{carry flag}
\end{array}
$$

The resulting sum is more than 8 bits and the carry flag receives the carryout. It can be used to signal an overflow problem (like an overflow light on a calculator) or it can be used to do multibyte (extended-precision) additions. The overflow problem can be sensed with a *Branch-on-Carry Set* (BCS) instruction (considered later in this book).

There exist instructions to manipulate the C bit separately from the accumulator:

1. CLC: *CLear the Carry flag.* OP Code = 18
   Makes $C = 0$ and is represented by $0 \rightarrow C$ in the operation column.
2. SEC: *SEt the Carry flag.* OP Code = 38
   Makes $C = 1$, or $1 \rightarrow C$.

Both of these instructions are only 1-byte instructions and require two cycles to complete, that is, one to get the instruction from memory and the other to do it. The OP code is listed under the *Implied* column because the destination of the operation is implied by the instruction.

If there is any doubt about the condition of the C bit before an addition is performed, it should be cleared by the CLC instruction so that a 1 is not incorrectly added into the sum. (However, it should not be cleared after the first addition in a multiple-precision situation.) Use of the CLC instruction is a general approach that is valid on any 6502 system. The KIM board permits an alternative method. After pressing GO on a KIM, the monitor loads the P register from the regular memory location 00F1 before causing the CPU to jump to the first instruction. This location generally contains random bits after power turn on, but it may be set to zero by using the keyboard and monitor *before* pressing GO so that the C bit is already clear (as well as the others) when the program commences. The SYM board uses memory location A65C for a similar purpose; moreover, the SYM monitor automatically clears this location at any reset.

A Complete Simple Program

Consider now a simple program to add together the numbers 2 and 4 and store the answer in memory location 0020_{16}. A typical *coding sheet* layout is used in Figure D7–5 for this program. Note the respective headings for the memory locations, the mnemonics, the hex codes, and the comments. As we first study 6502 programming, it is useful to write the mnemonics for the successive instructions next to the respective memory location numbers. Comments are *always* desirable to remind ourselves of what we want the microprocessor to do. After the program has been written out, we look up the OP codes for the various mnemonics on the programmer's reference card and enter the codes under the hex code column; this is called *hand assembly* of

Memory Location	Mnemonic	Hex Code	Comments
0005	LDA#	A9	LOAD 2 FROM NEXT LOCATION
6	$2	02	INTO THE ACCUM
7	CLC	18	CLEAR C SO DOESN'T ADD IN
8	ADC#	69	ADD 4 FROM NEXT LOCATION
9	$4	04	TO THE ACCUM
A	STA	8D	STORE (ABSOLUTE)
B	$0020	20	IN
C		00	LOCATION 20
D	JMP	4C	JUMP TO MONITOR
E	$1C4F	4F	(TO $1C4F
F	.	1C	FOR KIM MONITOR)
10	.	.	
.	.	.	
.	(DON'T	CARE)	
20	(DON'T	CARE)	RESULT PUT HERE BY PROGRAM

FIGURE D7–5. *Simple Program to Add 2 and 4*

the program. Finally, the program is loaded manually into the memory of the microcomputer and the program is run.

Notice that the program in Figure D7–5 begins in memory location 0005; this is simply an arbitrary choice. The purpose of the successive program steps should be quite evident from the comments given in the program. The actual data numbers 2 and 4 are placed in memory locations 0006 and 0009, respectively. They are "part of the instructions" because the immediate mode is used first to load the 2 into the accumulator and then to add 4 to the accumulator. Notice the *$ prefix* to the numbers 2, 4, 0020, and 1C4F in the program. This is a convention used to designate hexadecimal numbers. Although the traditional number-base designation in mathematics would be a subscript 16, this is not used in computing because subscripts cannot be readily entered on a computer terminal such as a teleprinter or a cathode-ray tube (CRT) terminal.

When the microprocessor reaches the STA instruction in MA 000A, the result of adding 4 to 2 is present in the accumulator. The STA instruction then causes the result to be stored to MA 0020, using the absolute addressing mode.

NOTE: It is true that a more efficient instruction to use here is the zero-page mode of the STA instruction. Why is this possible? Why is it more efficient?

Finally the program concludes, not with a halt instruction, but rather with its microcomputer board equivalent: Jump to the monitor program in ROM. An address for the KIM monitor ($1C4F) is given in the example of Figure

D7-5. If the SYM microcomputer were used, $8000 would be used rather than $1C4F.

Notice that the contents of the memory locations from MA 0010 and onward do not matter because the computer does not use them in this program. Furthermore, the number initially in MA 0020 does not matter because the computer places the result there, changing whatever was present before.

Running and Debugging a Program

To use a specific example in this section, let us assume that the program of Figure D7-5 is to be performed on a KIM or SYM microcomputer. After the program has been loaded into computer memory, the program has *not* yet been executed or *run*. The operator must set the program counter to the address of the first OP code in the program and issue a GO command to the CPU. The starting address of the program in Figure D7-5 is $0005. On the KIM program, executing would be initiated by pressing AD and entering 0005, followed by pressing GO. On the SYM this is done by pressing GO followed by 5 and carriage return CR. Note that the leading zeroes can be omitted on the SYM.

The computer then loads 2 into the accumulator, clears the carry flag, adds 4 to the accumulator, and stores this sum in memory location 0020. Finally, the program causes the CPU to jump to the KIM monitor entry address ($1C4F) in this example. (For the SYM, it should be $8000.) Subsequently, the microcomputer operator can examine memory at $0020 to see if the proper result is there. Students often expect the result (hopefully, 06) to appear in the KIM or SYM display, but this will *not* happen. Numbers and characters appear in the display only if a part of the program specifically causes this to happen, and there are no such directives in this simple program.

Of course, it is possible to add other numbers together simply by changing the contents of memory locations 6 and 9. Suppose a $07 and a $08 are put in these locations. On the KIM, the result (in MA 20) after running the program may be 0F, or it may be 15. (It is amusing to try this with perhaps a dozen KIMs.) Which is right? In fact $07 + 08 = \$0F$, but $07 + 08 = 15_{10}$. The 6502 microprocessor has the capability of performing addition (or subtraction) to the accumulator in normal binary, or in binary-coded-decimal (BCD). The microprocessor may be put into *decimal (BCD) mode* by setting the decimal-mode bit (D bit) in the processor status register (see Figure D7-4a) with the SED instruction—that is, *SEt Decimal mode*. Consequently, the 6502 treats the 8-bit accumulator as containing two 4-bit BCD digits and produces the appropriate carry into the left 4-bit group whenever the sum in the right 4-bit group exceeds 9. This feature is very convenient for performing arithmetic on BCD values, often obtained from digital voltmeters and similar digital instrumentation. The microprocessor remains in decimal mode as long as the D bit is set; it may be returned to binary mode by the CLD instruction

(*CLear Decimal mode*). Again as with the C bit, on the KIM the D bit may be set or cleared by adjusting that bit position in memory location $00F1 before running the program. Thus, if we wish D to be set and C clear, the number $08 should be loaded (this clears all other bits as well). The SYM always clears D mode on reset.

Some monitors have the ability to *single-step* through a program. This enables the operator to watch every step performed and to examine the accumulator or various memory locations to observe whether expected actions are occurring. This is very helpful in troubleshooting or *debugging* short programs with errors. Actually, the accumulator or other registers in microprocessors cannot be examined directly (as they can be in most mini-computers or larger computers). Rather, the monitor must have stored these registers in specific memory locations at each step.

In order to operate the KIM in *single-step mode,* the little switch *S* on its keyboard must be set to ON, and a *Non Maskable-Interrupt (NMI) pointer* at $17FA and $17FB must be first loaded into these memory locations *before* running the program. The NMI pointer address into the KIM monitor is $1C00, so that *00 must be loaded into $17FA and 1C into $17FB.* Then each pressing of GO causes one instruction to be completely executed and the *next* memory address, along with the instruction there, to show up in the display.

The registers are stored by the monitor in memory near the top of page zero on the KIM as given in Table D7–1. These may be examined while single-stepping a program by simply entering the address through the keypad and observing the contents in the right digit pair of the KIM display. To return to the next step in the program, simply press the PC key (program-counter-restore) and press GO to execute the next step.

The SYM may be single-stepped by pressing the *on* side of the *debug* key; then pressing GO and the starting address digits followed by CR causes the CPU to perform one step. The display shows the program counter after each step (along with *single-step-code* digit 2 in the right of the display). Remember that it represents the address of the next instruction to be done. Then press GO, CR repeatedly to cause the CPU to single-step along through the program. On the SYM the registers may be examined after any step by pressing the *REG*ister key. The PC is displayed first; successive registers are shown by pressing the *forward-arrow* button (→). At any time we may con-

MA	Contents
00EF	PROGRAM COUNTER, LOW BYTE
F0	PROGRAM COUNTER, HIGH BYTE
F1	STATUS REGISTER (P)
F2	STACK POINTER (SP)
F3	ACCUMULATOR (A)
F4	Y-INDEX REGISTER
F5	X-INDEX REGISTER

TABLE D7–1. *Registers Stored in Memory on KIM*

clude our examination of registers by pressing CR and then GO, CR for the next program step.

Let us consider how single-stepping the microprocessor through the example program of Figure D7–5 can be used to examine the operation of the microcomputer. It can also be used to catch program errors, program entry errors, and computer malfunctions. After the program has been loaded, the single-step mode should be established for the microcomputer as just described. Then after we issue a GO to the first instruction at MA 0005, the microcomputer stops with address 0007 in the display. This is proper because the first instruction (LDA# 02) is a 2-byte instruction, and the microcomputer executes the complete instruction before stopping. When GO is pressed again, the microcomputer address in the display advances to 0008 because CLC is only a 1-byte instruction.

At this point we might use the microcomputer monitor to examine the accumulator and check that it contains 02 as it should. Also, the processor status register may be checked to be certain that the C bit is now clear. The hexadecimal number appearing in the data portion of the display should be converted to binary in order to check the C bit in the rightmost or LSB position. Further, we may examine the contents of memory address 0020; we should find that it does not contain the result of 06 yet (unless the program has been run previously). Now we may continue through the program until the jump-to-monitor is evident by the appearance of the proper monitor address in the display. Note that if the microcomputer does not stop at a proper stopping point after each pressing of GO, it indicates some type of problem at that point in the program.

Essential Microcomputer Input and Output

A computer must communicate with the outside world to be useful. This communication in a computer center is often input from punched cards, punched paper tape, magnetic tape, teleprinter keyboards, and so forth; or it is output to line printers, punched tape, CRT displays, and the like. However, in the laboratory or in process control, the input and output take more general forms. The input may include data from A/D converters, or on/off conditions of "flags" (flip-flops) from devices connected to the experiment. Output may involve causing motors to start or stop, valves to open and close (via relays to handle the power), or linear voltage control through D/A converters.

In this final principal section of the chapter, we consider how to perform basic input and output operations with a microcomputer based on the 6502.

6502 Microprocessor Approach to Programmed I/O

Most computer input/output is performed in response to specific instructions in a program and occurs when these instructions are executed. This typical approach is called *programmed I/O.* Many minicomputers and microprocessors (for example, the PDP–8/E and HP2100 minicomputers and the Intel 8080 and Signetics 2650 microprocessors) have specific instructions or OP codes to cause binary data to pass out of the computer on some data bus, or else into the computer on the same or a different bus.

However, the 6502 and also the Motorola 6800 microprocessor borrow a technique made well known by Digital Equipment Corporation's PDP–11, called *memory-mapped I/O.* Devices that want to communicate with the CPU are connected to the same buses as memory. Each device must perform like memory at a certain memory location, or perhaps at several locations. Thus, the CPU sends a binary number to the device by *writing* a number (for example, by a STA instruction) to the address of the device. The device must recognize its "pigeonhole number" on the memory address bus and accept the 8-bit number (or perhaps part of the number) that then appears on the data bus.

On the other hand, if a device has data to send to the 6502, it must set up the data on the data bus when a *read*-from-memory at the specific address is executed (for example, by a LDA instruction). Thus, if a device has been designed and connected as memory location 0420, an LDA 0420 instruction will cause an 8-bit number from the device to be routed into the accumulator. The device must respond to the call as memory number 420 and produce the number for the 6502 to accept. The reader may reason at this point that designing the interconnection of input or output devices with the 6502 microprocessor is rather like designing additional memory locations and, in a sense, this is true. It is desirable to understand the purpose and some details of operation for the buses indicated already in Figure D7–3. However, almost all of the digital design work to accomplish I/O has been done through the availability of a family of general-purpose I/O integrated circuits from Mos Technology, Motorola, and other manufacturers. We see shortly that it is principally a matter of connecting proper pins on these ICs to the 6502 microprocessor, or to similar lines available in a 6502-based microcomputer.

Operation of 6502 Memory Communication Lines

Because the scientist is usually vitally interested in the connection of I/O devices to the computer, and because this connection must involve an interface to the memory communication lines of the 6502 microprocessor, we now discuss the lines involved, along with the voltage waveforms and protocol on these lines. In addition to the memory address bus (16 lines) and the data bus (8 lines) already mentioned, the $\phi2$ (phase 2) line and the read/write (R/W) line from the CPU chip are involved and must be connected to the I/O interface. Figure D7–6 shows the voltage waveforms or signals on these lines from the CPU chip to memory or I/O devices. The $\phi2$, R/W, and MA bus signals are all generated in the CPU and sent out in these lines. During a write-to-memory, the data bus signals are generated by the CPU and accepted by I/O memory, while during a read-from-memory, the signals are generated by I/O memory and accepted by the CPU.

The basic timing for the process is done by the CPU clock, which generates nonoverlapping square waves called $\phi1$ and $\phi2$. Clock $\phi1$ goes high during the first half of a machine cycle, while $\phi2$ goes high during the last half; these clock waveforms are pictured at the top of Figures D7–6a and b, respectively. The standard 6502 uses a maximum clock frequency of 1 megahertz and thus has a minimum period of 1 microsecond for either $\phi1$ or $\phi2$.

First we consider the signals during a read-from-memory operation, diagrammed in Figure D7–6a. When a read-from-memory is desired by the CPU, it brings the R/W line high (if not already high) within 300 nanoseconds from the beginning of the cycle. Memory must receive and recognize this feature; memory is now being called to output the number from some memory location to the data bus. Memory receives the memory address from the levels on the memory address bus lines, which the CPU establishes within 300 nanoseconds from the beginning of the cycle. Figure D7–6a thus shows the MA lines possibly changing (some to high and some to low) near the beginning of the cycle to communicate the binary memory address to memory. The data bus lines from the CPU are 3-state outputs and are maintained in *floating mode* by the CPU except during $\phi2$ (high) of a write-to device. During a read-from device (or read-from-memory), the device should take control of the data bus and assert highs and lows on the lines in accordance with the 8-bit number to be sent to the CPU chip. (The changing of the MA bus line, as well as data bus line levels, is indicated in Figure D7–6 as passing both high and low; of course, an individual line is to go to only high or low.) The data should be stable a minimum of 100 nanoseconds before the falling edge of $\phi2$ because the 6502 chip picks up the data at that time.

Therefore, when working with a standard 6502 running at top speed, the device or memory must be able to respond with data within 1000 nsec − 300 nsec − 100 nsec = 600 nsec after it receives a memory address number. This response time is called the *access time* and is characterized by memory manufacturers for their products. The shorter the access time, the more expensive (and usually power hungry) is the memory product.

The situation for a write-to-memory or peripheral device is pictured in Figure D7–6b. The write condition is conveyed to memory by the 6502 CPU bringing the read/write line low shortly after $\phi1$ goes high at the beginning of a cycle. The memory address lines then settle to tell which memory location

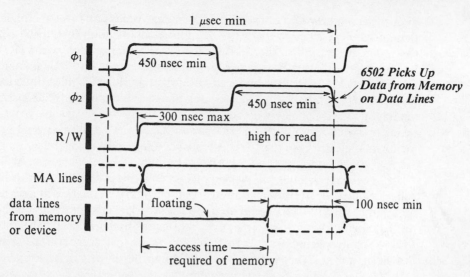

(a) Timing for a Read-from-Memory or Peripheral Device

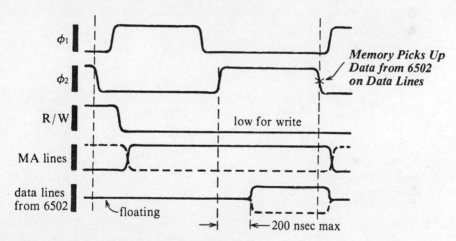

(b) Timing for a Write-to-Memory or Peripheral Device

FIGURE D7–6. *Timing for Memory Address Bus and Data Bus Relative to $\phi 2$ and Read/Write Control Signals*

or peripheral device should pick up the number on the data lines; and, of course, the peripheral devices must recognize their call numbers. The 6502 then asserts an output number within 200 nanoseconds after $\phi 2$ goes high during the second half of the cycle. This should be adequate time for the memory chips to recognize the low level of the R/W line and relinquish the data lines. The data line levels are maintained by the CPU until shortly after

D215

$\phi2$ goes low at the end of the cycle. The memory chips and peripheral device chips should *use the falling edge of $\phi2$* to clock the data into their storage registers; for example, *JK* flip-flops have this clocking behavior.

Notice that the data bus is bidirectional and that the CPU, memory, or device may all be senders or receivers of data on this bus, but only one at a time. Consequently, the outputs of any item connected to this line must be 3-state (or possibly open-collector outputs) with only one output enabled at any time to avoid contention. The memory address bus is unidirectional on the 6502 as typically only the CPU establishes addresses on this bus.

At this point it should be mentioned that for high-speed transfer of blocks of data, *direct memory access* (DMA) is often desirable. In this mode the peripheral device assumes control of all memory bus signals and transfers data to or from memory while the CPU is idled. Transfers can then take place at *memory speed*; for example, one transfer each microsecond, rather than, for example, waiting for data to pass from device to accumulator to memory in programmed I/O (requiring a number of machine cycles). Three-state buffer ICs must be connected between the MA lines of the 6502 and the MA bus to memory if DMA on the 6502 is to be implemented. The 6502 CPU is stopped when required by the DMA device by pulling the ready (RDY) pin on the chip to ground.

6530 Multipurpose Chip

Along with the 6502, Mos Technology introduced a multipurpose chip (IC) in 1975 called the 6530; a number of manufacturers have since added similar chips to the support family for their microcomputers. The intention of the 6530 is to make possible the implementation of a microcomputer in a small, low-cost application with a minimum of ICs. The chip connects directly to the data bus lines, several memory address bus lines, $\phi2$, and the reset line of the 6502 CPU chip; the chip includes the following:

1. 64 bytes of read/write memory (RWM, also called RAM),
2. 1024 bytes (1K) of read-only-memory (ROM),
3. Programmable timer with interrupt capability,
4. 8-bit I/O port,
5. 7-bit I/O port.

The read/write memory is the general sort of memory to which the computer may write data, or from which it may read data. This read or write may be done to any of its locations and hence is called *random access memory* or RAM. However, RWM would be a better term because read-only-memory (ROM) can also be directly read from any of its locations; that is, at random. The ROM contents of this chip are permanently established during the *masking* of the manufacturing process and therefore is appropriate only for large-quantity applications, such as the monitor for KIM or PET. ROMs do exist—though not the 6530—that may be programmed in the field by large electrical pulses that fuse appropriate links at the memory locations. Other ROMs may be erased by ultraviolet light for reprogramming. Indeed, Intel manufactures a version of the 8080 microprocessor with such a reprogrammable ROM available on the same IC.

The programmable timer can be used like a stopwatch to time intervals between events or cause the CPU to wait specific periods of time, rather like an egg timer timing hard-boiled eggs. It was one of the first available for a microprocessor, and the idea has since been picked up by virtually all the manufacturers of microprocessors because it is a very useful device. We discuss the programmable timer more completely later. (A somewhat similar device called the *programmable real-time clock* was introduced for the PDP–8/E and PDP–11 in 1971.)

The 8-bit and 7-bit parallel I/O ports are the principal topics of discussion in this section. The term *port* is often used for a specific I/O channel or capability. These ports permit easy and rather versatile communication with various kinds of devices, although their I/O possibilities are *not* as complete as those of the 6520 (Motorola M6820) peripheral interface adapter or PIA. The PIA is discussed in Chapter D10.

6530 Port Operation

The I/O ports of the 6530 chip work in conjunction with 4 contiguous memory addresses, shown in Figure D7–7a as XXX0, XXX1, XXX2, and XXX3. The X's here represent arbitrary hexadecimal numbers that depend on the manner of connection to the *memory address decoding* of the particular 6502 implementation. The 6530 chip available for experimentation on the KIM is arranged to use addresses 1700, 1701, 1702, and 1703, as shown in Figure D7–7b. I/O port A is located at address 1700. There are literally 8 wires leading from the 8 bit positions in this memory address to 8 pins on this 40-pin IC. These wires are drawn as two-way arrows leading from 8 boxes in *port A* (PA). The 8 boxes represent the bit positions of the memory address at 1700 and are labeled PA0, PA1, ... PA7 for port A; similarly we have PB0, ... PB7 for *port B* (PB) located at 1702. Notice that 0 denotes the least significant bit and 7 denotes the most significant bit. Furthermore, PB6 does not exist because there are not enough pins on the 6530 IC to make it available unless a *chip-select* pin is sacrificed; this can be done on special order, however.

Any individual wire may be programmed as an input wire (to the computer) or as an output wire by use of the corresponding bit in the *data direction register* (DDR) for the port. The wires, in fact, cannot be two-way arrows at a given instant, but only one-way. The reader should be able to discover the rule by studying Figure D7–7b, where an example port configuration is shown. Notice that the least significant 4 bits of port A are programmed as output (wire arrows lead away from the boxes) and the most significant 4 bits

Relative Memory Address

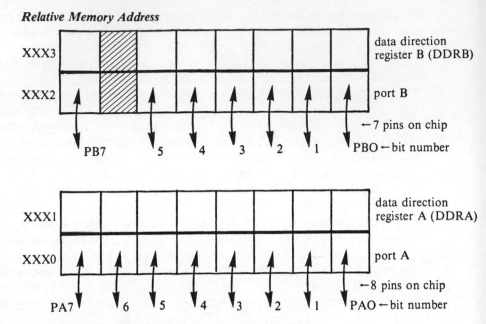

(a) Diagram of Two Parallel I/O Ports Available on 6530

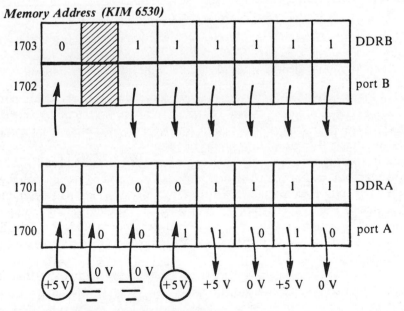

(b) Example of 6530 Port Addresses on KIM and a
Possible Input/Output Configuration

FIGURE D7–7. *Memory-Mapped I/O with the 6530 Chip*

are programmed as input. The rule, of course, is that a 0 in a DDR bit position causes the corresponding I/O pin to be an input pin, while a 1 causes the I/O pin to be output.

Suppose that pin PA4 has been programmed as input by placing a 0 in DDRA4 (data direction register A, bit number 4), as shown in Figure D7–7b. Then if the PA4 pin is connected to TTL high (for example, +5 V), the CPU will receive a 1 in bit position 4 of the accumulator if LDA 1700 is executed. This input of +5 V producing a 1 in PA4 is illustrated in Figure D7–7b. However, if an input line is connected to TTL low (for example, grounded), the CPU will receive a 0 in that bit position on a read from 1700. This situation is illustrated in Figure D7–7b for port lines PA5 and PA6.

On the other hand, if a line is programmed as output (by placing a 1 in the corresponding DDR bit position), the pin will present +5 V to the outside world when the CPU causes a 1 to be put to the port bit position. This situation is shown for PA1 in Figure D7–7b. It might be done by first loading the accumulator with a 1 in bit position 1 (for example, by LDA# 02), and then by storing the accumulator to port A (for example, by STA 1700). Of course, a pin presents near-zero volts as output if a 0 is placed by the 6502 CPU to an output port bit position. This situation is illustrated in Figure D7–7b for port lines PA0 and PA2.

The 15 I/O pins from the application 6530 IC are routed up to the 44-pin *application connector* at the left top edge of the KIM board. Figure 3.9 of the *KIM–1 User Manual* tells the pin assignments.

Programming 6530 Ports

Suppose a *reset* is sent to the 6502 microprocessor chip input pin with this name. This is done on the KIM (or SYM) microcomputer any time the RS button is pushed (for example, after a power-up) and causes the computer to begin running its monitor program. The reset line, which is active low, is generally also sent to peripheral devices such as the 6530 and 6520 chips. When the reset pin on these ICs is brought low, the port and data direction registers *are all reset to zero;* thus all I/O lines are established as inputs at reset, thereby preventing random numbers in the registers of these chips from going out of the ports at system turn-on. The user's program must initially load the DDRs with specific bit patterns to establish which pins will be outputs and which will be inputs.

A program sequence to set up the port configuration—that is, the DDR registers—shown in Figure D7–7b might be as follows:

```
LDA#    $0F     /PUT 00001111 INTO ACCUM
STA     $1701   /STORE IN DDR OF PORT A
LDA#    $3F     /PUT 00111111 INTO ACCUM
STA     $1703   /STORE IN DDR OF PORT B
```

Address	Contents	
M	A9	(LDA#)
M + 1	0F	
M + 2	8D	(STA)
M + 3	01	
M + 4	17	
M + 5	A9	(LDA#)
M + 6	3F	
M + 7	8D	(STA)
M + 8	03	
M + 9	17	

TABLE D7-2. *Actual Contents of Successive Memory Locations*

Notice that this program is written in the typical *compact form*. The actual contents of successive memory locations for this program would be as given in Table D7-2 (M is the first memory address).

Next is shown a program sequence to write data of 5 to port A, then read data from port A, and store this data at memory location 200.

```
LDA#    $X5      /LOAD ACCUM WITH 5
STA     $1700    /SEND TO PORT A
LDA     $1700    /READ PORT A
STA     $0200    /SAVE IN 0200
```

Notice that an X is used in line one; this indicates to the reader that *any* digit could be used here (but *not* X) because it will *not* be sent to that half of port A anyway (those pins are programmed as inputs). However, the reading of port A will now return Y5, where Y is the actual input data. Notice that the data existing on the output pins *will be read* as well as the input data. This behavior is explained next.

Model for 6530 Port Characteristics

A model for the electrical interconnections of the port registers is presented here. This model is very useful for understanding the characteristics for the I/O ports on the 6530 and also applies in most respects to the ports on 6520, 6820, 6821, and 6522 chips. The model is presented in Figure D7-8 and represents the arrangement for just *one bit;* for example, PA0. The arrangement is repeated for the others. The objective of this circuit is to make electrical connections between a data bus line of the 6502 (over which data passes between the 6502 and memory) and the actual I/O pin on the 6530 chip.

NOTE: The direction of passage is shown on most lines in the model by an arrow.

Of course, during a 6502 read-from-memory the direction must be to the 6502, while during a write-to-memory the direction is away from the 6502. The read/write line from the 6502 controls gating (drawn as switches with *W* and *R* positions) for this purpose. Also shown are switches that close only when the memory addresses (MA) appropriate to this device are detected on the memory address bus.

Besides the data direction register (one bit of the DDR is diagrammed as the top FF box in Figure D7–8), each port has an associated *data buffer register* (DBR) that receives and holds data presented by the 6502 CPU during a *write*-to-port instruction. One bit of this register is shown as an FF box near the center of the figure. Then if the I/O pin is configured as output, the DDR

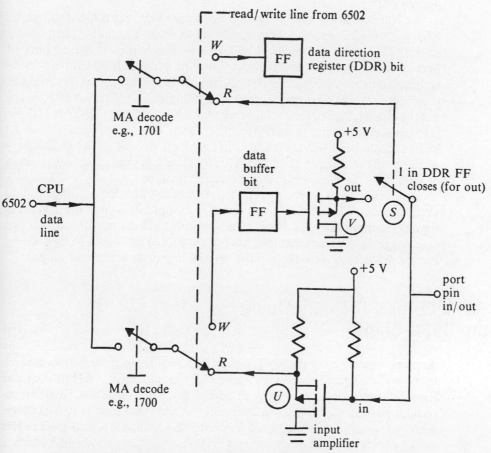

Note: FET Switches U and V Close for a Low Input

FIGURE D7–8. *Operation of an I/O Port Bit for the 6530*

FF causes switch S to close in order to connect the state of the data buffer register FF to the output pin. An FET switch labeled V, along with resistive pull-up, actually produces the low or high out. Notice that no matter what is written to a port data buffer, the voltage levels only appear at the port pins if they are configured as output. However, it is possible to read a port pin whether it is configured as input or output. An input amplifier (diagrammed as transistor U, Figure D7–8) senses the voltage level actually present at the I/O pin. Therefore, if a 1 is written to the particular bit position, but a circuit connected to the input pin for some reason shorts the pin to ground, the CPU will receive a 0 when reading this port pin (even when the port pin is configured as output so that a 1 might be expected). In general, of course, no circuit that actively presents low or high voltage levels should be connected to a port pin if it is configured as output. Why? How can transistor switch V be burned out?

Notice that the output drive is *not* totem pole, but rather through an FET switch to ground and resistive pull-up to +5 V. The outputs can drive 1 standard TTL load and behave like 1 TTL load as inputs. However, pin 0 of port A and of port B has extra capability of being able to source 3 milliamperes; thus they can supply base current drive for transistors. It should be commented that at reset, the ports are programmed as inputs, but assert highs out the pins because of the pull-up resistors. Therefore, if a high at an I/O pin is to cause some device to start operating, it will begin to operate at reset (!) and continue until the program is initiated on the 6502 that presumably would configure the pin as output. This practical but important feature must be considered in the microprocessor design process.

Notice that there are *no* flip-flop storage registers for latching the data that a *device* sends to a port when it is used as input. It is up to the device design to maintain the logic levels at port inputs until the microprocessor has detected them. The fact that they have been "picked up" could be signaled by the microprocessor through a pulse on one line programmed as output.

Basic Control Problem Using the 6530 Chip

As an elementary example of a program and circuitry to accomplish a control task by a 6502/6530-based microcomputer (for example, a KIM), consider the following problem. We have at hand 7 switches with which we desire to turn on and off 7 light bulbs individually. Assume that each switch has been arranged in conjunction with a 5-V source to produce 5 V or 0 V when the switch is flipped up or down, respectively. Assume that the 7 light bulbs are designed to operate from 4 to 5 V at 20 milliamperes.

Of course the elementary solution is merely to connect the switch outputs to the light bulbs as shown in Figure D7–9a. The much more expensive approach is to place a microcomputer between the switches and light bulbs as

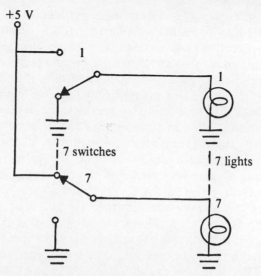

(a) 7 Switches Operate 7 Light Bulbs the Elementary Way

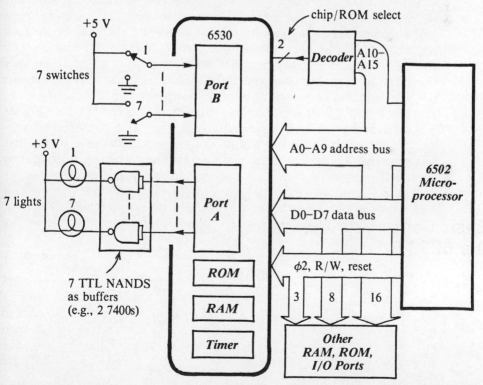

(b) 6502–6530 Microcomputer as a Programmable Connection Between Switches and Bulbs

FIGURE D7–9. *Connecting Switches to Light Bulbs (A Basic Control Example)*

shown in Figure D7–9b. The switch outputs are shown connected to port B of a 6530 chip, which in turn is part of a 6502 microcomputer. The light bulbs are connected, through a buffer, to port A. These ports must be respectively programmed as input and as output ports. The buffer is required on the output port because each port output can only drive 1 TTL load (source 100 microamperes and sink 1.6 milliamperes). The figure shows the use of 7400 NAND gates (readily available and inexpensive) that are capable of driving 10 TTL loads. Then, to light a bulb a NAND output goes low and about 20 milliamperes flow from +5 V through the bulb into the NAND. This current somewhat exceeds the TTL sinking specification (10×1.6 mA = 16 mA), but since a *logic-level* low is not required here, satisfactory operation can be expected.

Figure D7–9b also illustrates the nature of the electrical connections required between the 6502 microprocessor and the 6530 chip. These connections are already accomplished on the KIM microcomputer and are only discussed in general terms here. The types of lines involved should be comprehensible in light of the discussions of Figure D7–3 and Figure D7–6. The memory communication buses are used because the ports must function like memory locations; therefore, the 8-line data bus (D0–D7) is required in order to transfer data to/from the CPU. Further, the chip contains 1K bytes of ROM memory (plus some RAM), so 10 memory address lines (A0–A9) are required for ROM memory location specification. Note that $2^{10} = 1024 = 1$K. (Indeed, the KIM monitor program resides in a pair of 6530 ROMs.) The memory control lines $\phi 2$ and R/W are required, and reset is desirable for zeroing the port registers. Finally, the relative placement of the 1K+ addresses of the 6530 chip within the 64K address space of the 6502 microprocessor must be established; that is, the chip may be arranged to respond to the 1K addresses from $0000 to $03FF, or to those from $0400 to $07FF, and so forth. This is done with a decoder that watches the higher-order address lines (A10–A15) for a certain bit pattern and then activates the particular 6530 chip through use of *chip-select* and *ROM-select* pins on the 6530. More addressing details for the 6530 may be found in section 1.6 of the *6500 Microcomputer Family Hardware Manual,* which is available from the various 6500 manufacturers.

The design of the program is quite straightforward. The program shown in Figure D7–10 is arbitrarily begun in address $0020. First the "housekeeping chore" of establishing input ports and output ports is done (instructions in memory addresses 0020 through 0029). Then the bit pattern corresponding to switches that are on and off at port B is read into the accumulator. Next this pattern is sent to the port connected to the lights, and they respond to the switch configuration that occurred at the instant port B was read. Because output port bits are latched (by the data buffer in Figure D7–8), the lights would maintain this single on/off configuration if the program now went on to other activities. However, we want the lights to follow the switches from moment to moment, and this is accomplished by having the

MA	Instruction		Comments
0020	LDA#	$FF	SET UP PORTA (KIM)
0022	STA	$1701	AS OUTPUT PORT
0025	LDA#	$00	SET UP PORTB (KIM)
0027	STA	$1703	AS INPUT PORT
002A	┌►LDA	$1702	GET STATE OF SWITCHES AT PORTB (KIM)
002D	│ STA	$1700	SEND TO LIGHTS AT PORTA (KIM)
0030	└ JMP	$002A	GO DO IT AGAIN

FIGURE D7–10. *Program for Connecting Switches to Lights (I/O Port Address Assignments for KIM Application Connector Ports Are Assumed.)*

CPU jump back to MA 002A and read the switches again. The computer therefore remains in this loop indefinitely or until reset is asserted.

It is worth noting that on the KIM (or SYM) microcomputer boards, the 7-segment display will go dark during the execution of this program. The board display is multiplexed and requires rather continuous CPU participation; there is none in this program.

Further, the port addresses shown in Figure D7–10 are specifically those for the KIM. Although the application connector at the top edge of the SYM board is essentially pin-for-pin compatible with the KIM, and both boards use the 6502 as the CPU chip, it is *not* possible to take the program of Figure D7–10 and run it directly on a SYM. All the port addresses must be changed to those used by the SYM. This is a simple example of incompatibility often encountered between different computers, even when they are very similar. Of course, if a different CPU is involved (for example, a 6800 or an 8080), the differences are much more severe because the machine language instructions are quite different. Even when virtually identical operations are performed, the OP codes are almost certainly different. Machine language programs are therefore *not transportable* between different computers. One of the advantages of programming in a higher-level language (for example, BASIC, FORTRAN, PASCAL) is the greater transportability. However, I/O details such as those in this simple example would still generally require adaptation.

Use of SYM Application Connector Ports

Application ports for the SYM use a 6522 *versatile interface adapter* (VIA) chip. These ports have more sophisticated possibilities than the I/O ports of the 6530. However, they may be used in an elementary manner very much like the 6530 ports. In particular, the data direction register rules for usage of the respective ports are identical. Figure D7–11 illustrates the port A and port B

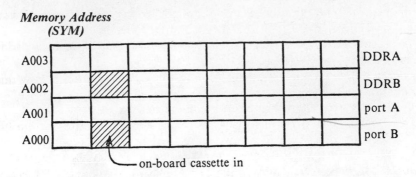

**Memory Address
(SYM)**

FIGURE D7-11. *Application Connector Ports for SYM Microcomputer Board with Memory Assignment*

(application connector) address assignments for the SYM. With the DDR address and port address information of Figure D7-11, it is a simple matter to modify the program of Figure D7-10 for proper operation on a SYM microcomputer. The actual pin usage of the 44-pin application connector on the SYM board is given in Table 4-2 of the *SYM-1 Reference Manual.* Since it is the same as for the KIM, a switch/light bulb circuit designed to plug onto the application connector of the KIM may also be plugged onto the A Connector of the SYM.

REVIEW EXERCISES

1. (a) Name the three principal parts of a computer.
   (b) What are the two principal sub-blocks of the CPU?
2. (a) What register in a classic microprocessor might be called the "running total" or "result" register?
   (b) Describe what is meant by the term *one-address instruction.* How is the register of part (a) involved?
3. What is the difference between a microprocessor and a microcomputer?
4. What is the essential difference between the classic microprocessor and the single-chip microcomputer?
5. (a) What is the difference between a memory address, and contents of a memory location?
   (b) Consider the notation (M) and M. What do the parentheses signify?
   (c) What is the direction of information flow during a memory-read operation and a memory-write operation, respectively?
6. (a) What is meant by the memory space of a microprocessor?
   (b) What is the size of the memory space for the 6502?

7. What is the size (in terms of the number of bits) of the accumulator register and the program-counter register for the 6502 microprocessor?

8. What is the address of the highest memory location that the 6502 can address? Give in binary, hexadecimal, and decimal forms.

9. Virtually all computers are sequential machines. Briefly describe how this accounts for the name *program counter* for this CPU register.

10. (a) What is meant by the term *bus* in computer usage?
    (b) Illustrate where the memory address bus and data bus exist in a microcomputer by placing them on an appropriate block diagram.
    (c) What functions do the two buses of part (b) perform, respectively?

11. Consider the data bus and the memory address bus on the 6502. Which is bidirectional and which is unidirectional? Explain why each has the particular directional character.

12. To what number is the program counter continuously being adjusted during the course of program execution?

13. (a) What is the difference between an OP code and a mnemonic?
    (b) What information is obtained from the columns headed, respectively, by OP, N, and # on the programmer's reference card of Figure D7–4b?

14. Consider the 3-byte instructions as a group for the 6502. What is always contained in the first byte?

15. Give the phrases for the operations with which the mnemonics ADC, LDA, STA, JMP, and CLC are associated.

16. (a) How many memory locations are on one "page" of memory for the 6502?
    (b) What are the addresses of the lowest memory location and highest memory location on page zero and on page one, respectively? Give each of the 4 addresses as a 4-digit hexadecimal number.

17. Three addressing modes are described in the chapter: immediate, absolute, and zero-page. From what does each of the respective descriptive terms derive?

18. (a) What is the difference between the operations of the LDA and the ADC instructions?
    (b) What instruction could be called the inverse of the LDA instruction?

19. (a) Discuss the typical use for a monitor program in a microcomputer.
    (b) What does ROM stand for?
    (c) Why is the monitor program usually placed in a ROM?

20. The 6502 microprocessor does not have a halt instruction. What then is used to terminate a program if it is not to run perpetually?

21. A program segment is written that adds two numbers from memory together. Why should the C bit be cleared before the addition steps in the program?

22. (a) A student has placed a KIM microcomputer in single-step mode and has executed several steps in a program. The student is now curious about the contents of the accumulator. Explain what he or she should do.
    (b) Repeat part (a) for the SYM microcomputer.

23. Single-step mode on the KIM is called debug mode on the SYM. Describe the operation of the microcomputer when placed in this mode. Why is this mode sometimes useful?

24. (a) What two little tasks must one attend to before it is possible to single-step a program on the KIM microcomputer?
    (b) What must be done before it is possible to single-step a program on the SYM microcomputer?
25. (a) In general terms, how does the 6502 microprocessor send a number to an I/O device? What type of instruction might be involved?
    (b) In general terms, how does the 6502 microprocessor receive a number from a device. What type of instruction might be involved?
26. (a) What is the difference between programmed I/O and direct memory access (DMA) I/O?
    (b) What is the possible advantage of DMA I/O?
27. (a) How are the $\phi1$ and $\phi2$ clock signals related on the 6502?
    (b) What is the state of the read/write line during a read operation?
    (c) What clock signal and what condition of this signal should be used by a memory device to pick up data during a write from the CPU?
28. The term *port* occurs in "airport," "heliport," "port authority of New York," and the "port of Dover." It is also used in computer jargon. What is the commonality of the term?
29. Describe why the 6502 and the 6530 chips make possible a small computer using only two integrated circuit packages.
30. What is the principal difference between port A and port B on the 6530 chip used in the KIM?
31. (a) What is the difference between a data direction register and a port?
    (b) How many of each are there on the 6530 chip?
    (c) What is the basic rule for using the data direction register in conjunction with a port?
32. (a) What is the electrical loading character of a 6530 port when programmed as input? Tell as number of TTL loads.
    (b) What is the output drive capability of a 6530 port when programmed as output? Tell as number of TTL loads.
33. What is the purpose of the data buffer register of a 6530 port? Is it put to use when a port is programmed as input or as output?

PROBLEMS

1. Convert the following decimal numbers to hexadecimal and then to binary.
   (a) 100
   (b) 236
   (c) 256
2. (a) Convert the following binary numbers to hexadecimal.
       (1) 01111000
       (2) 00011111000
       (3) 01101101010101110

(b) Convert the above numbers to decimal. Explain why the conversion to hexadecimal hastens the process over converting directly from binary to decimal.

3. Convert the following hexadecimal numbers to binary.
(a) F0
(b) 81
(c) A3
(d) 47

4. (a) Add the pairs of binary numbers to obtain the binary result in each case.

$$\begin{array}{ccc} 00101011 & 10101011 & 11010110 \\ \underline{01101101} & \underline{10110101} & \underline{00101010} \end{array}$$

(b) Add the pairs of hexadecimal numbers to obtain the result in hexadecimal in each case.

$$\begin{array}{ccc} 12 & B7 & 53 \\ \underline{43} & \underline{28} & \underline{A7} \end{array}$$

5. Most minicomputers have a specific instruction available to clear the accumulator (set the accumulator identically equal to zero). The 6502 does not have this instruction. Write an instruction that may be used for this purpose.

6. We want to add the number $20 to whatever is in the accumulator. Two possible instructions A and B will be considered:

(A)   ADC#
       $20

(B)   ADCz
       $20

Which instruction would almost certainly *not* work? Why?

7. How many microseconds are required to execute the three successive instructions illustrated?

Mnemonics

CLC
LDA#
$FF
STA
$1702

8. A student wishes to add one to a number already in the accumulator and does it with the instruction ADCz $01.
(a) Explain why this instruction would not be expected to work.
(b) Explain why it would work if the OP code for the instruction happened to be in the lowest possible memory location.

9. A student is puzzled by a program that contains the instruction ADC $1340 and says that this instruction should not work because it adds the 16-bit number $1340 to the accumulator, and the accumulator can only contain an 8-bit number. Explain the error in the student's reasoning.

10. Three short program segments A, B, and C are shown here.
(a) Assume each segment is to begin in memory location $0000. Find the re-

quired OP codes; write out the memory locations and their contents for each of the segments.

(b) Find the content of the accumulator after code segment A is executed and also after code segment B is executed. Explain why they are different numbers.

(c) Explain why it is not possible to predict the actual content of the accumulator after code segment C is executed unless additional information is given.

(A)	CLC	(B)	CLC	(C)	CLC
	LDA#		LDAz		ADC#
	$00		$00		$00
	ADC#		ADCz		ADC#
	$01		$01		$01

11. Consider the program illustrated.

(a) What is the purpose of the first instruction?

(b) After the program is run on a KIM microcomputer, what are the contents of memory location $001C?

(c) Will the microcomputer attempt to execute the codes found in memory locations $001A and $001B? Explain.

(d) How many microseconds are required by the KIM to run the program steps from the CLD instruction to the instant that it returns to monitor?

Memory Address	Mnemonic
0010	CLD
11	LDAz
12	$1A
13	ADCz
14	$1B
15	STAz
16	$1C
17	JMP
18	$1C4F
19	
1A	$08
1B	$04
1C	

12. Write a program that simply causes the contents of memory location $110 to be increased by $05. Let the program begin in memory location $12 and return to KIM monitor when it has completed its task. Write the program with the coding sheet layout shown in Figure D7–5; fill in all four columns.

13. Write a program that simply continuously sets and then clears the carry bit, or C bit. Have the program begin in memory location $0050. Write the program using four columns with headings *Memory Location, Mnemonic, Hex Code,* and *Comments* as shown in Figure D7–5.

14. Write a program that adds together whatever numbers are in the three memory locations $0020, $0037, and $0124. The result should be stored in memory location $0200. Have the program begin in memory location $0000. Use a coding sheet layout similar to that in Figure D7–5 and fill in all four columns.

15. Consider the program shown. A student hand assembles this program and enters it into program memory on a KIM. He or she also enters $08 into memory location $0000. Then the student runs the program three times in succession (by GO $0010, GO $0010, GO $0010).

(a) What does the student subsequently find in memory location $0000 if the KIM microcomputer is in binary mode?

Memory Address	Mnemonic
0010	LDAz
11	$00
12	CLC
13	ADC#
14	$04
15	STAz
16	$00
17	JMP
18	$1C4F
19	

(b) What would the student find in MA $0000 if the KIM had been in decimal mode?

16. Consider the program shown. It is hand assembled, loaded into memory, and placed into execution from address $0000.

(a) The program runs continuously. Why?

(b) Which memory address lines show activity or pulses? Justify your answer. Use the following notation for the 16 individual address bus lines: AB0, AB1,...AB15. AB0 is the line for the LSB.

(c) Are the remaining memory address lines continuously

Memory Address	Mnemonic
0000	LDA#
01	$20
02	ADC#
03	$04
04	STA
05	$0100
06	
07	JMP
08	$0000
09	

high or continuously low? Justify.

17. Consider the simple program shown. It is hand assembled and placed into execution from address $0020. Which data bus lines show activity or pulses? Justify your answer. Let the respective data bus lines be designated D0, D1,...D7. D0 is the line for the LSB.

Memory Address	Mnemonic
0020	LDA#
21	$08
22	JMP
23	$0020
24	

18. Explain why it is not good practice to place part of one's program in the memory locations $00EF through $00F5 on the KIM.

19. Rewrite the program of Figure D7–5 into the "compact form," such as that used in Figure D7–10.

20. We are presented with two types of memory ICs that are to be used in constructing additional memory for the KIM. The first, type A, is specified to have a maximum access time of 500 nanoseconds, while type B is specified to have a maximum access time of 1,000 nanoseconds. Which type should be chosen? Explain briefly the importance of this specification.

21. Suppose the program sequence (written in compact form) is executed on the KIM. The program is hand assembled and loaded into the KIM beginning at address $0010.

```
LDA#    $FF
STA     $1701
LDA#    $5A
STA     $1700
JMP     $1C4F
```

   (a) Show the contents of the relevant memory locations from MA 0010 and onward.

   (b) Suppose the program is executed. What are the respective readings of the 8 voltmeters V_0 through V_7 connected to the port A pins as illustrated in Diagram D7–1?

   (c) Suppose the program were loaded instead into MA 0050 and onward. Would it operate satisfactorily?

   (d) Suppose the JMP $1C4F instruction were omitted from the program. What would the KIM do differently? Can we really predict what it will do? Explain.

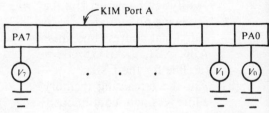

DIAGRAM D7–1.

22. Nothing is connected to the 6530 ports on a certain KIM. A student presses reset and then uses the monitor to examine the contents of memory location $1700. What does the student find in the data portion of the display? Explain.

23. Suppose a 6530 port is programmed as an input port. If a voltmeter is connected to a port pin, what voltage does it read? Explain why this reading occurs.

24. Suppose port pins PB0 and PB1 of a 6530 chip are both programmed as output ports. The bit pattern XXXX XX10 is sent to the port (the X's represent "don't care" bits). Someone unwisely connects pin PB0 to +5 V and also shorts pin PB1 to ground. One of the two connections may damage the port bit position. Explain which connection is damaging and which is not, and why this is so.

25. (a) Suppose port A of a KIM is connected (through a buffer) to 8 LEDs. Write a program that simply turns all 8 LEDs bright and then dark in rapid succession. Use the compact form similar to Figure D7–10 for your program.

Could you expect to actually see the lights turning on and off? Explain.

(b) Rewrite the above program so that it may be executed on a SYM rather than a KIM.

26. Suppose 8 lights are connected to port A of a KIM through a buffer. The lights operate from 12 V at 20 mA each.

(a) Explain why a buffer is required.

(b) Explain why a pair of 7400 quad-NAND-gate chips could *not* be used as the buffer.

(c) Look up the characteristics of the 7406. Explain why a pair of these devices could serve as buffers.

(d) Write a small program that turns on alternate lights; have the light from the least significant bit turned on. Leave the microcomputer back in monitor after establishing the lights. Use a compact form similar to that in Figure D7–10 for this program.

(e) Rewrite the above program so that it may be executed on a SYM rather than a KIM.

27. (a) Port A of a KIM is connected to an 8-bit D/A converter. Using instructions discussed in this chapter, write a program that causes the output of the D/A converter to produce a continuous staircase ramp like that shown in Figure D6–8. After reaching the highest step in voltage, the staircase is to begin again from 0 V.

(b) What is the time duration of each step in your ramp?

28. (a) The KIM microcomputer is to output 12-bit numbers on 12 lines to a port on a PDP–8/E minicomputer. Explain how this could be done with the application connector of the KIM. Make a diagram of the port usage.

(b) Can all 12 bits change to a new 12-bit number at the same instant? Explain.

29. Consider the above problem of 12-bit communication between a KIM and a PDP–8/E. In addition to the 12 lines used to communicate the data, let us use an additional port line (PB7) to tell the PDP–8/E that new data is ready. The PDP–8/E detects this by the fact that line PB7 makes a low-to-high transition. This should occur *after* the data has settled on all 12 data lines.

(a) Write a program that sends the two numbers $249 and $5FA to the PDP–8/E from the KIM ports; then the program exits to monitor. The ports should be initialized from within the program.

(b) Suppose the "ready signal" used above were a high-to-low transition. Explain how the PDP–8/E could get the erroneous impression that new data is ready just by the initialization process. (This could be avoided by loading the data buffers with the first number *before* port initialization.)

General Considerations of Hardware and Software

DIGITAL

The previous chapter introduced the central actor in the application of the microprocessor in the laboratory; namely, the microprocessor as the central processing unit that is supported by memory and input/output chips. A number of fundamental computer concepts and techniques were introduced; and, indeed, some basic microprocessor applications do not require devices or techniques significantly more elaborate than those of the previous chapter. However, there exist a number of supporting actors together with a more complex plot that are relevant to the larger microprocessor applications.

The application of the microcomputer in more extensive (and expensive) laboratory problems is not entirely novel, as the minicomputer has already been utilized in this regard since the late 1960s. Consequently, a considerable body of computer science practice has already been developed that is important to the scientific microcomputer user. Unfortunately, the collection of terms, equipment, and techniques can be rather bewildering to the new student of microcomputers. This book cannot discuss the constituents of larger laboratory computer systems in detail. Nevertheless, the first major section of the chapter—titled *Microcomputer Systems*—introduces important microcomputer equipment available to the scientific user. This section discusses the general categories of microcomputer systems and the purpose and capabilities of some major peripheral devices that may be incorporated into them. The general term *computer hardware* has evolved for the entire class of *physical* computer devices. But there is also a range of programming languages and program tools that are an important part of computer science.

The various forms of *programs* of any sort have come to be called computer *software*, and computer software forms an important part—indeed, sometimes the most expensive part—of any computer application. Consequently, the first section of this chapter also discusses the purposes and capabilities of some major types of software available to the scientific microcomputer user.

The second major section of this chapter—titled *Microcomputer Project Implementation*—discusses the general process of developing a laboratory microcomputer application. The process involves selection, design, and testing of both microcomputer hardware and software. This section stresses software, however, introducing the flowchart as a general program design technique for the programming of laboratory microcomputer projects. It also discusses the conventions of assembler language programming and, finally, how a microprocessor project (including assembler language programs) can be developed on a microcomputer development system.

Microcomputer Systems

Large Computers to Minicomputers as Backdrop

The first electronic computers were developed circa 1940 to numerically solve large and difficult mathematical problems in connection with scientific research. These evolved within a decade into large *mainframe* computers costing millions of dollars that were applied to data processing in large businesses, as well as the above sorts of scientific problems. Modern large computers continue to be manufactured in this price range for "computer center" applications.

They may be characterized as large because of the word size (32 to 64 bits), memory space (several million bytes), and physical size (room size). The large physical size is due in part to the many *peripheral devices* that are commonly connected to the main CPU. Always included is the provision for *mass storage* of many millions of bytes of programs and data; this is accomplished on *magnetic hard disc* and *magnetic tape* peripheral devices. Further, large computers customarily have the capability to input data/programs from many *terminals* that may be regarded as part of the computer (such as teleprinters and CRT terminals), as well as to output results to these terminals or to expensive high-speed *line printer* peripheral devices.

The *minicomputer* classification emerged in 1965, beginning with the PDP–8/E from Digital Equipment Corporation. Relative to the large computer, it may be regarded as "mini" in word size (8 bits to 24 bits), memory space (less than 64K words), physical size (less than 1 meter^3 for CPU and memory), and price (less than \$20,000 for a minimum usable configuration).

Typically, a rather smaller line of peripheral devices, which in turn have smaller capacities, is available for minicomputers as compared to large computers. However, upper-end minicomputers range into the domain held formerly by the large mainframe computer systems.

Because of their relatively mini price and mini size, minicomputers quickly grew to be an important segment of the computer industry. They were applied to data processing by smaller businesses (for example, with as few as 100 employees) and also applied to a new important area: *real-time* or *on-line* computer applications; that is, the minicomputer was connected directly to processes in an environment where its response in "real" time was important. The minicomputer became a building block in rather expensive and sophisticated laboratory equipment. Examples include the gas chromatograph, nuclear magnetic resonance spectrometer, nuclear particle accelerator, patient monitoring system, and centralized ECG system. The minicomputer was also placed into various industrial applications. Examples include machine tool controllers, steel-making machines, paper-making machines, and chemical process control.

In some of these applications, the minimum minicomputer configuration was adequate (about $6,000), consisting of the CPU + 4K memory box or mainframe, and teleprinter with low-speed paper tape reader/punch. Others required more extensive main memory, mass data storage on magnetic tape, fast-access mass data storage on magnetic disc, or faster printing capability. *Magnetic tape* is rather like the tape commonly used for audio purposes; for example, in cassettes. Ones and 0's are stored on digital magnetic tape by magnetizing tiny regions along a *track* on the tape in one direction or the other. These regions are sensed by the *head* when reading the tape. *Magnetic discs* use circular sheets of magnetic film and the digital bits are stored in concentric tracks on the disc. A *read/write head* moves over the disc to a given track in order to write or read the data to or from that track.

Many laboratory applications require A/D conversion, D/A conversion, and a timing capability in real time, called a *real-time clock*. Figure D8-1 diagrams a real-time system that incorporates many of these peripherals. Characteristics and typical prices (circa 1970 to 1980) for these devices are given in Table D8-1. From the above discussion and Table D8-1, it can be estimated that a moderately comprehensive minicomputer system typically costs some $15,000 to $25,000. Clearly the application must be such as to justify this expenditure.

Hardware and Software

Rather early in computer history, the term *hardware* came to be applied to the physical—often electronic—parts of a computer installation. Hardware includes the CPU and memory and various peripheral devices. Over the course of 1955 to 1975, the size and price of the CPU and memory hardware de-

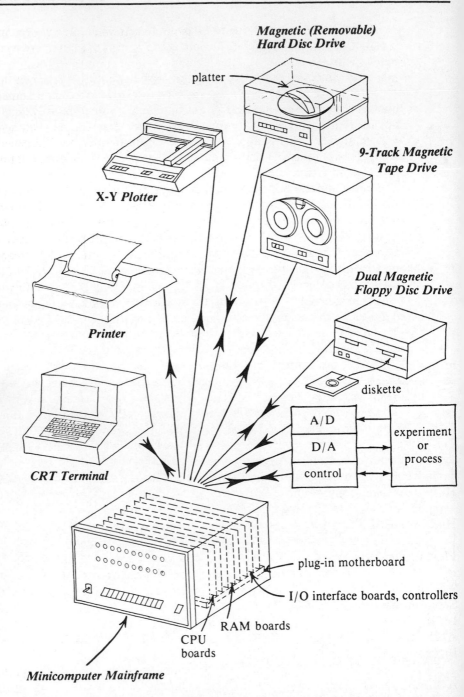

FIGURE D8-1. *Minicomputer in a Real-Time Application Shown with a Complement of Peripheral Devices*

creased by a factor of 100 due to innovations in semiconductor technology. The price of various peripheral devices also declined, although not nearly so dramatically.

An important part of any computer application is the program that the computer executes to accomplish the desired task. Any sort of computer program has come to be called *software* because it is not as physically tangible as the hardware and can also be changed rather readily. In many applications the computer software has become the most expensive aspect. The generation of a program remains very human-labor intensive, and human labor has become a very expensive commodity.

A rule of thumb that has persisted in the computer industry for decades is that a competent programmer can produce on the order of 10 lines of error-free, documented program per day! This number tends to hold true whether the programming is done in machine language (where each line is one OP code) or in a higher-level language. It is assumed that the reader already has acquaintance with some *higher-level language* such as BASIC, FORTRAN, or PASCAL; further, the previous chapter should give a good indication of the rather rudimentary operations involved in each line of a machine language program. Thus it should be clear that one line of a higher-level language pro-

TABLE D8–1. *Minicomputer Peripheral Devices*

Device	Typical Characteristics	Typical Price
Teleprinter (low-speed paper tape reader/punch)	10 to 30 characters/second (10 characters/second)	$1,200 ($200)
High-speed paper tape reader/punch	read 200 characters/second punch 50 characters/second	$1,500
Hard magnetic disc	5-megabyte capacity 10-millisecond random access	$5,500
Flexible magnetic disc	500-kilobyte capacity 250-millisecond random access	$3,000
9-track magnetic tape	40-megabyte capacity	$15,000
Serial printer	180 characters/second	$3,000
Line printer	300 lines/minute	$8,000
A/D and multiplexer	12-bit/16-channel	$1,600
Programmable real-time clock	4 modes/5 crystal frequencies	$1,000
A/D, two D/As, clock	10-bit, A/D, D/A	$2,000
X-Y plotter	programmable	$3,000
CRT terminal	20 lines × 80 columns	$1,000

gram must cause a computer to execute many (for example, 10 to 100) lines of machine code. This fact becomes a compelling economic argument for using a higher-level language in computer applications, because by utilization of a higher-level language, a programmer can ultimately produce many more machine instructions per hour of programming time than if direct machine language programming is used.

However, the higher-level language facility is generally not as efficient in producing machine code as a competent programmer is. On the order of 50% more memory may be required by code produced by the higher-level language. Further, the execution time may be slowed significantly, and this time may be critical in a real-time application.

These effects are especially important if the higher-level language is implemented as an *interpreter,* as is often the case for BASIC. When a computer executes a program through an interpreter, it examines each line of the program while the program is actually being executed, translates the various constructions into the machine code required, and then executes the instructions. This procedure is done for each line of the program, even if it has been translated before. Clearly this is a time-consuming process. Generally we cannot expect a BASIC program to accomplish successive actions in real time with any shorter time interval than 0.01 second. Further, the interpreter program itself must reside in a significant amount of memory, and this cost must be considered (for example, $100 for 8K ROM).

On the other hand, FORTRAN and PL1-type languages (PL/M, PL/Z, and so forth) are usually *compiled.* Thus a FORTRAN *compiler program* is run on some computer to translate the *source* FORTRAN program into actual machine code. This procedure is done only *once.* The code is then placed in the memory of the application computer and this *object program* may be executed. The code may be relatively compact and run with reasonable speed. However, if sophisticated mathematical constructions (for example, transcendental functions) are used in the source program, the object code can be expected to include mathematical subroutines of some size (for example, several kilobytes).

When a computer is utilized with a rather full range of peripherals and language possibilities, a significant amount of software is desirable simply to make these various facilities easy to access and use. Examples are *program routines* to operate a magnetic disc or a printer, or to keep a directory of stored programs and languages and make them accessible from mass storage a needed. Such software evolved from rather rudimentary "disc monitors" circa 1960 to sophisticated (sometimes expensive) computer *operating systems* (OS) in the 1970s. In the operation of large mainframe computers, the performance of the operating system is often as important as the performance of the computer hardware; indeed the operating system (software) may be nearly as expensive as the computer hardware. Sophisticated operating systems—called *multiprogramming*—provide for simultaneous use of the computer resources by many users. As minicomputer systems have become more sophisticated, the use of operating systems has become commonplace. Some of these operating systems are designed to support real-time communications with laboratory experiments.

Floppy Disc Devices

An important peripheral device that emerged approximately concurrently with the microprocessor is the *floppy disc* or *flexible disc* device. In terms of size and cost, the floppy disc low-cost storage device is particularly appropriate to microcomputer usage. A dual-drive (or two-disc) unit is sketched in Figure D8–1. A flexible magnetic disc or *diskette* is used to store 1's and 0's as tiny magnetized regions around concentric *tracks* on its surface. Two sizes of floppy discs and drives are available: the 8-inch *full-size floppy,* and the 5-1/4-inch *minifloppy;* these dimensions refer to the diameter of the diskette. The 8-inch diameter diskette has 76 tracks, while the 5-1/4-inch *minidiskette* has 23 tracks. The disc spins at 360 revolutions per minute within the *drive* (rather like a phonograph record in a phonograph) and the *read/write head* moves over the surface of the disc to read (pick up) or to write (record) data from or to various tracks. The phonograph analogy to the read/write head activity is that the pickup head of a record turntable may be moved over a phonograph record to play various parts of a record. 253K bytes may be stored on one side of an 8-inch standard diskette using *single-density* bit magnetization in each track; 89K bytes may be stored on one side of the 5-1/4-inch minidiskette. More recent *double-density* technology doubles the above disc capacities by using twice the bit density in each track. The capacity of one disc can also be doubled by use of recent *double-sided disc* technology; here both sides of a disc are recorded and read through the use of two read/write heads. If both of these technologies are used simultaneously, the capacity of one disc may be increased fourfold.

The average *access time* to read or write data to some track on a disc is important; this time is about 1/4 second (250 milliseconds) for the standard floppy drive and 1/2 second (500 milliseconds) for the minifloppy drive. Once accessed, the data transfer rate is 250K *bits*/second for the single-density standard floppy and 125K bits/second for the minifloppy. With the transfer rate the reader may readily calculate the approximate time required to transfer, for example, 16K *bytes* of data or program between a microcomputer memory and floppy disc. (Actually, a somewhat longer time is required due to additional "housekeeping" data that is placed between actual data blocks in each track.)

The floppy disc is very useful in minicomputer and microcomputer systems for storage of rather large programs or large amounts of data when random and rather quick access by the computer is required. Some examples are as follows:

1. Various collections or *files* of data, such as results from a number of experiments, are to be compared or analyzed in some way. The amount of data is too large to be economically placed in main memory, but the program operating in main memory may quickly access blocks of the data if it is available on a floppy disc peripheral device.

2. A number of different programs must be loaded into computer memory in order to perform various functions in a laboratory application. These programs are too large to fit in memory concurrently, but they may be quickly loaded into memory as they are needed if they reside on a floppy disc device.

3. In the development of programs, various languages may be used or different program segments and routines may need to be merged and compiled (possibly assembled) into machine code. For this application, magnetic disc storage becomes almost essential; these language compilers or program segments are stored on disc and rapidly brought into computer main memory as required.

Microcomputer Hardware and Software

A broad range of microcomputer hardware and software has evolved, and continues to evolve, to fit the microprocessor to an equally broad range of applications. Microcomputer hardware may be broadly organized into four categories:

1. Single-chip microcomputer,
2. Single-board microcomputer,
3. Mainframe-package microcomputer,
4. Single-package microcomputer system.

In this section the equipment found in each category is characterized, and the level of software commonly used with each is described.

At the very low end is the *single-chip microcomputer* that can serve as a control function in a device such as a hand-held game or even a food blender. 2K ROM, 64 to 128 bytes of RAM, and an interval timer are typically incorporated on the chip. Available memory generally dictates a machine language control program at this level. Rather large volume is needed to justify the ROM masking cost. I/O control lines emanate directly from the chip; some even incorporate an A/D converter.

Many *single-board microcomputers* have been introduced, of which the KIM and SYM are quite representative. These microcomputers have significant I/O capability and sufficient memory to use compact versions of higher-level languages. They are well suited to be incorporated in process control equipment, laboratory experimentation, and instrumentation of intermediate size.

Beginning with the 8080-based Altair microcomputer (first introduced as a kit in January 1975), a number of microcomputers have been produced in a *mainframe package* quite similar to that of the classic minicomputer pictured in Figure D8–1. Like the minicomputer, these microcomputers generally require an attached terminal for operation. A *motherboard* with plug-in connectors is placed along the bottom of the frame, and the CPU board, along with an ample power supply, is placed in the box. The motherboard permits easy expansion or tailoring to specific requirements because additional memory boards, parallel I/O and/or serial I/O boards, and peripheral controller boards are easy to plug in.

Altair used a bus of 100 lines (available through 2×50 pin connectors with 0.125-inch pin spacing) to carry memory address, CPU data-in, CPU data-out, and various control functions along the printed circuit motherboard. It has since become a bus standard as the *IEEE S–100 bus,* and a myriad of boards are manufactured to plug into this bus. However, its line functions were influenced by 8080 usage, and thus the S–100 bus is usually found in microcomputer mainframes based on the 8080 or its descendants— for example, the Z–80.

BASIC was the first higher-level language available for most of these mainframe-package microcomputers, although many other higher-level languages are now available from the microcomputer manufacturers or independent software houses. Furthermore, a rather complete line of peripheral devices is available for most of the microcomputers in this class, including floppy disc peripherals with an associated controller that plugs into the microcomputer motherboard. A CRT terminal is also typically connected to the mainframe to facilitate human interaction. In this case, a printer that can rapidly produce "hard copy" of programs and data for future study or reference is essential. The fully implemented microcomputer system then looks very much like the minicomputer system shown in Figure D8–1. Although prices for these peripherals have declined relative to 1970 minicomputer prices, a rather complete system may quite easily command a $10,000 price tag. Actually, there is little to distinguish between the expanded microcomputer system of 1980 and the minicomputer system of 1970. Consequently, a microcomputer configuration that includes floppy disc storage, a fast printer, and a CRT is often selected for small-business data processing.

As the number of languages, the number of supporting peripheral devices, and the scope of applications have increased, so also has the need for operating system software increased (just as it did earlier for the larger computers). A widely implemented microcomputer operating system is called CP/M; this software was originally developed for 8080-based microcomputer systems, although it has also been adapted for others. Most mainframe microcomputer manufacturers sell operating systems to be used on their larger microcomputer configurations; indeed, their capabilities and style for usage are rather similar to OS software available since 1970 for minicomputers. Unfortunately, some period of study and practice is generally required before an OS can be used effectively.

The *single-package computer system* is an important configuration made possible by the microprocessor and LSI technology. Beginning with the

6502-based Commodore PET in 1977, a number of microcomputers in this new style have appeared; these have been termed *personal computers.* A CRT display and full typewriter-like keyboard, as well as microcomputer board, are incorporated into a self-contained unit (although sometimes the CRT is cased separately) that often looks much like a simple CRT terminal. In some cases, even a floppy disc drive and small printer are incorporated. In less expensive models ($500 to $1,000), a cassette tape facility is universally provided for inexpensive "mass storage" for data or programs. However, with cassette usage a program or data access typically requires one or more minutes, versus perhaps a second for a floppy disc. Figure D8–2 illustrates some features of two single-package microcomputers.

Because a CRT and full-alphabet keyboard—also called an *ASCII keyboard*—are available, this microcomputer class is well suited to work with a higher-level language. BASIC implemented as an interpreter was almost universally the first language available, usually stored in ROM. The ability

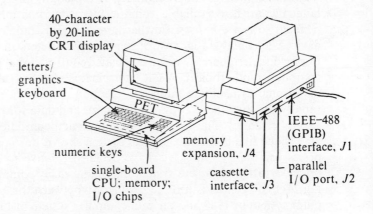

40-character
by 20-line
CRT display

letters/
graphics
keyboard

PET

numeric keys

single-board
CPU; memory;
I/O chips

memory
expansion, *J*4

cassette
interface, *J*3

IEEE–488
(GPIB)
interface, *J*1

parallel
I/O port, *J*2

(a) Commodore PET or CBM Microcomputer

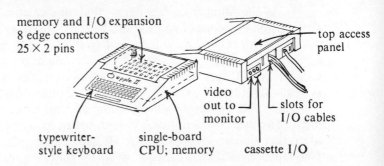

memory and I/O expansion
8 edge connectors
25 × 2 pins

top access
panel

video
out to
monitor

slots for
I/O cables

typewriter-
style keyboard

single-board
CPU; memory

cassette I/O

(b) Apple II Microcomputer

FIGURE D8–2.   *Features for Two Single-Package Microcomputers*

to handle stored data from within programs (as files) and also to work with groups of characters—that is, *strings*—under program control is typically available in these versions of BASIC. Of course, a variety of mathematical operations and functions are available.

Memory-mapped I/O can be accomplished in most microcomputer versions of BASIC with the PEEK and POKE instructions. Thus the memory location at *decimal* 3048 may be loaded with the binary equivalent of *decimal* 32—that is, with 00100000—through the BASIC statement: POKE 3048, 32. Conversely, the contents of this memory location will be assumed by the variable X through the BASIC statement: X = PEEK(3048). If the memory contents were $20, X would take the value 32.

Most microcomputers of the single-package class can be loaded with a machine language program and placed into execution of it. Knowledgeable users may make use of this high-speed execution capability and also of various machine language subroutines in the computer monitor ROM (for example, to exploit the keyboard, CRT, and other facilities), provided the manuals document such usage well.

Some single-package microcomputer systems have a motherboard arrangement within the case to accommodate expansion of memory, I/O facilities, device controllers, and so forth. The 6502-based Apple computer was perhaps first in this regard and has found wide use in scientific laboratories. Further, a number of higher-level languages—for example, PASCAL, FORTH, and "C"—were available rather early for the Apple.

Memory Hardware

Magnetic *core memory* dominated the random-access-memory (RAM) usage for computers until about 1976. A bit is stored by magnetizing a tiny toroid or "doughnut" of ferrite material in one direction or the other. It is a *nonvolatile* type of memory in that the bit is *not* lost when the power is turned off (the magnetization remains). However, core memory has been power hungry, rather bulky, and expensive to manufacture (4K words of memory for the PDP–8/E cost $3,000 in 1972).

Semiconductor memory uses integrated transistor circuitry to store data. More and more bits have been capable of manufacture on one IC and at a rather steeply declining price. Bipolar-transistor-type memory chips have the fastest access times (1 to 10 nanoseconds), but consume the most power. MOS-transistor-type memory chips—that is, *MOS* (metal-oxide-silicon) *technology*—have achieved rather rapid access times (50 to 500 nanoseconds) and have intermediate power requirements. CMOS-technology memory chips consume the least power and are well suited to battery operation; however, they are the slowest type (300 nanoseconds or more). In 1980 it was possible to purchase 4K bytes of memory for $100 to $200. RAM semiconductor memory is available in two types: *static* and *dynamic.* The *dynamic semiconductor memory* loses its bits (loses its "memory") after a few milliseconds unless "refreshed." The bits are stored as charge, and the charge leaks away. Proper pulses must be arranged to refresh these memories, during which time the CPU cannot use the memory. *Static semiconductor memory* chips use flip-flops to retain their bits as long as the power supply voltage is maintained to the chips and are easier to design into memory systems. However, not as many bits can be stored on one chip in the static case as in the dynamic, and they are more expensive. In 1980, 8K-bit static memories and 64K-bit dynamic memory chips were the largest commonly available. Unfortunately, semiconductor RAMs lose their memory when the power supply voltage is removed; that is, they are said to be a *volatile* type of memory.

Read-only-memories (ROM) are commonly available as integrated circuits and are of three types. The first is the *mask-programmed* ROM that is programmed by the manufacturer to user specifications. Typically the bit pattern in the ROM is determined by the final layer of metallization. The second type is the *programmable ROM* or PROM that is programmed by the user. Selected metal or polysilicon links are fused by a short high-current pulse. This process is irreversible. The third type is the *erasable-programmable ROM* or EPROM. In this type, bits are stored as charges in MOSFET cells and can be erased, typically by flooding the chip with ultraviolet light (a window exists on the top of the IC). The advantage of ROMs is that they do not lose their bit pattern when the power supply is turned off.

Semiconductor memories are widely used in microcomputers. In single-board microcomputer applications, the application programming or software is often placed in ROM. In this case, the program attains a curious status between software and hardware and has come to be called *firmware*. The application program is placed in ROM for two reasons. First, in very low cost control applications, there generally exists no keyboard or other facility for loading the program into RAM. Secondly, even if such a facility does exist, it is desirable to retain the program during power failure. However, in unattended operations we often want the CPU to resume running in an orderly fashion. To achieve this task generally requires hardware to assert a reset to the computer and software for new initialization. Notice that the CPU registers and any results in RAM memory would be lost, however. Therefore a *battery backup* sufficient to maintain +5 V during brief power failures (which are the most common) is often used.

A semiconductor memory IC that contains 1K bits is typically arranged as 1K×1 bit or 256×4 bits. (Recall that 1K is short for 1024.) The 1K×1-bit type has only 1 data line in/out, while the 256×4-bit type has 4 data in/out lines. Thus, 4 bits are available in parallel in the latter type. To specify any one of the 1K bits in the 1K×1-bit type requires a 10-bit binary number, so 10 memory address lines must lead into such a chip. On the other hand, 8 address lines are required to specify a memory address in the 256×4-bit type.

Since most classic microcomputers operate with 8-bit bytes, 1K-bit ICs are available organized as 128×8 bits. These have 8 parallel data in/out lines and require 7 address lines to specify the byte locations. (Notice that the number of lines or pins increases for the same amount of bit storage.) 1K×8-bit (8K-bit) and 2K×8-bit (16K-bit) static chips are also recently available, and larger chips are expected in the years ahead.

In addition to the memory address lines, semiconductor memory ICs almost always have one or more *chip-select* lines. These lines simplify construction of memory banks. No matter what address is present on the MA lines, these chips maintain their data-out lines in an off state (because they are typically 3-state), and they do not accept data in, unless the chip-select pin is active (typically low to activate the chip).

For example, suppose a 4K×8-bit (4K-byte) memory is to be constructed from 1K×1-bit chips. Eight of these chips in parallel constitute a 1K×8-bit memory (1K-byte memory block). Four of these 1K-byte memory blocks are required to construct a 4K-byte memory. The 10 *least* significant memory address lines are sent to *every* memory chip. The 2 *high-order* memory address lines (12 MAs in all for 4K) should go to a (2-bit-to) 1-of-4-line decoder. Each decoder output goes to one of the 1K memory blocks or *banks* so that 00 selects the lowest 1K bank, 01 selects the second 1K bank, 10 selects the third, and 11 selects the fourth (see Figure D8–3). If the data lines are 3-state, the data lines from one 4-chip column may simply be connected together to obtain 1 bit (of the 8). Only 1 chip of the 4 is ever selected at one time, so that no contention exists.

Character Communications and the ASCII Code

Microcomputer operation and application often involve communications with humans, peripheral devices, or other computers that make use of decimal numbers and groups of alphabetic characters (real, honest-to-gosh words). Thus, in addition to controlling a process, it may be desirable to convey information to an observer. A wind-energy data acquisition system might periodically print out on a printer or CRT display the information WIND SPEED IS 9 M/SEC. When using a higher-level language on a microcomputer, this periodic printout can often be accomplished quite easily without much knowledge of the actual internal mechanisms used. Thus, using the BASIC language on the PET, the statement

```
PRINT "WIND SPEED"; W;" M/SEC"
```

causes the desired phrase to appear on the CRT screen. *W* is assumed to be the variable used for the wind speed.

However, computers internally deal only with binary numbers (which may be compactly represented in hex). Therefore, various characters—letters,

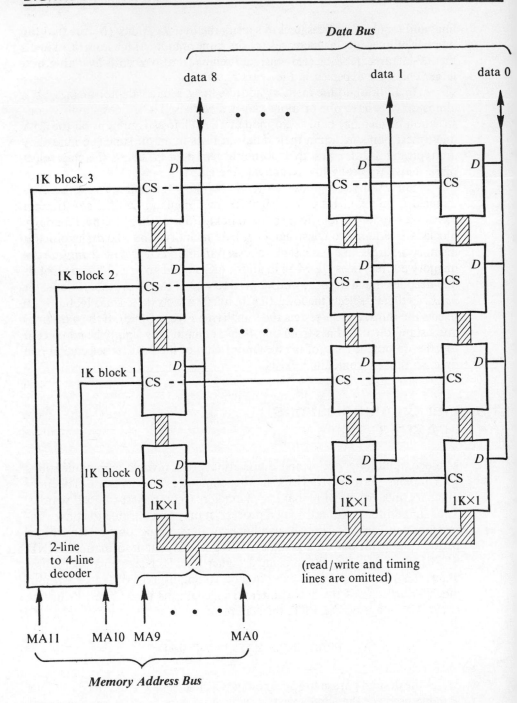

FIGURE D8–3. *Construction of a 4K-Byte Memory from 1K×1-Bit Memory ICs with Chip-Select (CS) Features*

numerals, symbols—must be input to the computer, and also stored within computer memory, in some form of binary code. When a person types a BASIC program into a computer (for example, on the PET or Apple keyboard), each key pressed causes a binary code for that character to be input to the CPU. A program running on the CPU must in turn interpret the codes and determine actions to be taken.

When a phrase such as WIND SPEED is printed on a printer, the CPU under direction of a program must send the code for W, then the code for I, and so on, to the printer. Even when the number 9.5 is printed, a code for 9, code for ".", and code for 5 must be sent.

There are all sorts of ways to code letters, numerals, and the like, into binary patterns. For many years IBM has used the EBCDIC (Extended Binary-Coded-Decimal Interchange Code). However, a widely used code is the ASCII code (American Standard Code for Information Interchange). For example, it is the code used by the ubiquitous Teletype, which was perhaps the paramount inexpensive computer terminal from 1965–1975. Virtually all modern CRT terminals transmit and receive characters in ASCII code.

ASCII code uses 7 bits to code the various characters; an eighth bit is generally appended in the most significant bit position to constitute the standard byte of data transmission. The eighth bit may be always set to 1, or always set to 0. However, it is more useful to let the eighth bit be a parity bit in order to catch transmission errors; for example, a changed bit. Then, in the *even parity* convention, this bit is made 0 or 1 in order to maintain the total number of 1's (in all 8 bits) always even.

A 7-bit code permits 128 different characters to be encoded. Figure D8–4 gives the code-to-character correspondence in a compact form (a look-up form rather like a multiplication table). Several examples are given. Note that the code for the numeral zero in *not* 00000000. Sending a 30 (hex) to a printer causes a single zero to be printed. The codes for the numerals and the letters of the alphabet are each in numerical order (A, B, C, . . . = 41, 42, 43, . . . and a, b, c = 61, 62, 63, . . .). Various commands to the terminal are also available. Thus, sending an OD (hex) to the terminal causes carriage-return (CR) of the printing head on a teleprinter; on a CRT the printing position for the next character is moved to the left of the screen. LF = OA (hex) causes a *line feed;* that is, the paper is advanced one line on a printer, or the printing position for the next character is moved downward one line on a CRT terminal. Finally, it should be pointed out that *if* even parity is used, A = 41, B = 42, (but) C = C3, D = 44, (but) E = C5, and so on.

Paper Tape Format

Paper tape has been used for many years as a simple and inexpensive way to store modest amounts of binary data and programs. Although floppy discs or cassette tapes are replacing paper tape, it is still used in some applications;

(most significant bit assumed
zero for hexadecimal case)

Hexadecimal → ↓ Binary ↓	0 000	1 001	2 010	3 011	4 100	5 101	6 110	7 111	◀ Most Significant
0 0000	NUL	DLE	SP	0	@	P	`	p	
1 0001	SOH	(DC1) X-ON	!	1	A	Q	a	q	
2 0010	STX	(DC2) TAPE	"	2	B	R	b	r	
3 0011	ETX	(DC3) X-OFF	#	3	C	S	c	s	
4 0100	EOT	DC4	$	4	D	T	d	t	
5 0101	ENQ	NAK	%	5	E	U	e	u	
6 0110	ACK	SYN	&	6	F	V	f	v	
7 0111	BEL	ETB	'	7	G	W	g	w	
8 1000	BS	CAN	(	8	H	X	h	x	
9 1001	HT	EM	)	9	I	Y	i	y	
A 1010	LF	SUB	*	:	J	Z	j	z	
B 1011	VT	ESC	+	;	K	[	k	{	
C 1100	FF	FS	,	<	L	\	l	|	
D 1101	CR	GS	–	=	M	]	m	}	
E 1110	SO	RS	.	>	N	↑	n	~	
F 1111	SI	US	/	?	O	←	o	DEL	

◀ Least Significant

Examples:

```
0(ZERO) = 0110000 = 30 (HEX)
B       = 1000010 = 42  (HEX)
b       = 1100010 = 62  (HEX)
LF (LINE FEED) = 0001010 = 0A (HEX)
```

FIGURE D8–4. *ASCII Code Table and Examples*

it also serves here to illustrate basic ASCII character storage. For example, a teletypewriter has a low-speed (10 characters per second) paper tape punch attached to the printing mechanism and also a paper tape reader. Commonly a row of holes is punched across the tape to constitute an 8-bit binary number, or possibly the ASCII code for one character (which may be one digit of a

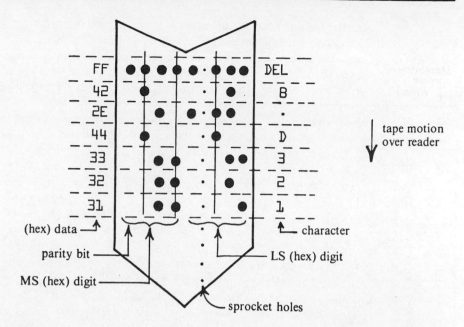

FIGURE D8-5. *Format of a Punched Paper Tape That Is Punched with ASCII Code for 123D.BDEL or Alternatively Binary Data 31, 32, 33, 44, 2E, 42, FF (Expressed Here in Hex)*

number or some letter). A hole is punched if the particular bit is a 1; no hole is punched for a 0.

Suppose a teletypewriter paper tape punch is turned on and the characters 123D.BDEL are typed on the teletypewriter. (Here *DEL* is the delete or rubout character.) The resulting punched paper type is shown in Figure D8-5. If this paper type is read back through the paper tape reader mechanism, these characters are printed on the printer if the teletypewriter is placed in *local mode* (except for the delete character); however, they are transmitted over the connecting communications lines if the teletypewriter is placed in *remote mode.*

Microcomputer Project Implementation

Hardware and Software Development

A successful microcomputer application involves the selection, design, and development of both hardware and software for the given application. Both must function properly and harmoniously. Essential characteristics of the various levels of both hardware and software have been discussed in the previous sections and must be brought into consideration.

Often there is a hardware-software trade-off decision to be made. The modern trend is certainly to put as many functions into software as possible. However, when very high speed responses are required, hardware must typically be used. The speed limitation upon the software approach, of course, is the cycle time of the microprocessor and the number of instructions required to generate the response.

For highest software speed, the bipolar *bit-slice microprocessor* approach may be considered (for example, Advanced Micro Devices Am2900 family). Bit-slice microprocessors use bipolar transistor technology rather than MOS technology in order to obtain higher operating speeds. These devices execute instructions with roughly a 100-nanosecond cycle time, but a number of chips are involved, along with more operating power and rather sophisticated microcoding and hardware design. If fast processing of floating point or of mathematical functions is required, mathematics hardware such as the Am9511 arithmetic processing chip may be connected to the microprocessor as a peripheral device. It possesses most of the functions of a scientific calculator; for example, use of the Am9511 for floating-point multiplication with 24-bit precision (7 decimal places) requires 84 microseconds, while a typical microprocessor software approach requires perhaps a millisecond.

Program Design: Algorithms as Flowcharts

The larger fraction of the design and debugging time for microcomputer applications is generally in the software. Its relatively high cost justifies a systematic approach. Indeed, the initial definition of the problem and the design of the algorithm to solve it generally require the most innovative thinking.

An *algorithm* is a specific method or set of rules for solving a problem in a finite number of steps. A *flowchart* or flow diagram is frequently used to represent an algorithm graphically. Visual representation of the sequence of steps can be very helpful in comprehending the interrelationships of the network of paths in a complex algorithm. In so-called *top-down design,* a general *flowchart* should typically be constructed first to show the principal features of the algorithm. One or a few blocks of the general flowchart can be taken as *modules* that are individually designed (often with *detailed flowcharts*) coded, and debugged. This approach is especially valuable if the software problem is a large one. The tested modules may finally be brought together as the program to accomplish the desired algorithm.

The symbols used in flowcharting have been standardized by the American National Standards Institute (ANSI). Figure D8–6a illustrates the most important symbols for our usage. Several of these symbols are used in the flowchart of Figure D8–6b, which illustrates the simple algorithm required to connect 7 switches to 7 light bulbs under microcomputer control. This is the I/O example that concludes Chapter D7. Note the flow arrows; the

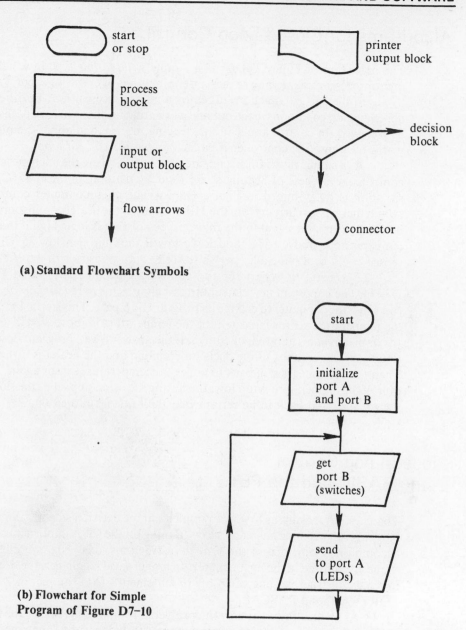

(a) Standard Flowchart Symbols

(b) Flowchart for Simple
Program of Figure D7–10

FIGURE D8–6. *Basic Flowchart Symbols and Usage*

rectangle is used to denote some sort of processing step, and the parallelo-gram is used to denote some manner of computer input or output. Connector circles may be used to avoid very long flow arrows or for continuation to another page; their use is illustrated later in Figure D8–9.

Algorithms for Closed-Loop Control

The algorithm of Figure D8–6b is a simple *straight-line* type in which the microprocessor unilaterally causes a definite series of events to occur. Often, however, the particular actions taken by a microprocessor may be different, depending on conditions in the outside world; that is, different flow paths may be followed. In control applications, feeding information about the outside world back into the controller is called *closing the control loop*.

As a simple illustration, consider a situation where the microprocessor controls the process of heating some fluid by maintaining it at 85°C. The situation is diagrammed in Figure D8–7a. The microcomputer controls a switch that passes current from the 110-V mains to the heater. A sensor placed in the fluid sends a signal to the microprocessor that is logic high if the fluid temperature is above 85°C, and logic low if the fluid is below 85°C. (The sensor could be a bimetallic switch in series with a resistor to +5 V.)

A general flowchart for the control algorithm is shown in Figure D8–7b. The important new element in this chart is the *decision diamond* that can cause the computer to change its program flow path. This step asks: "Does the temperature sensor indicate that the temperature is above 85°C?" Only a yes or no answer is allowed, of course. If the answer is yes, program flow continues out the *yes* apex of the decision diamond and the heater is turned off. Then the computer is sent back to check the temperature sensor again. However, if the temperature is too low, the testing/decision step sends the flow out the *no* apex and back to be certain that the heater is turned on.

Closed-Loop Control Using BASIC and the PET

The question remains as to how to implement the decision step in a computer language. In machine language programming on the 6502, implementation is accomplished with one of the *branch* instructions; this programming technique is discussed in the next chapter. In higher-level languages, the decision-making construct is quite often an IF statement—for example, in BASIC, FORTRAN, and PASCAL.

As an illustration of how the problem of Figure D8–7 might be implemented on a single-package microcomputer in higher-level language, let us assume that a PET is used. The 8-bit port A from a 6522 chip is available from the edge connector *J2* of the PET (see Figure D8–2a). Port B from this chip is *not* available, as it is used internally in the PET. Since a 6522 is used, the *relative* addresses for port A and its data direction register are the same as those for the SYM in Figure D7–11. On the PET, port A from *J2* is located at decimal address 59457, while the data direction register DDRA is at 59459 (see Figure D8–8a). We will connect bit number 4 to control a 110-V switch,

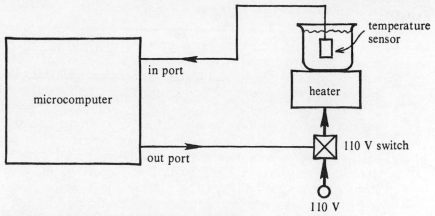

(a) **Microcomputer as a Temperature Regulator**

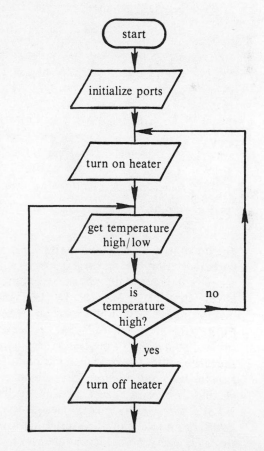

(b) **Flowchart for Temperature Regulation**

FIGURE D8-7. *Microcomputer in a Simple Closed-Loop Control Application, Requiring a Decision Step in the Algorithm*

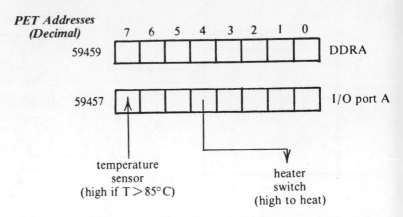

(a) PET 6522 I/O Port Model Applied to the Temperature Regulation Problem

```
10 POKE 59459 ,16  :REM**%00010000 TO DDRA
20 POKE 59457 ,16  :REM**TURN ON HEAT
30 LET A = PEEK(59457)  :REM**GET TEMP
40 REM**TEST IF TEMP>85C
50 IF (A-128)< 0 THEN 20
60 POKE 59457 , 00  :REM**TURN OFF HEAT
70 GO TO 30
80 END
```

(b) Temperature Regulation Program in BASIC for PET

FIGURE D8–8.   *Temperature Regulation Problem of Figure D8–7 Implemented on a PET in BASIC Language*

and the most significant bit from port A will be used as input from the temperature sensor. These features are all shown in Figure D8–7a.

The control flowchart of Figure D8–7b has been implemented in BASIC for the PET in Figure D8–8b. The single output wire is established in line 10 (the "%" found in the REM(ark) statement is often used to designate a binary number). Then a high is sent out on that wire in line 20. Note that the decimal equivalent of the desired binary number must be used. The state of the temperature sensor is then read into variable A by line 30. Now it is true that the state of the output bit to the heater will also show up in the value of A; thus the sensor bit must be isolated. To isolate the condition of any bit in BASIC, we generally must perform a decimal-to-binary conversion to obtain that bit, but to isolate the most significant bit is quite easy.

For an 8-bit binary number A, the most significant bit is 1 if the decimal number A is 128 or more. Thus, bit number 7 is 0 (and the temperature is less than 85°C) if quantity $(A - 128)$ is negative. Line 50 tests for this condition using an IF statement. If it is true, the CPU is sent back to turn on the heat. Otherwise, the heat is turned off in the next line-60 statement by sending 0 to the heater switch bit (and to all other bits, too). Finally, line 70 sends the computer back to test the temperature again.

As a postscript here it should be mentioned that isolating some interior bit at position N in most forms of BASIC is rather more effort. It could be done by realizing that bit N is 1 if the integer part of $A/2^N$ is odd. However, some versions of BASIC permit isolating a given bit very conveniently through the AND operation. Thus, PET and SYM BASIC perform a bit-by-bit AND of two arguments, which are taken to be *16-bit,* two's-complement numbers. (Two's-complement (negative) numbers as well as the AND, OR, and EOR instructions for the 6502 are discussed in the next chapter.) The SYM and PET BASICs also perform 16-bit OR and 16-bit NOT operations on a bit-by-bit basis.

Examples:

$$128 \text{ AND } 135 = 128$$

Since $128 = 10000000$ and $135 = 10000101$, the result of the bit-by-bit AND is $10000000 = 128_{10}$.

$$-1 \text{ AND } 4 = 4$$

Since $-1 = 1111111111111111$ (two's complement) and $4 = 0100$, the result of the AND is $0100 = 4_{10}$.

$$-1 \text{ OR } 8 = -1$$

Since $-1 = 1111111111111111$ and $8 = 1000$, the bit-by-bit OR results in "all one's" or -1.

$$\text{NOT } 8 = -9$$

Since NOT $0000000000001000 = 1111111111110111 = -9_{10}$.

In general, NOT $X = -(X + 1)$ because the negative (or two's complement) of a number is the (one's) complement of the number, plus one; that is, $-X = \text{NOT } X + 1$.

A More Elaborate Control Algorithm

Of course, the simple temperature regulation example of Figure D8–7b is a waste of microcomputer power. Why not let the temperature sensor (high/low indicator) control the 110-V switch directly? Therefore, the temperature-controlling requirement for Figure D8–7a is elaborated to a situation where the microcomputer becomes more desirable. Suppose the temperature is to be brought to 50°C for 1 hour, then to 85°C for 5 hours, and finally reduced to 30°C and held there. To accomplish this control requires either 3 high/low temperature sensors, or a general-purpose temperature transducer (such as a thermistor) in conjunction with an A/D converter. Further, some means of keeping track of real time is required, and is assumed to be available in our algorithm. This could be done with software timing loops; however, a hardware real-time clock is a very useful device. Hardware timers are available on both the 6530 and 6522 chips and may therefore be used on the KIM and SYM, respectively; Chapter D10 discusses how these timers are used. The PET has a built-in timer available to BASIC.

The flowchart for one algorithm to accomplish the temperature control required for the various time durations is shown in Figure D8–9. It should be emphasized that typically there are a number of possible algorithms to accomplish a given task; the one presented here represents one possibility for the case at hand. Notice that *two* decision-making diamond blocks are placed within a loop. Thus the computer continually keeps track of *both* time and temperature. The reader should trace through the actions of the algorithm and reason that the desired actions are accomplished. Note the use of *connectors* to avoid lengthy (and crossing) flow lines.

Assembler Language

The previous chapter introduced the essentials of programming a microcomputer in machine language. Although a microcomputer's central processing unit in fact only recognizes a sequence of 8-bit numbers as a sequence of instructions, we made life somewhat easier for ourselves by writing down mnemonics for these instructions as we developed programs. Subsequently we looked up the corresponding machine codes on a reference card. This procedure is often called *hand assembly* of the program. However, a computer can easily be programmed to perform such a tedious chore, and the use of an *assembler program* represented the first improvement in the lot of the computer programmer.

Another feature of the machine language programming discussed thus far is that specific memory address numbers are required when using absolute addressing or zero-page addressing. Thus, port address numbers and data direction register address numbers need to be specifically written in the program as it is written out. This is quite tedious. Why not use nicknames for the addresses—for example, PORTA or DDRA—rather than the actual numbers? The actual address numbers could be inserted later at the time the mnemonics are translated. The formal name for this approach is *symbolic addressing*. A word or *symbolic address* is used in the program rather than the actual number. Then in the process of assembling the numerical code, the assembler program inserts the actual number wherever the symbol appears in the program.

The assembler program must be able to determine the actual numerical address, of course. This can be done in two ways:

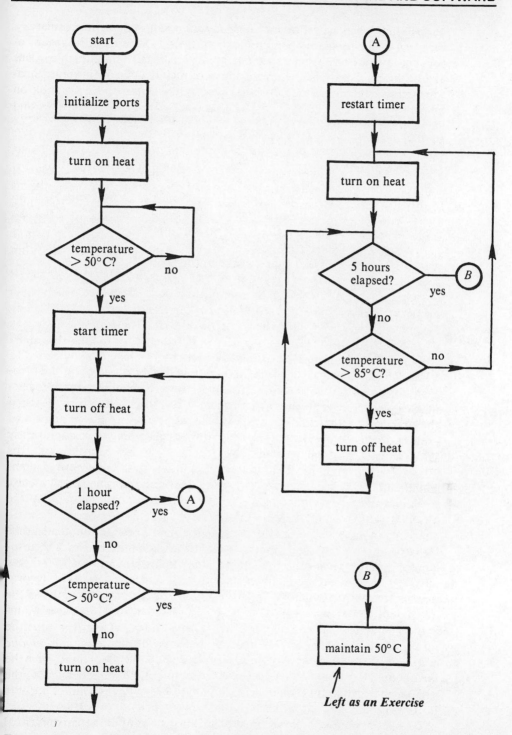

FIGURE D8–9. *Flowchart for a More Elaborate Temperature Regulation Process*

1. A symbol may be defined through an *assignment statement* at the beginning of the program—for example, PORTA = $1700.

2. The symbol may appear as a *label* to the left of a mnemonic somewhere in the program. The memory address of the OP code of this mnemonic becomes the numerical address.

These techniques of assembler language are perhaps best understood by example. Suppose we wish to write a program that sets up port A as an output port, reads the state of input port B into the accumulator, and then adds $0A and $20 to this value. Then it stores this sum in memory as a "result" as well as sending it to port A. Finally it goes back to read port B again, and repeats the entire procedure. Figure D8–10a illustrates how this program could be written in assembler language, while Figure D8–10b gives the same program written using the actual addresses (in the style of Chapter D7).

The assembler language program begins by *origining* the program with the line *$200; that is, the assembler program will arrange for the OP code of the first actual instruction ($A9 for LDA #%11111111) to be placed in memory address $200 (when the assembled program is ultimately loaded in memory). Next, 4 *symbols* are defined to the assembler program through assignment statements. Note the use of equal signs. These are the addresses of port B and port A, the address of the port A data direction register, and a constant (the hexadecimal equivalent of ten). Then the mnemonics begin with LDA. The comments at the right in each line are separated from the mnemonics by a semicolon in Mos Technology's convention. The assembler then ignores the characters between the semicolon and a carriage-return. Reading the comments in this example program should help determine what the program is doing. Comments are very important as program documentation for later changes and "maintenance."

The % sign in the first instruction indicates to the assembler that the number 11111111 is in binary. Binary usage is often useful when particular bit positions are to be emphasized. Next notice that the symbols DDRA and PORTB are used as operands in the STA and LDA instructions, rather than the actual numbers of these addresses. In the ADC# instruction, the symbol TEN has been defined previously, so that the assembler causes $0A to be loaded into the memory address immediately following the ADC# OP code.

NOTE: The convention used by Mos Technology to designate immediate addressing is to place the # sign next to the operand (*not* next to the mnemonic).

Next, we find the symbol DATA is used as the operand of an ADC instruction. To identify an actual address number for this ADC instruction, the assembler finds that the *label* DATA appears near the end of the program, to the left of $20. Indeed, because the number $20 appears after the JMP AGAIN, the number $20 will be arranged by the assembler to be loaded into

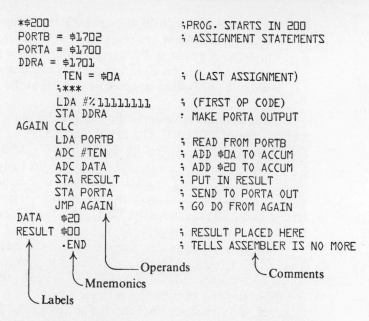

```
        *$200                   ;PROG. STARTS IN 200
        PORTB = $1702           ; ASSIGNMENT STATEMENTS
        PORTA = $1700
        DDRA = $1701
             TEN = $0A          ; (LAST ASSIGNMENT)
             ;***
             LDA #%11111111     ; (FIRST OP CODE)
             STA DDRA           : MAKE PORTA OUTPUT
        AGAIN CLC
             LDA PORTB          ; READ FROM PORTB
             ADC #TEN           ; ADD $0A TO ACCUM
             ADC DATA           ; ADD $20 TO ACCUM
             STA RESULT         ; PUT IN RESULT
             STA PORTA          ; SEND TO PORTA OUT
             JMP AGAIN          ; GO DO FROM AGAIN
        DATA    $20
        RESULT $00              ; RESULT PLACED HERE
             .END              ; TELLS ASSEMBLER IS NO MORE
                         Operands
                    Mnemonics                      Comments
             Labels
```

(a) A Program in Assembler Language

MA	Mnemonics/Operands	Comments
200	LDA #$FF	
202	STA $1701	MAKE PORTA OUTPUT
205	CLC	
206	LDA $1702	READ PORTB
209	ADC #$0A	ADD $0A TO ACCUM
20B	ADC $0217	ADD $20 TO ACCUM
20E	STA $0218	PUT IN "RESULT"
211	STA $1700	SEND TO PORT B
214	JMP $0205	GO DO AGAIN
217	$20	
218	$00	

(b) Same Program as in (a), but Using Explicit Addresses

FIGURE D8-10. *An Example Program Using Assembler Language Conventions*

memory just after the 3-byte JMP instruction. The number $20 then must be placed in memory address $0217 (see Figure D8-10b), and DATA becomes the label or nickname for $0217 to the assembler. Therefore $0217 is the address used for the ADC instruction, as shown in Figure D8-10b. The assembler will cause $0217 to be placed in memory (17 first and 02 second) following the OP code for ADC (absolute), and thus ADC DATA is assembled.

NOTE: There are three positions or *fields* for elements in one line of an assembler language program; they are the *label field, mnemonic field,* and *operand field,* in left to right order. One or more spaces are typed before a mnemonic to indicate to an assembler that the label field is to be skipped—that is, there is no label at the given mnemonic.

The program now stores the sum present in the accumulator into the address labeled RESULT. The assembler finds this address to be just after DATA, so it is $0218. Therefore this address is placed after the OP code for STA (absolute). Also, because $00 is placed to the right of the RESULT label (in the mnemonic position), the assembler will cause $00 to be placed in memory at location $0218 when the binary code for the program is ultimately loaded into computer memory. Of course, the content of memory address $0218 will change as the program runs.

Next the program stores the sum present in the accumulator to port A. The address to be used by the assembler is known to it through the second equivalence statement (PORTA = $1700). Finally, the program directs the computer to jump back to the address labeled by AGAIN and repeat the sequence of instructions from there. The address for the jump instruction is whichever address the CLC instruction occupies. The assembler finds this to be $0205 and assembles the code accordingly.

After the JMP instruction there exist two locations labeled DATA and RESULT. Their usage has already been discussed. Finally, the end of the program must be indicated to the assembler by the *pseudo OP* .END. It is not a mnemonic for an actual program operation, but rather a directive to the assembler that there is no more to the program; hence it is called a *pseudo* operation.

Microcomputer Development Systems

Software and hardware that facilitate the production of correctly functioning programs have existed in the minicomputer domain for many years. Important software includes an editor, an assembler, various compilers or interpreters, and debugging software. Minimum hardware consists of a minicomputer plus Teletype with paper tape reader/punch. If funding is available the project is greatly aided with a CRT, fast printer, floppy disc or hard disc mass storage, and an operating system to facilitate the use of these resources.

Since many aspects of microcomputer project development and usage are similar to those for the minicomputer, it is no surprise that we may now essentially substitute microcomputer for minicomputer in the above paragraph. The collection of hardware and software in the microcomputer case has come to be called a *microcomputer development system.* For low-budget applications this system can be as small as a KIM or a SYM board. A significant improvement involves use of an editor/assembler ROM on the SYM, along with a CRT or Teletype. If the budget and application warrant it, development systems that include a microcomputer mainframe, CRT, printer, and mass storage are available for most microprocessors, with a price tag of $5,000 to $25,000 and more. Indeed, this assortment of equipment is generally implied by the term microcomputer development system. It is much like the substantial minicomputer system of Figure D8-1. Some general-purpose products may be used for development for any one of several target microprocessors—for example, systems from Tektronix, Hewlett Packard, and GenRad.

Perhaps the principal difference between the minicomputer and microcomputer situations is that the target minicomputer application often includes many of the peripherals desirable for software development; therefore, the same system is used for both program development and application. On the other hand, the microcomputer application hardware may be as rudimentary as a few ICs and an on/off switch. It is quite clear that program development and debugging must be done on a computer other than the target microcomputer in this circumstance.

This section briefly examines the purposes of the software and hardware components of a development system. A general flow diagram of the development of a microprocessor project or application is used in conjunction with the discussion (refer to Figure D8-11).

First we must define the objectives that are desired for the microcomputer application. Then the software and hardware to accomplish these objectives must be designed. The project tends to split at this point into separate development flow paths, although trade-offs between the two must often be considered in the initial stages. Now the development system becomes involved, primarily on the software side of the development process. After the algorithm has been developed, it must be written as an assembler language or perhaps a higher-level language program; this is called the *source program*. Then it must be typed out for subsequent entry into the assembler program. A full alphanumeric keyboard is required for this. For example, a classical approach is to type the program on a Teletype with the paper tape punch turned on. Thus the ASCII codes for the characters of an assembler program are punched onto tape and exist in a *machine-readable form*. This program tape—called the *source tape*—may be run through a paper tape reader on the Teletype, and thus be fed to an assembler program running on a computer. If the source program is in a higher-level language, the tape is fed instead to a compiler or interpreter program. This step is labeled as block 2 in Figure D8-11.

However, computer assemblers or compilers do not tolerate typographical errors in the source program. Because a source program often consists of hundreds of typed lines, this task exceeds the typing talents of most computer users. For this reason editor programs were developed long ago. With an *editor program* running on a computer, we type the source program on a terminal (in either assembler language or a higher-level language), and

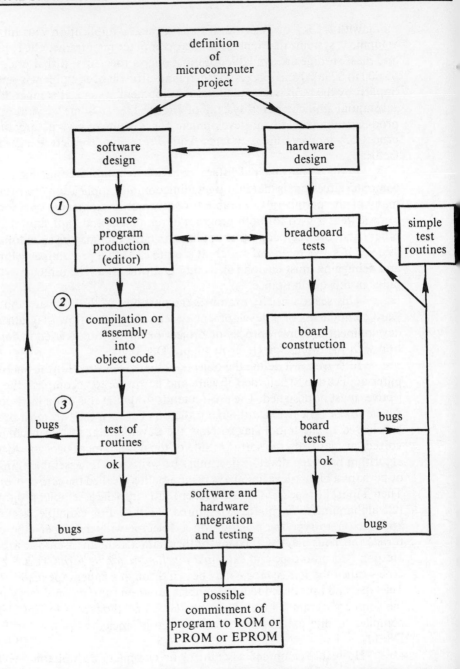

FIGURE D8–11. *Development of a Microcomputer Project or Application (Steps 1, 2, and 3 Are Facilitated with a Microcomputer Development System.)*

the editor program places the typed characters into computer read/write memory. The editor program includes the facility to later delete groups of characters or lines of characters, insert lines (or groups) of characters, and so on. Thus it is possible not only to eliminate all typographical errors, but also to make later additions or deletions in a program. This process is labeled as block 1 in Figure D8-11. When the source program is deemed to be correct, it may be output by the editor to punched tape, cassette tape, floppy disc, or even left in memory. These are all machine-readable forms and vary with the facilities at hand.

The source program in one of these forms is then fed into the assembler program. The assembler assembles the actual binary codes for the program; this is called the *object code* (or object program). Most assemblers are *two-pass* or even *three-pass* assemblers. As the assembler passes through the source program the first time, it finds where all the symbolic addresses are located and develops a table of all symbols used. The second pass then determines the actual binary codes. This object code may be output to punched tape, cassette tape, floppy disc, or directly into a region of RAM memory where it can perform the targeted tasks and be tested. Further, a program listing produced by the assembler is very useful and is obtainable during the second (or third) pass. A *program listing* is a list of sequential memory addresses and the codes placed therein as determined by the assembler. These are printed beside the source program mnemonics. Usually the program listing should be output to a *hard copy device* (teleprinter or fast printer) for use during debugging and testing and for later reference. For an example of an assembler listing, the reader is recommended to examine the listing of the respective monitor programs at the back of the KIM or the SYM reference manuals.

The object code produced by the assembler must be loaded into microcomputer memory and tested. This step is represented by block 3 in Figure D8-11. As a minimum debugging tool, the microcomputer should possess single-step capability for troubleshooting suspected problem areas. However, the number of instructions involved in certain parts of a program may be so many that single-stepping is not practical. Further, certain portions may need to run full speed to function properly in real time. For these reasons, a *break-point* capability is desirable. The 6502 microprocessor possesses the BReaK instruction with an OP code of $00. It is also called a *software interrupt* because normal program execution is interrupted when the microprocessor encounters the $00 OP Code. The *interrupt system* is discussed in the next chapter. Suffice it here to say that when the KIM or SYM computer encounters the break instruction, the computer exits to monitor in essentially the same fashion as it does after each step in single-step mode; then various registers and memory locations may be examined in the usual way. For break to flow to monitor properly on the KIM, however, the *IRQ (interrupt) vector* at memory locations $17FE and $17FF must be loaded with $00 and $1C, respectively. This number ($1C00) represents the address of the monitor single-step entry point and is very similar to the procedure required for single-stepping.

Larger development systems often include rather clever debugging facilities. One example is a *trace capability* where the OP codes of the last *N* steps before a certain breakpoint are recorded. (One firm refers to this capability as a "flight recorder." Recall that the flight recorder on an aircraft continuously maintains records of vital instruments for the previous few minutes before a crash.) A *disassembler* is then very useful when examining the trace codes. It clearly is an assembler in reverse. Through this facility the mnemonics for the last *N* steps, rather than obtuse OP codes, may be displayed for study on a CRT.

As routines are tested and as the hardware and software are tested together, changes in the software or the hardware are generally required. Perhaps a few more lines of code must be inserted in a few places, and some lines need to be changed. Retyping the entire program with these changes could be quite a task. Fortunately this can be avoided if the source program has been saved in some machine-readable fashion (paper tape, cassette, or floppy disc). The program may be input to editor and changes may be readily made using the editor facilities. Then the new program is assembled, and its object code output is again tested.

When the object code is finally satisfactory, it may be saved in some form for loading into microcomputer RAM when needed. In some cases it may be desirable or even necessary to place the code in PROM or EPROM chips for use in the target microcomputer.

REVIEW EXERCISES

1. What are hardware, software, and firmware, respectively?
2. Discuss the usage of the term *mainframe*.
3. Contrast the important characteristics of traditional large computers and of minicomputers.
4. What is meant by a real-time or on-line computer application?
5. (a) Compare the access time of a floppy disc with that of a hard disc.
   (b) Compare the storage capacity of a hard disc drive with a floppy disc drive.
   (c) What is a read/write head?
6. Suppose floppy discs are used for mass storage. Contrast the time for random access to a byte in mass storage as opposed to a byte in main memory.
7. Describe the advantages of programming in assembler language relative to machine language.
8. (a) What are the advantages of programming in a higher-level language relative to assembler language?
   (b) What are the advantages of using assembler language over a higher-level language?

9. Explain the difference between an interpreter and a compiler.

10. (a) Does an operating system represent hardware or software?
    (b) What does an operating system accomplish for a computer user?
    (c) Name an important operating system for 8080 (and Z–80) microcomputer users.
    (d) Describe a multiprogramming operating system.

11. (a) Explain the function of a motherboard in a minicomputer or micro-computer.
    (b) What is the IEEE S–100 bus?
    (c) What is an ASCII keyboard?

12. Explain briefly each of the following floppy disc terms:
    (a) single-density and double-density
    (b) single-sided and double-sided
    (c) mini-disc and full-size disc

13. (a) Contrast volatile memory with nonvolatile memory.
    (b) What type of memory is used in microcomputers to deal with the problem of memory volatility?

14. (a) Give the full names for the following acronyms:
        (1) ROM
        (2) PROM
        (3) EPROM
    (b) Describe in general terms what each is and the circumstances for which it is desirable.

15. (a) Explain the basic difference between static memory and dynamic memory. Does this question concern itself with core memory or with semiconductor memory?
    (b) Give advantages and disadvantages for static memory relative to dynamic memory.

16. Characterize the following semiconductor memory technologies with respect to access times and also relative power consumption:
    (a) MOS
    (b) bipolar
    (c) CMOS

17. (a) What does it mean to say that a memory chip is organized 1K×4 bits?
    (b) Discuss the function of a chip-select or chip-enable pin on a memory chip.

18. We would like a CRT to display the number 0. Tell why it would not work to send the binary number 00000000 to the CRT.

19. (a) Present the advantage and disadvantages of bipolar bit-slice micro-processors.
    (b) What is an arithmetic processing chip?

20. (a) Define the term *algorithm*.
    (b) Describe the relationship of a flowchart to an algorithm.
    (c) Give 4 basic flowchart symbols.
    (d) Discuss briefly top-down design.

21. What are PEEK and POKE instructions used for in the BASIC language? Why are they important to 6502-microcomputer I/O?
22. (a) What is assembler language programming?
    (b) Describe how symbolic addressing simplifies the writing of machine language programs.
    (c) Give a brief description of each of the following:
        (1) label
        (2) assignment statement
        (3) pseudo OP
23. (a) Present the typical hardware as well as software parts of a microprocessor development system.
    (b) Describe how a development system is used.
    (c) Why does a laboratory minicomputer project often not require the purchase of a separate development system?
24. (a) Describe the function of an editor program as well as an assembler program.
    (b) What is meant by a two-pass assembler?
    (c) Explain the nature and utility of a program listing.
25. Discuss briefly the use of each of the following in debugging a program:
    (a) software interrupt or breakpoint
    (b) trace capability
    (c) disassembler

PROBLEMS

1. Assume that the transfer rate from a floppy disc is 250 kilobits/second, and that the floppy disc's "controller" assembles the bits into bytes before presenting them to an I/O port of a microcomputer.
   (a) Since programmed I/O must be used to operate a standard I/O port, we must be concerned with the response speed of the microprocessor. What is the time interval, or latency, between arrivals of successive bytes at the port? Assume that an average instruction requires 3 cycles; how many instructions does a 6502 μP using a 1-MHz clock have time to execute in this latency?
   (b) Calculate the time interval required to fill 8K bytes of memory from a floppy disc.
   (c) Suppose the floppy disc were changed to double density. Discuss why a DMA technique probably must be used instead of programmed I/O.
2. The *2114 chip* is a widely used static semiconductor memory chip that is organized 1K×4 bits.
   (a) How many memory bits are on the chip?
   (b) How many memory address pins must the chip possess? Explain why.
   (c) How many data pins must the chip possess?

(d) Diagram the organization of a 4K-byte block of memory that is based on 2114 chips and a decoder that operate directly from the memory address bus of a microprocessor. Assume the memory block is positioned to occupy addresses $4000 through $4FFF. Illustrate the specific memory address lines required by both the chips and the decoder. We will assume that no memory exists in locations above $4FFF.

3. Write the successive ASCII codes required to send (CR) (LF) Micro (CR) (LF) to a terminal. (CR) and (LF) are carriage-return and line-feed, respectively.

4. Assume that a 6502 microprocessor is sending characters to a 30 character/second printer. Assume further that an average of 3 cycles per 6502 instruction are required, and that the 6502 uses a 1-MHz clock.

(a) Approximately how many instructions are executed by the 6502 in the time interval between the sending of characters to the terminal?

(b) Discuss whether it is possible for the microprocessor to accomplish other tasks while transmitting to the printer.

5. The algorithm for the temperature control problem as presented in Figure D8–7b can be criticized for turning the heater on initially, even if the temperature is already above the desired temperature. Develop a new flowchart that corrects this behavior.

6. Develop a general flowchart for the algorithm that the controller in a successive-approximation ADC may follow.

7. A microcomputer is to be used with a 7-bit DAC to implement an ADC by the staircase-ramp technique. The DAC output and the voltage to be measured are input to a comparator that outputs a logic-level high when the DAC voltage exceeds the voltage to be measured. The output of the comparator is presented to the most significant bit of an I/O port, while the remaining 7 bits of the port are used to send codes to the DAC.

(a) Develop a general flowchart for a program that achieves the ADC action. Include the possibility that an *overrange* exists with respect to the voltage to be measured.

(b) Assume a PET microcomputer (in conjunction with port A on connector *J2*) is used to implement this ADC. Assume further that the step size of the DAC output is 0.1 V. Write a program in BASIC that implements the algorithm to measure the voltage; it should print: "Voltage is XX.X volts." However, if the input voltage is greater than 12.7 V, the computer should print this overrange statement.

8. A microcomputer is often programmed to contain an elapsed time clock. Assume the number of seconds, minutes, hours, and days are respectively maintained in memory locations. Let us give the name SECONDS to the location with the number of elapsed seconds, and so on. The microcomputer receives a precision 1-Hz square wave on one line of an I/O port. Develop a flowchart for an algorithm to accomplish the desired task.

9. A microprocessor is to be used in an instrument that records the highest temperature and the lowest temperature since start-up. The microprocessor also records the time of occurrence for the respective high and low temperatures. The temper-

ature is input to a port by a digital temperature device. The time is input by a digital clock chip to a pair of additional ports as hours and minutes, respectively. Use the names HI TEMP, HI TEMP TIME, LO TEMP, and LO TEMP TIME for the respective locations. Develop a flowchart for the process to be followed by the microprocessor.

10. Frequently it is necessary to convert from binary to decimal; for example, we may want a microcomputer to display the decimal equivalent of a binary value of voltage that is input to the microcomputer by an 8-bit ADC. We will describe a convenient algorithm to convert an 8-bit binary number to BCD. Assume three locations named HUNDREDS, TENS, and ONES are used. First count the number of 100's in the given number; this is done by counting the number of times that 100 can be subtracted from the given number before a borrow out of the number occurs. This number of 100's shall be in the HUNDREDS location. (The borrow tells us that the result of the last subtraction is less than zero, or negative.) Next count the number of 10's in the number that remained after subtracting the 100's; this number is placed in the TENS location. The number that remains after subtracting 10's is placed in the ONES location. Develop a flowchart for this algorithm.

NOTE: In the next chapter we discuss the SBC or subtract instruction for the 6502, as well as how the carry bit is used to detect a borrow-out. However, these details need not concern us for the general flowchart. Also note that the binary equivalent of 100 or of 10 must be used in the actual machine language program, but this feature is not of particular concern to the flowchart either.

11. Rewrite the simple connect-switches-to-lights program of Figure D7–10 as an assembler language program. Only the operands $FF and $00 should remain as numeric operands.

12. Rewrite in a proper assembler language format the example "add 2 to 4" program of Figure D7–5. Use the label RESULT for location 20 and the symbol MONITOR for the monitor's entry address. Notice that through the use of descriptive names, the assembler language program becomes significantly more readable than the original. Also, it is possible to use the origining pseudo OP more than once in a program.

13. The nonlinear response of a transducer is a common problem in instrumentation. An example is the voltage output versus temperature for a thermistor in a Wheatstone bridge. If a calibration curve or table exists for the voltage as a function of temperature, it is possible for the user to read from the table the correct temperature corresponding to the given voltage. But a microprocessor can be programmed to perform the "table look-up" chore. Assume that an 8-bit ADC is used to input the uncorrected and unscaled temperature from the thermistor/ Wheatstone bridge; let the port connected to the ADC be called UTEMP. Assume further that the successive 256 temperature values (corresponding to the successive ADC codes $00, $01, ... $FF) are placed in page 2 of memory. The 6502 microprocessor should obtain the ADC value, then get the corresponding temperature from memory, and finally output the temperature to a port

called TEMP. (The TEMP port may be connected to a decimal readout if the temperature values are stored in BCD.) Let the data direction registers for the UTEMP and TEMP ports be called DDRUT and DDRT, respectively. Write an assembler language program that accomplishes the above task. The microprocessor should perform the temperature conversion continuously.

NOTE: It is necessary in the program to refer to an address immediately after an OP code; unfortunately, a label identifies the address of the OP code *itself.* Assemblers permit *operand arithmetic* that handles this problem. For example, if the label HERE appears in the program, the instruction STA HERE+1 accomplishes a store to the address immediately following that of the OP code labeled by HERE.

CHAPTER
D9

6502
Programming for
Algorithmic Processes

At this point we have examined the important components of a microcomputer and the character of 6502 machine-level programming. We have also seen how a microcomputer may be connected to an experiment or process, and how an algorithm for such application may be presented in terms of a flowchart. Some microcomputer programming for these *algorithmic processes* was presented using the BASIC language. In this chapter 6502 machine-level programming techniques for algorithmic processes are developed. However, some important matters of computer arithmetic must first be discussed.

Computer Arithmetic

Negative Numbers on Computers

Computers must manipulate negative numbers to be useful computational devices. Binary numbers can be positive or negative as easily as decimal numbers, of course. However, the plus or minus sign cannot be stored literally in the memory store. Nevertheless, it should be clear that one bit could be used to indicate the state of positive or negative. The left-most bit could be used as a *sign bit* (we commonly put + or − at the left) and the convention could be used that this bit be set to 1 if negative and 0 if positive. With 8-bit bytes this would leave 7 bits to indicate the magnitude of the number. This sign-and-magnitude convention is often called *signed binary*.

When a computer adds a number from memory to the accumulator, however, it will add the *entire* 8-bit number to the accumulator in the normal way, including the sign bit. Now it would be convenient if the addition process would take, for example, +2 and −1 and add them to produce +1. Let us examine this for a hypothetical computer that operates with 3-bit numbers. This case permits us to illustrate all the possibilities, and Figure D9–1a lists the unsigned binary numbers, while Figure D9–1b lists the signed binary numbers. In fact, a 3-bit microcomputer is not farfetched; the early Intel 4004 was a 4-bit machine.

Consider then +2 + (−1); to the left below is shown the familiar desired result, while on the right is shown the result that our computer's binary adding machine will produce:

$$
\begin{array}{ll}
 +2 & 010 \\
\underline{(+) -1} & \underline{ 101} \\
 +1 \quad \text{(desired)} & 111 = -3 \quad (\text{not } 001 = +1)
\end{array}
$$

The result is 111, which signifies −3 by our signed binary scheme and *not* the 001 = +1 we would prefer.

Let us try a different scheme. Suppose 000 is assigned to −4, with successive numbers being each unity larger. This scheme is shown in Figure D9–1c. It is called *offset binary* because the successive values ascend in the normal manner, but are all offset by 4 units to a more negative value than they have in the unsigned case. In fact, this approach is used rather often by A/D converters to represent negative and positive voltages. Let us try (+2) + (−1) with this representation:

$$
\begin{array}{ll}
 +2 & 110 \\
\underline{(+) -1} & \underline{ 011} \\
 +1 \quad \text{(desired)} & (1)\, 001 = -3 \quad (\text{not } 101 = +1)
\end{array}
$$

This time the binary adding machine produces the result 001 with a carry of 1. If the carry is ignored and only the result 001 in the accumulator is assumed, the result again represents −3 rather than +1.

As a third approach, suppose the most significant bit in the offset binary case is complemented; that is, $0 \to 1$ and $1 \to 0$. The resulting numbers are shown in Figure D9–1d and are termed the *two's-complement* representation. Notice that +1, +2, and +3 are just the same as in signed binary, while −1, −2, and so on, are the same as the states of a binary *down* counter as it counts down past zero. This pattern is the binary analog to a cassette magnetic tape counter when it goes past zero in a rewind: 0003, 0002, 0001, 0000, 9999, 9998, and so forth. Since +2 counts added to a down counter that is in state −1 will end up at +1, it may be anticipated that this approach will be useful. We have

$$
\begin{array}{ll}
 +2 & 010 \\
\underline{(+) -1} & \underline{ 111} \\
 +1 \quad \text{(desired)} & (1)\, 001 = +1 \quad (\text{if carry is ignored})
\end{array}
$$

1	1	1	7
1	1	0	6
1	0	1	5
1	0	0	4
0	1	1	3
0	1	0	2
0	0	1	1
0	0	0	0

(a) Unsigned Binary

0	1	1	+3
0	1	0	+2
0	0	1	+1
0	0	0	+0
1	0	1	−1
1	1	0	−2
1	1	1	−3
1	0	0	−0

(b) Signed Binary

1	1	1	+3
1	1	0	+2
1	0	1	+1
1	0	0	0
0	1	1	−1
0	1	0	−2
0	0	1	−3
0	0	0	−4

(c) Offset Binary

0	1	1	+3
0	1	0	+2
0	0	1	+1
0	0	0	0
1	1	1	−1
1	1	0	−2
1	0	1	−3
1	0	0	−4

(d) Two's-Complement Binary

1	1	1	7	0	0	0
1	1	0	6	0	0	1
1	0	1	5	0	1	0
1	0	0	4	0	1	1
0	1	1	3	1	0	0
0	1	0	2	1	0	1
0	0	1	1	1	1	0
0	0	0	0	1	1	1

(e) Binary   One's-Complement Binary

FIGURE D9–1. *Some Representations of 3-Bit Binary Numbers*

If carry is ignored the result of this addition is indeed +1, and the desired property is finally attained. In fact, two's-complement form is used almost universally by contemporary computers to represent negative numbers: It is important to notice that the left-most bit is set to 1 for all negative numbers in the two's-complement convention. This fact can be used as a quick indicator of whether a number is negative. However, comparing the bit patterns of the negative numbers for signed binary in Figure D9–1b and for two's-complement binary in Figure D9–1d reveals that they are *not* the same.

The two's-complement number can be readily computed from a binary number by the following rules:

1. *Change all bits that are 0 to 1, and all bits that are 1 to 0.* Thus all bits are complemented or inverted. This is called forming the *one's complement* of the number (see Figure D9–1e).
2. *Add one to this binary number.* The result is the two's complement of the number.

A computer can readily perform these two operations with logic circuits, and this accounts in part for its popularity.

Let us look at an 8-bit example. Given $00101110 = +46_{10}$

$$\text{one's complement} = \quad 11010001$$
$$\underline{+1}$$
$$\text{two's complement} = \quad 11010010 = -46_{10}$$

Notice that the most significant bit is 1, as it should be for a negative number. To check this result, mentally add $+46$ and -46 in these binary forms and note that zero results (with a carry, which is ignored). In fact, we can readily justify that if the binary number $-N$ is produced from N by the two's-complement rule given above, the sum $(-N) + (N)$ must always be zero (with a carry of 1). First notice that if the one's complement of N is added to N, the number $11111111 = -1$ must result. But when $00000001 = +1$ is in turn added to this number containing all 1's, the result is clearly zero, carry 1. Thus the desired *sum-to-zero* property must be attained.

Notice that with an 8-bit word size, the largest possible positive number is $0111\ 1111 = \$7F$. Thus the positive numbers go from $+1$ to $+127_{10}$. On the other hand, the negative numbers range from $-1 = 1111\ 1111 = \$FF$ down to $-127_{10} = 1000\ 0001 = \$81$ and finally $-128_{10} = 1000\ 0000 = \$80$ (there is one more negative number than positive!). See the following list:

hex	binary	decimal
$7F	0111 1111	+127
$7E	0111 1110	+126
.		
.		
.		
$03	0000 0011	+3
$02	0000 0010	+2
$01	0000 0001	+1
$00	0000 0000	0
$FF	1111 1111	−1
$FE	1111 1110	−2
$FD	1111 1101	−3
FC	.	−4
FB		−5
FA	.	−6
F9	.	−7
$81	1000 0001	−127
$80	1000 0000	−128

Now if numbers such as $+65_{10}$ and $+72_{10}$ are added together, an *overflow* into the sign bit will occur ($65_{10} + 72_{10} = 137_{10}$ is greater than $+127$). The result will appear negative when it is not. Similarly, if -65 and -72 are added together, the sign bit can be shown to become 0 because -137_{10} is too negative; again overflow occurs. However, a positive and a negative number added together will never give problems. The 6502 has a nice warning bit in the processor status register designated the *V bit*—called the *overflow bit*—that gets set if two's-complement overflow occurs. The V bit is set by the microprocessor if the sum of two positive numbers results in a negative number, or if the sum of two negative numbers results in a positive number. It is up to the programmer to test this bit and take corrective measures or issue an error warning. Of course, if the numbers are 8-bit positive only, the V bit should be ignored. The 6502 has another handy use for the V bit in connection with the 6520 PIA, as we see shortly.

Subtraction on the 6502

The PDP–8/E, the first minicomputer, does not have a subtract instruction. Rather, in order to subtract one number from another, the negative of the subtrahend is formed by a *Complement and Increment the Accumulator* (CIA) instruction. This number is then added to the minuend to obtain the result. Indeed, computers that possess a subtract instruction often perform it internally by the above *negate-and-add* sequence. In this way, special subtracting circuits are not necessary.

The 6502, however, does have a subtraction instruction: *SuBtract memory from the accumulator, including not Carry*. Its mnemonic is SBC, and the programmer's reference card shows the operation to be $A - M - \overline{C} \rightarrow A$. The $A - M$ portion is expected, but the instruction rather curiously also subtracts the complement of the carry from the expected difference. Recall that the ADC instruction also involved the carry bit. The next section demonstrates that the C-bit inclusion in both the ADC and the SBC instructions is useful for multiple-precision arithmetic. However, for a single-precision subtraction (and also for the *first* subtraction in the multiple-precision case), the programmer must cause the C bit to be set to 1 by an SEC instruction *before* doing the subtraction. Then the desired operation $A - M - 0 \rightarrow A$ is performed. Notice that if C were a 0, a 1 would be subtracted in the (first) SBC instruction and give an incorrect result.

The address M of the subtrahend number is determined by the particular addressing mode employed. The possibilities and usage are the same as those presented in Chapter D7 for the ADC instruction and are not repeated here.

Multiple-Precision Arithmetic

It frequently happens that an 8-bit binary number is not sufficient to represent a certain result. Recall that the largest possible value in the accumulator or in a single memory location for the 6502 microprocessor is only 255_{10}. For example, suppose we wish to accumulate the total solar energy density in each day. Assume that an A/D converter produces an 8-bit number that is proportional to the solar power density (for example, watts/meter^2) as sensed by a sun transducer or *pyranometer*. The converted pyranometer output may be read each minute by a microcomputer; then the sum of the 1,440 values obtained through a 24-hour period is proportional to the solar energy density in that day. However, if the A/D converter output is on the order of 250_{10} at high noon in midsummer, the sum for the day can be expected to be on the order of $(250/2) \times (1440/2)$ or 90,000. This sum is much greater than an 8-bit number can accommodate and also exceeds the capability of a 16-bit number (which is about 65,000). A 24-bit number can manage about $(4K)^2$ or 16,000,000 and is easily sufficient. Thus, 3 bytes of memory could be used to accumulate the total solar energy density for a day.

In *multiple-precision arithmetic* each number is stored in several (usually successive) bytes of memory; then a pair of 24-bit numbers, A and B (each consisting of 3 bytes), are added schematically as follows:

$$
\begin{array}{ccc}
\text{carry} & \text{carry} & \\
\textit{highest 8} \swarrow\ \textit{higher 8 bits} \swarrow\ \textit{lowest 8 bits} \leftarrow A \\
+\quad \textit{highest 8} \qquad \textit{higher 8 bits} \qquad \textit{lowest 8 bits} \leftarrow B \\
\hline
\text{Do last.} \qquad \text{Do second.} \qquad \text{Do first.}
\end{array}
$$

For addition the carry bit is first cleared, then the lowest 8 bits of A are loaded in the accumulator, and the lowest 8 bits of B are added to the accumulator. This first result should be stored as the lowest-order byte of the sum before the next byte of A is loaded into the accumulator. Then the next byte of B is added to the accumulator (but the C bit is left alone as a carry in) to obtain the next-order sum byte. This process continues for however many bytes of precision are used.

The procedure for subtracting two multibyte numbers is analogous to the above, except that C is set to 1 before the first (lowest-order) subtraction. Then "borrows" are correctly propagated through the subtractions of successively higher bytes, through the $-\overline{C}$ part of the SBC action.

At an early age we learn about the need to "borrow" from the digit of the next higher place if the subtracting digit (the subtrahend) is larger than the minuend digit at a given place. In the binary case it can be shown that $-\overline{C}$ is the equivalent of a *borrow in* to a higher-order byte from a lower-order byte. The rule with the 6502 is to set C to 1 before the subtraction of the lowest-order byte; then C is "left alone" as subtraction of the successively higher order bytes is done in a program.

Decimal Mode on the 6502

A digital laboratory instrument frequently makes the decimal digits in the display available from a jack at the rear of the instrument. As discussed in

Chapter D6, these digits generally exist within the instrument in BCD code; consequently, the digital output is also in this "quasi-binary" code.

Suppose two readings of 25_{10} and 37_{10} from an instrument are input to a 6502-based microcomputer. These readings might be DVM voltages. The respective codes are 0010 0101 and 0011 0111, and may be input byte-serial through an 8-bit port. Next consider that we wish the microcomputer to form the sum of these two numbers. Let us examine what the computer's binary adding machine would produce:

$$
\begin{array}{cc}
1 & 11 \\
25_{10} = 0010\ 0101 & \\
37_{10} = \underline{0011\ 0111} & \\
62_{10} & \underline{0101\ 1100} \\
\end{array}
$$

desired decimal   5   ? BCD (=\$C)

The result in the accumulator is *not* the correct BCD number for 62_{10} (which would be 0110 0010); neither is the 8-bit number a correct binary equivalent of 62_{10}. The problem is that no carry into the 10's place (which is the left 4-bit group) occurs; this carry should occur since $7 + 5$ exceeds 9. In essence, the right 4 bits accommodate the result, although 1100 is not a valid BCD digit.

However, the 6502 microprocessor has the capability of producing the correct BCD code for the sum, and this feature is very easy to use. Classic minicomputers cannot manage this feat so easily. First, simply *SEt the microcomputer to Decimal mode*; this is done with the SED instruction (OP code = \$F8). The fact that the 6502 is in this mode is indicated by a 1 in the D-bit position of the processor status register. As long as the microprocessor is in decimal mode, the microprocessor correctly generates a carry into the next BCD digit whenever an ADC instruction finds that the sum in a given BCD digit place exceeds 9. Further, the given digit is correctly adjusted to its decimal value. Multiple-precision BCD arithmetic is easily managed by simply leaving the C bit alone as the successively higher order bytes are added together. Finally, the D bit is cleared and the microprocessor reverts to normal binary addition mode after the CLD instruction.

When in decimal mode the subtraction instruction (SBC) produces the correct decimal result whenever a borrow is required for a given decimal place. If multiple-precision BCD subtraction is done, the carry bit should be left alone and it then correctly propagates the borrow condition to the higher byte. Again as in binary mode, the C bit should be *set* before the first (or the only) subtraction.

Suppose the subtrahend is greater than the minuend. For example, suppose the 6502 computer calculates $25 - 47$. What happens? The result in the accumulator will be 78, just as for the case $125 - 47$. A borrow will be generated, and this is indicated by the fact that the carry bit is *clear* (0). In fact, we have a negative result, of course, that is said to be the *ten's-complement form* for -22. It is as though the digital counter of a cassette recorder were put in reverse for 22 units after zeroing it. The counter would then read

78. To find the magnitude of this negative number, we subtract the result from zero (after first setting the carry bit). We get $00 - 78 = 22$ (and borrow 1, or $C = 0$), which is the correct answer.

Machine Language Programming for Process Control

Perhaps the most impressive aspect of computers is their ability to make decisions. Thus a computer may be programmed to play checkers or chess, and this "artificial intelligence" is sometimes actually frightening to humans. When a microprocessor is applied in laboratory experimentation or in process control, it often must be in *responsive* control. Depending on conditions that it senses in the experiment or process, it takes different courses of action according to some algorithm. This topic was discussed in general terms in connection with flowcharting in Chapter D8. Further, the IF-THEN construction in the BASIC language was applied to implement the decision diamond. This section considers the machine language decision-making instructions on the 6502. These are the *branch* instructions and must, in fact, be invoked by an IF-THEN or other higher-level-language decision construction. They are very important in machine language algorithms.

Decision Making on the 6502: Branch Instructions

A computer typically takes different courses of action depending upon whether a certain number is positive, negative, or zero. This number could correspond to the condition of a parameter in the outside world (for example, a temperature in an experiment) or it could be a test parameter in a computational process. In any case, the decision represents a fork or a *branch* in the path of flow of the program. For example, the computer follows one program path if the parameter is greater than zero and another path if the parameter is zero. The program flow can be diagrammed as shown in Figure D9–2a. The decision represents a "fork in the road"; shown here is a two-way or *binary fork*, which is the basic decision that the 6502—and most other computers—can make. More complex decisions like the one diagrammed in Figure D9–2b are often required in life and therefore in computer algorithms. They must be implemented on most computers by a *binary tree* of two-way branches as shown in Figure D9–2c. Notice how this decision diagram resembles the drawing of a branch of a tree. The term *branch instruction* derives from this fact.

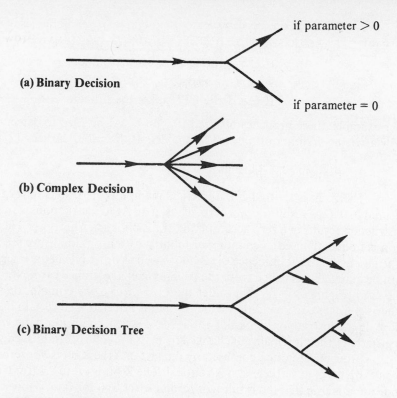

if parameter > 0

(a) Binary Decision

if parameter $= 0$

(b) Complex Decision

(c) Binary Decision Tree

FIGURE D9-2. *Branches in Program Flow*

The branch instructions of the 6502 number eight, and their mnemonics begin with B as might be expected. Each branch instruction works with respect to just one bit in the *processor status register* P. There are two instructions for each of the bits C, Z, V, and N in the P register. This register is simply a collection of 7 flip-flops or *flags* located within the 6502 chip; indeed, the SYM microcomputer presents it as the F register. We have already encountered the P register in the register model for the CPU on the programmer's reference card (see Figure 7–4a), and we have discussed the C and the V bits. The Z and N bits are discussed shortly in conjunction with their associated branch instructions.

In general, each branch instruction operates as follows: If the condition specified by the branch instruction for the particular bit in P *is* met, the CPU *takes the branch path* and jumps to a specific place in memory that may be either before or after the position of the OP code; however, if the branch is *not* taken, the CPU merely continues to the next instruction as usual. Let us first consider the particular branch instructions available and then see how the destination address is determined by the CPU if the branch is taken.

1. Branches on the C bit.

BCC: *Branch on Carry Clear.* OP Code = 90
       If C = 0 the CPU takes the branch.

BCS: *Branch on Carry Set.* OP Code = B0
       If C = 1 the CPU takes the branch.

For example, these branches off the carry bit could be used to detect overflow after the addition of unsigned numbers, as discussed earlier.

2. Branches on the Z bit.

The Z bit is set to 1 if a numerical manipulation results in zero. It is cleared to 0 if the result was *not* zero. Thus, if an ADC instruction or an LDA instruction results in a zero accumulator, the Z bit is set. This branch instruction is frequently used in counting or looping by a program, as we see later. The instructions that influence the Z bit (as well as other bits in the P register) can be quickly determined from the programmer's reference card. Notice on the card (Figure D7–4b) that under the *Condition Code* column, there are asterisks under each condition code bit that is affected by a certain instruction. If an instruction does not influence a given condition code bit (P-register bit), the bit remains unchanged from its previously established value.

Students are often confused by the fact that the Z bit is *not* zero if the result *was* zero; nevertheless, it is rational. The Z bit is set to a 1 (for true) to indicate it is *true* that the result *was* zero; it is set to 0 for false. However, in view of this possible confusion, the mnemonics do *not* use BZS or BZC. They rather represent a phrase that is straightforward in interpretation. It is certainly less confusing to think of the phrase for the mnemonic when using this instruction than to look at the operation shown under the operation column on the reference card.

BEQ: *Branch if result EQuals zero.* OP Code = F0
       If Z = 1, indicating the result *is zero,* the CPU
       takes the branch (branch on Z = 1).

BNE: *Branch if result Not Equal to zero.* OP Code = D0
       If Z = 0, indicating the result is *not zero,* the CPU
       takes the branch (branch on Z = 0).

3. Branches on the V bit.

The V bit in the P register indicates two's-complement overflow, as mentioned earlier, and is tested in two instructions. (There is also a convenient use of V to test the PIA I/O chips, in conjunction with the BIT test instruction. This usage is shown in the PIA discussion.)

BVC: *Branch if V is Clear.* OP Code = 50
       If V = 0 (so that no overflow occurred, for example)
       the CPU takes the branch (branch on V = 0).

BVS: *Branch if V is Set.* OP Code = 70
       If V = 1 (so that overflow occurred, for example)
       the CPU takes the branch (branch on V = 1).

4.   Branches on the N bit.

The N bit in the P register is set if the most significant bit in a result is set. This is the sign bit for a two's-complement number, so that this bit indicates that a number is Negative (N) if it is a signed number. In short, the N bit simply copies the most significant bit of the targeted number.

BMI: *Branch if result MInus.* OP Code = 30
       If N = 1, the result is negative and the CPU takes
       the branch (branch on N = 1).

BPL: *Branch if result PLus.* OP Code = 10
       If N = 0, the result is positive and the CPU takes
       the branch (branch on N = 0).

We have said that if the condition of a certain bit in the process status register is met, the CPU branches away, rather than simply going to the next address for its instruction. It remains to explain how the destination address is specified to the CPU. All branch instructions are 2-byte instructions. The first byte is the particular OP code and the second byte is a positive or negative (two's-complement) number that tells the number of memory locations forward or backward that the CPU must skip to find its next instruction. From there the computer continues in the normal sequential fashion. This mode for the specification of the destination address is called *relative addressing*.

The 6502 achieves its high-speed performance of a 2-byte instruction in 2 clock cycles by overlapping the fetching of the next memory location with interpreting the current data from memory.

NOTE: This technique is often called *pipelining*. The computer accomplishes more by sending two tasks down parallel "pipelines," doing them in parallel rather than serially.

Therefore, when the CPU obtains the amount of branch or *offset* from the second memory location, the program counter already gets incremented to the *next* memory address. Now if the branch *is* called for, the offset byte is added to the program counter (two's-complement addition with carry discarded) and the CPU goes to this memory address and fetches its next instruction. This CPU procedure explains the rule to compute the offset for the relative addressing mode used in branches: *The offset is always computed by counting to the destination address from the memory address following the offset byte.*

The following program form illustrates the computer's operation for a *branch forward* as well as a *branch backward*. To compute the value of the offset byte, we take the memory location *following* the offset byte location as zero and number backwards (negatively) or forwards (positively) to the desired destination OP code location. The negative numbers are two's-complement numbers, expressed as hex in the program.

memory address		
11	BRANCH code	
12	$02 (=+2)	← (offset byte)
13	instruction	(0) Next instruction
14	instr./data	(+1)
15	instr.	(+2)
16	instr./data	
17	instr./data	
18	instr.	(−4 = FC)
19	instr./data	(−3 = FD)
1A	BRANCH code	(−2 = FE)
1B	$FC (=−4)	(−1 = FF)
1C	instruction	(0) Next instruction
1D	instr./data	
1E	instr./data	

If the branch forward in memory address 11 is taken, the computer skips over the instructions or data in MAs 13 and 14 and does the instruction in MA 15; otherwise, the computer does the instructions/data in MAs 13 and 14 before doing that in MA 15.

If the branch backward in MA 1A is taken, the computer skips backward 4 locations (counting from the next instruction in MA 1C) to that in MA 18. The computer then repeats the 2 instructions/data that it recently did. For small displacements, down-counting in hex is convenient for deciding on the negative number (hex of the two's-complement number) needed in the displacement. As a check, we note that $FC + $04 = $100 = 00 when the carry is discarded, as it should be for −4 + 4 = 0. The SYM monitor has a convenient CALC command key that may be used to calculate the two's complement (negative) of a number, or to calculate the difference between two numbers. The latter can give the proper offset quite nicely. Thus, pressing CALC XX CR returns −XX in the display. Pressing CALC XX YY CR returns XX − YY in the display.

Notice that the destination address is always determined by the 6502 as a position relative to where the branch OP code is located. This is the reason for the name of the addressing mode, of course, and it can be a convenient addressing mode if we desire to relocate or reposition a group of code from one area of memory to another without adjustments to the code. Perhaps we wish to insert a few additional codes in the midst, for example. Unfortunately, examination of the programmer's reference card reveals that only the branch instructions have this addressing mode available to them.

Furthermore, no other addressing modes are available to the branch instructions. No branch-absolute, for example. This means that the farthest we can have the 6502 branch forward is 127 locations, and the largest backward branch is 128. However, we can use a jump-absolute at the destination of the branch in order to manage an arbitrary branch destination.

Doing Something More than Once: Looping

One of the very useful capabilities of a computer is that of doing something repetitively (without getting bored!) a specified and possibly large number of times. This is commonly done in a situation where a computer monitors various parameters in an experiment for some period of time. When the number of repetitions is specified, the computer must "keep count" and decide whether the task is completed; thus it becomes a basic example of decision making as well.

The topic is discussed by example. Suppose we wish to multiply a number A by number B. Notice that there are no multiply instructions in the 6502 instruction set. This was typical of early minicomputers as well, so that an *extended arithmetic element* was often purchased if rapid "hardware" multiplication was desired. Another solution is to multiply using repeated addition; that is, add A to the accumulator, B times. This is the approach of the "X" multiply key on the old mechanical adding machines.

The example program uses another new instruction besides the branch instruction called the *DEC instruction*. The mnemonic DEC comes from the phrase *DECrement the memory contents by one* and the reference card tells its operation succinctly as $M - 1 \rightarrow M$. DEC simply bumps the number in the destination memory location *down* by one. The accumulator is not involved in this, but examination of the condition code column on the reference card shows the N and Z P-bits are affected. Thus, if the result in the memory location is zero, the Z bit is set; also, the N bit mimics the most significant bit of the result. In this context the closely related *INC instruction* should also be mentioned. This instruction *INCrements the memory contents by one*. Its operation is represented as $M + 1 \rightarrow M$, so that the number in the destination location is bumped *up* by one.

The program is given in Figure D9–3. Notice that the numbers to be multiplied are $A = 2$ and $B = 3$ and that they are placed (rather arbitrarily) first in memory. They could have been deposited there previously by some larger program when it desires multiplication. The program itself begins in MA 0012. There the multiplier B (3 in this case) is loaded into the accumulator (actually the absolute addressing mode is not required here—why?), and then the STA instruction stores it as a *counter* (using the briefer zero-page mode). The counter will be used to keep track of the number of times the other multiplier A (2 in this case) gets added to the accumulator.

Memory Address	Mnemonic	Code	Comments
0010	$2	02	MULTIPLIER A
11	$3	03	MULTIPLIER B
12	LDA	AD	GET B INTO ACCUM
13	$0011	11	FROM
14		00	MA 11
15	STAz	85	SET UP AS
16	$30	30	COUNTER IN 30
17	LDA#	A9	CLEAR
18	$00	00	THE ACCUM
19	CLC	18	CLEAR CARRY, BE SAFE
1A	ADCz	65	ADD A TO ACCUM
1B	$10	10	FROM MA 10
1C	DECz	C6	DECREASE COUNTER
1D	$30	30	BY ONE (IN 30)
1E	BNEr	D0	IF COUNTER NOT ZERO,
1F	$Fa	FA	GO BACK (-6), ADD AGAIN
20	STAz	85	SAVE IN
21	$00	00	LOCATION ZERO
22	JMP	4C	RETURN TO MONITOR
23	($1C4F)	(4F)	($1C4F FOR KIM)
24		(1C)	

FIGURE D9-3. *Program that Involves Looping to Multiply Two Integers*

In MA 17 the accumulator is cleared and then the carry bit is cleared so that a 1 will not (incorrectly) be added to the result during the ADC instruction in MA 1A. This instruction causes 2 to be added to the previously zero accumulator. Next the counter in location 30 is decremented by 1 (from 3 to 2). The branch instruction in MA 1E then asks if this decrementing resulted in zero. This first time through, the *Branch if Not Equal to zero* or BNE instruction will cause the computer to branch back to $20 − $6 = 1A because the counter went from 3 to 2 (not zero).

NOTE: The Z bit will be zero in the status register.

Thus the computer returns to MA 1A and adds $02 to the accumulator once again, giving $2 + 2 = 4$. Then the counter is decremented from 2 to 1, which is still not zero, and the branch is taken again. Finally, 2 is again added to the accumulator, giving $2 + 2 + 2 = 6$, and the counter is next decremented from 1 to 0. Now the branch is *not* taken (because the Z bit gets set) and the CPU goes to the next instruction in location 20. There the current contents of the accumulator (which is $2 + 2 + 2 = 3 \times 2 = 6$) are stored in MA 30, and the program ends by exit to the monitor in this case.

Notice that the CPU went 3 times through the loop by checking the counter and using the branch instruction. The behavior of the counter and accumulator can be diagrammed as follows:

time through loop	1	2	3
accumulator	$0 + 2$	$2 + 2$	$2 + 2 + 2$
counter	$3 \rightarrow 2$	$2 \rightarrow 1$	$1 \rightarrow 0$

Also notice that the program could have been shortened by decrementing memory location 0011 directly; however, if we then wished to rerun the program, it would be necessary to reenter the 3 in MA 11 (why?). The program as written could be rerun immediately.

Index-Register Usage as Counters

The program could also be made more efficient by use of the *X index register* or the *Y index register*. These registers are introduced here in the rather elementary application of a counter. (They have more impressive applications in connection with various *indexed addressing* modes that permit efficient manipulation of tables of numbers in memory.) First notice on the register model of Figure D7–4a that the *X* and *Y* registers are 8-bit registers in the 6502 chip, rather like the accumulator. Just as the accumulator may be loaded through the LDA instruction, the *X* index register may be loaded using the LDX instruction, and the *Y* index register may be loaded using the LDY instruction.

A copy of the *X* or the *Y* index register may be placed in memory through the STX or the STY instruction, respectively. Again the operation is similar to STA for the accumulator. However, instructions to add or subtract memory to or from the index registers do not exist, so these registers are not true accumulators. Even so, increment index-register instructions exist as INX and INY; also decrement index-register instructions exist as DEX and DEY. Furthermore, the N and Z condition codes are affected by all of these index-register instructions. The *X* and *Y* index registers may therefore be conveniently used as counters. Since they exist within the CPU, INX and INY each require fewer bytes of memory and fewer machine cycles to execute than the INC (memory) instruction. The OP codes for INX, DEY, and so forth, are found under the *Implied* addressing mode column because the destination consequence is implied by the instruction to be in a certain CPU register. The reader should investigate these instructions on the programmer's reference card. How many cycles are saved by INX over INC (memory-absolute)?

Essentially two modifications are required in the multiply program of Figure D9–3 in order to utilize an index register rather than memory location 30 as a counter. Let us use the *X* index register. The index register *X* may be loaded with the initial value of the counter (a $03 in this case) by placing LDX (absolute) in MA 12 in place of the LDA (absolute). Now the STAz $30 instruction is no longer needed. The instructions for the remainder of the program beginning in MA 17 should all be moved to lower memory, beginning in MA 15. Fortunately, this shift can be done without changing any codes because the branch instruction uses relative addressing.

The SYM monitor includes a *BMOV (block-move) command* that speeds up this task greatly. Simply press (BMOV) (X) (−) (Y) (−) (Z) (CR) in order to relocate a block of codes from MA X through MA Y, to begin at MA Z. Here X, Y, and Z may each be up to 4 hex digits for the particular addresses involved, and the (−) key is used to delimit the parameters; that is to tell the monitor that X has been completed and Y begins next.

However, suppose that the program of Figure D9-3 is already in memory and we want to eliminate the instruction in MA 15 and MA 16 *without* moving the other instructions after it. The *No OPeration* code (NOP OP code = EA) may be placed in these addresses to cause the computer to do nothing during those machine cycles. Notice that the NOP code is *not* 00 (00 is the code for a *break* instruction, or *software interrupt*).

The second modification to Figure D9-3 is to change the "decrement the counter in MA 30" step, originally found in MA 1C and MA 1D. We now need rather to decrement the X index register, which is the counter; this is the DEX instruction, which requires only 1 byte. Therefore, either a NOP should be placed in memory in place of the $30 or the code beginning with BNE should be moved to directly after DEX. The program changes are now completed. Of course, if a SYM is used, the monitor entry address should be $8000 rather than the $1C4F entry shown, which is for the KIM.

A few concluding remarks about the increment/decrement instructions and index register manipulations should be made. First, it is important to realize that even when the 6502 is placed in decimal mode, the increment and decrement instructions operate in binary mode. Thus, if X contains the number $19 and the INX instruction is executed, the subsequent number in X is always $1A. Second, there are *transfer* instructions to copy the accumulator into either index register (TAX,TAY), and the reverse is also possible (TXA,TYA). Thus, the operation for *Transfer Accumulator to X* (mnemonic is TAX) is shown on the reference card as A → X.

Manipulate-Bits Instructions

There are several instructions that are useful for manipulating bit patterns. They include the rotate and shift instructions, and the AND, OR, and EOR instructions.

1. Two *shift instructions* exist:

ASL: *Arithmetic Shift Left the memory or accumulator contents.*

LSR: *Logical Shift Right the memory or accumulator contents.*

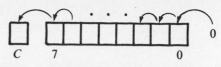

FIGURE D9–4. *ASL Instruction*   ***carry bit   accumulator or memory location***

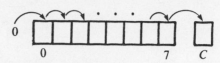

FIGURE D9–5. *LSR Instruction*   ***accumulator or memory location   carry bit***

Figure D9–4 illustrates the bit movement for ASL and Figure D9–5 illustrates the bit movement for LSR. These instructions may reference the accumulator (for example, ASL OP code = 0A) and cause the bits to move as in a shift register, with the carry bit C receiving the bit out of the end shifted toward, and *zero* shifted in at the other end. Or they may reference a memory location in one of several memory addressing modes (for example, zero-page and absolute); that is, the contents of a specified memory location get shifted (see Figure D7–4). Each time the instruction is executed, the bits are shifted one position. Note that the condition codes N and Z are also appropriately set or cleared by these instructions.

The logical-shift-right is *not* called arithmetic-shift-right because the latter implies preserving the sign bit during the shift; that is, bit 7 shifts to itself as well as to the right. Actually the arithmetic SL should probably be called a logical SL, too, since the sign bit is *not* preserved in bit 7 there, either.

2. Two *rotate instructions* exist that also shift the bits one place for each execution of the instruction. In this case the register and carry bit C work like a recirculating shift register in doing a "round robin" move of bits as diagrammed in Figures D9–6 and D9–7.

ROL: *ROtate Left the memory or accumulator contents.*

ROR: *ROtate Right the memory or accumulator contents.*

Figure D9–6 illustrates the bit movement for ROL and Figure D9–7 illustrates the bit movement for ROR. Again these instructions can work with the accumulator or with memory contents as the register being shifted; see Figure D7–4. Note that the condition codes N and Z are appropriately set or cleared by these instructions.

3. An instruction exists to *logical-AND* the contents of a specified memory location with the accumulator and leave the result in the accumulator. Memory is not changed.

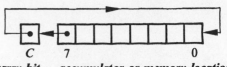

FIGURE D9-6.   *ROL Instruction*   **carry bit   accumulator or memory location**

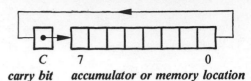

FIGURE D9-7.   *ROR Instruction*   **carry bit   accumulator or memory location**

AND: *AND memory with the accumulator.*

This instruction performs a bit-by-bit AND of the corresponding accumulator and memory location bits. Thus (Acc = 0101 1001) AND (Mem = 0000 1111) gives Acc = 0000 1001. From Figure D7-4 it can be seen that this instruction is available in many memory reference modes. Note that the operation is represented as $A \wedge M \rightarrow A$, since $\wedge$ or $\cap$ are commonly used to represent the notion of logical AND, or *intersection* of two sets. Also notice that N and Z bits are influenced.

4. An instruction similarly exists to perform a bit-by-bit *inclusive OR* of a specified memory location with the accumulator and leave the result in the accumulator; memory is not changed.

ORA: *OR memory with the Accumulator.*

Thus (Acc = 0101 1001) OR (Mem = 0000 1111) gives Acc = 0101 1111. Again Figure D7-4 reveals this instruction in many addressing modes. The operation is concisely represented as $A \vee M \rightarrow A$ since $\vee$ or $\cup$ are commonly used to represent the notion of logical OR or *union* of two sets. Again the condition code bits N and Z are influenced.

5. There is the other form of OR, namely the *exclusive OR,* also available.

EOR: *Exclusive-OR memory with the accumulator.*

Again a bit-by-bit exclusive OR of a specified memory location is made with the accumulator, and the instruction is available in many addressing modes. It should be noted that the common *complement-the-accumulator* instruction does not exist. However, it can easily be accomplished by the exclusive OR of all 1's with the accumulator: EOR #$FF. (Acc = 0010 1001) EOR (Mem = 1111 1111) gives Acc = 1101 0110.

Process Control Example

Most of the important machine language tools for the 6502 microprocessor have now been presented. These may be melded with the basic I/O port techniques presented in Chapter D7 to accomplish many useful and important microcomputer tasks. Perhaps the most typical microcomputer task in the laboratory is instrument and experiment control; in industry it is often *process control*. In many respects, the control example that is developed next may be considered to be the principal objective of the microprocessor chapters. Rather than an esoteric example, however, an example familiar to almost everyone is presented: the automatic clothes washer. Indeed, a typical clothes washer uses a surprisingly complex control function, and for pedagogical reasons this application is even simplified somewhat here.

Figure D9–8 is a quasi-pictorial diagram of the clothes washer and its functions important to our discussion. There are 7 devices controlled by the microcomputer. These are all on/off devices, and each is controlled by one bit from an output port. The output lines from the microcomputer are designated by the open arrows. Notice, for example, the microcomputer control to the fill valve that admits water to the tub, and the control to the motor and its connection to the washer agitator.

Typically, a solenoid that operates from 110 V ac is used to physically open the fill valve, or to manipulate a belt and pulley system from the motor to the agitator, or from the motor to the spin-dry tub. Suitable electronics must be arranged so that the weak dc drive (typically 1-TTL-load capability) from a microprocessor port line may control the 110 V ac to a solenoid. An electromechanical relay may be employed here, or even better, a *solid-state relay* with a TTL-sensitive input and sturdy ac switching capability at the output. Either device provides electrical isolation between the microcomputer electronics and the 110-V ac line voltage.

When a microcomputer is given a control function, it must generally receive information about the process that it is controlling. There are 4 sensors or input transducers that are illustrated in Figure D9–8. For example, there is a sensor to indicate if the drain is closed, or if the tub is full, and so forth. Each is a binary indicator (true or false) and is required to output a TTL high level for true and low level for false. Each indicator line is connected to one bit of the microcomputer's input port and is designated by a solid dark arrow in Figure D9–8.

Figure D9–9 illustrates the bit functions assigned to the input port, which is taken to be port A, and the bit functions assigned to the output port, port B. The true condition for each bit is also given in the figure. The output true conditions have been chosen so that the outputs at reset will produce desirable conditions; for example, the water fill valve will be closed so that no water will be filling, and the agitator will be stopped. Recall that at reset all port lines act high due to pull-up resistors.

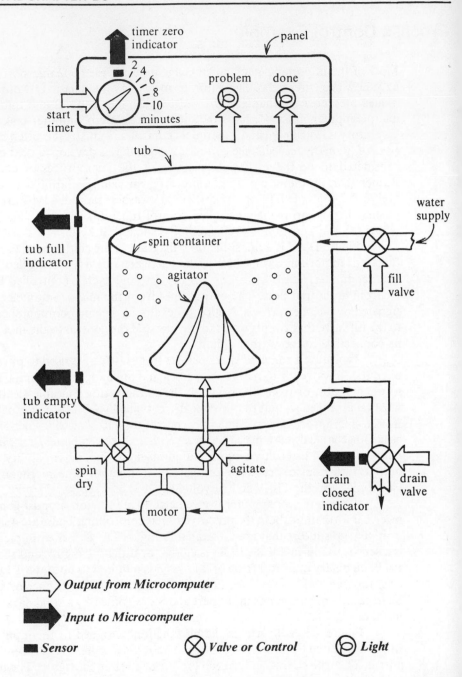

FIGURE D9-8. *Diagram of a Clothes Washer, Used as an Example of Process Control by Microcomputer (Sensors and Controlled Functions Are Illustrated.)*

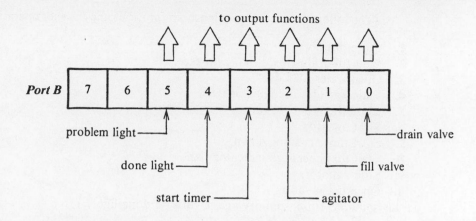

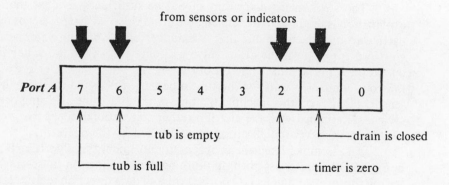

I/O Type	Name	Bit No.	True Condition
Outputs	open drain valve	PB0	high
	open fill valve	PB1	low
	run agitator	PB2	low
	start timer	PB3	low
	turn on done light	PB4	low
	turn on problem light	PB5	low
Inputs	drain closed indicator	PA1	high
	timer zero indicator	PA2	high
	tub empty indicator	PA6	high
	tub full indicator	PA7	high

FIGURE D9–9. *Input and Output Port Bit Assignments for the Clothes Washer Example (The True Condition for Each Bit Is Also Listed.)*

The following list gives an algorithm for the clothes washer operation:

1. Close drain valve,
2. Wait till drain-closed indicator true,
3. Open water fill valve,
4. Wait for tub-full indicator true,
5. Close the water fill valve,
6. Start agitator,
7. Start timer running down,
8. Wait for timer-zero indicator true,
9. Stop agitator,
10. Open drain valve.

(plus spin dry, rinse, spin dry again, turn on done light)

The steps in the algorithm should be sufficiently evident that little explanation is required. After closing the drain valve, we have a sensor on this particular machine to be sure that it actually closes. Thus the water need not go down the drain if the drain valve malfunctions. Also, the water filling operation is not a "timed fill" on our washer. Even if the water pressure is low, our controller waits for the tub to be truly full as indicated by the full sensor. Finally, on this machine the time duration for the agitating or wash cycle is determined with the aid of a rather conventional timer that ticks to zero from whatever initial setting is established by the operator.

An assembler language program to implement this algorithm is given in Figure D9–10. It is assumed that turning the appliance on causes a reset of the microprocessor and its I/O ports. Port and data direction register (DDR) addresses appropriate for the KIM are first defined (PORTA, DDRA, and so on); of course, these addresses could easily be changed to values for the SYM or some other 6502 configuration. The actual program begins in memory address $200. First the appropriate bits of port B are established as outputs, in agreement with Figure D9–9. Then the same bit pattern is written to port B (%00111111 will still be in the accumulator) so that the drain will be open, but the water fill valve closed, agitator stopped, timer stopped, and problem and done lights dark.

Next the microcomputer closes the drain valve. This instruction sequence, along with several others in the program, illustrates the manipulation of control bits through use of the AND and ORA instructions. First the LDA PORTB instruction loads the accumulator with the current bit-pattern in this control (output) port. In fact, the pattern that is returned should be $11111111. ("Extra credit": Why will the two 1's at the left of the number appear?) Next the AND #%11111110 performs a bit-by-bit AND between the *mask* pattern and the pattern in the accumulator. We have

$$
\begin{array}{r}
11111111 \quad \leftarrow \text{initial accumulator} \\
(\text{AND}) \quad \underline{11111110} \quad \leftarrow \text{mask} \\
11111110 \quad \leftarrow \text{final accumulator}
\end{array}
$$

```
PORTA = $1700
PORTB = $1702
DDRB  = $1701
DDRA  = $1703


          * = $200

          LDA  # %00111111    ;ESTABLISH OUT PINS
          STA  DDRB           ;FROM PORTB
          STA  PORTB          ;ALSO STOP THE OUTPUTS
          STA  PORTB          ;CLOSE DRAIN VALVE BY GETTING OUTS
          AND  # %11111110    ;AND ZERO THE DRAIN BIT
          STA  PORTB          ;OF THE OUTPUT
CHKDR ┌──LDA  PORTA           ;WAIT FOR DRAIN TO CLOSE BY
      │   AND  # %00000010    ;ISOLATING ITS INDICATOR AND
      └──BEQ  CHKDR           ; CHECK AGAIN IF NOT CLOSED
          LDA  PORTB          ;START WATER FILL BY
          AND  # %11111101    ;OPENING WATER VALVE,
          STA  PORTB          ;I.E., ZERO ITS BIT
CHKFL ┌──LDA  PORTA           ;WAIT FOR TUB FULL BY
      └──BPL  CHKFL           ;CHECKING BIT 7 (MINUS)
                             ;CHECK AGAIN IF NOT FULL

          •                  ;CLOSE WATER FILL VALVE
          •                  ;START AGITATION
          •                  ;START TIMER AND WAIT FOR TIMER ZERO

          LDA  PORTB          ;STOP AGITATOR BY BRINGING
          ORA  # %00000100    ONLY
          STA  PORTB          ITS BIT HIGH
          •
          •
          •
```

FIGURE D9–10. *Assembler Language Program to Implement the Clothes Washer Control Algorithm*

The consequence is that wherever a 1 existed in the mask, the accumulator bit is unchanged. Thus accumulator bits that were 1 in those positions remain 1, and those that were 0 remain 0 (although there were no 0's here). However, the 0 bit in the mask bit-pattern forces a 0 in that position in the accumulator. In this way, the drain valve will be closed and the other devices will be left in whatever condition they were in. Finally this control bit-pattern is sent to port B by the STA PORTB instruction, and the drain valve should actually close.

However, the microprocessor waits for this action to be evident through the drain-closed indicator before starting the water fill. A microcomputer decision is involved here. First the status of the indicators is obtained in the accumulator through the LDA PORTA instruction. However, we are interested *only* in the condition of the drain-closed indicator and wish to *mask off* the other indicator bits to zero. This is done with the AND #%00000010 instruction. Thus, let X represent either 0 or 1 in an accumulator bit position. We have

```
                              ┌─────── drain indicator bit position
                     XXXXXXXX  ← initial accumulator
         (AND)       00000010  ← mask
                    ──────────
                     000000X0  ← final accumulator
```

Notice that the resulting accumulator is entirely zero only if the drain-closed indicator bit (from PA1) was 0, indicating that the drain is *not* closed. In this case the BEQ CHKDR instruction—that is, *Branch if the result EQualed zero* to CHKDR—sends the microprocessor back to the instruction labeled CHKDR (CHecK DRain), and the microprocessor proceeds to obtain the indicator status for another check of the drain indicator. (Indeed, the assembler will calculate $F9 = -7$ for the relative address in this BEQ instruction.) In this way, the microprocessor runs in a *tight loop,* waiting for the drain to close. The arrow drawn in the program shows this loop. When the drain finally closes after perhaps 0.5 seconds, its indicator bit becomes 1, the masked accumulator will *not* be identically zero, and the branch back is *not* taken.

The microcomputer then proceeds to open the water valve by zeroing this control bit in port B and keeping the other bits as they are. For example, the drain should remain closed, the agitator stopped, and so on. The approach is generally like that already described for closing the drain valve.

Next the microcomputer waits for the tub to fill up. This time the tub-full indicator bit should be checked, and it happens to be in the most significant bit position, PA7. Our testing technique will exploit this fact. After loading port A into the accumulator, the N bit (negative flag) will be set if PA7 was set. But until the tub is full, PA7 is 0 and the N bit will also be 0 as for a plus number. Therefore, we use a BPL CHKFL instruction after the LDA PORT instruction. The microprocessor *Branches back on the PLus condition* to check the full indicator again. It remains in this loop waiting for the tub to fill. When the minus condition finally indicates that the tub is full, the microprocessor "falls through" to close the water fill valve and the subsequent operations.

Just one more control operation is detailed, and this is done to show a use of the ORA instruction. A specific bit can be made 1 (and the others maintained unchanged) through the ORA instruction. It is used to stop the agitator near the end of the program. The port B output status is read into the accumulator, and the number 0000 0100 is ORed to the accumulator to make bit number 2 high. When this is sent to port B, the agitator should stop; other outputs remain as they were.

It should be evident that the AND and OR operations available in machine language on the 6502 (and essentially on all computers) are very useful for the bit manipulations often required in laboratory real-time applications. Most implementations of BASIC make AND and OR functions available. However, many of them in the past have *not* performed the AND or OR on a bit-by-bit basis. For example, C = *A* AND *B* returns C = 1 if *A* and *B* are both equal to *or greater than 1*. However, the BASIC on the SYM and the PET treat *A* and *B* as 16-bit binary numbers and return for C an integer corresponding to the 16-bit result of a bit-by-bit AND between *A* and *B*. A similar behavior holds for OR.

Additional Hardware and Software Techniques for Laboratory Microcomputing

In the remainder of this chapter we consider some additional important hardware and software techniques that can be very useful for real-time microcomputing. They are associated especially with input/output processing, which is an important aspect of laboratory microcomputing. The principal hardware topic is the device flag, which is actually nothing more than a flip-flop. In the next chapter we look at support chips that provide flag flip-flops along with programmable I/O ports. This chapter concludes with the subject of the microcomputer stack and subroutine usage.

Device Flag and Asynchronous I/O

An orderly means of communication must be arranged between a computer and peripheral devices. For example, if a series of characters is to be sent by a computer to a Teletype, the transfer must take place at a rate determined by the Teletype because the computer could quickly "swamp" the relatively slow Teletype. Furthermore, if the computer is receiving characters from the Teletype, it must wait for a new character to be ready before reading a character from the input buffer (else it will read in the previous character again).

A simple but effective means of implementing programmed I/O is through the *device flag* technique. This is simply a flip-flop whose output Q can be read by the computer. It is called a flag because it is much like the red flag on a RFD mailbox. If a farmer (device) has a letter (byte) to send to the post office (computer), the farmer sets up the flag on the mailbox. The mail carrier, driving by the mailbox, can detect the fact that a new letter is ready by the fact that the flag is high. The carrier (computer) then stops, picks up the letter, and makes sure to put the flag down (clear the flag) in order not to mistakenly stop at the mailbox during the next round. This signal arrangement of "I tap you, you tap me back" is referred to as *handshake I/O*. The farmer (device) could further check that the mail has been picked up (as evidenced by the cleared flag) before putting a new letter into the mailbox. The analogy presented here, of course, is for an *input device* that sends data to the computer.

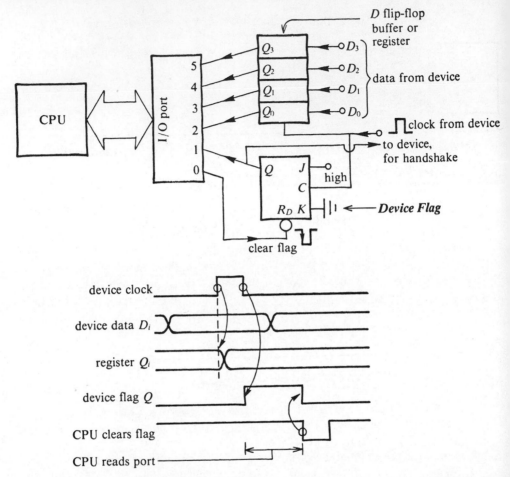

(a) Device Buffer, Flag, and Signals for Input to the Microprocessor from an Input Device

FIGURE D9-11. *Asynchronous I/O with Device Flag*

A series of *D* flip-flops can be the buffer or memory register (mailbox) that receives a binary number (letter) from the input device when clocked by a device-generated pulse (see Figure D9-11a). A *JK* flip-flop can be the device flag that is set by the trailing edge of the buffer clock pulse (now the data is settled in the buffer). The computer can clear this flag by a pulse to direct-reset after reading in the data. The register flip-flops should output to a port (such as a 6530 I/O port) that is read by the CPU under a read-from-memory instruction. Another pair of port bits are required to read the device flag bit (input) and to clear the flag (output). Figure D9-11a illustrates a 4-bit data buffer and flag, along with the timing of associated signals.

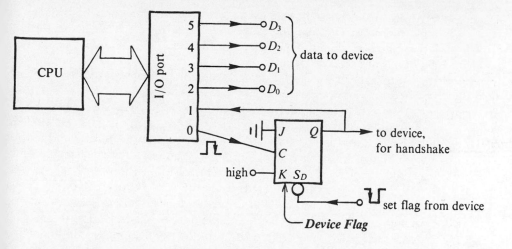

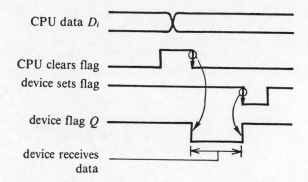

(b) Device Flag and Use of Port for Output from the Microprocessor to an Output Device

A device flag is also effective for an *output device*. The situation is like a farmer with a mailbox who only receives mail, at least in this particular mailbox. (If the farmer both sends and receives mail, *two* mailboxes are required in our analogy.) The mail carrier indicates a letter is in the box (which fills it—small mailbox!) by lowering or clearing the flag on the box. Then the farmer, when driving by, can see a letter must be in the box and stops to pick it up. In the process, the farmer makes certain to set the flag so that the mail carrier can see the box is available for another letter. If the flag is up during the next delivery attempt, the carrier drives by because stuffing in another letter pushes the first one out and it is lost to the wind!

Notice one simple rule used above, which gives some consistency to both situations: The *computer always clears the device flag,* whether the flag is associated with an input device or with an output device. Conversely, the device always sets the device flag. Thus, if the flag for a given device is set (be it an input or an output device), the computer always knows that the device is ready to be serviced.

Implementing an output port with a 6530 chip is quite easy since both port A and port B already possess flip-flops that latch the data sent to them by the CPU; that is, they contain buffers or registers for use as output (but *not* for input). An associated *JK* flip-flop is required for the device flag, however, and it is clocked to the low state (cleared) by a CPU pulse that is sent out by another port pin after data is loaded to the port. The device then can detect that the flag is low and pick up the data at its earliest convenience from the port outputs. The device then must set the flag. This is diagrammed for a 4-bit data transfer situation in Figure D9-11b. Bit 1 of the port is programmed as input to detect the device flag.

The flag-based I/O scheme just discussed is often called *asynchronous I/O* because the transfer of data (either in or out) may take place at quite random times. The other communication scheme is *synchronous I/O.* In this case data transfer always takes place at a prescribed time, and no flag is needed. It is like a mail carrier who delivers mail once an hour on the hour, and the farmer should then regularly go to the mailbox—for example, at 30 minutes past the hour—all day long. This mode of communication is typically used for rapid and rather sustained data transfer with computers. It does have the requirement (perhaps disadvantage) that both the mail carrier and the farmer have accurate clocks; that is, both the CPU and the device have accurate clocks, or perhaps access to a common clock.

A point is made here about the need for and function of the I/O port of a device like the 6530 in implementing the data transfer ports of Figure D9-11. On a memory-mapped I/O CPU such as the 6502, it is necessary to have gating that detects the memory address number of the device with which communication takes place. Only when this *ID number* of the device is present should data be taken from or passed to the CPU 3-state data bus. The 6530 chip performs the address bus decoding and data bus communication, but its cost also includes other features, especially ROM, which may not be needed. The 6532 chip exists that substitutes 128 bytes of RAM for the 1K ROM of the 6530 chip.

However, the versatile 6520 PIA has two 8-bit ports and incorporates 4 flag flip-flops, as well as 4 associated input/output lines. It is clearly a useful general-purpose I/O device and is discussed in Chapter D10. The 6520 and Motorola 6820 are identical (they do *not* incorporate a RAM or ROM). Furthermore, neither has a timer available, but the later 6522 VIA does include two programmable timers, in addition to the two versatile 8-bit I/O ports with flags, and a shift register.

Device Command Register in I/O Technique

It may be that the computer desires a peripheral to perform different operations with various data after they are transferred. This can be done by using some of the output bits as a command code; different binary numbers represent various commands to the device. This subgroup of bits may be regarded as a *command register* to the device. Indeed, if 8 bits of data must be transferred to the device in addition to a command code of, for example, 4 bits, 2 output ports are required, and one may be called the data port while the other is the command register to the device. Several instructions are needed to transfer the data as well as command to the device. This is always necessary if more than 8 bits are to be sent to the device by an 8-bit microprocessor such as the 6502, of course. Typically, the data should be established at the data port *before* the command and flag is established (why?).

Polling the Flags

When a number of devices are communicating with a CPU, it is necessary for the CPU to inspect the flags regularly to determine if one of them has data it wishes to communicate to the CPU or is ready to receive new data. (Even with just one device a regular inspection of its flag is necessary.) A routine to inspect all of the flags in turn (and attend to each that is found high) is often referred to as a *polling the flags* routine.

Figure D9–12 presents a flowchart for the general routine to poll the device flags and communicate with the devices. Each decision diamond represents a testing if the flag is set for a particular device.

The flowchart of Figure D9–12 is implemented by a rather general-form 6502 assembler language program in Figure D9–13. A number of assembler language conventions are used that actually make the program quite readable. Notice, for example:

1. Symbolic addresses: for example, DEVFLG1 for address of port that contains the flag for device #1;
2. Symbolic constants: for example, MASK1 = 00100000, if the flag bit for device #1 were in bit position 5;
3. Labels: for example, DEV1 is the label representing the first address of the routine (set of instructions) to communicate with device #1.

Examining the body of the program in Figure D9–13 shows that a byte that includes the flag bit is read from each device in turn. The flag bit is isolated with an appropriate mask and a branch to a routine to attend to the

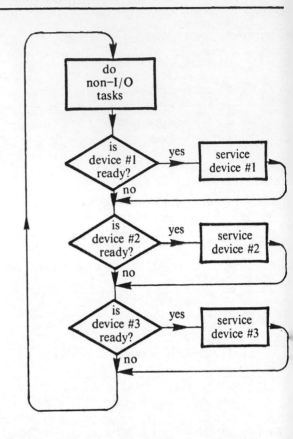

FIGURE D9–12. *Flowchart for Polling Flags and Attending to the I/O Device Associated with Each*

device is taken if that particular flag is high. Otherwise, the next flag is tested until all are examined and the computer may return to its principal activity.

It should be noted that if the flag bit is in bit 7, the mask operation can be avoided. The N bit would be set or cleared due to bit 7 under a LDA instruction, and a BMI (branch if minus) could be used to test this fact. However, a more convenient instruction from the LDA for this use is the BIt Test *instruction: BIT.* On the 6502 the BIT instruction may reference a memory location (for example, with absolute addressing), and the N condition code bit is set if bit 7 in the referenced location is 1; also the V bit is set if bit 6 is 1. The accumulator is *not* altered by the BIT instruction. Of course, the N and the V bit are each testable under branch instructions (for example, the BMI and BVS instructions), and again the mask operation can be avoided. Therefore, bit 6 and bit 7 are convenient flag positions, and we find them to be used as flags in the 6820/6821/6520 programmable interface chip (PIA).

Subroutine and Stack Usage

The subroutine is a very useful programming construction. The reader may have already learned its utility in programming with a higher-level language.

```
DEVFLG1 = XXXX                    ;ADDRESS OF PORT WITH FLAG 1
DEVFLG2 = XXXX                    ;ADDRESS OF PORT WITH FLAG 2
DEVFLG3 = XXXX                    ;ADDRESS OF PORT WITH FLAG 3
MASK1 = (1 ONLY AT FLAG BIT POSITION
MASK2 =  FOR PARTICULAR
MASK3 =  DEVICE)

BEGIN    LDA  DEVFLG1             ;GET WORD WITH DEVICE 1 FLAG
         AND  #MASK1              ;ISOLATE ITS FLAG BIT
         BNE  DEV1                ;IF NONZERO, GO ATTEND DEVICE 1
NEXT2    LDA  DEVFLG2             ;GET WORD WITH DEVICE 2 FLAG
         AND  #MASK2              ;ISOLATE ITS FLAG BIT
         BNE  DEV2                ;IF NONZERO, GO ATTEND DEVICE 2
NEXT3    LDA  DEVFLG3
         AND  #MASK3              .
         BNE  DEV3                .
         JMP  MAINTASK            .
DEV1     .                        ;CODE TO ATTEND TO DEVICE #1
         .
         .
         JMP NEXT2                ;GO CHECK NEXT FLAG
DEV2     .                        ;CODE TO ATTEND TO DEVICE #2
         .
         .
         JMP NEXT3
DEV3     .                        ;CODE TO ATTEND TO DEVICE #3
         .
         .
         JMP MAINTASK
```

FIGURE D9–13. *Typical Routine for Polling and Tending to Devices*

For example, BASIC contains the GOSOB and RETURN statements for subroutine programming. The JSR (*J*ump to *Sub*Routine) and RTS (*Re*Turn from *S*ubroutine) instructions on the 6502 perform very similar duties. Discussion of how the subroutine calls are actually managed on the 6502 leads to a discussion of the 6502 hardware stack. The *hardware stack* concept is a quite simple scheme for organizing a memory store, but it has surprisingly powerful applications. The first minicomputers did not possess a hardware stack, but the power of this technique became widely appreciated beginning in about 1970. Essentially all contemporary microprocessors have instructions and hardware to implement a stack. Students who use Hewlett Packard calculators must become familiar with stack operations because a stack is essential to the RPN technique.

First, the utility of the subroutine is illustrated. Suppose a program segment is required at several places in a program. For example, it may be necessary to multiply two numbers together at several points in the program. The same program code could be put into the program at each point that it is needed. However, this represents rather needless duplication and waste of program memory.

A *subroutine* is a program segment that is needed at several places in a program; however, the code is placed in memory only once, in a region separate from where it would be placed in the repetitive approach mentioned above. The program causes a *Jump to SubRoutine* (JSR) each time it is needed, and at the end of the routine's execution, a return must be made to the next instruction following the jump. However, the *ReTurn from Subroutine* (RTS) will be to different places in the program, depending on where the JSR was invoked. Figure D9–14 illustrates this in a diagram of the program flow for a program that uses a *multiply together two given numbers* (MLTPLY) subroutine at several points in the main program.

The JSR instruction is available on the 6502 in absolute addressing mode (OP code = \$20); JSR, therefore, is a 3-byte instruction and can jump anywhere in the 6502 address space. The first OP code of the subroutine must be placed at the address to which the computer jumps, of course. Then the 1-byte RTS instruction (OP code = \$60) is placed at the end of the subroutine code segment, and the 6502 automatically returns to execute the OP code in

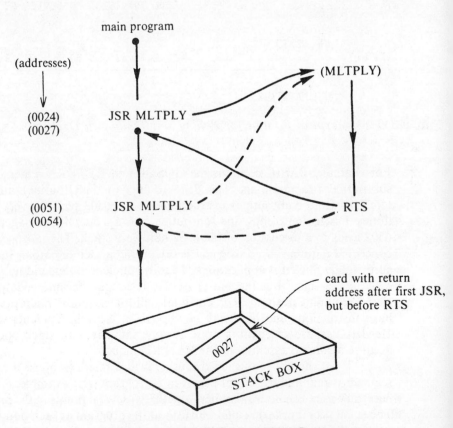

FIGURE D9–14. *Use of a Subroutine Call from a Main Program*

memory immediately following the particular JSR instruction that invoked the jump. It should be noted that a jump-absolute instruction is not particularly appropriate to return from the subroutine to the main program since the absolute address must be changed depending on the place in the program that called the subroutine. Indeed, if the subroutine existed in ROM, the return address would not be changeable (it is engraved in stone!).

The concept of a *stack* is very useful in handling this return address problem; therefore we first develop a model for its operation. Suppose the CPU takes note that a JSR is being requested, rather than a "plain JMP." The CPU could write the address of the next instruction beyond the JSR (the return address) on a card and place it in a box. At the end of the subroutine, the RTS instruction sends the CPU to the box and the CPU reads the number on the card to see where to return to. After reading the card, the CPU throws it away. This "stack box" is drawn at the bottom of Figure D9–14.

Even while the CPU is executing the subroutine, it could encounter a JSR to still another routine. This program flow situation is diagrammed in Figure D9–15. In response to the JSR, the CPU would again write the address of the next OP code on a card and place it on top of the previous card in a *stack*. When the last subroutine is completed, it should have an RTS instruction as its last instruction. This causes the CPU to take the top card off the stack and put the address written there into the program counter. The CPU thus returns to the instruction following the JSR and executes it. If that instruction was itself in a subroutine, the RTS instruction at its end causes another card to be taken from the stack and a return to its calling program. This technique permits an orderly procedure for returning from a subroutine, and subroutines may call subroutines, may call subroutines, . . . without losing the return trail. The stack condition for this card model is shown at the bottom of Figure D9–15; it represents the stack during the time that the CPU is executing the second subroutine (SBR2). Note the return addresses written on the cards.

Of course the 6502 does not actually use a box with a stack of cards, but rather must use read/write memory to save return addresses. They must be saved in a *last-in–first-out* scheme such as a stack of cards presents, however. This is done with the aid of a *stack pointer*. This is an 8-bit register in the CPU and is labeled S in the register model of Figure D7–4a. For the 6502 microprocessor, the stack is always on page 1 of memory (locations 0100 through 01FF) and builds from the top location (01FF) downward. When there are "no cards on the stack," the stack pointer should be adjusted to FF. Thus, after a reset the program for the 6502 should arrange to initially load the stack register with FF. The KIM and SYM monitors do this as an early order of business.

The stack pointer is always adjusted (usually automatically by the 6502) to contain the address of the next available memory for stacking of a number. We say it *points to* the available address. When a number is placed on the stack, the 6502 merely checks the stack pointer number to obtain the

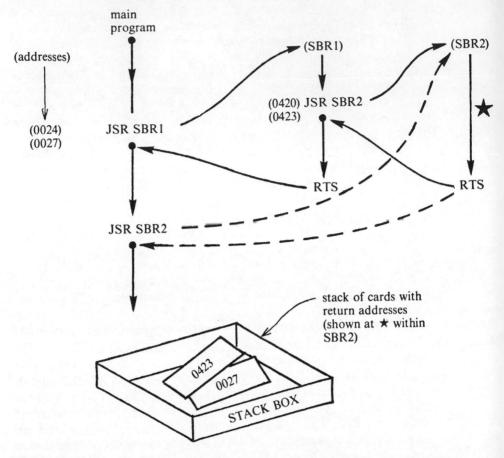

FIGURE D9–15. *"Stack" of Return Addresses When Two Subroutine Calls Are Pending*

address of the memory location into which the 8-bit number should be placed. The stack pointer is then decremented by 1 to point to the next available memory. If a 16-bit number is to be placed on the stack, it must be split and placed in 2 successive memory locations, of course. The stack pointer is accordingly decremented by 2 after stacking.

Assume that the stack pointer contains the value FF when a JSR occurs. The CPU automatically saves the 16-bit return address in the top 2 locations of page 1. The stack pointer is automatically decremented twice to point to the next available location (to 'FD). Additional JSRs cause additional pairs of bytes (16-bit return addresses) to be saved beneath the previous ones. Then when an RTS occurs, the PC is automatically loaded from the two locations just above the one *pointed to* by the stack register, and the stack register is automatically incremented by 2. The CPU then goes to the address

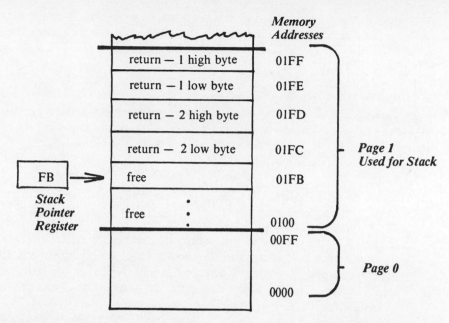

FIGURE D9–16. *Stack and Stack Pointer with Two Return Addresses Saved on the Stack*

in the PC and performs the next instruction. Figure D9–16 diagrams the stack and stack pointer with 2 return addresses saved on the stack. This corresponds to the condition of the stack model at the bottom of Figure D9–15.

The stack is automatically used by the 6502 whenever a subroutine call and return are invoked. However, the stack may also be conveniently used for temporary storage and later recall of the accumulator and other CPU registers. Specific instructions exist to "*push* data *onto* the stack" or to "*pull* it *off* the stack." This terminology follows from our card model of the stack. Thus, there exist:

PHA: *PusH the Accumulator on the Stack.* OP Code = 48

This causes the accumulator to be stored in the available location pointed to by the stack pointer, and the stack pointer register to then be decremented by 1.

PLA: *PulL the Accumulator from the stack.* OP Code = 68

This causes the stack pointer to be incremented by 1 and the accumulator to be loaded with the contents of the memory location pointed to by this value of S (that is, from the top of the stack).

There also exist instructions to push the processor status register on the stack (PHP) and pull the processor status register from the stack (PLP). If the X index register or Y index register is to be saved on the stack, each should first be transferred to the accumulator by the TXA or TYA instructions, respectively. Then the PHA instruction places the register on the stack. Restoring an index register subsequently involves the PLA followed by TAX or TAY.

Another use of the stack is in passing numbers (parameters) to a subroutine. These numbers are subsequently to be used by the routine, and presumably one or more numbers should be returned to the calling program as the results desired by it. Consider, for example, the routine presented in Figure D9–3 to multiply two integers. This could well be used as the subroutine to be called (by a JRS $0012) whenever the multiply operation is required. Merely replace the JMP MONITOR instruction at the end with RTS. The parameters passed to the routine are the two multipliers *A and B,* which are assumed by the routine to have been placed in MA 11 and MA 12. The calling program must know that the result is returned in MA 00.

However, use of specific memory locations for passing parameters to a subroutine can be inconvenient. The stack can be useful here. Thus, the two numbers to be multiplied can be pushed on the stack before the JSR. The subroutine must then retrieve the data from the stack; it will be "beneath" the return address bytes on the stack, and these must be removed and the data to be manipulated then removed. The result can be pushed on the stack and then the return address bytes pushed on the stack before an RTS is executed.

These steps involve *adjustment of the stack pointer* by the program. The stack pointer register itself may be loaded from the *X* index register through the *Transfer X to S* instruction (TXS). Of course, the *X* index register must first be loaded by either a LDX or a TAX instruction. Also, the stack pointer may be saved, examined, or adjusted through use of the *Transfer S to X* instruction (TSX). For example, it may easily be incremented or decremented after transfer to the *X* register and then returned again with TXS.

Subroutine Example

A program is presented next that illustrates a number of the concepts recently developed. This example assumes that 8 LEDs or indicators have been connected to port A (for example, of the KIM or SYM), and 6 switches have been connected to input high/low to the least significant 6 bits of port B. The objective of the program is to cause the LEDs to count up in binary-coded-decimal (BCD) at a rate that depends on the switch settings. A higher binary setting of the switches will cause a greater delay between changes of the LEDs; that is, the LEDs will count more slowly.

A general system diagram of this example is given in Figure D9–17. The algorithm for the program is as follows:

1. Establish I/O ports,
2. Put in decimal mode,

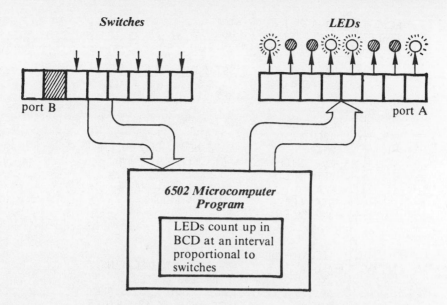

FIGURE D9–17.   *General System Diagram of the Example Using a Delay Subroutine (LEDs are shown in Highest Score (99_{10}) before "Rollover" to 00.)*

3. Get current LED number and add 1,
4. Read the switch setting,
5. Delay, proportional to switch value,
6. Send new number to LEDs,
7. Repeat from 3.

An assembler language program to implement this algorithm is given in Figure D9–18. The program uses a *software delay* to slow down the rate at which the LEDs count up, and this has been placed in a subroutine. We examine this delay subroutine first. Basically, the program calls for a delay by sending the 6502 into a "do nothing but count sheep" loop in order to waste a particular period of time.

Let T be the setting of the binary switches. This number will be in the accumulator as the 6502 enters the delay subroutine. The maximum value of T as input by the 6 switches is $00111111 = 63_{10}$. This number is shifted 2 places to the left at the beginning of the routine, which is equivalent to multiplying by 4. "ASL A" causes the shift to occur in the *accumulator*.

NOTE: Each shift to the left of a decimal number multiplies its value by the base, which is 10; similarly, each shift to the left of a binary number multiplies the value of the original number by 2.

```
LEDS = (PORT A OF KIM OR SYM)
DDRLEDS = (DAT. DIR. REG. PORT A)
SWITCHES = (PORT B OF KIM OR SYM)

              LDA #$FF        ;SET OUT PORT TO LEDS
              STA DDRLEDS
              SED             ;SET DECIMAL MODE
AGAIN       ► CLC
              LDA  LEDS       ;GET CURRENT LED VALUE
              ADC  #$01       ;ADD 01
              PHA             ;SAVE NEW VALUE ON STACK
              LDA  SWITCHES   ;GET SWITCH SETTING
            ◄ JSR  DELAY      ;GO WAIT
            ► PLA             ;GET BACK NEW VALUE
              STA  LEDS       ;SHOW ON LEDS
            ◄ JMP  AGAIN      ;REPEAT


              ;DELAY SUBROUTINE
DELAY       ► ASL  A          ;SHIFT SWITCH SETTING
              ASL  A          ;LEFT TWO PLACES
              ORA  #$03       ;MAKE RIGHT 2 BITS ONE
              TAX             ;USE X=INDEX AS COUNTER
LOOP        ► DEX             ;DECREMENT BY ONE
              BNE LOOP        ;DO AGAIN IF NOT ZERO
            ◄ RTS            ;X IS ZERO, RETURN
```

FIGURE D9–18.   *Assembler Language Program of Example Using a Software Delay Subroutine*

Next the right 2 bits are set to 1 by the ORA instruction. The resulting number is $4T + 3$. This number is placed in the X register and repeatedly decremented until zero. The machine cycles to execute these instructions yield a delay that may be computed using the number of cycles required for each instruction (found under the N column of the programmer's reference card, Figure D7–4b).

The computation of the time to execute the delay subroutine may be done as follows:

	ASL	2 cycles
	ASL	2 cycles
	ORA#	2 cycles
	TAX	2 cycles
repeated	DEX	2 cycles
$(4T + 3)$ times	BNE	3 cycles, except when "falls through" is 2
	RTS	6 cycles

The time to execute the subroutine is

$$2 + 2 + 2 + 2 + [(4T + 3)(2 + 3) - 1] + 6 = 20T + 28$$

The maximum delay possible is $20 \times 63 + 28 = 1,288$ cycles, or 1.288 milliseconds for the 1-microsecond clock cycle of the KIM or SYM. The minimum delay is 28 microseconds.

The operation of the main program should be quite clear from the comments in the program. Notice that the accumulator is temporarily saved on the stack by the PHA instruction before reading the switch setting into the accumulator, as the latter action would destroy the incremented LED value. Then the delay is accomplished by the JSR DELAY, after which the accumulator is restored by the PLA and then put out to the LEDs.

The assembler language program is not tied to specific memory locations, and the main program, as well as the subroutine, could be located nearly anywhere in available memory. However, memory near the top of page 0 should not be used on the KIM or the SYM (the monitor uses 00EF through 00FF on the KIM, and 00F8 through 00FF in the SYM), nor should memory near the top of page 1 be used (the stack uses it). Suppose the DELAY subroutine begins in $100. The 3-byte instruction for JSR DELAY would be coded as 20, 00, 01.

It is true that the delay achieved by the subroutine in Figure D9–18 is not large on the human time scale, and most of the LEDs will flash so rapidly that they appear to be continually on. Let us calculate the flashing rate of the slowest LED. The interval between the incrementing of the LED number is the delay time of $(20T + 28)$ cycles, plus the number of cycles in 1 loop of the main program. It is left as an exercise to show that the latter is 32 cycles. The incrementing period is then $20T + 28 + 32 = 20(T + 3)$ cycles. If T on the switches is set to $101111_2 = 47_{10}$, the incrementing period is $20 \times (47 + 3) = 1,000$ CPU clock cycles. Because the program causes the LEDs to count in BCD $(0, \ldots, 99, 0, \ldots, 99)$, the LEDs will all go dark every 100 increments or $100 \times 1,000$ cycles. With a 1.000-megahertz clock, this time interval is 0.1000 seconds, and the most significant LED will flash with this period. Changed to frequency terms, the slowest LED will flash 10.00 times per second. Note that the LEDs count up in BCD due to the ADC #01 in conjunction with decimal mode. However, the counter in the delay subroutine counts down in binary since the decrement (and increment) instructions *always* use this mode.

A larger delay could be achieved by placing a *loop within the loop* in the delay subroutine. Thus the Y index register could be used as a second counter and within the X loop. Only when it counts down from Y to zero would the X index register be decremented, and Y would be reloaded. The number of cycles involved would then be on the order of X times Y, rather than merely X. This change is left to the problems.

The need for a specified delay between microcomputer actions occurs rather frequently in laboratory microcomputing. The SYM monitor includes a delay subroutine that may be invoked from a SYM user's program to obtain a variable delay. In the next chapter we study the use of *hardware timers* to obtain delays.

REVIEW EXERCISES

1. (a)   What is the advantage of two's-complement binary numbers over signed binary numbers?
   (b)   Tell how a negative number is readily identified in either case.
2. Give the most positive and most negative 8-bit two's-complement numbers; give each in binary, hexadecimal, and signed decimal forms.
3. Describe the function of the N bit and the V bit, respectively, in the processor status register.
4. (a)   What is meant by multiple-precision arithmetic?
   (b)   Explain why the ADC instruction has a convenient property for multiple-precision addition, although it is not convenient for single-precision addition.
5. (a)   What must be done to the C bit if a single-precision subtraction is performed?
   (b)   Explain why the SBC instruction is convenient for multiple-precision subtraction?
6. (a)   Describe what the 6502 microprocessor accomplishes with an ADC instruction if the 6502 is in decimal mode.
   (b)   How is the 6502 microprocessor placed in decimal mode or removed from decimal mode?
7. (a)   A branch instruction could be called a conditional jump. Explain this statement.
   (b)   Which register is interrogated whenever a branch instruction is executed?
   (c)   What type of addressing is used by the branch instructions? Explain its method for determining the destination address.
8. What is the condition of the Z bit just after the instruction LDA #$00 is executed?
9. Explain the purpose of a counter in a program loop.
10. What is the operation of the DEC instruction and the INC instruction, respectively?
11. (a)   How many index registers does the 6502 possess?
    (b)   Give four similarities between an index register and an accumulator.
    (c)   Give an important difference between an index register and an accumulator.
    (d)   Give two reasons why an index register is more efficient than a memory location as a counter for a program loop.
    (e)   List four instructions that can change the contents of an index register.
12. (a)   Explain the difference between a shift instruction and a rotate instruction.
    (b)   Is the carry bit involved in the shift or the rotate instructions? Explain.
13. Explain how the condition of an arbitrary bit in a given memory location can be tested. Include a description of an appropriate mask.
14. Assume switch SWA is input to bit 0 (LSB) of a port, while switch SWB is input to bit 6, and switch SWC is input to bit 7 (MSB) of the given port.
    (a)   Explain how a 6502 program can test the condition of SWC without a masking operation. Give an example of the program segment required.

(b) Similarly explain how the condition of SWB can be tested without a masking operation. Give an example of the program segment required.

(c) The condition of SWA can also be tested without a masking operation on the accumulator, but rather through the use of a rotate instruction. Explain how this can be accomplished, including an example of the program segment required.

15. Give instructions that are convenient for adding 1 or subtracting 1 from a given memory location.

16. (a) Give an instruction sequence that is convenient for setting a given bit to 1 in a memory location, while the other bits remain unchanged.

(b) Give an instruction sequence that is convenient for clearing a given bit to 0 in a memory location, while the other bits remain unchanged.

17. What type of digital circuit is a device flag?

18. Suppose a device flag is used in connection with computer communication to an output device such as a printer.

(a) Who sets the device flag? Also tell when, and what it signifies to the other party.

(b) Who clears the device flag? Also tell when, and what it signifies to the other party.

19. Suppose a device flag is used in connection with an input device such as a printer.

(a) Who sets the device flag? Also tell when, and what it signifies to the other party.

(b) Who clears the device flag? Also tell when, and what it signifies to the other party.

20. (a) Explain the difference between asynchronous I/O and synchronous I/O.

(b) What is meant by handshake I/O?

21. What is the nature and purpose of a polling-flags routine?

22. What is meant by the term *nested subroutines*?

23. Describe the actions of the PHA and PLA instructions, respectively.

24. (a) How can the stack pointer be changed directly?

(b) Describe why this procedure should be invoked after a reset.

25. (a) What is the size of the stack pointer register on the 6502?

(b) Describe how this size in turn determines the size of the hardware stack on the 6502.

(c) Where is the hardware stack located on the 6502?

(d) Suppose the stack is empty; what is the number in the stack pointer register?

26. What is the common name for a last-in–first-out memory?

27. (a) What is the advantage and purpose of a JSR instruction relative to a JMP instruction?

(b) How is the stack involved with a JSR instruction?

(c) What is the purpose of the RTS instruction?

(d) How is the stack involved with an RTS instruction?

PROBLEMS

1. Express each of the following numbers as a 1-byte (8 bits) number using the two's-complement representation; express each in binary and in hex:
   (a) +1   (b) −1   (c) +9   (d) −9
2. Show that forming the two's complement twice on the number 01011101 returns the original number. Comment on this behavior as a property of negation.
3. Find the binary magnitude of each of the following two's-complement numbers:
   (a) 11001100   (b) 11100111   (c) 11000000
4. Consider the numbers 7F and 9A.
   (a) Tell if the number is positive or negative in each case (assuming two's-complement convention).
   (b) Find the two's complement of the respective numbers, expressing in binary and in hex.
5. The following calculation is to be performed on the 6502 microprocessor: $\$15 + \$46 - \$31$. Write a short program to accomplish this calculation.
6. (a) Only one of the following two program segments correctly develops (in the accumulator) the negative or two's complement of a number that is present in MA $20. Identify the correct case, and explain your choice.

(1) SEC	(2) CLC
LDA #$00	LDA #$00
SBC $20	SBC $20

   (b) Repeat question (a) for the following two segments:

(1) LDA $20	(2) LDA $20
OR #$FF	EOR #$FF
CLC	CLC
ADC #$01	ADC #$01

7 Consider the following arithmetic calculations to be carried out on the 6502 microprocessor. In each case tell the states of the C bit and the V bit after the calculation.

(a)	(b)	(c)	(d)
01000001	10010000	10010000	11000000
+01001001	+10000101	+00000101	+11100000

8. The double-precision number A is stored in MA $0000 and MA $0001 (least significant byte in $0000), while the double-precision number B is stored in MA $0002 and MA $0003 (least significant byte in $0002). Write a program segment that forms the sum $A + B$ and places the result in MA $0010 and MA $0011 (least significant byte in $0010).

9. Tell the contents of the accumulator after each of the following program segments is executed:

(a) CLD	(b) CLD	(c) CLD
LDA #$24	LDA #$24	LDA #$24
CLC	SEC	SEC
ADC #$37	SBC #$07	SBC #$37

(d) SED	(e) SED	(f) SED
LDA #$24	LDA #$24	LDA #$24
CLC	SEC	SEC
ADC #$37	SBC #$07	SBC #$37

10. Give the contents of the accumulator after each of the program segments given.

    (a) LDA #%01010011   (b) LDA #%01010011   (c) LDA #%01010011
        ORA #%11110000   AND #%11110000   EOR #%11110000

11. (a) The following two instructions could be called a "branch always"; explain why.

           SEC
           BCS $55

    (b) Does the branch occur to an earlier or later point in the program relative to the position of the branch instruction?

12. The multiply program of Figure D9–3 used a memory location for the counter. Suppose that an index register is used as the counter instead.

    (a) How much shorter is the program in terms of memory locations used?

    (b) How many machine cycles are saved for each passage through the loop?

13. Rewrite the multiply program of Figure D9–3 to use the X index register as a counter. Use assembler language (with labels and symbolic addressing) so that the program may begin in an arbitrary memory location on page 0.

14. Write a program that adds together 5 binary numbers from memory locations $200 and up (whatever has been placed in these locations). Have the program start in memory location $10 and store the resulting sum in $220. Use a program loop to accomplish this program. Present the program in typical coding sheet layout, including OP codes and comments. It is recommended that you run the program on a 6502 microcomputer to check that the program performs properly.

15. Write a program that adds together 5 double-precision numbers from memory locations $200 and up (whatever has been placed in these locations). Assume the least significant byte is first for each pair of locations. Use a program loop to accomplish this program. Have the program start in MA $10 and store the result in $240 (least significant byte) and $241. Present the program in typical coding sheet layout, including OP codes and comments.

16. One BCD digit exists in the right half—or least significant "nibble"—of a memory location named ONES, and another digit is similarly placed in a location named TENS. The left half or most significant nibble of each of these locations is zero. Write a program in assembler language that brings the digits together as a two-BCD-digit number and sends this number to an output port named SHOW. Thus, if the port is connected through BCD decoders to a decimal display, a two-digit number is displayed.

17. Write a machine language program to implement the temperature regulation algorithm of Figure D8–7. Note from Figure D8–8a that the temperature sensor input is on bit 7, while the heater control output is on bit 4 of I/O port A. Write the program in typical coding sheet layout, including OP codes. Assume DDRA and port A are at the same addresses as on the PET; however, note that the PEEK and POKE instructions use the *decimal* values for these addresses.

18. Write an instruction sequence starting at address $0220 that loads data into the accumulator from an input port at $A200 and then tests bit 3 of the data. If bit 3 = 0, the program must branch to $0240; otherwise it must branch to $0600.

19. The program in Figure D9-10 has a flaw that could be serious in other applications. For a few microseconds after the output port is first established, the fill valve is open and the agitator running (at least in principle). Further, the timer could actually be started.
    (a) Explain why this occurs for the program as it is written.
    (b) What small change could be made in the program to eliminate this behavior?

20. Write the assembler language program segment for the three steps of the algorithm mentioned in Figure D9-10; that is, write programming for: "Close water fill valve," "start agitation," and "start timer and wait for zero."

21. Assume that SW0 is input to bit 0 (LSB) and SW1 is input to bit 1 of port A on a KIM. Assume that LED0 is connected to bit 0 of port B, while LED1 is connected to bit 1 of port B. Write a program that begins with LED1 and LED2 off; the switches are initially off as well. When SW0 is turned on, both LED0 and LED1 are to turn on. The computer then waits for SW1 to be turned on (SW0 may or may not be on), at which time the LED0 should be turned off, but LED1 remains on. The program then exists to monitor.

22. Show that 1 loop of the main program in Figure D9-18 requires 32 cycles.

23. Write a software delay routine that employs a "loop within a loop" in order to achieve a longer delay than that obtained by the delay routine in Figure D9-18. Assume the delay routine uses two *delay integers* that it receives in the X and Y index registers, respectively; that is, the index registers have been loaded with these numbers prior to calling the routine. Write a formula for the total software delay of the subroutine in terms of the given initial values of X and Y.

24. From time to time a program requires 2 digits to be printed on a serial printer that receives characters in ASCII code from PORTA. It is convenient to use a "print-2-digits subroutine." Let the subroutine be entered with the 2 BCD digits present in the accumulator. Besides the 7 parallel lines for ASCII codes, the printer has 2 control lines: a READY line from the printer that is high when the printer is ready for another character; and a STROBE line to the printer that causes the printer to read an ASCII code and print it. The READY line is input on bit 7 (MSB) of PORTB, while the STROBE line is output on bit 0 (LSB) of PORTB.

    Assume the port lines have been properly initialized by the main program. Write the assembler language subroutine for this task. Do not assume the printer is necessarily ready when the subroutine is entered. Note that if the accumulator contains the number 49, the 4 should be sent to the printer first, followed by the 9. Assume the codes should be right justified in PORTA. Use the stack for any temporary storage required.

CHAPTER
D10

Characteristics and Application of 6502 Support Devices

One of the remarkable features of microcomputer usage is the family of versatile supporting integrated circuits that may be connected to the microprocessor. Each LSI device typically accomplishes one or more functions that would each require an entire board of SSI to MSI chips in the minicomputer of 1970. At that time, the science of laboratory minicomputing generally involved the design and operation of those function boards. On the other hand, applying the microcomputer involves study and use of the rules for choosing the particular desired functions on the support devices. They are generally *programmable* and can be adapted to a great variety of situations.

In this chapter we study the functions available on the 6530 and 6520/6820/6821 devices. The capabilities of the 6522 and 6850 devices are also introduced. These devices are indeed very versatile; however, this versatility implies a rather elaborate set of rules for the operation of each device, especially for the 6522 and 6850. Typically they must be read through several times before the various possibilities and usages become moderately clear. As always, experimenting with them results in the best understanding. In order to promote the understanding of the rules, they are presented in each case in quasi-pictorial form. These rule sheets, along with a copy of the programmer's reference card (instruction set), can be at hand in the laboratory and also during tests. It is hardly worthwhile for the user to memorize all the details.

We studied the essentially simple but important device flag concept in the last chapter. All of the support devices discussed in this chapter incorporate one or more flags. Furthermore, at the programmer's discretion they may actuate the interrupt system of the microcomputer. *Interrupt system hardware* in various forms has long been available on computers and can be particularly useful in real-time applications. In essence it is simply the computer's doorbell or telephone bell. When an external device wishes to communicate with the microprocessor in some way—for example, to exchange data or cause the microprocessor to do something other than its normal processing—it rings the interrupt doorbell to get the computer's immediate attention. The computer interrupts what it is doing to attend to the device.

The only other way external devices can get the microcomputer's attention is through their device flags and the polling-flags routine discussed in the last chapter. The computer must periodically check the flags in the normal course of executing the particular program. However, this can be rather time-consuming and inefficient, particularly if the computer has other useful things to accomplish and the external requests are infrequent. Further, the response to a device request may be too late. Thus, this chapter begins with a discussion of the interrupt system on the 6502. Although the essential idea is really quite simple, the actual system is somewhat involved; therefore, the interrupt section might be skipped in a short course. There are certainly many microcomputer applications that do not need to invoke it.

Interrupt-Driven I/O with the 6502 Microprocessor

The interrupt system of the 6502 (or any computer) is a particularly useful hardware facility for two situations:

1. The computer needs to carry out a particular task (for example, a lengthy calculation) and simultaneously attend to events in the outside world that occur infrequently;
2. The computer needs to manage several tasks in parallel (or simultaneously) that occur essentially asynchronously relative to each other.

The various actions of the 6502 interrupt system are quite reasonable when the practical matter of what must be done is considered. It might be helpful to continue the parable of the mail carrier and the farmer that was begun in the last chapter in order to illustrate the device flag concept.

Interrupt System Analogy

Consider the case of the mail carrier serving a number of RFD mailboxes. Working the route is only part of the job; the carrier has other important tasks to do most of the time back at the post office and would like to travel the route every two days to check mailbox flags. However, this does not satisfy the farmers. Some get angry if they have to wait more than one hour for letter pickup, even though they may mail a letter only once every few weeks! One solution to the problem is to wire each flag to a buzzer that is placed in the post office. When a flag is set up it rings the buzzer, and the mail carrier then interrupts his or her work. The carrier disconnects the buzzer and goes out on the route, checking flags and picking up mail from whichever farmer has the raised flag.

As soon as the flag is found, the carrier picks up the mail, lowers the flag (so the buzzer should not sound again immediately when reconnected later), and returns to the post office. However, if another farmer's mailbox flag was set almost simultaneously with the first (or perhaps while the mail carrier was out on the route), the buzzer sounds again as soon as it is reconnected upon the carrier's return to the post office.

Then the carrier immediately goes out on the route once more. In fact, it might be desirable to install a two-way radio in the car that would permit the carrier to reconnect the buzzer while out on the route and also to hear and respond to another buzz before returning to the post office.

Just driving around polling the flags takes up to two hours, and some of the farmers are particularly impatient. The mail carrier cleverly gives them higher *priority* by placing the impatient farmers first along the route (that is, in the polling-flags routine).

Now it is true that if the mail carrier is in the midst of a task when the interruption occurs, the task should be set aside in an orderly way so that it may be picked up again at the proper point and completed when the carrier returns. Furthermore, there may be times when the task is so important that the carrier does not wish to be interrupted. The carrier then merely opens the switch in series with the line to the buzzer in order to *disable interrupts*, or *mask out interrupts*. However, there are several very important people who can interrupt at any time (the governor and the president). They have *non-maskable interrupt* lines that lead to a second buzzer with a different tone. This buzzer cannot be disconnected; also, the carrier knows immediately that the interrupt is not one of the standard RFD farmers and that these VIPs should be called upon.

6502 Interrupt Protocols

All of these notions are implemented on the 6502 microprocessor. The reader should recognize them in the discussion of the 6502 interrupt system that now follows. The "standard buzzer" wire into the 6502 is the IRQ pin (pin number 4). It should normally stand high. When the *IRQ or interrupt-request* pin of the 6502 is brought low, the CPU finishes its current instruction and goes into an interrupt sequence *provided* interrupts are *enabled.* The *I bit in the processor status register* must be cleared to enable interrupts; if it is set, interrupts are disabled. The CLI instruction *CLears the Interrupt bit,* while the SEI instruction *SEts the Interrupt bit.* During a reset, the I bit is automatically set to disable interrupts at system start-up.

All devices that are to actuate the IRQ line are wire-ORed to this line (with open-collector outputs) so that any device can pull it low. The device should *keep it low* until the CPU has ascertained who is making the request. The usual technique is an arrangement whereby the device flag brings the IRQ line low when set; this may be done by connecting the Q of each flag flip-flop to an open-collector inverter and the inverter output to the IRQ line. Thus, only when the CPU clears the device flag will the interrupt request cease (see Figure D10–1).

There exists also a *nonmaskable-interrupt or NMI* line (pin number 6). A negative-going pulse on this line causes an interrupt, no matter what the state of the I bit. However, the response is somewhat different as we see shortly.

The NMI system responds only to a negative-going edge at the NMI input, and therefore it must return high before it will respond to a second interrupt.

When a normal interrupt occurs, the 6502 performs the next 5 steps *automatically:*

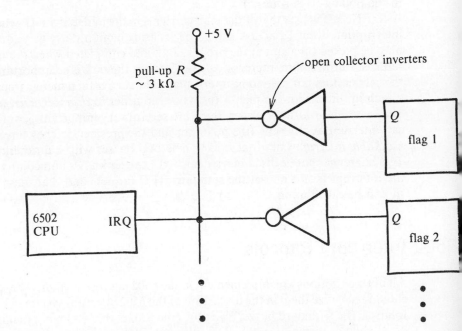

FIGURE D10–1. *Device Flag Connection to the IRQ Line*

1. The CPU finishes the current instruction so that the PC contains the address of the next instruction that must be performed.
2. The CPU sets the I flag to 1 to disable being interrupted again while attending to the cause.
3. The CPU pushes the program counter high byte and then low byte onto the stack and decrements the stack pointer by 2. This permits the 6502 to return later to the point where it was in the program when interrupted.
4. The CPU pushes the processor status register onto the stack and decrements the stack pointer. In this way, the state of the carry bit, N bit, and so forth, are automatically preserved for possible use when returning to the main program later. In general, we would expect them to be changed while servicing the interrupt.
5. The CPU goes to the top 2 locations of memory and finds the absolute address of where it should go in memory to obtain its next instruction (low byte is in FFFE and high byte is in FFFF). That is, the byte Y in FFFE and the byte X in FFFF are loaded into the program counter as the 16-bit address XY, and the 6502 therefore executes a jump to this destination address at which the interrupt-service program must begin. The interrupt-service routine's starting address (XY) must have been placed in FFFE and FFFF previously, of course. The 16-bit address in FFFE and FFFF is often called the *IRQ vector*.

At the address to which the CPU goes as a result of step 5, it is up to the programmer to have the first instruction of an *interrupt-service routine*. This routine should do the following:

1. Save the accumulator and index registers in some memory locations. This is done only if they are likely to contain information of importance to the main program, and if they will be modified by the interrupt service routine. Typically they are saved by pushing them on the stack.
2. Do a polling-the-flags routine to see who made the interrupt request. Clear the flag of the device that did it. This routine will be much like that in Figure D9–13.
3. Perform the I/O required by the device.
4. Restore the accumulator and index registers if saved; for example, pull them from the stack if they were saved there.
5. Do an RTI instruction (*ReTurn from Interrupt:* OP Code = 40). This instruction is rather like the RTS instruction placed at the end of a subroutine.

Next the CPU does the following *automatically* in response to the RTI:

1. Restores the processor status register from the stack.
2. Restores the program counter from the stack. The stack pointer is re-adjusted after these steps.

3. Goes to the address contained by the program counter and performs its instruction. Interrupts are also enabled.

If another device made an interrupt request after the CPU went into an interrupt-service routine, its flag will still be "ringing the buzzer" and the CPU will be interrupted immediately and go attend to it. In fact, the programmer could choose to enable interrupts again near the beginning of the interrupt-service routine if important and impatient devices are anticipated. Saving registers on the stack is a good way to retrace steps if interrupts pile up on interrupts. This is very much like the "subroutine-calling-subroutines" story presented in Chapter D9.

When a nonmaskable interrupt occurs, the action of the CPU is the same as that above, except that the CPU obtains the address of its first NMI service routine instruction from FFFA (low byte) and FFFB (high byte); this is the NMI *vector*. Therefore the CPU is sent directly to a different routine, which might be unique for one special device. In this way time is saved from polling the flags. However, since the NMI line cannot be disabled (at least by means internal to the 6502), in some cases care must be taken that the 6502 is not interrupted by an NMI too soon after system start-up. Typically there are initial "housekeeping" tasks that the microprocessor should do, such as establishing proper I/O lines.

The KIM and the SYM microcomputer boards use the NMI line to achieve the single-step behavior. When the board is placed in single-step mode, the *SYNC* pin signal from the 6502 is enabled back into the NMI input. Since the SYNC signal is a pulse that goes high for one cycle only during an OP code fetch, its falling edge can be used to interrupt the 6502 (when it finally completes the instruction). The 6502 must then jump to a single-step routine that saves registers, and so forth. This routine begins at $1C00 on the KIM. Therefore, on the KIM it is important that the NMI vector be the number $1C00, and in fact this is established when $00 is loaded into MA $17FA and $1C into MA $17FB on the KIM. It is explained shortly why memory addresses 17FA and 17FB are used rather than FFFA and FFFB; it is a practical RAM/ROM matter. The SYM automatically sets up the NMI vector at reset.

When a computer manages input and output through the use of the interrupt system it is said to be *interrupt driven*. There are certainly circumstances when this approach is the most natural and efficient. Manufacturers often place considerable emphasis on the speed with which a computer responds to an interrupt request. In fact, for devices that must be processed very quickly (very impatient farmers), it can be important to compute the estimated interrupt response time or *latency*. The automatic interrupt response consumes 8 cycles, while saving registers may require another 8 to 13 cycles; then, polling flags requires on the order of 5 cycles per flag, and finally the device service can begin. To this computation must also be added the fact that the interrupt may have occurred near the beginning of a many-cycle instruction; for example, 4 cycles for absolute addressing. Consequently, some 25 to 40 cycles may elapse before the interrupting device is serviced. Furthermore, restoring registers and returning from interrupt at the end of the interrupt routine requires time (6 cycles for the RTI and up to 5 cycles for restoring stacked registers). If the 6502 uses a 1-megahertz clock, the above numbers may be translated directly to microseconds, of course. The moral of this computation is that the interrupt system should not be used for devices that request repetitive service at a rate above 10 kilohertz.

For sustained transfer rates between 10 kilohertz and about 100 kilohertz, the microprocessor should not use the interrupt system, but should simply watch the ready flag for the particular device and then transfer the data. At data rates above about 100 kilohertz, programmed I/O is simply too slow. The instructions required to pass the data through the accumulator and out to memory require too much time. Transfer rates up to memory speed may be accomplished using *direct memory access (DMA)*. In this technique, the 6502 is "put to sleep" while the device transfers data directly to memory by use of the memory address bus, the data bus, and the memory read/write line. This rather sophisticated technique is discussed in Chapter 2 (section 2.3.4.2) of the *6500 Microcomputer Family Hardware Manual*. Clearly, the device must possess significant logic and counter circuitry to use the DMA approach.

If a number of devices are using the interrupt system so that the polling-flags routine becomes very lengthy, a shorter latency can be achieved through a *vectored interrupt system*. In the mail carrier/farmer analogy, a buzzer could be installed with a different signal for each farmer. Then the mail carrier would know which mailbox to go to directly, for the buzzer might buzz once per second for farmer number one, twice per second for farmer number two, and so on. Thus the interrupt system "points" (or *vectors*) the mail carrier directly to the interrupting farmer. In the microprocessor case, the device must input its code number to the microprocessor at the same time as it requests an interrupt. Also, some *priority hardware* must arrange for just one code to be input in the event that two devices interrupt simultaneously. Thus, more elaborate I/O hardware is required to implement the vectored interrupt approach. The *6502 Microcomputer Family Hardware Manual* discusses some possible vectored interrupt methods in section 2.3.3.2 of Chapter 2. Some microprocessors (for example, the Z–80) and minicomputers (for example, the PDP–11) customarily use the vectored interrupt approach.

Software Interrupts or Traps

If an interrupt sequence is initiated by an instruction, or by a condition that occurs because of instructions executed, it is frequently called a *trap*. Larger computers can have a number of trap types. The 6502 microprocessor possesses a *break instruction* (BRK) that causes an interrupt sequence just like a normal IRQ; its OP code is $00. Again, memory locations FFFE and FFFF vector the 6502 to the service routine.

The principal use of the break instruction is for program debugging. The break OP code can be inserted in place of an instruction at some point in a program to determine if the CPU reaches the place of insertion. This feature is particularly desirable in programs that are long or must be run at full speed for proper operation so that single-stepping is not possible. It is possible to program the interrupt-service routine so that it distinguishes between an actual IRQ interrupt and a break instruction interrupt. Then both types can occur without difficulty. The B bit in the processor status register (P) is set to 1 by the 6502 in response to a BRK. Recall that the P register is on top of the stack immediately after an interrupt. The B bit may be tested by an appropriate mask and branch placed at the beginning of the IRQ service routine.

6502 Reset

Because of the manner in which the reset operates on the 6502, it is reasonable to discuss it briefly at this point. It is necessary for any computer to begin executing instructions in an orderly manner. For the classical minicomputer the binary starting address of the program was set into a line of switches, and pressing the load switch caused this number to be loaded directly into the program counter. Then flipping the RUN switch to true caused the CPU to begin executing the program at the proper place. However, for a very low cost microprocessor application, there may well be *only* a single on/off switch. Some other approach must be used. Most microprocessors have a reset pin similar to that on the 6502.

The reset (RES) line, pin 40, should be held low until the +5-V power to the chip has stabilized. When this line is low, the microprocessor bus lines are inactive. On a positive-going edge, the CPU sets the I flag, runs 6 cycles and then loads the program counter from FFFC and FFFD. Consequently the CPU goes to this first memory address for program control. This program will typically be in ROM so that it is not lost on power-down. In the case of evaluation systems, the CPU goes to the *entry point* to a monitor that permits us to (at least) examine and change memory locations, as well as send the CPU to some address of our choosing and run a program.

After reset, only the I bit in the processor status register is defined. It is set automatically to 1 so that IRQ interrupts are disabled and the microprocessor has an opportunity to do some initial "housekeeping." This should include initializing the stack pointer to FF.

The manner in which RST, IRQ, and NMI use the top locations in memory has now been presented. These locations will be in ROM memory in most microprocessor applications so that they are not lost during power down. Certainly the RST vector must be in ROM or be arranged to be input from switches. Figure D10–2 diagrams the RST, IRQ, and NMI vector locations assumed by the 6502.

Memory
Address

Address		
FFFF	high-order byte	address of IRQ
FFFE	low-order byte	entry
FFFD	high-order byte	address of RST
FFFC	low-order byte	entry
FFFB	high-order byte	address of NMI
FFFA	low-order byte	entry
FFF9		
FFF8		

FIGURE D10–2.   *Diagram of Memory Locations Assumed by the 6502 for Interrupt Vectors*

Using the Interrupt System on the KIM and SYM

The KIM microcomputer board does not decode memory address lines 15, 16, and 17. Therefore, for any individual binary values of *X* and *Y,* the lower memory locations %000Y YYYY YYYY YYYY will respond to memory references to %XXXY YYYY YYYY YYYY. For example, if we use the KIM monitor to examine the memory locations FFFF and 1FFF, we find both contain 1C. Further FFFE and 1FFE both contain 1F, and when we try to change these values we find that we *cannot;* that is because the KIM monitor ROM exists up to 1FFF and "responds to the call" to the FFFF as well as to 1FFF.

Therefore, when an IRQ interrupt occurs (and the interrupt system is enabled), the 6502 on the KIM always receives the IRQ interrupt routine entry-point address from ROM as $1C1F. But if we are to be able to experiment with the IRQ system on the KIM, how can we have the 6502 go to an arbitrary IRQ entry point of our *own* choosing? In fact, the address 1C1F is again within KIM ROM. Let us examine the OP code that the 6502 receives when jumping to 1C1F; we may either use the KIM monitor to examine 1C1F, or we may refer to the KIM monitor listing found at the back of the *KIM-1 User Manual.* There we find the code 6C, followed by FE and 17. The OP code 6C is for a jump-*indirect* instruction.

This instruction uses *indirect addressing* and, in fact, is the only one possessing this addressing mode (somewhat unfortunate). It is called indirect because the jump destination is obtained by the CPU quite indirectly. The CPU takes the absolute address following the 6C OP code—which is 17FE in this case—and goes to this address to find the *final* destination address. Therefore, the two bytes at 17FE and 17FF are loaded into the program counter, with the low-order byte coming from the lower address 17FE (as usual). But

17FE and 17FF are located in a small amount of RAM that exists in the 6530 multipurpose chip. This permits the KIM user to load an IRQ entry-point address of his or her own choosing into 17FE and 17FF. Indeed, examination of the "special memory addresses" Figure 3.13 of the *KIM-1 User Manual* (next to the "memory map" figure) shows 17FE and 17FF designated as the IRQ vector.

Similarly, 17FA and 17FB are designated as the NMI vector. The actual NMI vector in FFFA and FFFB sends the KIM 6502 to address 1C1C, where the CPU finds a *jump indirect off 17FA*. Indeed, this is the reason we must load 17FA and 17FB, with the pointer $1C00 to the single-step handling routine, if we wish to use either the single-step mode or the *stop key* (ST). Both of these functions work the NMI line. The KIM stops with the registers saved in locations 00EF through 00F5 (also shown in the above-mentioned Figure 3.13), and the value of the program counter showing in the KIM display.

Suppose we wish to use the break command at some point in a program and have the registers saved as in single-step mode. Assume first that external interrupts are not used. Since break is a software IRQ, we see that we may simply load the IRQ vector at 17FE/F with the same pointer used for single-stepping, namely 1C00. However, if the IRQ pointer is being used for regular interrupts as well, we must test for break within our IRQ service routine and jump to 1C00 only if a break occurs.

Next we examine the SYM interrupt implementation. The SYM board does decode all of the memory lines. However, System RAM existing in memory addresses A600 through A67F (in a 6532 chip) is arranged to answer to addresses FF80 through FFFF.

NOTE: *System RAM* is RAM intended primarily for use by the SYM monitor program or system.

At a power turn-on or a reset, the 6502 is forced to retrieve the reset vector from 8FFC rather than FFFC. The reset monitor routine copies *default values* into the RAM addresses A620 through A67F from ROM locations 8FA0 through 8FFF. These values are listed in Figure 4-10 of the *SYM-1 Reference Manual* (on pages labeled "System RAM Memory Map, SY6532"), as well as on the SYM Reference Card.

To use the interrupt system on the SYM, we can do one of several alternatives. The direct approach is to load the IRQ routine entry address directly into FFFE and FFFF, either using the monitor or from within a program. This is possible because RAM at A67E and A67F answers to these addresses. (Or we can load A67E and A67F with the IRQ vector.) The default value of $800F placed by the monitor in these locations is then replaced, and the interrupt system in the SYM will operate as we have already described for the 6502.

However, a second approach permits convenient use of the BRK instruction while debugging. The default IRQ vector is left in location A67E/F or FFFE/F (called IRQVEC); it sends the 6502 CPU into the monitor IRQ interrupt handling routine. This routine traps out the fact that a BRK occurred and stops in a mode similar to the single-step mode if it was a software interrupt. The SYM display shows the PC in the left 4 digits and to the right the code of 0 for BRK. The registers, and so forth, may then be examined just as in debug mode. (GO), (CR) continues the program. However, if a BRK did not occur, the program executes a jump-indirect off the *User* IRQ vector (called UIRQ) in memory A678/9. Therefore, the *"normal"* interrupt vector should be placed in A678 and A679 rather than FFFE/F on the SYM.

Programmable Real-Time Clock and 6530 Timer

It often happens, particularly in laboratory applications, that computers must keep track of the actual time when various events occur, measure time intervals between events, cause events to occur at certain times, or produce delays between certain successive events. All of these involve time as it is actually passing in the real world, and a *real-time clock* has long been a computer accessory.

A commonly available real-time clock in the past operated from the line frequency to generate an interrupt every 1/60 second, and computer software (program) could then calculate the time of day and maintain this in appropriate memory locations. A significantly more versatile clock was made available about 1971 by DEC for the LAB−8/E system in the form of a *programmable real-time clock*. The timer on the 6530 and 6532 chips and two timers on the VIA 6522 provide some of this versatility at remarkably low cost. The 6530 (and 6532) timer is discussed here and the 6522 device functions are summarized later.

6530 Timer Rules

The operation of the 6530 programmable timer is much like the familiar "egg timer" that can be set to some initial reading—for example, 3 minutes—and the dial subsequently "ticks" toward zero; when it reaches zero the buzzer goes off. In this way we know the desired time interval has elapsed. Similarly, a down counter on the 6530 chip may be loaded with an initial count by storing an 8-bit number to one of several memory locations decoded by the 6530. The counter then counts down toward zero and, on reaching zero, sets its flag. This flag may or may not be enabled to the 6502's interrupt system (under program control) and may also be examined by reading a certain memory location. That is, even though the interrupt system of the 6502 is enabled, we may choose whether or not the flag from the 6530 timer works the IRQ line to the 6502. We might choose instead to merely check the 6530 timer flag periodically in order to learn if it has *timed out*. The period of the clock into the actual down counter may be chosen to be some multiple ($\times$ 1, $\times$ 8, $\times$ 64, $\times$ 1024) of the CPU clock, $\phi2$, which goes to the chip. Thus a *two-dimensional* adjustability of the *time-out interval* may be obtained. If the CPU clock is 1 megahertz, the time-out interval is conveniently some integer number of microseconds.

Figure D10-3 diagrams the parts of the 6530 programmable timer and illustrates the relative addresses involved in programming and using the timer. Notice that the "tick rate" of the clock into the down counter is determined by whichever address is used in writing the initial setting to the down counter. The drawing indicates that writing the number to an address between XXX4 and XXX7 will choose a period between 1 T and 1024 T, where T is the period of the 6502 clock, but the flag *will not* be enabled to the IRQ line. However, writing the initial counter setting to XXXC through XXXF will choose a corresponding clock period and *will* enable the flag to the interrupt line.

In the addresses given, XXX depends on the base memory address assigned to the particular 6530 chip. For the timer on the 6530 (chip number 002) available for experimentation on the KIM, XXX = $170. Thus writing $20 to address $1705 (for example, with a STA $1705 instruction) sets the initial number in the down counter to $20 = 32_{10} and sets the down-counter period to 8 microseconds. It also clears the timer flag. Then $32 \times 8 = 256$ μsec later, the timer flag will get set.

The flag can be examined by reading memory location XXX7. The state of the flag is returned in bit 7 and therefore can be conveniently examined by a branch off the N flag. In fact, the BIT instruction can be used to copy the timer flag into N without any register actually being loaded. If the flag is set, it automatically is cleared by reading this location.

The count state of the down counter can be examined at any time by reading XXX6 (which also disables interrupts), or by reading XXXE (which also enables interrupts). This read of the counter register also clears the timer flag. After the counter reaches zero, it continues counting past zero (FF, FE, ...) at the fastest rate ($\phi2$) and must be reloaded again to count from a particular initial value at some other clock rate. The fact that it continues counting past zero at the fast rate can be used to learn how many CPU clock cycles have elapsed since the counter flag was set (assuming it is less than 255), for then the register simply contains the two's complement or negative of the number of cycles since time out.

If the 6530 timer is to work the 6502 interrupt system, a somewhat curious connection must be made. The interrupt line from the flag is available from the bit-7 pin of port B (PB7) and goes low when the flag is set, as required by 6502 IRQ protocol. Therefore, the most significant bit wire from

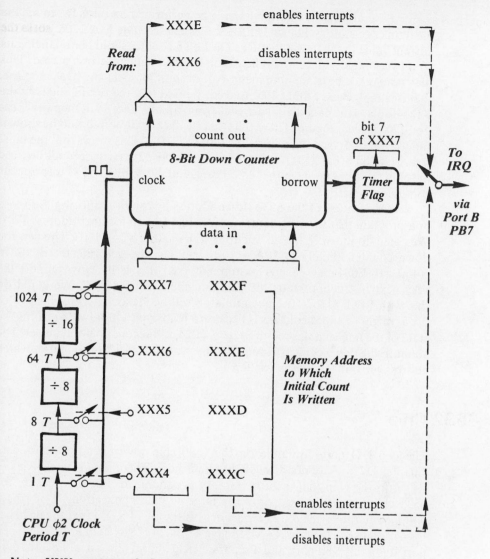

Note: *XXX represents the base address for the particular 6530,*
e.g., on KIM, XXX4 = 1704.

FIGURE D10–3. *Diagram with Relative Addresses of the Programmable Timer in the 6530 Chip*

port B for the particular 6530 chip must be connected to the IRQ line of the 6502 microprocessor system if the interrupt capability is to be used. Also, that particular bit must be programmed as *input* to permit the flag to work this I/O line.

Several simple experiments may be performed on the KIM to see the 6530 timer operating. Figure D10-3 shows that *reading* MA 1706 yields the current value in the down counter. The down counter should be changing its count very rapidly since it will be running with a 1-microsecond period. This may be checked by examining memory location 1706 using the KIM monitor; that is, simply press (AD) 1706. Indeed, we find that the right 2 digits in the KIM display (the data digits) are flickering rapidly. Second, if memory location 1707 is *read,* Figure D10-3 tells that the flag condition should be shown. Indeed, we find the data in location 1707 to be $80. This shows that the most significant bit is 1 and the flag is set. It gets set every 256 microseconds because the counter is operating at the fastest rate, and the display shows it to appear continuously set.

One feature of the 6530 timer addressing can be surprising. Suppose in a program that we write some number like $0A to memory address 1707. We could do this with the instructions LDA #$0A, STA $1707. This sets the down counter initially to $0A = 10_{10}, and sets the tick rate to the down counter to 1.024 milliseconds (assuming the KIM is used). Now suppose the very next instruction reads the same memory address 1707. We could do this with LDA $1707. The accumulator will be identically zero, instead of 0A as might be expected! This is because a read from 1707 always returns the state of the *flag,* and this requires 10×1.024 milliseconds before it is set. The count in the down counter is returned by a *read* from 1706, no matter which address the initial count is written to.

6532 Chip

The two I/O ports available on the 6530 chip were already discussed in Chapter D7 and are not discussed further here. There are also 1K bytes of ROM in the chip that must be factory programmed. For this reason, the 6530 chip is usually used only for large-volume applications. For small-volume situations, the *6532 chip* trades off the 1K of ROM that the 6530 has for 64 additional bytes of RAM, to give a total of 128 bytes of RAM. Further, port B is a full 8-bit port, and a separate IRQ output line is available for connecting the flags to the interrupt system. Also, an edge-sensitive flag (that uses PB7 as the flag-trigger input) is available besides the timer flag. Finally, a timer is available with rules of operation that are very similar to those for the 6530. Specification sheets for the 6532 chip are available in the *SYM-1 Reference Manual* since the 6532 ports are used by the SYM to operate its keyboard and display, and the 6532 RAM is used to provide System RAM for the SYM monitor.

The SYM 6532 addresses that are used to load the timer initial-count and disable timer interrupts are as follows: $A414 for 1 *T,* $A415 for 8 *T,* $A416 for 64 *T,* and $A417 for 1024 *T.* These addresses function like XXX4 through XXX7 in Figure D10-3. The SYM addresses that function like

XXXC through XXXF in Figure D10–3 and enable timer interrupts are SYM addresses $A41C through $A41F; however, the IRQ pin for the SYM 6532 is not wired to the interrupt system and consequently an interrupt cannot be generated. The current count in the SYM 6532 timer can be read from $A416, while the 6532 timer flag is present as bit 7 (MSB) in address $A417; these addresses are similar in function to XXX6 and XXX7 in Figure D10–3.

6530 Timer Examples

The following examples illustrate the use of the 6530 timer. The KIM addresses and its 1-megahertz 6502 clock are assumed.

Example 1: The following illustrates how the 6530 timer can be used to obtain a *delay segment* within a program. The tick rate is set to 8 microseconds, and the timer counts down from $20 = 32_{10}$. Then, by counting the number of cycles for each instruction as well as the delay introduced by the timer, the time required between instructions labeled DELAY and NEXT can be computed. This delay is about $(2 + 4 + 32 \times 8 + 4 + 2)$ microseconds.

```
DELAY    LDA #$20          ;(2) SET THE COUNTER TO
         STA $1705         ;(4) $20 = 32₁₀ ,TICK RATE = 8 µSEC

AGAIN  ┌─LDA $1707         ;(4) TEST THE FLAG
       └─BPL AGAIN         ;(2) TEST AGAIN IF NOT SET
NEXT     (NEXT INSTRUCTION)    ↑
                           └─ (microseconds per instruction)
```

The next example uses two subroutines in the KIM monitor that require some explanation. The first is a subroutine to briefly light up the 6-digit KIM display. A subroutine labeled SCANDS (*SCAN the DiSplay*) begins at $1F1F in the KIM monitor. If the instruction JSR $1F1F is executed, the subroutine references the contents of 3 memory locations on page 0 and causes each 8-bit content to be briefly displayed as a pair of hex digits. The memory location assignments are as follows:

MA $00F9: right pair of digits,
MA $00FA: middle pair of digits,
MA $00FB: left pair of digits.

NOTE: The *A, X,* and *Y* registers are modified when the SCANDS subroutine is executed.

The second KIM subroutine is used to read the calculator-like keyboard on the KIM. This subroutine is labeled *GETKY* in the monitor listing and begins at $1F6A; when executed, it returns to the calling program with the value in the accumulator of the key that is pressed. If no key is pressed at the time of JSR $1F6A, the value $15 is returned.

NOTE: The 6502 must be in binary mode for the keys above 9 to be returned with their proper value.

Example 2: In this example the programming of two *simultaneous activities* is illustrated. The left 2 digits of the KIM display are to continuously show the value of the current key being depressed, while the right 2 digits are to be counting up (in hexadecimal), with a time interval of 0.25 seconds between increments. We use the fact that $244_{10} \times 1.024$ msec = 0.2499 sec. Notice that reading the keyboard and lighting the display are done continuously within a loop that is waiting for the timer to "buzz." Also, the BIT test instruction is used to check the timer flag.

```
            CLD                 ;PUT IN BINARY MODE FOR GETKY
            LDA    #$00         ;ZERO OUT
            STAz   $F9          ;  RIGHT FOUR DIGITS
            STAz   $FA          ;  IN THE KIM DISPLAY
  RELOAD ┌─LDA    #$F4         ;LOAD TIMER WITH $F4=244
         │  STA    $1707        ;  AT TICK T = 1.024 MSEC
  GETKY  │┌─JSR    $1F6A        ;GET DEPRESSED KEY INTO ACCUM
         ││ STAz   $FB          ;PUT IN LEFT DIGIT PAIR
         ││ JSR    $1F1F        ;LIGHT UP THE DISPLAY BRIEFLY
         ││ BIT    $1707        ;SET N BIT IF TIMED OUT
         │└─BPL    GETKY        ;GET ANOTHER KEY IF NOT TIMED OUT
         │  INCz   $F9          ;TIME'S UP, BUMP UP RIGHT PAIR
         └──JMP    RELOAD       ;AND GO BACK TO RESTART TIMER
```

Example 3: This example illustrates the use of the *interrupt system*. The activity in the display should appear essentially identical to that in Example 2 just discussed. However, in this case the interrupt system is used to signal that 0.25 seconds has elapsed. The main program simply continuously reads the KIM keyboard and flashes the number in the display. When an interrupt occurs, the interrupt-service routine increments the digit pair in the right of the display and restarts the timer.

```
  * = $10            ;MAIN ROUTINE STARTS IN MA $0010
  CLD                ;PUT IN BINARY MODE FOR GETKY SUBROUTINE
  LDA    #$00        ;ZERO OUT
  STAz   $F9         ;RIGHT FOUR
  STAz   $FA         ;KIM DISPLAY DIGITS
  LDA    #$F4        ;LOAD TIMER WITH 244,
  STA    $170F       ;TICKS=1 MSEC, ENABLE TIMER INTERRUPTS
  CLI                ;ENABLE 6502 INTERRUPTS
```

```
GETKY1  ┌─JSR    $1F6A   ;GET KEY VALUE INTO ACCUM
        │ STAz   $FB     ;PUT IN LEFT DISPLAY PAIR
        │ JSR    $1F1F   ;FLASH THE DISPLAY
        └─JMP    GETKY1  ;DO AGAIN
        ;****INTERRUPT SERVICE ROUTINE****
        * = $200         ;BEGINS IN MA $200
        PHA              ;SAVE ACCUM ON STACK
        INCz   $F9       ;TIME'S UP, INCREMENT RIGHT DISPLAY PAIR
        LDA    #$F4      ;RELOAD TIMER, STILL
        STA    $170F     ;KEEPING TIMER FLAG TO IRQ
        PLA              ;RESTORE ACCUM
        RTI              ;RETURN TO MAIN ROUTINE
```

The main routine begins in location $0010, while the interrupt-service routine begins on page 2 in $0200. Notice that in this example the initial timer value is loaded into MA $170F (rather than $1707) so that the timer flag is connected to the IRQ line. Next, interrupts are enabled on the 6502 by the CLI instruction. For this program to operate, we must connect the flag-interrupt output from the 6530 to the IRQ line of the 6502; that is, we must connect a wire from PB7 (pin 15 on the application connector) to the 6502's IRQ input (pin 4 on the expansion connector).

Also, *before* running the program, we must load the interrupt pointer to our interrupt routine—that is, the starting address of the interrupt routine—into the KIM *IRQ-vector* locations. The low-order byte of $0200 must be put into MA $17FE, and the high byte into MA $17FF. Thus $00 goes into location $17FE and $02 goes into location $17FF.

Notice that the interrupt-service routine saves the accumulator on the stack just after entry. This is necessary because the interrupt routine modifies the accumulator, and it is being used in the main program. The accumulator is restored before returning from interrupt.

If this example is loaded into the KIM for experimenting, it is interesting to verify that the interrupt system is indeed a functional part. Simply disconnect the wire from PB7 to IRQ while the program is running. Then we see that the 2 digits in the right of the display "freeze," but the left 2 digits remain responsive to whatever key is pressed. We have indeed removed the timer flag from working the IRQ (the 6502 "doorbell"). Further, if we replace the CLI instruction with a NOP, the interrupt system remains disabled and the right-digit pair remains at 0.

6520/6820/6821 Peripheral Interface Adapter (PIA)

The *6520 peripheral interface adapter* (PIA) is an example of the type of powerful support chips that make input/output application of microprocessors quite easy and inexpensive compared to the minicomputer. These devices can be programmed to accommodate a variety of needs through the use of *control registers*. Furthermore, they are quite simple to connect to the microprocessor buses. Some rather simple memory address decoding may be needed, but the design process to develop an I/O port is much less elaborate than for the PDP-8/E, for example. The programmable versatility of these devices can at first appear confusing, however, and requires some study.

The 6820 was originally introduced along with the 6800 microprocessor by Motorola in the spring of 1974. Mos Technology/Commodore, Synertek, and Rockwell International manufacture the same part, but call it the 6520. Later Motorola introduced the 6821, which has the same pin functions and rules for operation, but has twice the output drive capacity. The 6520 is not available on the KIM or SYM boards for experimentation; however, a 6520 may be readily connected to either board, and this procedure is described later.

6520 PIA Programming Rules

Figure D10-4 diagrams the 6 addressable registers of the 6520 that are of concern to the programmer. It is desirable to examine the general features of the 6520 that are displayed in this diagram. The reader should examine it carefully. First we notice that there are two 8-bit ports, port A and port B, and a data direction register for use with each (DDRA and DDRB). The ports are sometimes called the data registers (DRA and DRB). Individual port lines may be programmed as either input or output, and again as in the 6530, the associated data direction register bit determines the direction. Therefore, this aspect should be quite familiar and is not described further.

An important new feature of the 6520 over the 6530 is the *control register* associated with each port. The control register associated with port A is called *control register A* (CRA) and that with B is called *control register B* (CRB). Of course, since memory-mapped I/O is used, these registers should respond to certain memory addresses. The relative memory addresses for the registers are shown to the left in Figure D10-4. The registers may be addressed at 4 successive locations. Port A is at the lowest address XXX0, while control register B is located at XXX3. The XXX value depends on the base address arranged for the chip, and how this is done is discussed later.

However, we should immediately wonder how six 8-bit registers can be addressed in 4 locations. In fact, Figure D10-4 shows data direction register A and port A are both addressed at MA XXX0. Also, DDRB and DRB are both addressed at MA XXX2. This situation appears to present a conflict; but indeed, only one of the two registers "answers the call" to the given address at one time. The one that responds is determined by the *data direction register access* (DDR-access) bit in the associated control register. Notice that this is bit 2 in each control register in Figure D10-4. If DDR-access = 0, the data direction register is accessed; if DDR-access is 1, the port (or data register) is accessed.

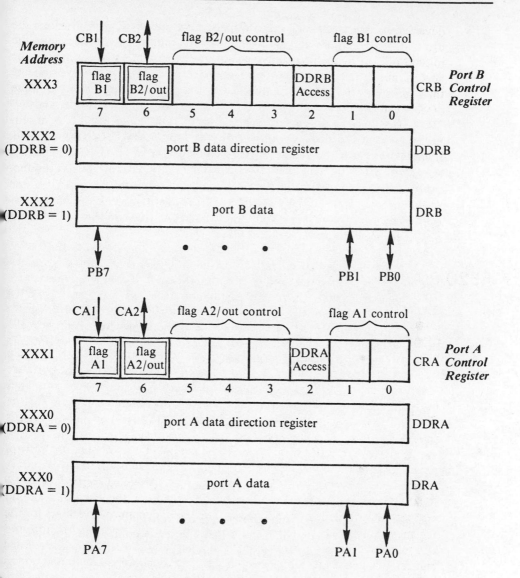

FIGURE D10-4. *Six Addressable Registers of the 6520/6820 Peripheral Interface Adapter (PIA) General-Purpose Interface Chip*

Now, at reset the reset line into the chip clears all 6 registers. This means that after reset the DDR-access bit is 0, and the data direction registers respond, rather than the ports. This is very appropriate, since the housekeeping instructions near the beginning of the program should initially establish port-line in/out directions by writing some bit-pattern to each data direction register (1 for out, 0 for in, of course). Later when housekeeping sets up the desired bit-pattern in each control register, bit number 2 should be set to 1. In fact, if we simply store $04 to each control register, the ports can now be used in the same manner that they are on the 6530.

The next feature to notice in Figure D10-4 is that there are 2 wires connected respectively to the 2 most significant bit positions of *each* control register (CR). These are in addition to the ordinary port I/O wires. The most significant bit position in each CR is a device flag for use with the associated port, and this is called *flag number 1* for each port. Each flag is simply a flip-flop to be used in the manner discussed in Chapter D9. Notice that an input-*only* wire leads to each flag number 1; in fact, this is simply a clock-input wire similar to that shown for the device flag flip-flop in Figure D9-11. One of the nice features of the 6520 is that we can program each flag to be set on either the rising edge or the filling edge of the flag-input signal. This is arranged by first placing the proper bit-pattern into the *control bits* associated with that flag. Thus, notice in Figure D10-4 that the flag-input wire or control wire CB1 passes into flag B1 in control register B (CRB), and that the right 2 bits of control register B are used to program the desired characteristics for this flag. Similarly, there is a control line CA1 that passes into flag A1 in CRA, and 2 control bits for this flag are at the least significant end of CRA.

Figure D10-4 shows that the control line connected to bit 6 in each control register is a *two-way wire*; this is because bit 6 may be used either as another device flag, called flag 2, or as an output line to output pulses from the microcomputer. When used as a flag, this control line 2 is a clock *input* to the flag flip-flop. However, it can be very useful to have another output wire in addition to the 8 port wires. For example, it can be very useful to *output* a pulse or level change to a device to signal that new data is now available on the 8 port wires. This is actually the *handshaking* technique discussed in Chapter D9 in connection with the device flag. The handshaking possibility is conveniently provided on the 6520 chip. The word *possibility* is used because we may choose the actual function desired for control line number 2 by placing the proper bit-pattern into a 3-bit control slot within the associated control register. Notice that the 3 bits for flag B2/control line B2 are near the center of control register B, while the 3 control bits for flag A2/control line A2 are near the center of control register A. The reason 3 control bits are required for the number 2 control line while only 2 are required for control line 1 is that it has more functions (input or output versus just input).

The rules for programming the desired control-line and flag behavior are presented in Figure D10-5. First, each flag is set by a certain level change to its control line. Also we may choose whether or not the flag is enabled to the IRQ line out of the chip. These two features are each controlled by a bit in the 2-bit control for flag A1 and also for flag B1. If bit 6 in either control register is to be used as a flag—that is, we choose to have flag A2 and/or flag B2—we must make bit 5 a *0* in that control register. This is indicated by the 0 in the dashed box at the top left of Figure D10-5. Then the 2 remaining bits in flag A2/B2 control have exactly the same rules as those for flags A1/B1. The

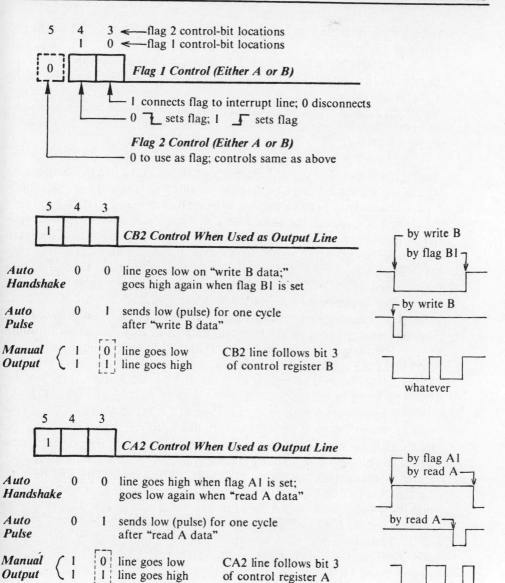

5   4   3 ←—flag 2 control-bit locations
    1   0 ←—flag 1 control-bit locations

| 0 | | | *Flag 1 Control (Either A or B)* |

— 1 connects flag to interrupt line; 0 disconnects

— 0 ⌐ sets flag; 1 ⌐ sets flag

Flag 2 Control (Either A or B)
— 0 to use as flag; controls same as above

5   4   3

| 1 | | | *CB2 Control When Used as Output Line* |

by write B
by flag B1

Auto   0   0   line goes low on "write B data;"
Handshake   goes high again when flag B1 is set

by write B

Auto   0   1   sends low (pulse) for one cycle
Pulse   after "write B data"

Manual ⎧ 1   0 line goes low   CB2 line follows bit 3
Output ⎩ 1   1 line goes high   of control register B

whatever

5   4   3

| 1 | | | *CA2 Control When Used as Output Line* |

by flag A1
by read A

Auto   0   0   line goes high when flag A1 is set;
Handshake   goes low again when "read A data"

by read A

Auto   0   1   sends low (pulse) for one cycle
Pulse   after "read A data"

Manual ⎧ 1   0 line goes low   CA2 line follows bit 3
Output ⎩ 1   1 line goes high   of control register A

whatever

Note 1: *All registers are zeroed by reset. Thus ports act as inputs, interrupts are disconnected, and DDRs are accessible.*

Note 2: *Flags are cleared by READ of corresponding data register only. Can't be set or cleared by writing to control register.*

FIGURE D10–5.   *Control Register Rules for Operation of the 6520/6820 PIA*

rules for manipulating any flag are the same and are presented in the top frame of Figure D10–5.

The right bit in the pair of flag control bits controls connection of the flag to the IRQ line. If this bit is 1, a set flag brings the IRQ line low. If the right bit is 0, the setting of the given flag cannot cause an interrupt. Therefore, the programmer can choose to have a given device flag *not* cause an interrupt, even though interrupts are enabled on the 6502. This feature is diagrammed in Figure D10–6.

The left bit of the pair of flag control bits controls the clocking behavior of the flag. The top of Figure D10–5 shows that a 0 in this bit position causes the associated flag to get set by a falling-edge voltage on its control line. Conversely, a 1 causes the flag to be set by a rising edge. A flag can *only* be cleared by a *read* of the associated port (that is, the associated data register). This read might be an LDA, LDX, BIT, INC, and so forth, of the given port since they each read a number from the memory address for at least part of their activity. Notice that a write to the port will *not* do. Thus, if a given port is used as an output port, the typical STA to the port will not clear its device flag. We must do a *fake read* or *dummy read* of the port. Also, a flag *cannot* be cleared by attempting to write a 0 to its bit position in the control register. Neither can it be set by attempting to write a 1 to its bit position.

The remaining rules in Figure D10–5 pertain to using control lines CA2 and CB2 as output lines. Then we no longer have the flag-2 function. This mode is obtained by placing a 1 in the left bit of the 3 control bits, and this 1 will be noted in the bit-5 boxes in the bottom portion of Figure D10–5.

The *manual-output* mode for CA2 or CB2 is easy to use. We set the middle control bit to 1; then the output line simply follows the state of the least significant bit of the group (CRA3 or CRB3). Should the program cause a 0 in this bit—for example, by storing XX110XXX at the control register address—the control line immediately goes low and stays there. On the other hand, storing a 1 in bit 3 of the control register causes its control-2 line to go high. Any pulse-form output could be generated in this way. This rule is the same for either CA2 or CB2 and therefore appears twice in Figure D10–5.

Just above the manual-output rules in Figure D10–5, we find the *automatic send-a-short-pulse* (auto pulse) mode. If the middle bit (bit 4) of the field is 0 and bit 3 is a 1, a one-cycle negative pulse—for example, 1-microsecond duration pulse if the CPU clock is 1 megahertz—is output on line CA2 *after* a *read*-port-A instruction. A similar pulse is output on line CB2 after a *write*-to-port-B instruction. Notice that they behave differently. This pulse behavior is diagrammed to the right of Figure D10–5. Such an *automatic pulse* on control line CB2 could be used to clock the latches of an output device after the data has been made available to the device on the port B lines. The automatic pulse on control line CA2 could signal an input device that data have been picked up from the device (by a read-port-A instruction).

The remaining rule to discuss is that for the *handshake I/O* mode for the CA2 and CB2 control lines. This behavior is essentially the same as the

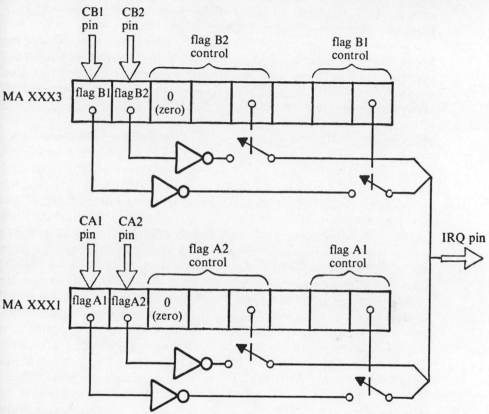

Note: **Open-collector inverters for wired-OR.**

FIGURE D10–6. *6520 Control-Bit Functions that Enable/Disable Any Flag to the Microprocessor IRQ Interrupt Line (The Inverters and Switches Modeled Here Are within the 6520 Chip, and the Broad Arrows Represent Chip Pins.)*

device flag handshake I/O technique illustrated in Figure D9–11. An essential feature there is that both the CPU and the device can monitor the device flag for orderly transfer of data. Remember that the *device always sets* the flag when it is ready, while the flag is always *cleared by the CPU* when it is ready.

Consider first the CA2 control-line handshake usage rule. This line is intended for handshaking with an input device. Indeed, this CA2 control-line mode is sometimes called *automatic handshake on read.* If the CA2 control field in control register A is set to 100, the state of flag A1 is simply connected to control line CA2; thus the peripheral device can monitor the state of its flag. When the device is ready—for example, after putting data on the port A lines—it sets flag A1 by working the CA1 control line, and the CA2 output follows this flag high. The 6502 program can note that the device is ready and read port A. This automatically clears flag A1 (recall that a given flag can always be cleared by *reading* its associated port), and control line CA2 follows the flag low on the next CPU cycle after the read. This is diagrammed on the Figure D10–5 rule sheet. Because the flag is low, the device knows that the computer has picked up the data and may proceed when ready with the input of new data to the port.

Consider next the CB2 control-line handshake usage rule. This line is intended for handshaking with an *output* device, and the mode is sometimes called *automatic handshake on write*. If the CB2 control field in control register B is set to 100, control line CB2 *almost* behaves as though it is simply connected to flag B2. First the computer should detect that the output device has accepted the previous data; this it learns by the fact that flag B2 is high. The CB2 line will similarly be high out to the device. The CPU then must clear the flag with a *dummy read* of port B. Next the CPU writes new data to port B. This automatically connects the flag B2 to control line CB2 on the next CPU cycle after the write, and CB2 consequently goes low. (If the flag B2 is not already low, the CB2 line will *not* go low because a write-port instruction does not clear the flag.) Because the CB2 line is low, the device knows that the flag is low and that new data is ready to be picked up from port B. After picking up the data, the device should work the CB1 line to flag B1. This sets the flag again, and control line CB2 follows flag B1 high. This behavior is diagrammed in Figure D10–5.

Electrical Characteristics of 6520 Ports and Control Lines

The electrical characteristics of the 6520 PIA require some comment. The port A lines and the CA2 in/out control line use pull-up resistors and can drive 1 TTL load. They also present 1 TTL load when programmed as inputs. Their electrical behavior is the same as that modeled in Figure D7–8 for *both* 6530 ports. Note that a port A pin will therefore present 5 V (through about 5 kilohms) to the outside world when programmed as input. Furthermore, a read from the port senses the actual logic-level voltage present on the pin. For example, if a given pin is shorted to ground, the bit value returned is always 0, even if the pin is programmed as output and a 1 has been sent to the port pin (that is, to the data output flip-flop). Similarly, if a given pin is shorted to +5 V, a read of the pin will return a 1, although the output transistor could be damaged if the pin is programmed as output (how?).

The port B lines and CB2 in/out control line are designed differently. They use a 3-state totem pole buffer (active pull-up, pull-down, and off) in the output mode. They can source 1 milliampere at a minimum of +1.5 V when outputting a 1 and therefore can provide modest base drive to a transistor or to a solid-state relay. Furthermore, since this 1 output level is not a "legal"

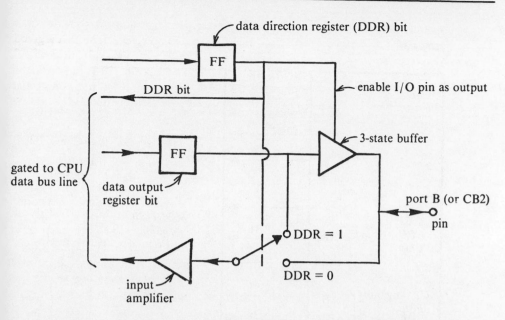

FIGURE D10-7. *Operation of a Port B I/O Pin for the 6520/6820 PIA (The CB2 Control Line Is the Same, except the Control Register Bit 5 (CRB-5) Is Substituted for the DDR Bit.)*

TTL high, a read is *not* done from the actual port pin when programmed as output. Rather, the read is done from the data output register bit or flip-flop. This is diagrammed in Figure D10-7. (Refer to Figure D7-8 for a model of port A behavior.) Thus, if a read is done from a pin that is programmed as output and is also shorted to ground, the bit returned will not necessarily be 0; it will be 1 if data of 1 has been previously stored to this port B data bit.

Finally, when port B pins and the CB2 pin are programmed as input lines, they present a high input impedance (greater than 1 megohm), rather like a good amplifier input. This is because no pull-up resistors are in parallel with the high impedance presented by the FET gate inputs. The model for port B and CB2 pin behavior in Figure D10-7 supports this fact. The same high input impedance characterizes control lines CA1 and CB1, which may only be used as inputs, of course.

Connecting the 6520/6820/6821 to 6502 Microprocessor Systems

The pin connections between the PIA and the microprocessor are typical of any device that is to communicate like memory to the CPU. Figure D10-8 diagrams the necessary connections. The data lines of the chip are connected

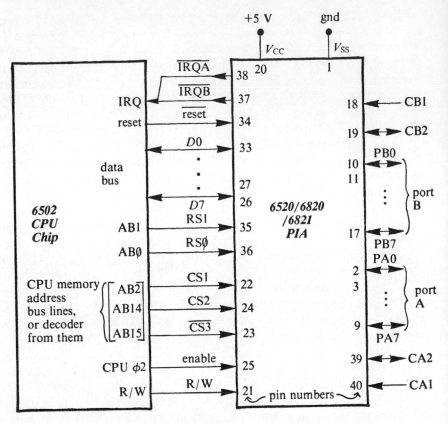

Note: *A simple connection possibility for the chip-select lines (CS1/2/3) to the 6502 is illustrated in brackets.*

FIGURE D10–8. *Pin Connections between CPU and PIA*

to the CPU data bus for two-way data communication. The IRQ line is connected to the corresponding CPU line if the interrupt system is to be used. Further, the reset line is connected to that system line for initialization. The R/W line is connected to the corresponding CPU line to indicate to the 6520 chip what type of operation is taking place; the 6520 must accept data during a write to it (releasing the data lines for CPU control) and assert data to the data lines during a read from it.

The $\phi2$ line from the CPU connects to the enable pin and, as usual with 6502 memory-like devices, the trailing edge of this pulse is used by the 6520 PIA to latch data from the CPU data lines (like an edge-triggered JK flip-flop). It is also used to enable PIA data to the lines during a read from the PIA (the CPU then does a latch of the data lines on the trailing edge of $\phi2$). The data lines from the PIA are always floating during $\phi1$ high and are always floating if the chip is not selected.

The *chip-select* pins (CS1, CS2, and $\overline{CS3}$) of the 6520 are used to "select" the PIA by certain codes on the memory address lines. Let the memory address bus lines be labeled AB15, AB14, ..., AB$\emptyset$. AB15 carries the most significant bit of the memory address number, while AB$\emptyset$ carries the least significant bit. Except for the fact that more chip-select pins may be present on a 6520, the chip-select PIA inputs act quite like those of any semi-conductor memory chip. Only if CS1 and CS2 are high and $\overline{CS1}$ is low will the PIA chip respond to the levels on the data pins, enable pins, and so forth. Thus it is "selected" for communication with the CPU from the many memory chips that might reside in the 6502's memory space. These lines are typically connected to higher-order memory address lines or to memory decoder lines that are derived from them. The *register-select* pins RS$\emptyset$ and RS1 are normally connected to memory address bus lines AB$\emptyset$ and AB1, respectively, as shown in Figure D10–8. These pins then provide the addressing of the 6 registers within the selected PIA, which in fact appear at just 4 memory locations. The reader should recognize that the use of AB$\emptyset$ and AB1 establishes the locations as consecutive.

A simple arrangement for connecting 6520/6820 PIA chip-select pins in a 6502 microcomputer system is illustrated in Figure D10–8. Let $\overline{CS3}$ be connected to AB15, and CS2 be connected to AB14. This can be done identically for a group of PIA chips if we need a number of ports. These PIAs then respond to memory addresses %01XX XXXX XXXX XXXX, which lie within the second 16K block of memory. We assume that RAM is decoded in the lowest 16K block of memory space so that page 0 and the stack on page 1 are operable. Further, ROM may be selected when AB15 is high. Then the reset, IRQ, and NMI vectors may be in this ROM at their normal positions at the top of the memory space. Finally, CS1 of a given PIA can be connected to any one memory address line between AB2 and AB13. This permits up to 12 PIA chips to be readily connected, providing up to *24* 8-bit ports. For example, CS1 of the first PIA could be connected to AB2; then its 4 addresses would be at %0100 0000 0000 0100 = $4004, up to $4007. CS2 of the second PIA could be connected to AB3; then its 4 addresses would be at %0100 0000 0000 1000 = $4008, up to $400B. Similar reasoning identifies the addresses for remaining PIAs that might be connected in this addressing scheme.

To connect PIAs to the KIM, the above decoding scheme cannot be used because the KIM does not decode the most significant 3 address lines AB13, AB14, and AB15. Consequently its on-board memory would incorrectly respond to addresses $4004, and so on. However, an even simpler scheme uses the 8 lines that come from the 74LS145 decoder on board the KIM. This 1-of-10 (or decade) decoder has the least significant 3 of its 4 input lines connected to AB10, AB11, and AB12; its open-collector outputs are active low and are used to select the memory on the board in 1K blocks. Its outputs are labeled K0 through K7 and are brought out to the application connector of the KIM so that additional 1K blocks of memory may be readily added. The 1K RAM on board the KIM is selected by K0, while the 6530 ROM chips are selected by K5, K6, and K7. We may use any one of K1 through K4 to select a PIA (if they are not already used for additional memory). However, a pull-up resistor in the range 1 kilohm to 4.7 kilohms *must* be connected between the particular K pin and the +5-V supply since none is provided on the KIM for K1 through K4.

Suppose just one PIA is to be connected to the KIM. We may connect $\overline{CS3}$ of the PIA to K1 from the KIM. Then CS1 and CS2 should be connected to permanent highs (they should not be left "floating"). Other PIA pins (enable, and so on) should be connected to the KIM memory expansion connector pins in the same manner as illustrated in Figure D10–8. Of course, we expect these 6502 CPU lines to be available on the memory expansion connector since they are required for operation of additional memory. The connections to the KIM are diagrammed in Figure D10–9. The PIA connected as above then responds to addresses % XXX0 0100 0000 0000 = $0400 through $0404. (The X's in this address specification are assumed to be zero for simplicity, although the PIA actually responds as well to $2400, $4400, and so on.)

Additional PIAs could be readily connected to the KIM. We may connect $\overline{CS3}$ from each PIA to K1. Rather than connecting CS1 permanently high (so that it is always true), CS1 from the first PIA may be connected to AB2, CS1 from the second PIA to AB3, and so forth. This permits a total of 8 PIAs to be readily connected since AB9 is the most significant address bus line that may be used (why?). It is left as a problem to determine the addresses to which these PIAs will respond.

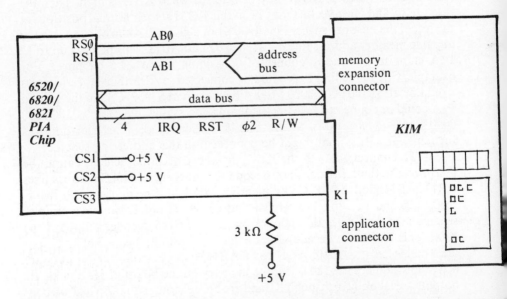

FIGURE D10–9.   *Diagram of Connection of a 6520/6820/6821 PIA Chip to a KIM Microcomputer*

To connect a 6520 PIA to a factory-supplied SYM microcomputer, the same pin connections may be used as have just been described because KIM-compatible edge connectors exist at the top of the SYM board. However, the K1 memory block-select pin cannot be used if this block of RAM has been populated on board the SYM. Rather, we may then use any one of K4 through K7 as none of these memory blocks are used by the SYM. A pull-up resistor is not required on the SYM K lines however. The SYM *does* completely decode the 16 memory address bus lines for activating the memory space that is occupied on the board.

Tests of PIA Functions

This section describes some very educational experiments that may be performed without any actual program being written; we simply use the KIM monitor and the fact that the PIA is memory mapped to the KIM. Indeed, it is a good idea to test if a PIA is operational after connection to the KIM by doing some of the exercises given here.

1. First we connect 4 switches (which output bounceless TTL levels) to the 4 control pins (CA1, CA2, CB1, and CB2). After pressing RS (reset), we examine memory locations $0400 through $0403 and find them to be zero (a consequence of the reset). At this point, we may write any number into MA 400 or MA 402 since they respond as data direction registers A and B, respectively. Using the KIM monitor, let us enter $00 into MA 400 (so port A will be an input port) and $FF into MA 402 (so port B will be an output port).

Next we will make the actual ports respond to MA 400 and MA 402 by setting the DDR-access bit to 1 in each control register. Thus we enter $ 0000 0100 = $04 into MA 401 and into MA 403. Now, when (input) port A is examined at MA 400, the display shows data of $FF if nothing is connected to the port pins. This is because of the pull-up resistors of the port A inputs. Further, even if we try through data-entry mode, we *cannot* write any different number to this *input* port address because the number merely goes to the output register, which is disconnected from the port A pins here. If we short a port A pin to ground, however, the display data for MA 400 changes; for example, shorting PA0 causes the KIM data display to change from $FF to $FE. On the other hand, we may enter any 8-bit number into MA 402, and a voltmeter or indicating lights connected to the port B pins show levels corresponding to the number.

Now let us examine MA 401, so that control register A shows up in the KIM data digits. It shows $04, which we entered previously. If a low-to-high transition is asserted by the switch into control line CA1, the display does not change; however, when the switch is flipped to produce the high-to-low transition, the display changes to show data = $84 = % 1000 0100. The flag A1 has been set, and indeed it was set on a *falling* edge to CA1 because the CA1 control bits are both 0 (refer to the rule at the top of Figure D10–5).

Continued flipping of the switch will not change the display from the $84 data value. If we next work the switch to CA2, we find the display data changes to $C4 = % 1100 0100. This shows that flag A2 is also set.

We next try to clear the flags A1 and A2 by putting the KIM in data-entry mode and entering $04 into MA 401; but the display refuses to change from the $C4 value in the right digit pair. Finally, we change to address-entry mode and examine MA 400. The monitor therefore is executing a read from port A. Advancing the memory address (by pressing +) to MA 401 now shows that the flags are cleared, evident by the presence of $04 in the data portion of the display. Indeed, the read of the port has cleared its flag. We could *not* clear the flags by attempting to write 0's to the control register in which they are located.

2. Analogous experiments may be conducted with the flags B1 and B2 in control register B by working the pair of switches connected to them.

3. We next change the edge response of flag A2 by using the KIM monitor to enter % 0001 0100 = $14 into MA 401. Now interrupts are still disconnected, flag A2 should be set by a rising edge, the port A data register remains accessible, and flag A1 should still be set by a falling-edge voltage transition. Indeed, keeping MA 401 in the display, we see that flag A2 sets immediately as the switch to CA2 asserts low to high (the display shows $54 = % 0101 0100), while flag A1 does not set when the switch to CA1 asserts low to high, but rather waits for high to low. The display data then immediately changes to $D4 = % 1101 0100. This time we check that the flags are cleared by reset; we press RS and note that the display immediately changes to 0401 00 (these are the 4 address digits and 2 data digits). The zeroed data shows that the flags are clear. Also, the data direction access bit is cleared and, therefore, the data direction registers now respond to MA 400 and MA 402.

4. As another experiment, we test the *manual-output* mode of CB2. The switch to CB2 is removed and an indicator light or a voltmeter is connected to it. Then the memory address $403 of control register B is set up (in address-entry mode), and % 0011 1100 = $3C is entered after placing the KIM in data-entry mode. The voltage from CB2 immediately rises to near +5 V. Remaining in data-entry mode, data % 0011 0100 = $34 is entered; the CB2 voltage falls to near zero. Just as the control rules in Figure D10-5 tell us, the CB2 output here follows the state of bit 3 (the fourth bit from the right).

5. As a final experiment, we test the *automatic-handshake* mode for the CB2 control line. The voltmeter or indicator light should still be connected to CB2 as in part (4) above. We press reset, set up the address to control register B—that is, to MA 403—and enter data % 0010 0100 = $24 to establish the handshake mode. We next work the switch to CB1 and observe that the flag B1 sets because the display data changes to $A4 = % 1010 0100. Further, the voltage from the CB2 pin is high (near +5 V). Next the address is changed to that for port B, which is $402. The monitor is reading port B, and this clears the flag (as we may check by advancing the memory address to

$403 and noting that data is $24). However, the voltage from CB2 remains high until we put the KIM in data-entry mode and press a digit key. Then a write to port B is executed and the CB2 line goes low, as specified by the Figure D10–5 rule for automatic handshake from CB2. Working the switch to CB1 sets flag B1, and the voltage from CB2 immediately goes high again. These actions agree with the negative pulse-like waveform (and notes) illustrated near the middle of Figure D10–5.

NOTE: The above experiment may also be performed with a PIA connected to a SYM. The principal difference is that the SYM does *not* read a memory address continuously as the KIM does. The SYM reads an address only when "first stepped into." It is necessary to step away from the port (for example, by pressing forward arrow or backward arrow) and then return to the address in order to read any change in the address.

Examples of 6520 PIA Use

In using the PIA in a laboratory control and communication situation, reset is first asserted to the microprocessor and PIAs. This zeros all the registers in the PIAs; thus we see that interrupts will *not* be enabled from the flags, the port lines are initially programmed as inputs, and the data direction registers (DDRs) are first accessible at XXX0 and XXX2 memory addresses. There must be an *initialization* procedure at the beginning of the program that first establishes port lines as inputs or outputs by writing appropriate bit-patterns to the DDRs. Next the control registers are loaded. Almost certainly the DDRB- and DDRA-access bits are made 1 so that the data ports become accessible at their locations. Further, if the flags are used, the flag control fields are programmed for: (1) the desired edge sensitivity of the control lines, (2) whether they should work the interrupt system (if the system is enabled by $I = 0$ in the P register of the CPU), and (3) whether CA2 or CB2 will be outputs. The actual process control and/or measurement programming begins after this initial housekeeping.

A number of examples are presented to illustrate PIA usage. They may readily be entered into a KIM or SYM to actually try them out (after a PIA has been attached). A KIM is assumed here, with the PIA base address arranged at MA $0400, as recently discussed.

Example 1: Assume that port B of the PIA has been connected to 8 LEDs. Since the output drive of a 6520/6820 PIA is sufficient for only 1 TTL load (for example, to sink 1.6 milliamperes to ground) some sort of driver must be arranged between the port pins and the LEDs. This might be NAND gates as diagrammed in Figure D7–9; however, a

---

current-limiting resistor should then be placed in series with each LED. Assume further that a push button with a bounceless TTL-level output is connected to the CB1 line and thus to flag B1. The push button outputs a high when pressed. This little system is diagrammed in Figure D10–10.

In this example, our task with this system is to cause the LEDs to count up in binary, incrementing by 1 at the instant the button is pressed. Holding the button down has no consequence. An algorithm for this task with our system would go as follows:

1. Initialize port B as output and flag B1 as rising-edge sensitive,
2. Turn the LEDs off,
3. Wait for flag B1 to set,
4. Increment port B to the LEDs (the *inherent read* of port B clears the flag),
5. Go to step 3.

We have port B at MA $402 and control register B at MA $403. The program could be written as follows:

```
                          ;RECALL THAT AFTER RESET, THE
      LDA #$FF            ;DATA DIRECTION REGISTER B RESPONDS AT PORT B
      STA  $0402          ;SET UP AS OUTPUT PORT
      LDA #%00000110      ;ACCESS BIT = 1, MAKE  B1 (+) EDGE
      STA  $0403          ;SENSITIVE, DISCONNECT INTERRUPTS
                          ;THIS COMPLETES HOUSEKEEPING
AGAIN BIT  $0403          ;COPY FLAG B1 INTO N BIT
      BPL  AGAIN          ;WAIT UNTIL FLAG SETS
      INC  $0402          ;BUMP UP THE NUMBER IN THE LEDS
                          ;THIS ALSO CLEARS THE FLAG B1
      JMP  AGAIN          ;REPEAT THE CYCLE
```

The comments should make the program quite self-explanatory. Note that MA 402 responds as data direction register B during the initial housekeeping, but MA 402 responds as port B after the %00000110 pattern is stored to control register B because the access B bit is then set. Further, since flag B1 appears in the most significant bit of control register B, a test of the N bit is done after the BIT instruction copies flag B1 into the N bit of the processor status register. If N = 0, the flag is *not* set and the program branches back—branch on plus (BPL)—to read the flag again. Finally, when the flag is set, the program falls through to increment the number at port B. Note that since the CPU must *read* port B in order to add 1 to the number, the flag B1 will be automatically cleared.

Example 2: In this example we assume the same task with respect to the LEDs as in Example 1. However, in this case the interrupt system is invoked when the button is pressed. The interrupt-service routine should then increment the LED count. To give the microprocessor something interesting to do the rest of the time, let us have the KIM display continuously show the current key depressed on the KIM keypad. The interrupt-service vector (the address of the interrupt-service routine) is set up in the initial housekeeping.

The main routine begins in MA 0200, while the interrupt-service routine begins in MA 0300. Then an assembler language program is as follows:

```
IRQL  = $17FE              ;KIM'S IRQ
IRQH  = $17FF              ;VECTOR LOCATIONS
CNTRLB = $403             ;CONTROL REGISTER B ADDRESS
PORTB = $402              ;PORTB ADDRESS
GETKY = $1F6A             ;KIM SUBROUTINE TO "GET A KEY"
SCANDS = $1F1F            ;KIM SUBROUTINE TO LIGHT THE DISPLAY
       ;BEGIN MAIN PROGRAM
       * = $200


       LDA #$00           ;SET UP THE IRQ VECTOR
       STA  IRQL          ;(FOR KIM) TO $300
       LDA #$03
       STA  IRQH
       LDA #$FF           ;ALL ONES TO DDRB
       STA PORTB          ;MAKING PORTB AN OUTPUT
       LDA #%00000111     ;ACCESS = 1, FLAG B1 (+) EDGE SENSITIVE,
       STA CNTRLB         ;CONNECT FLAG B1 TO IRQ
       CLD                ;PUT IN BINARY MODE FOR KIM SUBROUTINES
       LDA #$00           ;ZERO OUT LEFT
       STAz $FB           ;4 DISPLAY DIGITS
       STAz $FA
       STA  PORTB         ;AND THE 8 LEDS
       CLI                ;ENABLE 6502 INTERRUPTS
                          ;HOUSEKEEPING IS DONE
AGAIN  ┌─ JSR GETKY       ;GET VALUE OF DEPRESSED KEY INTO ACCUM
       │  STAz $F9        ;PUT IN RIGHT DIGIT PAIR
       │  JSR SCANDS      ;LIGHT THE DISPLAY BRIEFLY
       └─ JMP AGAIN


       ;****INTERRUPT SERVICE ROUTINE****

       * = $300           ;BEGINS AT MA $300
       INC PORTB          ;BUMP UP LED COUNT, CLEAR FLAG B1
       RTS                ;GO BACK TO WHERE WE WERE
```

Again the comments in the program should make it quite self-explanatory. Notice bit 1 is set to 1 in the control register for port B in order to connect flag B1 to the IRQ line. Also notice that no registers needed to be saved in the interrupt-service routine because the processor status register was automatically saved before entry to the routine. The INC instruction does not change any registers in the 6502 CPU other than the processor status register.

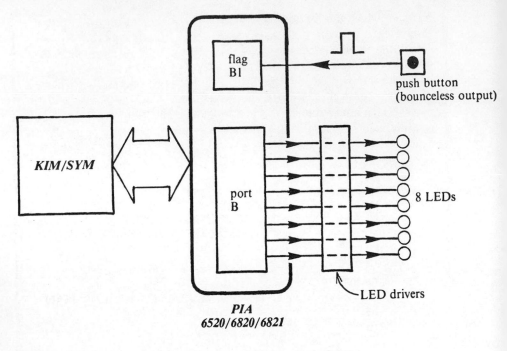

FIGURE D10-10. *Diagram of System Used in Examples*

Example 3: In this example the switch and LED system of Figure D10-10 is used again. In this case we desire all of the lights to change state at the moment the button is *released*; that is, on the *falling* edge of the pulse produced by the push button. The lights are initially all off. This program uses the following algorithm (which is *not* the most compact one possible):

1. Initialize port B and flag B1,
2. Turn all lights off,
3. Wait for flag B1 to set (button is released),
4. Clear the B flags,
5. Turn all lights on,
6. Wait for flag B1 to set,
7. Clear the B flags,
8. Go to step 2.

The program is as follows:

```
PORTB  = $402
CNTRLB = $403

       * = $200

              LDA   #$FF      ;SET DDRB FOR OUTPUT
              STA   PORTB
              LDA   #%00000100 ;FLAGS ARE (-) EDGE SENSITIVE,
              STA   CNTRLB    ;  ACCESS IS ONLY BIT = 1
AGAIN  ┌─►  LDA   #$00      ;TURN ALL LIGHTS OFF
       │      STA   PORTB
WAIT1  │  ┌─► LDA   CNTRLB    ;GET FLAGS
       │  └─  BPL   WAIT1     ;LOOK AGAIN IF FLAG B1 = 0
       │      LDA   PORTB     ;BUTTON IS RELEASED,
       │                      ;CLEAR FLAGS WITH DUMMY READ
       │      LDA   #$FF      ;TURN ALL LIGHTS ON
       │      STA   PORTB
WAIT2  │  ┌─► LDA   CNTRLB    ;WAIT FOR BUTTON RELEASE
       │  └─  BPL   WAIT2
       │      LDA   PORTB     ;OK, CLEAR FLAGS (BY DUMMY READ)
       └──  JMP   AGAIN     ;GO TURN LIGHTS OFF
```

Perhaps the principal feature of note here is that the flags must be cleared with a *dummy read* of port B, as the service of the port involved only a write to the port. Note that this in fact would clear *both* flag B1 and flag B2. Although of no consequence here, it could be a problem if both flags were being used. Finally, a more compact algorithm involving only one *wait loop* could be used if we would simply complement port B each time we want the lights changed. This can be done by using the exclusive-OR (EOR) instruction and is left to the problems.

Laboratory Microprocessor Application

This section illustrates a rather extensive possible laboratory microprocessor application. It illustrates how useful the various control-line functions for CA1 through CB2 can be; in fact, all 4 lines are put to work here.

In this example, it is desired to measure the analog voltage from some experiment once each minute and cause the value to be printed on a serial printer. The experimental voltage is in the range 0.00 V to 0.99 V, and the printer is to print the results in this format in a vertical column. The system is diagrammed in Figure D10–11.

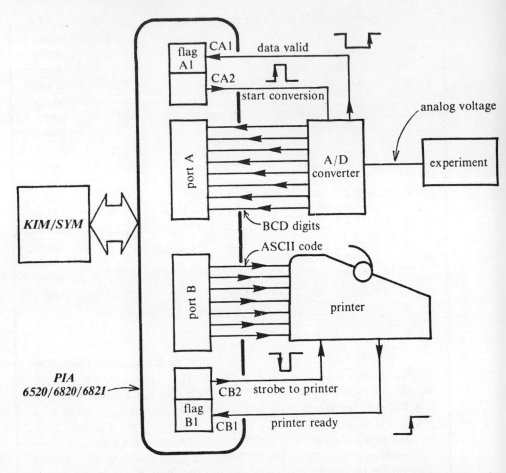

FIGURE D10-11. *Diagram for a System to Acquire and Print Once Each Minute the Voltage from an Experiment*

An A/D converter with 2 BCD-digits output (on 8 lines) is to measure the analog voltage. For the given voltage range, the A/D converter outputs a number from 00 to 99. We assume that the converter requires a positive-going edge to its *start-convert* input pin in order to begin a determination of the input analog voltage. After a conversion time on the order of 1 milli-second, the A/D converter changes the levels on its 8 data-output lines. During this brief interval, the *data-valid* output pin from the A/D chip goes low to show a false condition. When it rises again, the data on its data-output lines represent the newly determined voltage. In fact, the 3-1/2-digit 8750 A/D converter (Teledyne Semiconductor) operates in this manner. If it were used for this example, however, only the 2 least significant digits would be utilized.

We assume that the printer accepts each character in 7-bit ASCII code (no parity). A character is input over 7 parallel lines. The printer has an output line called *printer ready* that goes high (for true) when it is ready to accept another character for printing. This line goes low while the printing of a character is in process. To initiate the printing of a character, the *strobe* input line to the printer is brought low. On the falling edge of the strobe pulse, the printer latches the input character and begins printing the character. In fact, the Anderson-Jacobson 841 I/O terminal operates in the above manner.

Refer now to the system diagram in Figure D10–11. Notice that a single 6520 PIA, in conjunction with a KIM or a SYM, may be used to accomplish the desired I/O. Port A receives the A/D data, while control line CA2 is used as an output to send the start-convert pulse to the A/D. We use manual-output mode for this. Flag A1 is the device flag for the A/D converter. Control line CA1 receives the data-valid signal from the A/D converter so that flag A1 becomes the *A/D-done* flag. Notice that the *active edge* is shown by the arrow on each pulse form.

The least significant 7 lines from port B send the ASCII character to the printer. CB2 is used in automatic-pulse-output mode to strobe the printer, while flag B1 is the device flag for the printer. The printer-ready line is therefore input to control line CB1.

The algorithm for this example is as follows:

1. Initialize port A as input with CA2 as manual output (and initially low), flag A1 as (+) edge sensitive (no interrupts),
2. Initialize port B as output with CB2 as auto pulse out (on write), flag B1 as (+) edge sensitive (no interrupts),
3. Send carriage-return (CR) to printer,
4. Send a period to printer,
5. Get an A/D voltage,
6. Convert most significant BCD digit to ASCII,
7. Send to printer,
8. Convert least significant BCD digit to ASCII,
9. Send to printer,
10. Send letter "V" to printer,
11. Send CR to printer,
12. Wait 1 minute (less the time to print 4 characters),
13. Go to step 4.

This algorithm is implemented by the assembler language program of Figure D10–12. The numbered steps in the algorithm are placed in parentheses at the left of the program. Careful study of the system interconnections diagrammed in Figure D10–11, the algorithm, and the program with comments in Figure D10–12 should permit the reader to understand how the task is accomplished in this program. Pay particular attention to how the flags and control lines are programmed and used. However, a number of aspects of this program will be discussed further.

```
                PORTA = $400
                CNTRLA= $401
                PORTB = $402
                CNTRLB= $403


        (ALGORITHM STEP)

                        * = $200
    ( 1)            LDA #$00            ;INITIALIZE
                    STA  PORTA          ;PORT A AS INPUT
                    LDA #%00110110      ;CA1 ON (+)EDGE AS A/D DONE FLAG AND
                    STA  CNTRLA         ;CA2 MANUAL-OUT TO INIT CONV
    ( 2)            LDA #$FF
                    STA  PORTB          ;PORT B AS OUTPUT
                    LDA #%00101110      ;CB1 ON (+)EDGE AS PRINTER FLAG AND
                    STA  CNTRLB         ;CB2 AUTO PULSE TO PRINTER STROBE
    ( 3)            LDA #$0D            ;SEND CARR RETURN TO PRINTER
                    STA  PORTB          ;(ALSO, PRINTER FLAG WILL GET SET)
    ( 4) REPEAT     LDA #$2E            ;SEND PERIOD TO PRINTER
                    JSR  PRINT          ;(WAITS FOR PRINTER FLAG)
    ( 5)            LDA #%00111110      ;START A/D CONVERT
                    STA  CNTRLA         ;WITH MANUAL PULSE HIGH
                    LDA #%00110110      ;OUT CA2
                    STA  CNTRLA
        WAIT1 ┌──► BIT  CNTRLA         ;CHECK A/D DONE FLAG
              └─── BPL  WAIT1
                    LDX  PORTA          ;GET BCD VOLTAGE, CLEAR FLAG A1
    ( 6)            TXA                 ;VOLTAGE SAVED IN X, COPY TO ACCUM
                    LSR  A              ;MOVE TO RIGHT SIDE OF ACCUM
                    LSR  A              ;ENTERING ZEROS IN
                    LSR  A              ;LEFT 4 BITS
                    LSR  A              ;(NOTE: "A" SIGNIFIES ACCUM)
                    ORA #$30            ;MAKE ASCII DIGIT (01 to 31, etc.)
    ( 7)            JSR  PRINT          ;GO PRINT IT AS MSD
    ( 8)            TXA                 ;BCD VOLTAGE INTO ACCUM AGAIN
                    AND #$0F            ;CLEAR LEFT 4 BITS
                    ORA #$30            ;MAKE ASCII DIGIT
    ( 9)            JSR  PRINT          ;GO PRINT IT AS LSD
    (10)            LDA #$56            ;PRINT LETTER "V"
                    JSR  PRINT
    (11)            LDA #$0D            ;DO CARRIAGE RETURN
                    JSR  PRINT
    (12)            JSR  DELAY          ;WAIT ONE MINUTE (MINUS A LITTLE)
    (13)            JMP  REPEAT         ;REPEAT THE CYCLE
        ;****PRINT SUBROUTINE, PRINTS ASCII CHARACTER CURRENTLY
        ;      IN ACCUMULATOR****
        PRINT ┌──► BIT  CNTRLB         ;WAIT FOR PRINTER READY
              └─── BPL  PRINT
                    STA  PORTB          ;SEND CHARACTER, ALSO THE STROBE PULSE
                    LDA  PORTB          ;DUMMY READ TO CLEAR PRINTER FLAG B1
                    RTS                 ;RETURN

        ;****DELAY SUBROUTINE****
        DELAY       (SUBROUTINE FOR 1-MINUTE DELAY.  COULD BE SOFTWARE,
                    OR USE A TIMER.)
```

FIGURE D10–12. *Assembler Language Program*

Notice that when an output to the printer is desired in the program, this is done by a subroutine call—that is, JSR—to the PRINT subroutine that is placed near the end of the program. This subroutine prints whatever ASCII character is currently in the accumulator. This is a useful technique because the print process involves 4 instructions, and these would otherwise need to be replicated a number of times in the program.

The first pair of instructions in the PRINT subroutine causes the microprocessor *to wait* for the printer to signal that it is ready (via its printer-ready line to flag B1) before outputting the character presently in the accumulator to the printer. Note also that the subsequent STA PORTB instruction exploits the *automatic-pulse-output* mode from CB2 to strobe the printer. This 1-microsecond pulse conveniently occurs just *after* the port B lines are settled to the new ASCII character code. Then note that flag B1 must be cleared because it is *not* cleared automatically on a *write* to port.

However, a somewhat tricky point occurs at step 3 in the program. The *first* transmission to the printer is done *without* waiting for the printer-ready flag; this is because after the printer is first powered up, it is certainly ready and its printer-ready output line stands high. However, if the microprocessor is reset after printer power-up, *no rising edge* from the printer-ready line subsequently occurs to set the printer-ready flag B1. Consequently, the microcomputer gets "stuck" in the print subroutine waiting for the printer-ready flag, *even* though the printer is ready. (This sort of situation has embarrassed the author on occasion.)

In step 5 of the program, notice the coding used to send a short high pulse out CA2 to the start-convert pin of the A/D. This uses the manual-output mode. Then the CPU waits for the A/D-done flag (flag A1). Since approximately a millisecond (or 1,000 machine cycles) is required for a conversion, it is important that the CPU does *not* read the A/D output prematurely. When flag A1 finally sets, the 6502 knows that the A/D conversion is complete. Then, in reading port A to obtain the voltage value, the 6502 CPU automatically clears the A/D-done flag.

Notice the instructions in step 6 to change the left nibble of the BCD number (produced by the A/D converter) to an ASCII-coded digit.

NOTE: A *nibble* is a 4-bit binary number.

For example, if the A/D number were 46, we must first produce the number 34 (ASCII code for 4) and then send this to the printer in step 7. Indeed, the A/D number was initially loaded into the X index register to "save" it, because the accumulator is manipulated in order to obtain the ASCII digit desired. Similarly in step 8 the right nibble of the BCD number is converted to ASCII. To continue the example number 46, the 6 should be converted to 36 and then sent to the printer. Next the ASCII code for the letter "V" is sent to the printer, followed by the CR (carriage-return) code. Of course, the CR is sent to cause the printing mechanism to move to the left of the printing sheet in preparation for the next data printout. Recall that the various ASCII codes were presented in Figure D8–4.

Finally, a delay of nearly 1 minute is required before the read and print voltage cycle is repeated. This is assumed to be implemented in a subroutine that is placed at the end of the program. A software delay or a hardware timer delay could be used. For accuracy, this delay should take into account the printing time for 4 characters.

However, this printing time correction could be nicely avoided by use of a hardware timer that is capable of an accurate 1-minute time-out interval. Then the timer could be started just before step 4, and step 12 would simply wait for the 1 minute to time out, after which the CPU would return to reload the timer. For even greater accuracy the timer should be *free running*; that is, no instructions (and an attendant small time interval) are required to reload it to the initial setting. It does this automatically. The timers on the 6522 VIA chip have this capability and the VIA is considered next.

Other Supporting Device Chips

A number of modern integrated-circuit peripheral device chips are designed to connect directly to the memory communication bus of microprocessors. Some examples of these device chips are presented in Table D10–1; the chips presented are especially suitable for use with the 6502 or 6800 microprocessors.

ADC and DAC chips that are microprocessor compatible were mentioned in Chapter D6, and examples of this device type begin the table. Chips also exist that provide time-of-day and multiple-timer functions. Complex controller chips have been introduced to provide control and communications functions with floppy disc drives or to generate signals for a cathode-ray tube terminal.

Several manufacturers have introduced chips to implement the *IEEE–488* bus or *general-purpose instrument bus* (GPIB). The GPIB is an important standard interface first designed at Hewlett Packard (HP) in the early 1970s to interconnect their line of digital instrumentation with their minicomputers. The Institute of Electrical and Electronics Engineers (IEEE) established the IEEE–488–1978 standard in the year 1978 as a standard version of the HP-GPIB. This standard specifies a total of 24 lines to implement the interface: 8 lines for bidirectional transmission of data, 8 control lines, and 8 ground lines. A standard stacking-type interface plug is also specified. Transmissions can occur at a rate of up to 1 megabyte per second, with up to 15 devices connected to the bus (including the computer). A flexible control structure permits any device to be designated a "talker" on the bus, while

TABLE D10-1. *Selection of Microprocessor Support Chips*

Device	Function
74C911	4-digit LED display controller
DAC1000	10-bit DAC
ADC3511	3-1/2-digit A/D converter
MP20, ADC0816	8-bit A/D converter, multiplexer
MSM5832, MM58167	time-of-day clock
SY6551, MC6850	serial communications interface
MC6840	3 programmable timers
MC68488	IEEE-488 interface bus adapter
SY6545, MC6854	CRT controller
SY6591, MC6843	floppy disc controller

several devices can be simultaneous "listeners." The PET microcomputer uses an IEEE-488 interface as its standard interconnection to peripheral devices such as a printer or floppy disc drive.

6522 Versatile Interface Adapter (VIA)

The 6522 *versatile interface adapter* or VIA is a second-generation general-purpose support chip designed for the 6502; it is capable of all the functions of the 6520/6821 PIA and more. Similar to the PIA, the VIA is a 40-pin DIP device that is designed for memory-mapped operation and, therefore, direct connection to the 6502 memory bus. The VIA achieves its versatility through LSI technology and is comparable in price to the 6502 microprocessor chip.

The SYM microcomputer uses the 6522 VIA for I/O through the *application connector*. An additional VIA is supplied on the SYM board, while a socket is supplied for a third VIA chip; I/O pins from these 2 VIA chips are brought to the *auxiliary application connector* on the SYM. The PET microcomputer also uses a 6522 VIA for I/O through its parallel I/O port (*J2*).

The programmability of the many functions of the 6522 VIA involves a somewhat imposing set of rules. Therefore, only an overview of the VIA device is given here. A number of functions are similar to those on the 6520 and 6530/6532 chips. For the following discussion, refer to the model of the 16 VIA registers and various I/O lines that are presented in Figure D10-13.

Two 8-bit I/O ports (port A and port B) and attendant data direction registers are available as the lowest 4 locations. Associated flags A1, A2, B1, and B2 are in the *interrupt flag register* (IFR), and control lines CA1, CA2, CB1, and CB2 are connected to these flags; these 4 flags and control lines

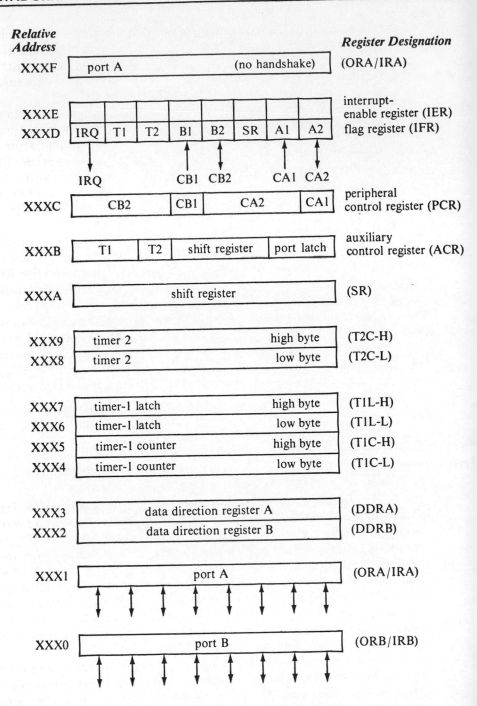

FIGURE D10-13. *Model of 6522 I/O Lines and Registers*

are similar to 6520/6820 PIA functions. Control-line behavior is determined by establishing proper control bits in the *peripheral control register*. However, the clearing of 6522 flags is more versatile than on the 6520; also latching input registers exist for each port so that an input device need only sustain data to a port near the instant that a port flag-1 is set.

Two 16-bit *timers* are available in the VIA. Both timers can operate in a *one-shot mode* similar to that for the 6530/6532 timer. In addition, timer 1 can automatically reload the 16-bit down counter to its initial count from the timer-1 latches after reaching zero; this is called the *free-run mode*. Both timers operate directly from the $\phi 2$ clock without predividers; however timer 2 can use an external clock from bit 6 of port B and therefore can function as a pulse counter. Furthermore, the borrow from timer 1 can be enabled out on bit 7 of port B.

An 8-bit *shift register* also exists in the VIA. This register can receive shift pulses from an external source (input on CB1), or timer 2 can be selected for use as the shift clock. The shift-register output is from control line CB2. Control bits to select the various modes of timer and shift-register operation are present in the *auxiliary control register*.

Individual timer and port flags may or may not be enabled through the IRQ output pin to the interrupt system. A given flag is enabled to the interrupt system if a directly corresponding bit is set in the *interrupt-enable register*. The reader is referred to the 6522 specification sheets for details on the various functions of the 6522; the *SYM-1 Reference Manual* includes the 6522 specification sheets.

Asynchronous Communications Interface Adapter (ACIA)

The utility of serial data transmission was described in Chapter D4. Teleprinters, CRT terminals, and serial printers often communicate in bit-serial mode. An early application of LSI technology was for a chip specifically designed for transmitting and receiving serial data: the *universal asynchronous receiver/transmitter* or UART. The classic UART is the 40-pin TR1602 device from Western Digital. This chip includes 2 shift registers for simultaneous transmitting and receiving of data. Various control input lines are connected to logic 0 or 1 values to select such attributes as parity, number of data bits, and number of stop bits. Further, a number of status lines tell if the chip is ready for new data.

Motorola introduced the 6850 *asynchronous communications interface adapter* or ACIA; this device is essentially a UART that is designed to connect directly to the microprocessor for memory-mapped I/O. The microprocessor communicates with an 8-bit *transmit-data register* as well as an 8-bit *receive-data register*. In addition, rather than using control lines and status lines, the 6850 chip includes an 8-bit *control register* and an 8-bit *status register*. These registers permit specific configuration and utilization of the chip through programming, rather like the programmability of the 6530 and 6520 functions presented earlier. A stable external clock signal must be input to the 6850; this clock establishes the *baud rate*—that is, the bit transfer rate—of the ACIA. The SY6551 ACIA is a device similar to the 6850, but the 6551 includes an on-chip programmable baud-rate generator. If a 1.8432-megahertz crystal is connected to the 6551, one of 19 baud rates from 50 to 19,200 baud can be programmed for chip operation.

REVIEW EXERCISES

1. Explain the utility of a computer interrupt system.
2. (a) Describe in general terms what happens when the 6502 microprocessor receives an interrupt.
   (b) Describe how the NMI interrupt differs from the IRQ interrupt in terms of:
      (1) input signal
      (2) response
      (3) maskability
3. What is the purpose of the I bit in the processor status register?
4. Why are the device flags connected as a wired-OR to the IRQ line of the 6502?
5. (a) What is an interrupt-service routine?
   (b) How does the 6502 microprocessor find its way to the interrupt-service routine?
   (c) Is the 6502 hardware stack used during an interrupt? Explain.
   (d) What is the purpose of the RTI instruction at the end of the interrupt service routine?
6. (a) What is a vectored interrupt system?
   (b) What is the advantage of a vectored interrupt system?
   (c) What is the disadvantage of a vectored interrupt system?
7. (a) What is a software interrupt?
   (b) How is a software interrupt caused on the 6502?
   (c) How does the 6502 respond to a software interrupt?
8. (a) Explain what is meant by the term *IRQ vector*.
   (b) Where does the 6502 microprocessor expect to find the IRQ, RST, and NMI vectors?
   (c) Since these memory locations are in ROM on the KIM, explain how adjustable IRQ and NMI vectors are made available to the KIM user.
9. (a) What is a real-time clock?
   (b) Explain the versatility of the programmable real-time clock relative to more elementary real-time clock approaches.
10. (a) The programmable timer on the 6530 chip can be said to have a two-dimensional adjustability. Explain this statement.

(b) What is the longest time interval that can be obtained from the 6530 timer? Does it depend on the CPU clock? Explain.

11. (a) The timer on the 6530 chip employs a counter. Is it an up counter or a down counter?

(b) The counter can be loaded using 4 addresses XXX4 through XXX7. What is the purpose for using 4 addresses?

(c) The counter can also be loaded using 4 different addresses from those in part (b). What is different about the alternate addresses?

(d) What is present in bit 7 of address XXX7 during a read operation?

(e) Tell two ways that the timer flag can be cleared.

(f) How can the state or count of the counter be determined?

(g) Address XXX7 behaves very differently for a write operation relative to a read operation. Explain.

12. What is the most important difference between the 6530 chip and the later 6532 chip?

13. (a) Name the 3 register types in the 6520/6820/6821 PIA.

(b) How many registers are present in the programmer's model for the PIA?

(c) How many addresses are used to access these registers?

(d) Explain how the disparity between (b) and (c) is solved for the register usage.

14. (a) How many possible flags are available to the user of the PIA?

(b) How many standard port lines are available from a PIA?

(c) How many control-line inputs are available?

(d) Two control lines serve only as input lines; explain what they input to.

(e) Two control lines are bidirectional; explain their purpose when used as inputs.

(f) Name the 3 mode types available to the PIA user if the bidirectional control lines are used as outputs.

15. (a) Control lines CA1 and CB1 are each defined by a pair of control bits. Tell precisely where these control bits are found in each case.

(b) Describe the function of each bit of the pair of control bits.

(c) Explain why control lines CA2 and CB2 are each defined by 3 bits rather than 2 bits.

(d) Explain how the programmer can obtain precisely the same type of behavior for control line CA2 as for control line CA1. Compare the programming rules for this case.

(e) Repeat question (d), substituting CB2 and CB1 for CA2 and CA1, respectively.

(f) How can the flags A1 and A2 be cleared?

(g) How can the flags B1 and B2 be cleared?

16. The interrupt system of a 6502-based microcomputer is enabled, and flag B1 in a PIA becomes set. Is the 6502 program execution necessarily interrupted by the given PIA? Explain.

17. (a) Describe the operational rules for obtaining the manual-output mode from control line CA2.

    (b)   What is the utility of this mode?

    (c)   Compare the manual-output mode for CB2 with that for CA2.

18. (a)   An output device requires a strobe pulse to cause the device to read the output of a PIA port. Describe a useful control-line possibility for this case.

    (b)   An input device requires a pulse to indicate that the 6502 microprocessor has read the data that is input by the device to a PIA port. Describe a useful control-line possibility for this case.

    (c)   What is the duration of the pulse for either case above?

    (d)   Is the pulse positive or negative in polarity?

19. (a)   Control line CA2 is used in automatic-handshake mode. Describe its behavior relative to flag A1.

    (b)   What is the general purpose of the handshake mode?

    (c)   Is the handshake mode for CA2 more convenient for use with an input device or an output device? Explain.

20. (a)   Control line CB2 is used in automatic-handshake mode. The CB2 line immediately moves high when the flag B2 is set, but CB2 does not immediately move low when flag B2 is cleared. What causes CB2 to go low?

    (b)   Is the handshake mode for CB2 most convenient for use with an input device or an output device? Explain.

    (c)   Explain why a fake read or a dummy read is required in the usage of port B.

21. (a)   Suppose port A and port B of a PIA are both programmed as inputs. Contrast their electrical characteristics.

    (b)   Suppose port A and port B of a PIA are both programmed as outputs. Contrast their electrical characteristics.

22. (a)   Explain the difference between the chip-select pins and the register-select pins for a PIA.

    (b)   Why is the microprocessor reset line connected to the PIA?

    (c)   What microprocessor line connects to the enable pin of the PIA? Give two actions accomplished by this connection.

PROBLEMS

1. (a)   Write a program segment for a KIM microcomputer that produces a delay or wait of 0.250-second duration. Use the 6530 timer to establish the timing.

    (b)   Extend the above program segment to produce a 10.0-second delay or wait.

2. Write a program by which a KIM microcomputer produces a 5.00-kHz square wave from the least significant bit of port A on the application connector. Use the 6530 timer to determine the output timing.

3. Write a program by which a SYM microcomputer produces a 5.00-kHz square wave from the least significant bit of port A on the application connector. Use the 6532 timer on the SYM to determine the output timing.

4. Write a program by which a KIM becomes a variable-frequency square-wave oscillator. Assume the 8-bit number N is input on port A of the application con-

nector. Then a square wave with a period of N milliseconds ($\pm3\%$) is to be developed out the least significant bit of port B of the application connector. If the input number N changes, the output frequency should change accordingly on the next half cycle. Use the 6530 timer to establish the square-wave period. Note that a binary number can be divided by 2 simply by shifting it right one place.

5. Write a program by which a SYM becomes a variable-frequency oscillator. Follow the instructions of Problem 3, except that the 6532 timer should be used rather than the 6530 timer.

6. The SYM monitor includes a subroutine called KEYQ that returns with the Z bit equal to 0 if any key is depressed on the SYM hex keyboard. The KEYQ subroutine begins at $8923. Write a program for a SYM microcomputer that produces a 200-millisecond ($\pm3\%$) positive output pulse each time someone presses a key on the SYM keyboard. Arrange the pulse to be output from the most significant bit of port B on the application connector. Use the 6532 timer to determine the time duration.

7. Write a program for a KIM microcomputer that produces a 200-millisecond ($\pm3\%$) positive output pulse each time someone presses the zero key on the KIM keyboard. Arrange the pulse to be output on the most significant bit of port B on the application connector. Use the 6530 timer to determine the pulse time duration.

8. Write an assembler language program for a KIM microcomputer that reads an 8-bit value from application connector port A once every 10 seconds and displays the number in the right 2 digits of the KIM display. Use the 6530 timer along with appropriate software to establish the 10-second intervals. Include comments in the program.

9. Write an assembler language program for a SYM microcomputer that reads an 8-bit value from application connector port A once every 10 seconds and displays the number in the right 2 digits of the SYM display; the previous readings shift left accordingly. Use the 6532 timer along with appropriate software to establish the 10-second intervals. Include comments in the program.

NOTE: A SYM subroutine called SCAND begins at $8906 and corresponds to the KIM subroutine with the same name. This SYM subroutine lights the display briefly to show the contents of the SYM *display buffer*. A SYM subroutine called OUTBYT begins at $82FA; when the OUTBYT subroutine is executed, the current 8-bit value in the accumulator is entered into the *right-most end* of the display buffer (corresponding to the right digit pair in the display). The 2 other 8-bit values are shifted left in the display buffer and consequently also in the display. (The OUTBYT subroutine also scans the SYM display once when it is called.) However, before any of these subroutines are called, it is necessary to execute a JSR to a subroutine called ACCESS that begins at $8B86; this subroutine "unprotects" system RAM so that it may be used by SYM monitor routines. JSR $8B86 needs to be done only once in the program.

10. A KIM microcomputer is to be used to check the shutter "speed" of a leaf-type camera shutter. A light source is placed on one side of the lens, and a light sensor is placed on the other. (A photoresistor with a 311 comparator could serve as the light sensor.) The light sensor produces a logic-high output when the shutter is open: this signal is input to bit 7 of port B on the KIM application connector. Write an assembler language program that measures the shutter time as a multiple of 64 microseconds. After pressing GO on the KIM, the camera shutter should be activated by the experimenter. Subsequently the KIM displays the shutter time in the right 2 digits of the KIM display. If the shutter time exceeds 255×64 microseconds, have the KIM display EE in the left 2 digits of the display.

11. The SYM board has an on-board "beeper" that uses a small peizoelectric speaker. The beeper produces a short beep any time the monitor routine called BEEP is entered. The BEEP subroutine begins at $8972.
    (a) Assume a push button is connected to control line CB2 of a 6520 PIA that is connected to the SYM. The base address (of port A) for the PIA is at address $0400. Assume the push-button output goes from low to high when the button is pressed; write a program that causes the SYM to beep at any instant that the button is pressed.
    (b) Repeat part (a), except have the SYM beep at the instant that the button is released.

12. A 6502 microcomputer and 1 PIA are to serve as a data transfer mechanism between 2 devices X and Y. The base address of the PIA is $0400. When a negative-going transition occurs on a line from device X, the 8 bits on 8 parallel lines from device X are to be read by the microcomputer. The computer then transfers the 8 bits to device Y; however, the most significant 4 bits are to be zero, while the least significant 4 bits remain as received from X.
    (a) Which port is most convenient as the input port from X? Explain why.
    (b) Make a diagram of the PIA registers; show the purpose of the various PIA lines as you have assigned them.
    (c) Write a program beginning in location $0010 to accomplish the stated task. Use typical coding sheet form; include OP codes and mnemonics.

13. Assume that a 6821 PIA is connected to a KIM microcomputer; the base address of the PIA is at MA $0800. Write a program that causes a square wave to be output on control line CA2. Tell the frequency of the square wave.

14. (a) The CB2 control line could be used in handshake mode with an input device to port B. However, a fake-write or dummy-write operation would be required in this usage. Explain why.
    (b) Consequently, the handshake mode should not be called automatic handshake in this case. Explain this statement.

15. A KIM microcomputer is to be used with a PIA to obtain a digital monostable multivibrator. The duration of the monostable is to be N milliseconds ($\pm 3\%$), where N is a binary number that is input by 8 switches connected to port A. The value of N may change from pulse to pulse. The monostable trigger-input line

should be positive-edge sensitive; use flag B1 as the monostable input. Use bit 0 from port B for the monostable output.

(a) Make a diagram of the PIA registers; indicate the usage of various PIA lines in this diagram.

(b) Design a flowchart for a program that implements the monostable behavior desired.

(c) Develop an assembler language diagram to implement the flowchart of part (b).

16. A KIM microcomputer is to continuously show in the right of the KIM display the last number input to port A of a PIA that is connected to the KIM. The number is to be read from port A only when the 6502 is interrupted by a negative pulse on the CA1 control line. Assume the base address of the PIA is $0400. Use the interrupt system in the program and load the necessary IRQ vector from within the program. Let the main program begin in MA $0030, while the interrupt-service routine is to begin in MA $0300. Write the program in assembler language.

17. Accomplish the task in Problem 16, but use a SYM microcomputer rather than a KIM microcomputer. See the note for SYM display usage given in Problem 9.

18. A 6502 microcomputer and 1 PIA are to count the number of pulses on control line CA1 that occur in the time interval between a start pulse and a stop pulse that are input to control line CB1. The total number is output to port B, after which the microcomputer waits for the next start pulse on CB2 and then repeats the counting process. Let both pulses be sensed on the positive-going edge. Assume the base address of the PIA is $0800.

(a) Design a flowchart of the required program.

(b) Develop an assembly language program to implement your flowchart.

Bibliography

It can be helpful to read about a topic when it is presented in a manner different from the student's own textbook. The presentation may be more elementary or more sophisticated. Furthermore, the reader may wish to study a topic in more depth, particularly if a certain project is being developed. Therefore a list of references follows. The first nine references pertain primarily to digital logic, while the remaining pertain to minicomputers and microprocessors. The references within each group are in chronological order, and brief comments are included with each to help in choosing a reference.

Malmstadt, H.V., and C.G. Enke. 1969. *Digital Electronics for Scientists*. New York: W.A. Benjamin.
   One of first texts to present digital electronics techniques for scientists with emphasis on use of integrated circuits. This material was updated in *Digital and Analog Data Conversions (Module 3)* by H.V. Malmstadt, C.G. Enke, and S.R. Crouch. 1974. Menlo Park, Calif.: W.A. Benjamin. The latest version of this material is in *Electronics and Instrumentation for Scientists* by H.V. Malmstadt, C.G. Enke, and E.C. Toren. 1981. Menlo Park, Calif.: Benjamin/Cummings.
Hughes, J.L. 1969. *Computer Lab Workbook*. Maynard, Mass.: Digital Equipment Corp.
   Introduction to digital logic techniques emphasizing TTL, including laboratory experiments.
Barna, A., and D.I. Porat. 1973. *Integrated Circuits in Digital Electronics*. New York: Wiley.
   Digital electronic devices and circuits presented at an intermediate level. Good reference for additional information.
Lancaster, D. 1974. *TTL Cookbook*. Indianapolis, Ind.: Sam.
   Useful for many "nuts and bolts" aspects of TTL digital logic usage.
Lee, S.C. 1976. *Digital Circuits and Logic Design*. Englewood Cliffs, N.J.: Prentice-Hall.
   Written for a senior level digital design course for electrical engineering/computer electronics programs.

Lancaster, D. 1977. *CMOS Cookbook.* Indianapolis, Ind.: Sams.

Williams, G.E. 1977. *Digital Technology.* Chicago: Science Research Associates, Inc.
Basic discussion of digital logic and some instrumentation, stressing I.C. devices.

Deitmeyer, D.L. 1978. *Logic Design of Digital Systems.* Boston: Allyn and Bacon.
Written for teaching digital design; includes more advanced techniques.

Horowitz, P., and W. Hill. 1980. *The Art of Electronics.* Cambridge: Cambridge University Press.
A compendium of modern scientific electronics practice, including both analog and digital techniques.

Soucek, B. 1972. *Minicomputers in Data Processing and Simulation.* New York: Wiley-Interscience.
Minicomputer topics relevant to laboratory applications.

Korn, G.A. 1973. *Minicomputers for Scientists and Engineers.* New York: McGraw-Hill.
Minicomputers and their application to laboratory problems.

Soucek, B. 1976. *Microprocessors and Microcomputers.* New York: Wiley-Interscience.
Update of earlier book with microprocessor emphasis.

Korn, G.A. 1977. *Microprocessors & Small Digital Computer Systems for Engineers and Scientists.* New York: McGraw-Hill.
Update of his earlier book to include microprocessors.

Osborne, A. 1976. *An Introduction to Microcomputers, Vol. I: Basic Concepts.* Berkeley, Calif.: Osborne/McGraw-Hill.
Discussion of various machine-language techniques and hardware approaches.

Osborne, A., and J. Kane. 1978. *An Introduction to Microcomputers: Some Real Microprocessors.* (Introduction to Microcomputers Series, Vol. II). Berkeley, Calif.: Osborne/McGraw-Hill.
Excellent source of information on the many microprocessors and support devices available.

——— 1978. *An Introduction to Microcomputers, Vol. III; Some Real Support Devices.* Berkeley, Calif.: Osborne/McGraw-Hill.
Useful source of information on general support devices and bus standards such as RS-232.

Peatman, J.B. 1977. *Microcomputer-Based Design.* New York: McGraw-Hill.
General text on microcomputer hardware and software.

Leventhal, L.A. 1978. *Introduction to Microprocessors: Software, Hardware, Programming.* Englewood Cliffs, N.J.: Prentice-Hall.
General text on microcomputer hardware and software; uses 8080 and 6800 microprocessors in examples.

Fisher, E., and C.W. Jensen. 1980. *PET and the IEEE 488 Bus (GPIB).* Berkeley, Calif.: Osborne/McGraw-Hill.
Good source of information on the IEEE 488 Bus and how to use it on the PET microcomputer.

Artwick, B.A. 1980. *Microcomputers Interfacing.* Englewood Cliffs, N.J.: Prentice-Hall.
Introduces concepts of interfacing microprocessors to various devices, including RS-232 basics.

Tocci, R.J., and L.P. Loskowski. 1982. *Microprocessors and Microcomputers: Hardware and Software.* Englewood Cliffs, N.J.: Prentice-Hall.
Introduction to microprocessors with use of 6502 as principal example.

Answers to Problems

The answers to odd-numbered problems, except for diagrams and lengthy discussions, are provided. In the case of derivations or discussion answers, only brief summary answers are given.

Chapter D1

1. (a) 2, 10, 8, 16; (b) 111111 (simply concatenate the two numbers); (c) 11100, 1100100, 101010101; (d) 13, 170, 12; (e) 10001, 10010, 10011, 10100; (f) 15, 252, 14; (g) D, AA, C

5. 64

7. (b) permanent high

9. (a) De Morgan's theorem $\overline{A} + \overline{B} = \overline{A \cdot B}$

   (b) De Morgan's theorem $\overline{A} \cdot \overline{B} = \overline{A + B}$

11. (a) $A \cdot \overline{C} + A \cdot B \cdot \overline{D}$

13. A logic level may be inverted or non-inverted (simply buffered) under control of a second logic level.

15. (a) $(A', B', C') = (A, B, C)$;
    (b) $(A', B', C') = (\overline{A}, \overline{B}, \overline{C})$

17. (a) T_A is off, T_B is off, T_C is on, out is low; (b) RTL; (c) NOR

19. (a) Assume inputs A, B and C, D to respective gates.
    Out $= \overline{(A \cdot B) + (C \cdot D)}$

    (b) Contention between totem pole outputs can damage the two gates.

21. (a) 10, 20; (b) 20 (determined by high output drive/load)

23. (a) L lights when S is closed; L is dark when switch S is open.

    (b) Closed switch S causes proper low; open switch S disconnects TTL input, which then acts high.

    (c) For positive logic 1, the output line is disconnected; hence no voltage to bulb exists to light it.

    (d) Switch S exercises inverter A as in part (b). But inverter A acts as switch to ground and similarly exercises inverter B.

25. (a) 1.1 mA; somewhat less than 1.6 mA, which is a max value; (b) 880 Ω

27. 33 nsec

29. 3.6 V, 0 V

Chapter D2

1. (a) Direct expression for output $= \overline{[A \cdot (\overline{A \cdot B}) \cdot (B \cdot (\overline{A \cdot B})]}$

5. (c) 8

7. (a) $\overline{A} \cdot \overline{B}$; (c) $A + B$; (e) $A + B$

11. (a) $\overline{A}\,\overline{B}C + \overline{A}BC + A\overline{B}C$

    (b) $(A + B + C)\,(A + \overline{B} + C)\,(\overline{A} + B + \overline{C})(\overline{A} + \overline{B} + C)(\overline{A} + \overline{B} + \overline{C})$

13. (a) $A \cdot B + C \cdot (A \oplus B)$

17. (b) Use 4 full adders. Invert the A bits before input to the adders, and input a 1 to the carry in of the LSB full adder.

    (c) Use 4 full adders and 4 X-OR gates. An X-OR gate is used to select inversion or noninversion of each A_i bit. The add/subtract control is input to each X-OR, as well as to the carry in of the LSB full adder.

23. demultiplexer (DEMUX) or data distributor
25. Connect data-in to logic 1.
27. (a) 32 data inputs, 1 data output, 5 line-select inputs;
    (b) Use four 8-to-1 MUX devices and one 4-to-1 MUX.
29. Use seven 2-input AND gates with an inverter at one input of each. Each gate outputs a true only if a corresponding sensor is high and the next higher-order sensor is low. The AND gate outputs are decoded through an octal-to-binary decoder. The output of sensor 8 can provide the 4th output bit (2^3).
33. (a) Thermostat A (T_A) connects directly to heater A control input (H_A). $\overline{A} \cdot T_B$ connects to H_B.
    (b) $\overline{H}_A \cdot T_B$ connects to H_B; $\overline{H}_B \cdot T_A$ connects to H_A

Chapter D3
3. (a) $Q = S + Q \cdot R$. If $S = 0$ and $R = 1$, $Q = 0 + Q \cdot 1$ is consistent for either value of Q.
   (b) Rules: Positive pulse to S sets FF; negative pulse to R resets FF.
5. Use 3-input NAND gates for the RS FF section of the gate design in Figure D3–4. The respective extra inputs to the NANDs become the direct-set and direct-reset inputs.
7. (a) high; (b) not known, except two outputs are opposite
9. Use 3-input NAND gates for the master RS FF section of the gate design in Figure D3–9a. The respective extra inputs to the NANDs become the direct-set and direct-reset inputs (active low).
13. (a) Q is low; (b) Q toggles; (c) Q goes high on first pulse

17. Toggle action is not involved.
19. Use 4 SPDT push-button switches. Three lines lead to each switch; ground, as well as S and R from an RS FF (to make each switch bounceless). Four RS FF outputs are ORed to clock of JK FF used in toggle mode. Q from JK FF drives solid-state relay that in turn controls room lamp.
21. Connect each line to data input of a data latch (D-type FF). Connect clock inputs of latches together; pull high through 5-kΩ pull-up. Normally open push button connected between clock input and ground.
23. (a) Use 3 RS FFs. Connect S of given FF through 5-kΩ pull-up to +5 V; also connect through bimetallic sensor to ground. Connect Q of FF to indicator light. Connect all R inputs together and through 5-kΩ pull-up to +5 V; connect R inputs through NO push button to ground for reset function.
    (b) Construct 20 circuits from RS FFs as in (a), but connect $\overline{Q}$ of each FF to indicator light. For example, 20°C light is at top of row of lights and 1°C light at bottom.
    NOTE: Octal D-type FFs could be used to reduce package count. Connect each D to high; clock of each FF through switch to high and 500 Ω to low.

Chapter D4
1. 16,383; 16,384
3. First-stage clock input receives pulses to be counted. Clock input to stage $n + 1$ receives $(Q_n \cdot \text{control}) + (\overline{Q}_n \cdot \overline{\text{control}})$. All J, K inputs connected high. (However, counter should be reset after change of control input.)
5. Use 4 JK FFs with $J = K = 1$ on all. Arrange gates so clock input to given stage receives up pulse if states of all

lower-order Qs are 1; or the clock input to given stage receives down pulse if states of all lower-order $\overline{Q}$s are 1. The first stage receives either up pulse or down pulse.

7. (a) three stages of JK FFs as in Figure D4–7. Connect $Q_C \cdot Q_B$ to direct resets.

 (b) Seventh state exists briefly.

9. (a) Connect 60 Hz to input of modulo-3 counter of Figure D4–5 and B output of this counter into clock of toggle-mode flip-flop. Q of latter is 10-Hz square wave.

 (c) Use SPDT push button in bounceless circuit of Figure D3–11 for start/stop push button. Bounceless pulse toggles T-type FF; Q of this FF enables 10-Hz pulses from circuit of part (a) to clock input of BCD counter as in Figure D4–10. Connect direct resets of BCD-counter FFs through 5-kΩ pull-up to 5 V, and through normally open push button to ground for reset function.

11. (b) $Q_A \cdot Q_D$ goes low on falling edge of 10th pulse and toggles Q_D to low.

 (c) $\overline{Q_A \cdot Q_D}$ is low after 9th pulse; dashed circuit expected to inhibit toggle of FFB from 0 to 1 on 10th pulse.

 (d) Q_A into FFB clock goes high before J, K of FFB goes low. Then master in FFB toggles before inhibit action is effective.

 (e) Connect $\overline{Q}$ of FFD into J, K of FFB.

13. (a) In Figure D4–7, disconnect output of NAND gate from direct resets and connect instead to J, K of FFA. Negative reset pulse is input to the R_D inputs.

 (b) Add a 2-input AND to circuit of part (a); output of the NAND as well as the pulse stream are

input to this AND, and the output of the AND has the 5-and-only-5 property.

15. Add gates to Figure D4–16a; let D_A be D input to FFA, D_i be new data-in, and R_c be recirculate-control. Gates accomplish $D_A = D_i \cdot R_c + Q_D \cdot \overline{R_c} = \overline{(\overline{D_i \cdot R_c}) \cdot (\overline{Q_D \cdot \overline{R_c}})}$. Three NANDs and an inverter implement the last statement.

17. (a) Construct 8-bit shift register as in Figure D4–16b. Use 8-input AND to form $Q_A \cdot \overline{Q_B} \cdot Q_C \cdot Q_D \cdot \overline{Q_E} \cdot \overline{Q_F} \cdot Q_G \cdot \overline{Q_H}$; output of AND connects to lock input. Push-button SPDT switch is connected in bounceless circuit of Figure D3–11b to provide shift clock; other SPDT switch connects to data-in (to FFA) to enter code.

 (b) Change Q, $\overline{Q}$ connections to flip-flops.

Chapter D5

1. Operate LM311 as zero-crossing detector by using $+$, $-$ power supplies and connecting inverting input to ground. Input sine wave to noninverting input. Output is unipolar (between ground and $V+$) square wave.

3. (a) Negative (-4.2 V) swing exceeds -0.5-V TTL input limit.

 (b) Have half-wave rectifier circuit with 500-Ω load.

 (c) Slow rise and fall character of sinusoidal waveform.

 (d) Connect half-wave rectifier circuit to 7414 input and 7414 output to clock input. 7414 Schmitt trigger squares up waveform.

5. Connect pins 4, 5, and 14 to +5 V and pin 7 to ground. Connect 0.014-μF capacitor between pins 10 and 11. Input pulses to pin 3; output is from pin 6.

7. Connect 20-V_{p-p} voltage through diode to factor-of-2 voltage divider constructed from two 500-Ω resistors

Connect 5-V_p half-wave rectified waveform from voltage divider to B input of 74121. Connect A_1 input or A_2 input low, and connect 0.072-μF capacitor between C and R/C pins. Connect pin 9 (R_{int}) to +5 V.

Chapter D6

1. Connect 1-MHz oscillator to 7 cascaded decade counters. Connect single-pole-5-position switch to outputs of last 5 stages.

3. Disconnect "enable" line from FF1/FF2; disconnect "load/hold" for data latches from MMVs. Connect these 2 lines to new "enable count events" switch. High from switch enables counting and the latches follow count. Low disables counting. Input pulses to be counted to f-input of f counter. Use halves of DPDT switch in "enable" and "load/hold" lines to give above optional connection.

5. (a) Time for measurement exceeds 1 second.

 (b) 10^3 times as many "ticks" from time base are measured.

 (c) Connect three ÷10 counters in series after Schmitt trigger.

7 Precision of output voltage depends on precision input voltages; TTL outputs only specified for high and low range.

9. (a) .02 μF; (b) 10 mV

1. (a) If ac signal is bipolar in voltage such that integration of $v(t)$ over period T gives 0, then integration over NT also gives zero.

 (b) 60-Hz line signal is symmetrically bipolar; since $T = 1/60$ sec, expect line signal to integrate to zero by part (a).

3. (a) Connect six 1-kΩ resistors in series with a 500-Ω resistor; connect between +.65 V and ground, with 500 Ω connected to ground. Connect inverting input of each of 7 comparators to successive resistor junctions, and all

noninverting inputs together as V_{in}. Use six 2-input AND gates; connect output of comparator and inverted output of next higher comparator to inputs of given AND. Only one AND gate output will be high, with centers of quantization intervals obeying relation $N_{out} = 10V_{in}$ as in Figure D6–12.

 (b) Connect output of AND gates to octal-to-binary encoder of Figure D2–13.

Chapter D7

1. (a) \$64, %1100100; (b) \$EC, %11101100; (c) \$10, %10000

3. (a) 11110000; (b) 10000001; (c) 1010011; (d) 01000111

5. LDA# \$00

7. 8 μsec

9. Eight bit contents of MA \$1340 are added, not \$1340.

11. (a) establish additions in binary; (b) \$0C; (c) no, exit to monitor occurs first; (d) 14 μsec

13. SEC, CLC, JMP \$0050

15. (a) \$14; (b) 20 (in BCD)

17. D0, D1, D3, D5, D6, D7

19. LDA# \$2, CLC, ADC# \$4, STA \$0020, JMP \$1CF4

21. (a) (all hex) A9, FF, 8D, 01, 17, A9, 5A, 8D, 00, 17, 4C, F4, 1C in locations 10 through 1C;

 (b) 0 V, 5 V, 0 V, 5 V, 5 V, 0 V, 5 V, 0 V;

 (c) yes;

 (d) execute unknown codes following STA \$1700; no

23. +5 V

25. (a) LDA# \$FF, STA \$1701, LDA# \$00, STA \$1700, LDA# \$FF, STA \$1700, JMP \$0005 (assume program begins in MA \$0000);

 (b) LDA# \$FF, STA \$A003, LDA# \$00, STA \$A001, LDA# \$FF, STA \$A001, JMP \$0005

27. (a) LDA# \$FF, STA \$1701, CLD, LDA# \$00, STA \$1700, CLC,

ADC #01, JMP $0008 (assume program begins in MA $0000);

(b)   11 μsec

29. (a)   LDA# $FF, STA $1702, STA $1703, LDA# $49, STA $1700, LDA# $02, STA $1701, LDA# $82, STA $1701, LDA# $FA, STA $1700, LDA# $05, STA $1701, LDA# $85, STA $1701, JMP $1C4F;

(b)   Port lines stand high after reset; go high-to-low when are initialized as output ports (since data buffers were zeroed by reset). Then PB7 would signal "data ready" to PDP–8/E prematurely.

Chapter D8

1. (a)   32 μsec, 10.7 instructions;
    (b)   0.26 sec;
    (c)   Latency of 16 μsec permits too few instructions for manipulating data and testing for completion of transfer.

3. (in hex) 0D, 0A, 4D, 69, 63, 72, 6F, 0D, 0A

5. In Figure D8–7, interchange turn-on-heater and turn-off-heater blocks; also interchange yes and no on decision diamond.

7. (a)   1. Initialize port; 2. Send zero to port; 3. Increment port value; 4. If comparator high, go 7; 5. If port value < 127, go 3; 6. Print overrange and stop; 7. Print port value and stop.

    (b)   10 POKE 59459, 127
          20 LET A = 0
          30 LET A = A + 1
          40 POKE 59457, A
          50 IF (PEEK(59457)) − 127 > 0 THEN 90
          60 IF A < 127 THEN 30
          70 PRINT "VOLTAGE EXCEEDS 12.7V"
          80 STOP
          90 PRINT "VOLTAGE IS" A/10 "VOLTS"
          100 END

9. 1. Initialize temp, time ports; 2. Get temp T; 3. Put T in HI TEMP and LO TEMP; 4. GET time TM; 5. Put TM in HI TEMP TIME and LO TEMP TIME; 6. Get temp T; 7. Is T < LO TEMP? Go 10 for no; 8. Yes, put T in LO TEMP; 9. Get time, put in LO TEMP TIME; 10. Is T > HI TEMP? Go 6 for no; 11. Yes, put T in HI TEMP; 12. Get time, put in HI TEMP TIME; 13. Go to 6.

11. PORTA = $1700
     DDRA = $1701
     PORTB = $1702
     DDRB = $1703
          *20
          LDA #$FF
          STA DDRA
          LDA #$00
          STA DDRB
     AGAIN LDA PORTB
          STA PORTA
          JMP AGAIN
          .END

13. TABLE = $0200
          LDA #$00
          STA DDRUT
          LDA #$FF
          STA DDRT
     REPEAT LDA UTEMP
          STA TBLOW+1
     TBLOW LDA TABLE
          STA TEMP
          JMP REPEAT

Chapter D9

1. (a) 00000001, $01; (b) 11111111, $FF (c) 00001001, $FF; (d) 11110111, $F

3. (a) 110100; (b) 11001; (c) 1000000

5. LDA #$15, CLC, ADC #$46, SEC SBC #$31

7. (a) C = 0, V = 1; (b) C = 1, V = (c) C = 0, V = 0; (d) C = 1, V = 0

9. (a) $5B; (b) $1D; (c) $ED; (d) ((BCD); (e) 17 (BCD); (f) 87 (BCD)

11. (b) later

15. LDA #$00, STA $240, STA $24 LDX #05, CLC, LDA $240, AD $200, STA $240, LDA $241, AD $201, STA $401, INCz $1F, IN(

$1F, INCz $28, INCz $28, DEX, BNE $E2, JMP (monitor)

17. LDA #$10, STA $E843, LDA #$10, STA $E841, LDA $E841, BPL $F6, LDA #$00, STA $E841, BPL $F4. (Last "branch always" makes position independent.)

19. (a) Data buffer for port is zeroed at reset. Low states occur briefly on pins when established as outputs.
    (b) Interchange STA DDRB and STA PORTB instructions.

21. LDA #$03, STA $1703, LDA #$00, STA $1700, STA $1701, LDA $1700, LSR, BCC $FA, LDA #$03, STA $1701, LDA $1701, AND #$02, BEQ $F9, LDA #$02, STA $1701, JMP $1C4F

23. (a) PHA, TYA, TAY, DEY, BNE $FD, DEX, BNE $F9, PLA, RTS
    (b) [X(54 + 6) + 14] cycles

Chapter D10

1. (a) LDA #$F4, STA $1707, BIT $1707, BPL $FB, RTS
   (b) LDX #$18, LDA #FY, STA $1707, BIT $1707, BPL $F8, DEX, BNE $F3, RTS

3. LDA #$01, STA $A003, LDA #$00, STA $A001, LDA $52, STA $A414, BIT $A417, BPL $FB, LDA #$01, STA $A001, LDA #$4F, STA $A414, BIT $A417, BPL $FB, BMI $ED
   NOTE: 18 cycles occur in addition to timer delay. BMI introduces 3 extra cycles in high duration.

5. LDA #$00, STA $A003, LDA #$01, STA $A002, INC $A000, LDA $A001, LSR A, STA $A417, BIT $A417, BPL $FB, BMI $EF

7. LDA #80, STA #1703, JSR $1F6A, ORA #$00, BNE $F9, LDA #$80,

STA $1702, LDA #$C8, STA $1707, BIT $1707, BPL $FB, LDA #$00, STA $1702, BEQ $E3
NOTE: Resistive pull-up required on PB7.

9. JSR ACCESS, LDA #00, STA DDRA, (GETA) LDA PORTA, JSR OUTBYT, (REPT) LDA #$18, STA CNT, LDA #$F4, STA TIMER, (WAIT) JSR SCAND, BIT TIMFLG, BPL WAIT; DEC CNT, BNE REPT, JMP GETA, (CNT) $00
NOTE: TIMER = TIMFLG = $A417

11. (a) LDA #%00010100, STA $0403, BIT $0403, BVC $FB, LDA $0402, JSR $8972, JMP $0015 (Assume program begins in MA $0010.)
    (b) Change first LDA to %00000100.

13. LDA #%00110000, STA $0801, LDXz $00, LDA #%00111100, STA $0801, JMP $0000 (Assume first instruction is in MA $0000. LDXz wastes 3 cycles for symmetrical square wave.) f = 55.55 kHz

15. LDA #$00, STA DDRA, LDA #%00000100, STA CRA, LDA #$01, STA DDRB, LDA #%00001100, STA CRB, (WAITP) BIT CRB, BPL $FB, LDA #$01, STA PORTB, LDA PORTA, STA $1707, BIT $1707, BPL $FB, LDA #$00, STA PORTB, LDA PORTB, JMP WAITP

17. *30, JSR ACCESS, LDA #$00, STA $A678 (or STA $FFFE), LDA #$03, STA $A679 (or STA $FFFF), LDA #%00000101, STA CRA, CLI, (AGAIN) JSR SCAND, JMP AGAIN
    *300, PHA, LDA #$00, JSR OUTBYT, JSR OUTBYT, LDA PORTA, JSR OUTBYT, PLA, RTI

Index

Analog Electronics
for Scientific Application

Analog Index

Index

Digital and Microprocessor Electronics for Scientific Application

Digital Index